A New Star-Rating System & Other Exciting News from Frommer's!

In our continuing effort to publish the savviest, most up-to-date, and most appealing travel guides available, we've added some great new features.

Frommer's guides now include a new **star-rating system.** Every hotel, restaurant, and attraction is rated from 0 to 3 stars to help you set priorities and organize your time.

We've also added **seven brand-new features** that point you to the great deals, in-the-know advice, and unique experiences that separate travelers from tourists. Throughout the guide look for:

Finds	Special finds—those places only insiders know about
Fun Fact	Fun facts—details that make travelers more informed and their trips more fun
Kids	Best bets for kids—advice for the whole family
Moments	Special moments—those experiences that memories are made of
Overrated	Places or experiences not worth your time or money
Tips	Insider tips—some great ways to save time and money
Value	Great values—where to get the best deals

We've also added a **"What's New"** section in every guide—a timely crash course in what's hot and what's not in every destination we cover.

Other Great Guides for Your Trip:

Unofficial Guide to the Mid-Atlantic with Kids

Frommer's Virginia

Frommer's Philadelphia & the Amish Country

Frommer's Washington, D.C., from $80 a Day

Maryland & Delaware

5th Edition

by Mary K. Tilghman

Here's what the critics say about Frommer's:

"The only mainstream guide to list specific prices. The Walter Cronkite of guidebooks—with all that implies."
—*Travel & Leisure*

"Complete, concise, and filled with useful information."
—*New York Daily News*

"Amazingly easy to use. Very portable, very complete."
—*Booklist*

"Detailed, accurate and easy-to-read information for all price ranges."
—*Glamour Magazine*

Hungry Minds™

Best-Selling Books • Digital Downloads • e-Books • Answer Networks
e-Newsletters • Branded Web Sites • e-Learning
New York, NY • Cleveland, OH • Indianapolis, IN

About the Author

Maryland native **Mary K. Tilghman** is a journalist and editor and has lived and worked all over the state, from small towns to a farm on the Eastern Shore. She and her family have seen just about every corner of the state, and Delaware by land and on their sailboat on the Magothy River. She lives in Baltimore.

Hungry Minds, Inc.

909 Third Ave.
New York, NY 10022

ISBN 0-7645-6614-8
ISSN 1072-8015

Editor: Kathleen Warnock
Production Editor: Tammy Ahrens
Cartographer: John Decamillis
Photo Editor: Richard Fox
Production by Hungry Minds Indianapolis Production Services

Front Cover Photo: Annapolis, U.S. Naval Academy, practice sailing
Back Cover Photo: Maryland Blue Crabs steamed with Old Bay seasoning

Special Sales

For general information on Hungry Minds' products and services, please contact our Customer Care department; within the U.S. at 800-762-2974, outside the U.S. at 317-572-3993, or fax 317-572-4002. For sales inquiries and reseller information, including discounts, bulk sales, customized editions, and premium sales, please contact our Customer Care department at 800-434-3422.

Manufactured in the United States of America

5   4   3   2

Contents

List of Maps

To my parents, Bill and Pat Tilghman, who taught me to love travel, and my husband, Ray Truitt, and our children Gina, Sean, and Brigid Truitt, who keep me on the go.

Acknowledgments

Special thanks to Deb Clatterbuck at Deep Creek Lake, J. Harry Feldman of the Greater Wilmington Convention & Visitors Bureau, Jennifer Boes of the Delaware Economic and Community Development office, and Mindy Bianco of the Maryland Office of Tourism Development.

—Mary K. Tilghman

An Invitation to the Reader

In researching this book, we discovered many wonderful places—hotels, restaurants, shops, and more. We're sure you'll find others. Please tell us about them, so we can share the information with your fellow travelers in upcoming editions. If you were disappointed with a recommendation, we'd love to know that, too. Please write to:

Frommer's Maryland & Delaware, 5th Edition
Hungry Minds, Inc. • 909 Third Avenue • New York, NY 10022

An Additional Note

Please be advised that travel information is subject to change at any time—and this is especially true of prices. We therefore suggest that you write or call ahead for confirmation when making your travel plans. The authors, editors, and publisher cannot be held responsible for the experiences of readers while traveling. Your safety is important to us, however, so we encourage you to stay alert and be aware of your surroundings. Keep a close eye on cameras, purses, and wallets, all favorite targets of thieves and pickpockets.

New! Frommer's Star Ratings & Icons

Every hotel, restaurant, and attraction listing in this guide has been ranked for quality, value, service, amenities, and special features using a star-rating scale. In country, state, and regional guides, we also rate towns and regions to help you narrow down your choices and budget your time accordingly. Hotels and restaurants in the Very Expensive and Expensive categories are rated on a scale of one (highly recommended) to three stars (exceptional). Those in the Moderate and Inexpensive categories rate from zero (recommended) to two stars (very highly recommended). Attractions, towns, and regions are rated according to the following scale: zero stars (recommended), one star (highly recommended), two stars (very highly recommended), and three stars (must-see).

In addition to the rating system, we also use seven icons to highlight insider information, useful tips, special bargains, hidden gems, memorable experiences, kid-friendly venues, places to avoid, and other useful information:

| Finds | Fun Fact | Kids | Moments | Overrated | Tips | Value |

The following abbreviations are used for credit cards:

AE	American Express	DISC Discover	V Visa
DC	Diners Club	MC MasterCard	

FROMMERS.COM

Now that you have the guidebook to a great trip, visit our website at **www.frommers.com** for travel information on nearly 2,500 destinations. With features updated regularly, we give you instant access to the most current trip-planning information available. At Frommers.com, you'll also find the best prices on airfares, accommodations, and car rentals—and you can even book travel online through our travel booking partners. At Frommers.com, you'll also find the following:

- Online updates to our most popular guidebooks
- Vacation sweepstakes and contest giveaways
- Newsletter highlighting the hottest travel trends
- Online travel message boards with featured travel discussions

What's New in Maryland & Delaware

Since Maryland and Delaware have so much water, water everywhere in the form of ocean, bay, rivers, and lakes, in Baltimore and Wilmington the focus is on the waterfront. Baltimore's been working on its Inner Harbor since the 1970s but old neighborhoods like Canton and Fells Point are getting new attention and a former industrial no-man's land is now the trendy Inner Harbor East.

Wilmington's new Riverfront project has achieved a similar transformation in Delaware.

GETTING THERE Amtrak's superfast Acela Express (© 800/USARAIL; www.amtrak.com) has been introduced in the Northeast Corridor, and now makes the trip from New York to Baltimore's Penn Station in about 2 hours (compared to 3 hours via regular service). The Acela also stops in Wilmington, Delaware, taking just over 90 minutes from New York.

GETTING ORIENTED Maryland's department of tourism has created some new driving tours in informative maps and brochures you can get from any visitor center. *Maryland Scenic Byways* is a guidebook with a map that details driving routes through the state's back roads, which are delineated with black-eyed Susan signs. If you don't want to drive a whole route, you can detour from the interstate for a few miles to drive past the parts that interest you.

Chesapeake Bay Gateways Network has a new guide that lists 89 Gateway sites and water and land trails. The sites are diverse: museums, historic houses, state parks, monuments—all of which have a Chesapeake Bay–related story. Hikers and boaters can use the map to explore the natural attractions. Get one at the visitor centers around the Bay, call © 800/YOUR-BAY, or visit www.baygateways.net.

MARYLAND

WHERE TO STAY More in Baltimore: a skyscraping **Baltimore Marriott Waterfront** now dominates the Inner Harbor East, an emerging neighborhood between the Inner Harbor and Fells Point. Call © 410/385-3000, fax 410/895-1900; www.marriott.com. **Courtyard by Marriott** (© 410/923-4000; fax 410/923-9970; www.marriott.com) has opened as well, and the Ritz Carlton has announced it will build a new hotel near Federal Hill. See chapter 4, "Baltimore."

The **Sleep Inn and Suites** has opened in Emmitsburg, near Frederick, and is already popular with visitors to the historic areas between Frederick and Gettysburg as well as visitors to the Shrine to St. Elizabeth Ann Seton and Mount St. Mary's College. Call © 800/SLEEP-INN or 301/447-0044; www.sleepinn.com. See chapter 7, "Frederick & the Civil War Crossroads."

WHERE TO DINE Baltimore chefs Cindy Wolf and Tony Foreman have two restaurants getting a lot of buzz: Southern-style **Charleston** (© 410/332-7373) in the Inner Harbor East; and **Petit Louis** (© 410/366-9393), a neighborhood bistro with a French flair in Roland Park.

Gertrude's (© 410/889-3399) at the Baltimore Museum of Art offers seafood with a pinch of Baltimore nostalgia. The nostalgia bug bit the elegant **Brass Elephant** (© 410/547-8480) on Charles Street, and the new menu and lower prices reflect the good old days. The **Petticoat Tea Room** (© 410/342-7884) in Fells Point has turned a storefront near the Admiral Fell Inn very pink and dainty.

Canton is a very hot neighborhood lately with busy cafes and nightclubs. At one end of O'Donnell Square, **Rick's Cafe Americain** (© 410/675-1880) offers casual dining, and at the other end **Sonar** (© 410/327-8333) stays cool with martinis and techno music. **The Can Company** has turned an old factory into an interesting mix of restaurants and businesses. See "Where to Dine" in chapter 4, "Baltimore."

Annapolitans love their restaurants and made room for a new bright spot on Main Street. **Aqua Terra** (© 410/263-1985) offers fresh variations on seafood. See "Where to Dine" in chapter 5, "Maryland's Two Capitals: Annapolis & St. Mary's City."

ATTRACTIONS   Vivat! St. Petersburg is coming. The Baltimore Symphony Orchestra's new director, Yuri Temirkanov, conceived a festival of Russian art, music, and culture to celebrate St. Petersburg's 300th anniversary. What's the connection? Temirkanov is director of both the St. Petersburg Philharmonic and the BSO. Art exhibitions, Russian opera, three BSO concerts, a Russian play at Center Stage, and many other events will be held February 13 to March 2, 2003. Call © 877/BALTIMORE or visit www.baltimore.org for details.

Seahorses are the new darlings at the **National Aquarium in Baltimore.** *Seahorses: Beyond Imagination* is the latest exhibit. The aquarium is about to break ground for a building devoted to Australia. Call © 410/576-3800; www.aqua.org.

The **Baltimore Museum of Art** (© 410/396-6310; www.artbma.org) has reinstalled its Cone Collection in elegant new quarters. Meanwhile, the **Walters Art Museum** (© 410/547-9000; www.thewalters.org) changed its name, built a new entrance, and turned the galleries themselves into works of art. The **Contemporary Museum** (© 410/783-5720) finally found a home. Though the staff was quite happy turning car dealerships and other old buildings into temporary museum space (and still does), they now have a permanent home near the Walters. See "Other Downtown Attractions" in chapter 4, "Baltimore."

Frederick's **National Museum of Civil War Medicine** has expanded with new exhibits on the tragedy and the triumphs doctors and nurses faced. Call © 800/564-1864 or 301/695-1864; visit www.CivilWarMed.org. See chapter 7, "Frederick & Civil War Crossroads."

AFTER DARK   Power Plant Live has brought new life to a formerly dark corner just north of the Power Plant complex in Baltimore. New restaurants and nightclubs are turning this into Party Plaza.

It's a bird. It's a plane . . . it's the **HiFlyer,** a tethered hot-air balloon flying next to the **Port Discovery Children's Museum.** This takes the prize for best view of Baltimore. And it looks quite ghostly at night. Call © 410/727-8120; www.portdiscovery.org.

OUTDOORS   Maryland has only one ski resort, but **Wisp** is expanding. Several trails and ski lifts have been lengthened, and a tubing park has been added. More development, including an indoor skating arena, is planned.

DELAWARE

WHERE TO STAY   Rehoboth Beach has a new hotel-cum-golf course. The 18-hole course at **Heritage Inn and Golf Club** on Route 1 is open to non-guests. Call ℂ **800/669-9399** or 302/644-0600; www.heritageinnand golf.com. See "Rehoboth Beach" in chapter 9, "Maryland & Delaware's Atlantic Beaches."

WHERE TO DINE   In Wilmington, the buzz is about **Deep Blue** (ℂ **302/777-2040**; www.deepblue barandgrill.com), a chic seafood restaurant set in a parking garage downtown. The restaurant is sleek, the cuisine trendy, and the tables full. Just as crowded, but more casual, is the **Backstage Café** (ℂ **302/778-2000**; www. welcomebackstage.com) on the Riverfront. This theme restaurant has a menu bigger than some books and offers live entertainment. See "Where to Dine" in chapter 10, "Wilmington."

ATTRACTIONS   The Delaware Center for the Contemporary Arts (ℂ **302/656-6466**; www.thedcca.org) has moved to impressive new digs on the Riverfront with plenty of room for its ever-changing shows. **Rockwood Museum,** housed in a Gothic-style mansion, was due to re-open in spring 2002 after extensive renovation. Call ℂ **302/761-4340**; www.rockwood.org.

Riverfront Wilmington is more than a pretty brick walkway on the Christina River. It's home to shops, museums, a small but lovely market, and a wildlife refuge. It's too new to compare with Baltimore's Inner Harbor, but it's worth a trip. See chapter 10, "Wilmington."

In the Brandywine Valley, **Hagley Museum** (ℂ **302/658-2400**; www. hagley.org) is reopening its Henry Clay Mill with new exhibits for DuPont's 200th anniversary. See chapter 11, "The Brandywine Valley & Historic New Castle."

1

The Best of Maryland & Delaware

I've always lived in Maryland and never wanted to live anywhere else. Delaware is tiny but it's a gem of a state right next door.

In either state it's easy to find fascinating places to visit: from historic sites dating back to the first settlements in the New World to high-tech attractions; good eating, from fresh seafood at local diners to fine dining; great natural beauty and lots of outdoor activity, from the ocean to the bay to the mountains.

The regions covered in this book can make a great day trip, weekend, or full vacation. A tourist at heart, I've spent my whole life visiting places around my state. I found myself awed while recalling the horror of Antietam, delighted by the iconoclastic home of American Red Cross founder Clara Barton, and invigorated by paddling a canoe down a tree-lined creek off the Patapsco River.

I can't wait for you to see the places I've always loved: the beautiful, hidden Cunningham Falls; the views from the rolling Appalachian Mountains; the friendly streets of Baltimore; and the bars and restaurants in Annapolis.

Don't be fooled by Delaware's size. Billing itself as the "Small Wonder," its coast hosts laid-back beach resorts, and the state is also a major destination for NASCAR and slots fans. It has an extraordinary number of finely preserved turn-of-the-century mansions, and a compact, cultured metropolis in Wilmington.

These two states have been touched by revolution, civil war, and world wars, and the people here don't forget. You can see places where George Washington stood, where brothers died, and where slaves ran for freedom. You can see silent monuments to those who defended the country in 1812, 1917, and 1945.

These states love the water that laps their shores. The Atlantic Ocean, the Chesapeake Bay, the rivers winding through valleys and flatlands, have given the people places to work, to play, and to stop and take in the beauty.

Bring your sense of wonder and your sense of humor. You'll learn something, maybe. You'll see something beautiful, of course. You'll have fun, definitely.

1 Frommer's Favorite Maryland & Delaware Experiences

- **The view from the Ocean City, Maryland, Ferris Wheel:** Fork over the $7 for a ticket and climb aboard the aging Ferris wheel. Ride just before sunset and you won't wait in line. That's the perfect time to watch the charter boats heading in for the night and to see the sun set over Assawoman Bay. As darkness falls, you can watch the lights begin to brighten the boardwalk. See chapter 9, "Maryland & Delaware's Atlantic Beaches."

- **The Star-Spangled Banner at Fort McHenry** (Baltimore): The park rangers ask visitors to help with the raising and the lowering of the huge flag each day. The little rooms, nooks and crannies, and views keep young ones interested. Outside the fort, the sprawling waterfront park is perfect for families and picnics. See chapter 4, "Baltimore."

- **Rafting the Yough:** The Youghiogheny River (generally just called the *Yock*) is Maryland's great white-water river. Its churning waters race through class III/IV rapids, with names like Gap Falls, Bastard, Triple Drop, Meatcleaver, Lost and Found, and Backbender. The water levels are controlled by dam release, so the river is runable almost year-round. See chapter 8, "Western Maryland."

- **Any Baseball Game:** Maryland has baseball's most beautiful stadium: Oriole Park at Camden Yards; and the best team in the world (the Orioles, of course!). Players toss balls to kids in the stands—and the Oriole Bird has been known to loft T-shirts or even (wrapped) hot dogs to the fans. The many minor league teams are also fun and more affordable. See "The Best Baseball in Maryland," later in this chapter.

- **Going "Downy Ocean":** Head for the crowded beaches of Ocean City, Maryland (with all those restaurants, shops, and golf courses), or to the quiet public beaches of Rehoboth or Bethany, Delaware. Both have their charms. The sand is white and clean; the waves can be gentle or furious (watch for the red warning flags). The sand crabs are used to being dug up and the seagulls will keep an eye on your snacks. (Don't give in and feed them. It can be pretty scary.) See chapter 9, "Maryland & Delaware's Atlantic Beaches."

- **Tea at Bertha's** (Fells Point, Baltimore; © **410/327-5795**): Bertha's tea is an afternoon delight. Cup after cup of Earl Gray with scones and clotted cream, Scotch eggs, and an assortment of savories and sweets are perfect in the shabby chic dining room of this Fells Point eatery. See "Where to Dine" in chapter 4, "Baltimore."

- **Crabbing on the Wye River** (St. Michaels, Maryland): Whether you are wading with crab pots or chicken-necking from a boat, the Wye River is the place to go crabbing. Crabs caught in this river are everyone's favorite. See chapter 6, "The Eastern Shore."

- **Preakness Week** (Baltimore): If you're young and want some serious partying, check out the infield. If you actually want to see the second jewel in the Triple Crown, head for the grandstand. The race, held the third Saturday in May, concludes a week of festivities. The party starts with hot air balloon races at Druid Hill Park and "balloon glow" events. If you want grandstand tickets to the Preakness, held at Pimlico Race Course (© **410/542-9400**), it's best to call up to a year ahead. Infield tickets are available up to the week before and are sold at some area gas stations.

- **Off-Road Vehicle Trips on Assateague Island:** Most people who visit Assateague see only the 4- or 5-mile (6 or 8km) stretch of guarded beach and federal and state camping facilities. They've missed the best part: the 20 miles (32km) of undisturbed beaches. This part of the island is only accessible on foot, by canoe or kayak, or over off-road vehicle trails, the fastest way to get to those secluded areas. See "Assateague Island National Seashore" in chapter 9, "Maryland & Delaware's Atlantic Beaches."

Maryland & Delaware

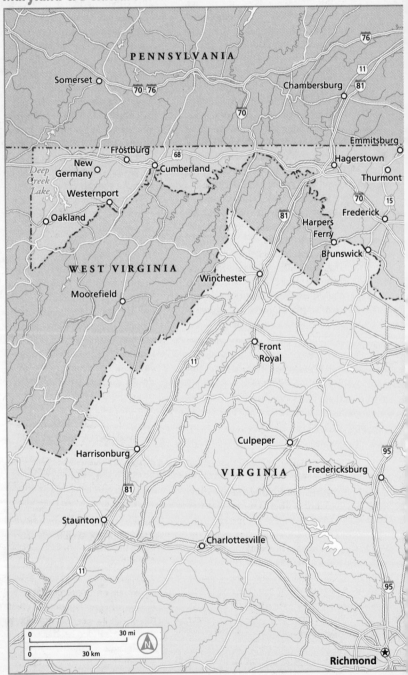

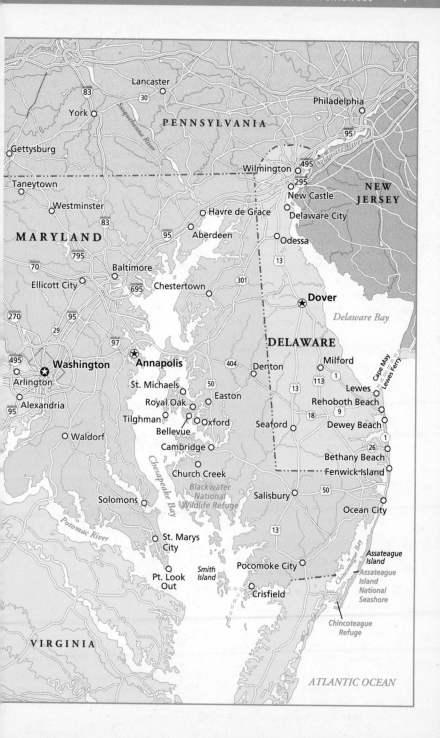

2 The Best Accommodations Bets

- **Harbor Court Hotel** (Baltimore; ✆ **800/824-0076**): It's a treat to walk in the door and you're pampered when you spend a night here. Rooms are exquisitely furnished with the ultimate in amenities, and the hotel contains some of Baltimore's best dining. See p. 69.

- **Hotel du Pont** (Wilmington; ✆ **800/441-9019**): Not only is this a showcase of marble, carved paneling, and DuPont's latest fibers, it's a hotel determined to bathe its guests in palatial surroundings, terrific amenities, and some of the best restaurants in town. See p. 287.

- **Tidewater Inn** (Easton, Maryland; ✆ **800/237-8775**): This is Eastern Shore hospitality at its best. The inn is noted for its gorgeous surroundings, careful attention to service, and location in the heart of Easton, which is perfect for a weekend getaway or even a hunting trip. See p. 147.

- **Inn at Montchanin Village** (Montchanin, Delaware; ✆ **800/ COWBIRD**): This cluster of buildings was once home for workers of the DuPont powder mills. Now they are charming guest rooms and suites, set in beautiful gardens, a few miles from the du Pont homes and gardens. See p. 288.

- **Annapolis Inn** (Annapolis, Maryland; ✆ **310/295-5200**): This sumptuous Georgian-style house was originally the home of Thomas Jefferson's physician in the 1770s. The three-course breakfast is served in the warm, cranberry-red dining room on fine china, silver, and crystal. There are Jacuzzis, a room with its own deck, a patio surrounding a koi fishpond, and experienced, welcoming hosts. See p. 112.

- **Elliott House Victorian Inn** (Grantsville, Maryland; ✆ **800/ 272-4090**): Western Maryland has always been a good place to get away from it all, but because of the bustling nature of the Deep Creek Lake area, there have been few tranquil places to stay. Enter the Elliott House, a restored 1877 Victorian home and outbuildings. Next to the Spruce Forest Artisan Village, less than a quarter mile from the highway, you needn't leave the grounds to commune with nature; just walk behind the inn through the wildflowers to the Casselman River. See p. 219.

- **Bluebird on the Mountain Inn** (Frederick, Maryland; ✆ **800/ 362-9526**): Reserve the room with the sun porch and make a beeline for the chaise longue. Or take your breakfast to the porch and listen to the wind rustle through the enormous trees. Hard to believe it's less than 2 hours from Baltimore or Washington. A massage therapist is only a phone call away. Just a few minutes' drive away are Frederick, the Civil War battlefields, and views of the Appalachians. See p. 200.

- **Waterloo Country Inn** (Princess Anne, Maryland; ✆ **410/651- 0883**): When Theresa and Irwin Kraemer moved from Austria to this 1775 Georgian manor on Maryland's Eastern Shore, their intention was to turn it into the quintessential country inn. Their hostelry on the banks of Monie Creek (which easily could qualify as a Most Elegant Inn) offers seclusion, peace, and tranquility, whether you're wandering the inn grounds, canoeing the lovely tidal creek, or biking the back roads of Somerset County. See p. 173.

3 The Best Dining Bets

- **Carrol's Creek** (Annapolis; © **410/263-8102**): The best views of the waterfront and Annapolis skyline are paired with imaginative food. Dine indoors or on the porch from a menu that is always changing but will match rockfish with polenta and free-range chicken with truffle-scented mashed potatoes. The cream of crab soup is always a winner. See p. 118.

- **Charleston** (Baltimore; © **410/332-7373**): Southern cuisine takes center stage at this restaurant in the trendy Inner Harbor East neighborhood. Expect to be treated like royalty while the wait-staff brings you your micro-green salad, grilled yellowfin tuna with Andouille sausage, and a perfect crème brûlée. See p. 76.

- **Green Room** (Wilmington, Delaware; © **302/594-3154**): Delaware's top restaurant impresses diners the minute they see the impressive decor. The impeccable service and classic continental cuisine, including Dover sole or filet of beef with Madeira truffle sauce, make the meal memorable. The sound of the harp in the background adds a touch of heaven. See p. 291.

4 The Best Affordable Dining

- **Harpoon Hanna's** (Fenwick Island, Delaware; © **800/227-0525**): The food is good, the fresh bread and muffins are outstanding. For a beach restaurant, this one is worth the trip. Set on a canal, its big windows let the sunset in. The fish is fresh, the staff hardworking. And children are always welcome. Come early or be prepared for a substantial wait. See p. 253.

- **Café Normandie** (Annapolis; © **410/263-3382**): This tiny venue on Main Street never fails to satisfy. From the baked Brie to the cinnamon-scented coffee, the food is good. Crepes have been on the menu for decades but there are plenty of other delicious choices. The atmosphere is intimate and rustic with a roaring fire in winter. See p. 119.

- **Gertrude's** (Baltimore; © **410/889-3399**): Which museum restaurant to choose: Gertrude's at the Baltimore Museum of Art, or Joy America at the American Visionary Arts Museum? Both are delightful, but Gertrude's always-satisfying seafood, its patio overlooking the sculpture garden, and that cup of crayons next to the salt and pepper make this one of Baltimore's best. See p. 85.

5 The Best Shopping Bets

- **Antique Row** (Baltimore): In one block of Howard Street a few blocks north of downtown, serious antiques fans can find old silver, chandeliers, assorted porcelains, and chairs of all sizes and shapes. See chapter 4, "Baltimore."

- **Rehoboth Outlets** (Rehoboth Beach, Delaware): Wear comfortable shoes; this is tax-free outlet shopping heaven. Four centers have everything from Waterford crystal to Oshkosh overalls. There's lots of clothing and home decor outlets, as well as books, food, and other stuff. See chapter 9, "Maryland & Delaware's Atlantic Beaches."

- **Downtown Annapolis:** Main Street and Maryland Avenue offer shoppers all kinds of choices in little shops. Tuscan kitchenware, Christmas ornaments, antique mirrors, and Navy sweatshirts are only a few of the items on these charming streets. There are a few chain stores but the best shops are locally owned. See chapter 5, "Maryland's Two Capitals: Annapolis & St. Mary's City."

6 The Best Views & Vistas

- **A Mountaintop at Wisp Ski Resort:** Ride the ski lift to the top, and before you go schussing down, take a good look. You'll see snow-covered slopes, the vast white expanse of Deep Creek Lake lined with the tracks of an occasional snowmobile, and a sky as blue as it can be. See chapter 8, "Western Maryland."
- **Severn River Scenic Overlook:** On Route 450 outside of Annapolis a beautiful stone porch offers stunning views of the Severn River and U.S. Naval Academy. It recently became the site of a World War II Memorial with summaries of the major battles, and obelisks bearing the names of Marylanders who gave their lives in World War II. See chapter 5, "Maryland's Two Capitals: Annapolis & St. Mary's City."
- **Great Falls of the Potomac:** On a sunny Sunday, the walkways are crowded, but who cares? Just outside of Potomac, a Maryland suburb north of Washington, D.C., on the C&O Canal, a series of walkways will take you over the Great Falls of the Potomac. Stand above the piles of jagged rocks as the Potomac River rushes over them and down to the sea, the steepest and most spectacular fall line rapids of any eastern river. See "Quick Stops Around the Capital Beltway" in chapter 5.
- **Bay Bridge:** When you get to the top, you get a wonderful view of the Chesapeake. Maryland's Eastern Shore stretches down one terminus, and the view of the western shore includes Annapolis south of the bridge and posh Gibson Island and two working but unstaffed lighthouses north of the bridge. The closest lighthouse is the Sandy Point light and the one farther away is the Baltimore light.

7 The Best Hiking

- **Calvert Cliffs State Park:** This park offers trails for moderate-length day hiking and a wide variety of wilderness scenery. The trails wind through forests and then descend into a primordial tidal marsh with grasses, waterfowl, and cypress trees. Most hikes include at least one view of the Chesapeake Bay from atop the cliffs or from a small beach at the base of the marsh. See chapter 5, "Maryland's Two Capitals: Annapolis & St. Mary's City."
- **Swallow Falls State Park:** A great place for families to hike in Garrett County, Maryland, this park's short trails wind through dark, peaty forest and offer relatively easy access to some stunning scenery. There are overlooks to three waterfalls—Swallow Falls, Tolliver Falls, and the 63-foot-high, cascading Muddy Creek Falls. See chapter 8, "Western Maryland."
- **Big Savage Trail:** This rugged trail extends 17 miles (27km) along the ridge of Big Savage

Mountain, passing impressive vistas along the way. A tough hike through almost total wilderness, it's our choice for serious backpack camping in Maryland. See chapter 8, "Western Maryland."

8 The Best Fishing & Crabbing

- **Point Lookout State Park** (Maryland): Location is everything at this peninsular park with the Chesapeake Bay on one side and the Potomac River on the other. Fish from the pier on the bay, or rent a boat at the camp marina. If they aren't biting in the bay, stroll over to the Potomac and try again. See chapter 5, "Maryland's Two Capitals: Annapolis & St. Mary's City."

- **Calvert County Charter Fleets:** For charter fishing on the Chesapeake, Calvert County south of Annapolis is the place to go. The small harbor of Chesapeake Beach is home to the largest charter fleet on the bay. With over 30 charter boats and a few headboats of its own, Solomons, south of Chesapeake Beach, has a good fleet, too. From either one, the captains are glad to take you trolling or chumming along the western and eastern shores of the Chesapeake. See chapter 5, "Maryland's Two Capitals: Annapolis & St. Mary's City."

- **Casselman River** (fly-fishing/near Grantsville, Maryland): Cleanup efforts in this area have paid off. The beautiful and wild Casselman River, once empty of fish because of local acid mining, is now teeming with trout. We've heard rumors of people catching as many as 40 fish a day (yeah, we believe that). One thing is for certain, though: The Casselman is once again a great place to fish. See chapter 8, "Western Maryland."

9 The Best Birding & Wildlife Watching

- **Blackwater National Wildlife Refuge** (Maryland): The Delmarva Peninsula is dotted with wildlife refuges and protected lands, havens for migrating waterfowl and other wildlife. Blackwater is the largest of these. During peak migration season, you'll see ducks, tundra and mute swan, and snow geese, as well as the ever-present herons, Canada geese, and osprey, and the occasional bald eagle. If you explore the wooded areas, you may even catch sight of the endangered Delmarva fox squirrel. See chapter 6, "Eastern Shore."

- **Bombay Hook National Wildlife Refuge** (Delaware): The largest of Delaware's wildlife refuges, Bombay Hook, northeast of Dover, has nearly 16,000 acres of tidal marsh, freshwater pools, and timbered swamps. You'll see a lot of migratory waterfowl, but after waterfowl season, in April, May, and June, migrant shorebirds and songbirds appear. See chapter 12, "Dover & Central Delaware."

- **Whale- & Dolphin-Watching on the Mid-Atlantic:** The Atlantic coast of Maryland and Delaware near Cape Henlopen State Park (Delaware), is a good place to spot whales and dolphins. The Great Dune at Cape Henlopen is a great vantage point (bring binoculars); there are also whale- and dolphin-watching cruises, even sea kayaking with the dolphins. See chapter 9, "Maryland & Delaware's Atlantic Beaches."

10 The Best Festivals & Events

- **Flower Mart** (Baltimore): This 1-day festival almost died a few years ago, but a group of Baltimoreans rescued it. On the first Wednesday in May, take a walk up Charles Street to the Washington Monument. The ladies wear flower-bedecked hats and there are plenty of flowers for your garden, as well as traditional Baltimore foods, including crab cakes and the yummy lemon stick. (Halve a lemon, stab it with a peppermint stick, and suck the juice through the candy.)
- **The Annapolis Sailboat Show** (Annapolis; ✆ **410/268-8828;** www.usboat.com): Boat dealers fill the city dock with an array of sailboats, some spartan racing boats and others luxurious floating living rooms. Wear sneakers or boat shoes and you can climb aboard them all and dream. Held the first weekend in October. The **Powerboat Show** is held the following weekend.
- **Waterfowl Festival** (Easton; ✆ **410/822-4567;** www.waterfowl festival.org): You'll see paintings of canvasbacks, herons, and Canada geese; decoys practical and fanciful; and sculptures so lifelike you'll want to smooth the feathers. There are sometimes even tiny sculptures worked in gold. Then for fun, stop by the duck-calling contest, held in Easton the first weekend in November.

11 The Best Family Activities

- *Harbor Queen* **Boat Ride** (Annapolis): The kids love leaning over the rail as waves hit the boat, and it's a great way to see the bay. There's a little history lesson but mostly this is a wind-in-your-face, sun-in-your-eyes ride. See chapter 5, "Maryland's Two Capitals: Annapolis & St. Mary's City."
- **B&O Railroad Museum** (Baltimore): When my children were old enough to venture away but not out of sight, I took them here all the time. I could stand in the middle of the roundhouse and watch them as they wandered among the iron horses. They loved the independence and I loved the museum. Still do. See chapter 4, "Baltimore."

12 The Best Camping

- **Janes Island State Park** (Maryland): For sunset views over the Chesapeake Bay, the campsites at this park north of Crisfield can't be beat. Many sites sit on the water's edge, offering unobstructed views and easy access to the canoe trail. If you prefer less primitive accommodations, there are a few waterside cabins. See chapter 6, "Eastern Shore."
- **New Germany State Park** (Maryland): This wooded campground is the cleanest, best-kept one we've stayed in. It's small, with only 39 well-spaced sites that offer easy access to hiking trails, fishing spots in the park lake, and the facilities of several other state parks and forests. There are also 11 cabins, which are great options for winter cross-country skiing trips. See chapter 8, "Western Maryland."
- **Potomac–Garrett State Forest** (Maryland): For primitive camping in the mountains, head to this little-known state forest in southern and western Garrett County. Nearly all the campsites are within walking distance of one of the

forest's mountain streams, and they're so spread out, you'll probably never know if you have camping neighbors. See chapter 8, "Western Maryland."

- **Cape Henlopen State Park** (Delaware): Summer beach camping is always a tenuous venture, with the heat, the bugs, and the sand. But the facilities at Cape Henlopen make for the best beach camping. There are 159 wooded sites, several with full hookups, and all with access to bathhouses and running water. Within the park, you'll find several miles of hiking and biking trails, guarded beaches, and great fishing. See chapter 9, "Maryland & Delaware's Atlantic Beaches."

13 The Best Curiosities

These are worth a look if you happen to be visiting the area:

- **The Fish That Didn't Get Away** (Ocean City, Maryland): At the south end of the boardwalk are a couple of stuffed prize fish caught off Ocean City. These record-breakers are pretty big, but the stories make a stop here even more worthwhile. You'll have to see for yourself.
- **Katyn Monument** (Baltimore): Next to the Marriott at the Inner Harbor East is a golden monument flashing in the sun. This 47-foot sculpture by Andrew Pitynski is dedicated to all prisoners-of-war as it memorializes Polish officers murdered by the Soviets in 1940 in the Katyn Forest.

- **Eye of Water** (Brandywine Valley, Delaware): A tiny feature in the Longwood Gardens, this strange little spot is where all the water circulates for the 50-foot waterfall a few paces west of it. It sits atop 90,000 gallons of water but you'd never know it, standing there in this little pavilion watching the Eye of Water.
- **Delaware Coast Watchtowers:** These tall, lonely towers stood sentry during World War II. Crews manned them 24 hours a day, on the lookout for German ships and submarines. The towers still look out to sea. You can't go inside then, but if you spot them as you drive along the coast, you'll know what they are.

14 The Best Picnic Places

- **Hagerstown Park** (Western Maryland): In the center of town, this is a gem. Its Victorian styling, playgrounds, and swans floating on the pond make it a great place to sit back and relax. There are concerts in the summer, a small Museum of Fine Arts, and the wonderful Hager House, built in 1739 when this was America's frontier. To get here, take the Sharpsburg Pike North exit off I-70, turn left on Wilson Boulevard, and turn right on Virginia Avenue.
- **Oregon Ridge Park** (Baltimore): The Baltimore Symphony Orchestra performs in this unassuming park off I-83 at Shawan Road in the summertime. Fourth of July concerts often end with fireworks. Bring your picnic and blankets or buy food here. Concerts begin about 8pm. See chapter 4, "Baltimore."
- **Quiet Waters Park** (© 410/222-1777): You can spend all day at this well-designed park south of Annapolis. Besides plenty of places to lay out your picnic, there are bike and walking paths, playgrounds, waterfront paths, boat and kayak rentals, gardens, and

The Best Baseball in Maryland

Marylanders love baseball. The Orioles are the big league team, of course, but the state is also home to six minor league teams, two baseball museums, and a monument to a storied slugger.

The **Baltimore Orioles** play at Oriole Park at Camden Yards. The stadium is easy to get to, right off I-95 to I-395 at the bottom of the ramp into town. The light rail stops here for every game. Parking in lots around the stadium (if not at the stadium) is close and usually costs less than $10. The stadium was designed to bring spectators closer to the action, and it does. Watch out for foul balls! A promenade follows the warehouse building along the outfield wall. Stop at the deck overlooking the bullpen to watch the pitchers warm up. The food is pretty good and ranges from hot dogs to Italian sausage to crab cakes. Former Oriole Boog Powell's barbecue stand sends a cloud of smoke up over the scoreboard wall and the pit beef sandwiches are worth the wait in line. The park also offers tours that give visitors a chance to sit in the dugout and in the press box from April to September. Call ℂ **410/547-6234** or visit www.TheOrioles.com.

An Orioles game might be a great place to bring a client (the stands are full of them), but a minor league game is the place to bring your family. In addition to lower ticket prices (less than $10) and more intimate stadiums, many teams have playgrounds, fireworks, and special events for families.

In **Aberdeen,** Maryland's newest team, a Class A squad affiliated with the Orioles, is owned by Aberdeen native Cal Ripken and his family. The brand-new stadium where the team will play is next to the Ripken Academy's six ballfields, each a youth-sized replica of other stadiums—Oriole Park at Camden Yards, Fenway Park, Wrigley Field, Memorial Stadium, Yankee Stadium, and Ebbetts Field. The Oriole Park field will be home to the Cal Ripken League World Series. For information call ℂ **410/575-7600** or visit www.ripkenbaseball.com.

The **Bowie Baysox,** a Class AA Orioles affiliate, has a fireworks display after every Saturday home game. The team plays in Prince George's Stadium. For tickets, call ℂ **301/805-6000** or visit www.baysox.com.

The **Delmarva Shorebirds,** of the Class A South Atlantic League, are an Orioles affiliate, and play near Ocean City at Arthur W. Perdue Stadium in Salisbury, Maryland. For tickets, call ℂ **888/BIRDS96** or 410/219-3112.

The **Frederick Keys,** a Class A Orioles affiliate, play at Harry Grove Stadium in Frederick, off Route 70. Current Orioles on the disabled list come here to get back into shape. The Keys even draw fans from the Baltimore area. For tickets, call ℂ **301/662-0013** or visit www.frederickkeys.com.

occasional art exhibits. In winter, there's an ice rink.

• **Trees of the States Arboretum:** This little haven at Delaware Technical and Community College's Georgetown campus is a pleasant place to stop on the way to or from the beach. Apart from the 51 trees representing the states and the District of Columbia, there's just a

The **Hagerstown Suns,** a Class A team of the San Francisco Giants, play at Municipal Stadium. For tickets, call ✆ **800/538-9967** or 301/791-6266, fax 301/791-6066, or visit www.hagerstownsuns.com.

Yes, the Babe was a Yankee but he was born in the narrow rowhouse that is now the **Babe Ruth Birthplace and Museum/Baltimore Orioles Museum.** Two rooms are set up as they would have looked when he was living here. Exhibits include a wall enumerating his home runs; and memorabilia from his career as well as from his days at St. Mary's Industrial School in Baltimore, where he learned to play the game. The Orioles and gone-but-not-forgotten Colts have their own exhibits. The Colts exhibit includes old films, ancient uniforms, and memorabilia from stars Johnny Unitas and Art Donovan. The Orioles' exhibit takes visitors up to today with mementoes of various World Series, All Star games and, of course, Cal Ripken. It's at 216 Emory St.; ✆ **410/727-1539;** fax 410/727-1652; www.baberuthmuseum.com. Admission is $6 for adults, $4 seniors, $3 ages 5 to 16. It's open April to October daily 10am to 5pm (until 7pm on Orioles' home game days; November to March daily 10am to 4pm. Closed January 1, Thanksgiving Day, and December 25. From Camden Yards, walk 2 blocks west on Pratt and south on Emory. It's a tiny street.

The **Ripken Museum** pays homage to more than Cal, Jr. It's a testament to the "Ripken Way," that took six Ripkens to professional baseball leagues. What makes this museum interesting is not just the exhibits, but the staff. They speak of the Ripkens as friends and knew one or all of them personally. Some of the most interesting items are from Cal, Sr. and his brothers who played minor league ball in its early days. It's at 3 West Bel Air Ave., Aberdeen, MD 21001, ✆ **410/273-2525;** www.ripkenmuseum.com. Admission is $3 adults, $2 seniors, $1 ages 6 to 18. It's open Memorial Day through Labor Day, Monday to Saturday 11am to 3pm, Sunday noon to 3pm; from Labor Day to May 1, Friday to Monday 11am to 3pm, Saturday 11am to 4pm, Sunday noon to 3:30pm; May, Thursday, Friday, Monday 11am to 3pm, Saturday 11am to 4pm, Sunday noon to 3pm. The last tour begins 30 minutes before closing. Take I-95 north to Exit 85 for Aberdeen. Turn right on Route 132 East. Go 1.6 miles (2.6km). The museum is on the left.

If you visit **Chestertown,** look for the life-sized statue of Bill Nicholson next to the town hall on Cross Street. The Chestertown native was a home run king in the 1940s with the Chicago Cubs. He led the majors in home runs and RBIs in 1943 and 1944. During the 1944 season, the New York Giants intentionally walked him with the bases loaded, rather than risk a grand slam. He died in his hometown, Chestertown, in 1996.

gazebo, a pond, and a picnic area. It's too small to make a special trip to, but if the baby's crying on Route 404, here's a lovely place to take a break. Each tree is marked with its species and state. Many have been growing here since 1976. For more information and large tour groups call ✆ **302/856-5400.**

2

Planning a Trip to Maryland & Delaware

Maryland and Delaware are relatively tourist-friendly states—they're compact and have good roads, fair public transportation, three international airports, and one national airport within a 3-hour drive. But even in such an accessible region, a little advance planning can make your visit run more smoothly. This chapter will answer many of the questions you may have while planning your trip: When is the best time to visit? Which festivals and events will coincide with my trip? How much time (and money) should I plan to spend? What's the best way to get there?

1 The Regions in Brief

MARYLAND

Maryland and Delaware, two of the smaller states, contain a wide variety of terrain, weather, topography, urban and rural areas. Here's a brief description of the major regions in the two Middle Atlantic States, starting from the mountainous west to the coastal east.

Western Maryland   Outdoor-lovers adore this part of Maryland. It has biking and hiking trails, lakes and white water. It has the Catoctin Mountains and Deep Creek Lake, charming towns and historic sites.

Everything west of Frederick County is considered Western Maryland. Although development is beginning to touch the area, particularly around Hagerstown and Cumberland, the atmosphere is peaceful. You can expect a smile and a welcome from the people you meet.

It used to take hours driving over small winding roads to get to the far reaches of Western Maryland. That's no longer true since the construction of Route 68, which continues westward when Route 70 heads north near Hancock. Route 68 bypasses the small towns and slices right through a mountain at Sideling Hill.

Now skiing at Wisp resort is a few hours away from the more populous eastern part of the state. Hiking a trail at Swallow Falls can take longer than driving to it. And many visitors frequent Deep Creek Lake and Rocky Gap State Park and Resort.

Summer and winter are the best times to visit. Spring is a little cold for most activities except shopping, limited sightseeing, and relaxing. Fall is the prettiest time for those sightseeing trips. Wisp Ski Resort has added an 18-hole golf course on its gentler slopes and made the ski lifts available for hikers and bikers once the snow melts. In the state parks, visitors can go cross-country skiing, snowshoeing, and tobogganing, or ride in a horse-drawn sleigh. Spring and fall are the seasons for hiking, biking, horseback riding, fishing, and sometimes boating. Summer offers warm breezes, hot sunshine, and cool shade for outdoor activities and relaxing afterwards.

Capital Region   A lot of territory is dumped into this region. All roads—or at least highways—go to Washington, D.C., and so do many of the people who live in these Maryland counties. But the counties of Frederick, Montgomery, Prince George's, Howard, and Carroll are distinctly different. Frederick's history is tied more to Western Maryland, though you'd never know it if you're driving the highways around rush hour. It's part of the Civil War crossroads, so you can't go far without finding another reminder of the War Between the States. The area is also home to Camp David, the presidential retreat, and rolling hills covered with orchards or dairy farms. A drive up Route 15 toward Gettysburg offers one of Maryland's best day trips.

The other four counties have mostly given themselves over to urban sprawl. There are still some gems to discover, like the Great Falls of the Potomac and, the home of Clara Barton, the founder of the American Red Cross. Roller coasters and space ships have made Prince George's County a destination for a visit to Six Flags America.

Southern Maryland Tobacco was king in Southern Maryland in the old days and still rules in some areas. As you drive down more rural routes through Charles, Calvert, and St. Mary's counties, you can see tobacco-curing barns with the long narrow slits that open them up to the air.

St. Clements's Island, where the first settlers first stepped upon the New World on March 25, 1634, is still a very remote place. St. Mary's City disappeared after Annapolis became the capital, but archaeologists are rediscovering and restoring the 368-year-old buildings in a fascinating work in progress.

Surrounded by both the wide mouth of the Potomac River and the Atlantic Ocean, this is fishing territory. At Point Lookout, anglers can try their luck in first one, then the other. In Calvert, Chesapeake Beach and Solomons offer many a fishing charter boat.

Eastern Shore This is the home of corn, oysters, and geese. On a flat spit of land that stretches up the eastern side of the Chesapeake Bay, from the Atlantic to the Susquehanna River, the Eastern Shore is different from the rest of Maryland. Natives have their own slow, thoughtful accent. They're sun- and wind-burned from long hours on a tractor or a workboat.

The Shore's flatness makes biking easy. There are rivers for fishing, boating, and swimming. Towns are small and though many are more businesslike than pretty, some have deserved reputations for charm and history. The wide-open spaces attract waterfowl from fall to spring (whether you're a hunter or a birder).

The mid-Shore—Talbot County, Kent Island, and Dorchester County along the Choptank—is the most developed part of the Eastern Shore and the most tourist-friendly. Though fishing and crabbing are important, the main industry here has historically been shipbuilding. Talbot County has the most hotels, inns, and restaurants.

Kent and Cecil counties comprise the North Shore, an area of highlands and rolling hills. The countryside is beautiful, but accommodations for travelers are few and far between.

Don't care about any of that? You'll love Route 50 because it will get you "downy ocean" in a hurry, hon.

Down the Ocean The Atlantic rules here. Sun, beach, and miniature golf as far as the eye can see! Here, too, are lifesaving stations that once housed the men who saved sailors in distress and the concrete watchtowers that once housed the men on the lookout for World War II enemy ships.

In Maryland, Ocean City's condos, shops, and highways dominate the state's coastline; it's Maryland's second largest city in the summer. South of the Inlet is Assateague Island, a

Wine, Maryland Style

Maryland has an interesting array of wineries from western Maryland to north of Baltimore City, with two in the D.C. area.

The largest winery is **Berrywine Plantations/Linganore Cellars,** which yields 300,000 bottles yearly and has visitors from all over the world. Combine this with a trip to New Market for lunch and antiques shopping for a day trip. Take I-70 to Route 75 and follow signs to New Market and Berrywine and continue north to Route 26 East to reach Elk Run and Loew.

At the farthest western point of Maryland you'll find the state's smallest winery. **Deep Creek Cellars** is literally a basement operation yielding 12,000 bottles a year, mostly dry red wines that are drinkable right away.

Visit the wineries while the grapes are growing in the summer or in September, when wine making begins. The tours are most interesting when you see those vats brimming with fermenting grape juice. On weekends, several wineries host festivals with live music, food, and their own wines. All are in picturesque country, filled with rolling hills and fresh air; and all have tastings and will help you choose a bottle or case to take home.

Berrywine Plantations/Linganore Cellars (13601 Glissans Mill Rd., © 410/795-6432), **Elk Run** (15113 Liberty Rd., © 410/775-2513), and **Loew** (14001 Liberty Rd., © 301/831-5464) are close enough to visit in a day. All are located off I-70, in Mount Airy, east of Frederick. Elk Run and Loew are nearby on Liberty Road, much smaller than Berrywine, but friendly and fun. All three have tours Saturdays 10am to 5pm and Sunday noon to 5pm. Berrywine has tours all week, too, 10am to 5pm. Berrywine hosts festivals with lots of music about twice a month.

Basignani Winery (15722 Falls Rd., Sparks, © 410/472-0703) produces lots of varietals, including Cabernet Sauvignon, Chardonnay, and Riesling. It's open weekends noon to 5pm. Take I-83 North to Exit 20B. Turn right on Route 25. It's on the left.

Woodhall Wine Cellars (17912 York Rd., Parkton, © 410/357-8644) is farther north on I-83 off Exit 27, next to the Gunpowder River. One of the oldest wineries in the state, Woodhall makes a wide variety of wines, including Gunpowder Falls Estate Chardonnay and Parkton Prestige, a red wine. Woodhall has festivals about once a month for special days or release of new wines. Tours are offered Tuesday to Sunday noon to 5pm. It's an easy drive from Basignani Winery to Woodhall.

Boordy Vineyards (12820 Long Green Pike, Hydes, © 410/592-5015), is also in northern Baltimore County. Boordy is one of Maryland's most highly regarded wineries. It hosts regular festivals and tastings. Tours are offered daily on the hour 1 to 4pm, though the winery is open Monday to Friday 5pm, Sunday 1 to 5pm. From the Baltimore Beltway (I-695) heading west, turn left at exit 29 (Cromwell Bridge Road), and go 2.9 mi. Bear sharp left over bridge onto Glen Arm Rd. Continue 3.2 mi. to stop. Turn left onto Long Green Pike and follow 2 mi. to Boordy's entrance on left.

Fiore Winery (3026 Whiteford Rd., Pylesville, © **410/879-4007**) is run by a wine maker whose family made wine in Italy for 400 years. The wines range from Chambourcin to Merlot and Chardonnay. It is about a half-hour drive from Woodhall or Boordy through the countryside or up I-95, off Exit 74. Turn left on Route 152, right on Route 165, left on Route 24, and right on Whiteford Road. It's about a 40-minute drive from the Beltway junction.

Penn Oaks (11 Midhurst Rd., Silver Spring, © **301/562-8592**) is a good place to stop if you're in the Washington, D.C. area. It's also one of the state's newest wineries, opened in 1997. German-style wines, from Riesling to Liebfraumilch, are featured here. Though usually open by appointment only, they offer tastings once a month. You have to call for the schedule.

Catoctin Winery (805 Greenbridge Rd., Brookeville, © **301/744-2310**) is fairly close to Penn Oaks. These are the only ones south of I-70. Catoctin is known for its Cabernet Sauvignon, Riesling, and especially Eye of the Oriole. Tastings are weekends noon to 5pm or by appointment. It's open for sales during the week. From the Capital Beltway, I-495, take Exit 28N Route 650, and continue 15 miles (24km) to Greenbridge Road.

Deep Creek Cellars (477 Frazee Ridge Rd., Friendsville, © **301/746-4349**) is interesting, if only because of its scale. A family-run operation, this one's just getting started as a full-time business. It's a nice diversion during a visit to the Deep Creek area. Tours are offered Saturday 11am to 7pm. Take I-68W to Exit 6. Go north on Route 42 and turn right on Frazee Ridge Road; the winery is on the left. If you want to make this part of a multi-winery trip, the owners will gladly offer directions to a couple of nearby wineries just over the Pennsylvania line.

In addition to winery tours, there are two festivals celebrating the grape.

The largest (drawing more than 20,000 people) is the **Maryland Wine Festival** held mid-September 10am to 6pm on Saturday and noon to 6pm on Sunday. It's at the Carroll County Farm Museum in Westminster and is a must for the state's wineries to attend. There are competitions among the pros, as well as amateur wine makers. There's also lots of great food, as well as the 10 tastings you get with the price of admission.

Wine in the Woods is a newer festival and follows the Maryland Wine Festival's formula. Its setting, under the trees of Symphony Woods in Columbia, makes it nice, too, especially since mid-May can be so humid. The festival is usually held on Preakness Weekend, noon to 6pm both Saturday and Sunday. Admission includes 10 tastings. For exact dates of both, call © **800/237-WINE** or visit www.Marylandwine.com.

seashore park renowned for its wild ponies and its pristine landscape.

DELAWARE

Down the Ocean, Continued In Delaware, much smaller resorts, such as Bethany and Dewey Beaches, are located between long stretches of public beach and national seashore. Rehoboth, Delaware's premier beach, retains its small town charm in spite of the crowds that can make north–south Route 1 impassable on holiday/summer weekends. An ever-expanding district of factory outlet stores on Route 1 makes the traffic worse (and the bargains more plentiful). Just north of Rehoboth is Lewes, a quaint Victorian town known as the terminus of the Cape May-Lewes Ferry. It's a nice diversion because of its shops, its (bay) beach at Cape Henlopen, or its location as a place to catch a charter fishing boat.

Central Delaware Kent County, which is primarily farmland, is Delaware's central county and home of Dover, the state capital. Bombay Hook National Wildlife Refuge on the Delaware Bay is a stop along the East Coast for migrating waterfowl and is less developed than Blackwater on Maryland's Eastern Shore. State capital Dover, a striking contrast to Annapolis, is a quiet town, with a few specialized museums and historic sites, but twice a year on race weekends Dover and most of the state fill up with fans of the big NASCAR auto races.

Brandywine Valley This is du Pont country. The American branch of the du Pont family has been in this region since E.I. du Pont opened his black powder mill on the banks of the Brandywine River in 1802. Their legacy is everywhere, from Longwood Gardens to the Nemours Mansion. You could easily spend a week here and not see all the sights.

It's not hard to see why the du Ponts, or anyone, would settle here: The rolling hills, fertile land, and the river itself have served as inspiration for the region's other famous family, the Wyeths. **Wilmington** lies at the mouth of the Brandywine River. It's a convenient spot for visiting the Brandywine Valley but it's also got interesting restaurants and museums of its own. The city's newly developed Riverfront is worth a visit, too.

2 Visitor Information

MARYLAND

For information about the entire state, call or write the **Maryland Division of Tourism, Film and the Arts,** 217 East Redwood St., 9th Floor, Baltimore, MD 21202 (© **800/MD-IS-FUN** or 410/767-3400). Its website has links to county websites at www.mdisfun.org. For information on Baltimore and the vicinity, contact the **Baltimore Area Convention and Visitors Bureau,** 100 Light St., 12th Floor, Baltimore, MD 21202 (© **877-BALTIMORE** or 410/659-7300; www.baltimore.org). For information on state parks, forests, and wildlife refuges, contact the **Maryland** **Department of Natural Resources,** Tawes State Office Building E-3, 580 Taylor Ave., Annapolis, MD 21401 (© **800/830-3974** or 410/260-8DNR), or visit www.dnr.state.md.us.

In addition, look for **Visitor Information** signs or blue question-mark signs near your destination. They are on all major highways and, especially in Frederick and Western Maryland towns, lead you to an office filled with knowledgeable people. I do this all the time and it works. If you are driving, **Maryland Welcome Centers** are on Interstate 95, Route 50, Route 68, Route 70, and Route 301, as well as at Baltimore–Washington International

Airport. Racks provide brochures, and maps. Staffers can also recommend accommodations.

DELAWARE

Delaware's tourism agencies are regional. **The Delaware Tourism Office,** 99 Kings Hwy., Dover, DE 19901 (℃ **800/VISITDE** or 302/739-4271; www.visitdelaware. com), can provide general information, calendar of events, and a map, but we suggest contacting local tourism offices and chambers of commerce, which provide more detailed information in a more timely fashion. In Southern Delaware (Sussex County), contact **Southern Delaware Tourism,** P.O. Box 240, Georgetown, DE 19947 (℃ **800/357-1818** or 302/ 856-1818). You can also get information, or request their publications, from their website (www.visit southerndelaware.com). For information on Wilmington and the Brandy-wine Valley, write or call the **Greater**

Wilmington Convention and Visitors Bureau, 100 W. 10th St., Suite 20, Wilmington, DE 19801 (℃ **800/422-1181** or 302/652-4088; www.visitwilmingtonde.com).

Since the terrorist attacks of September 11, 2001, a number of attractions have either closed temporarily—including Dover Air Force Base, the U.S. Naval Academy, the visitor center at the Calvert Cliffs nuclear power plant—or have made visiting more restrictive. At the very least, visitors are no longer allowed to carry large bags into public buildings and you may notice more guards, metal detectors, or other signs of tighter security measures. If you have any question about whether an attraction is open to the public, call ahead of time. In spite of the attacks, representatives at all these attractions made it clear they plan to continue as usual and hope to welcome as many people as before—with a little more caution.

3 Money

Prices in restaurants and hotels in the larger cities are higher than prices in small towns and roadside diners, as you might expect. Resort towns like Ocean City can be quite expensive in the summer, but far more reasonable in the shoulder and off-seasons. Expect expenses to rise the closer you get to Washington, D.C. As a corporate headquarters and destination for business travelers, Wilmington has many high-end hotels and restaurants. Baltimore is, overall, a less expensive city. Compared to New York in the U.S. and European destinations like London and Paris, both cities are much less expensive as tourist destinations.

ATMS

ATMs (automated teller machines) are linked to a national network that most likely includes your bank at home.

Cirrus (℃ **800/424-7787**; www. mastercard.com) and **PLUS** (℃ **800/ 843-7587**; http://usa.visa.com) are the two most popular networks; check the back of your ATM card to see which network your bank belongs to.

TRAVELER'S CHECKS

Traveler's checks are something of an anachronism from the days before the ATM made cash accessible at any time. The only sound alternative to traveling with large amounts of cash, traveler's checks were as reliable as currency but could be replaced if lost or stolen, unlike cash.

These days, traveler's checks seem less necessary because most cities have 24-hour ATMs that allow travelers to withdraw small amounts of cash as needed—and thus avoid the risk of carrying a fortune around an unfamiliar

What Things Cost in Baltimore	U.S.$	U.K.£
Shuttle from BWI to Inner Harbor	11.00	7.60
Economy class rental car from Avis for a week (unlimited mileage)	260	180
Double room at the Harbor Court Hotel (very expensive)	210–250	145–173
Double room at the Marriott Waterfront (expensive)	159–249	110–172
Double room at the Holiday Inn Inner Harbor (moderate)	89–174	62–120
Double room at Georgian House, a B&B in Annapolis	130–175	90–121
Lunch for one at Joy America Cafe at the Inner Harbor (moderate)	10.00	6.92
Lunch for one at Women's Industrial Exchange Tea Room (inexpensive)	7.00	4.84
Dinner for one, without wine, at Hamptons (very expensive)	45.00	31.12
Dinner for one, without wine, at The Prime Rib (expensive)	35.00	24.21
Dinner for one, without wine, at The Brass Elephant (moderate)	25.00	17.29
Dinner for one, without wine, at One World Café (inexpensive)	12.00	8.30
Full day's parking at the Inner Harbor	15.00	10.37
Orioles' game parking	6.00	4.15
Local phone call	0.50	0.35
Roll of ASA 200 Kodacolor film, 24 exposures	5.89	4.07
Adult admission to the National Aquarium	16.00	11.07
Inner Harbor water taxi fare, one adult, all day	5.00	3.46
Glass of Coca-Cola at bar or restaurant	1.50	1.04
Cup of espresso at PaperMoon Diner	2.00	1.38
Dessert at Vaccaro's	3.75–7.50	2.59–5.19
Movie ticket at the Senator theater	7.00	4.84
Upper reserve ticket to an Orioles' game	13.00	8.99
Pint of beer in Fells Point	2.50–5.00	1.73–3.46

environment. Many banks, however, impose a fee every time a card is used at an ATM in a different city or bank. If you're withdrawing money every day, you might be better off with traveler's checks—provided that you don't mind showing identification every time you want to cash a check.

You can get traveler's checks at almost any bank. **American Express** offers denominations of $10, $20, $50, $100, $500, and $1,000. You'll pay a service charge ranging from 1% to 4%. You can also get American Express traveler's checks over the phone by calling ✆ **800/221-7282;**

by using this number, Amex gold and platinum cardholders are exempt from the 1% fee. AAA members can obtain checks without a fee at most AAA offices.

Visa offers traveler's checks at Citibank locations, as well as several other banks. The service charge ranges between 1.5% and 2%; checks come in denominations of $20, $50, $100, $500, and $1,000. Call ✆ **800/732-1322** for information. **MasterCard** also offers traveler's checks. Call ✆ **800/223-9920** for a location near you.

CREDIT CARDS

Credit cards are a safe way to carry money and provide a convenient record of all your expenses. You can also withdraw cash advances from your credit cards at any bank (though you'll start paying interest on the advance the moment you receive it, and won't receive frequent-flyer miles on an airline credit card). At most banks, you can get a cash advance at the ATM if you know your PIN. If you've forgotten your PIN or didn't know you had one, call the phone number on the back of your credit card and ask the bank to send it to you, though some banks will tell you

over the phone if you answer a security question.

WHAT TO DO IF YOUR WALLET GETS STOLEN

Be sure to block charges against your account the minute you discover a card has been lost or stolen. Then be sure to file a police report.

Odds are that if your wallet is gone, it won't be recovered. However, after you cancel your credit cards, it is still worth informing the police. Your credit-card company or insurer may require a police report number.

Almost every credit card company has an 800 number to call if your card is stolen. They may be able to wire you a cash advance off your credit card, and in many places, they can deliver an emergency credit card in a day or two. Citicorp Visa's U.S. emergency number is ✆ **800/336-8472.** American Express cardholders and traveler's check holders should call ✆ **800/221-7282.** MasterCard holders should call ✆ **800/307-7309.** Otherwise, call the toll-free number directory at ✆ **800/555-1212.**

If you carry traveler's checks, keep a copy of the serial numbers separate from the checks so you're ensured a refund in just such an emergency.

4 When to Go

The resort towns on the Atlantic are most popular in the summer, and usually quite crowded. The fringe season, May and especially September, is the optimal time for cheaper rates, comfortable temperatures, and quieter beaches. Peak season for the Eastern Shore, Annapolis, and Southern Maryland is April through October,

when the weather clears up for boating and the fish start biting. Most everything is open in Baltimore year-round, though because of its boating culture and baseball season, summer is the most popular and crowded time to visit. I recommend visiting in May or fall when the weather is likely to be sunny but not so humid.

Baltimore's Average Monthly Temperatures & Precipitation

	Jan	Feb	Mar	Apr	May	June	July	Aug	Sept	Oct	Nov	Dec
Temp (°F)	31.8	34.8	44.1	53.4	63.4	72.5	77	75.6	68.5	56.6	46.8	36.7
Temp (°C)	0	1	6	11	17	22	25	24	20	13	8	2
Precip (in.)	3.05	3.12	3.38	3.09	3.72	3.67	3.69	3.92	3.41	2.98	3.32	3.41

Cumberland's Average Monthly Temperatures & Precipitation

	Jan	Feb	Mar	Apr	May	June	July	Aug	Sept	Oct	Nov	Dec
Temp (°F)	30.3	33.4	43.2	53.6	63.1	71.0	75.1	73.9	66.7	54.8	44.6	34.6
Temp (°C)	0	0	6	12	17	21	23	23	19	12	7	1
Precip (in.)	2.38	2.29	3.08	3.19	3.66	3.34	3.37	3.30	3.08	2.77	2.76	2.61

In Western Maryland, summer temperatures are generally 5° to 10° lower in the Allegheny Mountains than further east, offering a break from the summer heat of Baltimore and the shore areas. Peak time for fall foliage is about the third week in October, and you'll find a lot of local festivals this time of year. From the first snow in November to about mid-March, Garrett County has the state's only downhill skiing and cross-country skiing. Not much happens April through June but with good hotel deals and trees starting to bloom, it can be a good getaway in late spring. It seldom reaches 70° before July in Garrett County.

Wilmington and the Brandywine Valley are also year-round destinations. Most attractions offer festivals and events year-round. In the temperature chart, Baltimore information applies generally to Wilmington and the Brandywine Valley; expect summer temperatures to be slightly higher on the southern Eastern Shore and on the coast. Remember that monthly averages can be deceiving. Even though the average temperature in Baltimore during July is 77°, days in the 90s are common.

MARYLAND & DELAWARE CALENDAR OF EVENTS

January

Annapolis Heritage Antiques Show, Medford National Guard Armory, Annapolis. Third weekend in January. Fine country and period furniture and decorative arts to benefit London Town Foundation. ⓒ **410/435-1919;** www.armacost antiquesshows.com.

Chesapeake Bay Boat Show, Baltimore Convention Center, Baltimore. Begins last weekend in January, runs through following week. Dream of summer while climbing aboard all kinds of motor- and sailboats. Check out the latest equipment, too. ⓒ **212/922-1212;** www.boatshows.com.

February

Hunt Valley Antiques Show, Marriott's Hunt Valley Inn, I-83 and Shawan Road, Hunt Valley, MD. Last weekend in February. Couldn't make the Annapolis antique show? This one is filled with fabulous items, too. Call ⓒ **410/435-2292** for tickets; www.armacostantiques shows.com.

March

Maryland Day, Historic St. Mary's City. March 25. Several sites open with no charge. ⓒ **800/762-1634.**

April

My Lady's Manor Steeplechase Races and Champagne Reception, Route 146 and Pocock Road, Monkton, Baltimore County, MD. Saturday in mid-April. Annual running of the steeplechase, 3 miles (5km) over timber. Ladew Topiary Gardens. Call ⓒ **410/557-9466.**

Baltimore Waterfront Festival, Harborplace, Baltimore City. Last weekend in April. Begun as part of the festivities for the Whitbread Around the World Race in 1997, the festival has become an annual celebration of the Chesapeake Bay, boating, and seafood. Activities, food, entertainment. Free.

May

Maryland Film Festival, first week in May. Venues around Maryland. Check www.mdfilmfest.com for details.

Wings of Fancy Butterfly Show, Brookside Gardens, 1800 Glenallan Ave., Wheaton, MD 20902. Mid-May until July. See butterflies in this indoor show, along with fabulous flowers outdoors in the extensive gardens. Learn about plants that can attract these winged beauties to your garden. Call ℂ 301/949-8230.

Bay Bridge Walk, first Sunday in May. Begins 9am. Arrive early to walk the 4.3-mile (7km) span across the Chesapeake Bay. Call ℂ 877/BAYSPAN.

Preakness Celebration, Baltimore area. The Preakness Stakes, the second jewel of American horse racing's Triple Crown, is held the third Saturday in May at Pimlico Race Course. Gates open at 8:30am. It's not just a horse race, it's a week of celebration, beginning with a balloon race in Druid Hill Park the previous Saturday, just after sunrise. There's also a parade, concerts, and a 5k run. Call ℂ 410/542-9400; www.preaknesscelebration.com.

Wine in the Woods. Preakness Weekend (just by coincidence). Symphony Woods, Columbia, noon to 6pm. Sample Maryland wines and gourmet foods, and enjoy entertainment and arts and crafts. Call ℂ 410/313-7275.

Flower Mart, Mount Vernon, Baltimore City. Held on a Wednesday in mid-May, 11am to 8pm. A charming tradition around the Washington Monument, known for its flowers, lemon sticks, and crab cakes.

Chestertown Tea Party, Chestertown, MD. Bostonians weren't the only ones throwing tea overboard in

the 1770s. This festival, held the last weekend in May, re-enacts the 1774 Tea Party (on Saturday), with a colonial parade, crafts and art show, entertainment, and food. Call ℂ 410/778-0416.

A Day in Old New Castle, Delaware. Third Saturday in May. For more than 70 years, the residents of this historic district have opened their doors for an open-house tour of the town. On this day, the town's private homes, public buildings, gardens, churches, and museums are open to the public. Other events include maypole dancing, carriage rides, and musical programs. Call ℂ 302/328-2413.

Dover Downs NASCAR Weekend. Dover, DE. Late May or early June. This 2-day stock-car race draws dozens of top drivers from around the world to Dover Downs, nicknamed the "Monster Mile." Call ℂ 302/674-4600 for tickets.

June

Eastern Shore Chamber Music Festival: various sites in Queen Anne's, Kent, and Talbot counties, held two weekends in June. Call ℂ 410/819-0380 for the schedule of concerts of classical and contemporary music performed by internationally acclaimed musicians.

Columbia Festival of the Arts, Lake Kittamaqundi, Columbia, MD. 10 days in mid-June. Celebration of the arts with local and national stars of theater, music, dance, and visual arts. See www.columbiafestival.com for a schedule of events.

Delmarva Hot Air Balloon Festival, Milton, DE. Third Saturday in June. This annual event attracts over 20 balloons and features crafts, antiques, and food vendors; entertainment; and balloon rides. Call ℂ 302/684-3400 or 302/684-8404.

July

Salute to Independence, Antietam National Battlefield, Sharpsburg, MD. Held Saturday after Fourth of July. Annual Maryland Symphony Orchestra concert of classical and patriotic music with live cannon fire and fireworks. Call ⓒ **301/ 797-4000** or visit www.md symphony.com.

Artscape, Baltimore. Visual and performing arts celebrated in this weekend festival held in July. Nationally known performers join local artists. Children's activities are offered. Call ⓒ **410/396-4575;** www.artscape.org.

Delaware State Fair, State Fairgrounds, Harrington. Third week of July. Annual showcase for produce, agricultural wares, and crafts, as well as stock-car races, a demolition derby, harness racing, rides, games, and live concerts. Call ⓒ **302/398-3269.**

J. Millard Tawes Crab and Clam Bake, Crisfield, MD. Held on a Wednesday in mid-June, an all-you-can-eat celebration of crabs, clams, and corn. Call ⓒ **800/ 782-3913.**

Kunta Kinte Celebration, St. John's College, Annapolis. Mid-August. Cultural heritage festival with music, dance, arts, and crafts. Call ⓒ **410/349-0338** or see www.kuntakinte.org.

Maryland State Fair, Timonium Fairgrounds. Held from the week before Labor Day through the holiday weekend, daily 10am to 10pm. Eleven days of farm animals, crafts, produce, rides, entertainment, and thoroughbred racing. Call ⓒ **410/ 252-0200;** visit www.maryland statefair.com.

September

Star-Spangled Banner Weekend, Fort McHenry National Monument, Baltimore. Held weekend near Defender's Day, September 12, a Baltimore City holiday. Re-enactments of the War of 1812, with musket firing and children's activities. Call ⓒ **410/962-4290;** www.nps.gov/ fomc.

Maryland Wine Festival, Carroll County Farm Museum, Westminster, MD. Held a weekend in mid-September. Sample Maryland wines, food, and entertainment. Tour the farm museum. Call ⓒ **800/654-4645.**

Baltimore Book Festival, Mount Vernon Place, Baltimore City. Last weekend in September. Local bookstores and publishers, authors and storytellers, along with art, entertainment, and food. Call ⓒ **888/BALTIMORE,** or 410/ 837-4636; www.bop.org.

Bethany Beach Boardwalk Arts Festival. First Saturday in September. The major annual happening for the "Quiet Resorts" of Delaware's lower shore, this juried show attracts craftspeople, artisans, and spectators, and takes up the length of the boardwalk. There are competitions for woodcarving, photography, jewelry, batik, metal sculpture, calligraphy, oil and watercolor painting, toys, dolls, and painted porcelain. Call ⓒ **800/ 962-7873** or 302/539-2100.

Dover Downs NASCAR Weekend. Third weekend in September for tickets. This 2-day stock-car racing competition, like June's event, draws dozens of top drivers from around the world to Delaware. Call ⓒ **302/674-4600.**

October

United States Sailboat Show, City Dock, Annapolis. First weekend in October. Nation's oldest and largest in-water sailboat show. Call ⓒ **410/268-8828;** www. usboat.com.

United States Powerboat Show, City Dock, Annapolis. Second weekend in October. Nation's oldest and largest in-water powerboat show. Same contact information as Sailboat Show.

Autumn Glory Festival, Oakland, MD. Held Thursday to Sunday, second week in October. State banjo and fiddle championship, crafts, antiques. Call *C* **301/387-4386;** www.garrettchamber.com.

Catoctin Colorfest, Thurmont, MD. Held second weekend in October. Arts and crafts and the beauty of the mountains. Call *C* **301/271-4432.**

Tilghman Island Day, Tilghman Island, MD. Saturday in October. Local seafood, music watermen contests, and rides on skipjacks and workboats. Call *C* **410/886-2677.**

Maryland Million, Laurel Park, Laurel. Saturday in mid-October. Maryland's own are celebrated in this race of Maryland-bred, trained thoroughbreds. Call *C* **410/252-2100;** www.mdhorsebreeders.com.

November

Waterfowl Festival, Easton, MD. Second week of November. Decoys, artworks of waterfowl, duck calling contests, kid's activities, food. Call *C* **410/822-4567;** www.waterfowl festival.org.

December

New Year's Eve Extravaganza, Inner Harbor, Baltimore City. December 31. Parties suitable for families, non-alcoholic. Entertainment, food, fireworks. Call *C* **888/ BALTIMORE;** www.bop.org.

Yuletide at Winterthur. Mid-November through early January. Celebrate the holidays in 19th-century style, with a festive program at the Brandywine Valley museum, featuring decorations, entertainment, and guided tours. Call *C* **800/ 448-3883** or 302/888-4600.

Yuletide in Odessa, Odessa, DE. Mid-November through December. Holiday decorations and observances in 18th-century style in a small town in central Delaware. A house tour is held in early December. Call *C* 800/448-3883 or 302/ 378-4069.

5 The Active Vacation Planner

Between the Atlantic Ocean, the Chesapeake Bay, and the mountains of Western Maryland, there are a lot of outdoor activities to fill your vacation. The **Maryland Department of Natural Resources** is a good source of information for activities on state lands in Maryland, and they maintain a website at www.dnr.state.md.us. In Delaware, contact the state or local tourism agency and ask for *Delaware Eco-Discoveries* and *Delaware Outdoors.* The **Delaware Department of Parks and Recreation** also publishes a guide to all state parks and a listing of their summer programs. Maryland has a guide to help bikers, hikers, kayakers, and other outdoors fans find

Gateways to the Chesapeake. Get one from a welcome center or any local tourism office.

BICYCLING/MOUNTAIN BIK-ING Maryland and Delaware offer cycling options for all ages and abilities, and both states provide good maps for cyclists. March through October is the best time to cycle, although summer everywhere east of Hagerstown, Maryland, is generally hot and humid, with temperatures reaching the 90s, so bring plenty of water. Maryland law requires all cyclists under age 16 to wear helmets; otherwise, laws in both states are fairly standard. For a complete list of bicycle regulations, contact the **Bicycle**

and Pedestrian Program, State Highway Administration, 707 N. Calvert St., Baltimore, MD 21203 (© **410/ 545-5656**); or the **Bicycle and Pedestrian Coordinator,** Delaware Department of Transportation, P.O. Box 778, Dover, DE 19901 (© **302/760-2453**).

The Delmarva Peninsula—the Eastern Shore, Southern Delaware, and the Atlantic coast—is generally flat and light in traffic on the back roads. Southern Delaware is especially good to cyclists, with an excellent bicycle map of Kent and Sussex counties available. It's also home to Cape Henlopen State Park, a great place for family biking, with paved trails for cyclists and pedestrians only. On Maryland's Eastern Shore, the best places to ride are in the state parks and wildlife refuges, though the scenery is beautiful throughout the region. If you plan to cycle outside the parks, contact the county tourism agency and get a good map before you start out. In the more rural communities, roads are seldom marked and it's easy to get lost.

A unique bike trail in Maryland is the **C&O Canal towpath,** which runs along the Potomac River and the C&O Canal for 184½ miles (297km) from Georgetown to Cumberland. It's more challenging than bike routes on Delmarva but still a good family biking destination. The towpath is a wide dirt trail through floodplain forests, but it is mostly flat and closed to vehicular traffic. You can start in Georgetown or Cumberland but I recommend the C&O Canal Historical Park near Potomac, where you can take a ride on one of the canal boats and walk to the Great Falls of the Potomac.

Mountain biking is an emerging sport in Western Maryland. The state forests and parks of Garrett County offer miles of multiuse trails and designated mountain biking trails, and there are even a few guide services.

For experienced mountain bikers, try the trails at Potomac–Garrett State Forest or Savage River State Forest.

Cycling clubs throughout both states can provide information and maps. In Delaware, contact the **White Clay Bicycle Club,** 1016-1 McDowell St., Wilmington, DE 19805-2744 (www.whiteclaybicycleclub.org), for New Castle County; **Diamond State Bicycle Club,** P.O. Box 1729, Dover, DE 19903 (© **302/697-6400**), for Kent County; or **Sussex Cyclists,** Larry Wonderlin, 28 Marshall Rd., Rehoboth, DE 19971 (© **302/227-3697** or www.delawarewonder.com), for Sussex County.

Maryland has too many clubs to list here, but contact the Bicycle and Pedestrian Coordinator at the State Highway Administration (see above) and ask for *Bicycling in Maryland,* a helpful booklet that lists all the clubs in the state by region, as well as the government contact in each county. They also have a state bicycling map.

BIRDING & WILDLIFE WATCHING The Delmarva Peninsula is a prime location along the Atlantic Flyway, and as such, both Maryland and Delaware have many wildlife refuges for birding and wildlife watching. The best time to see migrating **waterfowl** is late winter to early spring (Feb and Mar) and fall. The largest and most visited of the refuges is Blackwater National Wildlife Refuge, just south of Cambridge on Maryland's Eastern Shore. In addition to flocks of Canada geese, tundra and mute swan, and several species of ducks and widgeons, you may also catch a glimpse of the endangered **Delmarva fox squirrel, peregrine falcon,** or **bald eagle.** At the smaller refuges you're likely to see the same types of wildlife with fewer humans around. In Maryland, these include Deal Island, south of Blackwater, and Eastern Neck, near Chestertown. Delaware's largest refuges are Bombay Hook and Prime Hook, but

Fort Delaware State Park on Pea Patch Island outside Wilmington is a good place to spot waterfowl, **muskrats,** and other mammals.

For information on birding in Delaware, contact the Delaware Audubon Society's **Birdline Delaware,** P.O. Box 1713, Wilmington, DE 19899 (© **302/428-3959;** www.audubon.org/chapter/de), or call the Delaware Birding hotline at © **302/658-2747.** In Maryland contact the **Audubon Society,** 23000 Wells Point Rd., Bozman, MD 21612 (© **410/745-9283**). You can also contact the **Maryland Ornithological Society,** Cylburn Mansion, 4915 Greenspring Ave., Baltimore, MD 21209 (© **800/823-0050;** www.mdbirds.org).

CAMPING The people of Maryland and Delaware love to sleep under the stars, so it can be difficult to find an empty campsite on a summer weekend. Accommodations throughout both states can be had for from $5 to $20 per night depending on amenities and location. RV camping is available at most parks, though not in state forests, and sites with full hookups are plentiful along the Atlantic coast in both states. You can always find a campground that's open year-round, but many parks along the coast close for the winter or offer limited sites. Several campgrounds are open during the winter in Western Maryland, though this certainly isn't the best time for camping unless you want to camp in the snow. Many beach campgrounds have significant mosquito and biting fly populations in summer. (We are among those who believe there are more mosquitoes per square foot on Assateague Island than any other place on earth.)

The largest campgrounds are at Assateague Island and Rocky Gap State Park in Maryland and at Cape Henlopen State Park in Delaware. Reservations are highly recommended at Rocky Gap and are a necessity if you want to camp at the federal campground at Assateague. Cape Henlopen and Assateague State Park do not accept reservations. For information about camping in Maryland, contact the **Maryland Department of Natural Resources,** State Forest and Park Service, Tawes State Office Building E-3, 580 Taylor Ave., Annapolis, MD 21401 (© **410/260-8DNR**), or the individual parks. In Delaware, contact the **Delaware Division of Parks and Recreation,** 89 Kings Hwy., Dover, DE 19901 (© **302/739-4702;** www.destateparks.com).

FISHING The region's fertile waters are one of its biggest attractions, and industries. Charter fishing, freshwater fishing, fly-fishing, deep-sea fishing, surf fishing, and even ice fishing—here's a quick rundown of the best places in both states.

On the Atlantic, **Ocean City** is the place to go for charter fishing in Maryland. Nearly all the charter operations run out of marinas in **Assawoman Bay** near the Inlet. In Delaware, nearly all the charter fishing operations are run out of **Lewes** and fish the Delaware Bay as well as the Atlantic. State lands along the coast, such as **Assateague Island** and **Delaware Seashore State Park,** offer the best surf fishing because the beach-going crowd is smaller.

Chesapeake Beach on the western shore of Chesapeake Bay, in Calvert County, has the bay's largest charter fishing fleet, and **Solomons** to the south is not far behind. If you prefer to fish from the shore, **Point Lookout State Park** in St. Mary's County has a large fishing pier on the bay as well as designated areas for shore fishing in the bay and on the Potomac.

For freshwater and fly-fishing, head west to **Deep Creek Lake** and the rivers of Garrett County. The **Casselman River** is reportedly the best place for fly-fishing in the area, but the **Youghiogheny** and the **North**

Branch of the **Potomac** are also good bets. Ice fishing is also growing in popularity in and around Deep Creek Lake.

For information and fishing regulations in Maryland, contact the **Department of Natural Resources Fisheries Service** at ⓒ 800/628-9944 or 410/267-7740. In Delaware, contact the **Delaware Division of Fish and Wildlife** at ⓒ 302/739-3498.

GOLFING   Maryland and Delaware have the Atlantic coast's highest concentration of courses. Most are in and around Ocean City, Maryland, or just across the border in Delaware. **Ocean City Golf Getaway** (ⓒ 800/4-OC-GOLF) publishes a guide to all the area courses and can arrange golf vacation packages with many area hotels and courses. Or visit www.oceancitygolf.com.

Rocky Gap Lodge and Golf Resort at Rocky Gap State Park near Cumberland, Maryland, is among the state's best. This 18-hole Jack Nicklaus signature opened in 2001. And it's in a beautiful location, next to Lake Habeeb in the Allegheny Mountains.

HIKING   &   BACKPACKING Opportunities for hiking abound in both states, but for serious hikers and backpackers, Western Maryland offers the most challenging and scenic trails. The **Appalachian Trail** runs through Maryland along the border of Frederick and Washington counties. Farther west, **Savage River State Forest** offers miles of hiking and multiuse trails and welcomes backcountry campers. The Big Savage Trail, a 17-mile (27km) hike along the ridge of Big Savage Mountain, is a good option for backpackers.

The **C&O Canal towpath**, a popular route for cyclists, is also a good place for a less strenuous hike. It runs along the canal and the Potomac River from Georgetown to Cumberland and

is generally flat. You can also pick up the trail from several places near Frederick. The **Mountain Club of Maryland** (MCM), 4106 Eierman Ave., Baltimore, MD 21206, provides information about specific trails and schedules hikes that nonmembers can participate in for a small fee. For information and a copy of the hike schedule, call ⓒ 410/377-6266 or visit their website at www.mcomd.org.

HUNTING   Hunting is a popular sport in both states. Because of its location on the Atlantic Flyway, the Eastern Shore, especially Talbot County and Cambridge, is a popular destination for autumn **duck** and **goose hunting.** Goose hunting has returned after a moratorium and the excitement level is high. Many hotels and inns there cater to hunters, and outfitters will plan hunting vacations.

Several state parks and federal wildlife refuges in Delaware are open at selected times for **small game, deer,** and wildlife hunting. For information on hunting in Delaware, contact the **Division of Fish and Wildlife,** 89 Kings Hwy., Dover, DE 19901 (ⓒ 302/739-3498).

RAFTING/CANOEING/KAYAK-ING   It's easy to find river trips for all ages and skill levels, from flat-water trips in Southern Delaware and the Eastern Shore to the raging class IV and V rapids of the **Youghiogheny** and **Savage** rivers in Western Maryland. The best time for river adventures is March through June, after the snow melts and the river levels rise. Summer trips are quite popular, but falling water levels make the trips much tamer.

There are many rivers on the Delmarva Peninsula good for flat-water canoeing. The **Nanticoke River** canoe trail in Southern Delaware at Trapp Pond State Park is perhaps the most beautiful, meandering through the northernmost stand of bald cypress in the country. On Maryland's Eastern Shore, the waters around **Blackwater National Wildlife Refuge** and the **Pocomoke River** north of Snow Hill are also good scenic canoe runs. On all flat-water trips in summer, you should come prepared to deal with the mosquito and biting fly populations.

Maryland is known for the abundance of white water in its western counties. In general, the farther west you go, the rougher the water; so for novices and first-timers, the creeks and rivers in Frederick and Washington counties are best. Several outfitters offer rafting trips down the **Shenandoah/ Potomac,** a class II/III river, as well as canoeing, kayaking, and tubing trips on nearby creeks. More experienced paddlers head for Garrett County, to the Youghiogheny and Savage rivers, both class IV/V. There are many outfitters in Maryland and nearby Ohiopyle, Pennsylvania, who offer rafting trips on the Youghiogheny and nearby rivers in West Virginia. The Savage is a dam-release river, only runable during snowmelt, after heavy rains, or following dam releases. For a release schedule, call ℂ **814/533-8911.**

You don't need any experience to take a raft trip with an outfitter. However, the Savage and much of the Youghiogheny are very dangerous and should not be run by inexperienced paddlers without a guide. If you are an experienced paddler and would like to run these or any of Maryland's and Delaware's rivers or creeks on your own, pick up a copy of *Maryland and Delaware Canoe Trails* (Seneca Press, 1996) by Edward Gertler. It is the definitive guide for this region.

SAILING   Annapolis is often called the "sailing capital of the world." In 2002, Annapolis hosted sailors from around the globe during the Volvo Ocean Race. Even on a regular day, sailing vessels fill the harbor. There are at least five sailing schools, countless places to charter bareboat or crewed sailboats, and companies that offer sailing/sightseeing trips on the harbor and nearby waterways. Some companies even offer overnight boat-and-breakfast trips and 2- or 3-day excursions on the bay.

SEA KAYAKING   With easy access to the ocean and the many bays and inlets along the coast, the beach resorts on the Atlantic coast offer a good base from which to do some sea kayaking. Chincoteague Bay at the Maryland end of Assateague Island is a favorite for kayakers with some paddling experience.

On the other side of the Chesapeake, a few companies offer sea-kayaking harbor tours in Annapolis and Baltimore as well as trips in different locations around the Bay. **Amphibious Horizons** (ℂ 410/267-8742; www. amphibioushorizons.com) operates out of Annapolis.

SKIING   Maryland is not a great skiing destination, but it does have one downhill ski resort and several miles of cross-country trails. **Wisp** near Deep Creek Lake has 23 trails and a vertical rise of 610 feet. It's a good place for beginners and intermediate skiers with only a few black-diamond trails. You'll find the best trails and facilities for cross-country skiing at **New Germany State Park** and **Herrington Manor State Park,** also in Garrett County. The season runs from about the end of November through mid-March. For ski conditions, call ℂ **301/387-4000.**

OUTFITTERS & ADVENTURE TOUR OPERATORS

Because the region is relatively compact and accessible, most outdoor adventures can be planned through local outfitters as day trips. Generally you'll have to make reservations a few days to a week in advance for sea kayaking and white-water rafting or kayaking trips. To charter a fishing boat or a sailboat, reserve farther in advance (a month or more) for peak season, especially summer weekends. Outfitters for specific sports are listed in the appropriate regional chapters.

If you're trying to plan a more extensive adventure vacation, there are a few places you can contact. The **Adventuresports Institute,** P.O. Box 151, 687 Mosser Rd., McHenry, MD 21541 (© **301/387-3032**), is actually a division of Garrett Community College, but its classes are open to the public. The institute offers weekend classes in white-water paddling, rock climbing, mountain biking, orienteering, camping, cross-country and Alpine skiing, sea kayaking, sailing,

and even fly-fishing. Classes cost about $300 for out-of-state students. The downside is that you have to plan your vacation to coincide with the class you wish to take.

Allegany Expeditions, Route 2, Box 88, Cumberland, MD 21502, can organize a variety of outdoor adventures, including hiking, biking, caving, canoeing, backpacking, and rock climbing. Call © **800/819-5170** or 301/722-5170 for information and reservations. Hunting and fishing trips on the Eastern Shore can be arranged through **Albright's Sportsman's Travel Service,** 36 Dover St., Easton, MD 21601 (© **800/474-5502**).

6 Insurance, Health & Safety

TRAVEL INSURANCE AT A GLANCE

Check your existing policies before you buy travel insurance to cover trip cancellation, lost luggage, medical expenses, or car rental insurance. You're likely to have partial or complete coverage. But if you need some, ask your travel agent about a comprehensive package. The cost of travel insurance varies, depending on the cost and length of your trip, your age and overall health, and the type of trip you're taking. Insurance for extreme sports or adventure travel, for example, will cost more than coverage for a cruise. Some insurers provide packages for specialty vacations, such as skiing or backpacking. More dangerous activities may be excluded from basic policies.

For information, contact one of the following popular insurers:

- **Access America** (© 800/284-8300; www.accessamerica.com/)
- **Travel Guard International** (© 800/826-1300; www.travelguard.com)
- **Travel Insured International** (© 800/243-3174; www.travelinsured.com)

- **Travelex Insurance Services** (© 800/228-9792; www.travelex-insurance.com)

TRIP-CANCELLATION INSURANCE (TCI)

There are three types of trip-cancellation insurance—one, in the event that you pre-pay a cruise or tour that gets cancelled, and you can't get your money back; a second when you or someone in your family gets sick or dies, and you can't travel (you may not be covered for a pre-existing condition); and a third, when bad weather makes travel impossible. Some insurers provide coverage for events like jury duty; natural disasters like floods or fire; even job loss. Some have provisions for cancellations due to terrorist activities. Check the fine print, don't buy trip-cancellation insurance from the tour operator that may be responsible for the cancellation; buy it from a reputable agency. Don't overbuy. You won't be reimbursed for more than the cost of your trip.

MEDICAL INSURANCE

Most health insurance policies cover you if you get sick away from home—but check, particularly if an HMO insures you.

Some credit cards offer automatic flight insurance against death or dismemberment in case of an airplane crash if you charged your ticket.

If you require additional insurance, try one of the following companies:

- **MEDEX International,** 9515 Deereco Rd., Timonium, MD 21093-5375 (℃ **888/MEDEX-00** or 410/453-6300; fax 410/453-6301; www.medexassist.com)
- Travel Assistance International (℃ **800/821-2828;** www.travel assistance.com), 9200 Keystone Crossing, Suite 300, Indianapolis, IN 46240. (For general information on services, call the company's Worldwide Assistance Services, Inc., at ℃ **800/777-8710.**)

Check to see if your medical insurance covers emergency medical evacuation: If you have to buy a one-way same-day ticket home and forfeit your nonrefundable round-trip ticket, you may be out big bucks.

LOST-LUGGAGE INSURANCE
On domestic flights, checked baggage is covered up to $2,500 per ticketed passenger. If you plan to check items more valuable than the standard liability, you may purchase "excess valuation" coverage from the airline, up to $5,000. Be sure to take any valuables or irreplaceable items in your carry-on luggage (security restrictions permitting). If you file a lost luggage claim, be prepared to answer detailed questions about the contents of your baggage, and be sure to file a claim immediately, as most airlines enforce a 21-day deadline. Before you leave home, compile an inventory of all packed items and a rough estimate of the total value. You will only be reimbursed for what you lost. Once you've filed a complaint, persist in securing your reimbursement; there are no laws governing the length of time it takes for a carrier to reimburse you. If you arrive at a destination without your bags, ask the airline to forward them to your hotel or next destination; they will usually comply. If your bag is delayed or lost, the airline may reimburse you for reasonable expenses, but is under no legal obligation to do so.

Lost luggage may also be covered by your homeowner's or renter's policy. Many platinum and gold credit cards cover you as well. If you choose to purchase additional lost-luggage insurance, buy it in advance from the insurer or a trusted agent (prices will be much higher at the airport).

CAR RENTAL INSURANCE (LOSS/DAMAGE WAIVER OR COLLISION DAMAGE WAIVER)
If you hold a private auto insurance policy, you probably are covered for loss or damage to the car, and liability in case a passenger is injured. The credit card you used to rent the card also may provide some coverage.

Car rental insurance probably does not cover liability if you caused the accident. Check your own insurance policy, the rental company policy, and your credit card coverage for the extent of coverage: Is your destination covered? Are other drivers covered? How much liability is covered if a passenger is injured? (If you rely on your credit card for coverage, you may want to bring a second credit card with you, as damages may be charged to your card and you may find yourself stranded with no money.)

This insurance costs about $20 a day.

THE HEALTHY TRAVELER
Maryland and Delaware don't pose any unusual health risks to the average visitor. If you're hiking or camping east of Washington, D.C., be aware that this is deer tick country, and deer ticks can carry **Lyme disease.** Wear

long sleeves and pants tucked into your socks, cover your head, and inspect yourself for ticks after the trip. Insect repellent containing DEET also helps repel the ticks. After your trip, watch for a bull's eye-shaped rash that can appear 3 days to a month following infection (but be aware that not everyone who is infected will get the rash). There is now a vaccine available for Lyme disease. Consult your doctor if you're planning to take an extensive trip to deer tick–infested areas.

Travelers to the Eastern Shore, especially anglers and boaters, should be aware of the occasional fish kills caused by *Pfiesteria* during the summer. *Pfiesteria* are microscopic marine organisms that under certain circumstances release a chemical toxin that causes lesions on fish and even large-scale fish kills. Some human health effects, including skin lesions, light-headedness, short-term memory loss, and headaches, have been documented among researchers working with high concentrations of the organisms and among watermen working in affected areas.

Pfiesteria have been detected in several parts of the Chesapeake Bay and nearby rivers, and are known to occur all along the coast from the Gulf of Mexico to the Delaware Bay. However, the presence of the organisms is not cause for alarm; certain conditions not yet understood must be met in order for them to become toxic to fish and harmful to humans. Visitors should simply avoid those waters recently affected by fish kills and use common sense. Do not swim or water-ski in an area closed due to a fish kill. Do not handle fish with lesions. Any fish or shellfish you buy in the grocery store or at restaurants are safe to eat, but if you're catching your own, never eat fish with sores or that seem diseased.

For more information on health issues related to *Pfiesteria*, call Maryland's Department of Health and Mental Hygiene for the county you are visiting. The general information number is ✆ **410/767-6860.** To report fish lesions in Maryland waters, call the Department of Natural Resources' 24-hour hotline at ✆ **888/584-3110.** Maryland DNR also has information about *Pfiesteria* on its website at www.dnr.state.md.us/pfiesteria.

WHAT TO DO IF YOU GET SICK AWAY FROM HOME

If you worry about getting sick away from home, consider purchasing **medical travel insurance** and carry your ID card in your purse or wallet. In most cases, your existing health plan will provide the coverage you need. See the section on insurance earlier in this chapter for more information.

If you suffer from a chronic illness, consult your doctor before your departure. For conditions like epilepsy, diabetes, or heart problems, wear a **Medic Alert Identification Tag** (✆ **800/825-3785;** www.medicalert.org), which will alert doctors to your condition and give them access to your records through Medic Alert's 24-hour hotline.

Pack **prescription medications** in your carry-on luggage, and carry prescription medications in their original containers. Bring copies of your prescriptions in case you lose your pills or run out.

And don't forget sunglasses and an extra pair of contact lenses or prescription glasses.

If you do get sick, you may want to ask your innkeeper or your hotel's concierge to recommend a local doctor. If you can't find a doctor who can help you right away, go to the emergency room at the local hospital or an urgent care center.

SAFETY

While most of Maryland and Delaware enjoy relatively low crime rates, Baltimore has a nagging problem with property and violent crime, and Wilmington also has neighborhoods where tourists are advised not to go. The major tourist areas of both cities are fairly well policed, but be alert and follow common-sense precautions.

If you're using public transport, it's best to travel during the day and to keep valuables out of sight. It is safer and smarter to drive or take a cab between neighborhoods (unless otherwise noted) rather than to walk, even when the distance is not too great. Keep a good city map at hand to help you out if you're lost. Neighborhoods go from safe to scary in a matter of a few blocks. It's best to keep on the main routes and turn around if anything looks worrisome.

In parts of Baltimore and Wilmington, panhandlers may approach you. Don't open your wallet or purse to give money. Offer only what's in your pocket. It's okay to say no, too.

7 Tips for Travelers with Special Needs

FOR TRAVELERS WITH DISABILITIES

Most hotels in Maryland and Delaware, including many bed-and-breakfasts and inns, offer accessible accommodations, but be sure to ask when you make reservations; we've noted B&Bs with accessible accommodations in reviews. Nearly all of the states' museums are accessible, with the exception of some historic buildings and sites. The state and county tourism offices listed in "Visitor Information" and in the individual chapters can help you locate accessible accommodations and answer any questions about specific historic sites.

The **Maryland Relay Service** (© **800/735-2258** TTY) and the **Delaware Relay Service** (© **800/ 232-5460** TTY) link standard voice telephones with text-telephone users. Several state parks in Maryland offer accessible facilities. A complete list is available from the Maryland DNR website at www.dnr.state.md.us/public lands/accessforall.html.

Many of the major car-rental companies now offer hand-controlled cars for disabled drivers. Avis can provide such a vehicle at any of its locations in the United States with 48-hour advance notice; Hertz requires between 24 and 72 hours of advance reservation at most of its locations.

Wheelchair Getaways (© **800/873-4973;** www.blvd.com/wg.htm) rents vans with wheelchair lifts and other features for the disabled in more than 100 cities across the United States.

You can obtain a copy of *Air Transportation of Handicapped Persons* by writing for Free Advisory Circular No. AC12032, Distribution Unit, U.S. Department of Transportation, Publications Division, M-4332, Washington, DC 20590.

Amtrak (© **800/USA-RAIL;** www.amtrak.com) and **Greyhound** (© **800/752-4841;** www.greyhound. com) offer discounts and services for the disabled. Call at least a week before your trip for details.

The **National Park Service** issues free "Golden Access Passports," which entitle disabled people and a guest of their choice to free admission into national parks, forests, and wildlife refuges. Get them at park entrances.

Vision-impaired travelers should contact the **American Foundation for the Blind,** 11 Penn Plaza, Suite 300, New York, NY 10001 (© **800/232-5463**), for information on traveling with Seeing Eye dogs.

AGENCIES/OPERATORS

- **Flying Wheels Travel** (© **800/ 535-6790;** www.flyingwheelstravel. com) offers escorted tours and cruises that emphasize sports and private tours in minivans with lifts.

- **Access Adventures** (© 716/889-9096), a Rochester, New York–based agency, offers customized itineraries for a variety of travelers with disabilities.
- **Accessible Journeys** (© 800/TINGLES or 610/521-0339; www.disabilitytravel.com) caters specifically to slow walkers and wheelchair travelers and their families and friends.

ORGANIZATIONS

- **The Moss Rehab Hospital** (© 215/456-9603; www.moss resourcenet.org) provides friendly, helpful phone assistance through its **Travel Information Service.**
- **The Society for Accessible Travel and Hospitality** (SATH) (© 212/447-7284; fax 212-725-8253; www.sath.org) offers a wealth of travel resources for all types of disabilities and informed recommendations on destinations, access guides, travel agents, tour operators, vehicle rentals, and companion services. Annual membership costs $45 for adults; $30 for seniors and students.
- **The American Foundation for the Blind** (© 800/232-5463; www.afb.org) provides information on traveling with Seeing Eye dogs.

PUBLICATIONS

- **Mobility International USA** (© 541/343-1284; www.miusa. org) publishes *A World of Options*, a 658-page book of resources, covering everything from biking trips to scuba outfitters, and a newsletter, *Over the Rainbow.* Annual membership is $35.
- **Twin Peaks Press** (© 360/694-2462) publishes books for travelers with special needs.

- *Open World for Disability and Mature Travel* magazine, published by SATH (see above), is full of resources and information. A year's subscription is $13 ($21 outside the U.S.).

GAY & LESBIAN TRAVELERS

In Baltimore, the main resource for gay and lesbians is the **Gay and Lesbian Community Center of Baltimore** (241 W. Chase St., Baltimore, MD 21201; © 410/837-5445). The center also produces the *Baltimore Gay Paper* (© 410/837-7748; www. bgp.org), twice a month, available for free at area restaurants, nightclubs, bars, and bookstores.

Rehoboth Beach, Delaware, calls itself the "Nation's Gay Summer Capital." The website www.gayrehoboth. com provides a list of gay-friendly hotels and B&Bs and information on nightlife and beaches.

The International Gay & Lesbian Travel Association (IGLTA) (© 800/448-8550 or 954/776-2626; fax 954/776-3303; www.iglta.org) links travelers with gay-friendly hoteliers, tour operators, and airline and cruise-line representatives. It offers monthly newsletters, marketing mailings, and a membership directory that's updated once a year. Membership is $150 yearly, plus a $100 administration fee for new members.

AGENCIES/OPERATORS

- **Above and Beyond Tours** (© 800/397-2681; www.above beyondtours.com) offers gay and lesbian tours worldwide and is the exclusive gay and lesbian tour operator for United Airlines.
- **Now, Voyager** (© 800/255-6951; www.nowvoyager.com) is a San Francisco–based gay-owned and operated travel service.

PUBLICATIONS

- *Out and About* (© 800/929-2268 or 415/644-8044;

www.outandabout.com) offers guidebooks and a newsletter 10 times a year with information on gay and lesbian travel issues.

- *Spartacus International Gay Guide* and *Odysseus* are annual English-language guidebooks focused on gay men, with some information for lesbians. You can get them from most gay and lesbian bookstores, or order them from **Giovanni's Room** bookstore, 1145 Pine St., Philadelphia, PA 19107 (© **215/923-2960;** www.giovannisroom.com).
- *Gay Travel A to Z: The World of Gay & Lesbian Travel Options at Your Fingertips,* by Marianne Ferrari (Ferrari Publications; www.ferrariguides.com), is a good gay and lesbian guidebook series.

FOR SENIORS

Mention the fact that you're a senior citizen when you make your travel reservations. All major airlines and many hotels offer discounts for seniors. Major airlines also offer coupons for domestic travel for seniors over 60. Typically, a book of four coupons costs less than $700, which means you can fly anywhere in the continental U.S. for under $350 round-trip. In most cities, people over the age of 60 qualify for reduced admission to theaters, museums, and other attractions, as well as discounted fares on public transportation.

Amtrak (© **800/USA-RAIL;** www.amtrak.com) and **Greyhound** (© **800/752-4841;** www.greyhound.com) offer discounts to persons over 62. And many hotels offer seniors discounts; Choice Hotels (Clarion Hotels, Quality Inns, Comfort Inns, Sleep Inns, Econo Lodges, Friendship Inns, and Rodeway Inns), for example, give 30% off their published rates to anyone over 50, provided you book your room through their toll-free reservations numbers (not directly with the hotels or through a travel agent). In most cities, people over the age of 60 qualify for reduced admission to theaters, museums, and other attractions, and discounted fares on public transportation.

Members of **AARP** (formerly the American Association of Retired Persons), 601 E St. NW, Washington, DC 20049 (© **800/424-3410** or 202/434-2277; www.aarp.org), get discounts on hotels, airfares, and car rentals. AARP offers members a wide range of benefits, including *Modern Maturity* magazine and a monthly newsletter. Anyone over 50 can join.

The Alliance for Retired Americans, 8403 Colesville Rd., Suite 1200, Silver Spring, MD 20910 (© **301/578-8422;** www.retiredamericans.org), offers a newsletter and discounts on hotel and auto rentals; annual dues are $13. *Note:* Members of the former National Council of Senior Citizens receive automatic membership in the Alliance.

AGENCIES/OPERATORS

- **Grand Circle Travel** (© **800/221-2610** or 617/350-7500; www.gct.com) offers package deals for the 50-plus market, mostly of the tour-bus variety, with free trips thrown in for those who organize groups of 10 or more.
- **SAGA Holidays** (© **800/343-0273;** www.sagaholidays.com) offers tours and cruises for those 50 and older. SAGA also offers a number of single-traveler tours and sponsors the "Road Scholar Tours" (© **800/621-2151;** sales info@sagaholidays.com), vacations with an educational bent. Order a brochure from the website.
- **Elderhostel** (© **877/426-8056;** www.elderhostel.org) arranges study programs for those aged 55 and over (and a spouse or companion of any age) in the U.S. and in more than 80 countries around

the world. Most courses last 5 to 7 days in the U.S. (2 to 4 weeks abroad), and many include airfare, accommodations in university dormitories or modest inns, meals, and tuition.

- **Interhostel** (© **800/733-9753**; www.learn.unh.edu/interhostel), organized by the University of New Hampshire, also offers educational travel for senior citizens. On these escorted tours, the days are packed with seminars, lectures, and field trips, with sightseeing led by academic experts. **Interhostel** takes travelers 50 and over (with companions over 40), and offers 1- and 2-week trips, mostly international.

PUBLICATIONS

- *The Book of Deals* is a collection of more than 1,000 senior discounts on airlines, lodging, tours, and attractions around the country; it's available for $9.95 by calling © **800/460-6676.**
- *101 Tips for the Mature Traveler* is available from Grand Circle Travel (© **800/221-2610** or 617/350-7500; fax 617/346-6700).
- *The 50+ Traveler's Guidebook* (St. Martin's Press).
- *Unbelievably Good Deals and Great Adventures That You Absolutely Can't Get Unless You're Over 50* (Contemporary Publishing Co.).

FAMILY TRAVEL

The family vacation is a rite of passage for many households, one that in a second can devolve into a *National Lampoon* farce. But as any veteran family vacationer will assure you, a family trip can be among the most rewarding times of your life.

Maryland and Delaware are very child- and family-friendly destinations (with a few exceptions noted in specific chapters) and you'll find many "family-style" restaurants and resorts, and even museums for young people, like Baltimore's Port Discovery and the Enchanted Garden in the Winterthur Estate in Delaware.

AGENCIES/OPERATORS

Familyhostel (© **800/733-9753**; www.learn.unh.edu/familyhostel) takes the whole family on moderately priced domestic and international learning vacations. The program staff handles all trip details, and a team of academic offers, talks and field trips. Trips are for kids ages 8 to 15 accompanied by their parents and/or grandparents.

PUBLICATIONS

Some publications you might find useful in preparing a family vacation to Maryland and Delaware include:

- *Frommer's Washington, D.C., with Kids*
- *The Unofficial Guide to the Mid-Atlantic with Kids*
- *How to Take Great Trips with Your Kids* (The Harvard Common Press) is full of good advice that can apply to travel anywhere.

WEBSITES

- **Family Travel Network** (www. familytravelnetwork.com) offers travel tips and reviews of family-friendly destinations, vacation deals, and thoughtful features such as "What to Do When Your Kids Are Afraid to Travel" and "Kid-Style Camping."
- **Travel with Your Children** (www.travelwithyourkids.com) is a comprehensive site offering sound advice for traveling with children.
- **The Busy Person's Guide to Travel with Children** (http://wz.com/travel/TravelingWith Children.html) offers a "45-second newsletter" where experts weigh in on the best resources for traveling with children.

TRAVELING WITH PETS

Many of us wouldn't dream of going on vacation without our pets. These days, more and more lodgings and restaurants are going the pet-friendly route. Many hotel and motel chains, such as Best Western, Motel 6, Holiday Inn, and Four Seasons-Regent Hotels, welcome pets. Policies vary, so always call ahead.

An excellent resource is www. petswelcome.com, which offers medical tips, names of animal-friendly lodgings and campgrounds, and lists of kennels and veterinarians. Also check out *The Portable Petswelcome. com: The Complete Guide to Traveling with Your Pet* (Howell Book House), which features the best selection of pet travel information anywhere. Another resource is *Pets-R-Permitted Hotel, Motel & Kennel Directory: The Travel Resource for Pet Owners Who Travel* (Annenberg Communications).

If you plan to fly with your pet, check the FAA's requirements for transporting live animals at www.dot. gov/airconsumer/animals.htm. You may be able to carry your pet on board if it's small enough to put inside a carrier that can slip under the seat. Pets usually count as one piece of carry-on luggage. *Note:* Summer may not be the best time to fly with your pet. Many airlines will not check pets as baggage in the summer. The ASPCA discourages travelers from checking pets as luggage any time, as storage conditions on planes are loosely monitored, and fatal accidents have occurred. Your other option is to ship your pet with a professional carrier, which can be expensive.

Dogs are prohibited on hiking trails and must be leashed at all times on National Park Service (national parks and monuments) lands. We've indicated in the listings for individual sites whether pets are permitted.

8 Getting There

BY PLANE

The gateway to Maryland is **Baltimore–Washington International Airport** (BWI), 10 miles (16km) south of Baltimore and 20 miles (32km) north of Annapolis. Hundreds of domestic and international flights arrive daily, and it is a hub for several airlines. Most cities and towns are also convenient to **Washington Dulles International Airport** and **Ronald Reagan Washington National Airport.**

Most major airlines fly into BWI, including **Air Canada** (© 800/776-3000), **American** (© 800/433-7300), **British Airways** (© 800/247-9297), **Continental** (© 800/525-0280), **Delta** (© 800/221-1212), **Northwest** (© 800/225-2525), **Southwest** (© 800/435-9792), **United** (© 800/241-6522), and **US Airways** (© 800/428-4322).

Commuter flights fly into **Wicomico Regional Airport** on Maryland's Eastern Shore and **Cumberland Regional Airport** in western Maryland.

Delaware does not have its own major airport. Located within easy reach is **Philadelphia International Airport,** 30 minutes from downtown Wilmington and 1½ hours from Dover; and **BWI,** approximately 1½ to 2½ hours to most points in Delaware; and **Dulles International Airport** and **Ronald Reagan Washington National Airport,** approximately 2½ to 3 hours to most points in Delaware. In addition, **New Castle County Airport,** about 10 miles (16km) south of Wilmington, serves private craft and some limited commercial flights.

Tips What You Can—and Can't—Carry On

The Federal Aviation Administration (FAA) has new **restrictions** for carry-on baggage, not only to expedite the screening process but to prevent potential weapons from passing through airport security. The agency has released a new list of items passengers may not carry onto an aircraft. For more detailed information, go to the FAA's website, www.faa.gov.

Not permitted: Knives and box cutters, corkscrews, straight razors, metal scissors, metal nail files, golf clubs, baseball bats, pool cues, hockey sticks, ski poles, ice picks.

Permitted: Nail clippers, tweezers, eyelash curlers, safety razors (including disposable razors), syringes (with documented proof of medical need), walking canes, and umbrellas (must be inspected first).

The airline you fly may have **additional restrictions** on items you can and cannot carry on board. Call ahead to avoid problems.

NEW AIR TRAVEL SECURITY MEASURES

In the wake of the terrorist attacks of September 11, 2001, the airline industry implemented sweeping security measures in airports. Expect a lengthy check-in process and extensive delays. Although regulations vary from airline to airline, you can expedite the process by taking the following steps:

- **Arrive early:** At least 2 hours before your scheduled flight.
- **Try not to drive your car to the airport.** Parking and curbside access to the terminal may be limited. Call ahead and check.
- **Don't count on curbside check-in.** Some airlines and airports have stopped it altogether, while others offer it on a limited basis. For information on its availability, check with the individual airline.
- **Be sure to carry plenty of documentation.** A government-issued photo ID (federal, state, or local) is required. With an E-ticket, you may be required to show printed confirmation of purchase, and the credit card with which you bought your ticket (see "All about

E-Ticketing," below). This varies from airline to airline, so call to make sure you have the proper documentation. Be sure that your ID is **up-to-date:** an expired driver's license, for example, may keep you from boarding altogether.

- **Know what you can carry on—and what you can't.** Travelers in the United States are limited to one carry-on bag, plus one personal bag (like a purse or a briefcase). The FAA has also issued a list of newly restricted carry-on items.
- **Prepare to be searched.** Electronic items, such as a laptop computer or cell phone, should be readied for screening. Limit the metal items you wear.
- **It's no joke.** When a check-in agent asks security-related questions, don't play the clown. You could end up not only missing your flight, but under arrest.
- **No ticket, no gate access.** Only ticketed passengers will be allowed beyond the screener checkpoints, except for those people with specific medical or parental needs.

FLYING FOR LESS: TIPS FOR GETTING THE BEST AIRFARE

Passengers within the same airplane cabin are rarely paying the same fare. Business travelers who need tickets at the last minute, change their itinerary at a moment's notice, or get home for the weekend pay the premium rate. Passengers who can book in advance, who can stay over Saturday night, or who are willing to travel Tuesday, Wednesday, or Thursday after 7pm, will pay a fraction of the full fare.

For example, a round-trip from Denver to Baltimore, booked 2 days in advance is $850; round-trip from Denver to Baltimore booked 3 weeks in advance is $328; round-trip from Denver to D.C. (Dulles), booked 3 weeks in advance, is $198.

- Airlines periodically lower prices on their most popular routes. Check the travel section of your Sunday newspaper or call the airlines directly and ask if any **promotional rates** or special fares are available. You'll almost never see a sale during the peak vacation months of July and August, or during the Thanksgiving or Christmas seasons; but in periods of low-volume travel, you should pay no more than $400 for a domestic cross-country flight. If your schedule is flexible, say so, and ask if you can secure a cheaper fare by staying an extra day, flying midweek, or fat less-trafficked hours. If you already hold a ticket when a sale breaks, it may even pay to exchange it, which usually incurs a $100 to $150 charge.

  Note: The lowest-priced fares are often nonrefundable, require advance purchase and a length of stay, and carry penalties for changing dates.

- **Consolidators,** also known as "bucket shops," buy seats in bulk from the airlines and then sell them back to the public at prices usually below even the airlines' discounted rates. Their ads usually run in Sunday newspaper travel sections. Before you pay, request a confirmation number from the consolidator and then call the airline to confirm your seat. Bucket shop tickets are usually nonrefundable or have stiff cancellation penalties. Protect yourself by paying with a credit card rather than cash. Keep in mind that if there's an airline sale going on, or if it's

---

Tips   All About E-Ticketing

Only yesterday **electronic tickets (E-tickets)** were the fast, ticket-free alternative to paper tickets. E-tickets allowed passengers to avoid lines at check-in, and saved airlines money on postage and labor. With increased security measures, however, an E-ticket no longer guarantees an accelerated check-in. You often can't go straight to the boarding gate, even if you have no bags to check. You'll need to show your printed E-ticket receipt or confirmation of purchase, as well as a photo ID, and sometimes the credit card with which you purchased your E-ticket. That said, buying an E-ticket is still a convenient way to book a flight; instead of having to wait for a paper ticket in the mail, you can book your fare by phone or on the computer, and the airline will confirm by fax or e-mail. In addition, airlines often offer extra frequent flier miles as incentive for electronic bookings.

Tips Don't Just Fly to BWI

Check all the airports in the Maryland/DC area: **Reagan National, Dulles,** and **BWI,** when scouting for low fares. With sales and promotions, the fare to one may be significantly lower than to the others. All three are accessible to the major destinations in the region.

---

high season, you can often get the same or better rates by contacting the airlines directly, so comparison shop.

Council Travel (© 800/226-8624; www.counciltravel.com) and **STA Travel** (© **800/781-4040;** www.sta.travel.com) cater to young travelers, but their bargain-basement prices are available to everyone. **The TravelHub** (© **888/ AIR-FARE;** www.travelhub.com) represents nearly 1,000 travel agencies, many of whom offer consolidator and discount fares. Other reliable consolidators are **1-800-FLY-CHEAP** (www.1800 flycheap.com); or "rebators" like **Travel Avenue** (© **800/333-3335;** www.travelavenue.com), that rebate part of their commissions to you.

- Search **the Internet** for cheap fares. Last-minute deals are available through weekly e-mail services provided by the airlines. See "Planning Your Trip Online," below, for more information.
- Join a travel club like **Moment's Notice** (© **718/234-6295;** www.moments-notice.com) or **Sears Discount Travel Club** (© **800/ 433-9383** or 800/255-1487; www.travelersadvantage.com), which supply unsold tickets at discounted prices. You pay an annual membership fee to get the club's hotline number. Of course, you're limited to what's available, so you have to be flexible.

- Join **frequent-flier clubs.** It's best to accrue miles on one program, so you can rack up free flights and achieve elite status faster. But it makes sense to open as many accounts as possible, no matter how seldom you fly a particular airline. It's free, and you'll get the best choice of seats, faster response to phone inquiries, and prompter service if your luggage is stolen, your flight is canceled or delayed, or you want to change your seat.

BY CAR

The eastern seaboard's major north–south link from Maine to Florida, **I-95,** passes through both states via Wilmington and Newark in Delaware and Baltimore and central Maryland. Other interstate highways that traverse Maryland are **I-83,** which connects Baltimore with Harrisburg and points north; **I-70** and **I-68,** which connect Western Maryland to the rest of the state and to Pennsylvania, West Virginia, and Ohio. There are no other interstates in Delaware, but to access the state from Maryland and points south, use U.S. **Routes 13** or **113.**

Tips DWI Gets Tougher in Maryland

As of January 1, 2002, a blood-alcohol level of .08 (lowered from .10) or greater will get you charged with drunk driving.

> **Tips On the Road to Maryland & Delaware**
>
> If you'll be driving to Maryland and Delaware, here are a couple of tips that can save you time and money:
>
> - **Keep the EZ-Pass in the window.** The computerized system for paying tolls (via a transponder tag on your windshield), called EZ-Pass in New York, Pennsylvania, Delaware, and New Jersey, and Fast Lane in Massachusetts, is accepted along most of the major highways along the East Coast, and can be used in the "M-Tag" lanes on toll highways, bridges, and tunnels in Maryland. Along with being able to use dedicated EZ-Pass lanes, you are charged a lower fee than the cash toll.
> - **The long way around may be the shortest way home.** Interstates in the Mid-Atlantic (particularly I-95) are frequently backed up to the point of paralysis, particularly on weekends and holidays. On a state map or road atlas, note which local roads parallel the major thoroughfares. They may only be two lanes with traffic signals and a 45 mph speed limit, but you'll still make better time on U.S. Route 40 from Baltimore to the Delaware Memorial Bridge than I-295 on a Sunday evening (with cheaper fuel and food available than at the rest stops on the interstates). U.S. Route 130 in New Jersey parallels I-95 (the Jersey Turnpike); and particularly when the backup at Exit 1 gets to be several miles long, it's far less frustrating to motor down a local highway, and cheaper (no tolls).

BY TRAIN

Amtrak (✆ **800/USA-RAIL;** www.amtrak.com) offers frequent daily service to Baltimore at Pennsylvania Station (downtown) and BWI Airport Rail Station and into Wilmington at the Amtrak station at Martin Luther King Boulevard and French Street. Amtrak also offers more limited daily service to Newark, Delaware; and Aberdeen and New Carrollton, Maryland; and limited service to and from the west at Cumberland and Rockville, Maryland. A new high-speed service, Acela, runs along the Northeast Corridor.

Maryland Area Rail Commuter (MARC; ✆ **800/325-RAIL**) service runs between Washington, D.C., and Baltimore during the week. MARC also serves Western Maryland in Brunswick and Frederick.

BY BUS

Greyhound (✆ **800/231-2222;** www.greyhound.com) serves major points in Maryland and Delaware, including Wilmington, Dover, Rehoboth Beach, Baltimore, Ocean City, Easton, Frederick, and Cumberland, with express service from New York City to Newark, Delaware, and Baltimore (downtown and East Baltimore's Travel Plaza) via Greyhound and Peter Pan/Trailways (use Greyhound phone/website for schedule information).

BY FERRY

The **Cape May–Lewes Ferry** travels daily between southern New Jersey and the lower Delaware coast. This 70-minute crossing is operated on a drive-on, drive-off basis and can accommodate up to 800 passengers and 100 cars. Full details on the ferry are given in chapter 9, "Maryland & Delaware's Atlantic Beaches."

9 Planning Your Trip Online

Researching and booking your trip online can save time and money. Then again, it may not. You don't always get the best deal online. Most booking engines do not include schedules and prices for budget airlines, and from time to time you'll get a better last-minute price by calling the airline directly, so don't restrict your search for bargains to the Internet.

On the plus side, Internet users can tap into the same travel-planning databases once accessible only to travel agents. Sites such as **Frommers.com**, **Travelocity.com**, **Expedia.com**, and **Orbitz.com** allow consumers to comparison shop for airfares, access special bargains, book flights, and reserve hotel rooms and rental cars.

But don't fire your travel agent just yet. Although online sites offer tips and data, they cannot endow you with the experience that makes a reliable travel agent an invaluable resource. For consumers with a complex itinerary, a good travel agent is still the best way to arrange the most direct flights.

Still, the benefits of researching your trip online can be well worth the effort.

Last-minute specials, such as weekend deals or Internet-only fares, are offered by airlines to fill empty seats. Most are announced on Tuesday or Wednesday and must be purchased online. They are only valid for travel that weekend, but some can be booked weeks or months in advance. Sign up for weekly e-mail alerts at airline websites or check mega-sites that compile comprehensive lists of last-minute specials, such as **Smarter Living** (smarterliving.com) or **WebFlyer** (www.webflyer.com).

Some sites, such as Expedia.com, will send you **e-mail notification** when a cheap fare becomes available to your destination. Some will also tell you when fares to a destination are lowest. Keep in mind that because several airlines are no longer willing to pay commissions on tickets sold by online travel agencies, these agencies may either add a $10 surcharge to your bill if you book on that carrier—or neglect to offer those carriers' schedules.

The list of sites below is selective, not comprehensive. Some sites may have evolved or even disappeared by the time you read this.

Tips Frommers.com: The Complete Travel Resource

For an excellent travel-planning resource, we highly recommend Frommers.com (www.frommers.com). We're a little biased, of course, but we guarantee that you'll find the travel tips, reviews, monthly vacation giveaways, and online-booking capabilities thoroughly indispensable. Among the special features are our popular Message Boards, where Frommer's readers post queries and share advice (sometimes even our authors show up to answer questions); Frommers.com Newsletter, for the latest travel bargains and inside travel secrets; and Frommer's Destinations Section, where you'll get expert travel tips, hotel and dining recommendations, and advice on the sights to see for more than 2,500 destinations around the globe. When your research is done, the Online Reservation System (www.frommers.com/booktravelnow) takes you to Frommer's favorite sites for booking your vacation at affordable prices. Travel Planning & Booking Sites

- **Travelocity** (www.travelocity.com or www.frommers.travelocity.com) and **Expedia** (www.expedia.com) are among the most popular sites, each offering an excellent range of options. Travelers search by destination, dates, and cost.
- **Orbitz** (www.orbitz.com) is a popular site launched by United, Delta, Northwest, American, and Continental airlines. (Stay tuned: At press time, travel-agency associations were waging an antitrust battle against this site.)
- **Qixo** (www.qixo.com) is another powerful search engine that allows you to search for flights and accommodations from some 20 airline and travel-planning sites (such as Travelocity) at once. Qixo sorts results by price.
- **Priceline** (www.priceline.com) lets you "name your price" for airline tickets, hotel rooms, and rental cars. For airline tickets, you can't say what time you want to fly—you have to accept any flight between 6am and 10pm on the dates you've selected, and you may have to make one or more stopovers. Tickets are nonrefundable, and frequent-flyer miles are not officially awarded (though we always ask at the airport, and have sometimes received the miles).

SMART E-SHOPPING
The savvy traveler is armed with insider information. Here are a few tips to help you navigate the Internet successfully and safely.

- **Know when sales start.** Last-minute deals may vanish in minutes. If you have a favorite site or airline, find out when last-minute deals are released to the public. (For example, Southwest's specials are posted every Tuesday at 12:01am central time.)
- **Shop around.** If you're looking for bargains, compare prices on different sites—and against a travel agent's best fare. Try a range of times and alternative airports before you make a purchase.
- **Stay secure.** Book only through secure sites. Look for a key icon (Netscape) or a padlock (Internet Explorer) at the bottom of your browser before you enter credit card information or other data.
- **Avoid online auctions.** Sites that auction airline tickets and frequent-flier miles are the number-one perpetrators of Internet fraud, according to the National Consumers League.
- **Maintain a paper trail.** If you book an E-ticket, print out a confirmation, or write down your confirmation number, and keep it safe and accessible—or your trip could be a virtual one!

ONLINE TRAVELER'S TOOLBOX
Veteran travelers usually carry some essential items to make their trips easier. Following is a selection of online tools to bookmark and use.

- **Visa ATM Locator** (www.visa. com), for locations of PLUS ATMs, or **MasterCard ATM Locator** (www.mastercard.com), for locations of Cirrus ATMs.
- **Intellicast** (www.intellicast.com) and **Weather.com** (www.weather. com). Give weather forecasts for all 50 states.
- **Mapquest** (www.mapquest.com). This best of the mapping sites lets you choose a specific address or destination, and creates a map and detailed directions.
- **Cybercafes.com** (www.cybercafes. com) or **Net Café Guide** (www. netcafeguide.com/mapindex.htm). Locate Internet cafes at hundreds of locations around the globe. Catch up on your e-mail and log onto the web for a few dollars per hour.

10 Getting Around

BY CAR

The most practical way to see both Maryland and Delaware is by car. Depending on traffic, it takes approximately 2 hours to get from Wilmington to Lewes; 1 hour and 15 minutes from Wilmington to Baltimore; 1 hour from Baltimore to Frederick; 2½ hours from Frederick to Cumberland; and 2½ hours from Annapolis to Ocean City.

If you are planning to drive on the Beltway (I-695), try to avoid it during rush hour. Congestion, particularly at the junctions north and south with I-95, has gotten terrible. Road widening is underway in some areas, but traffic is terrible from 7 to 9am and 3 to 6pm.

MAPS The tourism agencies in Maryland and Delaware both produce good, free maps. However, if you plan to do any extensive driving on Maryland's Eastern Shore, you'll need more detail than the state maps provide. Contact the county tourism agencies (especially Somerset, Dorchester, and Talbot) for free county maps. There are a couple of special interest maps, too. The best is the **Maryland Scenic Byways** map and guide, which offers ainw off-the-beaten-path routes with scenic stops. (Get them just so you can see what the black-eyed Susan signs along the road are referring to.) The state also puts out an excellent bicycle map.

BY PLANE

Commuter flights within Maryland are operated from Baltimore–Washington International Airport to Salisbury/Ocean City Regional Airport.

BY BUS/RAIL

You can travel in Baltimore on the metro, light rail, or bus, operated by the city's **MTA** (✆ **410/539-5000**). In Wilmington and the Brandywine Valley, **DART First State** (✆ **302/577-3278**) runs buses between the downtown business section and outlying suburbs and tourist attractions.

11 Tips on Accommodations

In Baltimore or Wilmington, your best bet is one of the big hotels in the tourist and business sections of town on a weekend or special package. They are pricier than the motels outside of town but you're closer to major attractions.

Baltimore has three Marriotts, a Hyatt, Sheraton, and a few non-chain hotels offering comfortable accommodation near the Inner Harbor.

If you prefer the suburbs, chain hotels/motels can be found near the Baltimore–Washington International Airport, along Route 40 and I-95, and around the Beltway which circles Baltimore City. The area boasts several Sheratons, a Hilton, and Embassy Suites. You can usually count on a clean, comfortable room at a Holiday Inn or Best Western, often with a simple continental breakfast. In most cases, children stay in their parents' rooms at no extra charge.

Wilmington also has a number of chain hotels in its business district—which usually have plenty of room on the weekends, often with free parking. Wilmington has some comfortable hotels on the outskirts of town. These are convenient to both Wilmington and the Brandywine Valley. Chain hotels include Holiday Inns, Embassy Suites, Quality Inn, and the Hilton.

For bed-and-breakfasts, head for Annapolis, Frederick, or Western Maryland. These areas are rich in B&Bs. Because they are old and often have delicate furnishings, innkeepers require children to be well behaved, if they are welcome at all.

There may be no TV, indoor pool, or hair dryer. But the bread at breakfast will be fresh from the oven and the furnishings usually reflect the locale. Lots of these places now have websites that are accurate, if a bit flowery.

In addition, many bed-and-breakfasts have made their accommodations as handicapped-accessible as possible. Call and check to see what can be done for you. Some innkeepers admit they haven't figured out how to accommodate a wheelchair while preserving a fine old house. But they're clearly working on it.

Smokers should be aware that their cigarettes are usually not welcome in the house, not even on the porches.

If you are going to a beach resort in Delaware or Maryland, you've got lots of choices: chain hotels, local hotels, or home and condo rentals. The chains offer predictable accommodations while the local hotels range from clean and comfy to dazzling. Generally, the lousy hotels just can't survive here.

What makes resort destinations really comfortable and economical for families are house and condo rentals. Real estate agents in each resort (listed in specific chapters) can help you find a place big enough for a family reunion or cozy enough for newlyweds. At the beach, you'll have to pack linens, towels, and paper products. These aren't provided. But you can count on a pretty well equipped kitchen, living areas with TVs and often VCRs, and sleeping space and bathrooms.

House rentals have become more popular in Deep Creek Lake, as well (chapter 8, "Western Maryland"). There are lots of choices; many come with hot tubs, boat piers, or beach access. Here linens are provided, so just bring paper products.

TIPS FOR SAVING ON YOUR HOTEL ROOM

The **rack rate** is the rate you'd get if you walked in and asked for a room for the night. Except at the height of the season or around major events, you can almost always do better.

- **Don't be afraid to bargain.** Most rack rates include commissions for travel agents, which some hotels may be willing to reduce if you make your own reservations. You may qualify for corporate, student, military, senior citizen, or other discounts. Mention membership in AAA, AARP, frequent-flier programs, or trade unions, which may entitle you to special deals as well. Find out the hotel policy on children—do kids stay free in the room or is there a special rate?

- **Rely on a qualified professional.** Certain hotels give travel agents discounts in exchange for steering business their way, so if you're shy about bargaining, an agent may be better able to negotiate discounts.

- **Dial direct.** When booking a room in a chain hotel, compare the rates offered by the hotel's local line with that of the toll-free number. Also check with an agent and online. A hotel makes nothing on a room that stays empty, so the local hotel reservation desk may be willing to offer a special rate.

- **Remember the law of supply and demand.** Resort hotels are most crowded and most expensive on weekends, so discounts are usually available for midweek stays. Business hotels in downtown locations are busiest during the week, so expect discounts over the weekend. Avoid high-season stays when you can; planning your vacation a week before or after peak season can mean big savings.

- **Avoid excess charges.** When you book a room, ask whether the hotel charges for parking. Many hotels charge a fee for dialing out on the phone in your room. A pay phone, may save you money, although many calling cards charge a fee when you use them on pay phones. Ask about local taxes and service charges, which could increase the cost of a room by 25% or more.

- **Consider a suite.** If you are traveling with your family or another couple, you can get more people into a suite (which usually comes with a sofa bed), and reduce your per-person rate. Remember some places charge for extra guests.
- **Book an efficiency.** A room with a kitchenette allows you to buy groceries and cook meals. This is a big money saver, especially for families on long stays.
- Join hotel **frequent-visitor clubs,** even if you don't use them much. You'll be more likely to get upgrades and other perks.
- Many hotels offer **frequent-flier points.** Don't forget to ask for yours when you check in.
- **Investigate reservations services.** These usually work as consolidators, buying up or reserving rooms in bulk, and then dealing them at a profit. You can get 10 to 50 percent off; but remember, these discounts apply to rack rates that savvy travelers rarely end up paying. You may get a decent rate, but always call the hotel to see if you can do better.

Among the more reputable reservations services, offering both telephone and online bookings, are: **Accommodations Express** (© 800/950-4685; www.accommodationsexpress.com); **Hotel Reservations Network** (© 800/715-7666; www.hoteldiscounts.com or www.180096HOTEL.com); **Quikbook** (© 800/789-9887, includes fax on demand service; www.quikbook.com). Online, try booking your hotel through **Arthur Frommer's Budget Travel** (www.frommers.com). **Microsoft Expedia** (www.expedia.com) features a "Travel Agent" that will also direct you to affordable lodgings.

LANDING THE BEST ROOM

Somebody has to get the best room in the house. It might as well be you.

Always ask about a corner room. They're often larger and quieter, with more windows and light, and they often cost the same as standard rooms.

When you make your reservation, ask if the hotel is renovating; if it is, request a room away from the construction. Ask about nonsmoking rooms, rooms with views, rooms with twin, queen-, or king-sized beds. If you're a light sleeper, request a room away from vending machines, elevators, restaurants, bars, and discos. Ask for one of the rooms that have been most recently renovated or redecorated. If you aren't happy with your room when you arrive, talk to the front desk. If they have another room, they may be willing to accommodate you. Join the hotel's frequent visitor club; you may qualify for upgrades.

- What's the view like? Cost-conscious travelers may be willing to pay less for a room facing the parking lot, especially if they don't spend much time in their room.
- Does the room have air-conditioning or just ceiling fans?
- Do the windows open?
- What is the noise level outside the room? If the climate is warm, and nighttime entertainment takes place alfresco, you may want to find out when show time is over.
- What's included in the price? Your room may be moderately priced, but if you're charged for beach chairs, towels, sports equipment, and other amenities, you could end up spending a lot more.
- Are airport transfers included?

- If it's off-season, will any facilities be shut down while you're there?
- If you're single, ask if there's a singles program. If it's off-season, inquire about the occupancy rate. (If you're looking for quiet, an empty resort may be fine; but if you're single and looking for fun, you may want to find a place a little more bustling.)
- Are there programs for children?
- How far is the beach?
- What is the cancellation policy?

12 Suggested Itineraries

A visit to Baltimore needs at least 2 full days, just to visit either the Inner Harbor or Baltimore's major museums. Plan on 3 if you also want to see Fells Point (highly recommended) or catch a baseball game. Add a day to see or Annapolis or Frederick.

Frederick is about 2 hours away. Although the city has plenty of charming sights, the attractions up Route 15 offer a glimpse of Western Maryland and are worth a day's excursion. It's going to be a long day, however, and you can't see everything and get back to the city until very late.

Annapolis can be a long day trip from Baltimore, or a destination of its own. You could spend at least 2 days if you want a tour of the U.S. Naval Academy, a ride on one of the excursion boats, and a visit to the historic homes and State House. Add a third day to see St. Mary's City.

A trip to the ocean needs a whole week to get the benefits of all that relaxation. A long weekend is fine and even a day trip will give you a chance to soak up some sun and jump the waves. But with a week or two, you'll have the opportunity to relax on the beach, spend a day on a fishing charter, see the ponies at Assateague, or wander through the shops of Lewes.

A weekend is not nearly enough time in Wilmington, especially if you use the city as a base for exploring the Brandywine Valley. Plan to stay at least 3 days: one for Wilmington's Riverfront and attractions, and another for the museums. Then plan a day at the du Pont homes: Winterthur, Hagley, Nemours, and Longwood Gardens. You'll have to pick, though, since each one takes about a half day; or spend part of a day at the Brandywine River Museum.

13 Recommended Reading

A number of books about the Chesapeake Bay region will give you historical and cultural perspective for your trip. The most well known is *Chesapeake* (Fawcett Books, 1990), James Michener's historical novel which he wrote while living on the Eastern Shore. It offers a good history of the area and the watermen who make their living on the Bay.

Beautiful Swimmers (Little Brown & Co., 1994), by William H. Warner, is a Pulitzer Prize–winning study of the blue crab and the culture around the prized crustacean. Gilbert Byron, a Chestertown native who once taught school in Lewes, Delaware, wrote several books about the waterman's life, as well as a volume of poetry about Delaware, titled simply *Delaware Poems*. Tom Horton's *An Island Out of Time* (Vintage Books, 1997), chronicles his 3 years living on remote Smith Island.

Anne Tyler's novels are usually set in and around Baltimore—*The Accidental Tourist* (Berkley, 1994) was made into a film with William Hurt and Geena Davis. Bethany Beach makes a cameo in the beginning of *Ladder of Years* (Ivy Books, 1997).

Speaking of movies, quite a few have been made in Baltimore, notably by Baltimoreans Barry Levinson and cult filmmaker John Waters, who still maintains a home in Baltimore. If you want to see Baltimore in the 1950s and '60s, check out Levinson's *Diner, Tin Men,* or *Avalon.* Waters's view of Baltimore is a bit more twisted, but *Hairspray* has some memorable moments (and is currently being turned into a Broadway musical); *Serial Mom* stars Kathleen Turner (who graduated from the University of Maryland–Baltimore County). *The Runaway Bride* takes place in Berlin, Maryland, called Hale in the movie.

On the small screen you can still catch repeats of *Homicide: Life On the Streets,* a television series based on the nonfiction book by David Simon (Ivy, 1993), shot on location in Baltimore.

 FAST FACTS: Maryland & Delaware

American Express In Baltimore, the office is located at 32 South St., Baltimore, MD 21202 (✆ **410/837-3100**); in Annapolis, contact the office in the Annapolis Mall on Bestgate Road (✆ **800/788-3559** or **410/ 224-4200**). In Wilmington, contact the Delaware Travel Agency, 4001 Concord Pike, Wilmington, DE 19803 (✆ **302/479-0200**). To report lost or stolen traveler's checks, call ✆ **800/221-7282**.

Area Codes The area code for all of Delaware is **302**. Some Brandywine Valley attractions are in Pennsylvania; their area code is **610**. Maryland has four area codes: **301** and **240** in the western half of the state, **410** and **443** in the eastern half, including Baltimore and Annapolis. Because there are two area codes in each region, you must dial the area code with every call, even if you're only calling next door.

Banks & ATM ATMs in both states generally use: **Most, Cirrus, PLUS, Novus,** and **MAC.** In addition, you can use MasterCard or Visa to get a cash advance from most machines.

Car Rentals See "Getting Around" earlier in this chapter.

Climate See "When to Go" earlier in this chapter.

Emergencies Dial ✆ **911** for police or to report a fire or medical emergency.

Newspapers/Magazines **The Baltimore Sun** and **The Washington Post** are the major newspapers in Maryland. In Annapolis, look for the **Capital,** and in the mid-Shore, the **Star Democrat.** You'll find the **Wilmington News-Journal** and the **Philadelphia Inquirer** in Delaware.

Police Dial ✆ **911** or, in Baltimore, ✆ **311** for nonemergency situations that require police attention.

Taxes State sales tax in Maryland is 5%. Delaware has no sales tax. Hotel tax in both states is between 7% and 8%.

Time Zone Maryland and Delaware are on eastern standard time. Daylight saving time is in effect from April through October.

Weather For Baltimore weather, call ✆ **410/936-1212**; for Wilmington, call ✆ **302/429-9000**.

3

For International Visitors

The pervasiveness of American culture around the world may make you feel that you know the U.S.A. pretty well, but leaving your own country still requires an additional degree of planning. This chapter will help prepare you for the more common problems that visitors may encounter.

1 Preparing for Your Trip

ENTRY REQUIREMENTS

Immigration laws have been a hot political issue since the terrorist attacks of September 2001, so it's wise to check at any U.S. embassy or consulate for current information and requirements. You can also plug into the U.S. State Department's Internet site at **www.state.gov**.

VISAS Canadians may enter the United States without passports or visas; you need only proof of residence. Citizens of Andorra, Austria, Australia, Belgium, Brunei, Denmark, Finland, France, Germany, Iceland, Ireland, Italy, Japan, Liechtenstein, Luxembourg, Monaco, The Netherlands, New Zealand, Norway, Portugal, San Marino, Singapore, Slovenia, Spain, Sweden, Switzerland, the United Kingdom and Uruguay need only a valid passport and a round-trip air or cruise ticket in their possession upon arrival to enter the United States for stays of up to 90 days. Once here, you may then visit Mexico, Canada, Bermuda, and/or the Caribbean islands and return to the United States without needing a visa. Further information is available from any U.S. embassy or consulate.

If you're from any other country, you must have: (1) a valid **passport** with an expiration date at least 6 months later than the scheduled end of your visit; and (2) a **tourist visa,** which may be obtained without charge from the nearest U.S. consulate.

Obtaining a Visa To obtain a tourist visa, submit a completed application form with a 1½-inch-square photo and demonstrate binding ties to your residence abroad. If you cannot go in person, contact the nearest U.S. embassy or consulate for directions on applying by mail. Your travel agent or airline office may also be able to provide you with the visa application forms and instructions. The U.S. embassy or consulate where you apply will determine whether you receive a multiple- or single-entry visa and any restrictions regarding the length of your stay. This could take weeks or even months depending on where you are applying, so file your paperwork well in advance.

British subjects can obtain up-to-date information by calling the **U.S. Embassy Visa Information Line** (© 0891/200-290) or the **London Passport Office** (© 0990/210-410 for recorded information).

DRIVER'S LICENSES Foreign
driver's licenses are mostly recognized in the U.S., although you may want to get an international driver's license if your home license is not in English.

MEDICAL REQUIREMENTS

Unless you're arriving from an area known to be suffering from an epidemic, inoculations or vaccinations are not required for entry into the United States. If you have a disease that requires treatment with narcotics or syringe-administered medications, carry a valid signed prescription from your physician to allay any suspicions that you may be smuggling narcotics (a serious offense that carries severe penalties in the U.S.).

For HIV-positive visitors, requirements for entering the United States are somewhat vague and change frequently. For up-to-the-minute information, contact the Centers for Disease Control's **National Center for HIV** (✆ **404/332-4559;** www.hivatis. org) or the **Gay Men's Health Crisis** (✆ **212/367-1000;** www.gmhc.org).

CUSTOMS REQUIREMENTS

Every visitor over 21 years of age may bring in, free of duty, 1 liter of wine or hard liquor; 200 cigarettes or 100 cigars (but no cigars made in Cuba) or 3 pounds of smoking tobacco; and $100 worth of gifts. You must spend at least 72 hours in the United States and must not have claimed the exemptions within the preceding 6 months. It is forbidden to bring in foodstuffs (particularly cheese, fruit, cooked meats, and canned goods) and plants (vegetables, seeds, tropical plants, and so on). Foreign tourists may bring in or take out up to $10,000 in U.S. or foreign currency; larger sums must be declared to Customs upon entering or leaving.

For more specific information regarding U.S. Customs, call your nearest U.S. embassy or consulate, or the **U.S. Customs** office at ✆ **202/ 927-1770;** www.customs.ustreas.gov.

What You Can Bring Home U.K. subjects returning from the U.S. can bring back 200 cigarettes; 50 cigars; 250 grams of smoking tobacco; 2 liters of still table wine; 1 liter of spirits or strong liqueurs (over 22% volume); 2 liters of fortified wine, sparkling wine, or other liqueurs; 60cc (ml) of perfume; 250cc (ml) of toilet water; and £145 worth of all other goods, including gifts and souvenirs. People under 17 cannot have the tobacco or alcohol allowance. For more information, contact **HM Customs & Excise,** Passenger Enquiry Point, 2nd Floor Wayfarer House, Great South West Road, Feltham, Middlesex, TW14 8NP (✆ **0181/ 910-3744;** from outside the U.K. 44/181-910-3744; www.open.gov.uk).

For a summary of **Canadian** rules, write for the booklet *I Declare,* issued by **Canada Customs and Revenue Agency,** 2265 St. Laurent Blvd., Ottawa K1G 4KE (✆ **800/461-9999** from within Canada, or 204/983-3500; www.ccra-adrc.gc.ca). Canada allows its citizens a $50 exemption if they are outside the country for 7 days or less, $200 for trips of 48 hours to 1 week, $750 for trips longer than a week. You can bring back, duty-free, 200 cigarettes, 2.2 pounds of tobacco, 40 imperial ounces of liquor, and 50 cigars. All valuables should be declared on the Y-38 form before departure, including serial numbers of valuables you already own, such as expensive foreign cameras.

The duty-free allowance in **Australia** is A$400 or, for those under 18, A$200. Personal property mailed back from the U.S. should be marked "Australian goods returned" to avoid payment of duty. Upon returning to Australia, citizens can bring in 250 cigarettes or 250 grams of loose tobacco, and 1,125ml of alcohol. If you're returning with valuables you already own, such as foreign-made cameras, you should file form B263. A brochure available from Australian consulates or Customs offices is *Know Before You Go.* For more information, contact **Australian Customs Services,** GPO Box 8, Sydney NSW 2001 (℃ **02/9213-2000**).

The duty-free allowance for **New Zealand** is NZ$700. Citizens over 17 can bring in 200 cigarettes or 50 cigars or 250 grams of tobacco (or a mixture of all three if their combined weight doesn't exceed 250 grams); plus 4.5 liters of wine and beer, or 1.125 liters of liquor. New Zealand currency does not carry import or export restrictions. Fill out a certificate of export, listing the valuables you take out of the country; that way, you can bring them back without paying duty. Most questions are answered in a free pamphlet available at New Zealand consulates and Customs offices: *New Zealand Customs Guide for Travellers, Notice no. 4.* For more information, contact New Zealand Customs, 50 Anzac Ave., P.O. Box 29, Auckland (℃ **09/359-6655;** www.customs.govt.nz).

INSURANCE Unlike many European countries, the United States does not usually offer free or low-cost medical care to its citizens or visitors. Doctors and hospitals are expensive, and in most cases will require advance payment or proof of coverage before treatment. You can get insurance to cover everything from the loss or theft of your baggage and trip cancellation to the guarantee of bail in case you're arrested. Good policies will also cover the costs of an accident, repatriation, or death. See "Insurance, Health & Safety" in chapter 2, for more information. Packages such as **Europ Assistance** (www.europ-assistance.com) in Europe are sold by automobile clubs and travel agencies at attractive rates. **Worldwide Assistance Services, Inc.** (℃ **800/821-2828;** www.worldwideassistance.com) is the agent for Europ Assistance in the United States.

Though lack of health insurance may prevent you from being admitted to a hospital in nonemergencies, don't worry about being left on a street corner to die: the American way is to fix you now and bill the living daylights out of you later.

Canadians should check with their provincial health-plan offices or call **HealthCanada** (℃ **613/957-3025;** www.hc-sc.gc.ca) to find out the extent of their coverage and what documentation they must take home if they are treated in the United States.

In Great Britain, many travel agents offer their own insurance, and will try to sell you a package when you book a trip. The **Association of British Insurers** (℃ **0171/600-3333;** www.abi.org.uk) gives advice by phone and publishes *Holiday Insurance,* a free guide to policy provisions and prices. You might shop around for better deals: Try **Columbus Travel Insurance Ltd.** (℃ **0171/375-0011**) or for students, **Campus Travel** (℃ **0171/730-2101**).

MONEY

The U.S. monetary system has a decimal base: 1 American dollar ($1) = 100 cents (100¢). Notes come in $1 (we call it a "buck"), $5, $10, $20, $50, and $100 denominations (the last two are not welcome when paying for small purchases and are not accepted in taxis or at subway ticket booths). There are also $2 bills, but you are unlikely to see one since some Americans consider them to be unlucky. There are six denominations of coins: 1¢ (one cent, known here as "a penny"), 5¢ (five cents, or "a nickel"), 10¢ (ten cents, or "a dime"), 25¢ (twenty-five cents, or "a quarter"), 50¢ (fifty cents, or "a half dollar"), and a $1 coin, the gold-colored "Sacagawea" (named for the woman portrayed on the coins), which you may receive as change from vending machines.

Changing foreign currency in the United States is a hassle, so leave any currency other than U.S. dollars at home. Even banks here may not want to change your home currency into U.S. dollars. The exceptions in Maryland and Delaware are the currency exchange desks at Washington Dulles International and Ronald Reagan Washington National airports, as well as Baltimore–Washington International Airport near Baltimore, operated by **Thomas Cook Foreign Exchange** (© 800/287-7362; www.us.thomascook.com).

Traveler's checks in U.S. dollars are accepted at most hotels, motels, restaurants, and large stores. Do not bring traveler's checks in other currencies. Sometimes a passport or other photo identification is necessary. The traveler's checks most widely recognized are **Visa, American Express,** and **Thomas Cook.** Be sure to record the numbers of the checks, and keep the information separate in case they get lost or stolen.

American Express, Diners Club, Discover, MasterCard (EuroCard in Europe, Access in Britain, Chargex in Canada), and Visa (BarclayCard in Britain) **credit and charge cards** are the most widely used form of payment in the United States, and you should bring at least one with you—if for no other reason than to rent a car, since all rental companies require them.

In Maryland and Delaware, some **automated teller machines (ATMs)** will allow you to draw U.S. currency against your bank and credit cards. When available, this is the easiest way to get U.S. dollars, and at the bank's rate of exchange, normally better than what you will receive at hotels and other businesses. You will need your personal identification number (PIN) to do so.

SAFETY

GENERAL While tourist areas are generally safe, and crime rates have been decreasing in the U.S., urban areas here tend to be less safe than those in Europe or Japan. Always stay alert. This is particularly true of large U.S. cities. It is wise to ask your hotel front-desk staff or the city's or area's tourist office if you're in doubt about which neighborhoods are safe.

Remember also that hotels are open to the public, and in a large hotel, security may not be able to screen everyone. Always lock your room door—don't assume that once inside your hotel you no longer need to be aware of your surroundings.

DRIVING Safety while driving is particularly important. Question your rental agency about personal safety in the area you are traveling in. When you pick up your car, ask for a brochure of traveler safety tips and for written directions or a map with the route clearly marked, showing how to get to your destination.

Many agencies offer the option of renting you a cellular phone for the duration of the car rental; inquire when you make your reservation.

Make sure that you have enough gasoline to reach your intended destination so that you're not forced to look for a service station in an unfamiliar neighborhood. If you do drive off a highway into a doubtful neighborhood, leave the area as quickly as possible. If you have an accident, even on the highway, stay in your car with the doors locked until you assess the situation or until the police arrive. If you are bumped from behind on the street or are involved in a minor accident with no injuries and the situation appears to be suspicious, motion to the other driver to follow you. *Never* get out of your car in such situations. If you see someone on the road who indicates a need for help, do *not* stop. Take note of the location, drive on to a well-lighted area, and telephone the police by dialing © **911** from any telephone.

Park in well-lighted, well-traveled areas if possible. Always keep your car doors locked, whether attended or unattended. Look around before you get out of your car, and never leave any packages or valuables in sight. If someone attempts to rob you or steal your car, do *not* try to resist the thief or carjacker—report the incident to the police department immediately.

2 Getting to & Around the U.S.

Most U.S. and several international airlines offer service from Europe to Washington Dulles International Airport and Baltimore–Washington International Airport (see "Getting There," in chapter 2). You can get here from Australia and New Zealand via **Air New Zealand** (www.airnz.com), **Qantas** (www.qantas.com), **American** (www.americanair.com), and **United** (www.ual.com), with a change of planes in Los Angeles. Call the airlines or contact your travel agent, and ask about promotional fares and discounts.

From Great Britain, **Virgin Atlantic Airways** (① 800/662-8621 in the U.S. or 01/293-74-77-47 in the U.K.; www.virgin-atlantic.com) has attractive deals from London and Manchester to Washington Dulles. British Airways (① **800/247-8726**) flies into Baltimore–Washington International.

Canadians should check with **Air Canada** (① **800/776-3000;** www.aircanada.ca), which flies to Washington Dulles International, Washington Reagan National, and Baltimore–Washington International.

AIRFARES Whichever airline you choose, always ask about **advance purchase excursion (APEX)** fares, which represent substantial savings over regular fares. Most require tickets to be bought 21 days prior to departure.

On the World Wide Web, the European Travel Network (ETN) operates a site at **www.discount-tickets.com**, which offers cut-rate prices on international airfares to the United States, accommodations, car rentals, and tours. Another site to click for discount fares worldwide is **www.etn.nl/ discount.htm**.

IMMIGRATION & CUSTOMS CLEARANCE When you arrive in the U.S., getting through immigration control can take 2 hours or more, especially on summer weekends. Accordingly, you should make very generous allowances in planning connections between international and domestic flights.

Air travelers from Canada, Bermuda, and some places in the Caribbean can sometimes go through Customs and Immigration at the point of departure, which is much quicker.

Wherever you are coming from, have your passport and other documents ready, and expect to be asked detailed questions about how long you intend to stay and what places you plan to visit. It's all part of the stepped-up security measures since September 11, 2001.

For further information, see "Getting There," in chapter 2.

GETTING AROUND THE U.S.

BY AIR You won't need to fly to reach all the regions described in this book once you're in Maryland or Delaware; if you're visiting other areas of the United States (one of the world's largest countries), you may wish to fly.

Some large airlines (for example, Northwest and Delta) offer travelers on their transatlantic or transpacific flights discount tickets allowing mostly one-way travel from one U.S. destination to another at very low prices. These discount tickets are not on sale in the United States and must be purchased in conjunction with your international ticket. This system

---

Tips   **The Right Side Is the "Right" Side**

In the United States we drive on the **right side of the road** as in Europe, not on the left side as in the United Kingdom, Australia, New Zealand, and South Africa.

---

is the best, easiest, and fastest way to see the United States at low cost. You should obtain information well in advance from your travel agent or the office of the airline concerned, since the conditions attached to these discount tickets can be changed without advance notice.

BY TRAIN   Long-distance trains in the United States are operated by **Amtrak** (© 800/USA-RAIL; www.amtrak.com). See "Getting There," in chapter 2, for information about service to and within Maryland and Delaware, especially Baltimore, Wilmington, and BWI Airport.

With a few notable exceptions (for instance, the Northeast Corridor line between Boston and Washington, D.C.), inter-city service is not up to European standards. Amtrak is a good way to get around the northeast and mid-Atlantic regions of the United States, but for longer trips, routes are limited, and fares seldom significantly lower than discount airfares.

International visitors can buy a **USA Railpass,** good for 15 or 30 days of unlimited travel on Amtrak. The pass is available through many foreign travel agents (see Amtrak's website for a complete list), and with a foreign passport, you can buy them at some Amtrak offices in the United States, including Boston, Chicago, Los Angeles, Miami, New York, San Francisco, and Washington, D.C. The prices are

based on a zone system—eastern, central, and western United States—and are highest in the peak summer months and at holidays. Reservations are generally required and should be made for each part of your trip as early as possible.

BY BUS   Although it's the least expensive way to get around the country, long distance bus service can be both slow and uncomfortable. It's not an option for everyone. **Greyhound** (© 800/231-2222; www.greyhound.com), the sole nationwide bus line, offers a discounted **International Ameripass** for unlimited travel ranging from 7 days to 60 days. Passes must be purchased online or at a Greyhound terminal at least 21 days before beginning travel. Special rates are available for senior citizens and students. Check Greyhound's website for fares and other special offers.

BY CAR   Traveling by car gives you the freedom to make (and alter) your itinerary to suit your own needs and interests. And especially in Maryland and Delaware, it offers the possibility of visiting some of the off-the-beaten-path locations, places that cannot be easily reached by public transport. For information on renting cars in the United States, see "Getting Around," in chapter 2, and "Automobile Organizations" and "Automobile Rentals," in "Fast Facts: For the International Traveler," below.

---

3 Shopping Tips

The U.S. government charges very low duties compared to the rest of the world, so you may find excellent deals on imported electronic goods, cameras,

and clothing. Of course, it depends on the value of your home currency versus the dollar, and how much duty you'll have to pay when you get home.

> ## *Tips* Telephone Tips
>
> - **To place a direct call from your home country to the United States:** Dial the international access code (0011 in Australia; 00 in Ireland, New Zealand, and the U.K.), plus the 3-digit area code and 7-digit local number (for example, 011-804/000-0000). Calls from Canada to the U.S. do not require a country code.
> - **To place a long-distance call within the United States:** Dial "1" followed by the 3-digit area code and the 7-digit local number (for example, 1-804/000-0000).
> - **To place a direct call from the United States to your home country:** Dial the international access code (**011**) followed by the country code (Australia 61, Republic of Ireland 353, New Zealand 64, U.K./Northern Ireland 44). For calls from the U.S. to Canada, just dial "1" followed by the area code and local number.
> - **To reach directory assistance ("information"):** Dial 411 for local numbers. For long distance information, dial 1 followed by the appropriate area code and 555-1212.

Many computers and most other electronic equipment here uses 110- to 120-volt AC (60-cycle) electricity. You will need a transformer to use them at home if your power is 220 to 240 volts AC (50 cycles). Be sure to ask the salesperson if an item has a universal power adapter.

Another popular source is **outlet malls,** in which manufacturers operate their own shops, selling directly to the consumer. Sometimes you can get very good buys at the outlets. Most lingerie and china outlets have good prices when compared to those at department stores, but that's not necessarily the case with designer clothing. In addition, some manufacturers produce items of lesser quality so that they can charge less at their outlets, so inspect the quality of all merchandise carefully. The main advantage to outlet malls is that if you are looking for a specific brand—Levi's jeans, for example—the company's outlet will have it.

You'll find national chain stores, department stores, and outlet malls throughout Maryland and Delaware. The most notable are the Rehoboth and Ocean City outlets at the ocean resorts, and Maryland's Arundel Mills. You will also find listings in the local telephone directory.

 ## FAST FACTS: **For the International Traveler**

Automobile Organizations Auto clubs will supply maps, routes, guidebooks, accident and bail-bond insurance, and emergency road service. The **American Automobile Association (AAA)** is the major auto club in the United States. Inquire about AAA reciprocity with your own auto club before you leave. You may be able to join AAA even if you're not a member of a reciprocal club; call AAA (✆ **800/222-4357**; www.aaa.com). AAA has a national emergency road service number: ✆ **800/AAA-HELP.**

Automobile Rentals See "Getting Around," in chapter 2.

Currency & Currency Exchange See "Entry Requirements" and "Money," under "Preparing for Your Trip," earlier in this chapter.

Electricity Like Canada, the United States uses 110 to 120 volts AC (60 cycles), compared to 220 to 240 volts AC (50 cycles) in most of Europe, Australia, and New Zealand. If your small appliances use 220 to 240 volts, you'll need a 110-volt transformer and a plug adapter with two flat parallel pins to operate them here. Converters that change 220 to 240 volts to 110 to 120 volts are hard to find in the United States, so bring one with you.

Embassies & Consulates All embassies are in the national capital, Washington, D.C., easily accessible from Baltimore: **Australia:** 1601 Massachusetts Ave. NW, Washington, DC 20036 (© 202/797-3000; www.austemb.org). There are Australian consulates in New York, Honolulu, Houston, Los Angeles, and San Francisco.

Canada: 501 Pennsylvania Ave. NW, Washington, DC 20001 (© 202/682-1740; www.cdnemb-washdc.org).

Republic of Ireland: 2234 Massachusetts Ave. NW, Washington, DC 20008 (© 202/462-3939). Irish consulates are in Boston, Chicago, New York, and San Francisco.

New Zealand: 37 Observatory Circle NW, Washington, DC 20008 (© 202/328-4800; www.emb.com/nzemb). New Zealand consulates are in Los Angeles, Salt Lake City, San Francisco, and Seattle.

United Kingdom: 3100 Massachusetts Ave. NW, Washington, DC 20008 (© 202/462-1340). Other consulates are in Atlanta, Boston, Chicago, Cleveland, Dallas, Houston, Los Angeles, and New York.

Emergencies Call © 911 to report a fire, call the police, or get an ambulance anywhere in the United States. This is a toll-free call (no coins are required at public telephones).

If you encounter traveler's problems, check the telephone directory to find the local **Traveler's Aid Society** (www.travelersaid.org), a national, nonprofit organization geared to helping travelers in difficult straits. Their services might include reuniting families separated while traveling, providing food and/or shelter to people stranded without cash, or even offering emotional counseling. If you're in trouble, seek them out.

Gasoline (Petrol) Petrol is known as gasoline (or simply "gas"), and petrol stations are known as both gas stations and service stations. Gasoline costs about half as much as it does in Europe. One U.S. gallon equals 3.8 liters or .85 imperial gallons. A majority of gas stations in Maryland and Delaware are actually convenience grocery stores with gas pumps outside; they do not service automobiles. Almost all stations have self-service gas pumps. Full service pumps come at a much higher rate.

Holidays Banks, government offices, post offices, and many stores, restaurants, and museums are closed on the following legal national holidays: January 1 (New Year's Day), the third Monday in January (Martin Luther King, Jr., Day), the third Monday in February (Presidents' Day, Washington's Birthday), the last Monday in May (Memorial Day), July 4 (Independence Day), the first Monday in September (Labor Day), the second Monday in October (Columbus Day), November 11 (Veterans' Day/Armistice Day), the last Thursday in November (Thanksgiving Day), and December 25 (Christmas).

Legal Aid The foreign tourist will probably never become involved with the American legal system. If you are "pulled over" for a minor infraction (for example, speeding), never attempt to pay the fine directly to a police officer; this could be construed as attempted bribery, a much more serious crime. Pay fines by mail, or into the hands of the clerk of the court. If accused of a more serious offense, say and do nothing before consulting a lawyer or your embassy or consulate. Here the government must prove a person's guilt beyond a reasonable doubt, and everyone has the right to remain silent, whether he or she is suspected of a crime or actually arrested. If arrested, a person can make one telephone call, and non-U.S. citizens have a right to call their embassies or consulates.

Mail Mail is delivered throughout the country by the **United States Postal Service** (www.usps.com). If you aren't sure what your address will be in the United States, mail can be sent to you, in your name, **c/o General Delivery** at the main post office of the city or region where you expect to be. You must pick it up in person and must produce proof of identity (driver's license, passport, and so on).

Generally found at intersections, **mailboxes** are blue with a red-and-white stripe and carry the inscription U.S. MAIL. If your mail is addressed to a U.S. destination, don't forget to add the five-digit postal code, or ZIP code, after the two-letter abbreviation of the state to which the mail is addressed (MD for Maryland, DE for Delaware).

Domestic postage rates are 21¢ for a postcard and 34¢ for a letter. Airmail postcards to Canada cost 50¢, while letters are 60¢. Airmail letters to other countries are 80¢ for the first ounce.

Newspapers/Magazines All over Maryland and Delaware, you'll be able to buy *USA Today,* the national daily, and *The Washington Post,* a highly respected daily paper. Every city has its own daily paper. Baltimore's paper is *The Sun,* Wilmington's is the *News Journal.*

Taxes In the United States there is no value-added tax (VAT) or other indirect tax at the national level. Every state, county, and city has the right to levy its own local tax on all purchases, including hotel and restaurant checks, airline tickets, and so on. Maryland sales tax is 5% on everything except food in a grocery store. Delaware has no sales tax.

Telephone, Telegraph & Fax The telephone system in the United States is run by private corporations, so rates, especially for long-distance service and operator-assisted calls, can vary widely. Generally, hotel surcharges on long-distance and local calls are astronomical, so you're better off using a **public pay telephone,** which you'll find clearly marked in most public buildings and private establishments as well as on the street. Many convenience groceries and packaging services sell **prepaid calling cards** in denominations up to $50; these can be the least expensive way to call home. Many public phones at airports now accept American Express, MasterCard, and Visa credit cards. Local calls made from public pay phones in Maryland and Delaware cost 50¢.

Calls to area codes 800, 866, 877, and 888 are toll-free. However, calls to numbers in area codes 700 and 900 (chat lines, bulletin boards, "dating" services, and so on) can be very expensive—usually a charge of 95¢

to $3 or more per minute, and they sometimes have minimum charges that can run as high as $15 or more.

For **reversed-charge** or **collect calls,** and for **person-to-person calls,** dial 0 (zero, *not* the letter O) followed by the area code and number you want; an operator will come on the line, and you should specify that you are calling collect, or person-to-person, or both. If your operator-assisted call is international, ask for the overseas operator.

Telegraph and telex services are provided primarily by **Western Union** (www.westernunion.com). You can bring your telegram into any Western Union office (there are hundreds across the country) or dictate it over the phone (② **800/325-6000**). You can also send money or have it sent to you very quickly via Western Union, but the fee can be as much as 15% to 25% of the amount sent.

Most hotels have **fax** machines available for guest use (be sure to ask about any charge to use it), and many hotel rooms are even wired for guests' fax machines. A less expensive way to send and receive faxes may be at stores such as **Mail Boxes Etc.** (www.mbe.com), a national chain of packing service shops (look in the Yellow Pages directory under "Packing Services"). Some Mail Boxes Etc. stores also have computers with Internet access for sending and receiving e-mail.

There are two kinds of telephone directories in the United States. The **White Pages** list private and business subscribers in alphabetical order. The inside front cover lists emergency numbers for police, fire, ambulance, and so on. The first few pages will tell you how to make long-distance and international calls, with country codes and area codes listed. Government numbers usually are on pages printed on blue paper. Printed on yellow paper, the **Yellow Pages** list all local services, businesses, industries, and churches and synagogues by type of activity, with an index at the front or back. The Yellow Pages also include city plans or detailed area maps, often showing postal ZIP codes and public transportation routes.

Time The continental United States is divided into four **time zones:** eastern standard time (EST), central standard time (CST), mountain standard time (MST), and Pacific standard time (PST). Alaska and Hawaii have their own zones. For example, noon in New York City (EST) is 11am in Chicago (CST), 10am in Denver (MST), 9am in Los Angeles (PST), 8am in Anchorage (AST), and 7am in Honolulu (HST). Both Maryland and Delaware observe eastern standard time.

Daylight saving time is in effect from 1am on the first Sunday in April through 1am on the last Sunday in October. Daylight saving time moves the clock 1 hour ahead of standard time.

Tipping Tipping is so ingrained in the American way of life that the annual income tax of tip-earning personnel is based on how much they should have received based on their employers' gross revenues. Accordingly, they may have to pay tax on a tip you didn't give them.

Here are some rules of thumb: **bartenders,** 10% to 15% of the check; **bellhops,** at least 50¢ per bag, or $2 to $3 for a lot of luggage; **cab drivers,** 10% of the fare; **chambermaids,** $1 per day; **checkroom attendants,** $1 per garment; **hairdressers and barbers,** 15% to 20% of the bill; **waiters and waitresses,** 15% to 20% of the check; **valet parking attendants,**

$1 per vehicle; **restroom attendants,** 25¢. Do not tip theater ushers, gas station attendants, or the staff at cafeterias and fast-food restaurants.

Toilets You won't find public toilets (referred to here as "restrooms") on the streets in most U.S. cities, but they can be found in hotel lobbies, bars, restaurants, museums, larger stores, railway and bus stations, or service stations. Note that restaurants and bars in resorts or heavily visited areas may reserve their restrooms for the use of their patrons.

4

Baltimore

A combination of interesting tourist attractions, historical sites, and friendly people in such picturesque old neighborhoods as Fells Point, Mount Vernon, Canton, and Federal Hill makes Baltimore an ever-more-popular tourist destination.

"Charm City" has welcomed visitors since 1729. Founded as a shipping and ship building town, manufacturing has always been a big part of this city. General Motors and Bethlehem Steel have been a part of the east Baltimore landscape for decades. Domino Sugar's sign dominates the Inner Harbor. More recently, Baltimore has welcomed a new wave of service industries and nonprofits. Tourism plays an ever-increasing role in the city's economy, and a laid-back population welcomes its visitors with a friendly "Hello, hon!" in the unique Bawlamer accent.

1 Orientation

ARRIVING

BY PLANE **Baltimore–Washington International Airport** (© 800/I-FLY-BWI or 410/859-7111) is 10 miles (16km) south of downtown Baltimore, off I-295 (the Baltimore–Washington Pkwy.). It's a major domestic and international hub. Domestic airlines serving Baltimore include **American** (© 800/433-7300); **Delta** (© 800/221-1212); **Continental** (© 800/525-0280); **Northwest** (© 800/225-2525); **Southwest** (© 800/435-9792); **United** (© 800/241-6522); and **US Airways** (© 800/428-4322).

To get to Baltimore from the airport, take I-195 west to Route 295 north, which will take you into downtown. **BWI Airport Shuttle** (known as Super-Shuttle; © 800/258-3826 or 410/859-0800; www.supershuttle.com) operates vans between the airport and all major downtown hotels. Departures are scheduled every 30 minutes between 5:45am and 11:15pm, and the cost is $11 per person one-way or $18 round-trip. The **Light Rail** also connects the airport with downtown Baltimore and the Amtrak stations at BWI and at Penn Station.

BY CAR **I-95** provides the easiest routes to Baltimore from the north and south. From the north, follow I-95 south through the **Fort McHenry Tunnel** ($1 toll) to Exit 53, I-395 north to downtown. Bear left off the exit and follow signs to the Inner Harbor. From the south, follow I-95 north to Exit 53, I-395 north to downtown. Bear left off the exit and follow signs to the Inner Harbor.

From the west, take **I-70** east to Exit 91, I-695 south (the **Baltimore Beltway**) heading toward Glen Burnie. Take Exit 11A, I-95 to I-395, north to downtown.

From **I-83** (Pennsylvania to the north), follow I-83 south to the merge with I-695 (the Baltimore Beltway). Continue on I-83 south for 1 mile (2km) to Exit 23A (I-83 south, downtown). Continue until the expressway (the Jones Falls Expressway) ends at President Street downtown. Once you arrive, you'll find lots of parking garages, as well as metered on-street parking throughout the downtown district. Garages charge about $15 a day, or $5 to $8 for special events or evening visits. Parking meters must be fed $1 an hour.

BY TRAIN   Baltimore is a stop on Amtrak's (© **800/872-7245;** www.amtrak.com) Northeast Corridor, between Wilmington and Washington, D.C. Trains arrive at and depart from Pennsylvania Station, 1500 N. Charles St., (north of the Inner Harbor), and BWI Airport Rail station (© **410/672-6169**), off Route 170 about 1½ miles (2km) from the airport. In addition, the **Maryland Area Rail Commuter Service** (MARC) provides rail service on two routes from Washington, D.C., stopping at BWI en route. One ends at Camden Station, closest to the Inner Harbor, and the other ends at Penn Station about 20 blocks north. From here you can take a taxi or the Light Rail Service, which runs Monday through Friday from approximately 6am to 10pm; the fare to the airport is $3.25 one-way. For more information, call © **800/325-RAIL.**

BY BUS   Regular bus service is provided to and from Baltimore via **Greyhound** and **Peter Pan/Trailways** (© **800/231-2222;** www.greyhound.com; www.peterpanbus.com). Buses arrive and depart from the **Baltimore Travel Plaza** (© **410/633-6389**), 5625 O'Donnell St. in eastern Baltimore; or downtown at 210 W. Fayette St. (© **410/752-7682**).

VISITOR INFORMATION   Call the **Baltimore Area Convention and Visitors Association** at 100 Light St., Baltimore, MD 21202 (© **877/ BALTIMORE;** www.Baltimore.org). BACVA has all sorts of information to help you plan your trip, including maps, brochures, and water taxi schedules. In town, visit the visitor center at Harborplace. It is located in a gray trailer just beside the Light Street Pavilion. You can also pick up a copy of the *Baltimore Quick Guide,* a purse-sized guide to what's happening in and around the city.

BALTIMORE'S NEIGHBORHOODS IN BRIEF

Baltimore has always been a hardworking town, home to fiercely loyal Orioles fans, proud residents of close-knit neighborhoods and families. Here are some neighborhoods you may wish to tour, and a few of the characteristics that make them unique.

Baltimore's **Inner Harbor** is the starting point for most visitors, and was the focal point of the town's turnaround beginning in the late 1970s. The National Aquarium is filled with fish, sharks, and dolphins, and topped with a rain forest. The Maryland Science Center's offers an IMAX theater and planetarium. Harborplace and The Gallery are shopping and dining extravaganzas that draw thousands of people every weekend.

The last freighters stopped coming in the 1960s but since the revitalization of the Inner Harbor, Baltimore has become a destination for pleasure boaters and tall ships.

The high-tech racing boats of the Whitbread Around the World Race were welcomed here in 1997 and the sailors will return in 2002 in the renamed Volvo Ocean Race.

Visitors can get a feel for Baltimore's seafaring days through its maritime museums on the Inner Harbor, from its harbor cruises, or even from its water taxis.

Just past the Inner Harbor are three of Baltimore's oldest neighborhoods:

Little Italy has been home to Italian immigrants and their descendants since the mid-1800s, when they opened the restaurants that continue to anchor the neighborhood.

These are charming, narrow streets filled with the aroma of cooking. Before or after dinner, take a walk to see the rowhouses and their famous marble steps that dominate the Baltimore streetscape—and notice the shrines with flowers and statues that grace a window here and there.

Fells Point was Baltimore's original seaport and home to the first shipyards. Baltimore clippers, a swift and elegant topsail schooner, were made here. For many years, immigrants arrived here. They stayed in Fells Point or moved to other Baltimore neighborhoods to make their mark in Highlandtown, Canton, and elsewhere.

The main pier is familiar to TV viewers as the site of the City Police Headquarters in the television series *Homicide*. The series is out of production, but *Homicide* is now part of Baltimore culture.

Fells Point has long been known as a rowdy part of town. It's packed with taverns, saloons, and bars. Restaurants and entertainment venues keep this neighborhood hopping all night long.

Canton is Baltimore's newest hot spot. Long a working-class neighborhood where brick and Formstone rowhouses line the straight streets, it was home to families whose breadwinners worked at nearby factories, canneries, and breweries. Today, technology firms rent office space. Families are moving in from other places, rehabbing or buying the homes. O'Donnell Square, an old city park, is now surrounded with places to stop for a drink and a bite to eat. The Can Company has turned an abandoned can-making operation into something new. It combines work—Dap Corporation is headquartered here—with play. Restaurants and a few shops have filled the first floor with patios surrounding the area outside.

The **Inner Harbor East** was formerly an industrial area; now the city's newest hotel and fine restaurants can be found here. Young adults moving to Baltimore want to live here among the old brick rowhouses and marble steps, not to mention their convenience to other harborside neighborhoods.

All these neighborhoods are connected by a new waterfront promenade as well as water taxis.

Mount Vernon surrounds the Washington Monument (which, as Baltimoreans will remind you, predates the one in the District of Columbia), and offers a collection of beautiful buildings from its heyday as the city's toniest neighborhood. It's home to the Walters Art Museum and the city's newest museum, the Contemporary.

Northern Baltimore City is mostly residential, though **Hampden** and **Mount Washington** offer their own charms, with interesting shopping and some small but good restaurants. If you happen to be in Baltimore during December, visit **34th Street** ★★ in Hampden to see how the neighbors dress their rowhouses up for the holidays with thousands of lights, model trains, and Santa Clauses; play Christmas music; and welcome the city to see this magnificent sight. People come from all over the city. It's one of the friendliest Christmas displays anywhere. Mount Washington is a short Light Rail trip from downtown, a good side trip if the glitz of the Inner Harbor is too much. It's small but offers a handful of fun restaurants, as well as some nice shops and a pottery studio.

Baltimore Neighborhoods

Canton **5**
Fells Point **4**
Hampden **8**
Inner Harbor **1**
Inner Harbor East **2**
Little Italy **3**
Mount Vernon **6**
Mount Washington **7**

2 Getting Around

BY CAR If you plan to stay near the harbor, it is much easier to walk or take one of the water taxi services than to drive and park. That said, driving in downtown Baltimore is fairly easy. The streets are on a straight grid. Many are one-way. The major northbound streets are Howard, Charles, and Calvert. Cathedral and St. Paul are southbound. Lombard and Pratt are the major streets east and west. Martin Luther King Boulevard on the west side connects the harbor with the cultural district. It runs both north and south.

Need to find an address? Buildings are numbered from Charles Street east and west. 100 East Lombard is in the block to the east of Charles. Baltimore Street is the dividing line for north–south addresses. 100 South Charles Street will be a block below Baltimore.

Note: Charles Street is undergoing massive reconstruction adjacent to the train station. Use Calvert or the Jones Falls Expressway as alternate routes until it opens late in 2002.

If you need to rent a car, the major agencies at Baltimore–Washington International Airport include **Avis** (✆ **800/331-1212** or 410/859-1680), **Alamo** (✆ **800/327-9633** or 410/850-5011), **Budget** (✆ **800/527-0700** or 410/859-0850), **Dollar** (✆ **800/800-4000** or 410/684-3315), **Hertz** (✆ **800/654-3131** or 410/850-7400), **National** (✆ **800/328-4567** or 410/859-8860), and **Thrifty** (✆ **800/367-2277** or 410/859-1136).

BY LIGHT RAIL, SUBWAY & BUS Baltimore's Mass Transit Administration (MTA) operates **Light Rail,** a 27-mile (43km) system of above-ground rail lines reminiscent of the city's old trolleys. It travels on one line in a north–south direction from the northern suburb of Timonium to Glen Burnie in the south, with a spur to Penn Station. The key stop within the city is Camden Station, next to the Orioles' ballpark. The Light Rail is the ideal way to get to a game or to travel within the downtown area between Camden Yards and the Inner Harbor to Lexington Market and the area around Mount Vernon Place.

Tickets are $2.50 round-trip and are dispensed at machines at each stop. Trains run every 15 to 30 minutes Monday through Friday between 6am and 11pm, Saturday between 8am and 11pm, and Sunday between 11am and 7pm.

Baltimore's MTA also operates **Metro,** a subway system that connects downtown with the northwest suburbs. Trains run from Johns Hopkins University Hospital in east Baltimore through Charles Center and north to the suburb of Owings Mills. Service runs Monday through Friday from 5am to midnight and Saturday from 6am to midnight. The fare is $1.35; you can also purchase a day pass that allows unlimited trips on the Light Rail, Metro, and city for $3. For information on both Light Rail and Metro service, call ✆ **800/543-9809** or 410/539-5000 or visit the MTA website at www.mtamaryland.com.

The MTA also operates a network of **buses** that connects all sections of the city. Service is daily, but hours vary. The base fare is $1.35 and exact change is necessary, or you can buy a day pass for $3. For information and schedules, contact the MTA at the numbers/website above.

BY TAXI All taxis in the city are metered; two reputable companies are **Yellow Checker Cab** (✆ 410/841-5573) and **Arrow Cab** (✆ **410/261-0000**). For airport trips, call **SuperShuttle** (✆ **410/859-4900**) or **The Airport Shuttle** (✆ **800/776-0323** or 410/381-2772).

BY WATER SHUTTLE & TROLLEY   Take the water taxi—either one—for a pleasant way to visit Baltimore's attractions or even go to dinner. Two companies operate water taxi service and both have different stops. But you can use either to get within walking distance of your waterfront destination.

Ed Kane's Water Taxi & Trolley (✆ **800/658-8947** or 410/563-3901) runs a continual service between about a dozen Inner Harbor locations including Harborplace, Fells Point, Little Italy, Canton, and Fort McHenry. The main stop at Harborplace is on the corner between the two pavilions. Tell the mate where you want to go. The cost is $5 for adults and $2 for children 10 and under for unlimited use of the water taxi and trolley to Fort McHenry for a full day. Tickets include a "Letter of Marque," a set of discount coupons for area restaurants, museums, and shops. Pick up a brochure at the main stop for schedule information for both the water taxi and the trolley. The 11 water taxis generally run about every 15 to 18 minutes 10 or 11am to 11pm or midnight April through October. Service is less frequent November through March, with runs 11am to 6pm. The trolley service runs daily 10am to 5pm May through August and Saturday and Sunday 10am to 5pm in April, September, and October.

The **Seaport Taxi** (✆ **410/675-2900**) goes to many of the same destinations as Ed Kane's, and their stops are usually next to each other. Adults can ride all day for $4 and children 10 and under for $2. For a good value, buy a Seaport Pass and combine this ticket with a visit to the *Constellation* and a ticket to ride all day on the Seaport water taxi. It costs $15.50 for adults, $13 for seniors, $8.50 youth 6 to 14. Children under 5 are free. The shuttle runs from April through October from 8 or 9am to 11pm or midnight. From November through March, service is offered weekdays 8am to 6:30pm and weekends 9am to 6:30pm.

ON FOOT   You really have to know only a few streets. The easiest is the **promenade** around the Inner Harbor. It will take you to Federal Hill and the American Visionary Arts Museum, the Maryland Science Center, Harborplace, the National Aquarium, the *Constellation,* and the Maritime Museum, as well as a few other shops and restaurants. The promenade extends along the water through Inner Harbor East to Fells Point and Canton. Because of construction, portions of the route are not quite finished. But it's a pretty walk, particularly around the Inner Harbor, Inner Harbor East, and Fells Point.

Pratt and **Lombard** streets are the two major east-west arteries just above the Inner Harbor. Pratt heads east to Little Italy and Lombard heads west to the stadiums. **Charles Street** is Baltimore's main route north and home to some good restaurants, Baltimore's Washington Monument, the Morris A. Mechanic Theatre, and the Walters Art Museum, all within walking distance of the Inner Harbor. **St. Paul Street** is the major route south.

 FAST FACTS: **Baltimore**

Airport   See "Arriving," earlier in this chapter.

American Express   The office is near the airport at 1302 Concourse Dr., Linthicum Heights (✆ **410/865-5300**).

Camera Repair   Try Service Photo Supply at 2225 N. Charles St. (✆ **410/235-6200**). For supplies go to Abbey Camera at 320 N. Charles St. (✆ **410/752-4475**).

Car Rentals In addition to airport locations, **Budget** offers car rental at the Hyatt Hotel at the Inner Harbor, 300 Light St. (© **410/783-1448**).

Emergencies Dial © **911** for fire, police, or ambulance.

Eyeglass Repair For Eyes is at 330 N. Charles St. (© **410/727-2027**). Sterling Optical has a shop at 22 Light St. (© **410/234-8398**).

Hospitals City hospitals downtown include Johns Hopkins Hospital, 600 N. Wolfe St. (© **410/955-5000**); University of Maryland Medical Center, 22 S. Greene St. (© **410/328-8667**); and Mercy Medical Center, 301 St. Paul St. (© **410/332-9000**).

Liquor Laws Restaurants, bars, hotels, and other places serving alcohol may stay open 6am to 2am. On Sunday and election days, some opt to close. You can purchase alcohol to take out at most bars. The legal age to buy or consume alcohol is 21.

Newspapers/Magazines The major daily newspaper is *The Baltimore Sun. The City Paper* is the city's weekly alternative. It's published Wednesdays and has excellent listings. *The Washington Post* is also widely available. The local monthly magazine is *Baltimore*.

Pharmacies Rite Aid is at 17 W. Baltimore St. (© **410/539-0838**). Walgreens is at 19 E. Fayette St. (© **410/625-1179**).

Police Dial © **911** for emergencies, **311** for non-emergencies requiring police attention.

Post Office The main post office is at 900 E. Fayette St. (© **410/347-4202**). It's open Monday to Saturday 6:30am to 11pm. Other area post offices are at 111 N. Calvert (© **410/347-4202**), and at 130 N. Greene St. (© **410/ 539-8575**). Both are open weekdays, 8:30am to 5pm.

Safety Baltimore has a nagging problem with property and violent crime. More police, along with the Downtown Partnership's safety guides, are doing a pretty good job of keeping the Inner Harbor and Mount Vernon areas fairly safe. But be alert and follow some common-sense precautions.

If you're using public transportation, try to travel during peak hours and keep valuables out of sight. It is safer and smarter to drive or take a cab between neighborhoods (unless otherwise noted in this chapter) rather than walk, even when the distance is not too great. Keep a good city map at hand. Neighborhoods go from safe to scary in a matter of a few blocks. Keep to the main routes and turn around if anything looks worrisome.

In some parts of the city, you're bound to be approached by a panhandler. Don't open your wallet or purse to give money. Offer only what's in your pocket. It's okay to say no, too.

Taxes The state sales tax is 5%. The hotel tax is an additional 7.5%.

Transit Information Contact the Mass Transit Administration (**MTA**) at © **800/543-9809** or 410/539-5000; www.mtamaryland.org, for bus, Light Rail, and Metro info.

Visitor Information In addition to the BACVA offices (see above), you can stop at the Downtown Partnership's offices at 217 North Charles St. for directions, maps, and other information. Or ask one of the Public Safety Guides wearing the purple caps.

Weather Call © **410/936-1212**.

3 Where to Stay

Baltimore is a town that caters to the business traveler—there are more than 5,600 hotel rooms, with all the amenities a business traveler looks for. There are almost no B&Bs, and only a few inns.

The new Marriott looms large over Inner Harbor East. Built with conventions in mind, it's got plenty of conference rooms and services for the businessperson. Next door is the Marriott Courtyard. On the horizon is a Ritz-Carlton, which will offer a luxury hotel and condos (in the million-dollar range) by Federal Hill. It's set to open in 2003 or 2004.

It can be hard to find a double for under $100 during the week; but that also means that some hotels offer weekend rates and packages that represent savings of 35% to 50% off normal Sunday through Thursday tariffs. So don't be scared off by midweek rates—try to time your visit for a weekend.

Every hotel listed is accessible to travelers with disabilities, although specific amenities vary from hotel to hotel.

INNER HARBOR
VERY EXPENSIVE

Baltimore Marriott Waterfront Hotel ★ *Kids* Baltimore's newest hotel, opened in February 2001, dominates a prime piece of waterfront—even though it's more than a few steps from the city's best-known attractions and the convention center. Luckily, the water taxi stops nearby. The hotel rises 32 floors in a developing area known as the Inner Harbor East. The rooms are pretty standard, with the added pleasures of down duvets and soft, pillow-top mattresses—and, of course, that skyline view. The best views are from the 30th, 31st, and 32nd floors and they come with a premium price. These concierge rooms have all the standard amenities plus deluxe continental breakfast and hors d'oeuvres and cocktails in the Concierge Lounge. Corner rooms offer two views of the city and cost extra. For children, the hotel offers cribs and rollaway beds at no charge and a kid's menu in the restaurants.

700 Aliceanna St., Baltimore, MD 21202. ✆ **410/385-3000.** Fax 410/895-1900. www.marriott.com. 750 units. $159–$249 double. AE, DE, DISC, MC, V. Self-parking $17, valet parking $23. Water taxi stop nearby. **Amenities:** Restaurant; delicatessen; lounge; exercise room; massage therapy room; business center. *In room:* A/C, dataport, minibar, iron.

Harbor Court Hotel ★★★ The Harbor Court strives for quiet dignity, refinement, and graciousness. It's a treat to walk in the door, and if you spend the night, prepare to be pampered. Rooms are exquisitely furnished, from suites with hand-painted decorations, marble bathrooms, kitchenettes, and canopy beds to large standard rooms outfitted in fine furnishings. The hotel overlooks the harbor but only a few rooms have a clear harbor view. Dining options include two first-rate restaurants: **Hampton's** (see "Where to Dine" below) and **Brighton's,** which serves a rich afternoon tea; and **the Explorer's Lounge,** which offers music every night and is popular with locals as well as hotel guests.

550 Light St., Baltimore, MD 21202. ✆ **800/824-0076** or 410/234-0550. Fax 410/659-5925. www.harbor court.com. 195 units. $220–$250 double, $375–$2,000 suite. AE, DC, DISC, MC, V. Self-parking $14, valet parking $18. **Amenities:** 2 restaurants; coffee shop; indoor pool; Jacuzzi; fitness center with racquetball, croquet, tennis and basketball; yoga and water aerobics; tanning; massage available. *In room:* A/C, fax, dataport, minibar, CD clock radio, trouser press.

Hyatt Regency Baltimore ★★★ The eye-catching all-glass Hyatt was the Inner Harbor's first hotel 20 years ago and it's still the best. Sure, Baltimore has more luxury hotels now, but the Hyatt still has the best location. It's a short walk across a skywalk to the Inner Harbor, another skywalk to the convention center, and a few blocks to the stadiums. Rooms have breathtaking harbor views and the amenities are terrific. It's often busy but not too noisy. Staff here couldn't be nicer. The rooms here are your standard hotel chain but there are several choices, including junior suites and VIP suites if you need the room. Kids under 18 stay free here but if your family needs two rooms, the second one's half-price.

300 Light St., Baltimore, MD 21202. ✆ **800/233-1234** or 410/528-1234. Fax 410/685-3362. 486 units. $125–$300 double. Ask for packages and discounts. AE, DC, DISC, MC, V. Self-parking $15, valet parking $20. **Amenities:** Rooftop restaurant; bar; indoor pool and Jacuzzi; recreation deck with jogging track, putting green, 2 tennis courts, and basketball court; health club; aerobics classes; executive level. *In room:* A/C, dataport and Internet access, minibar, iron.

Inner Harbor Courtyard by Marriott ✿   Overshadowed in size by its big sister, the Baltimore Marriott Waterfront, this Marriott won't be outdone for service or comfortable rooms, which are a good size with desks, comfortable beds, and well-equipped bathrooms. There are eight rooms with Jacuzzis and 10 corner suites. It's serious enough for business travelers but casual enough for families on vacation. Although it's is really not in the middle of major attractions, it's on the water taxi routes and located near the newly developing promenade, so getting to the Inner Harbor, Fells Point, or even Fort McHenry is easy.

1000 Aliceanna St., Baltimore, MD 21202. ✆ **410/923-4000.** Fax 410/923-9970. www.marriott.com. 205 units. $129–$209 double. AE, DC, DISC, MC, V. Self-parking $17, valet parking $23. Water taxi stop nearby. **Amenities:** Cafe; lounge; indoor pool; whirlpool; fitness center; business center; complimentary coffee in lobby. *In room:* A/C, TV with pay movies and Nintendo, dataport, minibar, coffeemaker, hair dryer, iron.

Pier 5 Hotel ✿ *Finds*   Be prepared for something wild when you walk into the lobby of the Pier 5. Painted in purple, yellow, and red, it features furniture in a style combining Art Deco and Cartoon Network. It works, though. It's bright and airy, and it's fun to settle back into those sofas. The rooms continue the color scheme, though much quieter and more refined. Standard rooms are quite comfortable and have lots of conveniences for both the business traveler and the tourist—even room service from the Cheesecake Factory. Suites are luxurious with one, two, or even three tiny balconies overlooking the water or the National Aquarium next door. Just about every room has a water view—and a much closer one than any of the other hotels because the hotel is only two stories high and right on the water. They offer lots of packages with local attractions that both adults and children will enjoy; and a few for romance, too.

771 Eastern Ave. (at the end of Pier 5), Baltimore, MD 21202. ✆ 410/539-2000. Fax 410/783-1469. www. harbormagic.com. 65 units. $149–$269 double, $375 suite. AE, DC, DISC, MC, V. Self-parking $16, valet parking $20. Pets welcome. Located on a water taxi stop. **Amenities:** 2 restaurants; coffee shop; exercise room access at Brookshire. *In room:* A/C, dataport and T1 Internet access, fridge, coffeemaker, bottled water, iron, robes.

Renaissance Harborplace Hotel ✿✿   The Renaissance is right in the middle of everything. Business travelers find it convenient to local firms, the convention center, and restaurants. Tourists like its location across the street from Harborplace and the Inner Harbor. It's part of The Gallery at Harborplace, five floors of shops and a food court topped by an office tower. Rooms are the biggest in Baltimore with comfortable furniture and wide windows that really open overlooking the Inner Harbor. (Its views are good; the Hyatt's are better.) There's a concierge level with a lounge where breakfast is served.

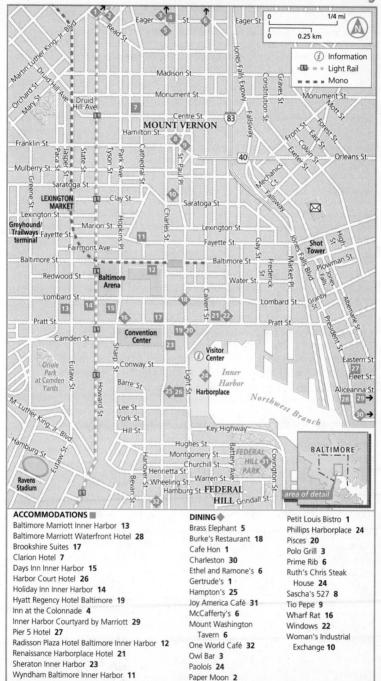

ACCOMMODATIONS ■
Baltimore Marriott Inner Harbor **13**
Baltimore Marriott Waterfront Hotel **28**
Brookshire Suites **17**
Clarion Hotel **7**
Days Inn Inner Harbor **15**
Harbor Court Hotel **26**
Holiday Inn Inner Harbor **14**
Hyatt Regency Hotel Baltimore **19**
Inn at the Colonnade **4**
Inner Harbor Courtyard by Marriott **29**
Pier 5 Hotel **27**
Radisson Plaza Hotel Baltimore Inner Harbor **12**
Renaissance Harborplace Hotel **21**
Sheraton Inner Harbor **23**
Wyndham Baltimore Inner Harbor **11**

DINING ◆
Brass Elephant **5**
Burke's Restaurant **18**
Cafe Hon **1**
Charleston **30**
Ethel and Ramone's **6**
Gertrude's **1**
Hampton's **25**
Joy America Café **31**
McCafferty's **6**
Mount Washington Tavern **6**
One World Café **32**
Owl Bar **3**
Paolo's **24**
Paper Moon **2**

Petit Louis Bistro **1**
Phillips Harborplace **24**
Pisces **20**
Polo Grill **3**
Prime Rib **6**
Ruth's Chris Steak House **24**
Sascha's 527 **8**
Tio Pepe **9**
Wharf Rat **16**
Windows **22**
Woman's Industrial Exchange **10**

202 E. Pratt St., Baltimore, MD 21202. ℂ **800/468-3571** or 410/547-1200. Fax 410/783-9676. http://
renaissancehotels.com. 622 units. $129–$309 double. Children under 17 stay free in parents' room. AE, DC,
DISC, MC, V. Self-parking $16, valet parking $20. **Amenities:** Restaurant overlooking harbor; lounge; access
to Gallery on first and fifth floor; indoor pool; courtyard; whirlpool; sauna; exercise room with bottled water
and fruit; business center; concierge level. *In room:* A/C, TV with Sega system, dataport, minibar, coffeemaker,
iron, robes.

EXPENSIVE

Baltimore Marriott Inner Harbor ✦   This hotel, with a dramatic 10-story
crescent-shaped facade, is a couple of blocks from Harborplace and the convention center, and across the street from Camden Yards. Don't confuse it with the
Baltimore Marriott Waterfront on Inner Harbor East. A waterfall dominates the
busy lobby. Guest rooms are designed in contemporary style and include all
the amenities the business traveler expects, including large desks.

110 S. Eutaw St., Baltimore, MD 21202. ℂ **800/228-9290** or 410/962-0202. Fax 410/625-7832. www.
marriott.com. 524 units. $179–$284 double. Weekend rates available. AE, DC, DISC, MC, V. Self-parking $8,
valet parking $12. **Amenities:** Restaurant; lounge; indoor pool; health club; whirlpool; sauna; business
center; game room; concierge level. *In room:* A/C, voice mail, dataport, high-speed Internet access, minibar,
coffeemaker, iron.

Wyndham Baltimore Inner Harbor (formerly the Omni Inner Harbor) ✦
You could get lost in here, but the staff is aware of how big their hotel is and are
quick to point a lost guest in the right direction. Just remember which tower
you're staying in. The Wyndham is Maryland's largest hotel, with two towers
housing 707 rooms. It's a popular place for conventions with lots of room for
meetings, banquets, and presentations. Guest rooms have lots of amenities for
business travelers. Don't be confused by the name. It's far more convenient to
the business district and the Baltimore Arena than to the harbor. The convention center is 3 blocks away and the harbor is 2 blocks farther down Pratt.

101 W. Fayette St., Baltimore, MD 21202. ℂ **800/WYNDHAM** or 410/752-1100. Fax 410/625-3805. www.
wyndham.com. 707 units. $125–$175 double. Weekend rates available. Children under 18 free in room. AE,
DC, MC, V. Self parking $16. **Amenities:** Restaurant; lounge with light fare; outdoor pool; exercise room.
In room: A/C, voice mail, dataport, Internet access, minibar, coffeemaker, iron, fridge on request.

MODERATE

Brookshire Suites ✦ *Kids*   This building was once a parking garage, but
probably only the tallest guests might notice the slightly lower ceilings. The
rooms are quite comfortable with room to spread out. The suites are even more
spacious, although bedroom space has been sacrificed for a bit more room in the
sitting area. The Cloud Club has a terrific view and lots of comfortable seating
and TVs if you need even more room to stretch out. What makes this an even
better deal for touring families is the full, hot breakfast buffet served here every
morning. The hotel sits a block away from the Inner Harbor on one of the city's
main arteries. It's easy to find and a good location for stepping out to see the
sights, whether it's the Inner Harbor or a trek up Charles Street.

120 E. Lombard St., Baltimore, MD 21202. ℂ **877/207-9047** or 410/539-200. www.harbormagic.com. 97
units. $120–$239 double; ask about packages. Rates include full breakfast in Cloud Club on top floor. AE, DC,
DISC, MC, V. Valet parking $20, parking in garage across street $15. Pets welcome. **Amenities:** Cloud Club
lounge; exercise room. *In room:* A/C, dataport and T1 Internet access, minibar, coffeemaker, iron.

Days Inn Inner Harbor *Value*   If you're willing to give up proximity to the
harbor (by 2 or 3 blocks), you can get a great deal at this modern nine-story
hotel. And if the stadium or convention center are in your plans, they are prac-
tically neighbors. It's got a great setup for business travelers, including "work

zone" rooms that offer large desks, a kitchenette, and plenty of room. But they all have the comfort you expect from this chain. It is located between the arena and convention center, and only 3 blocks from Camden Yards. Guest rooms offer standard chain-motel furnishings, plus hair dryers and iron and ironing board.

100 Hopkins Place (between Lombard and Pratt sts.), Baltimore, MD 21202. © 800/DAYS-INN or 410/ 576-1000. Fax 410/576-9437. www.daysinnerharbor.com. 250 units. $89–$174 double. Children under 17 stay free in parents' room. AE, DC, DISC, MC, V. Parking $11. **Amenities:** Restaurant; outdoor pool; complimentary access to nearby health club; patio courtyard; business center; work zone rooms. In room: A/C, TV with Nintendo 64, dataport, voice mail, minibar, coffeemaker, hair dryer, iron.

Holiday Inn Inner Harbor _(Kids_   You know what you get from a Holiday Inn, and for value and location, it's hard to beat this old-timer, the first major chain property in Baltimore. It's located between the Baltimore Arena and the convention center, a block away from Oriole Park and 3 blocks from Harborplace. It has an executive tower with 175 rooms geared to business travelers and has been updated and renovated regularly. Guest rooms are decorated in bright colors with traditional furniture including a desk, brass fixtures, and wide windows offering views of the city skyline.

301 W. Lombard St., Baltimore, MD 21201. © 800/HOLIDAY or 410/685-3500. Fax 410/727-6169. www. holiday-inn.com/bal-downtown. 375 units. $129–$189 double; $285 suite. Children under 18 stay free in parents' room. AE, DC, DISC, MC, V. Self-parking $8. **Amenities:** Restaurant; 50-foot indoor pool; exercise room; sauna. In room: A/C, TV with Sony Playstation, dataport and voice mail, coffeemaker, hair dryer, iron.

Radisson Plaza Hotel Baltimore Inner Harbor (formerly the Baltimore Hilton) _(Moments_   If you love grand old hotels with modern conveniences, this is the one for you. The former Lord Baltimore opened in 1928. Its ownership and name have changed several times but this 23-story French Renaissance–style hotel retains the old-fashioned charm that recalls the days when this was a refined part of town, filled with the genteel set. The entrance features marble columns, hand-carved artwork, brass fixtures, and chandelier. With the name change in mid-2001, the small but quiet guest rooms will receive new furnishings in 2002. Set in the heart of the theater and financial districts, it's particularly convenient to Mount Vernon attractions but the Inner Harbor is only 5 blocks away.

20 W. Baltimore St. (between Charles and Howard sts.), Baltimore, MD 21202. © **800/333-3333** or 410/ 539-8400. Fax 410/625-1060. www.radisson.com. 419 units. $79–$279 double. AE, DC, DISC, MC, V. Valet parking $22. **Amenities:** Restaurant; bar; exercise room; Jacuzzi; sauna; business center; concierge level rooms. In room: A/C, dataport, voice mail, coffeemaker, hair dryer, iron. Fridge or microwave available upon request.

Sheraton Inner Harbor   The Sheraton has a perfect location for conventioneers and fans of the Orioles or Ravens. Sports fans will like both the location and the packages with tickets for either baseball or football games. The rooms, though, are fairly dark and not as interesting as many other choices in the area. Its suites are a good idea, set up with Murphy beds so they can be turned into mini-conference rooms. The **Oriole Grill** has some interesting sports memorabilia, though no view out its picture window.

300 S. Charles St., Baltimore, MD 21202. © **410/962-8300.** Fax 410/962-8211. 337 units. $119–$249 double, $495–$1,500 suite. Children under 18 free in parents' room. AE, DC, DISC, MC, V. **Amenities:** Restaurant; casual grill and lounge; terrace; pool; exercise room. In room: A/C, dataport, minibar, iron. Fridge and microwave in suites.

FELLS POINT

Admiral Fell Inn ★★   Updated and expanded over the years, this charming inn sits just a block from the harbor in the heart of Fells Point. It is composed of seven buildings, built between 1790 and 1920 and blending Victorian and Federal-style architecture. Originally a boardinghouse for sailors, later a YMCA and then a vinegar bottling plant, the inn now includes an antiques-filled lobby and library and guest rooms individually decorated with Federal period furnishings. Some have canopy beds, and one suite has a fireplace and Jacuzzi. Two rooms feature balconies. A loft room is quite different from the rest, more rustic, with sloping ceilings that tall guests might not like. But from the three dormer windows, the views are among the best in the inn.

888 S. Broadway, Baltimore, MD 21231. ℂ 800/292-4667 or 410/522-7377. Fax 410/522-0707. www.AdmiralFell.com. 80 units. $215–$265 double. Pets (crate-trained dogs) permitted with additional fee. Rates include continental breakfast. AE, MC, V. Free self-parking, valet parking $7. **Amenities:** Hamilton's restaurant serving dinner and Sunday brunch; complimentary shuttle to downtown; coffee and tea in lobby. *In room:* A/C, dataport; iron available.

Celie's Waterfront Inn ★ *Finds*   Walk down the Sally walk of this 18th century town house and enter a quiet refuge. It's one of only a few bed-and-breakfasts in Baltimore and it's delightful. Each of the rooms has its own charms: two have a fireplace and whirlpool and harbor views. Two inside rooms are particularly quiet, as they overlook the courtyard filled with flowers in summer. Two rooms with city views as nice as the harbor view have private balconies and whirlpool tubs. One ground-floor room has its own courtyard. Furnishings were chosen with comfort in mind, with big beds, private bathrooms, and a homey parlor. The TVs are hidden in cabinets mounted on walls. Have breakfast in your room, on the deck, or in the garden.

1714 Thames St., Fells Point, Baltimore 21231. ℂ 800/432-0184 or 410/522-2323. Fax 410/522-2324. celies@aol.com. 7 units. $132–$242 double. Rate includes hearty continental breakfast. 2- or 3-night minimums may be required on weekends or holidays. AE, DISC, MC, V. Ask about parking arrangements. On water taxi route. **Amenities:** Roof deck with harbor views; access to conveniences such as fax, iron, coffeemaker, fridge, VCR. *In room:* A/C, telephone with answering machines and modem capability, whirlpools in some rooms, robes.

Inn at Henderson's Wharf ★   Not all the good waterfront hotels are in the Inner Harbor. The Inn at Henderson's Wharf offers gracious surroundings on the water at Fells Point, a few blocks from the Inner Harbor, with comfortable rooms facing either the water or a central courtyard with English-style gardens. Rooms have exposed brick walls, large windows, and feather beds. There are plenty of restaurants nearby, though the continental breakfast here is generous. Convenience is key here, from all the amenities in guest rooms to the free parking. You can even come by boat and dock in the marina at the front door. The inn takes up only part of this redevelopment of an old railroad warehouse. Condominiums fill the rest.

1000 Fell St., Baltimore, MD 21231. ℂ 800/522-2088 or 410/522-7777. Fax 410/522-7087. www.hendersonswharf.com. 38 units. $149–$259 double. Rates include continental breakfast. AE, DC, MC, V. Free parking. **Amenities:** 256-slip marina; free parking. *In room:* A/C, coffeemaker, hair dryer, robes, stereo with CD player.

NORTH OF DOWNTOWN

Clarion Hotel at Mount Vernon Square   This Mount Vernon–area hotel first opened in 1930 and still strives to offer old-fashioned service. The building has European-style ambience with a luxurious though small lobby and public

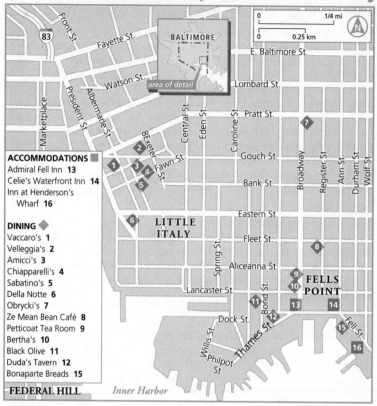

ACCOMMODATIONS ■
Admiral Fell Inn **13**
Celie's Waterfront Inn **14**
Inn at Henderson's
  Wharf **16**

DINING ◆
Vaccaro's **1**
Velleggia's **2**
Amicci's **3**
Chiapparelli's **4**
Sabatino's **5**
Della Notte **6**
Obrycki's **7**
Ze Mean Bean Café **8**
Petticoat Tea Room **9**
Bertha's **10**
Black Olive **11**
Duda's Tavern **12**
Bonaparte Breads **15**

FEDERAL HILL

Inner Harbor

rooms. Each of the guest rooms has period furniture, imported lamps, and a marble bathroom. A business center and dry-cleaning service are available. It's close to the Peabody Institute, Walters Art Museum, and Mount Vernon restaurants and shops. The walk to the Inner Harbor takes 20 minutes or so—and it's all downhill (which of course makes the walk back uphill).

612 Cathedral St., Baltimore, MD 21201. ℂ **800/292-5500** or 410/727-7101. Fax 410/789-3312. www. clarionhotel.com/hotel/md001. 103 units. $119–$219 double. Weekend rates available. Rates include continental breakfast. AE, DC, DISC, MC, V. Valet parking $18 a day. **Amenities:** 2 restaurants; business center; executive rooms stocked with office supplies. *In room:* A/C, speaker phones with dataport, fridge, coffeemaker, iron.

Inn at the Colonnade If your Baltimore visit will take you to the northern reaches of the city, to Johns Hopkins University right across the street, or the Baltimore Museum of Art; to take in a lacrosse game, or to visit friends in Homeland or Roland Park, this is a good choice. Sleek and elegant, the inn offers comfortable rooms, furnished in a Biedermeier style and plenty of amenities. The parking is a bit tricky and you'd do best to pull up and let the valet park your car.

4 W. University Pkwy., Baltimore, MD 21218. ℂ **800/222-TREE** or 410/235-5400. Fax 410/235-5572. www. doubletreehotels.com. 125 units. $135–$159 double; $175–$250 suite. Weekend rates and discounts available. AE, DC, DISC, MC, V. Self-parking $8, valet parking $10. **Amenities:** Polo Grill restaurant; indoor pool; whirlpool; exercise room; access to Johns Hopkins' jogging track and tennis courts; complimentary shuttle to Inner Harbor. *In room:* A/C, dataport, minibar in suites, fridge in some rooms, coffeemaker, hair dryer, iron.

4 Where to Dine

"Crabtown" has always been known for good seafood, but Baltimore is also home to a fair variety of ethnic and regional cuisines. In recent years, the Inner Harbor has become a bit overrun with chain restaurants serving mediocre fare; The Hard Rock Cafe and ESPN at the Power Plant continue to draw big crowds.

The newest dining and nightlife venue is Power Plant Live, a mix of night-clubs, chain restaurants, and some new local places. You can find it by looking for the Port Discovery's HiFlyer balloon hovering above it. Power Plant Live is located a block north of Pratt Street, a short walk from Charles Street and the Inner Harbor. Although the Port Discovery museum has been there since 1998, new restaurants have appeared through 2001.

There are plenty of good restaurants in Baltimore's main tourist area, and a wide variety of choices in nearby Little Italy, Fells Point, and Mount Vernon.

INNER HARBOR
VERY EXPENSIVE

Charleston ★★★ AMERICAN/SOUTHERN The Charleston is all the rage in Baltimore and a top choice for a special night out. With a beautiful set-ting and imaginative menu, the prevailing mood is "gracious," from the moment you are greeted. Chef Cindy Wolf's idea was to create a restaurant that celebrates Southern hospitality. With a cuisine based on the freshest possible ingredients, the menu changes every day. On a summer Saturday, the menu might include she-crab soup; a salad of kiwi, mango, baby arugula, and micro-greens dressed with lavender-honey and lemon vinaigrette; grilled yellowfin tuna with Andouille sausage; and fried green tomato and tomato-basil relish. A cheese course has become a big hit, with about a dozen cheeses to choose from. Por-tions aren't so big you can't enjoy dessert. Splurge on homemade ice cream or sorbet, Napoleons or crème brûlée with a Charleston touch. Can't decide? Charleston offers a five-course menu of the evening for about $60 a person or a seven-course tasting menu for about $70. The chef's husband and co-owner, Tony Foreman, has selected 500 bottles of wine that the service staff is ready to help you choose from. All the dining rooms are warm and inviting—the main room gives diners an opportunity to see the open kitchen. Wine lovers may want to make a reservation for the Wine Library. As you dress you might want to remember the room is slightly cool to protect the wines lining the walls.

1000 Lancaster St., Inner Harbor East. ✆ **410/332-7373.** Fax 410/332-8475. www.charlestonrestaurant. com. Reservations recommended. Main courses $20–$28. AE, DC, DISC, MC, V. Mon–Sat 5:30–10pm.

Hampton's ★★★ NEW AMERICAN Overlooking the Inner Harbor and the National Aquarium, this highly touted restaurant is the main dining room of the Harbor Court Hotel and worth a splurge for a special night out or sump-tuous brunch for its all-around fine-dining experience: elegant decor, great views, service, and cuisine. Dinner choices include Maine lobster *gratine;* pan seared tenderloin *au poivre;* and a trio of lamb consisting of roast rack, seared loin and braised *osso buco* with goat cheese polenta and zinfandel lamb jus. The brunch—appetizer, entree, dessert buffet, and flowing champagne—is quite popular, so be sure to make reservations.

In the Harbor Court Hotel, 550 Light St. ✆ **410/234-0550.** Reservations required. Jacket required. Main courses $28–$38; brunch $23–$33. AE, DC, DISC, MC, V. Sun, Tues–Thurs 5:30–10pm, Fri–Sat 5:30–11pm; brunch Sun 10:30am–2pm. Valet or self parking are complimentary for dinner and brunch guests.

EXPENSIVE

Pisces ⭐ *Moments* SEAFOOD In a city where lots of restaurants have good views, this view tops them all. Overlooking the Inner Harbor, Camden Yards, and the downtown skyline, this two-tiered rooftop restaurant was voted "Baltimore's best view" by the readers of *Baltimore* magazine. The interior is sleek and modern, the menu small but intriguing. Soups can range from cream of crab to grilled seafood miso, while entrees are mostly seafood wrapped in creative sauces and seasonings. Though the dining area is not particularly large, the well-spaced tables offer a pleasantly intimate dining experience. The waitstaff is quite knowledgeable, and service is anything but hurried. This is a place to relax and enjoy a spectacular view and a well-prepared meal.

In the Hyatt Regency Hotel, 300 Light St., 15th floor. ☎ **410/528-1234**. Reservations recommended. Main courses $15–$29. AE, DC, DISC, MC, V. Daily 4:30pm–1am.

Ruth's Chris Steak House ⭐⭐ AMERICAN Located between South Frederick and Market streets on the first floor of the Brokerage, the Baltimore branch of this national steakhouse chain is a favorite with the suit-and-tie crowd. Its dark wood furnishings, tiled floor, globe lanterns, and tree-sized leafy plants contribute to its clubby atmosphere. This is a place to come for beef—there are six choices of steak on the menu, all butter-bathed and prepared to order, plus prime rib and filet mignon. Alternatively, there are lobster, salmon, swordfish, and blackened tuna, as well as lamb chops and chicken.

600 Water St. ☎ **410/783-0033**. Reservations required Fri and Sat. Main courses $17.95–$33.95. AE, DC, DISC, MC, V. Mon–Thurs 5–10pm, Fri–Sat 5–11pm, Sun 4–9pm.

Windows ⭐ NEW AMERICAN The sweeping views of the Inner Harbor are only the beginning at this fifth-floor restaurant. The food is good enough for the locals, who know their seafood. Using fresh seasonal ingredients, especially Maryland-grown produce and seafood, the chef has created a delightful menu. Entrees vary widely, but recently included some wonderful grilled rockfish and lump crab grilled with charred tomato vinaigrette, as well as pecan-crusted cod and filet mignon with savory potato hash. Lunchtime is just as adventurous, with fresh ingredients and a touch of the unconventional. Even the turkey club was deliciously different, with smoked turkey, peppered bacon, and wheatberry toast.

In the Renaissance Harborplace Hotel, 202 E. Pratt St. ☎ **410/685-8439**. Reservations required. Main courses $15.95–$38.95; lunch $8.95–$14.95. AE, DC, DISC, MC, V. Daily 6:30am–11pm.

MODERATE

Burke's Restaurant INTERNATIONAL Located opposite Harborplace, this tavern-style restaurant has been a downtown fixture for more than 60 years. There are two rooms—one with a long, dark wood bar, ceiling fans, aged barrels, pewter tankards, and booth or stool seating; and another with a Tudor-style ceiling, wrought-iron chandeliers, framed prints depicting Old Maryland scenes, and traditional table seating. The menu here is extensive and the food particularly good. Crab cakes are a perennial standout, and the onion rings are legendary. Dinner entrees include steaks, beef ribs, barbecued chicken, and seafood platters.

36 Light St. (at Lombard St.). ☎ **410/752-4189**. Reservations recommended for dinner. Main courses $9.15–$20.95; lunch $3–$10; breakfast $2.60–$11.85. AE, MC, V. Daily 7am–2am.

Joy America Café ⭐ *Finds* AMERICAN "Nothing without Joy" isn't just a slogan at Joy America Café. The creative spirit that fills the American Visionary Arts Museum has spread to its cafe on the third floor. The hand-constructed

Kids **Family-Friendly Restaurants**

With the emphasis on seafood in Baltimore, finding an affordable family restaurant can be difficult. The restaurants and food courts at Harborplace are a good bet. Below are a few places where the younger set is quite welcome.

Amicci's (p. 80) It's casual; there are usually lots of other families so you don't have to worry about disturbing other diners; and there's a great selection of pasta dishes. If it's crowded, try Sabatino's or Vellegia's.

Phillips Harborplace (see below) Perhaps the city's most affordable good seafood, even if you're traveling with the whole family. The Harborplace location is ideal for lunch or dinner after a day at the Aquarium or the Science Center, and the children's menu includes seafood and non-fish favorites like burgers and fries and fried chicken.

Café Hon (p. 85) This Hampden eatery is so relaxed and offers so many comfort foods, you know a kid will like it. And the friendly staff will cater to them. The dining room is filled with knickknacks and other stuff to keep the little ones interested until the food arrives.

menus, sleek modern dining room, and creative food will bring joy. If the weather's nice, add to all this happiness by getting one of the small colored-glass–topped tables on the covered deck. Eat things like black bean and chevre burritos, enormous Spanish omelets with tomatillo sauce, sugar grilled Yucatán shrimp, or scrumptious salads while you watch tugboats steam past or ponder the movement of the sculpture in the plaza. The cafe is open whether or not you have time to see the museum. It's a nice place to stop after a visit to nearby Fort McHenry or the Baltimore Museum of Industry. Stop at the museum's front desk and get a sticker to go to the restaurant.

At the American Visionary Art Museum, 800 Key Hwy. 🕐 **410/244-6500.** Fax 410/244-6363. www. avam.org/joyamerica. Reservations accepted. Main courses $7–30; lunch $6–$11. AE, MC, V. Tues–Sat 11am–10pm; Sun brunch 11am–4pm.

Phillips Harborplace 🔹 *Kids* SEAFOOD   Of more than a dozen restaurants and sidewalk cafes in the festive Harborplace development, this is a standout, and the best place for good, reasonably priced seafood. It's a branch of the successful restaurant that has been an Ocean City, Maryland, landmark since 1956. Dinner is a feast of fresh seafood, featuring crab in many forms—soft-shell crab, crab and lobster sauté, crab cakes, crab imperial, and all-you-can-eat portions of steamed crabs. Other seafood dishes include salmon, swordfish, lobster, oysters, and snapper. Steaks and other meats are also available, and there's a good children's menu offering the usual burgers, chicken nuggets, and hot dogs as well as shrimp and fish, all served with side dishes. There's a lively sing-along piano bar and entertainment beginning at dinner. Phillips also has a seafood buffet outlet and a carryout in the Light Street Pavilion.

Level 1, Light Street Pavilion, Harborplace. 🕐 **410/685-6600.** Reservations not accepted but parties of 15 or more should call 🕐 **800/648-7067.** Main courses $14.99–$29.95; lunch $5.99–$12.99. AE, DC, DISC, MC, V. Sun–Thurs 11am–10pm, Fri–Sat 11am–midnight. Valet parking at the Harbor Court is discounted with validated ticket.

Wharf Rat BREWPUB   Located across the street from the convention center, the Wharf Rat has become a favorite with the business crowd and young sports fans during baseball and football season. The place is filled with paraphernalia from British, Scottish, and Irish beers and a glass wall in the dining room that allows diners to peek in on the beer making. The restaurant offers light entrees and sandwiches for dinner and lunch. The pub's Oliver Brewery offers a wide variety of ales and stouts, plus an especially good porter. Sandwiches and pub fare are more innovative and interesting than you might expect. Try the rich Wharf Club, a triple-decker sandwich with crabmeat, shrimp salad, bacon, and cheese; or the French Ambassador, country ham topped with melted Brie on French bread. For dinner, we recommend the London broil.

206 W. Pratt St. (at Hanover St. across from the convention center). ℂ **410/244-8900.** Main courses $12.95–$17.25; lunch $6.95–$9.95. AE, DC, DISC, MC, V. Daily 11:30am–2am.

LITTLE ITALY

In just a few packed blocks, you'll find all the pasta, cannoli, and lambrusco you could want. Make a reservation if you know where you want to eat. But if you want to wander first, plan to eat early or late and choose as you stroll through the basil-scented streets. If you can't find room for dessert, remember, there's always Vaccaro's to go. Parking has gotten easier here. On-street parking can be a headache and lots used to fill up quickly. A huge new lot has opened on Pratt at the entrance of Little Italy and many of the restaurants now offer valet parking.

EXPENSIVE

Sabatino's ✰✰✰ ITALIAN   Sabatino's still stands out for its exceptional Italian cuisine at reasonable prices. Everyone will tell you to get the house salad with the house dressing—it's thick and garlicky. Simple pasta dishes come in very large portions—but they are so good, you'll be happy to take home a little manicotti or gnocchi. The menu also has some seafood and meat dishes with pasta on the side. *Brasciole,* a roll of meat, prosciutto, cheeses, and marinara, is heavenly. Dining rooms fill three floors of this narrow building. It's worth the wait to be seated upstairs where it's quieter. This is a particularly good late-night dining spot, a good place to people-watch after the bars have closed.

901 Fawn St. (at the corner of High St.). ℂ **410/727-9414.** Fax 410/837-6540. www.sabatinos.com. Reservations recommended. Main courses $10–$17; lunch $8–$15. AE, DC, DISC, MC, V. Daily noon–3am.

Velleggia's ✰ ITALIAN   It's always crowded at Velleggia's. It's loud and fun, and you'll probably wait a few minutes. But then the food will come and you'll be glad you had patience. Fettuccini *al Mare Bianco* is wonderful, studded with shrimp, scallops, and crab. Lasagna Primavera skips the meat and adds vegetables. Cannelloni is rich and soothing. There are veal, beef, and chicken cooked the Italian way, too. It's all good.

829 Pratt St. ℂ **410/685-2620.** Reservations recommended. Main courses $10.95–$22. AE, DISC, MC, V. Sun–Thurs 11am–11:30pm, Fri–Sat 11:30am–1:30am.

MODERATE

Chiapparelli's SOUTHERN ITALIAN   In the heart of Little Italy, this restaurant is a longtime favorite. Southern Italian dishes in rich red marinara sauce, are the trademark here, with special plaudits for ravioli stuffed with spinach and ricotta and Italian wedding soup. Dinner is the main event, and veal is the star of the menu, cooked at least half a dozen different ways. You'll also find lots of tasty chicken dishes and classics as pescatore, shrimp parmigiana, and steak pizzaiola. The children's menu includes fusilli with a choice of sauce, chicken fingers, and pizza toast.

237 S. High St. (at Fawn St.). ✆ **410/837-0309.** Reservations recommended. Main courses $12–$25; lunch $5.95–$14.95. AE, DC, DISC, MC, V. Mon–Thurs 11:30am–10:30pm, Fri–Sat 11:30am–midnight, Sun 11:30am–10pm.

Della Notte ★★ ITALIAN   You might want to come to Della Notte just for the beautiful dining room. Banquettes line the circular dining room, and a huge tree rises in the center. It's a lovely backdrop for the great Italian food to come. Lunch is panini, pizza for one, and pasta. At dinner, pasta shines: *capellini al pomadoro* or fettuccini with a hint of nutmeg are among the tempting choices. The wine list goes on forever, with 16 champagnes alone. (Prices range from bargain to *wow!*) If you come late, you might want to stop at the piano bar in the Emperor's Lounge. Della Notte has that rare commodity in Little Italy: its own parking lot, free for guests while dining.

801 Eastern Ave. ✆ **410/837-5500.** Reservations recommended. Main courses $12–$22; lunch $8–$10.50. AE, MC, V. Sun–Thurs 11am–10pm, Fri–Sat 11am–midnight.

INEXPENSIVE

Amicci's *Value* ITALIAN   You'll almost certainly find Amicci's crowded with locals who don't want to spend a lot on good Italian food, and who also don't want to dress to the hilt. Amicci's bills itself as "a very casual eatery," and you'll likely find lots of young couples and children in jeans and T-shirts sitting down to big plates of pasta. The music piped in is likely to be B. B. King or Bob Marley. And don't be fooled by the small shopfront—the restaurant is a maze of small dining rooms. If you have to wait, it won't be too long. The antipasto for two or the *pane rotundo* (a creamy seafood dip served in a fresh-baked bread bowl) are superb starters. The sausage Marsala is a lovely take on the traditional chicken or veal dishes. Try the chicken and broccoli Alfredo or the gnocchi in a zesty sun-dried tomato and pesto sauce. Seafood lovers might consider the seafood special with mussels, shrimp and scallops in a Marsala sauce. Vaccaro's desserts are served here. So relax; have a cappuccino and some tiramisu.

231 High St. ✆ **410/528-1096.** Reservations accepted for parties of 6 or more. Main courses $7.90–$13.90. AE, DISC, MC, V. Sun–Thurs 11:30am–10pm, Fri–Sat 11:30am–11pm.

Vaccaro's ★ ITALIAN PASTRIES & DESSERTS   To top off a perfect day, stop at Vaccaro's, the always-busy restaurant for Italian desserts, coffee, and cappuccino. In addition to cannoli, rum cake, and tiramisu, it has decadently rich gelato. If you love gelato, you'll be thrilled by the huge servings of it. The Baci gelato combines the flavors of chocolate and hazelnut. (Can't decide on one? The menu doesn't tell you this but you can ask the waitress for a sampler and you'll get three different flavors.) Coffee is a standout here, too, plain or scented with cinnamon or vanilla. They even sell cannoli shells and the cream so you can assemble them yourself. They don't take reservations, but the wait is never too long. Visit on your birthday and you can choose a free dessert from their birthday menu. There's also a location at the Light Street Pavilion in Harborplace.

222 Albemarle St. ✆ **410/685-4905.** Desserts $3.75–$7.50. AE, MC, V. Mon–Wed 7:30am–10pm; Wed, Thurs, Sun 7:30am–11pm; Fri–Sat 7:30am–1am.

FELLS POINT
EXPENSIVE

Black Olive ★★ GREEK/SEAFOOD   This Greek *taverna,* just beyond the busier streets of Fells Point, is creating its own traffic. The combination of Greek fare and the freshest seafood have made this place a standout. Choose whatever the catch of the day is and trust the chef to make it wonderful. The restaurant has two small, intimate dining rooms, so small that reservations are a must. The service here is also top-notch and relaxed.

814 S. Bond St. ℂ **410/276-7141.** www.blackolive.com. Reservations required. Main courses $22–$32. AE, MC, V. Mon–Thurs 5–10pm, Fri–Sat 5–10:30pm, Sun 5–9pm.

Obrycki's ★★ SEAFOOD   Fells Point, the neighborhood where Baltimore began, is one of the city's best areas for seafood. The benchmark of all the eateries here is Obrycki's. Food connoisseurs Craig Claiborne and George Lang rave about this place. The decor is charming, with stained-glass windows, brick archways, and wainscoting along the walls. But the big attraction is the fresh seafood, especially crabs. This is the quintessential crab house, where you can crack open steamed crabs in their shells and feast on the tender, succulent meat. There's crab soup, crab cocktail, crab balls, crab cakes, crab imperial, and soft-shell crabs. The rest of the menu is just as tempting—shrimp, lobster, scallops, haddock, flounder, and steaks. Among the lunchtime choices are seafood salads and sandwiches. The service is extremely attentive.

1727 E. Pratt St., Upper Fells Point. ℂ **410/732-6399.** Reservations accepted only until 7pm Mon–Fri, and 6pm Sat–Sun. Main courses $14.95–$28.95; lunch/light fare $6.95–$13.95. AE, DC, DISC, MC, V. Open Mon–Fri 11:30am–10pm, Sat 11:30am–11pm, Sun 11:30am–9pm. Closed late Nov to mid-Mar.

MODERATE

Bertha's ★ INTERNATIONAL/SEAFOOD   Don't miss this Fells Point landmark, known for its mussels and music. The decor is shabby chic with dark walls and plenty of accessories proud of their age. It's a perfect place for a traditional afternoon tea, a dinner featuring Bertha's mussels in a variety of dishes, or a night of jazz or blues. Mussels headline the menu prepared in a dozen different ways, though they are delicious swimming in garlic butter. (You can also get a classic Baltimore souvenir, the EAT BERTHA'S MUSSELS T-shirt.) The rest of the menu is heavy on seafood, while at lunch you can get salads, omelets, sandwiches, burgers, and daily specials. Afternoon tea, with scones and clotted cream, Scotch eggs, and other tidbits, is a wonderful tradition. It's served daily 3 to 4:30pm and reservations are a must. After 9pm the music starts most evenings: jazz on Tuesday, Wednesday, and Thursday; and blues on Friday and Saturday.

734 S. Broadway. ℂ **410/327-5795.** Reservations accepted only for parties of 6 or more for lunch and dinner; reservations required for afternoon tea. Main courses $8.75–$18.75; lunch $5.25–$9.95; afternoon tea $9.75. MC, V. Sun–Thurs 11:30am–11pm, Fri–Sat 11:30am–midnight.

Ze Mean Bean Cafe AMERICAN   Though this cozy little place hasn't strayed too far from its Eastern European roots, it's traveled a bit and now has 100 bottles of wine. In addition to the always wonderful *pierogi, holupki* (two cabbage rolls stuffed with beef and rice and topped with light tomato sauce), or chicken Kiev, the chef has added veal chops, Kodiak salmon, tilapia stuffed with crab, and a wonderful filet mignon topped with a Stilton cheese sauce. The lunch and light fare menu includes salads and sandwiches. Brunch is served a la carte on Saturday and Sunday, with jazz on Sunday. The restaurant has two dining areas, one upstairs and one downstairs. Soft jazz or classical guitar plays nightly in the downstairs dining room. Make reservations if you wish to sit nearby.

1739 Fleet St. ℂ **410/675-5999.** Reservations recommended. Main courses $7.95–$21.95; lunch $4.95–$7.95. MC, V. Mon–Thurs 10am–11pm, Fri 10am–1am, Sat 9am–1am, Sun 9am–11pm.

INEXPENSIVE

Bonaparte Breads FRENCH/BAKERY   This wonderful little spot is part bakery, part cafe, all French. You can stop for freshly baked pastries or bread studded with fruit, olives, or herbs. Or you can stop for breakfast or lunch. It's *prix fixe*. Breakfast is about $6 and lunch about $8. Be prepared to make lots of decisions. You walk up to the counter and choose between three kinds of sandwiches and two quiches (seafood quiche is creamy, rich, and filled with all kinds of seafood, even octopus). Then have a seat at one of the tables surrounded by leather-upholstered chairs to wait for your lunch. If you're lucky, you'll get a table by the window so you can look out at the harbor while you eat. After lunch, which includes salad, you have to decide again among the fresh pastries in the case. Filled with fruit and sugar, they're all good. Bonaparte has a second restaurant in Savage Mill with the same kind of arrangement.

903 South Ann St., Fells Point. ✆ 410/342-4000. MC, V. Daily 8am–7pm. Lunch served only until 3pm but breads and pastries available until 7pm.

Duda's Tavern *Finds* PUB FARE   From the outside, this is an unassuming little place and looks like dozens of corner bars around Baltimore. Inside, it's dark, with eight small tables and a big bar. But around Fells Point, it's got a great reputation for food. Specials change for lunch and dinner every day. Look for crab cakes and fresh fish and probably something unexpected. On a recent afternoon, specials included smoked chicken and apple sausage, tangy pulled barbecue sandwich, and red local tomatoes stacked with smoky mozzarella. Also on the menu are raw bar items, fresh salads, and 15 or more appetizers. It's not your usual pub fare. Duda's has 100 different beers to pair with their great food.

1600 Thames St., Fells Point. ✆ 410/276-7555. No reservations. Main courses $5.99–$15.99. DC, DISC, MC, V. Daily 11am–1am (kitchen closes at midnight).

Petticoat Tea Room   Everything about this new little restaurant is sweet. Dressed in pink and lace, the small dining room is pretty. Teacups are filled with fresh roses, and humorous little books sit on every table. Tea comes in dainty teacups and sandwiches are arranged on a plate. You can get hot or cold tea, and jasmine and mint are among the many blends. Among the food choices are little finger sandwiches, all so good you'll wish they were bigger. In summer, the tomatoes are local, cucumber is fresh and delicate, shrimp salad savory. They come with spicy cheese sticks, fresh fruit, and a perfect little praline. It doesn't look like a lot of food but when you've finished, you'll be content. If not, there's always a wonderfully sweet dessert waiting. Afternoon tea is $15.95 and High Tea (reservations required) is $19.95. Both are served whenever you want. Saturday breakfast and Sunday brunch are also offered.

814 S. Broadway, Fells Point. ✆ 410/342-7884. Reservations suggested but required for tea. Lunch $8.95–$12.95. AE, DISC, MC, V. Sun–Thurs 11am–6pm, Fri–Sat 11am–8pm.

CANTON

Rick's Café Americain AMERICAN   Don't look for Ilsa or Captain Renault to come sauntering into Rick's Café Americain. It really is an American cafe. But the decor of this brand-new eatery recalls those romantic days in Casablanca. So do the sandwiches. How about a Blue Parrot, chicken with jerk spices, or Captain Renault's grilled fish sandwich? The fish sandwich is quite good, a thick slab of fresh fish between slices of rosemary-scented bread. Dinner entrees include pasta, lamb chops, and steaks. The casual cafe is on O'Donnell Square. Although it can be quiet at lunchtime, it's filled to capacity and quite noisy at night.

2903 O'Donnell St., Canton. ☎ **410/675-1880.** No reservations accepted, but for large parties call ahead for preferred seating. Main courses $11–$18, sandwiches and light fare $6–$10. AE, DC, DISC, MC, V. Daily 11am–2am.

FEDERAL HILL

One World Café VEGETARIAN   Popular with the Gen-X crowd, this Federal Hill spot serves vegetarian and vegan fare, along with coffee, wine, and microbrews, in a relaxed setting. Don't miss the hummus dip. Taking a chance on the daily specials is a good idea. The veggie burger and quesadillas are quite good. Though most of the menu consists of sandwiches and soups, there are a few dinner entrees such as pasta primavera and Thai tempeh. Dining rooms are on three floors; the second is a bit roomier.

904 S. Charles St. ☎ **410/234-0235.** Main courses $2.95–$11.95; breakfast $2.75–$7.95. AE, MC, V. Mon 7am–10pm, Tues–Fri 7am–11pm, Sat 8am–11pm, Sun 8am–10pm.

MOUNT VERNON/CHARLES STREET
EXPENSIVE

Prime Rib ★★ STEAK HOUSE   In the heart of Mount Vernon, this restaurant—a standout for fine beef since 1965—aims to spoil beef-lovers. Their prime rib is the best around. In fact, it could spoil you for all other steaks. The pork chops are huge; the Caesar salad's crisp Romaine is dressed to perfection; The lobster bisque is rich and creamy. If you want seafood, there are crab cakes, and a variety of fish dishes, such as blackened grouper. Everything is a la carte. It's so good, it's popular. Tables are squeezed together and intimate conversation is impossible. In fact, the dining room can be quite noisy. But people come here for the food, not the conversation.

1101 N. Calvert St. (between Biddle and Chase sts.). ☎ **410/539-1804.** Reservations recommended. Main courses $16.95–$39. AE, DC, DISC, MC, V. Daily 5pm–midnight.

MODERATE

Brass Elephant ★★ ⓥalue AMERICAN   The Brass Elephant returned to its 1981 menu for its 20th anniversary, and the response was so enthusiastic, they've kept it. Lower prices and hearty American food have replaced the fancy entrees. So now you spend about $30 per person for some wine, some crab chowder, rockfish or stuffed pork chops. And all of this comes in one of Baltimore's most elegant restaurant settings, an 1861 town house with fireplace, chandeliers, and gold-leaf trim. Valet parking is complimentary.

924 N. Charles St. ☎ **410/547-8480.** Reservations required. Main courses $12.50–$24. AE, DC, DISC, MC, V. Sun–Thurs 5:30–9pm, Fri–Sat 5:30–11pm.

Owl Bar AMERICAN   Housed in the wedding-cake-fancy Belvedere, the Owl Bar exudes a long-ago charm with its brass rail bar, paneled walls, leather furnishings, and an owl here and there. Yet it's a more casual place than all that, especially as the older diners give way to a younger crowd around 9pm. The menu bows to contemporary tastes, with a brick oven that turns out such trendy creations as white pizza (made with all white cheeses) and the Owl (made with grilled chicken, caramelized onion, and mozzarella). Specialty pastas are also appealing, including blackened chicken farfalle. Other choices include Black Angus steaks, roasted portobello mushrooms, and coconut peanut chicken.

1 E. Chase St. ☎ **410/347-0888.** Reservations recommended for dinner. Main courses $9.95–$24.95; lunch $5–$10. AE, DC, DISC, MC, V. Mon–Thurs 11:30am–11pm, Fri–Sat 11:30am–midnight, Sun 11am–10pm.

Sascha's 527 ★★ AMERICAN   In a colorful but sophisticated dining room with high ceilings and velvet banquettes, Sascha's has put together an eclectic menu. Dinner choices range from burgers to "pizzettes" (like gourmet pizzas) to several meat and seafood entrees. But their "taste plates" are where they shine. Small, appetizer portions priced at $4 to $9 a plate give diners a chance to try a few adventurous dishes. The Acapulco High Rise is Sascha's answer to nachos, but don't miss the Indonesian chicken canes that come with an Asian slaw. At lunch, the restaurant goes buffet style. Choose from a variety of offbeat sandwiches, vegetarian side salads, panini sandwiches, or rich soup.

N. Charles St., Mount Vernon. (*C*) 410/539-8880. Main courses $6.50–$15, lunch $4.25–$6.75. AE, DC, MC, V. Daily 11am–4pm, 5:30–11pm.

Tío Pepe ✫✫✫ MEDITERRANEAN/SPANISH   Walk down the stairs into the Tío Pepe's whitewashed, arched rooms that resemble a wine cellar. Spanish artwork, wrought iron, and gaily-colored pottery decorate the tiny dining rooms that seem to go on and on. Start with the wonderfully fruity sangria. It's the perfect beginning for a dinner from the Catalan region of Spain. The menu's highlights include irresistible shrimp in garlic sauce, filet of sole with bananas and hollandaise sauce, tournedos Tío Pepe, and beef in a sherry sauce with mushrooms. Dessert is a standout: smooth flan or chocolate soufflé and their wonderful roll cakes. The servers are so professional you'll feel like royalty. Tío Pepe is a big special-occasion restaurant with Baltimoreans so reservations are a must. Call as far ahead as 3 weeks if you want a table on Saturday at 7:30pm.

10 E. Franklin St. (just off Charles St.). (*C*) 410/539-4675. Reservations required. Jackets suggested. Main courses $18–$25; lunch $11–$20. AE, DC, DISC, MC, V. Mon–Fri 11:30am–2:30pm; Mon–Thurs 5–10:30pm, Fri 5–11pm, Sat 5–11:30pm, Sun 4–10:30pm.

INEXPENSIVE

Woman's Industrial Exchange Restaurant ✫ *Finds* AMERICAN   Housed in an 1815 brick building, where you're greeted by a gracious doorman, this restaurant, along with the craft shop, has been helping women help themselves since post–Civil War days (there's a listing for the craft shop in the "Shopping" section of this chapter). The waitresses, wearing big white bows around their blue uniforms serve up delicious breakfasts and lunches. (In the movie *Sleepless in Seattle,* waitress Miss Marguerite made her acting debut at age 92.) The menu is simple with homemade soups, salads, sandwiches, omelets, meat or fish platters, and luscious desserts (charlotte russe is a specialty). The chicken salad is terrific. Afterward, take time to browse in the shop.

333 N. Charles St. (*C*) 410/685-4388. Main courses $3.95–$6.95. MC, V. Mon–Fri 7am–3pm.

NORTH OF DOWNTOWN
EXPENSIVE

Polo Grill ✫ AMERICAN   Often compared to New York's 21 Club in atmosphere, this clubby restaurant is ensconced in the main dining room at the Inn at the Colonnade, opposite Johns Hopkins University. The menu changes regularly, but don't be surprised to find triple-cut Colorado rib lamb chops with a black currant sauce, or roasted Long Island duck breast. Signature dishes include fried lobster tail with drawn butter and honey mustard sauce; penne pasta with blackened chicken; and Asian-style salmon with warm sesame spinach leaves. Fresh lobster by the pound and prime cut-to-order steaks are also popular.

4 W. University Pkwy., Homewood (in the Inn at the Colonnade). (*C*) 410/235-8200. Reservations required. Main courses $16.95–$35.95. AE, DC, DISC, MC, V. Mon–Thurs 6:30am–10:30pm, Fri–Sat 7am–11:30pm, Sun 7am–9:30pm.

MODERATE

Gertrude's ★★ SEAFOOD   Pause at Gertrude's during a visit to the Baltimore Museum of Art. John Shields, the chef and cookbook author has created a restaurant filled with local delights, some touched with nostalgia and all prepared with great care, enough that the restaurant has become a destination in itself. Baltimoreans fondly remember the Hutzler's Tearoom Club, which recalls a beloved restaurant in a downtown department store. If you're feeling adventurous, you might like the small plates that include citrus barbecue shrimp or portobello crab imperial. There are soups (rich cream of crab) and sandwiches (plenty of Old Bay on the shrimp); or maybe you're ready for Crab Cake Heaven, three crab cakes made using two traditional recipes and the third more up to the minute. There's also a seafood bar. The restaurant itself is sleek, with tall windows overlooking the sculpture garden and outside seating in warm weather. But this is a museum too, so the tables are covered with white paper and a cup of crayons is nestled among the salt and peppershakers and sugar bowl.

At the Baltimore Museum of Art. Ⓒ **410/889-3399**. Reservations. Main courses: dinner $8.95–$33.50, lunch $6.50–$10.50. Tues–Fri 11:30am–9pm, Sat 5–9pm, Sun 5–8pm.

PaperMoon Diner DINER   This funky diner/health food restaurant has been a favorite of the college crowd for years. The first thing you'll notice when you walk in is the collection of toys and antiques everywhere. The next thing you'll notice is that all the servers appear to be waiting on you. The food is good and it's a fun place to eat. It's not the usual diner fare, although you can get burgers, sandwiches, and breakfast all day. There's an assortment of vegetarian options, including the veggie cheesesteak and the black-eyed quesadilla—black olives, artichoke hearts, tomato, and mushrooms between two tortilla shells with melted cheese and salsa. Or try the spinach, portobello, and Swiss omelet.

227 W. 29th St., Remington (between Remington Ave. and Howard St.). Ⓒ **410/889-4444**. www.papermoon diner.com. Reservations required for parties of 5 or more. Main courses $7–$14. MC, V. Daily 24 hours.

Petit Louis Bistro Kids FRENCH   A little bit of Paris has come to Roland Avenue. Petit Louis offers great bistro food such as escargots, foie gras terrine, and cassoulet for two in a noisy, friendly, neighborhood setting. The menu changes every day in order to use the freshest ingredients available. Though the bistro looks old and established, it's only about a year old. Already, the locals consider it their place to go. As a neighborhood place, it's okay to bring the kids. The chef will improvise a dish they'll like and the waiter will bring crayons. The adults can focus on a menu filled with French classics and a respectable wine list.

4800 Roland Ave., Roland Park. Ⓒ **410/366-9393**. Fax 410/366-9019. www.petitlouis.com. Reservations recommended. Main courses $8–$18. AE, DC, DISC, MC, V. Lunch Tues–Fri 11:30am–2pm; dinner Tues–Thurs 5–10pm, Fri–Sat 5–11pm, Sun 5–9pm.

INEXPENSIVE

Cafe Hon Kids AMERICAN/DINER   It didn't take long for Cafe Hon to become a Baltimore institution. This kitschy little diner serves homey comfort food: The specialty is their "Much Better than Mom's" meat loaf, served with mashed potatoes and the vegetable of the day. At dinner you'll also find spaghetti, sour beef, pork chops, and hot roast beef. The lunch menu includes all the traditional sandwiches you'd expect from a diner: chicken salad, grilled cheese, burgers, Reubens; there are even blue plate specials. Come for breakfast and get their killer coffee and "Hon Buns," cinnamon rolls as big as your hand and smothered in cinnamon and icing. It's a great place to bring the family because you can always find something on the menu any kid will eat.

1002 36th St. (at Roland Ave.), Hampden. ✆ 410/243-1230. Main courses $8.95–$13.95; lunch $3.95–$8.95. AE, DC, DISC, MC, V. Mon–Thurs 7am–10pm, Fri 7am–10pm, Sat 9am–10pm, Sun 9am–8pm. Parking in lot behind restaurant.

MOUNT WASHINGTON

Ethel and Ramone's ✪ CAJUN/AMERICAN   On a little street in Mount Washington you're confronted with at least three intriguing restaurants on the same block. This one had a table open one sunny lunchtime, and turned out to be a good choice. Tables are set in a narrow dining room or on the porch and the sidewalk so you'll hear everything going on. Your waiter will take care of you at this casual, offbeat eatery where they know good food. Get the gumbo. It's rich with Andouille sausage and chicken, spicy and filling. There are lots of Louisiana favorites, including red beans and rice and jambalaya, plus entrees like vegetarian lasagna, chicken Marsala, and fettuccini with mushrooms. Lunch is mostly overstuffed sandwiches with side salads, such as potato salad with zing.

1615 Sulgrave Ave. ✆ 410/664-2971. Fax 410/664-2971. Reservations recommended. Main courses $11.95–$19.95, lunch $5.95–$8.95. AE, V. Tues–Sat 11am–3pm and 6–11pm.

McCafferty's ✪ BEEF/SEAFOOD   You get the impression at first that this is a man's restaurant. The menu focuses on beef, prime rib, and seafood. The restaurant lobby focuses on baseball and football memorabilia. But the dining room is elegant—even if the sign at the front door says CASUAL DRESS RECOMMENDED. The food is first-rate, from the Caesar salad to the entrees to desserts made in the restaurant: bread pudding, Key lime pie, Chocolate Oblivion.

1501 Sulgrave Ave. ✆ 410/664-2200. www.marylandnightlife.com. Reservations required on weekends. Main courses $16.95–$28.50; lunch $6.95–$24. AE, DC, DISC, MC, V. Weekdays 11:30am–10pm, Sat–Sun 5:30–10pm. Valet parking available.

Mount Washington Tavern ✪✪ AMERICAN   This sprawling restaurant, beloved by locals, has bars to watch ball games, casual wood-paneled nooks for intimate dining, and a garden room elegant enough for a special occasion. It's big enough that if the Ravens score, you'll never know it in the dining room. The menu is eclectic with some seafood, steaks, and a raw bar. Light fare is available at lunch. If you are a nacho fan, try their fowl nachos. It's a huge mound of tortilla chips smothered in salsa, shredded chicken, guacamole, and sour cream, which are perfect with a beer or while you wait for your crab cake. Sunday brunch is available until 3pm.

5700 Newbury St. ✆ 410/367-6903. Reservations recommended on weekends. Main courses $16–$26. AE, DE, DISC, MC, V. Mon–Sat 11:30am–2am, Sun 10:30am–2am.

5 The Top Attractions

Although much of Baltimore's business activity takes place along Charles Street, the city's focal point for tourism is the **Inner Harbor** ✪✪✪, home of the Baltimore Convention Center and Festival Hall Exhibit Center, the Harborplace shopping pavilions, the National Aquarium and other museums, Oriole Park at Camden Yards, Ravens Stadium, and the Pier 6 Concert Pavilion.

First and foremost, the Inner Harbor is a deepwater port. Boats from all over the world dock here, and it's not unusual on summer weekends for the harbor to be overrun with the white dress uniforms of sailors from here or across the seas. Here's what you can see, starting with the National Aquarium and going counterclockwise around the harbor.

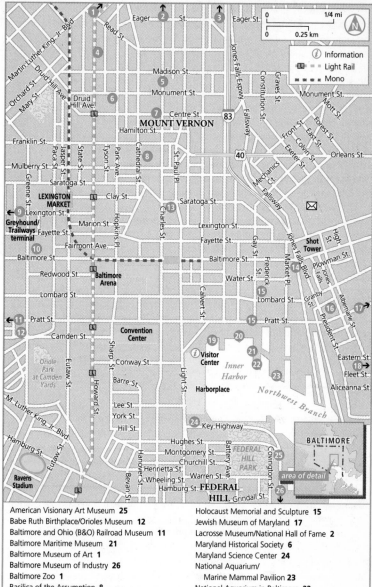

American Visionary Art Museum **25**
Babe Ruth Birthplace/Orioles Museum **12**
Baltimore and Ohio (B&O) Railroad Museum **11**
Baltimore Maritime Museum **21**
Baltimore Museum of Art **1**
Baltimore Museum of Industry **26**
Baltimore Zoo **1**
Basilica of the Assumption **8**
Civil War Museum at President Street Station **18**
Contemporary Museum **7**
Edgar Allan Poe House **9**
Edgar Allan Poe's Grave Site and Memorial **10**
Eubie Blake National Jazz Institute
 and Cultural Center **4**
Fort McHenry **26**
Great Blacks in Wax Museum **3**

Holocaust Memorial and Sculpture **15**
Jewish Museum of Maryland **17**
Lacrosse Museum/National Hall of Fame **2**
Maryland Historical Society **6**
Maryland Science Center **24**
National Aquarium/
 Marine Mammal Pavilion **23**
National Aquarium in Baltimore **22**
Old St. Paul's Church **13**
Port Discovery **14**
Star-Spangled Banner Flag House/
 1812 Museum **16**
Top of the World **20**
USS *Constellation* **19**
Walters Art Museum **7**
Washington Monument & Museum **5**

National Aquarium in Baltimore ★★★   Visitors can walk into a room surrounded by patrolling sharks, wander among the coral reefs, follow the yearly migration of fish, and visit a rain forest on the roof at one of best aquariums in the country. In addition to the watery denizens, exhibits include a popular puffin display; *Maryland: Mountains to the Sea;* and a new Amazon River Forest filled with plants and animals as well as fish. The sharks are a main attraction, as is a dolphins exhibit/performance. You can easily spend a day here. On a cold day, it's a joy to skip to the top of the aquarium and bask in the Amazon heat that envelops the brightly colored birds, the shy iguana, and the sloth. (For the best views, come straight here when the aquarium opens, as that's when the animals are most active.) Though you walk in front of most of the exhibits, you actually walk inside the doughnut-shaped Coral Reef and the Open Ocean (shark) tanks, getting up close with these exotic creatures. New for 2001 was the small seahorse exhibit; these delicate, colorful little animals are a delight.

The Marine Mammal Pavilion is connected by covered bridge to the main hall. It's where you'll find the dolphins: three generations from one family. Don't miss the presentations; reserve a seat when you get your tickets at no additional fee. There are also talks by aquarium staff, and feeding time in the coral reef draws a crowd. There are two gift shops and a refreshment area.

Insider tip: The aquarium draws huge crowds in summer. The best way to beat the crush is to buy timed tickets in advance and/or visit during non-peak times, especially weekday mornings, Friday evenings, or after 3pm. Construction of a new Australian exhibit is due to begin in fall 2002, though all the present exhibits are expected to remain open. The new building is to open in 2005.

501 E. Pratt St., on the harbor. ⓒ 410/576-3800. www.aqua.org. Admission $16 adults, $13 seniors, $9.50 ages 3–11. July–Aug daily 9am–8pm; Mar–June and Sept–Oct Sat–Thurs 9am–5pm, Fri 9am–8pm; Nov–Feb Sat–Thurs 10am–5pm, Fri 10am–8pm. Hours and prices subject to change. Exhibits are open 2 hours after last ticket is sold.

Baltimore Maritime Museum   It's called a museum, but it's really three boats and a lighthouse that tell some recent maritime history. The Coast Guard Cutter *Taney* survived the bombing of Pearl Harbor. The submarine USS *Torsk* sank the last two Japanese merchant ships of World War II and still holds the record for the most dives and resurfacings of any submarine. The Seven-Foot Knoll Lighthouse is worth a climb up the steps to see the Fresnel light and learn about the lighthouse that once welcomed immigrants here. The lightship *Chesapeake* spent 40 years anchored near the mouth of the Chesapeake Bay. Each provides an interesting glimpse into the lives of 20th century sailors.

Insider tip: For a good value, buy a **Seaport Pass** and combine this ticket with a visit to the USS *Constellation* and a ticket to ride all day on the Seaport water taxi for $15.50 adults; $13 seniors; $8.50 ages 6 to 14; free under 5.

Piers 3 and 5, Inner Harbor. ⓒ 410/396-3453. Admission $6 adults, $5 seniors, $3 ages 5–14. Buy tickets at the booth near the National Aquarium, on board the *Taney,* or at the lighthouse.

Top of the World Observation Level   For a 360-degree view of Baltimore city, head for this sky-high observatory on the 27th floor of the World Trade Center, the world's tallest pentagonal building, next to Harborplace. In addition to the fine view, you can acquire a bit of background about Baltimore from the exhibits, hands-on displays, and multimedia presentations. Try to visit during some of their annual special events, such as Saturday Sunsets, featuring live jazz and refreshments. Renovations have improved viewing conditions and made it more accessible to disabled visitors. The only way to reach a higher altitude is Port Discovery's HiFlyer. This costs less and the floor doesn't move.

401 E. Pratt St., on the harbor. © 410/837-4515. Admission $4 adults, $3 seniors and ages 5–15. Mon–Sat 10am–5:30pm, Sun noon–5:30pm. Tickets are sold in the lobby up to a half hour before closing.

USS Constellation ★★ *Kids* You can't miss the *Constellation,* docked for years at the Inner Harbor (pre-dating Harborplace). Baltimoreans did miss it when it underwent repairs several years ago. A stunning triple-masted sloop-of-war originally launched in 1854, the *Constellation* is the last Civil War–era vessel afloat. Tour her gun decks, visit the wardrooms, see a cannon demonstration, and learn about the life of a sailor. Demonstrations begin with the raising of the colors at 10:30am and continue on the hour. Special events include a Fourth of July picnic and a New Year's Eve champagne reception, both ending with fireworks over the harbor. Tickets are required. A free birthday party is held the Saturday closest to August 26.

Pier 1, 301 E. Pratt St. © 410/539-1797. www.constellation.org. Admission $6.50 adults, $5 seniors, $3.50 ages 6–14. Admission includes audio tour. Daily May to mid-Oct 10am–6pm, mid-Oct to Apr 10am–4pm.

Maryland Science Center ★★ *Kids* The Maryland Science Center doesn't shy away from anything scientific. Three floors of exhibits include the popular Outer Space Place, home of the Hubble Space Telescope National Visitor Center and Space Link, which offers a live connection to NASA. In October 2002, look for an exhibit called "Grossology: The Impolite Science of the Human Body." Sometimes the exhibits are too crowded or have limited interest, but the IMAX theater and planetarium are always worth a visit. The IMAX theater presents shows as diverse as *Beauty and the Beast* and *Space Station 3D.* Lightspeed Laser Theater uses lasers to tell a scientific tale. The 3-D movies are breathtaking. IMAX is so popular, extra screenings are available Thursday and Sunday evenings. The stars are on display at the David Planetarium or The Crosby Ramsey Memorial Observatory (open Thurs nights free of charge).

601 Light St., Baltimore, MD 21230 (south side of the Inner Harbor). © 410/685-5225. www.mdsci.org. Admission varies according to the special exhibits. A recent trip cost $18 for adults, $14 for children, and $15 for senior citizens. Mon–Fri 10am–5pm; Sat, Sun 11am–6pm with extended hours in summer. Call ahead, as hours change with some exhibits. Metered on-street parking and paid lots on Light St. and Key Hwy. Water taxi stop.

American Visionary Art Museum ★ Look for the "Whirligig," a 55-foot multicolored, wind-powered sculpture at the front of this curvaceous building housing some of the most interesting art you're bound to see. Visionary art is made by people who aren't trained as artists but feel compelled to draw, paint, or create a ship with matchsticks. Everything is fascinating; some is quite troubling. And the artists' stories can be as interesting as their art. "The Art of War and Peace" opened by coincidence soon after the September 11, 2001 attacks. The paintings, sculptures, Hmong war quilts, and other pieces were drawn from the memories of soldiers and victims of war. Their visions are quite dark, filled with horrific images. On the other hand, a 10-foot model of the *Lusitania* dominates a first-floor gallery. It's made from 193,000 matchsticks. The museum's three stories are painted mostly in pastels with blond wood floors, an occasional plain bench, and some indirect natural light. The rooms are as soothing as the art is vivid. From the moment you set your eyes on Emery Blagdon's "Healing Machines" mobile hanging down three floors, you'll be entranced. Some of the exhibits are certainly too strong for children, and the museum will alert you about that. Other exhibits are a joy that children would love. A sculpture barn and sculpture garden are filled with other delights. The AVAM is also home to Joy America cafe on the third floor (see "Where to Dine" earlier in this chapter) and an offbeat (of course) gift shop on the first floor.

800 Key Hwy. ✆ 410/244-1900. Admission $6 adults, $4 seniors and children. Tues–Sun 10am–6pm. Closed Thanksgiving and Dec 25. Take Light St. south, turn left onto Key Hwy. (at the Maryland Science Center); museum is about 3 blocks on right.

Baltimore Museum of Industry *Finds*   Housed in a former cannery in a still-industrial part of Baltimore, the museum gives visitors a look at industries that made Baltimore a great city in the 1880s—canning, printing, and clothing. This museum is geared to children. Wall-sized pictures recall the days before child labor laws, and exhibits are set up so kids can get their hands on oyster-shucking stations, antique irons, and moveable type. Tour guides are sensitive to children's attention spans and adjust their talks toward younger visitors. Other exhibits include one of only two working steam tugboats in the country. The museum is a few blocks from Fort McHenry; a visit to both—with a picnic on Fort McHenry's lawn—could make a great day. One of the city's least known museums, it's one of the best for children and anyone who loves industrial history.

1415 Key Hwy., Baltimore, MD 21230. ✆ 410/727-4808. www.thebmi.org. $6 adults, $4.50 students and seniors, $20 family. MC, V. Open Sun noon–5pm, Mon–Sat 10am–5pm. Free parking. Water taxis stop nearby. No. 1 bus stops on Fort Ave., 1 block south of the museum.

Fort McHenry ★★★ *Moments*   The flag that flies at Fort McHenry is 30 feet by 42 feet, big enough for Francis Scott Key to see by the dawn's early light and write "The Star-Spangled Banner." The flag's 15 stars and stripes still fly as boldly as they did that terrible night when soldiers here stood once again to reclaim American independence.

The star-shaped fort looks much as it did in 1814, the year of the British attack. Its buildings, repaired in the days following that attack, still stand.

The star spangled banner is central to this fort, which is a national park. Visitors are invited to take part in the daily changing of the flag. In fact, because the flag is so big, about 20 people are needed to keep it off the ground and fold it. Stop by at 9:30am or 4:30pm (7:30pm June–Aug) to join in. The large flag flies only during daylight hours but a smaller flag flies over the fort at night. The rangers conclude this ceremony with a short historical talk about the fort, the flag, or the national anthem. Two special weekends are worth a trip: **Star Spangled Banner Weekend** held in mid-September recalls the British attack on the fort; and **Civil War Weekend** recalls the days when Union soldiers and Confederate prisoners of war filled these same buildings.

On selected Sundays, from 6 to 8pm, military bands perform with a color guard, drill teams, and the Fort McHenry Guard dressed in 1814-style uniforms, a ceremony which began in 1803. Admission to the ceremony is free. Call for a schedule. Exhibits recall Baltimore under siege during the War of 1812, the fort's Civil War service, and its use as an army hospital during World War I. A visit takes about 90 minutes. The fort sits on a point in the harbor, where visitors can see the Inner Harbor, the Patapsco River, and down to the Chesapeake Bay. Visits to the park outside the fort are free and picnicking is allowed.

Fort McHenry National Monument and Historic Shrine, E. Fort Ave. ✆ 410/962-4290. Admission $5, free for under age 17. Sept–May daily 8am–5pm; June–Labor Day 8am–8pm. Free parking. Stop on water taxi and Seaport Taxi routes.

6 Other Downtown Attractions

NEAR LITTLE ITALY

Port Discovery ★★ *Kids*   This is a kid-powered museum where in exhibits covering three floors, kids of all ages (though mostly ages 6–12) can cross the Nile to explore ancient Egypt, climb through a kitchen drain as they solve a mystery in Miss Perception's Mystery House, and climb and play on the three-story-high Kidworks. Walt Disney Company "Imagineers" designed most of the exhibits. Adding to the activity are some high-tech toys in the PD Kid Club, where children use computers to compose music, shoot digital videos, or produce their own cartoons. Blackberry PDAs add a new dimension to the ancient Egypt exhibit as children gather clues as they wander through the exhibit. The high-tech gizmos will also be used in the Mystery House by 2002 and enable kids to instant-message other children throughout the museum.

Insider tip for parents of toddlers: Port Discovery offers a free storytime presented by the Enoch Pratt Free Library. Sign your kids up, and they can also spend some time in Sensation Station, a toddler room filled with stuff that fascinates very young children. This program, called the Pratt Exploration Center, has its own entrance. It is open to everybody on Wednesdays and Fridays. Call for exact times.

As part of a visit—or as its own attraction—visitors can take a trip on a tethered helium balloon that rises 500 feet above Baltimore. The **HiFlyer** ★★ can carry 25 to 30 passengers (including up to three wheelchairs) for the 20-minute ride. It flies noon to 8pm (and until midnight on summer weekends) every day from April through December. You can see to the city's limits.

35 Market Place (part of the Power Plant Live complex). ℂ **410/727-8120.** Fax 410/727-3042. www.port discovery.org. Admission $10 adults, $7.50 ages 3–12. HiFlyer $12 adults, $11 seniors, $8.50 ages 3–12 during the day; $15 for all riders 8pm–midnight. Daily 10am–5:30pm, except HiFlyer which is open until 8pm (except Thurs–Sat when it's open until midnight).

Holocaust Memorial and Sculpture   In the heart of downtown near the Inner Harbor, this open-air memorial and sculpture stands as a stark reminder of the 6 million Jews murdered by the Nazis in Europe between 1933 and 1945.

Corner of Water, Gay, and Lombard sts. Free admission. Daily 24 hours.

Jewish Museum of Maryland   For insight into local Jewish history, stop in here. The museum consists of two restored 19th-century synagogues: the Lloyd Street Synagogue, built in 1845 (the oldest in Maryland), and the B'nai Israel Synagogue, built in 1876 and still in use as Baltimore's only downtown synagogue. Also here are exhibit galleries, a visitors' orientation center, a museum shop, and a new permanent children's exhibit, "The Golden Land: A Family Learning Center." Exhibits focus on culture, as well as religion. A 2001–2002 exhibit looks at the golden age of the department store.

15 Lloyd St. ℂ **410/732-6400.** Fax 410/732-6451. www.jewishmuseummd.org. Admission $4. Sun and Tues–Thurs noon–4pm. Travel east on Pratt St.; turn left on Central St., left on Lombard St., and then right onto Lloyd St.

Star-Spangled Banner Flag House and 1812 Museum   Everyone remembers Betsy Ross and the first American flag. Baltimoreans recall Mary Pickersgill and the gigantic 15-star flag she sewed. It flew over Fort McHenry during the bombardment of the War of 1812 that inspired Francis Scott Key to write "The Star Spangled Banner." Though the flag is now part of the Smithsonian, the seamstress who made the heavy, woolen flag is memorialized in the

1793 house where she lived from 1807 to 1857. Guides offer visitors a glimpse of her life and times. See period furniture and artifacts of the war. A new War of 1812 Museum is due to open Flag Day (June 14), 2003, adjacent to the existing buildings. It will be the only museum in the country dedicated to this second war for independence.

844 E. Pratt St., at the corner of Albemarle, 2 blocks from the National Aquarium. (410/837-1793. Fax 410/837-1812. www.flaghouse.org. Admission $5 adults, $4 seniors, $3 children. AE, MC, V. Tues–Sat 10am–4pm. Closed major holidays.

WEST OF DOWNTOWN

Babe Ruth Birthplace and Museum/Baltimore Orioles Museum ★ George Herman "Babe" Ruth was born in this rowhouse. Two rooms are recreated as they would have looked when the Sultan of Swat was a boy. Other exhibits include a wall enumerating all his home runs, and memorabilia from his major league career as well as from his days at St. Mary's Industrial School in southwest Baltimore, where he learned to play the game. The Orioles and gone-but-not-forgotten Colts have their own exhibits here, as well.

216 Emory St. (410/727-1539. Fax 410/727-1652. www.baberuthmuseum.com. Admission $6 adults, $4 seniors, $3 ages 5–16. Apr–Oct daily 10am–5pm (until 7pm on Orioles home game days); Nov–Mar daily 10am–4pm. Closed Jan 1, Thanksgiving, and Dec 25. From Camden Yards walk 2 blocks west on Pratt and south on Emory. It's a tiny street.

Baltimore and Ohio (B&O) Railroad Museum ★★ *Kids* In 2002 and 2003, the museum will celebrate 175 years of railroading with special exhibits, rail excursions, and a Fair of the Iron Horse 175. Locomotives from around the world are coming for the fair, which will run from June 27 to July 6, 2003. American railroading got its start at this site when the B&O Railroad was chartered in 1827. The first locomotive, *The Tom Thumb,* was built here and a 1926 replica is still operating. This whole place is a celebration of railroading. It's housed in a marvelous roundhouse with a humongous turntable even a kid can turn, tracks filled with old trains, memorabilia from dining cars and train stations, and a wonderful model railroad that will make you nostalgic for the days of train travel. If you can, come on a weekend when for an extra $3 you can take a short train ride through the 175 years of railroading history that began here.

901 W. Pratt St. (410/752-2490. Fax 410/752-2499. www.borail.org. Admission $8 adults, $7 seniors, $5 ages 2–12. Museum daily 10am–5pm. Closed Easter, Thanksgiving, Dec 24, Dec 25, Jan 1. Bus: 31.

Baltimore Civil War Museum at the President Street Station *Finds* Tucked beside the Marriott Inner Harbor is a small brick structure with a curved roof. The first bloodshed of the Civil War occurred when Union soldiers arrived in April 1861 on their way south, a mob of Southern sympathizers attacked them as they marched from this railroad station to Camden Station (now near Oriole Park). The little building, one of the country's oldest railroad stations, has been restored and now has exhibits about that awful day and Maryland's railroad history, as well as an exhibit on the Underground Railroad.

601 President St., Inner Harbor East. (410/385-5188. www.mdhs.org. Admission $3 adults; $2 children 13–17, students with ID and seniors; free for Maryland Historical Society members and children 12 and under. Group rates available with prior reservation. Open Tues–Sun 10am–5pm.

Edgar Allan Poe's Grave Site and Memorial *Moments* Three modest memorials in this small old graveyard recall the poet who wrote "The Tell-Tale Heart" and "The Raven" (the only poem to inspire an NFL team's name). After his mysterious death in 1849, Poe's relatives erected a small gravestone. Before

Only in Baltimore, Hon!

- **Cannoli at Vaccaro's,** Little Italy. All the desserts are scrumptious, but the cannoli is a tradition. Skip dessert wherever you're having dinner and come here, or stop by the annex at the Light Street Pavilion.
- **The View from the Glass Elevators at the Hyatt.** Short of a harbor-view room, this is the best view in the city, especially at night, and it's free!
- **The Seventh-Inning Stretch at Camden Yards.** There's nothing like a crowd of 45,000 uniting for a rousing rendition of "Thank God I'm a Country Boy."
- **Spring in Sherwood Garden.** This community garden in north Baltimore (Highfield Rd. and Greenway) is out of the way and hard to find, but an oasis in May when the tulips are blooming. The trip will take you through lovely neighborhoods that tourists seldom see.
- **Taking a Water Taxi to Fells Point/Little Italy.** It's an inexpensive way to see the harbor, and, if you're staying in the Inner Harbor, a great way to avoid the hassle of parking.
- **Ice-skating at Rash Field.** The best ice-skating in town is right on the harbor near the Maryland Science Center during cold weather. It's a sight to see all of Baltimore lit up at night as you glide along on the ice.

the stone could be installed, a train crashed through the monument yard, and destroyed it. In the century since, the site has been adorned with three newer monuments: the main memorial, which features a bas relief bust of Poe; a small gravestone adorned with a raven at Poe's original burial lot; and a plaque placed by the French, who, thanks to the poet Baudelaire, enjoy some of the best translations of Poe's works. The poet is remembered on his birthday every January when a mysterious visitor leaves half a bottle of cognac and roses at the grave. On the weekend closest to Poe's birthday, a party is held in his honor.

Westminster Cemetery on the southeast corner of Fayette and Greene sts. ☎ 410/706-2072. Daily 8am–dusk. Closed major holidays.

Edgar Allan Poe House   In this tiny west Baltimore house, Edgar Allan Poe wrote many of his great works. Poe lived here for 3 years (1832–35) while courting his cousin, whom he later married. The building contains Poe memorabilia, period furniture, changing exhibits, and a video presentation. The house is located on a tiny, one-way street heading south. There is no house number but you will see a black antique street lamp out front and two markers on the house. Don't try to walk here from downtown. Take a car or cab.

203 N. Amity St. ☎ 410/396-7932. Admission $3 adults, $1 under age 13. Apr–July and Oct to mid-Dec Wed–Sat noon–3:45pm; Aug–Sept Sat noon–4pm. Closed mid-Dec to Mar.

MOUNT VERNON

Basilica of the Assumption of the Blessed Virgin Mary ★★   This church been a monument to religious freedom since 1806. As it nears its 200th birthday, this cathedral of the Catholic Archdiocese of Baltimore is undergoing restoration from its dome to its rarely-seen undercroft. Designed by Benjamin

Latrobe—who was designing the U.S. Capitol at the same time—the neoclassical basilica is considered one of the most beautiful churches in the country. A national shrine and historic landmark, it was the first cathedral built in the United States. In the fall of 2001, work began to return the oft-renovated structure to its original light-filled splendor. Visitors will be welcome during the restoration. However, do call ahead or check the website as some parts of the renovation may require that the building be temporarily closed. It's a beautiful neoclassical gem visited by Mother Teresa of Calcutta, Saint Elizabeth Ann Seton, and Pope John Paul II, as well as numerous other religious and political figures.

400 block of Cathedral St. ℂ **410/727-3564.** Free admission. Masses daily; tours offered after the 10:45am Sun Mass and by appointment. Take Charles St. north; turn left on Franklin St. and left again onto Cathedral St. Parking garage located on Franklin and Cathedral is convenient.

Contemporary Museum Though the museum has been around for 10 years, it just got a home of its own. Its exhibits have appeared in a variety of places: a bus terminal, a bank building, a former car showroom. In a small storefront near the Walters, the Contemporary is turning three small rooms into galleries for shows distinctly contemporary, the art of our time. Photography, video, painting, and performance art have all been the focus of past shows. About four shows per year are planned. It's a nice counterpoint to its neighbors, the elegant Walters and the eminent Maryland Historical Society, both a block or so away.

104 W. Centre St., in Mount Vernon. ℂ **410/783-5720.** Fax 410/783-5722. Hours vary with exhibitions so calling ahead is a must. Admission $3 adults, $1 children.

Eubie Blake National Jazz Institute and Cultural Center Baltimorean Eubie Blake, ragtime pianist and Broadway composer, is remembered in this small museum nestled in Howard Street's Antique Row. A long-term exhibit of photographs, "The Storm is Passing Over," remembers the heyday of Pennsylvania Avenue, a vaudeville theater district where local and national musicians played, particularly the Royal Theatre, where Billie Holiday, Chick Webb, Eubie Blake, and Cab Calloway all played. A front gallery has changing exhibits, and the sculpture garden is under development. Because the focus here is music, most of the space is devoted to recitals and programs for children. There usually isn't a lot to see, and not really very much about Blake himself. *Insider tip:* Talk to the docents here; many of them knew Blake or Calloway personally.

847 N. Howard St. ℂ **410/225-3130.** www.eubieblake.org. $2 for adults, $1 for school-age children.

Maryland Historical Society ★★ *Kids* You can find all kinds of stuff here: Cal Ripken's bat, Baltimore painted furniture, Stieff silver, a recording of Eubie Blake playing the piano, Tench Tilghman's Revolutionary War officer's uniform. These represent some part of Maryland's 350-plus years of history in a sprawling museum that takes up a city block and includes the town house of Baltimore philanthropist Enoch Pratt which served as the MHS's first home, and the old Art Deco Greyhound bus terminal, as well as several other buildings. Among the many highlights are the original manuscript of "The Star Spangled Banner" and an Early American Life gallery filled with portraits and artifacts from Maryland's first residents. For children there is the Child's World Exhibition with dolls, toys, and furniture they can touch. The museum offers History Haversacks, bags filled with activities like scavenger hunts and crafts projects the kids can make as they look through the museum. Don't miss the shop. It's part consignment/part gift shop. There are plenty of antiques and other interesting items. It's easy to spend a couple of hours here. It's close enough to the Walters and Contemporary for a full day in the museums. And it's not far from the Eubie Blake Cultural Center and the antiques shops of Howard Street.

201 W. Monument St. ✆ **410/685-3750**. www.mdhs.org. Admission $4 adults, $3 seniors, $3 ages 13–17; family rate (2 adults and 3 children 18 or younger) $12. Tues–Fri 10am–4:30pm, Sat 9am–5pm, Sun 11am–5pm. Some parking on Howard St. Near Light Rail stop.

Old St. Paul's Church   Originally founded in 1692 as one of Maryland's first Anglican parishes, this building dates to 1856. The church was built in Italian Romanesque style and is filled with Tiffany stained glass windows and mosaics. A brochure outlining some of the treasures is available in the back of the church. The Tiffany rose window, which crowns the entrance, is a jewel many people miss. In addition, two friezes salvaged from the previous church, which burned in 1817, have been incorporated into the portico. In addition to Sunday services, the church is the site of a Tuesday noontime music series October through May.

Charles and Saratoga sts. ✆ **410/685-3404**. www.oldstpauls.ang-md.org. Free admission. Sun services at 8am, 10am, and 5pm. Call for weekday services. Church often open during the week for quiet visits.

Walters Art Museum ★★★ *Value*   The Walters, with its collections of ancient art, medieval armor, and French 19th century painting, has always been one of Baltimore's great attractions. Begun with the 22,000-object collection of William and Henry Walters, it has always been a delight, but with a 3-year renovation ended in late 2001, the galleries for ancient and medieval art have been reorganized and renewed. Utilizing dark walls and pinpoint spots, the works of art glisten like jewels. Walk through the galleries of sculpture, paintings, gold jewelry, mummies, and sarcophagi and see the progress of fine art through 50 centuries. It tells the story of Western civilization through its permanent collection as visitors progress through each gallery. The exhibits end with objects from the Middle Ages in the Knight's Hall, with tapestries, furnishings, and suits of armor. Exhibitions will include images from the "Crusader Bible," animals carved by Fabergé from semiprecious stones, and masterworks of ancient art from the British Museum, in 2003. The cafe serving light fare and expanded museum store have moved to the new, bright and airy lobby. Free admission days make it easier for parents to bring their children to this wonderful place.

600 N. Charles St. ✆ **410/547-9000**. www.thewalters.org. Admission $8 adults, $6 seniors, $5 students and young adults, 17 and under free. No admission charged first Thurs or Sat. Tues–Sun 10am–5pm. Bus: 3, 11, or 22; Light Rail to Centre St.; or take Charles St. north to the Washington Monument.

Washington Monument and Museum   This column, 178 feet tall, stands as the country's first major architectural memorial to George Washington. Begun in 1815, it was designed by Robert Mills, who also designed the Washington Monument (begun in 1848) in Washington, D.C. To learn the whole story, step inside this building and have a look at the exhibit "The Making of a Monument." The physically fit can also climb the 228 steps to the top of the tower and see why this spot is often called the best view in Baltimore.

Mt. Vernon Place. ✆ **410/396-0929**. Donation $1 per person. Summer Tues–Fri 10am–6pm, Sat–Sun 10am–4; winter Tues–Fri 10am–4pm, weekend hours vary. Take Charles St. north to the monument.

NORTH OF DOWNTOWN

Great Blacks in Wax Museum   In the northeast corner of the city, this is the nation's first and only wax museum dedicated to famous African-American heroes and historical legends. Displays are in chronological order, and each highlights a period in African-American history, from ancient Africa to slavery and the Civil War to the Civil Rights era. The people portrayed include black inventors, pilots, religious and educational leaders, scientists, and more. Quite a few Marylanders are among these, such as Frederick Douglass and Thurgood Marshall. Plans for expansion are underway, with a phase devoted mostly to staff and visitors' comfort to be completed in 2003. The second phase will add gallery space, a restaurant, and the Royal Theatre Heritage Center. Look for it in 2005.

1601–03 E. North Ave. © 410/563-3404. www.greatblacksinwax.org. Admission $6 adults, $5.75 seniors and college students, $4.25 ages 12–17, $3.75 ages 2–11. Jan 15–Oct 14, Tues–Sat 9am–6pm, Sun noon–6pm; Oct 15–Jan 14, Tues–Sat 9am–5pm, Sun noon–5pm. Closed Mon except during Black History Month in Feb, July, and Aug.

Baltimore Museum of Art ★★★   The BMA is famous for its Matisse collection, assembled by Baltimore sisters Claribel and Etta Cone, who went to Paris in the 1920s and came back with a collection of great art. These sisters have been honored with a new $4 million Cone Wing which showcases their collection of paintings by Matisse, Cezanne, Gauguin, van Gogh, and Renoir. Visit the special room set up to remember these fascinating women: drawers filled with their personal things, pieces of furniture, and a virtual tour of their Baltimore apartments. The largest museum in Maryland, the BMA it boasts galleries dedicated to modern and contemporary art; European sculpture and painting; American painting and decorative arts; prints and photographs; arts of Africa, Asia, the Americas and Oceania; and the 2.7-acre sculpture garden with 35 major works by Alexander Calder, Henry Moore, and others. Highlights include the 35,000-square-foot West Wing for Contemporary Art with work by Andy Warhol, Jasper Johns, and Baltimorean Grace Hartigan; early American decorative arts with an emphasis on Maryland and a wonderful gallery of miniature rooms; and European art that includes Impressionist painting by Monet and Degas's "Little Dancer, Age Fourteen." A new wing featuring the collection of Old Masters opened in late 2002. Younger visitors can borrow the BMA-FUN-ART packs to show them museum pieces on their own level as they listen to music or draw themselves. **Freestyle at the BMA** is a free event held first Thursdays until 8pm with gallery tours, music, and special activities for families. A summer jazz series in the sculpture garden is another delight.

10 Art Museum Dr. (at N. Charles St. and 31st St.). © 410/396-7100. www.artbma.org. Admission $7 adults, $5 seniors and students with ID, free for ages 18 and under, free admission on first Thurs of the month. Wed–Fri 11am–5pm, Sat–Sun 11am–6pm. Bus: 3 or 11. Take Howard St. north; bear right onto Art Museum Dr., about 3 miles (5km) north of the harbor.

Baltimore Zoo *Kids*   It may be the third oldest zoo in the United States, but the staff here is doing their best to make it one of the most modern. Some 2,000 animals live here, including a beloved polar bear, prairie dogs, and tigers. As part of a $60 million renovation, cages in the Main Valley will be replaced with more modern habitats, and visitors will get a better look behind the scenes. Several exhibits have already been renovated, including the Chimpanzee Forest, Leopard Lair, and African Watering Hole. The children's zoo is a must-see for kids with its lily pads, tree slide, farm animals, and Maryland wilderness exhibit. Plan to spend a few hours here. Bring a stroller for the little ones since that last hill to the exit can be a daunting on a hot summer day. **Zoolights** ★, the zoo's wonderful walkthrough holiday light display, is open nights Thanksgiving to New Year's.

Druid Hill Park. © 410/366-LION. www.baltimorezoo.org. Admission $10 adults, $6 seniors and ages 2–15. Daily 10am–4pm. Take Exit 7 (Druid Hill Lake Dr.) off I-83 and follow the signs for the zoo.

Lacrosse Museum and National Hall of Fame   This museum offers a look at 350 years in the history of lacrosse, America's oldest sport. Displays include photographs and murals of athletes at play, sculptures and paintings, vintage equipment and uniforms (how this sport has changed its look!), a multimedia show, and a documentary, "More than a Game: A History of Lacrosse." In the Hall of Fame room, a computer kiosk gives visitors access to data on the honorees. Hours of operation occasionally change, so call before you visit.

113 W. University Pkwy. ⑦ 410/235-6882. www.lacrosse.org. Admission $3 adults, $2 ages 6–15. Feb–May Tues–Sat 10am–3pm, June–Jan Mon–Fri 10am–3pm.

7 Organized Tours & Cruises

LAND & SEA TOURS

Amphibious sightseeing vehicles take visitors on a cruise of the harbor after touring the city's neighborhoods. **Ride the Ducks tours** are conducted in converted 1945 DUKWs that accommodate 38 passengers. For information call ⑦ **410/ 727-DUCK.**

SPECIAL-INTEREST WALKING TOURS

A number of organizations offer specialized tours of specific neighborhoods or sites. **Concierge Plus, Inc.** (⑦ **410/580-0350**) provides "A Taste of Little Italy" and "Hollywood on the Harbor" walking tours, which give interesting and fun perspectives on the city. The Little Italy excursion takes you on a lunch tour ($45 per person), coupling good food with insight into the history of the neighborhood. The "Hollywood on the Harbor" tour ($40 per person including lunch) explores Fells Point, pointing out sites used in the filming of *Homicide, Sleepless in Seattle,* and other movies and shows filmed in Baltimore. Tours for groups only are offered on weekends year-round, and you must make reservations.

The **Fells Point Visitor Center** (808 S. Ann St.; ⑦ **410/675-6750;** www. preservationsociety.com) offers several historical tours of some of Baltimore's oldest streets. The "Paths of Freedom Walking Tour," which focuses on events in the life of Frederick Douglass, is offered on second Saturdays March through November 10am to noon for $5. A "Maritime History Walking Tour" is offered on fourth Sundays 10am to noon for $5. Around Halloween, "Ghost Tours" are offered for several weekends after dark for $10. Children 7 and older are asked to join the 7pm tour. Reservations are a must; call the center.

Baltimore Architecture Foundation Walking Tours are offered in Mount Vernon the first Saturday of the month and in Federal Hill on the second Saturday. Call ⑦ **410/539-7772.**

African American Cultural Tours focus on contributions of local African Americans, as well as important landmarks. Call ⑦ **410/727-0755.**

Baseball fans should not miss a tour of **Oriole Park at Camden Yards.** Well-informed tour guides fill you in on where Eddie Murray hit his 500th home run, why there are no bat racks in the dugout, and how many miles of beer lines run under the stadium seats. You get to go places the average fan can't see: the dugouts, the umpires' tunnel, and the press box. Tickets are $5 for adults and $4 for seniors and children, and can be purchased at the Fan Assistance Lobby at the north end of the warehouse building at the ballpark. Buy tickets at least 30 minutes before the tour. Tours are conducted weekdays 11am to 2pm on the hour, Saturday 11am to 2pm on the hour, and Sunday 12:30 to 3pm on the hour. Hours change during baseball season and aren't offered when the Ravens play at home. Call ℂ **410/547-6234** to confirm the tour schedule and other information.

CRUISES & BOAT TOURS

There's no shortage of options for seeing Baltimore from the water. Several touring boats will inevitably be docked at the Inner Harbor during your visit, but the cheapest way to get on the water is to take **Ed Kane's Water Taxi & Trolley** (ℂ **800/658-8947** or 410/563-3901) or the **Seaport Taxi** (ℂ **410/675-2900**). Both provide transportation to various destinations, including Harborplace, Little Italy, Fells Point, Canton, and Fort McHenry, but you are welcome to stay on for the entire route. See "Getting Around," earlier in this chapter, for more details.

You can't miss the *Bay Lady* and *Lady Baltimore,* two 450-passenger three-deck luxury ships docked outside the Light Street Pavilion. Harbor Cruises, Ltd. (ℂ **800/695-BOAT** or 410/727-3113; www.harborcruises.com) offers 2-hour lunch, 3-hour dinner, and 2½-hour moonlight excursions on both ships, as well as themed cruises such as bull roasts and crab feasts. Prices range from $25 to $50 per person. The food is passable but the cruise is well worthwhile.

For a tall-ship adventure, come aboard the *Clipper City* (ℂ **410/539-6277**; www.sailingship.com), a 140-passenger topsail schooner. This ship offers 2-hour afternoon excursions, 3-hour evening trips with live calypso and reggae music, and 3-hour Sunday champagne brunch sails, all departing from the dock next to the Maryland Science Center. Afternoon sails cost $12 for adults, $2 for children under age 12; calypso and reggae sails and Sunday brunch cost $30 for adults.

From Fells Point, ride aboard the *Nighthawk,* run by A-1 Nighthawk Cruises (ℂ **410/276-7447**; www.a1nighthawkcruises.com). This 82-foot 49-passenger schooner offers 3-hour excursions into the waters of the Inner Harbor and Patapsco River. The schedule includes moonlight sails with buffet dinner and live music. "Murder mystery" cruises are offered occasionally as well as crab feast cruises. Prices range from $40 to $50 per person.

For a view of the water from a skipjack, take a ride on the *Minnie V,* a 1906 skipjack built on the Eastern Shore. This boat, unlike the other, larger boats, is the real thing. Living Classrooms, the boat's owner, expects guests to work (if they want to), raising the sail or even steering the boat. Tickets for the 90-minute cruises are $13 for adults and $3 for children 12 and under. Tours are offered summer weekends when weather permits. Call ℂ **410/685-0295.**

8 Sports & Outdoor Activities

BASEBALL From April to October, when the Baltimore Orioles play ball, the city catches "Oriole fever"—everyone wants to go to the games and everyone talks about the results. If there's a home game during your visit, do whatever you have to do to get a ticket: It's a real Baltimore experience. The team plays at **Oriole Park at Camden Yards,** 333 W. Camden St. (ℂ **410/685-9800**). Afternoon games are usually at 1:35pm and evening games are slated for 7:35pm. Ticket prices range from $9 to $32.

BOWLING Duckpin bowling is a Baltimore original—invented here around the turn of the 20th century. The balls fit in your hand (no holes) and the pins are about the size of a Natty Boh beer bottle, hon (translation: the 7-oz. bottles of locally brewed National Bohemian beer). If you like strikes and spares, go find a tenpin alley; they're tough to get in duckpins. If you'd like to try it out yourself, here are a few alleys: **Seidel's Bowling Center,** 4443 Belair Rd. (© **410/ 485-5171**); and **Pinland Bowling Lanes,** 10 N. Dundalk Ave. (© **410/ 285-0135**).

FOOTBALL   The Baltimore Ravens play at Ravens Stadium (formerly PSINet Stadium) next door to Camden Yards. There are about 5,000 seats sold per game (the rest are held by season ticket holders). Ticket prices average about $35 and range from $17 to $75. For information or tickets call © **410/261-RAVE,** or visit www.ravenzone.net.

HORSE RACING   Maryland's oldest thoroughbred track and the site of the annual Preakness Stakes is **Pimlico Racecourse,** Park Heights and Belvedere avenues (© **410/542-9400**), about 5 miles (8km) from the Inner Harbor on the city's northwest side. The racing season is from mid-March to mid-June. The Preakness, the middle jewel in racing's Triple Crown, is held the third Saturday in May. Post time for regular racing days is 12:35pm, and admission is $3 for the grandstand and $5 for the clubhouse. Self-parking is free, valet parking is $1.50.

INDOOR SOCCER   A **Baltimore Blast** (© 410/73BLAST; www.baltimore blast.com) game combines sport with show business during introductions and half time. But the play is always competitive and the team has had a loyal following for more than 20 years. The season lasts October through April and games are played at the Baltimore Arena.

LACROSSE   Baltimore's pro lacrosse team is the **Baltimore Bayhawks** (© **410/560-3511;** www.baltimorebayhawks.com) made it to the MLL finals in 2001. Games are played June to September at Johns Hopkins University.

PADDLEBOATS & ELECTRIC BOATS   Beside the World Trade Center, you can rent paddleboats or little electric boats for a spin around the harbor. Hours vary according to season. Spend a half hour on the water. Paddleboats, some built as dragons, cost $7 to $10 a half hour per boat, depending on the number of people riding. Not that energetic? Electric boats can be rented for $12 for two passengers or $18 for three for half-hour rides.

PUBLIC PARKS

Baltimore has many green spaces but a couple are worth special mention:

Federal Hill ★★★   It's that big hill that overlooks the Inner Harbor. Take the 100 steps on the Battery Avenue side, the east side; or enter from Warren Avenue on the south side and you won't have any steps to contend with at all, except maybe a curbstone. The hill has been valued for its scenic views since the first Baltimoreans came here to watch construction around the harbor. A single black cannon recalls the Civil War when federal guns were trained on this city. Take your dog (on a leash) or take your children. Once they get tired of the view, they can play in the fenced-in playground.

Federal Hill Park, Battery and Warren Avenues, Baltimore. No phone. Best to visit during daylight hours. Free.

Cylburn Arboretum (Moments)   You'll have to look for this one but when you find it (just off Northern Parkway, a quick run up the Jones Falls Expressway), you'll be thrilled with the fascinating gardens and fancy, if a little timeworn, mansion. A patchwork of gardens covers part of the grounds: a formal Victorian garden, as well as gardens devoted to butterflies, shade, roses, and vegetables. A children's garden pays tribute to a local TV personality, Stu Kerr. Woodland trails wind 2 ½ miles (4km) through the forests of Cylburn. There's a bird sanctuary where 161 species have been spotted, including the Baltimore oriole and bald eagle. The house, an ornate stone building with mansard roof, tower, and cupola, has an equally ornate interior with inlaid floors, mosaics, and plasterwork. It houses a horticultural library, nature museum, and bird museum. Tucked in the woods off two very busy thoroughfares, the park is a peaceful retreat from urban life.

4915 Greenspring Ave., Mount Washington. ℂ 410/367-2217. Fax 410/367-7112. www.cylburnassociation. org. Grounds open daily 6am–9pm, or until dusk in winter. Museums in mansion open Tues and Thurs 1–3pm.

9 Shopping

INNER HARBOR

Harborplace (ℂ 410/332-0060; www.harborplace.com) is actually three separate locations: two stand-alone pavilions on Light and Pratt streets; and **The Gallery,** a mall in the Renaissance Harborplace Hotel. Between them, they sell everything from onion rings to diamond rings. The Light Street Pavilion has the most food stalls and restaurants, with some souvenir shops. The Pratt Street Pavilion offers specialty stores, clothing and jewelry shops, and more restaurants. The Gallery's shops fill three floors, with the fourth floor reserved as a food court. More than 160 shops are packed into the two levels of the Harborplace pavilions and the four floors of The Gallery. Most of the stores are open Monday through Saturday 10am to 10pm and Sunday noon to 6pm.

Among the choices, most are franchises of national chains but a few offer some local color. **The Fudgery** in the Light Street Pavilion once employed Baltimore native and rap singer Sisqo. Employees make amazing music while they make the fudge. **Lee's Ice Cream,** also in the Light Street Pavilion, is made in west Baltimore. The **White House** and **Black Market** clothing shops have stores all over the country, but the originals are in the Pratt Street Pavilion.

The Pratt Street Pavilion is connected via skywalk The Gallery. The latest addition to Harborplace, added in 1987, The Gallery is a four-story atrium trimmed in brass and mahogany, that contains more than 75 fine shops, including Banana Republic, Brooks Brothers, Ann Taylor, and the Disney Store. During the winter holidays, Santa's magical house is located between the Harborplace pavilions between Thanksgiving and Christmas Eve.

SHOPPING THE NEIGHBORHOODS
HAMPDEN

Fat Elvis   This tiny shop in Hampden houses a good selection of unusual antiques, but you'll also find some great coats and dresses, as well as old LPs, glassware, and other collectibles. Usually open Friday to Saturday 10am to 6pm, Sunday noon to 4pm. 833 W. 36th St. ℂ 410/467-6030.

Hometown Girl   If you want a real Baltimore souvenir, Hometown Girl probably has it. There are books about Baltimore and/or books written by Baltimoreans, fun shirts, posters and mugs, even screen painting kits. (If you've walked past the old rowhouses of Little Italy or Highlandtown, you've probably seen a window screen sporting a painted landscape.) The shop has moved to larger quarters across the street and added a soda fountain (more nostalgia for old Baltimoreans). Hours are Sunday 11am to 6pm, Monday to Wednesday 11am to 8pm, and Thursday to Saturday 11am to 9pm. 1001 W. 36th St. ℂ 410/ 662-4438. www.celebratebaltimore.com.

Mud and Metal This great little shop specializes in functional art—lamps, tables, business card holders, jewelry—often created from recycled materials. Local artists make all items and the selection is constantly changing. Open Monday to Wednesday 11am to 6pm, Thursday to Friday 11am to 7pm, Saturday 10am to 7pm, Sunday noon to 5pm. 813 W. 36th St. ⓒ 410/467-8698.

Paper Rock Scissors These galleries and shops are filled with the works of 100 local and regional artists. The art varies widely from painting to stained glass and home decor. And it's affordable. Open Tuesday to Saturday 10am to 6pm, Sunday noon to 5pm. 111 West 36th St. ⓒ 410/235-4420. www.paperrockscissors.com.

Wild Yam Pottery Hampden is becoming a center for local artists, and this shop was the first to arrive in the mid-1990s. Pottery items are handmade in the shop. Most pieces are practical—lamps, baking dishes, vases—in soothing, earthy tones. Special orders and handcrafted jewelry are also available. Open Monday to Friday 10am to 5pm and sometimes on Sunday. 1013 W. 36th St. ⓒ 410/662-1123.

FELLS POINT

Angeline's Art Gallery & Boutique Located in the Brown's Wharf complex, this shop specializes in paintings and drawings by local and national artists, especially Baltimore and Fells Point scenes. Open Monday to Thursday 11am to 6pm and Friday to Saturday 11am to 8pm. 1631 Thames St. ⓒ 410/522-7909.

Art Gallery of Fells Point This cooperative gallery features works by Maryland and regional artists, from oil paintings, watercolors, drawings, sculpture, photography, pastels, and fibers, to jewelry. Open Tuesday to Friday 11am to 5pm, weekends 10am to 6pm. 1716 Thames St. ⓒ 410/327-1272.

Brassworks Company Brass glistens from every shelf here. Fine-quality items include lamps, candlesticks, doorknockers, and a lot more. Open weekdays 8:30am to 5pm, Saturday 10am to 6pm, and Sunday noon to 6pm. 1641 Thames St. ⓒ 410/327-7280. www.baltimorebrassworks.com.

Minás This place houses more than just clothes, but vintage clothing, especially worn-in jeans, are the specialty. Open daily except Tuesday, 11am to 8pm. 733 S. Ann St. (at Lancaster St.). ⓒ 410/732-4258.

Ten Thousand Villages Using the "Body Shop" model of commissioning indigenous peoples for handmade products, this large shop (for Fells Point, anyway) is filled with textiles, pottery, baskets, and religious icons, even coffee, all fairly traded and affordably priced. 1621 Thames St. ⓒ 410/342-5568.

MOUNT VERNON

Beadazzled Be dazzled by the array of beads. They come from everywhere—Europe, South America, Africa—and in every color. There's usually a crowd of people looking for just the right combination for their next pair of earrings or necklace. They offer classes too, and have all the equipment you'll need to utilize the beads in your own craft projects. 501 N. Charles St. ⓒ 410/837-2323.

A People United This nonprofit shop features a variety of goods made by women who are part of development cooperatives in India, Nepal, Thailand, Guatemala, Kenya, and other lands. You'll find a colorful selection of clothing, jewelry, and accessories. Sweaters here are not your average pullovers. A new section featuring Indo-Asian wood and marble furnishing has been added. Open Monday to Saturday 11am to 6pm and Sunday noon to 5pm. 516 N. Charles St. ⓒ 410/727-4470.

Woman's Industrial Exchange Founded in 1880, this shop's mission has always been to help women by selling their handiwork, originally as part of a national movement after the Civil War. Baltimore's effort continues today with its charming craft shop and tearoom. (See "Where to Dine," earlier in this chapter.) The work is finely done: smocked dresses, handmade afghans and quilts, baked goods. The wares, which come from women around the country, change all the time. Open weekdays 9am to 3pm. 333 N. Charles St. ✆ **410/685-4388**.

MOUNT WASHINGTON

Baltimore Clayworks In two buildings, they hold classes, rent studio space, and offer artistic outreach to children. They also have a gallery and shop. The main building, a former convent, has a warren of little rooms turned over to gallery space where the works change frequently but are often art pieces rather than mugs and pitchers. The shop has functional pottery, made by local potters. Open Monday to Saturday 10am to 5pm. 5706 Smith Ave. ✆ **410/578-1919**. www. baltimoreclayworks.org.

Jurus I go out of my way to shop at this elegant little store filled with jewelry crafted by the owners, tableware, scarves, and Third World crafts. Many of these are one-of-a-kind items. Open Tuesday to Saturday 10am to 5:30pm. 5618 Newbury St. ✆ **410/542-5227**. www.jurusjewelry.com.

OXOXO Gallery Hugs and kisses for this tiny little shop in the heart of Mount Washington. There's lots of handcrafted jewelry here—not the kind you'd see in Tiffany's—but clever twists of metal, gems, and sometimes found objects, as well as sculpture and other treasures, too. New shows are scheduled about every 6 weeks. Bring your sense of humor. Open Tuesday to Saturday 11am to 6pm. 1617 Sulgrave Ave. ✆ **410/466-9696**.

Something Else You won't find the clothing here in any department store. Flowing dresses, exotic jewelry, colorful scarves, and heavy South American sweaters are made of flax, wood, and cotton. Open Monday to Friday 11am to 6pm, Saturday 10:30am to 6pm. 1611 Sulgrave Ave. ✆ **410/542-0444**.

Sunnyfields With so many funky little shops in Baltimore, it's nice to see this one, filled with Williamsburg reproduction furniture and accessories, porcelain and crystal, lamps and party furnishings. It even has a bridal registry. (The party napkins, however, will make you laugh.) Open Monday to Thursday 10am to 6pm, Friday to Saturday 10am to 5pm. 6305 Falls Rd. ✆ **410/823-6666**.

ANTIQUE ROW

In 1 block—the 800 block of Howard Street—lies an amazing string of antiques shops. It's fun and addictive to go from shop to shop, looking at both junk and treasures. There are a lot of treasures here.

Most of the shops are open from about 10am to 5pm, although Sunday hours may not begin until noon. Parking on the street is metered at $1 an hour, so bring lots of quarters. Or take the Light Rail; it runs up this street. Many of these shops keep their doors locked. Just ring the doorbell. Here's a sampling of the shops.

Imperial Half Bush (✆ **410/462-1192**) specializes in old silver. It fairly glitters with both Baltimore and imported flatware and hollowware.

Amos Judd and Sons, Inc. (✆ **410/462-2000**) is a dark little store but is filled with cases of elegant jewelry and some unique lamps and chandeliers.

Alice S. Marks at the Antique Treasury (✆ **410/728-6363**) keeps her cases crammed with Staffordshire and Transferware.

E. A. Mack (© 410/728-1333) specializes in 19th century furniture, all of it in lovely condition. You can also get custom reproductions made here.

Connoisseur's Connection (© 410/383-2624) has a little of everything: from furniture to curiosities. It's eclectic and fun.

Regency Antiques (© 410/225-3455) seems to go on and on with furniture for every room, sparkling chandeliers, sculpture, paintings, tapestries, and all kinds of mirrors.

MARKETS

Baltimore still has several old-fashioned markets with vendors selling seafood, baked goods, produce, and sweets. The Farmer's Market held under the Jones Falls viaduct is a Sunday tradition for many people.

Baltimore Farmers' Market   For a look at Old Baltimore, stop at this weekly outdoor gathering, a great source for crafts, herbs, jams, jellies, baked goods, and smoked meats, local produce and flowers. Open June through mid-December, Sunday 8am to noon. Saratoga St. between Holliday and Gay sts. © 410/752-8632 (for office at 200 W. Lombard St.). www.baltimoreevents.org.

Broadway Market   Smell and taste the flavors of Baltimore's original seaport at this 200-year-old market, which has two large covered buildings staffed by local vendors selling fresh produce, flowers, crafts, and an assortment of ethnic and raw bar foods, ideal for snacking, a quick lunch, or a picnic. You'll even find an old-fashioned Baltimore tradition: "sweet potatoes," soft white candies powdered with cinnamon. Open daily 8am to 6pm. S. Broadway between Fleet and Lancaster sts., Fells Point. No phone.

Cross Street Market   First opened in 1846, Cross Street Market is one of Baltimore's oldest continuously operating public markets. Come for the fresh flowers that seem to be everywhere. Local vendors also have fresh produce, seafood, meats, flowers, candy, baked goods, and much more. Cross St. between S. Charles and Light sts., Federal Hill. No phone.

Lexington Market   Established in 1782, this Baltimore landmark claims to be the oldest continuously operating market in the United States. It houses more than 140 merchants, selling prepared ethnic foods (for eat-in or take-away), fresh seafood, produce, meats, baked goods, sweets, even freshly grated coconut. It's worth a visit for the aromas, flavors, sounds, and sights, as well as good shopping. Bring cash, as credit cards are not accepted. Open Monday to Saturday 8:30am to 6pm. 400 W. Lexington St. © 410/685-6169. www.lexingtonmarket.com.

Arundel Mills   This is not in Baltimore proper, but if you are a shopaholic, you might find your Nirvana here. It's like a combination theme park/mall, and it's *huge,* with some 200 shops. Superstores such as Off 5th Saks Fifth Avenue Outlet, Bass Pro Shops Outdoor World, and Burlington Coat Factory are joined by plenty of smaller shops, an Egyptian-themed 24-screen movie theater, and lots of restaurants. Jillian's combination of bowling, arcade, games, and food is an afternoon's diversion all by itself. Off Rte. 295, 10 miles (16km) south of Baltimore. © 866/MD-MILLS. www.arundelmillsmall.com. Take Rte. 295 south, pass BWI exit to exit for Arundel Mills.

10 Baltimore After Dark

Baltimore used to be very quiet after dark. Fells Point's bars always drew a crowd, and the streets were busy when a concert, or play was scheduled. Not any more. The Inner Harbor, Federal Hill, Canton, Fells Point, and Mount Vernon have developed lives after dark.

For major events, check the arts and entertainment sections of *The Baltimore Sun* and *The Washington Post*. *The City Paper,* a free Baltimore weekly, has very complete listings down to the smallest local bars and clubs.

Tickets for most major venues are available at the individual box offices, at **TicketMaster** (℗ 410/481-SEAT; www.ticketmaster.com), or at **Baltimore Tickets** (℗ 410/BALT-TIX) at the visitor center at the Inner Harbor.

THE CLUB & MUSIC SCENE

Baltimore has a nice variety of small live-performance venues. National acts come to the **Baltimore Arena** near the Inner Harbor and to the **Pier Six Concert Pavilion** at the Inner Harbor. A number of smaller, local clubs welcome smaller touring acts and local performers, from rock to jazz to folk.

COMEDY CLUB

Comedy Factory Above Burke's Restaurant, this club presents live comedy Friday and Saturday at 8:30 and 10:30pm and offers half-price admission with a hotel key. 36 Light St. (at Lombard St.). ℗ **410/752-4189**. Cover $10.

DANCE CLUBS

Baja Beach Club Located at the Brokerage, opposite Harborplace, this club presents rock/alternative deejay dance music Wednesday through Sunday, 8pm to 2am, often hosted by deejays from "alternative" station WHFS. True to its name, in addition to the music, you'll also find lots of bikini-clad women. The club is popular with locals and draws a crowd of energetic 20-somethings. 55 Market Place (at E. Lombard St.), Inner Harbor. ℗ **410/727-0468**. No cover.

The Depot North of the Inner Harbor, this club draws a mostly young crowd with its house and retro music. Friday night features '80s music, Saturday is house remixes, and Sunday is gothic. 1728 N. Charles St. ℗ **410/528-0174**. No cover.

FOLK/TRADITIONAL

Cat's Eye Pub A Fells Point bar with an Irish feel, Cat's Eye is known for its traditional Irish music, but you'll often hear blues, bluegrass, zydeco, and jazz. In addition to the nightly live music, there's a back room with chessboards and game tables. Open noon to 2am. 1730 Thames St. ℗ **410/276-9866**. www.catseyepub. com. Occasional $5 cover, mostly free.

Mick O'Shea's Irish Pub If you're in a St. Patrick's Day mood on any weekend, come to this pub for traditional Irish music. You might be lucky enough to hear O'Malley's March. Baltimore Mayor Martin O'Malley fronts the band. There's live music Thursday through Saturday nights, and food starting at 11:30am: sandwiches, soups, and Irish specialties. 328 N. Charles St. ℗ **410/539-7504**. Cover for special occasions and performances $5–$20.

JAZZ & BLUES

Bertha's The Fells Point bar/restaurant is not only a great place to eat mussels—it's also a great venue for live jazz and blues every day of the week. 734 S. Broadway. ℗ **410/327-5795**.

Buddies Pub & Jazz Club This informal, lively place is known for its live jazz on Friday and Saturday nights from a house band that starts about 9:30pm and continues to 1:30am. If you get hungry, the kitchen serves burgers, sandwiches, and crab cakes. The restaurant is also open for lunch on weekdays. 313 N. Charles St. ℗ **410/332-4200**. No cover.

Explorer's Lounge In the Harbor Court Hotel The crowd is middle-aged, the music mellow, and the environment sumptuous with cozy chairs and sofas, and small tables by the windows. Jazz combos or pianists play cool music nightly Tuesday through Saturday. 550 Light St. ℂ **410/234-0550**. No cover.

ROCK

Bohager's Bohager's is the place to hear known-but-not-arena touring rockers, along with local bands. David Byrne, Ben Folds, and They Might Be Giants have appeared recently. Bohager's Caribbean themed bar/island between Fells Point and Little Italy boasts harbor views in summer and a controversial giant inflatable dome in winter. 701 S. Eden St. ℂ **410/563-7220**. www.bohagers.com. Cover $15 Thurs–Sat beginning at 9pm includes open bar. Cover for concerts varies.

Eight by Ten The musically savvy have followed this much-loved little gem from Fells Point to its new location in Federal Hill. The emphasis is on blues, but rock groups also play here regularly, and there's an occasional jazz performance. The Eight by Ten feels like a neighborhood party with really good music. It's open 9pm to 2am. 10 E. Cross St. ℂ **410/625-2000**. Cover varies.

Hammerjacks Hammerjacks is back. The original, a storied and rowdy local club that featured national rock acts, was torn down to make way for the football stadium, but it has been revived in a new location. It's open Thursday night at 9pm, Friday with a local radio deejay at 9pm, and Saturday at 7pm. It closes at 2am. 316 Guilford Ave. ℂ **410/234-0044**.

The Horse You Came In On This Fells Point bar is popular with the local college and post-college crowds. It features live rock or acoustic music nightly. 1626 Thames St. ℂ **410/327-8111**. Cover only on Tues, Fri and Sat.

Sonar Creative martinis and coffee-based cocktails, DJ or special concerts most nights with an emphasis on tech and house music. 3000 O'Donnell St. ℂ **410/327-8333**. Cover varies.

BEER, BILLIARDS & CIGARS

Baltimore Brewing Company The home of DeGroen's beer, this microbrewery is part German restaurant, part beer hall. Its large drinking area is lined with sturdy picnic tables and wicker bottom chairs. On the side is one very long copper-lined bar where the staff serves up DeGroen's five main beers on tap. You can even purchase any of the beers to go in growlers. 104 Albemarle St. (between Little Italy and the Inner Harbor). ℂ **410/837-5000**.

Bay Café This waterfront bar in Canton is Baltimore's Margaritaville, with a laid-back Caribbean atmosphere. There's indoor and outdoor seating, and on weekends you'll find a deejay playing top-40 pop or zydeco or something good for a party. 2809 Boston St. ℂ **410/522-3377**. No cover.

Edgar's Billiards Club & Bar This upscale day-and-night club offers 17 full-size pool tables as well as smoking and nonsmoking areas and a fine selection of cigars. 1 E. Pratt St., at Light St. ℂ **410/752-8080**.

John Steven, Ltd When you enter this establishment on the eastern edge of Fells Point, you'll be greeted by the fragrant smell of steamed shrimp. It's a great place to sit down and have a beer and a pound or so: medium, large, or jumbo. There's also a great sushi bar. 1800 Thames St. ℂ **410/327-5561**.

Max's on Broadway Max's is a Baltimore institution known for its tremendous beer selection. This cigar-friendly bar caters to the young conservative

---

⌒ *Tips* **A Guy Walks into a Bar . . .**

Baltimore has two distinct bar scenes: sports bars, where fans gather to watch the game or to discuss the results, and the Fells Point scene, which includes some bars that have music (listed above). Sports fans can stroll into any of a dozen bars in the vicinity of Camden Yards for lively game conversation, but try **Downtown Sports Exchange,** 200 W. Pratt St. (✆ 410/659-5844); **Pickles Pub,** 520 Washington Blvd. (✆ 410/752-1784); or **Orioles Bar** in the Sheraton Inner Harbor (✆ 410/962-8300).

Fells Point, a combination of pubs in historic rowhouses and hip clubs in old industrial buildings, is a focal point of Baltimore's nightlife and a favorite among the college students and young professionals. But the bar scene has expanded, and **Federal Hill's** narrow streets have a number of great spots for a beer and some music. **O'Donnell Square** in Canton is ringed with nightspots. Once you park space, you can walk from place to place.

The newest place to go is **Power Plant Live.** A combination of restaurants and bars, it's busy on Saturday nights. Some of the tenants are old-timers, including **Ruth's Chris Steak House** (see "Where to Dine,"); **Havana Club,** a cigar bar; and **Maryland Art Place,** a gallery featuring local artists. Newcomers include the **Improv,** a comedy club; **Babalu,** a Cuban grill with salsa music; **Howl at the Moon,** a rock-and-roll piano bar; **Have a Nice Day Café,** a '70s-style disco; **McFadden's Irish pub** (self-explanatory); and **Mondo Bondo,** an Italian bistro. Power Plant Live is up the street from the power plant, north of Lombard Street at Marketplace.

---

crowd. On the lower level, you'll find several pool tables as well as the main bar. Upstairs are comfy tables and chairs and Max's Mobtown Lounge, a turn-of-the-20th-century parlor lounge with rich leather seats and original artwork. 737 S. Broadway. ✆ 410/675-MAXS.

Wharf Rat This small Baltimore favorite is also a frequent stop for conventioneers looking for a drink. It has a pool table and a dining area adorned with the paraphernalia of traditional English, Scottish, and Irish beers. It's also a brewpub, so you can sip an Oliver ale or stout and look in on the brewery through large windows in the dining area. For information on the menu, see "Where to Dine," earlier in this chapter. There's a second location in Fells Point at 801 S. Ann St. (✆ 410/276-9034). 206 W. Pratt St. (at Hanover St. across from the convention center). ✆ 410/244-8900.

COFFEEHOUSES

Spoons In addition to brewing coffee, they roast their own, here, too. There's a full breakfast menu and light fare such as soups, panini, and sandwiches all day. Hours are Sunday to Tuesday 7am to 5pm, Wednesday to Saturday 7am to 10pm. 24 E. Cross St. ✆ 410/539-6751.

Donna's Donna's started out in this Mount Vernon location, but has grown into a local chain. It offers an upscale coffeehouse environment with a wide variety of both coffees and light cuisine. You'll also find Donna's in The Gallery. 800 N. Charles St. ℭ 410/385-0180.

THE GAY & LESBIAN SCENE

Along with the *Baltimore Gay Paper* and its website at www.bgp.org, you can find information and listings for events of interest to the LGBT community at the **Out in Baltimore** website (www.outinbaltimore.com); and from the **Gay, Lesbian, Bisexual & Transgender Community Center of Baltimore,** 241 W. Chase St. (ℭ **410/837-5445;** www.glccbaltimore.org).

Refer to these directories for a complete directory of nightspots. Below are three longtime community favorites:

Coconuts Café   This small bar attracting a primarily lesbian crowd is comfy and friendly. Deejays play the tunes on weekends, with occasional live music. 311 W. Madison St. (at Linden Ave.). ℭ 410/383-6064. Cover varies.

Central Station   This Mount Vernon pub has a video lounge on the second floor for its patrons, and a restaurant with cuisine a few notches above bar food. 1001 N. Charles St. ℭ 410/752-7133. www.centralstationpub.com. No cover.

The Hippo   This Baltimore mainstay has three rooms with pool and pinball, constant music videos, and a dance floor that attracts a primarily gay and lesbian clientele, but all are welcome. The music is mostly house and techno. There's a piano bar on Thursdays and Fridays, a video bar on Saturdays. 1 W. Eager St. (at Charles St.). ℭ 410/547-0069. Cover varies.

FILM

IMAX Theater/Maryland Science Center   Even if you have no interest in the science center, you can still see IMAX movies. If you don't make it to the Science Center during the day, there are double features each weekend on the theater's five-story-high, 75-foot-wide screen. Admission to the "NightMAX" shows is $9 for one show or $12.50 for two. Call for show times. 601 Light St., on the harbor. ℭ 410/685-5225.

The Senator ☆   This 1930s Art Deco movie house was rated as one of the best motion picture theaters in the country by *USA Today.* It has hosted the world premieres of many Baltimore-based flicks such as *Serial Mom, Diner, Liberty Heights,* and *Cecil B. Demented.* The Senator's regular programs include high-quality first-run films, classics, and art films, and also occasional live musical performances. 5904 York Rd. ℭ 410/435-8338. www.senator.com.

The Charles   In an industrial-style building, The Charles offers films not showing anywhere else in town (first-run independent and foreign films, in particular). Its five auditoriums are big and comfortable, with stadium seating. Cinema Sundays, when the films come with bagels, coffee, and conversation, are presented September through December, about every other week. The Charles is also a venue of the annual Maryland Film Festival, held for a week in April or early May. 1711 N. Charles St. ℭ 410/727-FILM. Parking garage across the street.

Little Italy Open Air Film Festival   On summer Fridays you can catch a feature-length movie on a blank billboard on the side of a restaurant. Bring your chair, or use the ones already set up, to see movies with an Italian accent, like *Cinema Paradiso* and *Spartacus.* Movies are projected from the bedroom window of a house near the corner of High and Stiles streets. It's free.

THE PERFORMING ARTS

Baltimore has a solid range of resident performing arts companies: a nationally recognized symphony; an opera company; a major regional theater; and a national touring house in the **Morris A. Mechanic Theater** (✆ 410/625-4230) at Baltimore and Charles streets, a block from the harbor; and several local professional theater companies.

THEATER

Center Stage ✦✦✦   Many major American plays have been developed at Maryland's state theater (including works by August Wilson and Eric Overmyer), which has been presenting new and classic work since 1963. The theater has two spaces, one a traditional proscenium stage and the other offering directors more flexibility in set design and staging. Theatergoers can see re-imagined revivals like the recent version of *The Pajama Game,* or new drama such as August Wilson's prize-winning *Jitney.* The theater offers childcare at several matinees and "Nights Out" for its gay and lesbian fans. 700 N. Calvert St. ✆ 410/332-0033. www.centerstage.org. Tickets $10–$38.

For entertainment by local professional actors at affordable prices, check out these area theaters: the **Fells Point Corner Theater,** 251 S. Ann St. (✆ 410/276-7837; www.fpct.org), presents eight productions a year. The **Vagabond Players,** 806 S. Broadway (✆ 410/563-9135), presents a variety of classics, contemporary comedies, and dramas.

The city's prominent black theater company **Arena Players** (801 McCulloh St., off Martin Luther King Blvd.; ✆ 410/728-6500) presents contemporary plays and romantic comedies.

Everyman Theatre is another solid local company that presents classics and new works. It's at 700 N. Calvert St. (✆ 410/332-0033).

The Theatre Project ✦, 45 W. Preston Street (✆ 410/752-8558), is the city's professional company presenting experimental and avant-garde work.

CLASSICAL MUSIC & OPERA

The world-class **Baltimore Symphony Orchestra** (✆ 410/783-8000; www.baltimoresymphony.org) performs several concerts a week at the Joseph Meyerhoff Symphony Hall from September through June. Each season brings classical and pops concerts. In the summertime, you'll find the BSO outside at Oregon Ridge Park, north of the city off I-83. Their Fourth of July concerts are terrific fun. Conductor Yuri Temirkanov has won rave reviews in Baltimore and during the 2001 European tour. Tickets range from $15 to $60. In addition, the **Peabody Symphony Orchestra** (✆ 410/659-8124) is a performing unit of the Peabody Institute of Music at the Johns Hopkins University in Friedberg Hall.

The **Baltimore Opera Company** (www.baltimoreopera.com) has been a tradition in the city for almost 50 years. Its slogan, "It's better than you think—It has to be," has helped it create a solid audience. The company presents five productions each year. The December opera is always one children will like, with ticket prices discounted for young people. All operas are performed with supertitles. Performances are at the **Lyric Opera House,** 140 W. Mt. Royal Ave. (✆ 410/494-2712). Acoustics are so good, even spectators in the last row of the balcony hear every note. Ticket prices range from $35 to $124. Contact the Lyric for schedule information and tickets.

Maryland's Two Capitals: Annapolis & St. Mary's City

Maryland's two capitals, present-day Annapolis and the state's first capital, St. Mary's City, are only 86 miles (138km) apart. People seeking a place to practice their faith in a time when religious persecution was a serious business founded both. While Annapolis continues to thrive, St. Mary's City gradually disappeared. But the oldest city is re-emerging as a historical site with archaeological digs and reconstruction of the town that was the first city of the old colony.

While it's a working state capital, Annapolis retains much of its colonial past: It's where George Washington resigned as commander-in-chief and where Congress ratified the treaty to end the Revolutionary War. More than 1,500 historic buildings are scattered among the narrow brick streets and alleys. (There are more colonial buildings in Annapolis than in any other town in the country.)

It's also a college town, home to the United States Naval Academy and to historic, eccentric St. John's College.

After more than 350 years, Annapolis keeps moving. Politicians hold the General Assembly from January to April. Midshipmen march in "The Yard." Marylanders arrive by land and sea all year round.

Its streets bustle most weekends with packed restaurants, bars, and shops. The pleasure boats arrive like clockwork every spring. Warm weather brings the festivities to the water's edge, and downtown takes on the air of a casual long-running party.

1 Orientation

ARRIVING

BY PLANE Annapolis is served by **Baltimore–Washington International Airport** (© 800/I-FLY-BWI or 410/859-7111; www.bwiairport.com), about 20 miles (32km) northwest of the city. Minibus shuttles between the airport and the major hotels and the Naval Academy are operated by **Airport Shuttle** (© 410/381-2772) or **SuperShuttle** (© 800/BLUE-VAN). Reservations aren't necessary but advance notice will help you get away from the airport more quickly. The fare is about $30 each way. Transfer by taxi is about $40 one-way. Contact **BWI Taxi Service** at © 410/859-1103.

BY CAR From Baltimore and points north, take I-695 (the Baltimore beltway) to I-97 south and U.S. Route 50 east. Rowe Boulevard from U.S. Route 50 will take you into downtown. From Washington, D.C., take U.S. Route 50 east off the Washington beltway (I-495) to Rowe Boulevard.

It's best to walk the historic district because parking is difficult. **Parking garages** are next to the visitor center off Northwest Street, on Duke of Gloucester Street behind City Hall, on Washington Street, and on South Street. You can also park at the Navy/Marine Corps Stadium (off Rowe Blvd. at Taylor Ave.)

and ride the Downtown Parking Shuttle into the historic district. (See information below under "Getting Around.")

BY BOAT   To secure a boat slip or mooring during a visit to Annapolis, call the Harbormaster's Office at © **410/263-7973** or e-mail harbormaster@ci. annapolis.md.us.

BY BUS   **Greyhound** (© **800/231-2222;** www.greyhound.com) offers service from all over the Eastern Seaboard; buses depart from and arrive at the Navy/Marine Corps Stadium on Rowe Boulevard. **Baltimore MTA** (© **800/ 543-9809** or 410/539-5000; www.mtamaryland.com) provides weekday service to and from Baltimore; buses stop at College Avenue by the state office buildings and the Navy/Marine Corps Stadium. **Dillon's Bus Service** (© **800/ 827-3490** or 410/647-2321; www.dillonbus.com) offers commuter service to D.C. every morning and back to Annapolis every afternoon, with buses stopping at the Navy/Marine Corps Stadium, Harry S. Truman Park, and several other places downtown. The rate is $3.35 one-way.

VISITOR INFORMATION

The **Annapolis and Anne Arundel Conference and Visitors Bureau** (© **410/ 280-0445;** www.visit-annapolis.org) runs a visitor center at 26 West St., just west of Church Circle, with maps and brochures on just about everything. Bus and walking tours (see "Organized Tours & Cruises," later in this chapter) leave from here daily; there's also a gift shop and the volunteers are helpful with recommendations and reservations for dinner or accommodations. The center is open daily 9am to 5pm. The bureau also runs an information booth at the City Dock during the summer. Pick up a free copy of *Destination Annapolis,* a magazine produced by the Visitors Bureau with a good map of the downtown area. You can get *Inside Annapolis,* a free bimonthly magazine listing local events as well as area businesses, at most restaurants and hotels.

CITY LAYOUT

The streets of downtown Annapolis radiate from two circles: **State Circle** and **Church Circle.** The three main streets are Main, Maryland, and West. Main Street leads from Church Circle to the City Dock. Maryland Avenue stretches from State Circle to the walls of the U.S. Naval Academy. West Street runs from Church Circle all the way to Route 2 and beyond. The U.S. Naval Academy, surrounded by a high, gray wall, is in its own enclave, east of downtown.

2 Getting Around

BY PUBLIC TRANSPORTATION

BY SHUTTLE   The **Annapolis Department of Parking and Transportation** (© **410/263-7964** on weekdays, 410/263-7994 on weekends) operates a shuttle-bus service between the historic/business district and the parking area of the Navy/Marine Corps Stadium. The no. 11 shuttles depart every 15 minutes and run to Church Circle weekdays 6:30am to 8pm and on weekends May to October 10am to 6pm. Extended service around the historic district is offered weekdays 9am to 3pm and 5pm to 8pm, and weekends May to October 10am to 6pm. The fare is 75¢ (exact change) at the stadium, at the Department of Natural Resources, and at Courts of Appeal (all on Rowe Blvd.). Once downtown, the shuttle is free to board at all downtown stops.

BY BUS   From Monday through Saturday, Annapolis Transit runs commuter bus service from the historic district to other parts of the city such as the

Annapolis Mall or Eastport. Base fare is 75¢ and exact change is required. Buses run every half hour, from 5:30am to 7pm. (Get a route schedule at www.ci. annapolis.md.us.)

BY CAR

CAR RENTALS   Car-rental firms in Annapolis include **Budget,** 2002 West St. (© **410/266-5030**); **Discount,** 1032 West St. (© **410/268-5955**); and **Enterprise,** 1023 Spa Rd. (© **410/268-7751**).

PARKING   With much of its 18th-century layout intact, midtown Annapolis is very compact, with narrow streets; consequently, parking in the historic district is limited. Visitors are encouraged to leave their cars in a park-and-ride lot on the edge of town off Rowe Boulevard just west of the Navy/Marine Corps Stadium, and take the shuttle (see above). Other parking garages are located behind the visitor center off Northwest Street, on Duke of Gloucester Street behind City Hall, on Washington Street, and on South Street. You can also try your luck at metered parking at the City Dock or on the street. Be aware, however, that many downtown streets have parking restrictions. Look for the signs.

BY TAXI

If you need transportation once you are in town, call **Annapolis Cab Company** (© **410/268-0022**), **Arundel and Colonial Cab** (© **410/263-2555**), or **Yellow Checker Cab** (© **410/268-1212**).

BY WATER TAXI

From late May through Labor Day, the **Jiffy Water Taxi** (© **410/263-0033**) operates from the City Dock to restaurants and other destinations along Spa and Back creeks. You can also call them, as you would a land taxi, and they will pick you up from your boat or waterfront location for a ride to a specific destination. At a restaurant, ask the waiter to call for a ride back. It's a handy way to avoid the parking hassle and a pleasant sightseeing experience. Fares range from $1.50 to $4. Hours are Monday through Thursday from 9:30am to midnight, Friday from 9:30am to 1am, Saturday from 9am to 1am, and Sunday from 9am to midnight. There is also limited service in early May and in September and October.

 FAST FACTS: Annapolis

American Express In the Annapolis Mall on Bestgate Road (© **410/ 224-4200**). Open 10am to 6pm Monday through Friday, 10am to 8pm Thursday, 10am–5pm Saturday.

Area Code The area codes in Annapolis are **410** and **443**.

Emergencies Dial © **911** for fire, police, or ambulance.

Hospitals **Anne Arundel Medical Center** recently moved to 2001 Medical Parkway off Jennifer Road (© **443/481-1000**).

Liquor Laws Places serving alcoholic beverages may stay open from 6am to 2am, except on Sunday and election days. The minimum age for buying or consuming alcohol is 21.

Newspapers/Magazines The local daily newspaper is the *Annapolis Capital*. *The Baltimore Sun* and *The Washington Post* are also widely available. The leading monthly magazine is *Annapolis*.

Pharmacies There's a Rite Aid at 2027 West St. near Parole (✆ **410/266-5055**).

Police For nonemergency police assistance, dial ✆ **311**. For emergencies, dial ✆ **911**.

Post Office The main branch is on Church Circle (✆ **800/275-8777**). It's open Monday through Friday 9am to 5pm, Saturday from 9am to noon.

Taxes The local sales tax is 5%; the local hotel tax is an additional 7%.

3 Where to Stay

There are many convenient accommodations downtown, though families may find the hotels along Route 50 easier on their wallets and quieter, as well.

There are many bed-and-breakfasts, historic inns, and hotels within walking distance of all the attractions and restaurants. However, they are expensive. It is hard to find a double-occupancy room in Annapolis for under $100. To lessen the dent in your wallet, many properties offer packages at reduced rates during slower times; be sure to ask about special offers when you reserve.

Special events—USNA parents' weekend and Commissioning Week in May, Army/Navy games, the Annapolis Boat Show (which runs 2 weeks in Oct), to name a few—send hotel prices skyrocketing.

A number of hotel chains have properties right off Route 50 in the Parole area of Annapolis. These are much more reasonably priced and some offer shuttles into downtown. It's only a few minutes by car from downtown—but again you have to worry about parking.

All the major hotels have rooms accessible for travelers with disabilities, but most of the inns and bed-and-breakfasts do not.

EXPENSIVE

Annapolis Inn ★★★ It was good enough for Thomas Jefferson's doctor in the 18th century, now it's a perfect spot for a romantic getaway or moment of pure luxury in the 21st century. The three bedrooms are separate and private. While the public rooms are Georgian in their decoration and elegance, the private rooms are shrines to comfort with big, cozy beds, lush seating areas, and bathrooms with Jacuzzis and heated marble tile floors. There are no phones to trouble you, televisions if you must, and modem ports if absolutely necessary. A three-course breakfast is served in the dining room with scones, a fruit course, and something hot. Elegance rules, as each course comes on fine china and crystal. In warm weather, breakfast is also served on the intimate patio. Check the website or call to learn more about murder-mystery or romantic weekend packages or cooking weekends. If you can pry yourself from the surroundings, the Annapolis attractions are all quite close.

144 Prince George St. ✆ 310/295-5200. www.annapolisinn.com. 3 units. $250–$475 double. Rates include full breakfast. AE, DISC, MC, V. Parking on street. *In room:* A/C, TV, Jacuzzis, dataport available.

Annapolis Marriott Waterfront ★★ The only waterfront hotel in Annapolis, and the only one with boat docks for guest use, this modern six-story property attracts (duh) the boating crowd. It sits in Annapolis's best location, beside the City Dock overlooking "Ego Alley" and Spa Creek. Guest rooms are decorated in an elegant, contemporary style enhanced by floor-to-ceiling

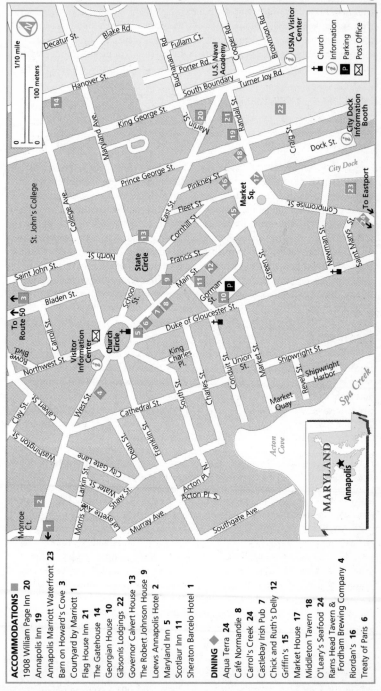

ACCOMMODATIONS

1908 William Page Inn **20**
Annapolis Inn **19**
Annapolis Marriott Waterfront **23**
Barn on Howard's Cove **3**
Courtyard by Marriott **1**
Flag House Inn **21**
The Gatehouse **14**
Georgian House **10**
Gibsonis Lodgings **22**
Governor Calvert House **13**
The Robert Johnson House **9**
Loews Annapolis Hotel **2**
Maryland Inn **5**
Scotlaur Inn **11**
Sheraton Barcelo Hotel **1**

DINING

Aqua Terra **24**
Café Normandie **8**
Carrol's Creek **24**
Castlebay Irish Pub **7**
Chick and Ruth's Delly **12**
Griffin's **15**
Market House **17**
Middleton Tavern **18**
O'Leary's Seafood **24**
Rams Head Tavern &
  Fordham Brewing Company **4**
Riordan's **16**
Treaty of Paris **6**

113

windows. About three-quarters of the rooms have balconies on the waterfront or with water views, and the rest overlook the historic district. Besides standard rooms, some rooms have Jacuzzis, and one suite is available. If you have a few minutes, stop by the hotel's gallery to see the collection of historic photographs and ship models, including *Old Ironsides* and the *African Queen*. It's open to the public.

80 Compromise St., Annapolis, MD 21401. ℭ **800/228-9290** or 410/268-7555. Fax 410/269-5864. www. annapolismarriott.com. 150 units. $129–$269 double; $219–$499 upgraded rooms. AE, DC, DISC, MC, V. Valet parking $12 overnight. **Amenities:** Pusser's Landing; indoor and outdoor restaurant and lounge; boat dock; exercise room; sun deck; 300-foot boardwalk. *In room:* A/C, dataport, fridge and microwave available, coffee-maker, hair dryer, iron, robes.

Loews Annapolis Hotel ★★★ *Kids*   The Loews Annapolis is loaded with amenities (except for boat slips—see the Annapolis Marriott for those) and an exceedingly friendly staff. Located near Church Circle, within walking distance of the main attractions of the historic district, this modern six-story hotel with a redbrick facade and a tree-shaded courtyard entrance fits in well with the historic buildings. It has a spacious lobby and skylit public areas. Guest rooms, furnished in dark woods, quilted plaid prints, and nautical art, offer views of the city skyline and historic area. Ask about special grandparents' packages.

126 West St., Annapolis, MD 21401. ℭ **800/526-2593** or 410/263-7777. Fax 410/263-0084. www.loews annapolis.com. 217 units. $109–$239 double; $169–$409 suite. AE, DC, DISC, MC, V. Self-parking $10; valet parking $13. Pets accepted. **Amenities:** Restaurant; bar; fitness center. *In room:* A/C, dataport, minibar, fridge and microwave available, coffeemaker, iron.

MODERATE

1908 William Page Inn ★   In a town that lives and breathes colonial style, here's a Victorian marvel, all cedar shake and wraparound porch. The first-floor room even has direct access to the porch. Each spacious room has its own character. The quietest room has a private bathroom with shower and whirlpool, and the attic suite with chaise and couch is far enough away that guests can disappear for days—and some do. Breakfast is always tempting, served in the big, comfortable common room every day from 8 to 10am.

8 Martin St., Annapolis, MD 21401. ℭ **800/364-4160**. www.williampageinn.com. 5 units (3 with private bathroom). $130–$260 double. Rates include full breakfast. Parking available. *In room:* TV available, standard in attic room. No telephone but all rooms wired for phones and modems.

Flag House Inn   With a gingerbread-trimmed front porch and the state or country flags of current guests flying beneath a mansard roof, this three-story Victorian house (ca. 1858) is nestled on a street between the City Dock and the main gate of the Naval Academy. Inside, the guest library with a working fireplace and the dining room display period naval and maritime art and antiques. Guest rooms (including a two-room suite) have a king-sized bed or twin beds, antique and reproduction furniture, private bathrooms, comfortable seating, and good reading lamps. Breakfast includes fruit, cereals, fresh baked breads or pastries, and a hot main dish. The innkeepers, Bill and Charlotte Schmickle, proud parents of a 1999 USNA graduate and members of the Naval Academy Sailing Squadron, are particularly good hosts for prospective students and sailors of all abilities.

26 Randall St., Annapolis, MD 21401. ℭ **800/437-4825** or 410/280-2721. Fax 410/280-0133. www. flaghouseinn.com. 5 units (shower only). $95–$200 double. Rates include full breakfast. MC, V. Free parking. No children under age 10.

The Gatehouse   Sitting in the shadow of the U.S. Naval Academy, this brick town house combines colonial style with modern conveniences. Often filled with USNA relatives, this bed-and-breakfast is most convenient to the Naval Academy but is only a short walk from the historic district. It is far enough out of the way to be a bit quieter than places near Main Street. The rooms with queen beds and cable TV are comfortable. The best rooms are two mini-suites with four-poster or sleigh bed, private sitting area, and in-suite baths. All come with fresh flowers, robes, and special bath soaps, as well as fresh cookies and bottled water upon arrival. The deck out back offers a quiet place to relax in the sun or under the stars.

249 Hanover St. ℂ 888/254-7576 or 410/280-0024. www.gatehousebb.com. 5 units, 4 with private bath. Rates include full breakfast. 2-night minimum stay required some weekends. Whole-house rentals available. MC, V.

Georgian House ⚑   This bed-and-breakfast is housed in one of the oldest structures in Annapolis. Its historic charm is enhanced by the modern conveniences and its location. Walk through the back gate and you're on your way down Main Street. The four rooms each have their own ambience. One room has its own deck, the suite has a working fireplace in the sitting room, and another room has a double shower. Breakfasts include fresh-baked muffins or rolls and a hot entree such as the popular crab quiche or strawberry crepes.

170 Duke of Gloucester St. ℂ 800/557-2068 or 410/263-5618. www.georgianhouse.com. 4 units. $130–$175 double. AE, MC, V. Rates include full breakfast. Parking on street or for nominal charge in Hillman Garage just behind house. **Amenities:** Video/book library; microwave; fridge on second floor. *In room:* TV/VCR, telephone outlet with Internet access.

INEXPENSIVE

Barn on Howard's Cove ⚑   Just a few minutes out of town, you can stay in a barn. But this isn't just a barn, it's a refuge. It's a little hard to find: set back on a driveway, the house sits on a quiet cove. Relax on the deck or in the gazebo overlooking the water, or launch a canoe or kayak and go exploring. A stone fireplace dominates the sprawling common room of this converted 1850 horse barn. Breakfast is served on the deck or in the solarium. Climb the spiral staircase to two delightful rooms, both with private bathrooms. One suite has a queen bed and a sleeping loft for those willing to climb a ladder to the double bed. There's also a sitting room with a balcony overlooking the water. The second room is large, with a queen bed and pullout loveseat. In the hallway is a small kitchenette with refrigerator, microwave, coffeemaker, and library of videos. If there's no room here but you want to stay on Howard's Cove, ask about Meadow Garden. The neighboring home is also a bed-and-breakfast. In addition to two rooms and access to the cove, Meadow Garden has a swimming pool and hot tub.

500 Wilson Rd., Annapolis, MD 21401. ℂ 410/266-6840. 2 units. $125 double. No credit cards. Rates include full breakfast. **Amenities:** Use of canoe; kayak. *In room:* TV/VCR.

Country Inns and Suites ⚑ *Kids*   Though not in downtown Annapolis, this family-friendly hotel has the advantage of being just off Route 50 and across the street from the Westfield Shoppingtown Annapolis. A complimentary shuttle bus gets you into town pretty quickly. The hotel, which opened in 1998, has a mix of standard rooms with two queen beds and suites. One-bedroom suites offer refrigerator and microwave, two televisions, and pullout sofas. The double queen suite sleeps six. King suites overlook the woods (instead of the highway in front). The whirlpool suite also has a working fireplace. Ask about romantic getaway packages in the whirlpool suite. In the high summer season, a 2-night minimum stay may be required. With children, this might be the most comfortable choice.

2600 Housely Rd., Parole. ⓒ 800/456-4000 or 410/571-6700. Fax 410/571-6777. www.countryinns.com. 100 units. $109 double queen standard, $134–$189 suite. Rates include continental breakfast. AE, DISC, MC, V. Free parking. **Amenities:** Coffee and snacks available anytime in lobby; pool and whirlpool; exercise room; fax; complimentary shuttle to historic district; laundry and dry cleaning service. *In room:* Free local calls, dataport, coffeemaker, hair dryer, iron, fridge and microwave (suites only).

Courtyard by Marriott   In a quiet setting about 5 miles (8km) west of the historic district, this contemporary three-story facility is a favorite with business executives on weekdays and families on weekends. The rooms follow the usual Courtyard plan, with sliding glass windows and balconies or patios facing a central landscaped terrace. Guest units are spacious, with a separate sitting area, sofa, and desk. Some rooms have balconies.

2559 Riva Rd., Annapolis, MD 21401. ⓒ 800/321-2211 or 410/266-1555. Fax 410/266-6376. www.courtyard. com. 149 units. $79–$149 double. Children stay free in parents' room. AE, DC, DISC, MC, V. Free parking. **Amenities:** Breakfast buffet; indoor pool; whirlpool; exercise room. *In room:* A/C, TV with pay movies, coffeemaker, hair dryer, iron, fridge and microwave in suites.

Gibson's Lodgings *Value*   An exceptional value, this three-building complex (two restored town houses and a modern three-story annex) is within walking distance of the harbor, the historic district, and the Naval Academy. The Patterson House (dating from 1760) is a Federal–Georgian house with a Victorian facade. The adjacent Berman House is a tri-gable variation of a 19th-century stucco homestead-style dwelling. The annex (or Lauer House) was built of brick in 1988 to blend in with the older buildings, and has meeting and seminar rooms. A central garden and courtyard serve as a common area for all three buildings.

110 Prince George St., Annapolis, MD 21401. ⓒ 877/330-0057 or 410/268-5555. Fax 410/268-2775. www. avmcyber.com/gibson. 20 units (17 with private bathrooms). $79–$99 double with shared bathroom, $89–$189 double with private bathroom. Rates include continental breakfast. AE, MC, V. Free courtyard parking.

Scotlaur Inn   The Scotlaur is perhaps the best value in the historic district. You can get a room—with a full breakfast—for under $100. The inn is housed in the top two floors of a three-story brick building; the ground floor belongs to Chick and Ruth's Delly (see "Where to Dine," below) The Levitt family, who always offer a warm welcome, owns both the eatery and the inn. The guest rooms are handsomely furnished in a turn-of-the-20th-century style, but require walking up one or two flights of stairs (no elevator). Antique bookshelves have been filled with volumes for visitors. Unfortunately, the Scotlaur suffers a bit for its location: Even though the public garage is behind the inn, it (and every other lot and garage in the city) often fills up on weekends. Avoid the rooms that face onto the back alley, or loud passersby in the alley below may wake you or keep you up.

165 Main St., Annapolis, MD 21401. ⓒ 410/268-5665. www.scotlaurinn.com. 10 units. $75–$150 double. Rates include full breakfast. MC, V. Self-parking in adjacent public garage $8. Pets accepted. *In room:* Hair dryer, iron.

Sheraton Barcelo Hotel   The Sheraton Barcelo was a newcomer to Annapolis with renovations newly completed in 2001. It took over a site vacated by the Wyndham Garden, in the Parole section west of downtown Annapolis. It offers lots of modern conveniences right off Route 50. Besides, it's only a hop and a skip to downtown. The spacious rooms are your standard Sheraton rooms, freshly decorated with new furniture.

173 Jennifer Rd., Annapolis, MD 21401. © **800325-3535**, 410/266-3131. Fax 410/266-6247. www.sheraton. com. 196 units. $89–$229 double, $139–$279 suite. Club level rates include continental breakfast. Free parking. AE, DC, DISC, MC, V. **Amenities:** Restaurant; bar; indoor pool; exercise room; Jacuzzi; business center; shuttle to historic district. *In room:* A/C, TV/VCR, pay movies, fax, dataport, coffeemaker, hair dryer, iron, safe, kitchenette and fridge in suites only.

HISTORIC HOSTELRIES

Clustered around the city's two key traffic circles, the **Historic Inns of Annapolis** are an attractive option. The old-fashioned decor provides an enjoyable taste of the historic. Some of the buildings have antique fireplaces in the rooms, carved wooden banisters, and wide porches suitable for enjoying the evening. If you have a preference for a specific amenity, ask when making reservations.

Although they are separate properties, the inns are run as a single entity; to reserve a room at any of them, contact the **central office** in the Governor Calvert House, 58 State Circle (© **800/847-8882** or 410/263-2641). Rates range from $129 to $199 for a double, with the possibility of higher rates on holiday weekends. Rates are dependent on several factors—to get the best rate, call a few times and asking for their lowest available rate. Check-in must be done at the Governor Calvert House, where free shuttle service is provided to the other inns.

Governor Calvert House is at 58 State Circle. Both a conference center and a hotel, this lodging is composed of several restored and integrated colonial and Victorian residences. One public room, which dates from 1727, contains an original hypocaust (a warm-air heating system), now covered with a huge sheet of tempered glass and used as a display area. The 55 bedrooms are furnished with antiques. This property has underground parking and a sunny ground-floor atrium.

Maryland Inn is at 16 Church Circle. This flatiron-shaped structure has been operating as an inn since the 1770s. As pretty as the outside and public rooms are, the 44 rooms are small. The location at the corner of Church Circle and Main Street, as well as the helpful staff, makes this a good place to stay, though. Even better, the charming Treaty of Paris restaurant and King of France Tavern where jazz is king every weekend are right here.

The Robert Johnson House is at 23 State Circle between School and Francis streets, overlooking the governor's mansion and the Maryland State House. This lodging consists of three adjoining Georgian homes dating from 1773. The 30 artfully restored and furnished guest rooms are individually decorated with four-poster beds and antiques; each unit also has a private bathroom.

Historic Inns of Annapolis, 58 State Circle, Annapolis, MD 21401. © **800/847-8882** or 410/263-2641. Fax 410/268-3613. www.annapolisinns.com. 124 units in 3 properties. AE, DC, DISC, MC, V. Valet parking $12. **Amenities:** Restaurant; 2 bars (See "Where to Dine," "Annapolis After Dark," later in this chapter); local health club privileges; complimentary coffee/tea; local shuttle van. *In room:* A/C, TV or TV/VCR, dataport, coffeemaker, hair dryer, iron.

4 Where to Dine

You can eat in Annapolis at colonial dining rooms, taverns, bistros, and waterside seafood houses. Many choice dining spots are located in the city's hotels and inns. For families and travelers on the go, there is **Restaurant Park,** a complex of fast-food and family-style eateries at the intersection of Routes 50, 301, and 450, about 4 miles (6km) from downtown, opposite the Annapolis Shopping Plaza.

EXPENSIVE

Carrol's Creek ★★★ SEAFOOD   For the best views of the waterfront and Annapolis skyline, along with imaginative food, head for this sleek waterfront restaurant in the Eastport neighborhood. Seating is available in a wide-windowed setting indoors or on an umbrella-shaded outdoor porch. Start with a bowl of cream of crab soup—it's one of Maryland's best. Though this is definitely a seafood restaurant, the kitchen is quite adventurous, pairing rockfish with parmesan polenta and ratatouille, shrimp with crabmeat and vegetables in a stir-fry, free-range chicken with truffle scented mashed potatoes, and duck with lingonberry chutney. A couple of special dinners are offered seasonally, such as the crab dinner with cream of crab soup, salad, crab cakes, and dessert for $40. Come by water taxi for the full waterfront effect. Come at lunchtime for their delicious food at a fraction of dinner prices (and a sunny view).

410 Severn Ave., Eastport. © **410/263-8102.** Reservations accepted only for indoor weekday lunches and dinners; priority seating on weekends. Main courses $14–$33; lunch $7.95–$14; brunch $18.95. AE, DC, DISC, MC, V. Mon–Sat 11:30am–10pm, Sun 10am–10pm.

Middleton Tavern ★★ AMERICAN/SEAFOOD   Established in 1750 by Horatio Middleton as an inn for seafaring men, this restaurant's patrons included Washington, Jefferson, and Franklin. Restored and expanded, this City Dock landmark offers dinner entrees such as crab cakes, roasted salmon, and lobster tails, as well as steaks and chateaubriand for two. It's a nice mix of historic location and good food. At lunch, the menu includes pizzas, pastas, fajitas, and sandwiches. Stopping for a drink on the tavern's front porch is a favorite summer evening activity for both locals and visitors.

2 Market Space (at Randall St.). © **410/263-3323.** Fax 410/263-3807. Call ahead for priority seating. Main courses $13.95–$49.95; lunch $5.95–$15.95. AE, MC, V. Mon–Fri 11am–midnight, Sat–Sun 10am–midnight.

O'Leary's Seafood ★★ SEAFOOD   Located just over the Spa Creek Bridge, this spot has been a local dining favorite for over 20 years. Those in the know come here for the freshest seafood. Served in a swank, warm dining room, it's prepared to order in a variety of ways. Or choose one of the creative menu selections, such as crispy grouper with fresh Gulf shrimp or sautéed shellfish with polenta. Some find it noisy, so if that bothers you, come on a weekday or ask to sit in the back dining room. But don't miss great seafood, prepared with panache.

310 3rd St., Eastport. © **410/263-0884.** Fax 410/263-5869. www.olearys-seafood.com. Reservations strongly recommended. Main courses $19.95–$29.95. AE, DC, MC, V. Sun–Thurs 5–11pm, Fri–Sat 5pm–midnight.

Treaty of Paris ★ AMERICAN   Come hungry to Sunday brunch, when you'll find everything from made-to-order omelets and Belgian waffles to mussels and Alaskan crab legs, plus a range of luscious desserts. Centrally located in the Maryland Inn, this cozy dining room exudes an 18th-century ambience with a decor of brick walls, colonial-style furnishings, and an open fireplace, all enhanced by the glow of candlelight. The eclectic menu offers such dishes as sautéed rockfish, veal sweetbreads, smoked breast of duck, crab imperial, veal Oscar, blackened steaks, and beef Wellington (always a wonderful choice).

16 Church Circle. © **410/216-6340.** Reservations recommended for dinner and Sun brunch. Main courses $16.95–$34.95; lunch $6.95–$13.95; brunch $19.95. AE, DC, DISC, MC, V. Mon–Sat 7–10am, 11:30am–2:30pm, and 5:30–9pm (open to 10pm Fri–Sat); Sun 10am–2pm and 5:30–9pm.

MODERATE

Aqua Terra ★ INTERNATIONAL   Here's a new dining experience tucked into a storefront on Main Street. Not only are the furnishings sleek and modern,

Jugglers, dancers and an assortment of acrobats fill the street.

She shoots you a wide-eyed look as a seven-foot cartoon character approaches.

What brought you here was wanting the kids

to see something magical while they still believed in magic.

America Online Keyword: Travel

With 700 airlines, 50,000 hotels and over 5,000 cruise and vaca-

tion getaways, you can now go places you've always dreamed of.

Travelocity.com
A Sabre Company
Go Virtually Anywhere.

"WORLD'S LEADING TRAVEL WEB SITE, 5 YEARS IN A ROW" WORLD TRAVEL AWARDS

the food is, too. Don't look for everyday crab cakes or grilled salmon here. The ever-changing menu always has pasta, seafood, meat, and vegetarian choices. But the pasta will be *buccatini* tossed with shrimp, mussels, and a garlicky marinara; and the tuna *au poivre* might be served with lemongrass risotto. Everything is fresh and inventive. Come if you're adventurous.

164 Main St. © 410/263-1985. Reservations recommended. AE, DISC MC, V. Lunch Wed–Sun noon–2:30pm; dinner Sun–Mon 5–9pm, Tues–Thurs 5:30–10pm, Fri–Sat 5:30–11pm.

Café Normandie ★★ FRENCH   This rustic storefront in the heart of Annapolis's historic district serves up the tastes and atmosphere of a French country restaurant. From its hearty onion soup to the delicate baked Brie, every starter is a hit. The entrees are classics, including shrimp Provençal, trout amandine, and beef bourguignon. A delightful pasta dish combines linguini with chicken, shrimp, and walnuts in a basil and cream sauce. The menu continues to include the wonderful main course and dessert crepes that put this restaurant on the map many years ago. Check in advance for early-bird specials from 5 to 6:30pm. Breakfast is served Friday through Sunday.

185 Main St. © 410/263-3382. Reservations recommended for dinner on weekends. Main courses $12.95–$27.95; lunch $8.75–$12.95; breakfast $7.50–$12.50. AE, DC, DISC, MC, V. Mon–Thurs 11am–10pm, Fri 9am–10:30pm, Sat–Sun 8am–10:30pm.

Castlebay Irish Pub IRISH   In a town brimming with Irish pubs, here's one that stands out. Specialties are shepherd's pie, fish-and-chips, and corned beef and cabbage. The beef and lamb stews are exceptional. The lunch/sandwich menu is a little lighter. You'll find burgers and fries, corned beef, and a BLT piled high with thickly sliced bacon. There's also a reasonably large children's menu, featuring smaller portions of their traditional fare, chicken tenders, grilled cheese, and even a few pasta dishes. At the bar, you'll find all your favorite Irish brews.

193 Main St. © 410/626-1065. www.castlebayirishpub.com. Main courses $8.95–$18.95; lunch $5.95–$11.95. AE, DISC, MC, V. Mon–Fri 11am–midnight, Sat–Sun 10am–midnight.

Griffin's AMERICAN   Service is swift and attentive at this busy restaurant, in keeping with the rhythm of the rock music that blares in the background. It has a long turn-of-the-20th-century-style bar specializing in microbrews, and two dining areas with vaulted ceilings, exposed brick walls, tile and marble flooring, mounted animal heads, and a collection of framed feathered masks surrounding several dozen small, tightly packed tables. The menu changes regularly, but you're likely to find such specialties as grilled yellowfin tuna with Hawaiian barbecue glaze; Caribbean jerk chicken breasts; peppercorn beef tenderloin, served with caramelized onions and port wine mushroom sauce; and Griffin's Seafood Pasta—mussels and clams in an herb tomato broth over penne.

22–24 Market Space, City Dock. © 410/268-2576. Fax 410/280-0195. Reservations accepted Mon–Thurs only. Main courses $12.95–$19.95; lunch $5.95–$8.95. AE, DC, DISC, MC, V. Mon–Sat 11am–2am, Sun 10am–2am.

Rams Head Tavern & Fordham Brewing Company ★★ INTERNATIONAL   Whether you come for dinner in one of the cozy dining rooms or have a drink and appetizers on the sidewalk, this is a great stopping place. This storefront pub/restaurant serves more than 170 beers—including seasonal selections from its microbrewery, the Fordham Brewing Company. It's also a venue for music and comedy acts (see "Annapolis After Dark," later in this chapter). The restaurant offers several different settings, ranging from little rooms with brick walls and working fireplaces and/or views of the microbrewery to a wisteria-covered, heated outdoor patio. On a summer evening, the front sidewalk is the place to be. The menu is the same all day, but smaller "lunch" portions of their entrees are available. The Jamaican Jerk Rasta Pasta—jerk chicken with tricolor fettuccini—is excellent and very spicy. The menu also includes more traditional regional fare, such as jumbo lump crab cakes and rockfish Silopanna; lots of burgers, steaks, and sandwiches; and a large selection of appetizers including a wonderful crab dip. The waitstaff is young and usually witty.

33 West St. ⓒ 410/268-4545. www.ramsheadtavern.com. Reservations recommended but not always needed for dinner. Main courses $5.95–$24.95; lunch $5.95–$10.95. AE, DISC, MC, V. Mon–Sat 11am–2am, Sun 10am–2am.

Riordan's AMERICAN   Riordan's serves traditional American cuisine and seafood, including sandwiches, seafood, and pasta all day. There's a selection of penne platters, and unusual sandwich offerings like the grilled salmon BLT and the Crisfield chicken sandwich, a grilled chicken breast topped with pepper jack cheese and spicy crab dip. The main bar and dining area, which seem to be busy all the time, are on the first floor, but for a quieter setting, you can sit in the smaller dining room on the second floor. There's also a small bar on the second floor.

26 Market Space. ⓒ 410/263-5449. Fax 410/268-5867. www.riordans.com. Main courses $11.95–$19.95; lunch $5.95–$8.95. AE, DC, DISC, MC, V. Mon–Sat 11am–2am, Sun 10am–2am.

INEXPENSIVE

Chick and Ruth's Delly AMERICAN   An Annapolis tradition, this ma-and-pa establishment has been run by the Levitt family for more than 30 years. The small deli/restaurant, decorated in true diner fashion—orange is the dominant color—is famous for its 50 or so sandwiches named after local and national political figures and local attractions. The current governor could order a namesake Parris Glendening (baked potato stuffed with broccoli and cheese), and the diminutive Maryland senator could have a Barbara Mikulski (open-faced tuna with melted cheese on a bagel). A local favorite is the Main Street (corned beef and coleslaw). There's even a Bill Clinton: turkey breast, lettuce, and tomato on whole wheat. Platters, pizzas, salads, sundaes, and milk shakes are also available.

165 Main St. ⓒ 410/269-6737. www.chickandruths.com. Main courses and lunch $2.95–$7.95. No credit cards. Daily 6:30am–4pm. Open to 10pm Wed, Thurs, Sun; and to 11:30pm Fri–Sat.

Market House DELI/FAST FOOD   Originally a farmers' produce station built in 1784 and rebuilt in 1858, this place retains some of the flavor of a market, with open stalls and a variety of foods, although the wares now fall mostly into the fast-food category. Stroll around and order raw bar items, sandwiches, deli food, pizza, desserts, cheeses, salad bar, breads and pastries, espresso, and more. It's the ideal spot to grab a quick meal, browse, or stock up for a picnic.

City Dock. ⓒ 410/269-0941. All items $2–$8. No credit cards. May–Oct Mon–Thurs 9am–6pm, Fri–Sun 9am–7pm; Nov–Apr Wed–Mon 9am–6pm, Tues 9am–3pm.

5 The Top Attractions

The central area of Annapolis is a National Historic District, with over 1,500 restored and preserved buildings. Since the streets are narrow and parking is difficult, the ideal way to see it is on foot. Several guided tours are described below; self-guided walking tour maps are available free from the visitor center.

Plan to spend some time around the **City Dock** along the waterfront. This is a yachting hub, with craft of all sizes in port. Sightseeing harbor cruises are

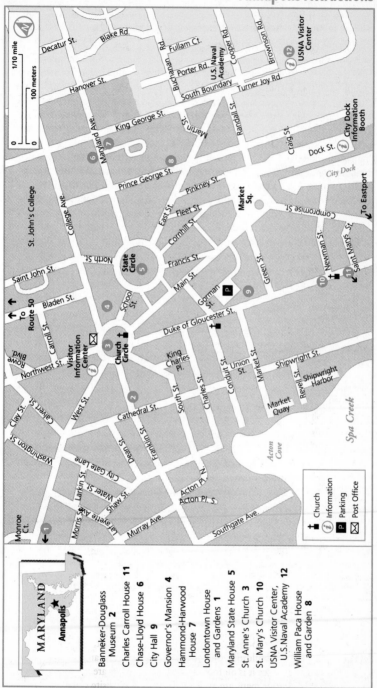

Annapolis Attractions

MARYLAND
★ Annapolis

Banneker-Douglass Museum **2**
Charles Carroll House **11**
Chase-Lloyd House **6**
City Hall **9**
Governor's Mansion **4**
Hammond-Harwood House **7**
Londontown House and Gardens **1**
Maryland State House **5**
St. Anne's Church **3**
St. Mary's Church **10**
USNA Visitor Center, U.S.Naval Academy **12**
William Paca House and Garden **8**

† Church
ⓘ Information
P Parking
⊠ Post Office

available in spring, summer, and fall. The City Dock is also home to fine seafood restaurants, lively bars, specialty shops, galleries, and a summer theater.

U.S. Naval Academy ★★★   Since 1845, Annapolis has been the home of the U.S. Navy's undergraduate professional college, spread over 338 acres along the Chesapeake Bay and Severn River on the eastern edge of town. To acclimate yourself and join a guided tour (see "Organized Tours & Cruises," later in this chapter), step into the Armel–Leftwich Visitor Center at the Halsey Field House, just inside Gate 1. Here you can view a 12-minute orientation film, see exhibits on the life of a midshipman, and browse the gift shop. Among the attractions on the academy grounds are the chapel, which contains the crypt of John Paul Jones; and the U.S. Naval Academy Museum in Preble Hall, which contains collections of nautical relics, paintings, ship models, and other items.

Try to plan your trip to see noon formation (held in Tecumseh Court at 12:05pm Mon–Fri), when the midshipmen line up and are accounted for before marching in for the noon meal. **Commissioning Week,** usually the last week in May, is a colorful time of full-dress parades; it is also a busy period for Annapolis hotels, as relatives and friends of the midshipmen pour into the city. No cars are permitted on academy grounds. Please call in advance to confirm hours.

Armel–Leftwich Visitor Center, 52 King George St. (enter via Gate 1 at intersection of King George and Randall sts.). ✆ 410/263-6933. www.navyonline.com. Free admission to grounds and visitor center; guided walking tour $6 adults, $5 seniors, $4 students. Mar–Dec daily 9am–5pm, Jan–Feb daily 9am–4pm. Closed Jan 1, Thanksgiving, and Dec 25.

Banneker–Douglass Museum   Named after two prominent local African-American residents, astronomer and inventor Benjamin Banneker and abolitionist Frederick Douglass, this museum presents exhibits, lectures, and films portraying the historical life and cultural experiences of African Americans in Maryland. The site was formerly the Old Mount Moriah African Methodist Episcopal Church.

84 Franklin St. (off the south side of Church Circle). ✆ 410/216-6180. Free admission. Tues–Fri 10am–3pm, Sat noon–4pm.

Charles Carroll House   Built in 1721–22, and enlarged in 1770, this is the birthplace and home of Charles Carroll of Carrollton, the only Catholic to sign the Declaration of Independence. It sits on high ground overlooking Spa Creek, a block from City Dock. Visitors can tour the house plus the 18th-century terraced boxwood gardens and a 19th-century wine cellar. The Charles Carroll House hosts several public programs throughout the year. Recent programs have included mother-daughter high teas, an 18th-century dress workshop, a Celtic music concert on the terraced lawns, and a candlelight Christmas dinner.

107 Duke of Gloucester St. (behind St. Mary's Church at Spa Creek). ✆ 410/263-1737. www.carrollhouse. com. Admission $5 adults, $4 seniors, $2 ages 12–17, free for under age 12. Mar–Dec Fri noon–4pm, Sat 10am–2pm, Sun noon–4pm; Tues–Thurs tours by appointment. Closed Easter, Thanksgiving, Dec 24, and Dec 25.

Hammond–Harwood House ★★   Built in 1774, this house is one of the finest examples of Georgian architecture in the United States. It's a unique example of the Maryland five-part Palladian mansion that connects the central main section of the house by hyphens (smaller sections consisting of a hallway and small rooms) to semi-octagonal wings. Famous for its center doorway of tall Ionic columns, the interior is a showcase of decorative arts and paintings, as well as ornamentation and woodcarvings. The house is named for its owners Mathias

Frommer's Favorite Annapolis Experiences

- **Noon Formation at the Naval Academy.** Don't miss this daily ritual, when midshipmen assemble at Bancroft Hall and march in to lunch.
- **Milk Shakes at Chick and Ruth's Delly.** Anything on the menu at this homey diner is a treat, but we highly recommend the chocolate shakes.
- **Sailing, Sailing, Sailing.** A trip to Annapolis is not complete without a view of the city from the water, the dome of the State House rising majestically above the harbor. Take a narrated tour on the *Harbor Queen* or the *Annapolitan* for a view of the city, the Naval Academy, and the Bay Bridge (© 410/268-7601).
- **Sitting on the Dock of the Bay.** On a sunny afternoon, pick up a lunch at The Market and head to the City Dock to watch the boats.

Hammond, a Maryland member of the Provincial Assembly, and the Harwood family, who owned the house before it became a museum. The newest addition to the house is a photo exhibit documenting it from the 1920s to the present.

19 Maryland Ave. (northeast of State Circle, at the corner of King George St). © 410/263-4683. Admission $5 adults, $3 ages 6–18. Tours top of the hour Mon–Sat 10am–3pm, Sun noon–4pm. Closed Jan 1, Thanksgiving, and Dec 25.

London Town House and Gardens ★★   Just south of Annapolis, across the South River, stands the 1760s Georgian home of William Brown, the only remaining structure from what was once a bustling trade town called London Town. The London Town Foundation, with Anne Arundel County, continues the enormous archaeological task of unearthing the 23 acres around the William Brown House and rebuilding the lost town. Visitors can check the progress—which will include a re-construction of several buildings. The first will be a 1690 structure, the Lord Mayor's Tenement. Don't miss the house that sits on the South River and the 8-acre wild and lovely woodland gardens. It, like the archaeological sites, is quite accessible; the foundation wishes to educate the public about the social history of the town and times, as well as the process of restoration and excavation. So don't expect a du Pont estate—this is a work in progress.

839 Londontown Rd., Edgewater. © 410/222-1919. Admission $5 adults, $4 seniors and children ages 7–12. Mon–Sat 10am–4pm, Sun noon–4pm. Take Rte. 50 to Rte. 655 (Exit 22), then take Rte. 2 south, over the South River Bridge. Turn left at light on Mayo Rd., left at light on Londontown Rd. Go 1 mile (1.6km).

Maryland State House ★★★   This is the oldest U.S. capitol in continuous legislative use (built 1772–79). The building also served as the U.S. Capitol from 1783 to 1784. In the Old Senate Chamber, you'll see where George Washington resigned his commission as commander-in-chief of the Continental armies. This was also where the Treaty of Paris, which ended the Revolutionary War, was ratified. It remains the site of the Maryland General Assembly, which fills these halls January through April. Come then if you want to see the place in action. You can see the House and Senate chambers and changing exhibits on your own, or take the free 30-minute guided tours of the first-floor rooms at 11am and 3pm from the visitor center on the first floor. The State House dome, the wooden one of its kind, is made of cypress beams held together by wooden pegs.

State Circle. ℂ 410/974-3400. www.mdisfun.org. Free admission. Daily 9am–5pm. Tours daily 11am and 3pm. The building is closed only on Dec 25, but the visitor center is closed Jan 1, Easter, Thanksgiving, and Dec 25.

William Paca House and Garden ✦✦✦ The home of William Paca, a signer of the Declaration of Independence and a governor of Maryland during the Revolutionary period, this estate was built between 1763 and 1765 and restored by Historic Annapolis from 1965 to 1976. It's one of two such houses in Annapolis. Another, the Brice House, is around the corner but isn't open to the public. Tours are offered on the hour, and on the half hour during the summer. The five-part structure, with a stalwart central block, hyphens, and wings, contains 37 rooms. Behind the Paca estate is a 2-acre terraced garden with a fish-shaped pond, a Chinese Chippendale bridge, a summerhouse, and a wilderness garden. All by itself, the gardens are a joy to wander through (in season).

186 Prince George St. ℂ 410/263-5553. www.annapolis.org. House and garden tours $8 adults, $5 ages 6–18. Mon–Sat 10am–5pm, Sun noon–4pm; Jan–Feb, Fri–Sat 10am–5pm, Sun noon–5pm. Closed Thanksgiving and Dec 25. Last house tour at 4pm.

6 Organized Tours & Cruises

WALKING TOURS

To hit the high points of Annapolis, take a **Historic Annapolis Walk with Walter Cronkite,** a self-guided audiocassette walking tour narrated by the TV news broadcaster. The tour takes in 19 historic and architectural sites with 45 minutes of commentary that can be completed at a leisurely pace in 1½ hours. It is available only at the Historic Annapolis Museum Store, 77 Main St. (ℂ **410/268-5576**), Monday through Saturday from 10am to 5pm, Sunday from noon to 5pm. The cost per rental is $5. The Historic Annapolis Foundation also offers an **African-American Heritage Audio Walking Tour** (also $5), which covers 15 sites in the historic district, including the Banneker–Douglass Museum, the Matthew Henson Memorial, and St. John's College. Tours take approximately 1½ hours and are also available at the Museum Store.

Three Centuries Tours of Annapolis, 48 Maryland Ave. (ℂ 410/263-5401), offers informative tours with guides in colonial costume. Their historic district tours, which include the Naval Academy, are 2 hours in length and operated on a turn-up-and-go basis, with no reservations required. Tours depart daily, April 1 to October 31, at 10:30am from the visitor center at 26 West St. and at 1:30pm from the City Dock information booth. From November 1 to March 31, there is only one tour a week, on Saturday at 2:30pm, departing from Gibson's Lodgings. The price is $10 for adults and $5 for students. *Note:* You must bring a picture ID to gain access to the Naval Academy and State House. (If you take a morning tour, the guides try to get you to the Naval Academy in time for the midshipmen's noon formation.) Three Centuries Tours also offers group-specific tours, focusing on such topics as colonial life (for young visitors), historic mansions, and bay cruises.

The **U.S. Naval Academy Walking Tours** depart from the Armel–Leftwich Visitor Center of the U.S. Naval Academy, Gate 1, King George and Randall streets (ℂ 410/263-6933), every day of the year except January 1, Thanksgiving, and December 25. From June through Labor Day, tours depart every half hour Monday through Saturday from 9:30am to 3:30pm and Sunday from 12:30 to 3:30pm. From September through November and April through Memorial Day, tours are hourly Monday through Friday from 10am to 3pm, and every half hour

Saturday from 10am to 3:30pm and Sunday from 12:30 to 3:30pm. From December through March, tours are Monday to Saturday at 10am, 11am, 1:30pm, and 2:30pm, and Sunday at 12:30pm and 2:30pm. The price is $6 for adults, $5 for seniors, and $4 for students. Bring picture ID with you.

BUS TOURS

Discover Annapolis Tours, 31 Decatur Ave. (℃ **410/626-6000;** www.discover-annapolis.com) offers a coach tour of the city and some outlying areas. An air-conditioned 25-passenger minibus takes visitors through the historic district—by the State House, the Chase–Lloyd House, the Hammond–Harwood House, and St. Johns College, to name a few—and some areas not covered by the walking tours: Eastport, the Charles Carroll House, and the Severn River Scenic Overlook. The narrated tours last about an hour. The tour guides also give tips on how to see the town on your own. Tours operate year-round, departing from the lot behind the visitor center at 26 West St. several times daily April through November, and most weekends December through March. The cost is $12 for adults, $6 for children ages 11 to 15, $3 for children 10 and under (preschoolers are free).

CRUISES & BOATING TOURS

To see the sights of Annapolis from the water, **Watermark Cruises** ✦ at the City Dock (℃ **410/268-7600**) operates a variety of cruises along Annapolis Harbor and beyond. Choices include a 40-minute narrated cruise that covers the highlights of Annapolis Harbor, the U.S. Naval Academy, and the Severn River; a 40-minute tour of the residential waterfront along Spa Creek and the Naval Academy shore; the Thomas Point Lighthouse Cruise, a 90-minute trip on the Severn River; and the 90-minute Severn River Ecotour. **Chesapeake Tours** also offers a Day-on-the-Bay excursion to St. Michaels. Prices for the 40- and 90-minute tours range from $7 to $14 for adults and $4 to $7 for children 3 to 11; children under 2 are free. Sailings are daily from Memorial Day through Labor Day, with abbreviated schedules in the spring and fall.

7 Outdoor Activities

With the Chesapeake Bay and Severn River at its doorstep, Annapolis is the pleasure boating capital of the eastern United States. The city offers many opportunities to enjoy sailing and water sports, as well as other outdoor activities.

BICYCLING   Though the streets are often too crowded for a leisurely excursion, just outside the city are several parks and paths for cycling. A good place to bike is the **Baltimore and Annapolis Trail** (℃ **410/222-6244**), a smooth, 13.3-mile (21km) asphalt route that runs from Annapolis north into the suburbs. Formerly a rail corridor, it's considered a "community sidewalk" by the locals and is ideal for biking, walking, jogging, in-line skating, or meandering. It begins at Ritchie Highway, at the U.S. Route 50 interchange, and ends on Dorsey Road at Route 648 in Glen Burnie. It's open daily from sunrise to sunset.

Just outside the city, on the South River and Harness Creek, **Quiet Waters Park** (℃ **410/222-1777**) has 6 miles (10km) of biking/hiking trails with an overlook along the South River. You can rent bicycles at the visitor center from spring through fall. A skating rink is set up in winter. The park is open from 7am to dusk, 6 days a week (closed on Tues), and there's a $4-per-vehicle entrance fee.

Visitors who want to bike the Eastern Shore can cross the Chesapeake Bay using the Annapolis Transit system. Bike racks have been added to the Kent Island commuter buses. Buses leave Kent Island and Annapolis every weekday morning and return each evening. Fare is $1.50. The bike goes for free. Call ahead to be sure there's room on the bus and to confirm the return trip (© **410/ 263-7964**).

SAILING SCHOOLS & SAILING TRIPS   Learn to sail at the oldest and largest sailing school in America: the **Annapolis Sailing School,** 601 6th St. (P.O. Box 3334), Annapolis, MD 21403 (© **800/638-9192** or 410/267-7205; www.annapolissailing.com). With more than 120 boats and a huge support staff, this facility offers a wide range of instructional programs for novice and veteran sailors, including a KidShip program for children ages 5 to 15. Courses range from a weekend beginner's course for $295 to a 5-day advanced course in preparation for bareboat (skipper-less) charters for $835 and up.

Womanship, 137 Conduit St., Annapolis, MD 21401 (© **800/342-9295** or 410/267-6661; www.womanship.com), is a sailing program for women. Instruction is available from novice to advanced levels, in daytime or live-aboard settings. Learning cruises range from 2 to 7 days, and from $395 to $1,595. There are courses for mothers and daughters, families, and youths (ages 10–17). A new program, Young Womanship, is for seventh to eleventh graders.

There are many sailing schools in the area, so call around to find the best rate and a schedule that suits your needs. Some others in the area are **Chesapeake Sailing School** (© **800/966-0032** or 410/269-1594), which offers a teen sailing course; and, just for adults, **Tradewind Yachts** (© **410/267-9151**) and **J World Annapolis** (© **800/966-2038** or 410/280-2040).

If you prefer to let a captain and crew sail the boat, you can board the 36-foot sloop *Beginagain,* 1056 Eaglewood Rd., Annapolis (© **800/295-1422** or 410/ 626-1422; www.beginagain.qpg.com), at the City Dock. The *Beginagain* can carry only six passengers, so it has an intimate feel. Operating from May through September, this vessel offers 3-hour trips, departing daily at 9am, 1pm, and 6pm (May–July) or 5pm (Aug and Sept). The cost is $60 a passenger.

The 74-foot schooner *Woodwind* and her sister ship the *Woodwind II,* 80 Compromise St., Annapolis (© **410/269-4213;** www.schooner-woodwind.com), depart from the Marriott Hotel side of the City Dock for 2-hour sailing trips several times daily, April through November. Departure times vary, so check the website or call for times. Sunset cruises, which depart daily at 6:30pm or 5:30pm depending on the season, have a different theme each day, such as a beer tasting or ecotour. If you like sailboat racing, don't miss watching the Wednesday night races aboard the *Woodwind.* The cost is $24 to $27 for adults, $22 to $25 for seniors, and $15 for children under 12. Special destination cruises and overnight trips are scheduled regularly. Check the website for upcoming events.

SEA KAYAKING Amphibious Horizons (© **888/ILUV-SUN** or 410/ 267-8742; www.amphibioushorizons.com) offers 3-hour sunset kayak tours in the South River Fridays at 6pm. Your fee covers kayak, soda and snack, and guide. These trips cost $25 for adults, $20 for ages 12 to 17, $15 for ages 5 to 11. Amphibious Horizons also offers a variety of trips in creeks on both sides of the bay, as well as instruction and kayak rentals at Quiet Waters Park south of Annapolis. Pre-registration is necessary for sunset paddles. Admission to Quiet Waters Park is $4 per vehicle, though walk-ins and bike-ins are free.

WATER-SPORT RENTALS & CHARTERS   To charter a sailboat, you can contact most of the sailing schools in the area, including all the ones listed above. In addition, **Annapolis Bay Charters, Inc.,** P.O. Box 4604, Annapolis, MD 21403 (© **800/292-1119** or 410/269-1776), offers both bareboat and crewed charters on both sail- and powerboats.

For speedboats, contact **Suntime Boat and Jetski Rentals,** 2822 Solomons Island Rd., Route 2, Edgewater (© **410/266-6020**).

8 Shopping

Shops in Annapolis are filled with nautical-themed merchandise. You could redecorate your house from the shops on Maryland Avenue. Navy T-shirts, the classic visitor souvenir, are everywhere.

The historic district has three main streets filled with shops. **Main Street,** which runs from Church Circle to the City Dock, has many apparel and gift shops. **Maryland Avenue** has shops in the block just below the State House and State Circle where you might find home accessories or an antique or two. There are shops around the **City Dock** itself, mostly nautical in nature. Shops are usually open every day from 10am. Most are closed by 9pm, some earlier.

It's a friendly place—and picturesque in December. With greenery draped around every window, white lights on the trees, and a huge decorated tree at the market (which everybody will compare to the tree filled with farm implements a few years back), it's a delightful, old-fashioned place to buy those last-minute items. Finish with a drink at McGarvey's or a meal at one of the casual restaurants.

Here are some of the standouts on Main Street and Maryland Avenue.

Jewelry that combines elegance with nautical themes is a reality at **LaBelle Cézanne,** 117 Main St. (© **410/263-1996**).

Get your *de rigueur* NAVY T-shirt at **Peppers,** 133 Main St. (© **800/254-NAVY** or 410/267-8722), or at **Fit to a Tee,** 107 Main St. (© **410/268-6596**).

At **Plat du Jour** (© **410/269-1499**; www.platdujour.net), you'll be convinced you walked off Main Street and into Tuscany or Provence. It's filled with tableware, linens, toiletries, and a cookbook or two. Lovers of the Emerald Isle should head for **Avoca Handweavers,** 141–143 Main St. (© **410/263-1485**; www.avoca.ie), with its Irish clothes, linens, and other decorative items. Visit the **Sign O' the Whale** at 99 Main St. (© **410/268-2161**) for all kinds of clothing and home decor with a nautical flair.

Handmade pottery is available in several places. **The League of Maryland Craftsmen** carries pottery, carved wood, and all kinds of handmade items at 216 Main St. (© **410/626-1277**; www.annearundelcounty.com/art/league.htm). **The Annapolis Pottery,** at 40 State Circle (© **410/268-6153**), sells wares made on the premises. You can even watch the stock being made.

For housewares, head for Maryland Avenue. Some stores sell new stuff, including **Evropa** at 62 Maryland Ave. (© **410/268-4400**), or **Peake House** (© **410/280-0410**) for Herend and Spode; try **Penny Randall** (© **410/268-0050**) for Mackenzie-Child's pottery and accessories. For antiques visit **Hobson's Choice Antiques,** 58 Maryland Ave. (© **410/280-2206**), featuring 18th and 19th century items, including silver, porcelain, furniture, and model trains.

For something to hang on the walls, check out **McBride Gallery,** 215 Main St. (© **410/267-7077**; www.mcbridegallery.com). **Nancy Hammond's** brightly colored multi-media pieces are displayed at her gallery at 64 State Circle

(© **410/267-7711;** www.nancyhammondeditions.com). **Circle Gallery** is at 18 State Circle between School and Franklin sts. (© **410/268-4566**).

There are lots of galleries with prints, posters, and paintings; expect a nautical theme—sailing is a passion here. Check out **Annapolis Marine Art Gallery,** 110 Dock St. (© **410/263-4100;** www.annapolismarineart.com), and **Moon Shell Gallery,** 8 Fleet St. (© **410/263-5970**).

For gifts and collectibles, stop by the **Annapolis Country Store,** 53 Maryland Ave. (© **410/269-6773;** www.annapoliscountrystore.com) for Classic Pooh, Raggedy Ann, Madeleine, and Curious George items. You can get holiday baubles from **Christmas Spirit** at 180 Main St. (© **410/268-2600**) year-round.

Most stores in the historic district are open Monday through Saturday 11am to 5 or 6pm and Sunday from noon to 5pm. Many stay open until 8 or 9pm on Friday and Saturday, and several open at 10am or earlier during the week.

MALLS & MARKETS

Annapolis Harbour Center   West of downtown at the junction of Routes 2 and 665, this shopping center is laid out like a maritime village, with more than 40 shops, services, and fast-food eateries, as well as nine movie theaters. Open Monday to Saturday 10am to 9pm and Sunday noon to 5pm. 2512A Solomons Island Rd. © **410/266-5857.**

Westfield Shoppingtown Annapolis   Situated off Route 50 between West Street and Bestgate Road, this mall has five department stores (Nordstrom, Lord & Taylor, Hecht's, JCPenney, and Sears) as well as more than 175 specialty shops and a big food court. Open Monday to Saturday 10am to 9:30pm, Sunday 11am to 6pm. 2002 Annapolis Mall (Bestgate Rd.). © **410/266-5432.**

Pennsylvania Dutch Farmers Market   Opposite the string of shops at Annapolis Harbour Center (see above), this market is run by Amish and Mennonite families from Lancaster County, Pennsylvania. Wares range from sausages and pickles to organic produce, as well as homemade jams, fudge, cakes, pies, and soft pretzels, all ideal for a picnic or snack. Handmade quilts are available in a crafts section. Open Thursday 10am to 6pm, Friday 9am to 6pm, and Saturday 9am to 3pm. 2472 Solomons Island Rd. © **410/573-0770.**

9 Annapolis After Dark

Annapolis is a town of small venues: most local bars feature live music on weekends—everything from pop to classic rock to blues and funk—and there are a few good local theater companies.

For up-to-date weekly listings of concerts and other entertainment events in the Annapolis area, check the "Entertainment" section of the *Capital* newspaper on Friday. *Inside Annapolis,* a bimonthly publication distributed free throughout the city, also gives a summary of entertainment venues and upcoming events and other information of use to visitors. The Visitors Bureau publishes seasonal event calendars; you can pick these up at the visitor center on West Street.

BARS & CLUBS

Armadillo's   This place offers a variety of live entertainment—jazz, blues, funk, classic rock, acoustic rock, and oldies. Music usually starts at 9:30pm daily. 132 Dock St. © **410/280-0028.** Cover $2–$4.

King of France Tavern ★★★   The low-ceilinged room of the Maryland Inn's colonial kitchens make this a cozy setting for jazz, big band or the occasional folk, classical, or chamber music most weekends. The light-fare menu usually has something that goes well with the music and a drink. Music usually starts at 8:30pm. Reservations are a good idea. 16 Church Circle. © 410/269-0990. www.annapolisinns.com. Cover $3–$10, depending on the music.

McGarvey's Saloon   McGarvey's, O'Brien's, and Riordan's, three bars near the City Dock, make up the most happening area of Annapolis at night. McGarvey's doesn't have live music, but draws a crowd for its seafood, especially oysters, and beer. They even have their own private-label Aviator Lager. It's loud, friendly, and fun anytime. 8 Market Space. © 410/263-5700. www.mcgarveyssaloon.com. No cover.

O'Brien's Oyster Bar and Grill   Located near the City Dock on Main Street, O'Brien's has live music most nights; on Thursdays there's usually a deejay spinning Top 40 tunes. Music begins around 9:30 or 10pm. 113 Main St. © 410/268-6288. www.obriensoysterbar.com. Cover about $3–$5 Thurs–Sat.

Pusser's Landing   The entertainment here is the boat traffic. Boaters just have to bring their boats up "Ego Alley" to the City Dock only to turn around and head back into the harbor. A warm summer evening on Pusser's deck with one of their specialty rum drinks and boat traffic—this must be Annapolis. Pusser's also serves meals all day. 80 Compromise St. in the Annapolis Marriott Waterfront Hotel. © 410/626-0004.

Rams Head Tavern ★★★   The Rams Head has become the top nightspot in town, hosting such national acts as Arlo Guthrie, Phoebe Snow, and Leon Redbone. Dinner and show packages are available. Ticket-holders must be 21 or older (and the audience usually does range from young adult to middle-aged). 33 West St. © 410/268-4545 for information or tickets. www.ramsheadtavern.com. Cover varies.

Riordan's Saloon   Popular with the postcollege crowd, Riordan's aims to be the friendly neighborhood bar, and it is. With four TVs, if there's a game on, you can expect the usual cheers and moans. 26 Market Space. © 301/261-1524.

COFFEEHOUSES & WINE BARS

49 West Coffeehouse, Winebar, Gallery ★   49 West is a welcome addition to Annapolis nightlife. Located a block or so west of Rams Head Tavern, this coffeehouse/wine bar features live classical, jazz, and folk music every night. 49 West St. © 410/626-9796. Cover usually runs about $5 or $8.

THE PERFORMING ARTS

The town's largest venue, the **Maryland Hall for the Creative Arts** ★, 801 Chase St. (© 410/263-5544), presents performances by the Annapolis Symphony Orchestra, the Annapolis Opera, the Annapolis Chamber Orchestra, and the Ballet Theater of Annapolis, as well as one-person shows. You can check out the calendar of events at www.mdhallarts.com. Performances are nightly at 7 or 8pm and tickets range in price from $10 to $30.

In the summer, there are several free outdoor concert series and theater productions. The **Naval Academy Summer Serenade** (© 410/203-1262), held weekly at the City Dock, features the USNA groups Next Wave, the Electric Brigade, and concert band. Concerts are free, but bring your own seating. Quiet Waters Park, south of Annapolis, also hosts a concert series (free for walk-ins, admission charged for cars). Call © 410/222-1777 for more information.

Since 1966, the **Annapolis Summer Garden Theatre** ★★, 143 Compromise St. at Main Street across from the City Dock (© 410/268-9212), has staged musical and theater performances with local talent at its outdoor theater at reasonable prices every summer. Shows are daily at 8:30pm. Reservations are encouraged, and tickets cost $10 for adults and $8 for students and seniors.

Colonial Players Theater, 108 East St. (© **410/268-7373**), also offers year-round theater in a 180-seat theater-in-the-round setting. The company performs five plays each year. Shows are Thursday through Saturday at 8pm and Sunday at 2:30 or 7:30pm, and ticket prices range from $8 to $11.

10 Quick Stops Around the Capital Beltway

Baltimore, Annapolis, and Washington form a triangle filled with suburbs and small towns, connected by state roads, interstates, and beltways. The attractions below are easy day trips from Baltimore or Annapolis, though they are closer to the District of Columbia. Going counterclockwise around the Capital Beltway:

Six Flags America *Kids* Roller-coaster fans, pay attention. Six Flags has some "awesome" coasters. Just ask the 27 teenagers I joined for a day here. The Joker's Jinx had them screaming. Superman had them flying and Typhoon Sea Coaster sent them through the dark and into water. Unfortunately, the lines are awesome, too. During peak times, waits for the popular rides can be as long as a hour. Take a break and go to Paradise Island water park. The wave pool, water slides, and Crocodile Cal's Outback Beach House will cool you off. *Note:* the park requires visitors to go through metal detectors; don't take anything valuable—you have to put down backpacks and bags for some of the rides and to go in the water.

13710 Central Ave., Mitchelleville, MD 20721. © **301/249-1500.** www.sixflags.com/america. Admission $36 adults, $27 seniors and handicapped, $18 kids (48" & under), free ages 3 and under. Parking $9. Open weekends Apr–May and Sept–Oct 10am–6pm; daily Memorial Day–Labor Day, 10:30am–6pm or later. AE, DISC, MC, V. From Washington, D.C., take I-495/I-95 to Exit 15A to Rte. 214 east to the park 5 miles (8km) on the left. From Baltimore and areas north, take I-695 to I-97 south (Exit 7), then Rte. 3/301 south to Rte. 214 west to the park 3 miles (5km) on the right.

Savage Mill This restored cotton mill has all kinds of antiques shops, as well as fine arts, crafts, and clothing boutiques and a couple of places to stop for a bit of refreshment. It's an interesting old building that keeps its heritage alive by using the names of the buildings' original purposes in all its signs and maps. Need a baguette? Go to Bonaparte Breads in the Spinning Building. In the Carding Building, Old Weave Building, and a couple more, you can find Irish goodies, antique jewelry, furniture and dolls, eye-catching handmade sweaters, needlework supplies, and something for your sweet tooth. It's easy to spend a day here.

8600 Foundry St., Savage, MD 20763. © **800/788-6455.** www.savagemill.com. Mon–Wed 10am–6pm, Thurs–Sat 10am–9pm, Sun 11am–6pm. Closed Dec 25, Christmas, Easter, and Thanksgiving. Off Rte. 32 to Rte. 1 south. Turn right at Howard St. Follow the signs.

Brookside Gardens It's just 50 acres, but it's a gem. The top draws are the conservatories with their tropical plantings and the summertime butterfly show, but don't overlook the rose and aquatic gardens, which are wonderful places to stroll. The serenity of the Japanese Tea House is something you'll remember. Paths are accessible for wheelchairs and strollers, and some wheelchairs are available at the visitor center. There's no picnicking, but take your lunch to the neighboring **Wheaton Regional Park** (2000 Shorefield Rd.; © **301/946-7033**). With lots of trees and playgrounds, it's a great place for kids to run.

1800 Glenallan Ave., Wheaton, MD 20902. © **301/962-1400.** www.brooksidegardens.org. Gardens open daily sunrise to sunset except Dec 25; conservatories 10am–5pm; visitor center 9am–5pm. Admission free. To

Brookside: From I-270 and points west, take Exit 4A, Montrose Rd. east, which turns into Randolph Rd. Go 7 miles (11km) and turn right onto Glenallan Ave. From I-495, the Capital Beltway, take Exit 31A (north on Georgia Ave./Rte. 97) toward Wheaton. Drive 3 miles (5km) north on Georgia Ave. to Randolph Rd. and turn right. At the second traffic light, turn right onto Glenallan Ave. Park at the visitor center at 1800 Glenallan Ave. or at the conservatories at 1500 Glenallan.

Clara Barton's Home ★ *Finds* The Red Cross was everything to its founder.

You can tell by looking at her house in Glen Echo. The halls are lined with closets, filled with (what else?) blankets, lanterns, and other supplies for disaster relief. Her office is no-nonsense, including her chair. She cut off the back so she wouldn't rest while hard at work. The home, built in 1891 and now a National Historic Site, is a quirky thing, its design unusual inside and out, but as you wander through the rooms that sheltered Clara and her Red Cross staff, you'll get to know more about the woman who made Red Cross her mission and her life. There are only 11 rooms so it's a short visit, but it's fascinating. The ranger/ guides are great with kids and never fail to keep them interested.

5801 Oxford Rd. at MacArthur Blvd., Glen Echo, MD 20812. © 301/492-6245. www.nps.gov/clba/. Free admission. Open daily. Tours every hour on the half hour 10:30am–4:30pm. Closed Thanksgiving, Dec 25, and Jan 1.

Glen Echo Park Combine a visit to Clara Barton's house with a trip here. It's

just across a parking lot. The carousel is a hand-carved Dentzel carousel, built in 1921 and it still takes riders May to September. The rest of the amusement park is gone but the park has lots of arts programs. It was built as a Chautauqua meeting ground, and emphasis on the arts continues today. There's a children's theater, a puppet theater, and a children's museum. There are also dances (swing, contra and square) for adults held Fridays, Saturdays and Sundays in the Spanish Ballroom. Lessons are offered, too. Call ahead for an up-to-date schedule. But if you're going to Clara Barton's house, stop here for a ride on the carousel.

7300 MacArthur Blvd., Glen Echo, MD 20812. © 301/492-6282. www.nps.gov.glec. Admission free but tickets required for carousel. Admission to arts events varies.

C&O Canal Museum at Great Falls of the Potomac ★ This is *the* stop

on the C&O Canal. Visitors board the *Canal Clipper* for an hour-long ride. Stop at the visitor center in the Great Falls Tavern. Then it's time for a boat ride, or to watch the lock operate. Mules pull the boat, as they did in the 1870s. Park rangers are dressed in period clothing. Definitely stop by the Great Falls. The Olmsted Island Boardwalk is wheelchair-accessible and runs through woods to a bridge overlooking one branch of the falls, and then to the overlook where the falls crash over the rocks. The boardwalk is crowded on nice days, but when you get there, you'll have plenty of space to catch your breath and take in this incredible sight.

11710 MacArthur Blvd. near Falls Rd. (MD Rte. 189), Potomac, MD 20854. © 301/767-3714 or 301/ 299-3613. www.nps.gov/choh. Open daily 9am–5pm. Park admission $4 per vehicle, $2 for walk-ins. Admission valid for 3 days. Boat fare about $8. Take Exit 41W off I-495.

11 From Annapolis & St. Mary's: Solomons & Calvert County

For over 100 years Calvert County has been the Chesapeake playground of citizens of Baltimore, Western Maryland, and Washington, D.C. At the center is the town of Solomons, which offers history, outdoor activities, and marine sports.

Solomons, often (mistakenly) called "Solomons Island" after the island that makes up its center, is a town dominated by water. It's an island and the end of two peninsulas formed by the Patuxent River, Back Creek, and Mill Creek (the

Patuxent's mouth into the Chesapeake is visible from the town's southern end). The island is connected to land by a bridge so short if you blink you'll miss it, but you still feel surrounded by water. A walk through town will take you past numerous sailboats, yachts, and charter fishing boats, as well as old and modern watermen's homes, the century-old Drum Point Lighthouse, and Solomons's wide public pier, the place to see beautiful sunsets over the Patuxent.

The rest of Calvert County offers hiking, fossil-hunting, access to the historical sites of St. Mary's County, and charter fishing on the Chesapeake.

ESSENTIALS

GETTING THERE Solomons is at the southern tip of the peninsula of Calvert County. Maryland Routes 2 and 4 merge and run north–south across the county, giving access to all the sights. To reach Solomons from Washington, D.C., and points south, take I-95 to the exit for Route 4 south and follow Route 4 all the way to Solomons. From Annapolis and points north, take the exit for Route 2 south off U.S. Route 50 and follow Route 2–4 to Solomons.

VISITOR INFORMATION Write to the **Calvert County Department of Economic Development,** Courthouse, Prince Frederick, MD 20678, or call ⓒ **800/331-9771** or 410/535-4583 (www.co.cal.md.us/cced). Once there, stop by the information center just outside Solomons at the base of the Governor Thomas Johnson Bridge on Route 2–4.

ATTRACTIONS

Calvert County offers a combination of attractions and scenery. St. Mary's County's historic sites are close, so you can combine visits over a few days.

Battle Creek Cypress Swamp Sanctuary ★★ In 1957, the Nature Conservancy bought this 100-acre parcel of land as a sanctuary on the northernmost limit of the natural range of the great bald cypress trees that once dominated the swamps of the southern states. A quarter-mile elevated boardwalk allows visitors to explore this primeval environment of ferns, flowers, and ancient cypress trees. You might also spot frogs, turtles, crayfish, and raccoons. Inside the visitor center are exhibits on the natural and historical heritage of the swamp area, including an interesting display on animal tracks and a rare albino turtle.

Grays Rd. (mailing address: 175 Main St.), Prince Frederick. ⓒ 410/535-5327. www.calvertparks.org. Free admission. Apr 30 to Oct 1 Tues–Sat 10am–5pm, Sun 1–5pm; Oct–Apr Tues–Sat 10am–4:30pm, Sun 1–4:30pm. Take Rte. 506 west from Rte. 2–4, then turn left onto Grays Rd.; the sanctuary is one-quarter mile on the right.

Calvert Marine Museum and Drum Point Lighthouse ★★ _Kids_ This gem of a museum explores the area's relationship with the sea. Visitors can see exhibits on marine paleontology and local fossils from Calvert Cliffs (see "Other Outdoor Activities," below), including the jaws of extinct varieties of the great white shark, and an estuary aquarium showing examples of life in the Patuxent, with the opportunity to touch turtles and horseshoe crabs. You'll also find exhibits on local maritime history, from the British fleet's defeat of the American flotilla during the Revolutionary War to modern recreational boating. Children will love the Discovery Room, filled with hands-on activities. Outside you'll find two playful river otters, and the Drum Point Lighthouse, which you can tour if you're willing to brave the very steep stairs. Drum Point is one of the three remaining screwpile lighthouses (they look like hexagonal cottages mounted on metal poles) that served on the Chesapeake around the turn of the

20th century. The other two are Thomas Point Lighthouse, in the bay near Annapolis, and Hooper Straight Lighthouse, now housed at the Chesapeake Bay Maritime Museum in St. Michaels (see chapter 6, "Eastern Shore"). The museum also offers harbor cruises aboard the bugeye *Wm. B. Tennison* Wednesday to Sunday, May to October.

14200 Solomons Island Rd. (P.O. Box 97), Solomons. ℂ 410/326-2042. Admission $5 adults, $4 seniors, $2 ages 5–12. Cruise tickets are an extra $5 for adults and $3 for children 5–12. Daily 10am–5pm. Closed Thanksgiving, Dec 25, and Jan 1.

CHARTER FISHING ✦

One of Calvert County's biggest draws is its fleet of charter fishing boats. Rockfish (striped bass or stripers if you're from north of the Chesapeake) are frequently the main quarry, but bluefish, Spanish mackerel, white perch, spot, croaker, flounder, sea trout, and black drum are also sought, depending on the time of year. Check with the charter boat captain to find out what is in season before you plan your trip.

Charter fishing is organized in two ways: through loose affiliations of captains and through organized operations. It's easy to charter a boat either way. In the case of an organized operation such as Bunky's Charter Boats, Inc. (see below), call the office, and they will supply a boat. If all their boats are full, they will contact a local captain from outside their fleet and have him run the charter.

It works a little differently with captains' associations. In this case, you call a contact person for the association, usually one of the captains. If that captain has an opening, he will offer to take you out on his boat. If he doesn't, he will either arrange for another captain to take you out or give you the names and telephone numbers of captains in the association who might be available.

Here are a few things to remember when you go on a charter boat: Ask the captain what you will need to bring. Most charters include fishing gear; some supply bait for free, some don't. Bring a cooler to take your catch home. The mates on charter boats work for cash tips, which should be at least 15%.

IN SOLOMONS

Bunky's Charter Boats, Inc.　Bunky's operates out of a well-stocked bait-and-tackle shop across from the walking pier on Solomons Island. They have a fleet of 10 charter boats, including one 48-foot headboat, the *Marchelle*. Charter rates for up to six passengers on all boats except the *Marchelle* are $375 per half day (6 hr.) and $450 per full day (8 hr.). There's a per-person charge of $40 for extra people. Rates for eight people on the *Marchelle* are $450 per half day and $500 per full day; again, extra passengers $40 each. Nonfishing cruises on the *Marchelle* are available for $175 per hour with a 2-hour minimum. Bunky's also rents 16-foot power skiffs for those who want to go it on their own, but you need a license to fish if you are not on a charter boat.

14446 Solomons Island Rd. S. (P.O. Box 379), Solomons, MD 20688. ℂ 410/326-3241. www. bunkyscharterboats.com.

Fin Finder Charters and Solomons Charter Captains Association　Sonney Forest is your contact for the SCCA. The association runs many of its 42 boats out of the Calvert Marina Charter Dock on Dowell Road (ℂ **410/ 326-2670**), where Captain Forest is the dock master. Eight of the SCCA's boats can carry more than six people; some can carry as many as 30. Standard association rates are $350 for a half day and $450 for a full day for six passengers, with extra passengers charged $40 for a half day and $60 for a full day.

The *Fin Finder,* a 46-foot Chesapeake-style workboat, is Captain Forest's own charter boat. It carries up to 30 passengers. In addition to standard daily charters, Captain Forest also offers cruise tours and packages complete trips.

Box 831, Solomons, MD 20688. ✆ 800/831-2702. www.finfinder.com or www.fishsolomons.com.

IN CHESAPEAKE BEACH

Chesapeake Beach has the largest fleet on the bay, with over 35 boats. To get there from Annapolis, take Route 2 south to Maryland Route 260 west, which ends just north of the harbor at Maryland Route 261. From Washington, D.C., take Route 4 west to Route 260 west and follow the directions above. At the harbor, there's a water slide on the north side; everything else (**Rod 'N' Reel** and the **Chesapeake Beach Railway Museum**) are on the south side of the harbor and on the bay side of Route 261. **Seaside Charters** is on the inland side of Route 261, just behind Abner's Crab House.

Rod 'N' Reel Charter Fishing   Rod 'N' Reel is the largest single charter fishing operation in Maryland's share of the Chesapeake, with 30 boats; the 55-foot *Bounty Hunter* is the largest craft. Charter rates for up to six people are $370 per 6-hour trip and $515 per 8-hour trip. It is $50 per person extra for over six people. Or get on a headboat for $35 per person.

P.O. Box 99, Chesapeake Beach, MD 20732. ✆ 800/233-2080 or 301/855-8450. www.rodnreelinc.com.

Chesapeake Beach Fishing Charters   Seaside Charters is an association of charter captains with 18 boats and some of the best rates in the area. Rates are $350 for six people per half day (6 hr.) and $480 per full day (8 hr.). There are evening outings and fishing trips, as well.

P.O. Box 757, Chesapeake Beach, MD 20732. ✆ 301/855-4665.

OTHER OUTDOOR ACTIVITIES

HIKING & BIRD-WATCHING   Calvert County's topography of rolling hills and tidal marsh estuary offers some prime spots for communing with nature.

Battle Creek Cypress Swamp Sanctuary's half-mile nature loop (see "Attractions," above) is a good, nonstrenuous walk.

If you're up for a brisk 2-mile (3km) hike, **Calvert Cliffs State Park** ★ (✆ 301/872-5688) has long been one of Maryland's favorite outdoor destinations. A winding trail follows a brook as it travels down from the hills to a lush tidal marsh. At the end of the trail, the tidal marsh opens across a small beach into the Chesapeake Bay; on either side stand the 30-foot-tall eroding hillsides known as Calvert Cliffs. These multicolored cliffs, first noted by English explorer John Smith, expose several layers of sediment that were once at the bottom of a prehistoric ocean. As the winds and water erode them, they yield ancient secrets—fossils. Because of recent landslides the park has restricted access to the bottoms of the cliffs. Fossil hunting is allowed on the beach and wire sieves are provided to make your search easier. Typical finds include fossilized shells and crustaceans and the occasional prehistoric shark's tooth, but dinosaur bones are not unheard of. (For more on Calvert Cliff's paleontology, see the Calvert Maritime Museum listing, above.) The park is open daily from dawn to dusk, $3 per vehicle.

Flag Ponds Nature Park, off Route 2–4 (✆ 410/586-1477 or 410/535-5327), has several trails offering access to the forested heights of Calvert Cliffs, sandy beaches, and freshwater ponds with observation platforms for spotting waterfowl. Flag Ponds is open Memorial Day to Labor Day, Monday through Friday 9am to 6pm and Saturday and Sunday 9am to 8pm. From Labor Day to Memorial

Day the park is open Saturday and Sunday only, from 9am to 5pm, although during daylight saving time it stays open on weekends until 6pm. Admission fees (per vehicle) are $4 for Calvert residents and $6 for nonresidents April through October, and $3 for all visitors the rest of the year.

SPORTFISHING   Although charter fishing is this area's forte, there are also several choice locations for sportfishing, including **Bay Front Park,** Chesapeake Beach; the **fishing pier** at Flag Ponds Nature Park (see above); and **Solomons Fishing Pier,** under the Gov. Thomas Johnson Bridge (Rte. 4) in Solomons.

  Bait and tackle are available at Bunky's Charter Boats, Inc., 14448 Solomons Rd. South, Solomons (© **410/326-3241**); and at Rod 'N' Reel, Harbor Road and the Bay, Chesapeake Beach (© **301/855-8450**).

SWIMMING   Both Flag Ponds Nature Park (Rte. 2–4) and Chesapeake Beach's Bay Front Park offer pleasant unguarded beaches for bay swimming. Remember that whenever swimming in the Chesapeake, you should be wary of **sea nettles,** small, jellyfishlike stinging creatures that are especially common after the Fourth of July, especially if the weather's been dry.

WHERE TO STAY

Back Creek Inn Bed & Breakfast ★★   Housed in an expanded blue 1880 waterman's house, this inn offers travelers a relaxing stay in a serene waterfront setting. Innkeeper Carol Pennock has decorated the home with antiques, hand-made quilts, flowers from the inn's garden, and original paintings. From the cozy sitting room, you can watch boats drift by the patio and garden in the waters of Back Creek . The Lavender Room is a small cottage newly redecorated with a Jacuzzi and a screened porch overlooking the creek. The Tansy, Chamomile, and Peppermint rooms also enjoy water views. Both Thyme and Peppermint are suites. Thyme has a fireplace, too. The inn has Garden Tea Thursdays 3 to 5pm. The full breakfast, which often includes fresh baked goods, is quite good.

Alex and Calvert sts. (P.O. Box 520), Solomons, MD 20688. © **410/326-2022.** Fax 410/326-2946. http:// bbonline.com/md/backcreek. 7 units. $95 double, $125 suite, $145 cottage. Additional guests $25. Rates include full or continental breakfast. MC, V. Only children over 12. **Amenities:** TV; outdoor Jacuzzi (in season); bikes; picnic baskets (requires 48 hours notice). *In room:* A/C, coffeemakers in suites and cottage, hair dryer.

Comfort Inn Beacon Marina   Completely updated in 2001, this two-story hotel is geared toward nautical enthusiasts as well as average travelers. The hotel complex includes a 187-slip marina, with 40 covered slips. The rooms are clean and comfortable and have been modernized from the windows to the bathrooms. Best of all, guests can open the windows to enjoy the breezes off Back Creek.

255 Lore Rd. (P.O. Box 869), Solomons, MD 20688. © **800/228-5150** or 410/326-6303. 60 units. $69–$149 double, $129–$149 suite. AE, DC, DISC, MC, V. Rates include continental breakfast. **Amenities:** Waterfront restaurant and bar; pool; hot tub; passes to nearby health club; 187-slip marina. *In room:* Dataport, fridge, microwave, coffeemaker, iron.

Holiday Inn Select Solomons ★   The biggest hotel in Solomons, the Holiday Inn was revamped in 2000. Many rooms have good views, particularly on the second floor or above and on the southern ends of the hotel's guest wings.

155 Holiday Dr. (P.O. Box 1099) off Rte. 4, Solomons, MD 20688. © **800/356-2009** or 410/326-6311. Fax 410/326-1069. www.hiselect.com/solomondsmd. 326 units. $94–$129 double, $149–$229 suite. AE, DISC, MC, V. **Amenities:** Waterview restaurant; marina with 90 slips; dockside bar; outdoor pool; tennis courts; health club; sauna; volleyball courts; business center; executive level. *In room:* A/C, dataport, coffeemaker, hair dryer.

Solomons Victorian Inn ⚐　Known locally as the Davis House, this late Victorian structure was built by Solomons shipbuilder Clarence Davis, who built President Kennedy's yacht, the *Manitou*. All but one of the rooms enjoy a view of Back Creek Harbor or the Patuxent River. The inn is decorated in antiques and reproductions and has four public spaces: a living room, a sitting room, a library, and a glassed-in porch where breakfast is served. Try to get the Solomons Sunset suite, which features a king bed, microwave and galley area, a whirlpool tub, and great views of the harbor on two sides. Two new suites in the Carriage House have private entrances, whirlpool tubs, and harbor views. Minimum 2-night stays apply on certain holiday and event weekends.

125 Charles St. (P.O. Box 759), Solomons, MD 20688. ✆ **410/326-4811.** Fax 410/326-0133. www.solomons victorianinn. 8 units. $90–$175 double. Rates include full or continental breakfast. AE, MC, V. Children over 12 welcome. *In room:* A/C, whirlpool tubs or microwaves in some rooms.

WHERE TO DINE

C.D. Cafe, Inc. CONTINENTAL　Everybody around here recommends the C.D. Cafe for lunch. This tiny, relaxed restaurant in the Avondale shopping center just off Solomons Island, offers a nice range of continental dishes, from smoked salmon cakes to a really spicy Cajun shepherd's pie. They open every morning at 9am for newspaper reading, coffee, and pastries. Lunch starts Monday through Saturday at 11:30am and Sunday brunch is served 11:30am to 2:30pm.

Avondale Center, 14350 Solomons Island Rd., Solomons. ✆ **410/326-3877.** Reservations not accepted. Main courses $8.25–$18.95; lunch $4.25–$11.95. MC, V. Mon–Sat 9am–2:30pm and 5:30–9:30pm, Sun 11:30am–2:30pm and 5:30–9pm.

Lighthouse Inn SEAFOOD　Fine dining with a view of a picturesque harbor is what you get at this popular eatery near the heart of Solomons Island. The dining room is divided into a lower floor and a loft, both offering a view of Back Creek Harbor out floor-to-ceiling windows. The bar is a replica of a Chesapeake Bay skipjack. Dinner specials include baked stuffed shrimp, but the lightly broiled crab cakes are excellent. In summer, the deck is a great place to dine.

14636 Solomons Island Rd. S., P.O. Box 178, Solomons. ✆ **410/326-2444.** Reservations strongly recommended. Main courses $16.95–$28.95. AE, DC, DISC, MC, V. Mon–Thurs 5–9pm, Fri–Sat 5–11pm, Sun 4–9pm.

Rod 'N' Reel SEAFOOD　If you're planning to stop or sail here—it's right at the marina—come hungry. Crabs and oysters get special treatment here. Crabs appear in every course and you can get your oysters on the half shell or fried or paired with a crab cake. There's plenty of fish, shrimp, and steak, too. There are also about a dozen huge seafood combinations to fill even the hungriest fisherman. This is a waterfront, casual place, perfect for celebrating after a day in the sun. They're open for breakfast, too. Check out the weekend breakfast buffet with goodies like homemade doughnuts, creamed chipped beef, and hominy.

Rte. 261 and Mears Ave., Chesapeake Beach. ✆ **877/763-6733,** 410/257-2735, or 301/855-8351. www. rodnreelinc.com. Reservations accepted for parties of 8 or more. Main courses $12.99–$39.99; lunch $5.99–$18.99. AE, DISC, MC, V. Mon 11am–9pm, Tues–Fri 11am–10pm, Sat–Sun 8am–10pm.

Smokey Joe's Grill AMERICAN　Smokey Joe's is a favorite of Chesapeake Beach charter captains because of its barbecue and its location on the charter dock next to Rod 'N' Reel. This casual bar/restaurant has several windowside tables where you can watch the boats at their moorings. It's a great place to stop for a beer and a sandwich after a day on the bay. If you're planning a day on the water, call 24 hours ahead and they'll make you up a boxed lunch with beer and/or soda.

Rte. 261 and Mears Ave., Chesapeake Beach. (© **410/257-2427.** Reservations not required except for parties of 8 or more. Main courses $8.99–$23.99. AE, MC, V. Sun–Thurs 11am–10pm, Fri–Sat 11am–11pm.

Stoney's Seafood House SEAFOOD   Take Maryland Route 264 west off Route 2–4 to get to Broomes Island Road for this great little seafood house in Broomes Island. It has a large porch for outdoor dining and sits right on the water. Stoney's, like every other seafood place in Maryland, purports to have the "best crab cakes in the world"; the difference is that Stoney's may be right. They make a fine filet mignon sandwich, too. The same menu is offered at the Prince Frederick location in Fox Run Shopping Center on Route 4 (© **410/535-1888**).

Oyster House Rd., P.O. Box 41, Broomes Island, MD 20614. (© **410/586-1888.** Reservations accepted for large parties only. Main courses $3.95–$15.95. AE, DISC, MC, V. Apr 1 to Nov 1 Sun–Thurs 11am–9pm, Fri–Sat 11:30am–10pm.

12 St. Mary's County: Where Maryland Began

The Free State got its start here in 1634 where the Potomac River meets the Chesapeake Bay. It's a lovely but remote peninsula, still dotted with tobacco barns and laced with rivers and creeks. Lexington Park is the county's biggest town and the home of the Patuxent River Naval Air Station.

Most visitors come to St. Mary's County for the fishing—there are two big bodies of water to choose from—or to see St. Mary's City, the state's first capital.

It's a long, lovely drive down Route 5—although pockets of suburbia are popping up all over. It's a quicker trip, though not as pretty, down Route 4. It's an easy day trip from Annapolis, Washington, or Baltimore. Or, combine a visit to St. Mary's with a stay in Solomons for a quintessential Chesapeake Bay vacation.

ESSENTIALS

GETTING THERE   Maryland Routes 5 and 235 run the length of St. Mary's County, providing access to all the major sites of interest. You can get to Route 5 from I-495 (the Washington beltway). From Annapolis, take Maryland Route 2 south to Solomons, then Maryland Route 4 across the Governor Thomas Johnson Bridge; it will intersect with Route 235 a few miles past the bridge. If you want a more scenic drive, take Route 50 to Route 301 to Route 5 all the way to St. Mary's City—it is slow and meandering. St. Mary's City is 86 miles (138km) from Annapolis, 69 miles (111km) from Washington, D.C., 101 miles (163km) from Baltimore, and 173 miles (279km) from Wilmington.

VISITOR INFORMATION   For information before setting out, contact **St. Mary's County Division of Tourism,** 23115 Leonard Hall Dr., Leonardtown, MD 20650 (© **800/327-9023** or 301/475-4411). You can also stop by the **St. Mary's County Chamber of Commerce Visitor Information Center** at 28290 Three Notch Rd., Mechanicsville, MD 20659 (© **301/884-5555**).

DISCOVERING MARYLAND'S FIRST CAPITAL

Historic St. Mary's City was Maryland's capital city for only a few years. In that time, the town and its people were responsible for some significant "firsts" for both the state and the nation: the first laws were enacted establishing religious toleration and separation of church and state; the first Catholic chapel in English America was established here; the first African American voted in a legislature here; women first sought the right to vote here. But by the end of the 17th century, the capital had moved to Annapolis and St. Mary's City began to disappear.

Though the buildings fell, they left the marks that have given archaeologists clues about the early colonial town. In the 21st century, visitors can see a re-created early plantation, view the inns and public buildings, and visit a reproduction of one of the ships that brought the first Marylanders here.

Plan to spend at least 4 hours visiting the town's sights. If you're going to drive this far, make sure you have time to enjoy the visit. Wear comfortable shoes and bring the baby's stroller. Many paths are paved for the benefit of both disabled and walking visitors, but a couple are gravelly or steep. Bring water. It can get very hot and humid here and soda machines are as absent as they were in 1634.

Historic St. Mary's City is more archaeological dig than town. Once the town was abandoned, the area was developed as farmland so lots of clues to the state's first city remained underground. The buildings that have been reproduced are small and simple except for the **State House**—and look as they would have when this area was first settled by English colonists. You'll also see "ghost frames," wooden frames of buildings whose foundations have been discovered but which aren't completely rebuilt or whose purposes are still unknown. They help give you a sense of the mix of farm and village that once was. There are also lots of signs and guides, who will help you get a feel for 17th century Maryland.

Once you arrive, stop at the **visitor center** to see the exhibits, get the gear for the state-of-the-art audio tour, watch the introductory video, and see the exhibit "And Once a Metropolis," which chronicles the rise and fall of St. Mary's City.

Don't miss the State House or **Godiah Spray's 17th century tobacco plantation.** While the public building is formal, the plantation shows how hard life was for the early colonists. The house is simple, the fields rough.

Smith's Ordinary, a 17th century inn, with its medieval-style fireplace and tiled inglenook, is the newest building. The second inn, built in the 1600s, **Farthings Ordinary,** has pre-packaged refreshments and drinks for sale to modern-day visitors. Don't miss the **Brick Chapel.** Archaeologists were surprised to discover three lead coffins here. Reconstruction of the church has begun and an exhibit nearby relates the archaeologists' discovery.

Walk down to the water to see the *Dove.* Along with the much larger *Ark,* it brought Maryland's first settlers here on March 25, 1634. This 76-foot ship is a 1978 reproduction of the pinnace, a square-rigged merchant ship of the day. Children love to board the boat and talk with the costumed sailors aboard.

Walking trails through woodlands and near the water stretch 3½ miles (5.6km) and still recall how this area must have looked to early settlers.

Special programs are offered on **Maryland Day** (Mar 25); **Community and Trail Day** in June (exhibits are open free of charge and there are special events); **Tidewater Archaeology Dig** in late June (when you can join the archaeologists); **Woodland Indian Discovery Day** the weekend after Labor Day (with storytelling, Native American crafts, and exhibits); and **Grand Militia Muster** in late October (a gathering of 17th century re-enactment units).

P.O. Box 39, St. Mary's City, MD 20686. ✆ 800/SMC-1634 or 301/862-0990. www.stmaryscity.org. Admission $7.50 for adults, $6 for seniors and students, $3.50 for ages 6–12. All the sites are open mid-June to mid-Sept Wed–Sun 10am–5pm. In spring, mid-Mar to mid-June, and fall, mid-Sept to mid-Nov, all sites are open Tues–Sat 10am–5pm. On Sun, only the tobacco plantation, visitor center, and exhibit hall are open. The museum closes mid-Nov to mid-Mar.

OTHER HISTORIC SITES

Also in St. Mary's County, **Sotterley Plantation** ✯, is worth a visit. The 1717 Tidewater plantation house tells a story 3 centuries in the making. The manor house includes an intricately carved Chinese Chippendale staircase and gorgeous shell alcoves. In the 19th century, this was home to the largest group of enslaved African Americans in the state. Reminders of these times include a slave house built in the 1849s. The last owners restored the house and gardens in the 20th century. Most of the Colonial Revival furnishings in the house belonged to them. The house, a National Landmark, has been undergoing restoration since 2000. All the furnishings have been removed but tours continue which feature the architecture and restoration work. The furniture (accompanied by an expanded tour) was due to be returned by the end of 2002. In 2003, look for the new boat dock on Sotterley Creek and plan to sail to Sotterley.

Rte. 245, Hollywood, MD. © 800/681-0850 or 301/373-2280. www.sotterley.com. $7 adults, $5 ages 6–16, free for ages 5 and under. Open Tues–Sat 10am–4pm, Sun 10am–4pm for grounds only. Closed Nov–May.

OUTDOOR ACTIVITIES
POINT LOOKOUT STATE PARK ⚓   Located at the tip of St. Mary's County, at the confluence of the Potomac River and the Chesapeake Bay, **Point Lookout State Park** (© **301/872-5688**) offers visitors a chance to see both bodies of water at one time. The park's 1,046 acres offer a beach on the Potomac, and a fishing pier on the Chesapeake, Civil War monuments dedicated to prisoners of war who died when this site was a POW camp, and docks for boating and catching the ferry to Smith Island across the bay, as well as campsites and cabins. Day use is $3 on weekends and holidays, May through September.

Visitors interested in **fishing** can cast their lines just about anywhere during the day except the beach swimming area. Favorite areas are the pier on the bay side, and the point on either the bay or riverside. Campers can also fish at designated piers near campsites. A fishing license is required only for the bay shoreline. Rowboat, canoe, and motorboat rentals are available at the camp store off Route 5 near the boat launch. You can also catch a ride to Smith Island on the *Capt. Tyler* (© **410/425-2771**) from here. From Memorial Day to mid-October, boats depart at 10am Wednesday through Sunday and return to Point Lookout at 4pm. For more information on Smith Island, see "Crisfield & Smith Island," in chapter 6.

The park offers 147 wooded **campsites** (26 with full hookups). Prices range from $18 to $33 per site, depending on hookup services. Cabins sleeping four cost $40 a night and a cottage that sleeps six costs $60 for a weekend (© **888/432-CAMP**). The office (© **301/872-5688**), at the entrance to the camping area, is open from 8am to 11pm. Day-use facilities with a guarded beach for swimming and picnicking are on the Potomac side, past the fishing pier.

FISHING CHARTERS
Chesapeake Bay Fishing Parties (© **301/872-5815**) has several charter boats and headboats for both day and night fishing. Charters run about $50 to $60 and headboat rates run about $35 for a day trip or night fishing.

For gear, snacks, and the scoop on where to eat, stop at **Rick's Marine** (© **301/872-5156**) in Scotland on Route 5, near Point Lookout State Park.

WHERE TO STAY
St. Mary's City doesn't have too many options for lodging. **Lexington Park** has some chain hotels and restaurants, including Best Western and Hampton Inns,

There is one bed-and-breakfast within walking distance of the historic town.

Brome–Howard Inn   The rich and the famous drop in here—or have their weddings or parties. (Lots of Washingtonians have summer or retirement homes in the area.) The innkeepers will treat you with the same hospitality. The four guest rooms vary widely in decoration but all are elegant. Three have fireplaces. Two third-floor rooms combine for a suite for families or couples who need to stretch out. The views are as beautiful as the antiques decorating the rooms.

18281 Rosecroft Rd., P.O. Box 476, St Mary's City, MD 20686. ℂ **301/866-0656.** Fax 301/866-9660. www. bromehowardinn.com. Rates $80–$160. Rates include hot or continental breakfast or Sun brunch for Sat-night guests. AE, MC, V. **Amenities:** Restaurant; parlor with television; bicycles. *In room:* A/C, TV available, CD players.

WHERE TO EAT

A couple of restaurants are located near one another down Route 252 (Wynne Rd.) in **Ridge.** They're all near the water and seafood is the specialty.

Courtney's Restaurant SEAFOOD   Nothing's fancy at Courtney's. It's a cinderblock building and simple dining room with red tablecloths and a bar with the TV going. But after a day of fishing or hiking around St. Mary's you might be hungry for some good home cooking. That's what Courtney does best. How do you like your crabs? You can get steamed, crab cakes, or soft-shells. Want fresh fish? Courtney's husband comes home every morning with the day's catch. They offer carryout, too.

48290 Wynne Rd., Ridge. ℂ **301/872-4403.** No reservations. Open 7am–9pm. Cash only. Main courses $11–$13.95; lunch $4.75–$6.95.

Spinnakers Restaurant SEAFOOD   Tucked in a corner of a huge marina, Spinnakers looks unassuming. The nautical theme might make you want another crab cake, but this is a good place for a culinary adventure. The menu changes quite a lot to include the freshest fish, but it's always interesting. If you aren't ready for trout fettuccini, perhaps, or fresh fish in parchment, or shrimp and chicken *étouffée*, there's always steak or maybe duck. This is a casual place to eat but your taste buds will be convinced this is fine dining.

Point Lookout Marina, Wynne Rd., Ridge, MD 20680. ℂ **301/872-4340.** Fax 301/872-0260. www.spinnakers restaurant.com. Reservations recommended. Main courses $16–$21. AE, MC, V. Summer open daily except Tues, 5–9pm (till 10pm Fri–Sat). Winter open Thurs–Sat 5–9pm. Take MD Rte. 5 or MD Rte. 235 south to Ridge. Turn onto Wynne Rd. (Rte. 252) and go 1.6 miles (2.6km). Turn right onto Millers Wharf Rd. Restaurant is on the marina at end of road.

6

Eastern Shore

Across the Chesapeake Bay Bridge, life slows down. Turn off Route 50 or Highway 301 and go down a country road past cornfields. Pause by rivers and marshes where birds and rustling grass are the only sounds. Stop in small towns that have fought the intrusion of chain stores so Mom-and-Pop shops could survive. If you love to watch trees light up with fireflies on a summer night; cycle down a country lane; let the breeze take your boat past farms as old as America, you'll love the Eastern Shore.

Easton is the unofficial capital of the Eastern Shore. It's the largest town (Ocean City swells larger with visitors in the summer), and its colonial roots are evident on picturesque streets.

In nearby Talbot County are three waterfront communities within easy driving distance. **St. Michaels** has the most shops, the shore's most interesting museum (the Chesapeake Bay Maritime Museum), and plenty of charm. Boaters clog the harbor on summer weekends, but on pretty spring and fall days or in mid-week during the summer, its charms are more accessible. **Oxford** is much quieter with fewer tourist attractions but attractive for its slower pace, shady Strand, and narrow, colonial streets. **Tilghman** (my favorite place!) hasn't bothered to beautify for the tourists—but its unique, waterman's lifestyle is enough to make visitors come.

Cambridge, on the Choptank River, hasn't gotten the attention it deserves. Its historic district, shopping, and nearby outdoor activities make it a place to go—and the new Hyatt resort will make it even more popular.

North of the Bay Bridge, **Chestertown** is not only a colonial town, it's a college town. George Washington allowed the college founders to use his name for Washington College, which lies near the heart of downtown.

The southern areas of the Shore, including **Smith Island** and **Crisfield,** are the ultimate in waterman villages. Change comes slowly to these remote parts of Maryland, and residents like it that way. That very attitude draws visitors to these hard-to-reach spots.

1 Talbot County ★★

40 miles (64km) SE of Annapolis, 60 miles (97km) SE of Baltimore, 71 miles (114km) SE of Washington, D.C., 110 miles (177km) SW of Wilmington

Set in the middle of the Eastern Shore, Talbot (it's pronounced *Tall*-but) County has the most popular towns for visitors north of Ocean City. Easton is the county seat. Filled with pretty residential streets and historic colonial buildings, it's all business during the workday, but on weekends, the streets, restaurants and watering holes fill up. St. Michaels clings to its maritime tradition. Lots of visitors arrive by boat to one of the town's many marinas. Whether you come by land or water, you'll find quaint streets, lots of spots for admiring the Miles

River, and the Chesapeake Bay Maritime Museum. Continue down Route 33 to Tilghman, where watermen are king. Housing developments are on the horizon for this remote spot, but it remains a great place to see watermen's boats and enjoy fresh seafood. Oxford has a place in colonial history as a busy seaport, home of Revolutionary War financier Robert Morris, and as the resting place of George Washington's trusted aide, Tench Tilghman.

For a fun side trip, head over Route 404 to Wye Mills, home of one of Maryland's tiniest state parks (see "A Drive to Wye Mills," later in this chapter).

ESSENTIALS

GETTING THERE   The best way to get to the Easton area is by car, via U.S. Route 50 from all directions. St. Michaels, Tilghman, and Oxford are reachable by boat with plenty of dock space.

Easton Municipal Airport (© 410/822-0400), about 3 miles (5km) north of the city on U.S. Route 50, services local charter planes, including a charter service operating there. **Greyhound** (© 800/231-2222) offers regular bus service into its depot at the junction of U.S. Route 50 and Cordova Road.

VISITOR INFORMATION   For maps, brochures, and complete lodging and restaurant information about Easton and environs, contact the **Talbot County Office of Tourism,** 11 N. Washington St. (right inside the county courthouse), Easton, MD 21601 (© 410/770-8000; fax 410/770-8057; www. talbotchamber.org or www.talbgov.org).

GETTING AROUND   The only way to get around Talbot County is by car, or if you're lucky, by boat (though Easton is fairly landlocked). Maryland Route 33 from Easton will take you to St. Michaels and Tilghman Island, and Maryland Route 333 goes to Oxford. The shortest and most scenic route from Oxford to St. Michaels is via the **Oxford–Bellevue Ferry** (© 410/745-9023; www.oxfordmd.com/obf), across the Tred Avon River. Established in 1683, this is the country's oldest privately operated ferry. The trip is three-quarters of a mile (1.2km) long and takes 7 minutes. You can catch the nine-vehicle ferry either from Bellevue, off Routes 33 and 329, near St. Michaels, or at Oxford (off Rte. 333). The ferry runs every 25 minutes March through November, from 7 am to sunset, Monday through Friday; 9am to sunset Saturday and Sunday from March through November. It doesn't run December through February. Rates for a car and two persons are $5.50 one-way and $9 round-trip; extra car passenger, 50¢; walk-on passengers, $1.25; and bicyclists, $2.50 one-way. Trailers and RVs can be accommodated, but call first. If you're driving with kids, go out of your way to ride this ferry—unless you've been on countless ferries elsewhere. It's so tiny it can't even compare to the Cape May–Lewes Ferry but it's a short, fun ride to a long country road leading either to St. Michaels or Easton.

If you don't bring your own car to the Easton area, you can rent one from **U-Save Rental,** Matthewstown Road (© 410/822-4118); or **Enterprise Rental,** Route 50 near Dutchman's Lane (© 410/822-3260). For local cab service, try **Scotty's Taxi** (© 410/822-1475).

SPECIAL EVENTS   The **Waterfowl Festival** ★★★, held the second week in November, turns Easton into a celebration of ducks, geese, and other birds. The 3-day festival draws as many as 20,000 visitors. Venues around the town display Federal Duck Stamp paintings, duck decoys, carvings so realistic you'll want to smooth those ruffled feathers. Some 400 artists' works are displayed. Don't miss

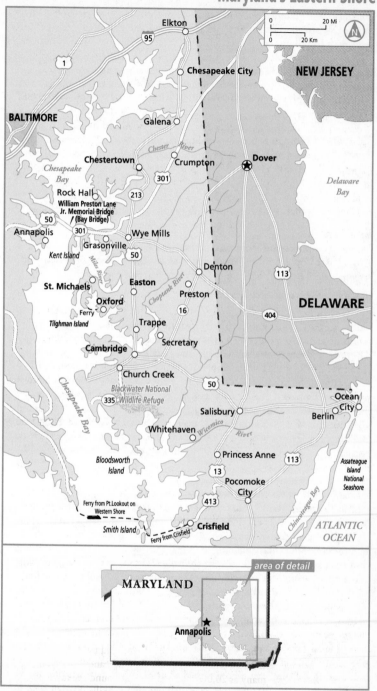

the duck-calling contest—a fascinating performance. You don't have to like hunting to attend. The entrance fee is $12 for adults (children under 12 are free); with free shuttle buses shuttling running to the different sites. If you visit wildlife refuges around Maryland, you'll see where the proceeds of this event are used. Nearly $4 million has been raised over the years to protect and conserve wildlife habitats. For information, contact Waterfowl Festival, 40 S. Harrison St., P.O. Box 929, Easton, MD 21601 ((C) **410/832-4567**; fax 410-820-9286; www.waterfowlfestival.org).

The county's other major event, the **Mid-Atlantic Maritime Festival** ★★★ ((C) **410/820-8606**), is held in St. Michaels annually the third weekend in May. The 3-day festival packs the town as tourists and natives celebrate the area's maritime history with displays of ship models, photographs, nautical arts, and crafts, as well as music, seafood, and a parade of tall ships.

Oxford Day ((C) **410/226-5730**; www.oxfordmd.com/oba), held the last Saturday in April, is a fun local fest, with music, entertainment, and crab races.

EASTON

Visitors to the Eastern Shore usually start at Easton. Dubbed the "Colonial Capital of the Eastern Shore," this town values its visitors. Route 50 is filled with reasonably priced chain hotels and good restaurants are everywhere.

WHAT TO SEE & DO

Take a walk through the downtown district; it's filled with history. Start at the **Talbot County Courthouse,** at 11 N. Washington St. Not only is the building a historic landmark erected in 1710, it's the home of the local tourism office. They've got plenty of brochures, maps, and recommendations.

Stop and look at the **Bullitt House,** on Harrison Street. It was built in 1790; an investment firm's offices are now there. Then walk down Washington Street to see the **Thomas Perrin Smith House,** built in 1803. Once a newspaper office, it is now the Chesapeake Bay Yacht Club. The **Brick Hotel** was built in 1812 and is now an office building. The **Shannahan and Wrightson Hardware Building** may be the Court House Square Shops now, but in 1791, Owen Kennard was opening the town's oldest store. It grew over the years and the grand opening of one of its additions was momentous: December 7, 1941, Pearl Harbor Day.

The **Historical Society of Talbot County,** 25 S. Washington St. ((C) **410/822-0773**) offers guided tours through three historic homes and a museum surrounding a Federal-period garden Tuesday through Saturday, 11am to 3pm.

The **Academy Art Museum** ★ ((C) **410/822-ARTS**; www.art-academy.org) transformed 18th-century buildings on the corner of Harrison and South streets into a gallery. Nearly 100,000 visitors annually see its shows of works by regional and national artists and its performing arts presentations. Exhibitions are free.

Avalon Theatre ((C) **410/822-0345**; www.avalontheatre.com) has been providing entertainment since its vaudeville days in 1921. Silent films are screened in the Art Deco theatre at 40 E. Dover St. Since its restoration in 1989, it's been the site of three world premieres, as well as performing arts programs.

A little farther out of the downtown area is **Third Haven Meeting House,** 405 S. Washington St. ((C) **410/822-0293**). Built in 1682, the meetinghouse once hosted William Penn, who preached while Lord Baltimore was present. It's still in use today. Admission is free but donations are welcome. It's open 9am to 5pm daily with Sunday service at 10am.

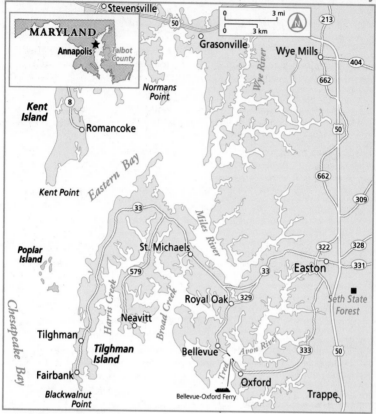

SHOPPING

The Easton–St. Michaels–Oxford area is full of craft, antiques, and specialty shops. Talbot Street in St. Michaels, lined with stores for about 6 blocks, is the best place for shopping, with a good selection of work from local artists and studios. Most shops in the area are open weekdays from 10am to 6pm; many are open weekends, but expect reduced hours in winter.

Albright's Gun Shop Located across from the Tidewater Inn, this shop stocks guns and accessories, bow-hunting supplies, sport clothing and watches, canvas goods, and fishing tackle. It is also the home of Albright's Sportsman's Travel Service (see "Hunting," later in this chapter). Custom repair and gunsmithing are done on the premises. Open weekdays 9am to 5:30pm, Saturday 9am to 3:30pm, with extended hours in the waterfowl-hunting season. 36 E. Dover St., Easton. ✆ **800/474-5502** or 410/820-8811.

Antiques & Rare Books A small assortment of rare books, furniture, antiques, and odds and ends stock this under-decorated store. Owners and watchcat Sam are friendly and encourage browsing. Closed Wednesdays. Call for winter hours. 13 N. Harrison St., Easton. ✆ **410/763-9030.**

Where to Dine Near the Bay Bridge

If you cross the Bay Bridge and can't wait another minute for some fresh seafood, there are some good restaurants are close to the eastern terminus of the bridge.

Fisherman's Inn ✦ SEAFOOD   Set among the marinas of Kent Narrows, the Fisherman's Inn offers casual dining in its big dining room or on the Crab Deck in warm weather. The Crab Deck, where an old crab picking shed once stood, is open from the end of April to the end of October and has a similar menu to the Fisherman's Inn, plus steamed crabs. You'd better want seafood—a single crab cake or a whole platterful of fish and shellfish. How about a Caesar salad topped with lump crabmeat or fried oysters? The dinner menu is available all day, and there's a lunch menu of salads and sandwiches and a casual fare menu after 4pm which looks like a smaller version of the lunch menu. Come by car or by boat—there are plenty of boat slips. 3116 Main St. (Rte. 50), Grasonville. ℂ 410/ 827-8807. www.fishermansinn.com. No reservations accepted. AE, DISC, MC, V. Entrees $13.99–$24.99, lunch $5.50–$15.99. Open daily 11am– 10pm, except Dec 24–25.

Harris Crab House SEAFOOD   This informal indoor-outdoor waterfront restaurant is a typical crab hous, nestled among the marinas by the Kent Narrows bridge. Long tables covered with brown paper jam the lower hall, and you might find yourself sharing a table with another group. Now this is a crab feast: no cloth or china, only paper, paper towels, and crab mallets. Since crabs take so long to pick, there's plenty of time for talking and the mood here is jovial. Other entrees are simple, fried, and good. Besides plentiful portions, diners get a lovely view of the

Cherry's   Since 1926, this store has been a favored spot for ladies' and men's quality sportswear, outdoor wear, and work and sporting shoes. It looks like a surplus store but carries all the better name brands. Monday to Saturday 9am to 5pm. 26 W. Dover St., Easton. ℂ 410/822-4750. Fax 410/822-4751.

Crackerjacks   This children's store stocks all sorts of books, toys, games, dolls, stuffed animals, pinwheels, crafts, and more. 7 S. Washington St., Easton. ℂ 410/822-7716. Fax 410/822-7716.

Rowen's Stationery and Bookstore   Two entrances lead to this book and stationery store. It stocks a wonderful variety of books about the Eastern Shore, Chesapeake Bay, Maryland, sailing and nautical topics, wetlands, waterfowl, bird-watching, and decoys. It also sells stationery, artists' supplies, prints, housewares, kitchen gadgets, gifts, and souvenirs with crab-design motifs. 14 N. Harrison St. and 10 N. Washington St., Easton. ℂ 410/822-2095.

WHERE TO STAY
Talbot County offers accommodations from basic of a chain hotels on Route 50 to high style and luxury on the waterfront. You pay for the luxury, especially on busy weekends during the Waterfowl Festival or hunting season, though you can park for free. In St. Michaels, Oxford, and Tilghman, there's room for your boat.

sunset. The menu features crabs by the dozen; all-you-can-eat shrimp and crab; and various broiled, steamed, or fried combinations of hard and soft crabs, crab cakes, hard- and soft-shell clams, oysters, and scallops—depending on what's in season. The menu also offers barbecued chicken and ribs and some unusual items like crab nuggets. Lighter items, such as sandwiches and burgers, are popular at lunchtime. Get here early and sit downstairs. Upstairs may seem like a better view, but the downstairs atmosphere is better. Kent Narrows Way N., Grasonville, MD 21638. © 410/827-9500. Reservations not accepted. Main courses $11.95–$20.95; lunch $3.95–$9.95. MC, V. Daily 11am–10pm. Off Rte. 50 at Exit 42.

Kent Manor Restaurant INTERNATIONAL Overlooking more than 200 acres of farmland and waterfront on the east side of Kent Island, this manor house restaurant is an attraction in itself. Settle into one of four cozy, Victorian dining rooms or the enclosed water-view solarium, and select from traditional Eastern Shore fare, including crab cakes and crab imperial or, try the wild boar tenderloin, herb-encrusted ostrich, and buffalo medallions in a wild forest mushroom and onion glaze. On Sunday there's an a la carte brunch with dessert bar. 500 Kent Manor Dr., Stevensville. © **800/820-4511** or 410/643-5757. Reservations recommended for dinner. Main courses $19–$32; lunch $8–$14. AE, DC, DISC, MC, V. Mon–Sat 11:30am–4pm and 5–9pm, Sun 10am–2pm and 4–9pm. Closed Mon and Tues in winter only. Turn south on Rte. 8, Exit 37 off Rte. 50/301.

Comfort Inn This two-story hacienda-style property is set back from busy Route 50, surrounded by trees, and has a brigh, airy lobby with lots of light woods and plants. The guest rooms, many of which surround a central courtyard, are furnished with pastel tones and waterfowl art. Rooms open to the outside and there is no elevator.

8523 Ocean Gateway (Rte. 50), Easton, MD 21601. © **800/228-5150** or 410/820-8333. Fax 410/820-8436. 84 units. $79.95–$99.95 double. Rates include continental breakfast. AE, DC, DISC, MC, V. **Amenities:** Outdoor pool; coffee in lobby. *In room:* A/C, dataport, iron available. Pets welcome.

Days Inn *Kids* Set back from Route 50 in a shady setting, this motel is a favorite with families. The guest rooms offer a well-maintained contemporary decor with coffeemakers, standard furnishings, and a choice of bed sizes.

7018 Ocean Gateway (Rte. 50), Easton, MD 21601. © **410/822-4600.** Fax 410/820-9723. www.daysinn. com. 80 units. $70–$105 double. Rates include continental breakfast. AE, DC, DISC, MC, V. Pets accepted for a fee. **Amenities:** Outdoor pool. *In room:* A/C, dataport, coffeemaker, hair dryer.

Tidewater Inn *★★★* This luxuriously appointed hotel is in the heart of Easton, and is a prime venue for Waterfowl Festival events. It has far more character than your average hotel, with open fireplaces, paintings of 18th-century Easton, and a well-regarded restaurant. Special touches abound, such as the on-site kennels for hunting dogs; horse and carriage rides; and the special-made ballroom chandelier, imported from Spain. Bedrooms are furnished with reproduction pieces. The emphasis here is on hospitality. They'll treat you right.

101 E. Dover St., Easton, MD 21601. (✆) **800/237-8775** or 410/822-1300. Fax 410/820-8847. www.tide waterinn.com. 114 units. $85–$186 double; $240–$558 suite. AE, DC; MC; V. Pets accepted (in on-site kennels). Complimentary valet parking. **Amenities:** 2 restaurants; 1 bar; outdoor pool; access for fee to nearby health club; business center; babysitting available; kennels for pets. *In room:* A/C, TV/VCR with movies, dataport, fridge available, hair dryer available, iron available, robes.

WHERE TO DINE

Seafood lovers, rejoice. Crabs, oysters, and fish (especially rockfish) reign supreme in Talbot County. Crab in all forms is the main attraction—you'll find it served as plump crab cakes, spicy crab soup, and crab imperial, a rich, creamy crab dish. But if you don't care for seafood, don't despair. Many restaurants also serve up juicy prime rib and crispy Delmarva fried chicken.

Legal Spirits AMERICAN   The owners are new and the menu has changed, but this is still a good spot for lunch or dinner. This tavern-style restaurant is housed in the historic Avalon Theater complex, and a Prohibition theme dominates, complete with gangster accessories and old newspaper articles on the walls. A tin ceiling, stained-glass windows, and brass fixtures are reminiscent of an era synonymous with silent movies, vaudeville, and Art Deco.

42 E. Dover St., Easton. (✆) 410/820-0765 or 410/820-0747. Reservations recommended for dinner. Main courses $8.25–$22.95; lunch $6.75–$10.95. AE, DISC, MC, V. Daily, 11am–10pm.

Rustic Inn *(Finds* INTERNATIONAL   A longtime favorite, this eatery sits in the midst of a string of shops. Although it can easily be overlooked, it is a hideaway worth finding. The decor features farm implements, fishing gear, and tobacco-growing tools, surrounding a wood-burning fireplace. Entrees include surf and turf, lobster tails, crab and oyster imperial, veal, chicken, and flounder. Sandwiches, salads, and pasta make up the lunch menu.

Talbottown Shopping Center, Easton. (✆) 410/820-8212. Reservations recommended for dinner. Main courses $10.95–$23.95; lunch $4.95–$13.95. AE, MC, V. Tues, Thurs, and Fri 11:30am–2pm; Mon–Sat 5–10pm, Sun 4–9pm.

ST. MICHAELS

Since its founding in the late 1700s, **St. Michaels** has looked to the water for its livelihood. Shipbuilding made it famous. Log canoes were first workboats and then became better known as racing boats. Bugeyes and Baltimore Clippers were built here, too. Watermen came to sell their catch, and canneries and oyster-packing plants sprang up. Ask a local to tell you the story of how, long ago, residents fooled the British and saved their town during the Revolutionary War. For the Cliffs Note version, see "What to See & Do," below.

Today, St. Michaels is an enormously popular destination for boaters willing to cram their boats into the crowded harbor on a sunny weekend. It's also bed-and-breakfast heaven; many establishments look out to the beautiful Miles River. Make time for the **Chesapeake Bay Maritime Museum,** where the town's history—in fact, the history of the whole Chesapeake Bay—is celebrated. St. Michaels' streets also offer a variety of shops and restaurants.

WHAT TO SEE & DO

The Miles River Yacht Club and Chesapeake Bay Maritime Museum sponsor **log canoe races**—just about the oldest class of boat still sailing around here. Usually sailing races are more exciting for the sailor than for the spectator. But these boats—big on sail, small on hull—have to be seen to be appreciated. Races are usually held on several summer weekends. For information contact Miles River Yacht Club (✆ **410/745-9511;** www.milesriveryc.com or www. logcanoe.com).

Make sure you make time to visit **The Cannonball House,** Mulberry Street at St. Mary's Square. The house isn't open to the public, but you can examine the exterior. When the British attempted to shell the town during the War of 1812, the townspeople outsmarted them. They blacked out the town and hung lanterns high in the trees so the British overshot the houses. Only one cannonball hit the town, striking the chimney of this house. The town was saved and the "blackout strategy" was born.

Chesapeake Bay Maritime Museum ★★★ Dedicated to the preservation of maritime history and to the Chesapeake Bay, this waterfront museum has the largest collection of Chesapeake Bay watercraft in existence (76 boats). The comprehensive collection is comprised of many floating exhibits, including a skipjack and a restored log-bottom bugeye, as well as crabbing skiffs, workboats, and log canoes. The centerpiece is the Hooper Strait lighthouse, an authentic 1879 screwpile lighthouse. The museum is also home to a working boatyard, an extensive waterfowl decoy collection, and a 4,000-volume library—James Michener relied upon it when writing his best-seller *Chesapeake.* "The Steamboat" focuses on steam and mechanical propulsion on Chesapeake Bay.

Mill St., Navy Point, St. Michaels. ✆ **410/745-2916.** www.cbmm.org. Admission $7.50 adults, $6.50 seniors, $3 ages 6–17. Summer daily 9am–6pm, spring/fall daily 9am–5pm, winter weekends and holidays 10am–4pm. Closed Jan 1, Thanksgiving, and Dec 25. Take Rte. 33 into St. Michaels; turn right at Mill St. and follow signs to the museum.

SHOPPING

Shops in St. Michaels are concentrated along Talbot Street, and usually are open 10am to 6pm weekdays and most weekends. Hours are shorter during winter.

Artiste Locale A range of local artwork is displayed here, including pottery, original-design T-shirts, soaps, candles, paintings, jewelry, and stationery. There are all kinds of home furnishing and gift items, many with an Eastern Shore flair. 112 N. Talbot St., P.O. Box 743, St. Michaels. ✆ **410/745-6580.**

Hodgepodge Garden decorations, as well as a great variety of accessories, baskets, decoys, throw blankets, mirrors, and more, poke out from every angle in this interesting shop. 308 S. Talbot St., St. Michaels. ✆ **410/745-3062.**

The Mind's Eye This store's business card proclaims "incredibly neat stuff," and we agree. Don't miss this unique gift gallery filled with folk art: wood carvings, pottery and glassware, jewelry, cards, sculpture, and wall hangings, all by American artists. 201 S. Talbot St., St. Michaels. ✆ **410/745-2023.**

St. Michaels Candy Company For those with a sweet tooth, here is a shop stocked with handmade chocolates, truffles, novelty candies, gourmet ice cream, teas, yogurt, and unique gift items such as chocolate crabs and oysters, cookbooks, beer-making kits, kitchen accessories, and barley candy. 216 S. Talbot St., St. Michaels. ✆ **888/570-6050** or 410/745-6060. Fax 410/745-6311. www.candyisdandy.com.

Talbot Ship and Rail If you didn't come to town in a boat, then how about going home with one you can carry in the car? Model ships, NOAA charts, and nautical books and art fill this store at the end of town. They will also restore old models. New here are the model trains, from G to Z scale, from Marklin, LGB and Micro-Trains. 211 N. Talbot St., St. Michaels. ✆ **410/745-6268.** www.talbot-ship-and-rail.com.

WHERE TO STAY

Hambleton Inn   Every room has a water view, a private bathroom, and antique furnishings at this immaculate Victorian-style bed-and-breakfast. An open second-floor porch, enclosed lower porch, and small harborside deck provide three more spots from which to view the boats docked at St. Michaels. Complimentary bicycles are also available for guests' use. If you stay here, tell the innkeeper of any special needs, especially dietary, in advance.

202 Cherry St., St. Michaels, MD 21663. © **866/745-3350** or 410/745-3350. Fax 410/745-5709. www. hambletoninn.com. 5 units. $125–$275 double. Rates include breakfast. MC, V. **Amenities:** Bike rental. *In room:* A/C.

Inn at Perry Cabin ✦✦   Now owned by the Orient Express, this proper English country inn set on the Miles River aims for the highest luxury standards and charges accordingly. Pampering sets this place apart from other local properties: the luxurious touches include a full-time concierge, fresh flowers in every room, and afternoon tea in the drawing room. We've been told that if the service is less than exemplary, the management will make every effort to correct it, even up to offering a complimentary return trip. Facilities include an outdoor terrace, rose and herb garden, and boat dock. There's also access to golf, fishing, horseback riding, hunting, and a helicopter pad.

308 Watkins Lane, St. Michaels, MD 21663. © **800/722-2949** or 410/745-2200. Fax 410/745-3348. 41 units. $295–$695 double. Rates include afternoon tea. AE, DC, MC, V. Pets accepted for fee. **Amenities:** Restaurant; bar; indoor pool; exercise room; sauna; bikes available; business center; massage available; babysitting available. *In room:* A/C, TV/VCR, dataport, fridge available, hair dryer, iron.

Parsonage Inn ✦   The Parsonage, a red-brick Victorian home built in 1883, is a beauty. It served as the parsonage to the United Methodist Church from 1924 to 1985. Today, it's a respite for travelers willing to exchange a water view for the delicious breakfasts, cozy decor, and creature comforts. Each room contains brass beds, Laura Ashley linens, and private bathrooms. Many rooms also have ceiling fans, access to a sun deck, and fireplaces. Guests can take advantage of the inn's complimentary bicycles. Special touches during the off-season, such as wine and cheese in the evenings or restaurant gift certificates, entice visitors in the winter months.

210 N. Talbot St., St. Michaels, MD 21663. © **800/394-5519** or 410/745-5519. Fax 410/745-6869. www. parsonage-inn.com. 8 units. A/C. $100–185 double. MC, V. Rates include gourmet breakfast. Minimum 2-night stays required most weekends. Children welcome by prior approval. **Amenities:** Bikes available. *In room:* A/C, TV in some rooms, dataport, iron.

St. Michaels Harbour Inn ✦   It's hard to beat this inn for views of the water and boats. It's right by the 60-slip marina, a modern hotel with both rooms and suites, almost all with sweeping views of the water and most with private balconies or terraces. Each room has contemporary furnishings with maritime-themed art. The suites also have kitchenettes, wet bars, and sitting rooms. The restaurant is particularly romantic at dinner when the sun sets over the marina.

101 N. Harbor Rd., St. Michaels, MD 21663. © **800/955-9001** or 410/745-9001. Fax 410/745-9150. www. harbourinn.com. 46 units. $149–$475 double. AE, DC, DISC, MC, V. **Amenities:** Boat slips; 2 restaurants; outdoor pool; exercise room; spa; water-sports equipment rental; bikes; business center; babysitting available. *In room:* A/C, fax, dataport, kitchenette in some rooms, fridge, coffeemaker, hair dryer, iron.

Wades Point Inn on the Bay ✦✦   A long country road leads to this grand old house, set on a curve of land overlooking both the Chesapeake and Eastern bays. Surrounded by a sprawling lawn and 120 acres of fields, woodlands, and nature trails, you can find seclusion, peace, and some great sunset views. The inn was built in the early 19th century by Thomas Kemp, a shipbuilder credited with creating the famous 19th-century Baltimore clipper, the *Pride of Baltimore*. His family turned the house into a resort popular for 100 years. The main house offers varied guest rooms (with private or shared bathrooms), all furnished with antiques and cooled by the cross-ventilation of bay breezes, ceiling fans, and screened porches. For modern comforts mixed with reproduction furnishings and decor, request a room in the newer adjacent Kemp Building. Its 12 rooms have private bathrooms and air-conditioning, and most have private porches or balconies; four have kitchenettes. Breakfast is served in a bright wicker-filled room in the main house overlooking the bay.

Wades Point Rd. (at the end of the road), St. Michaels, MD 21663. © **888/923-3466** or 410/745-2500. Fax 410/745-3444. www.wadespoint.com. 24 units (6 with shared bathroom). $120–$230 double. Rates include continental breakfast. No extra charge for children under 12. 2-night minimum stay on weekends and holidays. Discounts available for stays of 3 days or more. MC, V. 5 miles (8km) west of St. Michaels, off Rte. 33. **Amenities:** Dock; walking trails; canoe/kayak launch; water sports equipment and bike rentals; executive level rooms. *In room:* A/C, kitchenettes (in some units), balconies, coffeemaker, hair dryer available, iron.

WHERE TO DINE

Bistro St. Michaels ✦ FRENCH/SEAFOOD   This busy restaurant captures the ambience of a Parisian-style bistro. The small downstairs dining room can be noisy but the upstairs dining room and garden patio are more quiet and intimate. On a busy night, service can be slow. Chef David Stein changes the menus with the seasons and his offerings are creative, hardly the usual broiled crab cake or fried fish. Soups vary from an excellent potato-and-onion to intriguing black bean with crème fraîche and smoked ham. Entrees can include delicate shrimp on a skewer or a cornmeal and horseradish crusted rockfish.

403 S. Talbot St., St. Michaels. © **410/745-9111**. Reservations recommended. Main courses $22–$29. AE, DC, DISC, MC, V. Thurs–Mon 5:30–9pm.

Crab Claw ✦ SEAFOOD   For many Marylanders, this is a destination restaurant. They come by the busloads for the fresh seafood, hot steamed crabs, and cool river breezes. It's casual and fun. And it's right near the Chesapeake Bay Maritime Museum. The emphasis of the all-day menu is on crabs served in all styles—you'll find backfin crab cakes, crab soup, soft crab, crab fluff (batter-dipped and fried crab cakes), and crab imperial. But what the Crab Claw does best is steamed crabs. If you're looking for something more creative, you'd do better at other area restaurants. Other seafood and fried chicken are also available.

Navy Point, Mill St., St. Michaels. © **410/745-2900**. Reservations accepted. Main courses $12.50–$22.95. No credit cards. Mid-Mar to mid-Dec daily 11am–10pm.

St. Michaels Crab House *(Kids)* SEAFOOD   Located on the marina, this casual, family-friendly restaurant offers a choice of indoor (air-conditioned) seating amid a nautical decor or a large outdoor area lined with picnic tables and umbrellas. The building dates from the 1830s, when it was an oyster-shucking shed. The menu, which includes a children's menu, features steamed crabs, crab cakes, soft-shell crabs, and snow crab legs, as well as stuffed flounder, fried shrimp, fried oysters, and an extensive raw bar. The crab imperial and Cajun tuna get a thumbs-up. For landlubbers, there are steaks and barbecued or grilled chicken. Lunch items range from soups and salads to sandwiches and burgers.

305 Mulberry St., St. Michaels. © **410/745-3737**. www.stmichaelscrabhouse.com Reservations recommended for dinner. Main courses $9.95–$18.95; lunch $5.25–$12.95. DISC, MC, V. Mid-Mar to mid-Dec Mon–Sat 11am–11pm, Sun 11am–10pm.

Town Dock Restaurant ★★ AMERICAN/SEAFOOD This bustling restaurant overlooking the harbor offers some of the finest dining in the area. In the main dining room, candlelit tables retain their intimacy even when the place is busy. Chef Michael Rork (who has been featured in gourmet magazines) presents a "new Eastern Shore" cuisine that puts a twist on traditional favorites. Foodies will love the pork chops with pecan-encrusted mango-cranberry chutney, salmon grilled with black bean and corn salsa, and potato-encrusted rockfish with tomato piccalilli (a kind of relish). This flair extends to the lunch menu, too. A selection of indulgent but light desserts ends the meal on a high note, followed by chocolate-covered strawberries presented with your check. There are two dining levels inside and outdoor seating on the deck. Upstairs at John and Mike's, you'll find a limited menu, live entertainment and even a humidor on weekends. Town Dock has an unusual commodity in St. Michaels—a parking lot.

125 Mulberry St., St. Michaels. © 410/745-5577. www.town-dock.com. Reservations recommended for dinner. Main courses $16–$25; lunch $8–$14. AE, DC, DISC, MC, V. Mon–Thurs 11:30am–9pm, Fri–Sat 11:30am–10pm, Sun 11am–9pm.

208 Talbot *Finds* AMERICAN This restaurant is on a busy thoroughfare at the end of town and offers no water views, but the food draws a crowd every night. The menu emphasizes Eastern Shore seafood, produce, and herbs, but served with panache. Tuna is paired with potato-apple puree, or rockfish comes with wild mushrooms, potato fritter, and oyster cream. Entrees change often but usually include several seafood dishes, chicken, rack of lamb, and steak. Your best bet is to call or visit their website for the current menu. On Saturday nights, you'll be offered a fixed-price menu with four courses to try their creative cuisine. The decor is relaxing and intimate, with exposed brick walls, crisp white linens, and an oyster plate collection.

208 N. Talbot St., St. Michaels. © 410/745-3838. www.208talbot.com. Reservations recommended. Main courses $23–$29; fixed-price 5-course dinner $50 (Sat only). DISC, MC, V. Wed–Thurs 5–9pm, Fri–Sat 5–10pm, Sun 5–9pm. Closed mid-Feb to mid-Mar.

TILGHMAN ISLAND

Keep driving on Route 33, the road from Easton to St. Michaels, and you'll arrive in **Tilghman,** on Tilghman Island in the middle of the Chesapeake Bay. The island's rugged beauty is slowly giving way to development, as more and more visitors decide to stay. Seafood restaurants are good all along the Eastern Shore—but when you see those boats just beyond a Tilghman restaurant's front door, you know the crabs, fish, and oysters are the freshest. After a meal at one of the local seafood houses, be sure to wander by those boats, part of the last commercial sailing fleet in North America. These beauties head out every dark winter morning to "drudge" oysters the old-fashioned way. The boats see a lot of hard work, and some of them are beautifully painted.

Tilghman is a good place to spend a day with a camera; if you want a real escape, come here for the quiet and the seafood. Bring your fishing pole; there are plenty of places on the island—not to mention charter boats for hire—if you want to cast your line.

OUTDOOR ACTIVITIES Eating isn't the *only* thing to do in Tilghman (see "Where to Dine," below). If you want to ride on a skipjack, several are available for group charters, sunset cruises, or ecotours. The *Rebecca T. Ruark,* with Wade Murphy Jr. at the helm, is the oldest working skipjack on the bay. Call © 410/829-3976 or visit www.skipjack.org. Fishing packages are available from

Harrison's Chesapeake House Sportfishing Center (© 410/886-2121; fax 410/886-2599; www.chesapeakehouse.com). Kayakers can rent equipment or take a tour with **Island Kayak** (© 410/886-2083). If you'd prefer to fish or crab yourself, call **C.R. Duck's** at © 410/886-2483 or rent a boat from **Deep Reef Small Craft Rental** at © 410/886-2545. All require advance reservations.

WHERE TO DINE

The Bridge Restaurant ★★ *Kids* SEAFOOD   You can order typical Chesapeake seafood dishes here: steamed crabs, oysters on the half shell, crab imperial. Or you could be adventurous and choose seafood cooked in a spicy coconut milk sauce, cooked with Cajun spices, or sautéed South Carolina style. If you must, there are a few meat entrees, too. Children's entrees come with games to keep them entertained and happy. Sitting at a water-view table with a plate full of creatively prepared seafood is sure to make you happy, too.

6136 Tilghman Rd., Tilghman Island. © 410/886-2330. www.bridge-restaurant.com. Reservations accepted—even for steamed crabs. Main courses $13.50–$$23.50, lunch $5–$13.50. AE, DC, DISC, MC, V. Open daily noon–10pm.

Harrison's Chesapeake House ★★★ SEAFOOD   The granddaddy of Tilghman Island restaurants is this one and there's a good reason they've been so successful: Eastern Shore hospitality and plates full of Eastern Shore fare. This family-style restaurant offers simply prepared seafood with a wonderful view of the waters from whence it came. Try the Chesapeake House Special: fried chicken, crab cakes, fresh vegetables, and homemade bread. Crab, fish, clams, oysters, or whatever else is in season, along with beef and chicken, are on the menu. Kids have their own choices, too, from fried chicken to crab cakes to PB&J, if they prefer. Harrison's also has an inn and charter fishing.

21551 Chesapeake House Dr. © 410/886-2121. www.chesapeakehouse.com. Reservations accepted. Entrees $11.95–$22.95. MC, V. Hours vary according to season, but always open weekends, closed Mon–Tues in Dec.

OXFORD

Oxford is a refined place, with a shady park and beach in the center of town. It wasn't always so quiet. One of the state's oldest towns, it was the Eastern Shore's first port of entry. In the 1700s, shipping made this a very busy place. It was home to many of Maryland's prominent citizens, including Robert Morris, a shipping agent, and his son Robert Morris, "financier of the Revolution," as well as Tench Tilghman, George Washington's aide-de-camp who carried the news of Cornwallis's surrender to the Continental Congress in Philadelphia. Tilghman is remembered with a monument in Oxford Cemetery.

Although it is quieter than St. Michael's and Tilghman Island, it's a pretty place to visit, walk, and enjoy a picnic under the trees on the serene Tred Avon River. The beach at The Strand is small and quiet enough for dipping your toes.

You can also ride the **Oxford to Bellevue Ferry** ★ (see "Getting Around," at the start of this section). This tiny ferry, one of the oldest in the country, will take you and your car across to one of the sleepiest parts of Talbot County.

The ferry runs March 1 to mid-December. Call the owners, Captains David and Valerie Bittner (© 410/745-9023), for the schedule. The fare is $4 per car and driver; 25¢ for each additional passenger, or $5.75 round-trip. Without a car the trip is 75¢ per passenger; or bring your bike for $1.50.

The country drive that follows is quiet and completely undeveloped. Of course, you also take the ferry going the other way, making Oxford your destination. What a fun way to spend a day!

OUTDOOR ACTIVITIES ON THE EASTERN SHORE

BICYCLING **St. Michaels Town Dock Marina,** 305 Mulberry St., St. Michaels (© **410/745-2400**), rents bikes for $4 an hour, $6 for 2 hours, or $16 for a full day April to November. In Oxford, stop at Mears Yacht Haven on the Strand (© **410/226-5450**), where bikes are $2.95 an hour, $9.95 half day, or $14.95 all day from April to November.

CRUISING To see the highlights of the area by boat, **Patriot Cruises Inc.,** P.O. Box 1206, St. Michaels (© **410/745-3100;** www.patriotcruises.com), offers 1-hour narrated cruises on board the *Patriot,* a 65-foot two-deck vessel with indoor and outdoor seating. The cruise plies the waters of the Miles River and the shoreline off St. Michaels, passing historic homes, waterfowl, and working watermen. Operating from April through October, the trip costs $10 for adults and $4.50 for children under 12. The boat sails from the dock next to the Chesapeake Bay Maritime Museum at 11am, 12:30pm, 2:30pm, and 4pm. If you prefer the quiet of sailboats and the beauty of sunset cruises, here are two different choices. The bronze and teak *Lady Patty,* a pretty 45-foot classic bay ketch, and the skipjack ***Herman M. Krentz*** ★ offer 2-hour cruises for $30 per person from April through October. Private half- or full-day charters are also available. The *Lady Patty* (© **800/690-5080** or 410/886-2215; www.Lazyjack inn.com or www.sailladypatty.com) leaves from the Knapps Narrows Marina April to October at 11am, 2pm, and sunset. (Call first since charter cruises can pre-empt a scheduled sail.) The *Herman M. Krentz* (© **410/745-6080;** www.oystercatcher.com) sails daily from St. Michaels between oyster seasons. Two-hour trips leave daily at 10:30am, 2pm, and sunset.

FISHING Fishing excursions on the Chesapeake are the specialty of **Harrison's Sport Fishing Center,** 21551 Chesapeake House Dr., Tilghman Island (© **410/886-2121** or 410/886-2109), a family enterprise more than 100 years old. Packages are available from $209 per person per day, including all fishing, tackle, boat transport, a room at the nautically themed Harrison's Chesapeake House Country Inn, and meals (a boxed lunch, plus a huge fisherman's breakfast and dinner at the Harrison's Chesapeake House restaurant). Depending on the time of year, the catch can include rockfish (striped bass or stripers), sea trout, blues, croakers, spot, or perch. **Albright's Sportsman's Travel Service** (© **800/474-5502**) can also help you plan your fishing trip.

GOLF The **Hog Neck Golf Course,** 10142 Old Cordova Rd., Easton (© **410/822-6079**), is rated among the top 25 U.S. public courses by *Golf Digest.* This par-72, 18-hole course and par-32, 9-hole executive course is north of town off Route 50. Rates for nonresidents are $29 Monday to Thursday and $36 on weekends, plus $14 for carts. Open February to December, weekdays 7am to sunset, and weekends 8am to sunset.

Harbourtowne Golf Resort (© **800/446-9066;** www.harbourtowne.com), in St. Michaels, is a par-70 course, designed by Pete Dye. Greens fees for hotel guests are $55; $65 for nonguests, including cart. Harbourtowne offers 1- and 2-night golf packages, too.

The Easton Club's par-72 18-hole course is open to the public. Fees are $34 for 18 holes plus $14 for cart. The course is open 8am to 7pm weekdays and 7am to 7pm weekends during peak season. Call © **800/277-9800** or see www.eastonclub.com.

HUNTING After a 6-year moratorium, hunters can once again hunt Canada geese. Maryland's Eastern Shore has long been considered the finest duck- and goose-hunting region on the Atlantic Flyway, with hundreds of thousands of migratory game birds flying through. More than 20 local organizations conduct guided waterfowl hunts for Canada geese (late Nov through late Jan), ducks (late Nov through mid-Jan), and sea ducks (early Oct through mid-Jan). Some quail and pheasant hunting is also available. White-tailed and sika deer may be hunted September to December. The Department of Natural Resources publishes an annual guide with all the regulations, including bag limits and season dates; call © **877/620-8DNR** or see www.dnr.state.md.us/wildlife/. **Albright's Sportsman's Travel Service,** 36 Dover St., Easton (© **800/474-5502** or 410/820-8811), can help plan any sort of hunting or fishing trip you have in mind.

SHOPPING

Oxford shops are usually open weekdays 10am to 6pm, and most stay open on weekends. In the winter, hours may be cut back.

Crockett Bros Boatyard, Inc. A wide selection of seafaring clothes and collectibles makes this one of the best-stocked chandleries on the Eastern Shore. The wares range from nautical necessities and yachting apparel to gifts and games. Also boat slips and boat repair. 202 Bank St., Oxford. © **410/226-5113.** www.crockettbros.com.

Oxford Mews Emporium The bikes are gone, alas, but the shop lives on selling gifts, necessities, and non-necessities. 105 S. Morris St., Oxford. © **410/820-8222.**

Silent Poetry Inspired by a 4th-century Greek poet who declared that art is "silent poetry," this shop stocks original paintings by regional artists, etchings and prints, nautical items, and decoys and carvings by local craftspeople and other gift items. 201 Tilghman St., Oxford. © **410/226-5120.**

WHERE TO STAY

Oxford Inn *Value* Surrounded by a picket fence, this circa-1900, three-story Victorian house sits beside Town Creek, close to everything. This inn is a good value; the cozy guest rooms are tastefully furnished with antiques, quilts, armoires, and dressing tables. Many rooms have window seats and/or views of the water, and families should ask for the larger third-floor suite, which is quite roomy. The only drawback is that sometimes the noise from adjoining rooms carries. A second-floor sitting room with bay windows overlooking the water has a telephone, TV, and VCR, as well as coffee and tea, sherry, and games.

504 S. Morris St. (P.O. Box 627), Oxford, MD 21654. © **410/226-5220.** www.oxfordmd.com/oxfordinn/. oxfordinn@friend.ly.net. 11 units (2 share a private bathroom). $90–$150 double. Rates include continental breakfast. 2-night minimum stay on some weekends. DISC, MC, V. **Amenities:** Pope's Treasures coffee shop with Internet connection; gift shop. *In room:* A/C.

Robert Morris Inn ★★ This historic inn overlooking the Tred Avon River was once the home of Robert Morris Jr., a financier of the American Revolution. Built in 1710 by ships' carpenters, the inn retains much of the original flooring and staircase. When author James Michener came to the Eastern Shore to write *Chesapeake,* this is where he came to eat crab cakes and outline the historical novel. The Robert Morris offers a relaxed setting, ideal for intimate weekend getaways. The romantic rooms are filled with antiques and reproductions. Bathrooms are a special feature—many rooms have large footed tubs with movable faucets and come complete with bubble bath. Though some of the rooms are small, many have separate sitting rooms, river views, and, large

Kids A Drive to Wye Mills

Three places in this hamlet make a detour worthwhile. If you bring children, this could be one of those trips they talk about for a long time. The mill, the big tree, and those hard little rolls are things that make an impression.

From Route 50, go to Route 663 to Wye Mills, about 13 miles (21km) north of Easton or about 14 miles (23km) southeast from Kent Island. This tiny burg is famous for a number of things: the Wye Mill, the Wye Oak, and Orrell's Beaten Biscuits.

Flour ground at **Wye Grist Mill** was sent to George Washington's troops at Valley Forge during the Revolutionary War. The building itself has been in operation since 1671 and is considered the earliest industrial building in Maryland. Visitors can see it in operation today, the first and third Saturdays of the month. There are guides on hand to show all the gear that made the waterwheel and grinding stones work, and they're good at explaining it on a child's level. After a visit, you can buy wheat flour or corn meal ground right here. Or take home a recipe or two. The mill is on at Route 662, off Route 50, Wye Mills (© 410/827-6909). Admission is free, but suggested donation is $2. Hours are mid-April to mid-November Monday to Friday 10am to 1pm, Saturday to Sunday 10am to 4pm.

You can't miss the **Wye Oak.** The largest white oak in the country and Maryland's official state tree, this enormous beauty is 450 years old. It was growing long before European settlers came. It dominates its own 20-acre state park at 37 feet in circumference and 96 feet high. You'll find it at 13070 Crouse Mill Rd. (© 410/634-2810). Free admission. Picnic tables and restrooms are available.

You can't leave without getting a taste an old Maryland tradition. **Orrell's Maryland Beaten Biscuits,** in business since 1935, has limited hours, but try to schedule a stop. The dough really is beaten—usually with a hammer, though the back of an ax works as well—to get the biscuits to rise. The method was used in a time when leavening was in short supply. You can even try the finished product or buy some and take them home. Orrell's is at 14124 Old Wye Mill Rd. (Rte. 662), Wye Mills, MD 21679 (© 410/827-6244; www.beatenbiscuits.com). Free admission. Open Tuesday to Wednesday (phone for hours); tours are available.

bathrooms. Two rooms are more like small apartments. There are also rooms with private porches at the Sandaway, a nearby lodge situated on a private beach. The inn's restaurant reputedly has the best crab cakes on the Eastern Shore (see "Where to Dine," below). Just across the Strand is the Oxford–Bellevue Ferry, which makes several trips daily (in-season) to nearby St. Michaels.

314 N. Morris St. and The Strand, P.O. Box 70, Oxford, MD 21654. © **410/226-5111.** Fax 410/226-5744. www.robertmorrisinn.com. 35 units. Apr–Nov $130–$280; Dec–Mar winter rates vary. AE, MC, V. **Amenities:** Restaurant; kayaks available. *In room:* A/C.

WHERE TO DINE

Robert Morris Inn ★★★ AMERICAN/SEAFOOD   Crab is the specialty here; James Michener rated the crab cakes the best on the Eastern Shore. He's right. Dating from the early 18th century, the dining room and tavern of this old inn (see "Where to Stay," above) are attractions in themselves, featuring original woodwork, slate floors, and fireplaces. The murals of the four seasons were made from wallpaper of 140 years ago. The many varieties of crab cake are exceptional: baked seafood *au gratin* cakes (crab and shrimp with Monterey Jack cheese, cheddar, and seasonings), Oxford crab cakes (seasoned, breaded, and fried), and Morris crab cakes (oven baked without the breading). Lunch items range from sandwiches and salads to omelets, burgers, seafood platters, and hot entrees. Jackets are required for men in the main dining room except from Memorial Day to Labor Day.

314 N. Morris St. and The Strand, P.O. Box 70, Oxford. © 410/226-5111. www.robertmorrisinn.com. Reservations for parties of 8 or more only accepted. Main courses $18–$34; lunch $5.74–$12.95. AE, MC, V. May–Nov daily 8am–10am, noon–3pm, 3–8:30 for light fare in the taproom and 5:30–8:30pm. Closed Dec–Mar.

Schooner's Llanding SEAFOOD   Yes, the spelling is correct; it's an old Welsh spelling of "landing." This informal spot is on a marina with great views of the water and tables on the deck in season. Schooner's offers prime rib, crab, oyster, and shrimp; sandwiches; seafood soups; and catch-of-the-day specials. It's a good place for lunch or for a boisterous evening of telling sailing stories, aided by several draft beer options. Seafood entrees are fairly good though some complain they're overpriced. A champagne brunch is offered on Sunday.

Foot of Tilghman St., Oxford. © **410/226-0160**. No reservations accepted. Main courses $10.95–$22.95; lunch $4.95–$10.95. MC, V. Sun–Mon and Wed–Thurs 11:30am–3pm, 5–9:30pm; Fri–Sat 11:30am–10pm; but hours vary in winter.

CAMBRIDGE

Cambridge lies just across the Choptank River Bridge. It's a sleepy town, far quieter than Easton or St. Michaels. High Street leads to the Choptank—a lovely stroll with a great water view at the end. History buffs, especially those interested in the Civil War era, may be interested in the town's connections with the Underground Railroad. Nature-lovers find it a nice stop on their way to Blackwater Refuge or to a hunting or fishing trip. Visitors planning a mid-shore visit to Easton, St. Michaels, and Tilghman may prefer this quiet place as a base.

Since its foundation in 1684, Cambridge has drawn those who love the water and the earth. Once a harbor for trading ships taking tobacco to England and later a deepwater port for 20th-century freighters, Cambridge was also a ship-building town. Skipjacks, bugeyes, and log canoes were made here. The town still draws boaters—but now they are pleasure boaters.

In its prosperity in colonial times and again in the early 20th century, Cambridge became the home of governors, lawyers, and landowners. Their beautiful homes line High Street, Water Street, Mill Street, and Hambrooks Boulevard. Sharpshooter Annie Oakley built her house at 28 Bellevue Ave. on Hambrooks Bay. The roofline was altered so Oakley could step outside her second-story windows and shoot waterfowl coming in over the bay. The house is privately owned, but the owners have erected a small sign in Annie's memory.

Harriet Tubman's home no longer exists but she often walked the streets and country roads around here as she led more than 300 slaves to freedom on the

"Underground Railroad." She is remembered in monuments, markers, a museum in Cambridge, and a driving tour.

Anyone who has read James Michener's *Chesapeake* or John Barth's *Sotweed Factor* may recognize some of the places they read about—this is one of the towns to inspire these novels.

ESSENTIALS

GETTING THERE   Come by boat (your own, there aren't any ferries)—from the Chesapeake Bay east on the Choptank River—or come by car. Cambridge is on Route 50, 15 miles (24km) south of Easton. Once you cross the Sen. Frederick Malkus Bridge over the Choptank, you're there. The historic district is east of the highway, called Ocean Gateway here.

VISITOR INFORMATION   In Sailwinds Park, just east of the bridge at 2 Rose Hill Place, the **Route 50 Visitors Center** is full of information and staff who can provide information about Cambridge and some of the quaint, small—and I mean small—towns surrounding it, as well as the Blackwater National Wildlife Refuge south of town. Call © **410/228-1000** or visit www. tourdorchester.org.

GETTING AROUND   The quickest way to get around is by car but since the area is so flat, many prefer bicycle. The roads are fairly quiet, making it a pleasure to drive or bike.

At the visitor center, be sure to get a couple of good brochures. *Historic Walking Tour of Cambridge* shows visitors around some of the most significant buildings, houses, and churches in town. The pocket-sized *Museum Guide, A Passport to History* describes seven museums around town and has directions to the outlying Dorchester Heritage Museum and the Spocott Windmill Complex. (Don't miss this, especially if you're a kid.)

WHAT TO SEE & DO

Historic High Street ⚓, which ends at the Long Wharf, is lined with 19th-century homes from a variety of periods, including French Second Empire, Queen Anne, and Federal. An informative brochure offers details about the history of these homes, most of which are privately owned. Stop in the **Dorchester Arts Center,** 120 High St. (© **410/228-7782**), to see the exhibits, which change monthly, and browse the gift shop. Both feature local artists and artisans. Volunteer docents staff the center Monday to Saturday 10am to 2pm.

At Long Wharf, check out the *Nathan of Dorchester* (© **410/228-7141;** www.skipjack-nathan.org), a living museum built by local volunteers. Visitors can even sail the 63-foot skipjack and learn how to handle her. Saturday walk-on cruises are offered twice a month in June, July, and August. Cruises on the Choptank last 2 hours. Just stop by or call for a reservation.

Brannock Maritime Museum   This is at the Commodore's Cottage B&B and its artifacts have been lovingly collected and displayed by the Brannocks themselves. There are ship models, captain's caps, and books and photos that tell the story of Cambridge's shipbuilding industry from colonial times to recent merchant marine days, along with memories of past wars. Ask about the photos of Japanese sailors planning the attack on Pearl Harbor. There's also an extensive library often in use by people researching their families or maybe a book.

215 Talbot Ave., Cambridge. © **410/228-1245.** Open daily by appointment or Fri–Sat 10am–4pm, Sun 1:30–4pm.

Neild Museum and Herb Garden This is one of several museums operated by the Dorchester County Historical Society. This museum focuses on agricultural history of the county, including a colonial herb garden.

902 LaGrange Ave. ℰ **410/228-21613**. daviddelaria@hotmail.com. Open Thurs, Fri, Sat 10am–3pm.

James B. Richardson Maritime Museum Come here to find out what a bugeye is or how a log canoe sails or what a skipjack was built to do. With builder's models, hand tools, and building plans, the museum focuses on all the boats used on the Chesapeake Bay for fishing, oystering, and trading.

410 High St. ℰ **410/228-3967** or 410/228-4185. Free admission. Open Wed, Sat, Sun 1–4pm.

The Underground Railroad Gift Shop/Museum This pays tribute to Harriet Tubman, a former slave known for her part in the Underground Railroad. The small storefront museum offers tours of places in Dorchester County where she lived, prayed, and worked. Only a few of the actual buildings still exist, but tour guides use the locations to tell stories about Tubman's life and efforts.

424 Race St. ℰ **410/228-0401** or 410/228-3106. tubman@shorenet.net. Free admission. Mon–Fri 9am–5pm.

OUTSIDE OF TOWN

A side trip worth taking is to see the **Spocott Windmill** ★★. It isn't far from Cambridge, 7 miles (11km) west of town on Route 343. The windmill, the only existing post windmill for grinding grain left in Maryland, is still operated at least twice a year. It's not the original—three others have been on this site since the 1700s. This one was built in 1972 by shipbuilder James Richardson who also built the replica of *The Dove,* one of two ships that brought the first settlers in Maryland in 1634. That ship is docked in St. Mary's City.

Also at the site are three other historic buildings. These include a **tenant house,** a humble 1½-story wood dwelling built about 1800; and **Castle Haven School House,** a one-room schoolhouse built in 1870, which has photographs of the students who attended in the early part of the 20th century. Both were moved here from other parts of the county. The schoolhouse exhibits include rosters of past classes and photos of teachers. Research is underway to learn more about Adeline Wheatley, who lived in the tenant house for 50 years. Her husband Columbus was a Union soldier during the Civil War. A country Museum Store open by appointment only evokes an old-time feeling with the potbellied stove surrounded by benches, cases filled with World War II–era merchandise, and a model of the windmill.

The sites are on Hudson Road (Rte. 343) and are open seven days a week, 9am to 5pm. Admission is free. Call ℰ **410/228-7090** to make arrangements for tour guides (available by appointment).

The **Dorchester Heritage Museum at** 1904 Horn Point Rd. (ℰ **410/228-1899**) is also a short drive from Cambridge. The tiny converted aircraft hangar features tools for farming and fishing as well as antique toys, Native American artifacts, a waterfowl exhibit, and an archaeological dig of a 1608 home. It is connected by breezeway to a pilot's house that features a 1914 kitchen with a broom machine. It's open April 15 to October 31 on Saturday and Sunday.

A VISIT TO A NATURAL REFUGE

Blackwater National Wildlife Refuge ★★★, just 12 miles (19km) south of Cambridge, gives waterfowl a place to land and bald eagles and endangered

Delmarva fox squirrels a safe haven. It gives humans a place to stand in awe of nature. Some 23,000 acres of marsh, freshwater ponds, river, forest, and field were set aside in 1933 for the migratory birds which use the Atlantic Flyway.

The most popular time to visit Blackwater is autumn. During fall migration, which peaks in November, some 35,000 geese fill the refuge; 15,000 ducks join them. An enormous variety of birds come: mallards, black ducks, blue-winged teals, wood ducks, widgeons, and pintails. Blackwater's free open house held the second weekend in October is a great time to see some of the refuge's residents up close. Programs held throughout the day focus on the birds, including peregrine falcons, and on the wildlife, including deer, fox squirrels, and nutria.

Winter is the best time to see the bald eagles. Some 18 nesting pairs have set up homes high in the trees, the greatest number of bald eagles on the east coast north of Florida. As many as 150 eagles have been seen at Blackwater. Golden eagles stop by in winter, too, though sightings are rare.

Visitors in the spring will see lots of birds headed north. Marsh and shorebirds arrive, as do the ospreys who to set up house for their new families. The ospreys, or "fish hawks," build huge nests on platforms in the middle of the marsh. They swoop and dive into the water for fish and then fly back to feed their noisy offspring. A note for eagle fans: An Eagle Festival is held in March.

If that isn't enough nature, in spring 2002 the Dorchester Garden Club will dedicate a new butterfly garden near the visitor center.

In summer, birders can find warblers, orioles, blue herons, and even wild turkeys. (Be prepared: Biting bugs, such as flies and mosquitoes, can be fierce here in summer. Wear a hat and be on the lookout for ticks in early summer.)

VISITOR CENTER   The visitor center is located off Key Wallace Drive. It's open year-round Monday through Friday 8am to 4pm and weekends from 9am to 5pm. Staff members can provide all kinds of information, including maps, bird lists, and calendars of events. A small exhibit explains who lives at the refuge and a huge picture window gives visitors a view of the geese and other waterfowl browsing in the field behind the center. Look for the real-time camera trained on the osprey nest. Since the nests are pretty high, most people don't get to see inside one of these. Ospreys live here only in the spring and summer. There are plans to mount a camera above an eagle's nest in 2002.

GETTING THERE   From Route 50, take Route 16 southwest out of Cambridge, and turn south on Route 335. Turn right onto Key Wallace Drive and right again into the visitor center.

FEES & REGULATIONS   Admission is $3 per vehicle and $1 per pedestrian or cyclist. (Fee allows entry of all accompanying family if on foot or bicycle.) Pets are not permitted on the trails but are allowed—on leashes—on the wildlife drive.

A WILDLIFE DRIVE   Though the refuge belongs to the wildlife, the park has set aside hiking paths and a short wildlife drive for cars and bicycles so visitors may see and hear these amazing crowds of birds. These are open dawn to dusk. After paying the admission at a self-service pay station, visitors reach a fork in the road about a third of a mile into the drive. Turn left for the Marsh Edge Trail and Observation Site. Then head back to up the road for the rest of the drive.

The 5-mile (8km) ride meanders past pools and marshes and through woodlands. Much of the drive is through flat marshes that stretch to the horizon. It's quiet, except for the buzzing insects and calling birds. Bring your binoculars and camera. You may see any number of birds, deer, or even the rare Delmarva fox squirrel.

Want to stretch your legs and see everything a little more closely? You can park at one of the two walking trails. **Woods Trail** is a half-mile (0.8km) long and runs through a mature forest. **Marsh Edge Trail** is a third of a mile (0.5km) and begins in the woods and ends with an 80-foot (24m) boardwalk extending into Little Blackwater River. If you visit in the spring or summer, look for the osprey. In the fall, you'll see the waterfowl.

An observation site has been set up at the end of this part of the drive with an information kiosk. The view over the Blackwater River is incredible, and the sights and sounds of all those migrating waterfowl can be awe-inspiring. In the fall and winter of 2001, work was underway for a new photo blind at the edge of a pond and connected by a boardwalk to the drive overlooking the Little Blackwater River. Ask about it at the visitor center.

OTHER OUTDOOR ACTIVITIES

BIKING　　The 5-mile (8km) wildlife drive is an easy ride on flat, mostly quiet roads. If you plan to bike from Cambridge (about 10 miles/16km) or Vienna (about 15 miles/24km), bring water and anything else you might need because there aren't many places to stock up between Cambridge and Blackwater. Before you go, get a "Cycling Trails of Dorchester County" map (available at the visitor center in Cambridge, or call ℂ **800/522-TOUR** or 410/228-1000; www.tourdorchester.org). In addition, Blackwater has its own bike map with two suggested loops. One 20-mile (32km) loop takes bicyclists from Cambridge's public high school into the refuge. A 5-mile loop crosses the refuge in two locations while winding through several miles of beautiful country roads. Ask about that at the visitor center.

BIRDING　　The refuge offers bird walks on weekend mornings throughout the year. They last about 2 hours. Meet at the visitor center.

BOATING & FISHING　　A launching ramp for canoes and kayaks is open from April 1 to September 30. Get a "Water Trails of Dorchester County" map (available at the visitor center in Cambridge, or call ℂ **800/522-TOUR** or 410/ 228-1000; www.tourdorchester.org). Several local groups rent canoes and kayaks or offer tours.

Fishing and crabbing are also permitted from April 1 to September 30 from small boats and bridges, but note that state laws apply here. A state sportfishing license is required for fishing in the Blackwater and Little Blackwater rivers. No fishing is allowed from the shores.

HUNTING　　Deer hunting for both white-tailed and sika deer is allowed in the refuge, but is quite limited. Hunters must mail in applications between July 1 and September 15. Only 415 hunters are be allowed each day. Locations and dates are limited. Archery permits are more readily available with many more dates for hunting available. Hunting licenses are required as well as valid archery, youth, muzzleloader, or shotgun hunt permits. For applications and all the regulations, write to **Blackwater Refuge Hunts,** 2145 Key Wallace Dr., Cambridge, MD 21613; or pick up an application at the visitor center beginning July 1. Archery permits are available after September 15 on a daily basis, at 2145 Key Wallace Dr., off Route 335 (ℂ **410/228-2677**; www.fws.gov). Admission is $3 per car or $1 for pedestrians or bicyclists. Admission is free to anyone holding a federal duck stamp or a Golden Eagle Passport, a Golden Age Passport, or a Blackwater National Wildlife Refuge Pass. The fee is good all day.

SHOPPING

Cambridge is not about shopping—stores cater to locals who need groceries, and sundries. Quaint shops are scarce; if that's what you're looking for, head to Easton and St. Michaels. **Bay Country Shop,** Route 50, a half-mile south of the Choptank River Bridge (© **800/467-2046** or 410/221-0700), offers some mementoes with Eastern Shore flair. This shop is filled with everything with a duck or goose on it: clothing, artwork, decoys, and home decor. If you like model boats, stop here; their sailing ships are built by local craftspeople. Hours are Monday to Saturday from 10am to 6:30pm and Sunday from 1 to 5pm.

TOURS

Muddy Marsh Outfitters (© **410/228-2770;** sikadeer@muddymarsh.com) offers canoe and kayak tours, both guided and unguided, and rentals. **Loblolly Landings and Lodge,** 2142 Liners Rd., Church Creek (© **410/397-3033;** www.loblollylandingsbandb.com) also rents canoes and kayaks; half-day and full-day rentals range from $15 to $35; a bicycle rents for $10 a day.

   Crabmania Tour ✖, offered June through mid-October by the county Department of Tourism, gives visitors a chance to spend a day learning about the life of a waterman. It starts with a ride aboard the 47-foot *Cambridge Lady* to cruise the Choptank River while learning the history of the Chesapeake. Tour stops include Hoopers Island, the A. E. Phillips Crab Processing Plant, lunch at a local restaurant, Blackwater National Wildlife Refuge, and historic Cambridge. The tour costs about $45 a person. Call © **800/894-5806** for reservations.

WHERE TO STAY

The big news in Cambridge is the Hyatt. Designed to be a destination in itself, this brand-new resort on 342 acres on the Choptank River opened in March 2002. There are also a couple of hotels on Route 50 worth checking into. Cambridge also has some beautiful B&Bs. The visitor center can lead you to some, and I've included a few nice ones below.

Cambridge House ✖ This Queen Anne–style sea captain's mansion, next to Long Wharf, puts visitors in the middle of Cambridge's most beautiful street. Rest and watch the tourists go by as you sit on the inn's front porch or get away from it all in the Victorian gardens. Its elegant rooms feature queen- and king-sized beds, fireplaces in some of the rooms, and formal breakfast each morning either in the dining room or on that porch.

112 High St., Cambridge, MD 21613. © 410/221-7700. www.cambridgehousebandb.com. 6 units. $120 double. Rates include breakfast and high tea at 3pm for guests only. AE, MC, V. *In room:* A/C.

The Cambridge Inn Don't judge this hotel by its worn exterior or lobby; it offers clean, spare rooms, recently updated. Built in 1986 as an Econo Lodge, it's independently owned now. Rooms are reached by indoor corridors on two floors. It's certainly not a place to go out of your way for, but it's fine for staying the night with the kids and even a pet.

Ocean Gateway, Cambridge, MD. © 410/221-0800. www.marylandcambridgeinn.com. 96 units. Weekend $50–$89; weekdays $50 single, $60 double. AE, DISC, MC, V. **Amenities:** Bar; indoor pool; coffee in lobby 24 hours a day. *In room:* A/C, dataport, hair dryer and iron available at front desk.

Commodore's Cottage ✖ *Kids* This is two comfortable homes set in the shaded garden of a 1916 home. One, the home's original carriage house, has one bedroom with a king canopy bed and a queen sleeper sofa in the living room. There's a dining room and a kitchen, too. Earl and Shirley Brannock, Cambridge natives, built the second cottage with room for six. It has two bedrooms, a huge living room with a bay window, and its own patio. It has its own kitchen, too, but the Brannocks deliver an extended continental breakfast to the cottages each morning. The neighborhood itself is charming, with big, old houses facing tree-lined streets. There's a maritime museum on the property.

215 Glenburn Ave., Cambridge, MD 21613. ℂ **800/228-6938** or 410/228-6938. 2 cottages. $85–$95 double, $15 per additional person though children under age 6 are free. Rates include continental breakfast. MC, V. **Amenities:** Garden; maritime museum. *In room:* A/C.

Glasgow Inn ★★ This 1760 whitewashed brick house on the National Register of Historic Places lies at the end of a row of reproduction colonial bungalows. But it's the real thing, a plantation house that once had commanding views of Hambrooks Bay. Though there are houses built between the Glasgow Inn and the water now, the setting in a 3-acre park is relaxing. The house, which has its Christmas tree decorated in the center hall year round, has big, comfortable rooms on three floors. The third floor with its slanted ceilings and dormer windows has great views—but taller guests may want the headroom offered by rooms on the other two floors. The rooms share hall bathrooms, except the only room with a king-sized bed. If the house is filled up, a small bungalow just up the road has three more rooms. Every room is simply furnished and comfortable—forget the fragile antiques here. Quilts on the beds add a warm, homey touch.

1500 Hambrooks Blvd., Cambridge, MD 21613. ℂ **410/228-0575.** 10 units. $100–$150 double. Credit cards accepted only to hold a reservation; bill must be paid with check, cash, or traveler's check. Rates include full country breakfast. *In room:* A/C, TV in some rooms, phone outlets but no phones in rooms.

Holiday Inn Express ★ Except for the Hyatt, it's Cambridge's newest hotel at 2 years old. The staff gives this chain hotel an Eastern Shore hospitality. The Jacuzzi rooms combine the usual room with a tub big enough for two right next to the king-size bed. For romantic getaways, robes hang in the closet, and flowers and a box of candy arrive before the guests. For everybody else, there's a bowl of fruit in the lobby, a big-screen TV, and a microwave in the breakfast area by the pool. Golf packages with the Hyatt's golf course are planned, and restaurant-hotel packages for New Year's. Details were not set at press time.

2715 Ocean Gateway, Cambridge, MD. ℂ **877/432-7832** or 410/221-9900. www.hiexpresscambridge.com. 86 units, including 4 Jacuzzi rooms. $89–$199 double. Rate includes continental breakfast. AE, DC, DISC, MC, V. Baby cribs free; rollaway cots available for about $10. **Amenities:** Pool; exercise room; spa. *In room:* A/C, dataport, coffeemaker, hair dryer, iron.

Hyatt Regency Chesapeake Bay ★★ This brand new resort on 342 acres on the Choptank River opened in March 2002. The facilities go beyond any other resort in the area, with enough amenities to keep families occupied on site, as well as a variety of packages take advantage of the surrounding countryside: area hunting and Blackwater packages, for instance. Its European-style spa, restaurants, marina, and 18-hole golf course designed by Keith Foster are open to the general public.

2800 Ocean Gateway, Cambridge. ℂ **800/233-1234** or 410/901-1234. www.hyatt.com. 400 units, including 16 suites and 40 "mini-suites." $325 double. AE, DC, DISC, MC, V. Call for policy on pets. **Amenities:** 5 restaurants; 2 bars; general store; indoor pool; 2 outdoor pools; 18-hole golf course; 4 tennis courts; beach; bicycle and water sports equipment rental; 150-slip marina; health club; Camp Hyatt children's program; business center; massage. *In room:* TV with movies and games, dataport, fridge, coffeemaker, hair dryer, iron.

WHERE TO DINE

Snappers Waterfront Café ★★ SEAFOOD/INTERNATIONAL   Come for the crab dip, served in a crusty French loaf. Add a couple of friends or your family, a cold drink, and a view of Cambridge Creek. You're going to like it here. The casual cafe, with a deck overlooking the creek, has an enormous menu. There's lots of seafood, Jamaican jerk chicken, pastas, and quesadillas, even an Italian night on Thursdays. Kids have a menu of their own—and a couple of video games they'll like just past the front door. Sunday brunch is offered 11am to 3pm—but no champagne or bloody Marys until after noon, thanks to the liquor laws. Snappers is a casual, come-as-you-are kind of a place with friendly staff.

112 Commerce St., Cambridge, MD 21613. ✆ 410/228-0112. Reservations only for 5 or more, recommended Fri and Sat. Main courses $6.95–$26.95, lunch $4.75–$12.75. AE, DC, DISC, MC, V. Open daily, Labor Day to Memorial Day 11am–9pm, summer 11am–10pm.

Suicide Bridge Restaurant ★ SEAFOOD   This is the place to be on a Saturday night. The lobby, bar, and benches outside are filled with people waiting as long as 45 minutes for their turn at fresh seafood and crab cakes. It's popular for good reason. A few chicken and steak dishes are on offer, but the very fresh seafood here is cooked simply and well. Its popularity makes service a little slow sometimes, so come with your patience. Although there are no reservations, diners can call for "preferred seating" and that puts them at the top of the wait list for the time they say they're arriving—that can cut the wait to less time than you can have a drink. The restaurant overlooks the suicide bridge—its sad history is printed on the menu—and has a marina for those who sail to dinner. Boats must be less than 50 feet tall to fit under the Choptank River Bridge. Picture windows on both floors allow diners to enjoy the sunset while enjoying dinner.

The restaurant also operates the *Dorothy-Megan,* an 80-foot paddle wheeler, for 2-hour lunch and 3-hour dinner cruises. Lunch cruises cost about $28. Dinner cruises cost about $40. Sightseeing only is $12. Call ✆ 410/943-4775 for schedules and rates.

6304 Suicide Bridge Rd., Hurlock. ✆ 410/943-4689. Fax 410/943-1663. www.suicidebridge.com. Reservations not accepted but a priority seating system is in place. Main courses $12.95–$28.95, kids' menu $3.95–$4.95. MC, V. Open Apr–Dec, Tues and Wed 11am–9pm, Fri and Sat 11am–10pm, Sun noon–10pm.

2 Chestertown

55 miles (89km) E of Baltimore, 70 miles (113km) NE of Washington, D.C., 50 miles (81km) SW of Wilmington

Chestertown, founded in 1706 on a hill overlooking the Chester River, exudes history and beauty. Walk down Water Street and High Street to see the, ornate brick homes, many of which date from the mid-1700s, when this was a great port that rivaled Annapolis. You can drive across the Chester River bridge and see the grand sea captains' homes and, if it's in town, the pretty yellow reproduction of the schooner *Sultana.* Now, this once-thriving seaport is a quiet retreat for vacationers. Area attractions are limited. The town can be seen in 1 day, but pilgrimages to Eastern Neck National Wildlife Refuge or Rock Hall, or further south to Talbot County, can fill a weekend. Chestertown is also home to Washington College, established in 1782.

ESSENTIALS

GETTING THERE The only way to get to Chestertown is by car. From Easton, follow U.S. Route 50 north to Route 213 and then follow Route 213 north into Chestertown. From I-95 and U.S. Route 40, take the Elkton exit and follow Route 213 south into Chestertown.

VISITOR INFORMATION For a map and travel brochures about Chestertown and the surrounding area, contact the **Kent County Office of Tourism,** 400 High St., Chestertown, MD 21620 (*C* **410/778-0416;** www.kentcounty. com). The office is open for walk-in visitors Monday through Friday 9am to 4pm.

GETTING AROUND Since there is no public transport in Chestertown, touring by car or walking through the historic streets are the best ways to see the sights. High Street is Chestertown's main thoroughfare. A self-guided driving tour and walking tour brochure is available from the tourism office.

SPECIAL EVENTS On Memorial Day weekend each year, Chestertown reenacts one of its contributions to the cause of independence, the **Chestertown Tea Party** ★★. On May 23, 1774, after hearing of the closing of the port of Boston, Chestertown citizens boarded a British ship in the harbor and tossed its tea overboard. The festival—which gets bigger every year—includes a reenactment, boat rides, colonial parades with costumed participants, crafts, buggy rides, and ragtime bands. For information, call *C* **410/778-0416.**

WHAT TO SEE & DO

Take a walk down High Street and across Water. The neatly laid out streets are lined with gracious brick townhouses, built by shipbuilders, lawyers, merchants, and naval officers. On High, make sure to stop near the **White Swan Tavern,** 231 High St. George Washington used to stop here when he was visiting the town. It was restored in the 1970s, and is open for tours most afternoons. Call *C* **410/778-2300.** The **Geddes–Piper House,** down Church Alley, is impressive. It's open on Saturday and Sunday from 1 to 4pm for a $3 donation. (Call the Kent County Historical Society at *C* **410/778-3499.**) The **Courthouse,** on Cross Street, stands on the site of a 1706 courthouse and jail. Down Water are some of the most beautiful houses: **Widehall,** the **Hynson–Ringgold House,** and the **River House.** If you've been to Winterthur, you've seen paneling and woodworks removed from this house for the Chestertown Room.

The Kent County Office of Tourism has some great brochures about the area, with information about walking and driving tours. One explains the differences between Georgian, Federal, and Queen Anne styles for the architecturally challenged. (Plaques also offer hints to the buildings' significance.)

If you like trees or you need an excuse for walking around Washington College, check out the **Virginia Gent Decker Arboretum.** It's really not a park because the trees have been planted along college walkways. The various trees—from Japanese pagoda trees to American lindens—have been labeled and are located on a map available on campus. Call *C* **800/422-1782,** ext. 7726, or 410/778-7726, or visit the website at http://arboretum.washcoll.edu.

Southwest of Chestertown is the old, tiny town of **Rock Hall,** which sits right on the Chesapeake, across from Annapolis and Baltimore. Boaters have considered this a good place to stop for the night for a long time. In fact, in colonial times, Rock Hall was *the* place to stop on the way to Philadelphia. George Washington, Thomas Jefferson, and James Madison all stopped here.

In the 21st century, lots of new people are stopping here. Many boaters take advantage of the terrific marinas and the picturesque Rock Hall Harbor. Shops, restaurants, and small inns are beginning to appear, too. Rock Hall looks like it will be the next St. Michaels, and heaven knows the Eastern Shore—and Maryland—will always welcome another pretty weekend destination.

About halfway between Chestertown and Rock Hall, off Route 20, is **St. Paul's Church,** erected in 1713 and one of Maryland's oldest churches in continuous use. The church is open daily 9am to 5pm; donations are welcome. The church served as a barracks for British soldiers during the War of 1812. Actress Tallulah Bankhead is buried in the church cemetery.

Just south of Rock Hall, **Eastern Neck National Wildlife Refuge** is little known—but that's okay with the bird-watchers and nature lovers who come here. Migrating waterfowl rest here for the winter, and butterflies heading to South America for the winter. The refuge's website even has a toll-free phone number (© **877/477-9267**), so tundra swan fans can keep on top of their arrival here. Like Blackwater National Wildlife Refuge near Cambridge, this wooded island is a winter haven for migratory birds, from Canada geese to the large tundra swan. The four walking trails and one handicapped-accessible boardwalk are a nice diversion. In spring and fall, bald eagle sightings are not uncommon. It's at 1730 Eastern Neck Rd., Rock Hall (© **410/639-7056;** www.easternneck.fws.gov).

SHOPPING

From antiques to New Age books, High, Cross, and Cannon streets are lined with enticing shops. Most stores are open during the week and on Saturday from 9 or 10am until 5pm. A few stores are open Sunday, but most are closed.

Blue Heron Antiques and Collectibles, 204 High St. (© **410/778-8118**), is one of the larger and more reasonably priced antiques stores, offering several small rooms of mainly glassware, dishes, frames, and artwork. Some furniture and unusual pieces can also be found. It's open every day. A few doors away, the **Kerns Collection, Ltd.,** 210 High St. (© **410/778-4044**), displays contemporary prints, clocks, lamps, ties, clothing, jewelry, and accessories—all by designers or artists—in a gallery setting. Pieces range from the sophisticated (sleek cobalt and gold decorative bowls) to the humorous (papier-mâché dog-shaped wall clocks).

For a peek at a craftsperson in action, step inside the **Chester River Knitting Company,** 306 Cannon St. (© **800/881-0045** or 410/778-0374; www.sweater makers.com), where Bill and Beth Ruckelshaus produce hand-framed cotton, wool, and cashmere sweaters with distinctive designs, such as a crab or waterfowl motif, or knit to order. Leather accessories are also available.

Twigs and Teacups, 111 S. Cross St. (© **410/778-1708**), lives up to its name by carrying a huge assortment of gifts including stationery, books, soaps, bathroom accessories, toys, pottery, joke items, and (of course) teas, coffees, and teacups. Sit down and have a cup of tea across the street at **Play It Again Sam,** 108 S. Cross St. (© **410/778-2688**), a popular coffeehouse that serves salads, sandwiches, and homemade desserts and sells antiques and a few CDs.

The **Compleat Bookseller,** 301 High St. (© **410/778-1480**), one of the better bookstores on the Eastern Shore, offers a collection of classics, children's books, and bestsellers. It's where to find books of local interest, from histories of the Oyster Wars to coffee-table books about the Shore.

If you're up for a shopping trip outside of town, **Dixon's Auction Sales,** about 10 miles (16km) northeast of Chestertown at Routes 544 and 290, Crumpton

(© **410/928-3006**), has weekly outdoor furniture auctions spread over 15 acres. Inside a large barnlike structure, smaller items are auctioned. You might find antiques, brass doorknobs, 19th-century harpoons, musical instruments, or records. Auctions are held every Wednesday from 9am until the last item is sold.

WHERE TO STAY

Brampton Inn ★★   A curving tree-lined driveway leads to this three-story redbrick inn, a mile southwest of town (off Rte. 20). Built in 1860 and listed |on the National Register of Historic Places, it sits on 35 acres surrounded by gentle hills and farmland. Guests enjoy the use of two sitting rooms, a wide front porch, and extensive spruce-shaded grounds with lawn furniture. Rooms are furnished with authentic period antiques and canopy or four-poster beds; all have private bathrooms, five with whirlpools. Nine rooms have fireplaces. The suites have a sitting room and private TV. Afternoon tea is served every day.

25227 Chestertown Rd., Chestertown, MD 21620. © **866/305-1860** or 410/778-1860. www.brampton inn.com. 10 units. $125–$225 double; $185–$225 suite. Rates include full breakfast. 2-night minimum stay on weekends and 3-night minimum stay on holiday weekends. DISC, MC, V. *In room:* A/C, hair dryer, iron.

Imperial Hotel ★★   With a fanciful gingerbread-trimmed triple-porch facade, this three-story brick building is a focal point along the main street of Chestertown. The interior includes a Victorian-style restaurant (see "Where to Dine," below), parlor and lounge/bar, and courtyard garden. Guest rooms are furnished with brass beds, period antiques, armoires, and colorful wallpapers. One suite is on the third floor with a private porch, parlor, and kitchen; the other occupies the top floor of an adjacent 18th-century carriage house.

208 High St., Chestertown, MD 21620. © **410/778-5000.** Fax 410/778-9662. www.imperialchester town.com. 13 units. $95–$150 double; $150–$200 suite. Rates include continental breakfast. AE, MC, V. **Amenities:** Restaurant. *In room:* TV, hair dryer and iron available.

Inn at Mitchell House   If you are looking for a quiet Old World retreat surrounded by remote farmland and habitats for birds, migrating geese, white-tailed deer, and red fox, try this three-story 1743 manor house with a screened-in porch. Nestled on 10 acres overlooking Stoneybrook Pond, it sits midway between Chestertown and Rock Hall off Routes 21 and 445; Tolchester marina is half a mile away. The guest rooms, named for historic people or places, are furnished with four-poster beds, hooked rugs, antiques, and framed old prints. Most rooms have a fireplace or sitting area; all have private bathrooms. On Friday and Saturday nights, dinner is also available to guests in the dining room (reservations are required 24 hours in advance).

8796 Maryland Pkwy., Chestertown, MD 21620. © **410/778-6500.** www.chestertown.com/mitchell. 6 units. $95–$120 double. Rates include breakfast. MC, V. **Amenities:** Dinner served Fri and Sat (reservations required). *In room:* A/C.

Lauretum Inn   Crowning a 6-acre spot on a shady knoll at the edge of town, this three-story 1881 Queen Anne Victorian (listed on the National Register of Historic Places) was named Lauretum, meaning "Laurel Grove" in Latin, by its first owner, Harrison Vickers. The downstairs decor—fully restored—is lovely, featuring a formal parlor with painted ceiling medallion and fireplace, reading room, screened porch, and sitting room, all open to guests. The rooms are bright and large. All have private bathrooms. Every room has a TV for viewing videos from the inn's 600-movie library.

954 High St. (Rte. 20), Chestertown, MD 21620. © **800/742-3236.** www.chestertown.com/lauretum. 5 units. $65–$140 double. Rates include continental breakfast. AE, DISC, MC, V. *In room:* A/C, TV/VCR, hair dryer, iron.

WHERE TO DINE

The Feast of Reason *Value* SANDWICHES   This airy little sandwich shop is a favorite of the college crowd and a great place to grab a bite while touring the historic district. The menu changes daily but you can always expect tasty gourmet sandwiches, soups, and salads.

203 High St. (across from the Imperial Hotel). © **410/778-3828.** Sandwiches $4.25–$5. No credit cards. Mon–Sat 10am–4pm.

Imperial Hotel ★★ AMERICAN   This inn offers fine cuisine and an elegant ambience in two intimate dining rooms: the Hubbard Room and the Barroll Room. Seating is also available on the patio in the summer (with live jazz some weekend evenings). The menu changes seasonally, but house favorites often include a selection of seared seafood and roasted meats, all accompanied by seasonal vegetables. When it's in season, the rockfish is delectable. Sunday lunch offers the same kinds of foods: quail, scallop, and tuna salad; and risotto with lobster and spinach were on a recent menu, along with several egg dishes.

208 High St. © **410/778-5000.** Reservations suggested. Main courses $16–$28; lunch $12–$18. AE, MC, V. Fri–Sat 5:30–9:30pm; Wed–Thurs 5:30–9pm; Sun noon–3pm, lunch only.

Old Wharf Inn *Finds* AMERICAN/SEAFOOD   Locals come here for good value and good views of the Chester River. The food is simply prepared, though not as dazzling as the view. The restaurant has an informal "Old Chesapeake" atmosphere, with captain's chairs, ceiling fans, a row of paned windows overlooking the water, and ships' wheels adapted into lighting fixtures. The menu features Eastern Shore traditions such as fried chicken, Smithfield ham, crab cakes, clams, and several kinds of shrimp dishes (from fried and coconut battered to scampi). Monday through Thursday nights offer changing dinner specials for $10.95. Sunday brunch offers everything from eggs Benedict to crab cakes. The inn is usually crowded, so come early.

98 Cannon St. (on the water). © **410/778-3566.** Fax 410/778-2989. Reservations not accepted. Main courses $8.25–$19.50; lunch $3.75–$14.25. AE, MC, V. Daily 11am–9pm.

CHESTERTOWN AFTER DARK

Although there really isn't what could be called "nightlife" in Chestertown, there is one local hot spot. **Andy's**, 337½ High St. (© **410/778-6779;** www.andys-c town.com), features live music—everything from rock to jazz to bluegrass, usually with a cover charge, on Friday and Saturday nights starting around 8:30pm in a back room filled with couches, chairs, and a fireplace. The bar carries several local microbrews on tap. They've just added a nonsmoking brick lounge, too. The atmosphere is low-key with most age groups represented.

3 Chesapeake City

54 miles (87km) NE of Baltimore, 40 miles (64km) SW of Wilmington, 25 miles (40km) NE of Chestertown

The first thing you notice when driving over the Chesapeake and Delaware (C&D) Canal Bridge is the fascinating view of the canal itself. With a width of 800 feet, private boats and commercial ships use this connection between the Chesapeake Bay and Delaware River, passing the small, historic town of Chesapeake City. As the canal was built in the early 1800s, this port town grew and eventually changed its name from the Village of Bohemia to Chesapeake City. Its inhabitants built beautiful homes, most of which still survive, and several restored Victorian dwellings now house shops and bed-and-breakfasts. Though it's easy to see everything in a day, the city's pleasing views and laid-back manner make it a tempting spot to linger for some relaxation. Boaters find it to be a great destination or place to stop on a cruise along the inland waterway.

ESSENTIALS

GETTING THERE   From Easton and other points on the southern Eastern Shore, take Route 301 northeast to Route 213, which leads directly into Chesapeake City. From Baltimore, take I-95 or U.S. Route 40 to the Elkton exit, and follow Route 213 south. You can also sail into town along the canal.

VISITOR INFORMATION   For brochures about the Chesapeake City area, contact the **Cecil County Office of Economic Development,** Tourism Department, 1 Seahawk Dr., Suite 114, North East, MD 21901 (© **800/232-4595** or 410/996-6292).

GETTING AROUND   Although the downtown area of Chesapeake City lends itself to walking, the best way to see the surrounding sights is by car. There is no public transportation.

ORIENTATION   The C&D Canal divides the city into north and south sides. The main commercial and historic area is on the south side of the canal. Free parking under the bridge and further in town is clearly marked. South Chesapeake City is walker friendly, with one main street, Bohemia Avenue, where most stores and businesses are located. Look for free walking and shopping brochures in any shop.

WHAT TO SEE & DO

To learn more about the town's focal point, head to the **C&D Canal Museum** 😊, 815 Bethel Rd. (© **410/885-5622**). Located on the waterfront at 2nd Street, it features an enormous waterwheel and two-story steam engine that once worked a lock on the canal, as well as a series of exhibits on the canal's history and operation. The museum's grounds house a reconstructed 30-foot-tall lighthouse (really more like a beacon). The museum is open Monday through Friday 8am to 4pm and is closed all federal holidays. Admission is free.

To soak up the ambience of this canal-side town, stroll through **Pell Gardens,** a peaceful, grassy setting overlooking Back Creek on Rees Wharf at the end of Bohemia Street. You can sit in the gazebo, or on one of the many benches. You might contemplate the canal with a snack or homemade ice-cream from the tiny **Canal Creamery** (© **410/885-3314**), next to the park (open seasonally).

Chesapeake City also serves as an excellent point of departure for excursions into the surrounding countryside. To see more of the canal and other local waterways, arrange a cruise on board the *Miss Clare* cruise boat, which sails on Saturday and Sunday, spring through fall. For $10 per hour for each adult, with reduced rates for children, you can ride the boat and hear a historical narrative of the area. Your itinerary can vary depending on time and interests, although popular options include trips to the Elk River and back (1 hour round-trip) or to the Turkey Point Lighthouse (2 hours round-trip). Call about weekday cruises. Cruises are arranged by calling © **410/885-5088.**

On land, visitors can select from a number of itineraries offered by **Hill Travel,** 200 Bohemia Ave., Chesapeake City, MD 21915 (© **800/466-1402** or 410/885-2797; www.uniglobehilltravel.com). You can also create a custom tour that includes local destinations, including museums, churches, and historic sites. Their most interesting tours are the walking tour of Chesapeake City's historic district and a narrated motor tour of the thoroughbred horse farms nearby—some quite famous. Tours start at around $20 per person and require reservations.

SHOPPING

Shopping is one of the main attractions in Chesapeake City; most stores are open from 10am until 9 or 10pm on Friday and Saturday, and until 5pm on Sunday. Winter hours tend to be more limited. Bohemia Avenue is the major thoroughfare and begins at the waterfront with a collection of art galleries offering original and local art, as well as limited-edition prints. The oldest of these, **Canal Artworks,** 17 Bohemia Ave. (© **410-885-5083**), is also the most charming. It's run by friendly staff and provides framing services.

Back Creek General Store, 100 Bohemia Ave. (© **410/885-5377**), is housed in a restored 1861 vintage building and is packed with throw rugs, pottery, candles, gourmet foods (featuring fudge), soaps, and the largest collection of miniature houses by Sheila and Byers Choice (one-dimensional, painted cutouts), including ones of Chesapeake City, that we've seen anywhere. Looking deceptively small from the front, **Marens,** 200 Bohemia Ave. (© **410/885-2475**), contains several rooms full of collectibles, cards, local folk and wildlife art, and home furnishings. Persevering shoppers will find floor-to-ceiling Christmas ornaments and decorations in the back room.

At the corner of 3rd Street and Bohemia Avenue is **Black Swan Antiques** (© **410/885-5888**). Cozy and crowded, every corner is jammed with dinnerware, jewelry, home furnishings, linens, and nautically themed antiques.

Back to Nature, 1074 Augustine Herman Hwy. (© **410/885-3148**), has an Elkton address, but has moved just outside of Chesapeake City on Route 213. It still carries clothing, jewelry, crafts, Christmas decorations, and specialty items (you'll laugh at the funny dog-food dishes), all with a nature or animal theme. Since the shop has moved near a golf course, golfing items are big, too.

WHERE TO STAY

Blue Max Inn ⭐ Built in 1844, this house was once occupied by author Jack Hunter while writing his book *The Blue Max.* Decorated in period style, the large bedrooms have private bathrooms. Thoughtful touches include chocolates, flowers, and complimentary beverages. Guests can enjoy the cozy parlor with a fireplace, a dining room, a gazebo, and best of all, first or second-floor porches overlooking the historic district. Breakfast can be served in the solarium, which offers views of the gardens and fishpond.

300 Bohemia Ave., Chesapeake City, MD 21915. © 877/725-8362 or 410/885-2781. Fax 410/885-2809. www.bluemaxinn.com. 8 units. $110–$185 double. AE, DISC, MC, V. **Amenities:** Jacuzzi; bikes. *In room:* A/C, dataport, hair dryer, iron, robes, CD player.

Inn at the Canal ⭐ This three-story house dates from 1870 and its Victorian charms have been preserved through antiques and family heirlooms. Set back from the canal, the house offers guest rooms with some water views of Back Creek Basin. Guest rooms are decorated with antiques and quilts. Guests enjoy the turn-of-the-20th-century dining room, the guest parlor, and two wicker-filled porches where you can sit and watch the boats breeze by on the canal. In the old milking room of the house, the innkeepers run a store, **Inntiques,** specializing in restored furniture and tools; inn guests get a discount.

104 Bohemia Ave. (P.O. Box 187), Chesapeake City, MD 21915. © 410/885-5995. Fax 410/885-3585. www. innatthecanal.com. 7 units. $85–$175 double. Rates include breakfast and afternoon refreshments. AE, DC, DISC, MC, V. *In room:* A/C, dataport.

WHERE TO DINE

Bayard House ⭐⭐⭐ AMERICAN Few people come to Chesapeake City without stopping for a meal at this acclaimed restaurant, perched beside the canal in the oldest building in Chesapeake City. It dates from the early 1780s when Samuel Bayard built a manor home on this site. Two dining areas are offered: a glass-enclosed dining room with wide windows overlooking the water, and an outdoor canal-side patio. A signature dish is the tournedos Baltimore (twin petit filet mignons, one topped with a crab cake and the other with a lobster cake, served with Madeira-cream and seafood-champagne sauces).

11 Bohemia Ave. ☎ 410/885-5040. www.bayardhouse.com. Reservations strongly recommended for dinner. Main courses $19.95–$27.95; lunch $9.95–$13.95. AE, DC, DISC, MC, V. Daily 11:30am–3pm and 5–9pm.

Chesapeake Inn Restaurant and Marina SEAFOOD   Walk or sail to this modern building (there are 60 boat slips) for a trio of dining locations, all with waterfront views. Casual dining, with a light-fare menu and live bands, is offered on the lower-level deck. The upper-level dining room and deck feature fine dining. A well-rounded wine list accompanies the menu of seafood, steak, veal, chicken, and pasta, with an emphasis on seafood combinations. From the buttery bisque to the crab cakes, the crab dishes were hearty and delicious.

605 2nd St., Chesapeake City, MD 21915. ☎ 410/885-2040. Fax 410/885-2620. www.chesapeakeinn.com. Reservations recommended for dinner. Main courses $18.95–$29.95; lunch $7.50–$15. AE, DC, DISC, MC, V. Mon–Thurs 11am–9pm, Fri–Sat 11am–11pm, Sun noon–10pm (call ahead, hours change in winter).

Schaefer's Canal House ★★ AMERICAN   First opened in 1908 as a general store, this wide-windowed restaurant sits on the north side of the canal facing Chesapeake City's historic district. From June through August, seating is available on the dockside terrace. The menu offers quite a variety, including wonderful crab cakes, fresh fish, prime rib, and surf-and-turf. (You won't be hungry when you leave.) On Thursday night, there's a seafood buffet for $19.95. As ships sail through the canal past the restaurant, the dining room lights dim and the ship's name, port of origin, and cargo are announced. Come by boat—there's a marina. The gift shop is open in summertime.

208 Bank St. ☎ 410/885-2200. Reservations recommended. Main courses $20–$33; lunch $7–$14; brunch $15.95. DISC, MC, V. Mon–Fri 11am–10pm, Sat–Sun 8am–10pm; Sun brunch 10am–3pm.

4 Crisfield & Smith Island

138 miles (222km) SE of Baltimore, 54 miles (87km) SW of Ocean City, 135 miles (217km) S of Wilmington

The remote town of Crisfield, on the extreme southern end of the Eastern Shore, was once to Chesapeake Bay seafood what Chicago is to meat packing—integral. Millions of oysters came through the town, their empty shells piling up to create a new shoreline. Once, Crisfield was the "seafood capital of the world."

Since then, economic winds have changed, and Crisfield has shrunk considerably. However, the town's heart still beats for the seafood trade. Every day its plants ship out their daily harvest of crabs and oysters around the world. The harbor and seafood processing area are still paved with oyster shells. Crisfield and its neighbor Smith Island offer an insider's look at the lives of the watermen and the seafood industry and some of the best seafood around. Everybody still talks about Mrs. Kitching's cooking. (Her cookbook is a great souvenir to take home.) It is also a great place from which to launch a fishing or touring boat trip on the deep waters of the southern Chesapeake.

ESSENTIALS

GETTING THERE   Crisfield is accessible by car via Maryland Route 413 from Route 50 or U.S. Route 13. You can also get to Crisfield by boat past

Smith Island. (Tangier Sound looks like a good bet but the water gets quite shallow.)

VISITOR INFORMATION   For brochures, maps, and all sorts of helpful information about Crisfield and the surrounding countryside, contact the **Somerset County Tourism Office,** P.O. Box 243, Princess Anne, MD 21853 (© **800/521-9189** or 410/651-2968), or stop by the office right on Route 13 in Princess Anne—look for flags flying. You can also contact the **Crisfield Chamber of Commerce,** J. Millard Tawes Museum, Somers Cove Marina (P.O. Box 292), Crisfield, MD 21817 (© **800/782-3913** or 410/968-2500), for brochures and information from the helpful staff.

SPECIAL EVENTS   Crisfield's two biggest events are the **National Hard Crab Derby and Fair** ⭐ and the **J. Millard Tawes Crab and Clam Bake.** The Hard Crab Derby and Fair is a 3-day event, with a crab-cooking contest, a crab-picking speed contest, country music, and of course, the crab race. It's held Labor Day weekend every year, and admission is usually around $4. Make hotel reservations well in advance. The Crab and Clam Bake, held 1 to 5pm on the third Wednesday in July, is an outdoor all-you-can-eat affair featuring crabs, clams, fish, corn on the cob, and watermelon, and in election years, lots of politicians. Tickets must be purchased in advance. For either event, call © **800/782-3919** or 410/968-2500.

WHAT TO SEE & DO

The **J. Millard Tawes Museum,** 3 9th St. (© **410/968-2501**), at the Somers Cove Marina, was founded in 1982 to honor a Crisfield-born governor of Maryland. It also houses the chamber of commerce offices. The exhibits detail the history of Crisfield and development of its seafood industry. The museum offers an escorted **walking tour** ⭐ of the port, which is the best way to see the town. Visitors can to see soft-shell crabs as they peel from their hard shells and watch lightning-fast workers pack crabmeat or oysters (depending on the season). Open daily April through October, Monday through Friday 9am to 4:30pm, Saturday and Sunday 10am to 2pm; November through May, Monday through Friday 10am to 2pm. Admission to the museum is $2.50; children under 12 get in free. The walking tour costs $2.50 for adults and is free for children under 12.

About 15 miles (24km) north of Crisfield on U.S. Route 13 is **Princess Anne,** a small country town with 38 historic homes, businesses, and churches. If you have time, take a moment to drive through the town, which is listed on the National Register of Historic Places. All the homes are privately owned except the **Teackle Mansion** (© **410/651-2238;** www.teacklemansion.org), at the end of Prince William. Built in 1801 and patterned after a Scottish manor house, this was the residence of Littleton Dennis Teackle, an associate of Thomas Jefferson and a shipping magnate, and his wife Elizabeth. With two entrances, one fronting the Manokin River (now obscured by trees) and one facing the town, this grand house measures nearly 200 feet in length and is symmetrically balanced throughout. Though the mansion suffered through some financial hard times, its care has now been taken over by sponsors of Olde Princess Anne Days and repairs are underway. Color analysis of the interior rooms has been completed and the first room, the main hall, gets the first new paint job. Outside, there's a new roof, repointed bricks, restored shutters, and "grained" door. It's open for guided tours April through mid-December, Wednesday, Saturday, and Sunday 1 to 3pm; mid-December through March,

Sunday from 1 to 3pm. Inside you'll see elaborate plaster ceilings, mirrored windows, a 7-foot fireplace, a beehive oven, American Chippendale furniture, a Tudor–Gothic pipe organ, an 1806 silk world map, and a 1712 family Bible. The admission and tour charge is $4 per person; free for children under 12.

OUTDOOR ACTIVITIES

The **Somers Cove Marina,** 715 Broadway, Crisfield (✆ **410/968-0925**), with 450 berths, is one of the largest facilities in Maryland. The marina is able to accommodate both sailboat and motor yachts from 10 feet to 150 feet. There are boat ramps, tiled showers, a laundry room, swimming pool, boat storage, electricity, water, and a fuel dock.

Fishing trips leave from the marina and the nearby town dock each day in pursuit of flounder, trout, spot, drum, blues, and rock. To book a headboat or charter, walk along the waterfront and talk with the various captains or call any of the following: **Charter Fishing Center** (✆ **800/967-FISH**), which has several charter and headboats from which to choose; **Capts. Robert Parks** and **Gilbert Howard** (✆ **410/968-1779**); **Capt. Keith Ward** (✆ **410/968-0074**; www.crisfield.com/prim); or **Capt. Charlie Coiro** (✆ **410/957-2151**; www. crisfield.com/good). Charters cost about $60 a person.

Janes Island State Park, 26280 Alfred Lawson Dr., Crisfield (✆ **410/ 968-1565**), gives nature lovers a place to **hike, camp, canoe,** and **powerboat.** Sitting on the edge of the Tangier Sound, Janes Island has excellent scenery, beautiful sunsets, and a winding canoe/boat trail, the only way to see the island portion of the park. In warm weather, the park rents canoes and kayaks for $6 an hour or motorboats for $10 an hour. Campsites are also available. Most are closed in the winter but four full-size cabins can be rented year-round.

SHOPPING

Besides shellfish and fishing, this area's other claim to fame is the **Carvel Hall Factory Outlet,** Route 413, Crisfield (✆ **410/968-0500**). Carvel Hall was started in 1895 when a blacksmith hammered out his first seafood-harvesting tools on a borrowed anvil. Today, discounts of up to 50% are given on brand-name cutlery made in this Crisfield plant, plus hundreds of other gift items such as glassware, pewter, sterling silver, plated hollowware, brass, and crystal. Open daily from 9am to 5pm (closed major holidays).

WHERE TO STAY

Choosing where to stay is easy in Crisfield. There are a couple of motels in town, all in the moderate category with basic accommodations. The best choice, however, is a nearby country inn in Princess Anne.

Somers Cove Motel   Views of the water add to the setting of this modern two-story facility. Opened in 1979, it was refurbished in 2001 with new carpet, bigger TVs, refrigerators, and microwaves, and new furniture. Each room also has a balcony or patio. Its biggest asset is its location in the middle of everything.

700 Norris Harbor Dr., Crisfield, MD 21817. ✆ **410/968-1900.** Fax 410/968-3448. www.crisfield.com/somers cove. 40 units, including 4 with kitchenettes. $45–$150 double. DISC, MC, V. Pets accepted for fee. **Amenities:** Outdoor pool; patio; picnic tables; grills; boat docks; boat ramps. *In room:* A/C, coffeemaker and iron available.

Waterloo Country Inn ★★★   The Waterloo Country Inn, a dignified brick manor house built in the Federal style in 1775, is one of the most elegant and charming accommodations on the Delmarva Peninsula. Surrounded by farmland and overlooking a tidal pond on Monie Creek, this small inn's amenities are gracious and numerous. Most of the rooms have hardwood floors and are decorated with antiques and sophisticated artwork. All rooms have full bathrooms. The Chesapeake Suite features a whirlpool for two. Dinner can be arranged for guests; locals claim that the Waterloo offers the best fine dining in the area. Grab a bike or canoe to explore the roads and waterways. Located about 30 minutes from Crisfield, the Waterloo is a great place from which to stage a visit to the southern Eastern Shore. Or, if you're looking for a little seclusion, the innkeepers here have made this a first-class place to get away from it all.

28822 Mt. Vernon Rd., Princess Anne, MD 21853. ℂ 410/651-0883. Fax 410/651-5592. www.waterloo countryinn.com. 6 units. Apr–Oct $125–$245 double; Nov–Mar $105–$225 double. 2-night minimum June–Oct. Rates include full breakfast. AE, DISC MC, V. Pets accepted with prior arrangement. **Amenities:** Outdoor pool; Jacuzzi; bikes; canoes. *In room:* A/C, dataport, hair dryer.

WHERE TO DINE

Not surprisingly, the focus of attention here is seafood, and plenty of it. This is the place to have your fill of crab, from crab omelets for breakfast, to crab soup and crab sandwiches for lunch, to crab cooked in a dozen different ways for dinner. Most restaurants in town serve an inexpensive breakfast starting between 5:30 and 6am to cater to the resident and visiting fishermen.

Original Captain's Galley ⭐ SEAFOOD   Overlooking the City Dock, this contemporary-style wide-windowed restaurant is the ideal place to watch the boats in the harbor and enjoy fresh seafood. Dinner entrees include crab cakes, crab imperial, crab au gratin, and a gargantuan seafood feast (soft crab, crab cake, fish fillet, scallops, shrimp, and oysters), as well as steaks and fried chicken. Lunch choices are mainly sandwiches, such as crab cake, oyster fritter, crab imperial, soft crab, shrimp or tuna salad, and assorted meats. The restaurant offers **ecotours** daily April through November at 10am and 1:30pm. Tickets are $20 for adults and $10 for kids under $10. For reservations, call ℂ **410/968-9870.**

1021 W. Main St. ℂ 410/968-3313. Reservations recommended for dinner. Main courses $6.95–$18.95; lunch $2.95–$7.95. AE, MC, V. Daily 11am–10pm.

Watermen's Inn AMERICAN   Although this eatery does not boast water views, the food here is the prime attraction, with an ever-changing menu of cooked-to-order dishes. Dinnertime choices focus on baked stuffed jumbo soft crabs, crab cakes, baked stuffed flounder, jumbo fantail shrimp, crab au gratin, fried chicken, baby-back ribs, charbroiled steaks, vegetarian plates, and a signature cream of crab soup that's not to be missed.

9th and Main sts., Crisfield. ℂ 410/968-2119. Fax 410/968-3970. Reservations recommended for dinner. Main courses $8.95–$19.95; lunch $2.95–$8.95. AE, DISC, MC, V. Wed–Thurs 11am–9pm, Fri–Sat 11am–10pm, Sun 8am–9pm.

AN EXCURSION TO SMITH ISLAND

Located 13 miles (21km) west of Crisfield in the midst of Chesapeake Bay's Tangier Sound, Smith Island is Maryland's largest inhabited offshore island. It's really a cluster of islands, including the Martin National Wildlife Refuge. Three tiny towns are located on two other parts of Smith Island. Ewell and Rhodes Point are on one and Tylerton is on the third.

Conveniences the rest of us take for granted—sidewalks, traffic lights, bars, shopping centers—just don't exist here. You can't even drive here—there's no bridge to the mainland. The people make their living primarily from the sea, by crabbing and tonging or dredging for oysters.

Many Smith Islanders are direct descendants of British colonists who came in the early 1700s. Their isolation and speech patterns handed down since the 1700s have given residents here an accent all their own. The isolation here is lessened a bit by radio, TV, and telephone. Older children go to school on the mainland. The islanders welcome visitors all summer long.

A visit to Smith Island must be taken in the warm weather. Winters are hard and spring and fall are busy times, so the boats stop coming from October to April. The restaurants and inns close, waiting for another summer season.

GETTING THERE   Go to Crisfield to take one of the passenger ferryboats that depart from the City Dock or from Somers Cove Marina, or take your own boat. The trip takes approximately an hour, depending on the route and time of year. Boats sail weekends in late May and early September and daily through the summer. The round-trip costs $20 to $25 and children ages 3 to 11 are half-price. All boats usually depart Crisfield around noon and return from the island around 5pm. The *Captain Tyler* departs from the Somers Cove Marina at 12:30pm and docks in Ewell. Overnight packages with motel accommodations and meals are also available. Contact **Smith Island Cruises** (© 410/425-2771) for reservations. They're a must. Smith Island Cruises' twin-hulled *Chelsea Lane Tyler* makes the trip daily from Point Lookout for $30 for adults. The trip across the bay takes 1½ hours. See chapter 5 for details.

Capt. Otis Ray Tyler (© **410/968-1118**) goes year-round. His boat is the mail boat and leaves Crisfield's City Dock at 12:30pm and departs Ewell at 4pm. From Virginia you can catch the *Spirit of the Chesapeake* (© **804/453-3430**) at Virginia KOA Campground. The 90-minute cruise leaves Reedville around 10am.

Only one boat goes to Tylerton. The *Captain Jason II* goes to both Ewell and Tylerton from Crisfield. To catch a ferry to someplace on Smith Island besides Ewell, you have to travel with **Capts. Terry and Larry Laird** (© **410/425-5931** or 410/425-4471) on the *Captain Jason I* or *II*. Both boats depart from the City Dock and dock at Ewell and Tylerton (in the summer).

You can bring your own boat, but check the charts carefully for shallow spots. Smith Island Harbor at Ewell can be 4½ feet at low tide. Water is deeper if you come from Tangier Sound via Big Thorofare. Smith Island has no marinas, but the gas dock in Ewell is open Monday through Saturday 8am to 5pm. (Avoid gassing up in late afternoon; the watermen use the pumps then.) If you plan to stay, there is some overnight docking. Call Ruke's Store (© **410/425-2311**) or Driftwood General Store (© **410/425-2111**) for dock rental.

VISITOR INFORMATION   You can pick up information about Smith Island in Crisfield at the **Crisfield Chamber of Commerce,** 906 W. Main St., Crisfield, MD 21817 (© **800/782-3913** or 410/968-2500). Before your trip you can contact the **Somerset County Tourism Office** (© **800/521-9189;** www.intercom.net/npo/smithisland/), which offers a self-guided walking tour.

Once you arrive in Ewell, the island's largest town, visit the **Smith Island Center** (© **800/521-9189** or 410/425-3351) to get a sense of how the island is laid out, learn a little history, and see exhibits about the island. It's open daily noon to 4pm April through October and is located just up Smith Island Road from the Bayside Restaurant.

GETTING AROUND   No cars are permitted on the island. Everything is within walking distance. You can bring your bike on the ferry or rent one right beside the County Dock. They run $3 for a half hour and $5 for an hour. Golf carts for two are also available for $8 per half hour or $10 per hour. Or maybe you'd like the 20-minute bus tour that offers a glimpse at the Smith Island lifestyle. It costs two bucks to find out how the townspeople deal with necessities such as school, electricity, and telephone service.

ORIENTATION Smith Island boats three harbor towns. **Ewell,** the "capital" of Smith Island, is the largest town. It's where most cruise boats dock and has the majority of the island's seafood-packing houses. **Rhodes Point,** about a mile south of Ewell and the island's center for boat repair, used to be called Rogues Point because of all the pirates who came here. It's a marshy place, reachable via a wooden bridge from Smith Island or March Roads. **Tylerton** may be the most remote place in Maryland, accessible by only one boat. It's home to the state's last one-room school—which closed in 1996. The architecture here is the most ornate on Smith Island and it's the main reason to visit.

PREPARING FOR YOUR VISIT

The attraction of Smith Island is its isolation. These three tiny towns—Tylerton has about 90 residents—have no shopping malls, fast food restaurants, or sidewalks. Residents here do their best to make your visit enjoyable, and their welcome is always warm. So is the weather. In fact, it's probably going to be quite hot and humid. The mosquitoes will drive you crazy if you don't douse yourself with bug repellent, and you might find yourself getting bored before the boat leaves to take you home. When you come, bring water to drink, wear a hat and sunscreen, and dress for a hot day.

That said, visitors should plan for a lazy day of strolling or biking, maybe even a hike from Ewell to Rhodes Point. Spend lots of time enjoying the bay's breezes and admiring the town's quaint charms. Stop in one of the two country stores to see what's on the shelves and chat with the townspeople. Maybe you'll find some fig preserves or pomegranate jelly made by islanders from local trees. If it's Sunday, go to church. These are church-going people and they welcome visitors.

Besides the Smith Island Center, visitors can visit the **Middleton House** on Caleb Road, which serves as an interpretive center for the Martin National Wildlife Refuge. The refuge, the third of Smith Island's islands, is too fragile for visitors, but this center's exhibits offer a look at some of the wildlife there. Those are the big attractions. You might want to wander by Smith Island Motel, operated by Frances Kitching and her son Harry. Mrs. Kitching's *Smith Island Cookbook* is a Maryland favorite. Signed copies are available in town.

You might as well get to know your fellow visitors, too. You'll keep seeing them once you get off the boat. All the cruise boats arrive and depart at the same time and a couple dozen tourists all want to eat at the same restaurants and see the same sights at the same time.

WHERE TO STAY & DINE

Ewell is home to two restaurants, and each of the ferries sends its passengers to a different one: **Bayside Inn** (© 410/425-2771) and **Ruke's Seafood Deck** (© 410/425-2311). Both are quite used to the sudden dash of hungry visitors piling in all at once. If you don't want to eat with a crowd, bypass the restaurants until later in the day and pop into one of the general stores for a snack. An ice cream shop and snowball stand are by the county dock, as well. In Tylerton the only place to eat is the **Drum Point Market** (© 410/425-2108).

The towns of Smith Island are so tiny there isn't much room for hotels. But if you want to stay, there are a few bed-and-breakfasts as well as Mrs. Kitching's

Smith Island Motel (© 410/425-3321). The motel has only eight rooms, each with a TV and A/C. There are two shared bathrooms (one for men, one for women), and guests have use of a refrigerator, coffeemaker, toaster and microwave in the lounge. It's open mid-April to mid-October.

The Inn of Silent Music   Visitors can find respite in this old-fashioned farmhouse, surrounded on three sides by water. Three rooms have private bathrooms. The thoughtful innkeepers pick up their guests at the Tylerton dock, and will cook dinner for $15 a person. They have canoes and kayaks and bikes.

2955 Tylerton Road, Tylerton, Smith Island, MD 21866. © 410/425-3541. www.innofsilentmusic.com. 3 units. $105–125 double. Gourmet breakfast included. 2-night minimum some weekends. Rain checks if the ferry doesn't run. No credit cards. Children over age 6 welcome. **Amenities:** 2 canoes; 2-person kayak; bikes; dinner available. *In room:* A/C.

7

Frederick & the Civil War Crossroads

Frederick's citizens have found themselves at the crossroads of American history several times. This was especially true in August 1862, during the Civil War, when Frederick became a major hospital site for thousands of wounded soldiers who were brought in from the Battle of South Mountain. The next month, Union and Confederate soldiers clashed near Sharpsburg at Antietam Creek, in the bloodiest fighting in the whole war. There were so many casualties that after the battle, there were more wounded soldiers residing in Frederick than there were citizens.

In 1862, Barbara Fritchie confronted Stonewall Jackson and was immortalized in poetry ("*Shoot if you must this old grey head/but spare your country's flag, she said.*"). Two years later, Confederate General Jubal Early demanded ransom that saved the town from destruction. Clashes at Harpers Ferry and Gettysburg again brought wounded soldiers into the town before the Battle of the Monocacy was waged southeast of the town.

Reminders of these sad days remain in the historic sites, battlefields, and museums around the area. The National Park Service maintains the four battlefields. Antietam will mark the 140th anniversary of the battle in September 2002. Gettysburg is the most popular of the battlefields, with plenty of crowds around the monuments and reminders of the battle. Harpers Ferry's reminds visitors of its past in a beautiful setting overlooking the Potomac River. The Monocacy site has changed very little since the battle in July 1864, except for a few monuments and a visitor center.

Frederick remembers the war with its Barbara Fritchie House and the National Museum of Civil War Medicine. But Frederick isn't stuck in the past. Maryland's second largest city, it continues to grow, with suburbs extending down toward Washington, D.C., and a downtown area that shines as a place to shop, dine, or relax.

Outside of town are rolling fields and orchards, the foothills of the Catoctin Mountains, and plenty of green space for picnicking and hiking.

1 Frederick ⟨★

47 miles (76km) W of Baltimore, 45 miles (72km) NW of Washington, D.C., 34 miles (55km) S of Gettysburg

In recent years, Frederick has grown from a largely agricultural community to the second largest city in the state—a bustling Washington suburb with a population of over 45,000—and it's still growing. Despite this, the city has managed to maintain its small-town charm. The 33-block historic district with its 18th- and 19th-century buildings and the clustered church spires that make up

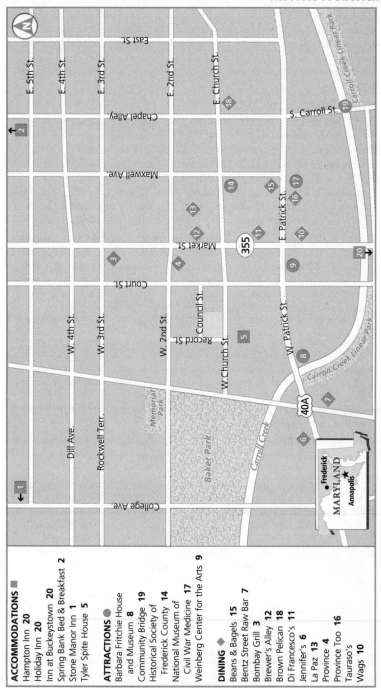

Historic Frederick

ACCOMMODATIONS
Hampton Inn **20**
Holiday Inn **20**
Inn at Buckeystown **20**
Spring Bank Bed & Breakfast **2**
Stone Manor Inn **1**
Tyler Spite House **5**

ATTRACTIONS
Barbara Fritchie House
  and Museum **8**
Community Bridge **19**
Historical Society of
  Frederick County **14**
National Museum of
  Civil War Medicine **17**
Weinberg Center for the Arts **9**

DINING
Beans & Bagels **15**
Bentz Street Raw Bar **7**
Bombay Grill **3**
Brewer's Alley **12**
Brown Pelican **18**
Di Francesco's **11**
Jennifer's **6**
La Paz **13**
Province **4**
Province Too **16**
Tauraso's
Wags **10**

Frederick's skyline are still a main attraction. Antiques and craft shops dominate the downtown shopping area, and Frederick has a vibrant restaurant and bar scene. North and west of the city, the agricultural community still thrives: Fresh produce from local orchards and farms is available all summer, and in early spring newborn foals can be seen romping in the pastures of the county's horse farms.

ESSENTIALS

GETTING THERE   From Washington, D.C., take I-270 to Frederick, where the interstate becomes U.S. 15 and continues north to Gettysburg. From Baltimore, take I-70 west. From points west, take I-68 east to I-70.

Greyhound (✆ **800/231-2222**) operates daily bus service to Frederick into its depot on 27 E. All Saints St. (✆ **301/663-3311**).

Maryland's **MARC** train to Frederick from Washington, D.C., on the Brunswick line opened in December 2001. Since this is a commuter line, service is available only on weekdays. Call ✆ **800/325-RAIL** for information.

VISITOR INFORMATION   The **Tourism Council of Frederick County** operates an efficient, helpful visitor center at 19 E. Church St., Frederick, MD 21701 (✆ **800/999-3613** or 301/663-8687; www.visitfrederick.org). This office not only supplies maps, brochures, and listings of accommodations and restaurants but also conducts walking tours of the historic district. Tourist information booths are also in the rest areas on I-70 west of Frederick and on U.S. 15 south at Emmitsburg. All of these facilities are open daily from 9am to 5pm.

GETTING AROUND   The best way to get around in Frederick is by car— that is, if you're not walking through the historic district. Parking is cheap, when it isn't free. Downtown has metered parking and parking garages that run about $5 during the week, $1 on Saturday, free on Sunday. Stop at the visitor center to have your parking garage ticket validated for up to 3 hours of free parking on weekdays. If you park in a residential district, check for the restricted parking signs that limit nonresident parking.

SPECIAL EVENTS   The most popular and beautiful time of the year is mid- to late October, when fall colors are at their peak. That's also the peak time for special events. **Catoctin Colorfest** in nearby Thurmont is a craft show of enormous proportions, filling the town's parks and public areas and lining the streets. It's held annually in mid-October. Call ✆ **800/999-3613** or 301/663-8687 for information and exact dates.

Haunted Rail and Trail will take you, if you dare, on the Walkersville Southern Railroad Train for a ride to Fountain Rock Park for creepy fun. It's held in late October. Call ✆ **301/696-2936.**

A couple of events mark the anniversary of **Civil War dates.** The commemoration of the Battle of Monocacy is held in early June (✆ **301/662-3515** for information). The Battle of Antietam is recalled in September (✆ **301/432-5124** for information).

WHERE TO STAY

Surprisingly for a city its size, Frederick has only one choice in the historic district. Other hotels and bed-and-breakfasts are spread throughout the county. Most moderately priced chain hotels are just outside the city limits, or you can head north on Route 15 to Thurmont, where you'll find a cluster of small hotels. All the hotels in the area have free parking.

EXPENSIVE

Inn at Buckeystown ✪   Set in a quiet country village on the Monocacy River, this restored three-story mansion dates from 1897. The building is rich in Italianate Victorian details, with a wraparound porch, widow's walk, gables, bay windows, and ornate trim. Here, you'll get both bed and board (breakfast and dinner), in the true country inn tradition. Dinner is served on Victorian china with period silver and glassware. (Nonguests can also eat dinner here; make a reservation 24 hours in advance.) The interior is rich with antiques, Oriental rugs, chandeliers, and hand-embroidered fabrics. There are five working fireplaces. The five rooms and suites located in the main house have varying amenities and unique touches, including fireplaces and balconies and/or bay windows. All arrangements for lodging or dining must be made by advance phone reservation.

3521 Buckeystown Pike (Rte. 85, 4 miles [6km] south of Frederick), Buckeystown, MD 21717. ✆ **800/272-1190** or 301/874-5755. Fax 301/831-1355. 7 units. $170–$300 double. Rates include breakfast and dinner for 2; $110–$240 for bed-and-breakfast only. AE, DISC, MC, V. Children welcome. **Amenities:** Restaurant. *In room:* TV/VCR.

Stone Manor Inn ✪   If you're planning a quiet, romantic getaway in the country, this is the inn for you. This historic manor, parts of which date from the 1760s, is surrounded by a 114-acre working farm with open fields, walking trails, wooded nooks, and gardens for you to roam about undisturbed. The house, which opened as an inn and restaurant in 1991, offers suites individually decorated with antiques and reproductions, including canopy or carved poster beds, and several feature one or two of the house's 10 original fireplaces. Each suite has also been equipped with modern amenities, including whirlpools and double multihead showers. The Trillium Room, with its antique quilts, toys, and vintage clothing, is a favorite. The Hibiscus suite is wheelchair accessible and features a private entrance, a fireplace, and two porches.

5820 Carroll Boyer Rd., Middletown, MD 21769. ✆ **301/473-5454.** Fax 301/371-5622. www.stonemanor.com. 6 units. $150–$275 suite. Rates include continental breakfast and chef's welcoming plate. AE, DC, DISC, MC, V. **Amenities:** Restaurant; bar. *In room:* A/C, TV/VCR, hair dryer, iron.

Tyler Spite House ✪   In the heart of Frederick's historic district, opposite City Hall, this three-story Federal mansion dates from 1814. Dr. John Tyler built it for the sole purpose of preventing the city from building a thoroughfare through the property; hence the word *spite* was added to the name. The house has 14-foot ceilings with intricate moldings and eight working fireplaces. Guest rooms are furnished with antiques, down comforters, and Oriental carpets. Tours of the house are offered so guests can see where the country's first cataract surgery took place, as well as items that once belonged to Barbara Fritchie, John Hanson (first president of the U.S. under the Articles of Confederation), and Maryland's Governor Thomas Johnson, among others. Horse-drawn carriage rides can be arranged for an additional fee.

112 W. Church St., Frederick, MD 21701. ✆ **301/831-4455.** Fax 301/662-4185. www.selectregistry.com. 5 units. $200–$250 double. Rates include full breakfast and afternoon tea. AE, MC, V. **Amenities:** Outdoor pool; whirlpool; patio; walled garden.

MODERATE

Hampton Inn   Located 2 miles (3km) south of downtown Frederick, this modern six-story hotel is a former Quality Inn with a dark brick facade—not the customary Hampton style. It is nestled beside an artificial lake and is connected by footbridge to a replica of a lighthouse that serves as an informal crab restaurant in the summer months. Many guest rooms also overlook the lake.

5311 Buckeystown Pike, Frederick, MD 21704 (Exit 31B off I-270 at Rte. 85). (C) **800/HAMPTON** or 301/698-2500. Fax 301/695-8735. www.hamptoninnfrederick.com. 160 units; 15 suites have kitchenettes. $79–$135 double. Rates include continental breakfast; pets accepted for additional charge. AE, DC, DISC, MC, V. **Amenities:** Restaurant; indoor pool; exercise room; business center; executive level. *In room:* A/C, TV with pay movies; dataport, coffeemaker, hair dryer, iron.

Holiday Inn *Kids*   This modern two-story brick hotel is first and foremost a conference facility; public areas are often bustling with activity. However, except for the handful of rooms that overlook the courtyard/restaurant, most guest rooms are separated from the public areas and are relatively quiet. Rooms are slightly above standard Holiday Inn size and decor and the indoor pool and exercise area are in a big, airy space. Attention, shoppers: The hotel is adjacent to the Francis Scott Key Mall. It's also just a short drive from the historic district.

5400 Holiday Dr. (I-270 at Rte. 85), Frederick, MD 21701. (C) **800/HOLIDAY** or 301/694-7500. Fax 301/694-0589. 155 units. $84–$89 double. Rates include continental breakfast. Pets accepted. AE, DC, MC, V. **Amenities:** Restaurant; lounge; indoor pool; whirlpool; sauna; exercise area; video game room; miniature golf course; board games available for children; shuttle to local sites. *In room:* A/C, TV/VCR with pay movies, dataport, voice mail, fridge, microwave, coffeemaker, hair dryer, iron.

Spring Bank Bed & Breakfast   Dating from 1880 and listed on the National Register of Historic Places, this sprawling redbrick Italianate and Gothic Revival bed-and-breakfast inn exudes a homey feeling. Its three stories are bedecked with gables, cupolas, double porches, bay windows, and a fish scale–patterned slate roof. Inside are high ceilings with frescoes, intricate stenciling, faux-marble mantles, antique furnishings, and William Morris wallpaper. The inn is located north of downtown Frederick, just off Route 15, in a country setting on 10 acres. Innkeepers Beverly and Ray Compton do a great job of making you feel at home.

7945 Worman's Mill Rd., Frederick, MD 21701. (C) **301/694-0440.** www.bbonline.com/MD/springbank. 5 units (3 with shared bathroom). $90–$120 double. Rates include continental breakfast. AE, DISC, MC, V. *In room:* A/C, fax available, dataport in 1 room, hair dryer and iron available.

WHERE TO DINE
EXPENSIVE
Brown Pelican ★★ INTERNATIONAL   Located in the historic district, this basement restaurant is decorated in a nautical style, with vibrant sea tones, driftwood, and yachting collectibles. The dinner menu is extensive and emphasizes seafood and veal. Some of the specialties include a delightful "Veal Brown Pelican" (with ham, mushrooms, and cream); veal Nicholas, which combines veal with shrimp; blackened salmon; and jumbo lump crab cakes. For lunch, there are sandwiches, soups, and salads.

5 E. Church St. (C) **301/695-5833.** Fax 301/695-5876. Reservations recommended for dinner. Main courses $16.95–$29.95; lunch $6.95–$10.95. AE, DISC, MC, V. Mon–Thurs 11:30am–9:30pm, Fri 11:30am–3pm and 5–10pm, Sat 5–10pm, Sun 5–9:30pm.

MODERATE
Bombay Grill INDIAN   Bombay Grill offers traditional Indian cuisine in a formal but relaxed setting. Although just across the street from a popular brewpub, the restaurant feels as though it is a thousand miles away. The decor features light woods, exposed brick walls, and a long bar. Tables are set with pink tablecloths and candle centerpieces. The menu covers a wide range of vegetarian and meat-based options, with a focus on grilled dishes. Some choices include shrimp *masala*, shrimp curried in a spicy sauce; and vegetarian *korma*, fresh

vegetables in a creamy, nutty raisin sauce. Try the chicken *tikka,* a tasty dish of chicken marinated in yogurt and herbs, served sizzling from the charcoal grill.

137 N. Market St. ⓒ **301/668-0077.** Reservations recommended for dinner. Main courses $7.25–$16.95; lunch buffet $7.95. AE, DC, DISC, MC, V. Sun–Thurs 11:30am–10pm, Fri–Sat 11:30am–11pm.

Brewer's Alley AMERICAN/PIZZA   Wood-fired pizza and beer brewed on-site make this place a winner. The food is consistently good here: standard pub fare such as sandwiches, burgers, and daily specials. But the specialty, the pizza, is creative and fun. Pizzas are topped with everything from barbecued chicken to a double layer of pepperoni and cheese, with inventive names like Grecian Formula. There's a pizza of the day, too. The brewpub is popular to a fault, and on busy weekends the wait for a table can be long.

124 N. Market St. ⓒ **301/631-0089.** Reservations recommended on weekends. Main courses $7.25–$16.95; lunch $4.95–$10.95. AE, DC, MC, V. Mon–Thurs 11:30am–9pm, Fri–Sat 11:30am–10:30pm, Sun noon–9pm.

Di Francesco's ITALIAN   Decorated like a country villa, with whitewashed walls and lots of plants, this restaurant exudes the flavors and ambience of Italy. The dinner menu offers more than a dozen pastas in full or half-size orders, such as fettuccini with smoked salmon and lasagna. Entrees shrimp marinara or scampi, and filet mignon. Lunch features salads, omelets, pizzas, and pastas.

26 N. Market St. ⓒ **301/695-5499.** Reservations recommended for dinner. Main courses $11.95–$16.95; lunch $4.95–$9.95. DC, DISC, MC, V. Mon 5–9:30pm, Tues–Thurs 11:30am–3pm and 5:30–9:30pm, Fri–Sat 11:30am–3pm and 5–10pm, Sun 4–8:30pm.

Jennifer's ⭐ AMERICAN   This neighborhood favorite is definitely worth a venture off Frederick's Restaurant Row on Market Street. Just about a block from the county courthouse, Jennifer's is seldom crowded and attracts mostly a local crowd: lawyers and businesspeople for lunch, and downtown Fredericktonians for dinner. A slate fireplace facing the restaurant's two dining rooms, exposed brick walls, and a large oak bar create a warm, comfortable atmosphere, and the myriad of flags (city, state, and country) hanging from the ceiling reflects the restaurant's varied menu. Their extensive lunch menu has the usual burgers, pizza, salads, and soups. The lunch food is okay, but dinner is exceptional, especially the fish and seafood. Hot and crunchy Creole catfish with honey-pecan butter is a winner, and so is the crab dip. If these sound too rich or calorie-laden, try their $11 spa menu entrees based on Weight Watchers recipes.

207 W. Patrick St. ⓒ **301/662-0373.** Main courses $11–$24; lunch $5–$9. AE, DC, DISC, MC, V. Mon 11:30am–9:30pm, Tues–Sat 11:30am–11pm, Sun 4–9:30pm.

La Paz *(Value* MEXICAN   Tucked away behind the parking deck on Market Street, this local favorite offers good value for an extensive menu of Mexican fare. The two smallish dining rooms fill quickly and can be a bit loud, especially on weekends. From the main menu, you can get fajitas, flautas, or a vegetable burrito. Or build your own dinner with tacos, burritos, enchiladas, or tostadas. And of course the margaritas are quite good. There's a limited children's menu.

18 Market Space. ⓒ **301/694-8980.** Reservations accepted for parties of 6 or more only on weekdays. Main courses $6–$12.50; lunch $4–$5.25. AE, DC, DISC, MC, V. Mon–Thurs 11am–10pm, Fri 11am–11pm, Sat 11:30am–11pm, Sun 4–11pm.

Province ⭐ AMERICAN/INTERNATIONAL   One of Frederick's oldest houses (ca. 1767) is the setting for this restaurant, consisting of a small bistro-style front room and a bright brick-walled room in the rear. The latter overlooks the herb garden, which produces ingredients for the kitchen. The furnishings include snowshoe chairs and paintings by local artists. Dinner specials change daily, but a few favorite dishes are pistachio-encrusted veal saltimbocca; grilled Asian marinated salmon and spicy shrimp; and Andouille sausage. Lunchtime selections focus on salads, quiches, crab cakes, and creative combination sandwiches. And, whether visiting for dinner or lunch, be sure to save some room for Province's desserts—they're the best in town.

131 N. Market St. ⒸⒶ **301/663-1441.** Fax 301/663-1596. www.provrest.com. Reservations required. Main courses $14–$20; lunch $7–$10. AE, DC, DISC, MC, V. Mon 11:30am–3pm, Tues–Thurs 11:30am–3pm and 5:30–9pm, Fri–Sat 11:30am–3pm and 5:30–10pm, Sun 11am–2pm and 4–8pm.

Tauraso's ✿ AMERICAN/ITALIAN   Bright and busy, this restaurant is the main dining choice at the Everedy Square shopping complex. Tauraso's is often thought of as Frederick's premier restaurant, which is a reputation it does a pretty good job of living up to. There are three settings—a more formal dining room, an outdoor patio, and a casual pub—but one extensive menu. Entrees range from Italian choices such as pastas, Tauraso's original seafood sausage, and Italian bouillabaisse to international favorites such as crab cakes, charcoal-grilled chicken, and steaks. For lunch, you'll find sandwiches, frittatas, pastas, and salads. Pizzas made in a wood-burning oven are also featured throughout the day.

6 N. East St. (at Everedy Square). ⒸⒶ **301/663-6600.** Fax 301/663-6677. Reservations recommended for dinner on weekends. Main courses $7.95–$23.95; lunch $4.95–$9.95. AE, DC, DISC, MC, V. Sun–Thurs 11am–10pm, Fri–Sat 11am–11pm.

INEXPENSIVE

Beans & Bagels DELI   This unpretentious little coffee shop is one of the few places in Frederick where visitors can sit, read the paper, and enjoy gourmet coffee and a fresh bagel. The menu of coffees and coffee-related specialty drinks is impressive. You can also get soups and sandwiches served on sourdough or seven-grain bread, croissants or, of course, bagels. Breakfast is served all day.

49 E. Patrick St. ⒸⒶ **301/620-2165.** All items $1–$6.95. No credit cards. Mon–Fri 7am–3pm, Sat–Sun 8am–4pm.

Province Too DELI   Good for breakfast or lunch, or to stock up for a picnic, this deli offers fresh baked goods, stews, soups, made-to-order sandwiches, and combination salads, plus gourmet teas and coffees. There's a small seating area, or you can get your food to go. Province Too has some great desserts as well.

12 E. Patrick St. ⒸⒶ **301/663-3315.** All items $1.50–$6. AE, DC, DISC, MC, V. Mon–Fri 7am–4pm, Sat 9am–4pm.

Wags *(Finds)* AMERICAN   At only about 15 feet across at its widest, this tiny basement bar is the smallest of Frederick's favorite nightspots. It can't seat more than 35 people comfortably, but that's part of the appeal. The other part can be summed up in four words: Wags's burgers and fries. The fries are served boardwalk style: greasy and in a heaping basket. The burgers are the stuff of cardiologists' nightmares: big, fattening, and dripping with cheese, sour cream, or Wags's special sauce. They've been voted the best burgers in Frederick 7 years in a row. There are other equally distressing (and wonderful) sandwiches on the menu, including the classic Reuben and ham and cheese.

24 S. Market St. ⒸⒶ **301/694-8451.** Main courses $3.75–$6.95. Mon–Sat 11am–2am. AE, DISC, MC, V.

WHAT TO SEE & DO

The focus of Frederick is its 33-block **historic district.** Many of the buildings been carefully restored, and the street layout today is much as it was in the early days. With Courthouse Square and Old Frederick City Hall at its heart, this city is a showcase of mansions and elegant brick townhouses. The sites also include 18th- and 19th-century church spires and eye-tricking murals of angels, birds, and the **Community Bridge** ✦. Once adorned with the words "This is a Shared Vision," the Community Bridge is actually a concrete structure, but it's now completely disguised as a stone-arch bridge by phantom perspective paintings of engravings, statues, and other images by artist William M. Cochran. All of this stuff looks real at a distance and some of it you have to touch to believe. The Frederick Visitor Center, 19 E. Church St. (✆ **301/663-8687**), distributes a map of the district and coordinates a program of **walking tours.** Tours depart from the visitor center each Saturday and Sunday, April through December, at 1:30pm. The price is $4.50 for adults, $3.50 for seniors, and free for children under 12.

DOWNTOWN MUSEUMS & HISTORIC SITES

Barbara Fritchie House and Museum This house, built in 1926, is a replica of the home of Frederick's Civil War heroine and uses materials from her house. At age 95, Barbara Fritchie bravely waved the Stars and Stripes in the path of Confederate soldiers and was immortalized in a poem by John Greenleaf Whittier as the "bravest of all in Fredericktown." A visit includes a video presentation of her life and times; a collection of mementoes including quilts and linens made by Barbara; her caps, shawls, and dresses; and her desk, tables, chairs, and china.

154 W. Patrick St. ✆ 301/698-0630. Admission $2 adults, $1.50 seniors and under age 12. Apr–Sept Mon and Thurs–Sat 10am–4pm, Sun 1–4pm; Oct–Nov Sat 10am–4pm, Sun 1–4pm. Closed Dec–Mar.

Historical Society of Frederick County ✦ This Federal-style landmark (ca. 1820) is a good place to broaden your knowledge of area history. Exhibits focus on local notables such as Roger B. Taney, chief justice of the U.S. Supreme Court and author of the *Dred Scott* decision; Francis Scott Key, author of "The Star-Spangled Banner"; Thomas Johnson, first governor of Maryland; and Barbara Fritchie. There's also a genealogical library and a formal garden.

24 E. Church St. ✆ 301/663-1188. www.fwp.net/hsfc. Admission $2 adults, free for under age 17. Mon–Sat 10am–4pm, Sun 1–4pm. Library Tues–Sat 10am–4pm. Guided tours available year-round, except first 2 weeks of Jan.

National Museum of Civil War Medicine *(Finds)* For a brief respite from a day of antiquing, stop by this newly expanded museum. Opened in 1996, its exhibits fill two floors of a three-story building that holds a macabre place in Civil War history. Several thousand dead from the Battle of Antietam were housed and embalmed here. Exhibits tell the story of army life and doctors' and nurses' attempts to aid wounded and dying soldiers, as well as the medical advances they made as the war progressed. The exhibits use dioramas, artifacts, and photographs. Special attention is given to the role of women in hospitals, and, of course, to the Battle of Antietam, fought in nearby Sharpsburg. An expanded gift shop has also been added.

48 E. Patrick St. ✆ 800/564-1864 or 301/695-1864. Fax 301/695-6823. www.CivilWarMed.org. Admission $6.50 adults, $6 seniors, $4.50 ages 10–16. Mon–Sat 10am–5pm, Sun 11am–5pm.

Rose Hill Manor ✦ *(Kids)* Kids love this place, but adults do, too. The 1790s manor house was the last home of Maryland's first elected governor. You can take a tour of this historic home, but the manor also acts as a children's museum. Kids can learn about early America as they play with period toys or learn how to use household tools. Also in the 43-acre park are an icehouse, early American garden, log cabin, blacksmith shop, farm museum, and carriage museum that has some wonderful sleighs on display. The lawns invite picnickers to set a spell. The house tour takes about 1½ hours.

1611 N. Market St. ℂ **301/694-1646** or 301/694-1648. $3 adults, $2 children and seniors. Apr–Oct tours Mon–Sat 10am–4pm, Sun 1–4pm. Mar, Nov, and Dec tours Sat 10am–4pm and Sun 1–4pm. Closed Jan, Feb.

Schifferstadt   On the western edge of town, you'll find Frederick's oldest standing house, one of America's finest examples of German colonial architecture. Built in 1756 by the Brunner family, who named it for their homeland in Germany, it has stone walls more than 2 feet thick and hand-hewn beams of native oak pinned together with wooden pegs. Unusual original features include an enclosed winding stairway, a vaulted cellar and chimney, wrought-iron hardware, and a perfectly preserved five-plate jamb stove. Guided tours are given throughout the day. A gift shop, featuring arts and crafts, is adjacent in a 19th-century addition. German celebrations are held throughout the year.

1110 Rosemont Ave. ℂ **301/663-3885**. Admission $2 adults. Apr to mid-Dec Tues–Sat 10am–4pm, Sun noon–4pm. Closed mid-Dec to Mar, Easter, July 4, and Thanksgiving.

TOURS

To learn about Frederick's history, join a **guided walking tour** of the historic district Saturday or Sunday (and some Monday holidays). Tours, conducted by certified guides, leave from the Frederick Visitor Center, 19 East Church St. at 1:30pm. Tours are $4.75 for adults, $3.70 for seniors, and free for children under 12. Call ℂ **301/694-7433** or see www.visitfrederick.org. If you can't make a tour, you can buy a self-touring brochure at the visitor center.

If wineries or breweries are more your thing, or if you'd like a Ghost Tour or maybe some insight into the Civil War, the folks at the visitor center can help you find a tour you'd like. There are plenty of them.

A CIVIL WAR BATTLEFIELD

Monocacy National Battlefield   This stretch of farmland was the site of a little-known but important Civil War encounter, the Battle of the Monocacy. General Jubal Early led 18,000 Confederates against a Union force of 5,800 under General Lew Wallace. The Confederates won but their forces were weakened so that Union troops at Fort Stevens could push them back from Washington and save the Union capital late in the war. Today, the battlefield remains virtually unchanged since the battle on July 9, 1864. The visitor center at the beginning of the Gambrills Mill trail has displays and artifacts, and an electronic map detailing the battle. An auto tour is 4 miles (6km) round-trip, and two other trails offer historic and scenic vistas. From May through August, special events are scheduled on the first weekend of the month, and a commemoration of the battle is held on a weekend near July 9.

4801 Urbana Pike. ℂ **301/662-3515**. www.nps.gov/mono. Free admission. Open daily 8am–4:30pm (5:30 on summer weekends). From the north, east, or west, use I-70. Take Exit 54 and proceed south on Rte. 355; the visitor center is on the left one-tenth mile south of Monocacy River bridge. From the south, use I-270. Take Exit 26 and turn left onto Rte. 80; then turn left onto Rte. 355 north; the visitor center is 3.7 miles (6km) north.

SPECTATOR SPORTS & OUTDOOR ACTIVITIES

BASEBALL   Frederick has its own Orioles farm team, the **Frederick Keys.** They play in Harry Grove Stadium, off I-70 and Route 355 (Market St.), from May to August or early September. General admission is about $10. For tickets or information, call ℂ **301/662-0088.**

BIKING   Bicyclists and hikers can access the towpath of the **Chesapeake and Ohio Canal (C&O)** in several places in Frederick County: Point of Rocks, off Route 15 South; Brunswick, Route 79 off Maryland Route 340; and Sandy Hook, left off Route 340, before you cross the Potomac River. The canal runs along the Potomac for 184½ miles (297km) from Georgetown to Cumberland and its towpath is great for biking. Bicycle bells are required on the towpath.

Nearby, both Antietam National Battlefield and Gettysburg National Military Park are terrific sites to tour on bike.

HIKING   The **Appalachian Trail** runs along the border of Frederick and Washington counties, through **Washington Monument State Park, South Mountain State Park, Greenbrier State Park,** and **Gathland State Park,** where hikers can easily access the trail. You can hike the entire Maryland portion in 3 or 4 days, but any section of it makes a great 1-day excursion.

North of Frederick, **Catoctin Mountain Park,** Route 77, Thurmont (© **301/ 663-9388**), adjacent to Camp David, and **Cunningham Falls State Park** (© **301/271-7574**) offer several miles of easy to moderately strenuous hiking trails. Both are off Route 15 north. (See "Serenity & Apples on Route 15," later in this chapter.)

A final great place for a day hike is the rocky **Billy Goat Trail** at Great Falls of the Potomac. Here, a somewhat strenuous hike through woods and over boulders guides you along the cliff walls above the emerald waters of the Mather Gorge.

PADDLING   Though Frederick is landlocked, the Potomac River isn't far. It's an easy trip down Route 340 to Knoxville, almost to Harpers Ferry, West Virginia. There you can get access to both the Potomac and the Shenandoah for canoeing, tubing, white-water rafting, or kayaking. See "Harpers Ferry National Historical Site" later in this chapter.

SHOPPING

Besides the sightseeing, two primary reasons to visit the Frederick historic district are dining and shopping. The continuing restoration of downtown has led to an ever-increasing population of antiques stores, gift shops, and boutiques. The two main shopping areas are within easy walking distance of each other.

Everedy Square and **Shab Row** comprise the first of these shopping areas, beginning at the corner of Patrick and East streets and continuing north about 2½ blocks. The ratio of antiques stores to specialty shops is much lower here; there are several gift shops specializing in country crafts and Christmas decor, a Talbot's store (selling women's clothing), and just a few antiques stores.

For the full Frederick shopping experience, you'll have to go a block or so southwest, to the main shopping district. Start at Carroll Street, and shop your way down Carroll to Patrick Street. Be sure to stop and take a look at the **Community Bridge** on Carroll Street. Turn left on Patrick. From Patrick to Market Street there's virtually nothing but antiques stores and a few restaurants. Below, we've listed only the largest and most unusual shops in both districts; this is by no means a comprehensive list. **Business hours** at most downtown stores are 10 or 11am to 5pm on weekdays and noon to 6pm on weekends.

Because Frederick County is such a fertile area, it's an ideal place to shop for local produce, fruits, jams, jellies, ciders, baked goods, and more. But in most cases, you'll have to leave the historic district and head into the countryside to reach the produce markets (one exception to this is listed below).

ANTIQUES

Antique Cellar   This crowded shop has some of the best prices in town on Victorian, Empire, and primitive furnishings, furniture, frames, and trunks, though some merchandise may need repair and refinishing. Closed Wednesday. 15 E. Patrick St. ✆ **301/620-0591.**

Antique Imports   Located in Shab Row, this shop houses the largest collection of British antique furniture, framed art, and lamps in the region. It is rather pricey, but the quality here is quite good. 125 N. East St. ✆ **301/662-6200.**

Antique Station   Outside the historic district, housed in an old roller-skating rink, this 35,000-square-foot market contains the wares of more than 200 dealers, with an emphasis on glassware and dishes, jewelry, sports memorabilia, and other smaller items. 194 Thomas Johnson Dr. ✆ **301/695-0888.**

Cannon Hill Place   The highlight here is two rooms crammed with vintage clothing. The rest of this large shop is filled with glassware, sports memorabilia, and in general, small, inexpensive items ranging from junk to antiques. 111 S. Carroll St. ✆ **301/695-9304.**

Edward & Edward Consignments   This is a good place to get one-of-a-kind bits and pieces to finish off renovation projects. They carry lots of reasonably priced furniture, lamps, and trunks, as well as ironwork, shutters, ceramic tiles, and wooden trim work. 35 S. Carroll St. ✆ **301/695-9674.**

Emporium Antiques at Creekside   This spacious market, housed in the old Buick dealership, displays the wares of over 130 dealers, with a large collection of light oak furnishings, glassware and china, Fiestaware, vintage clothing, records, books and magazines, and lots more. 112 E. Patrick St. ✆ **301/662-7099.**

ART & GIFTS

Flights of Fancy   Situated in the heart of Everedy Square, this fun, colorful shop carries a little of everything: toys, jewelry, pottery, cards, candles, holiday decor, garden sculptures, and much more. 20 East St. ✆ **301/663-9295.**

OUTDOOR ACCESSORIES

Trail House   This shop offers clothing and equipment for backpacking, camping, hiking, rock climbing, and other sporting pursuits. It also stocks local and regional maps and books, handy for walkers. Hours are Monday to Thursday 10am to 7pm, Friday 10am to 8pm, Saturday 9:30am to 5:30pm, and Sunday noon to 4pm. 17 S. Market St. ✆ **301/694-8448.** Fax 301/694-8448. www.trailhouse.com.

PRODUCE MARKETS

McCutcheon's Factory Store   Downtown, off South Street, this is one of the oldest local enterprises, founded in 1938. It sells a full range of apples, nuts, and dried fruits but is best known for its apple butter, preserves, jellies, and jams, as well as honey, mustards, salad dressings, relishes, hot sauces, ciders, and juices, which are now sold throughout the state. There is also a mail-order service, if you'd like to ship your purchases. Hours are Monday to Friday 8am to 5pm. Weekend hours vary; call ahead. 13 S. Wisner St., Frederick. ✆ **800/888-7537** or 301/662-3261. www.mccutcheons.com.

VINTAGE CLOTHING

Venus on the Half Shell   For casual clothing from the '60s and '70s, stop by this shop. You'll find a good selection of jeans, men's shirts, ladies' suits and dresses, and some nifty coats and jackets. Open Sunday to Monday noon to 5pm, Tuesday to Saturday noon to 9pm. 151 N. Market St. ✆ **301/662-6213.**

FREDERICK AFTER DARK
THE BAR SCENE

Frederick's bar scene has been compared to Georgetown's and is often visited by Washingtonians. The Frederick bar crawl begins at the north end of Market Street at **Olde Town Tavern,** 325 N. Market St. (© 301/695-1454), home of cheap beer and the local college crowd. It then proceeds south down Market, passing other establishments: **Bushwallers,** an Irish bar, 209 N. Market St. (© 301/695-6988); **Brewer's Alley,** a large brewpub, 124 N. Market St. (© 301/631-0089); **Province,** an almost microscopic bar, 129 N. Market St. (© 301/663-1441); **Firestone's,** 105 N. Market St. (© 301/663-0330), whose claim to fame is the live music Wednesday through Saturday, with music ranging from jazz to R&B to classic rock (check www.firestonerestaurant.com for a schedule); **Wags,** a basement bar with good hamburgers (see "Where to Dine," earlier in this chapter), 24 S. Market St. (© 301/694-8451); and **Griff's Landing,** a bar with passable seafood, 43 S. Market St. (© 301/694-8696).

The crawl often ends 2 blocks off Market Street, at the **Bentz Street Raw Bar,** 6 S. Bentz St. (© 301/694-9134). Housed in an old firehouse garage down the street from Baker Park, the Raw Bar is kind of a dive. The decor features cement floors and a mix-and-match assortment of tables, plastic chairs, and booths, but this is the place for live music any night of the week. You might hear blues, jazz, R&B, classical, or sometimes rock. It really is a raw bar, with all kinds of seafood, and the kitchen's open late.

MUSIC & THE PERFORMING ARTS

Because in one sense Frederick is a suburb, it really doesn't have much in the way of an arts scene. However, the **Weinberg Center for the Arts,** 20 W. Patrick St. (© 301/228-2828; www.weinbergcenter.org), a vintage 1920s movie theater that serves as Frederick's cultural arts center, offers a wide variety of musical and comic entertainment, as well as a twice-monthly movie series that even children will like. Local talent, including the Fredericktowne Players and the Maryland Regional Ballet, perform here, too. Call or check the website for performance and ticket info.

In June, July, and August, there are free open-air concerts at the **Baker Park Bandshell,** 2nd and Bentz streets (© 301/662-5161, ext. 247). Concerts are scheduled for 8pm on Sunday evening and feature a variety of local and military bands as well as touring musical acts.

If you are looking for live blues, rock, or folk music, check out the **Bentz Street Raw Bar** (see "The Bar Scene," above).

2 Antietam National Battlefield ⭐

22 miles (35km) W of Frederick, 10 miles (16km) S of Hagerstown, 57 miles (92km) SW of Gettysburg

Antietam (or Sharpsburg to Southerners) is one of the saddest places you can visit in Maryland. A walk down Bloody Lane will send shivers up your spine—especially if you've seen the photographs of the corpses piled up on this road. More than 23,000 men were killed or wounded here when Union forces met and stopped the first attempted Southern invasion of the North in September 1862. It is the site of the bloodiest single-day battle of the Civil War—with more Americans killed or wounded than on any other single day of combat, including D-day. President Abraham Lincoln made a rare battlefield appearance shortly after the battle at Antietam to confront the Union's reluctant General George McClellan over his unwillingness to pursue the retreating Confederate

---

Moments **A Candlelight Remembrance**

On the first Saturday of December, Antietam battlefield is illuminated with 23,000 candles, for all those killed, wounded, or missing after the battle. People come from everywhere, willing to wait an hour or more, for the chance to drive past this sad but beautiful sight. Cars start moving through the park at about 6:30pm and continue until midnight.

---

army. Clara Barton, who founded the American Red Cross 19 years later, nursed the wounded at a field hospital here.

Today, the battlefield is marked by rolling hills and farmland, attended only by a visitor center, a cemetery, modest monuments, and the gentle waters of Antietam Creek. The mood at Antietam is somber. Gettysburg has all the monuments and displays but this is the place to come to consider the tragedy, rather than the triumph, of war.

ACCESS POINTS   The battlefield lies on Maryland Route 65, just north of Sharpsburg. It can also be approached from the east on State Route 34. For a scenic trip from Frederick, take alternate Route 40, which takes you through Middletown and then over South Mountain ridge, where the Battle of South Mountain occurred; then turn right on Route 34 in the town of Boonsboro; this will take you into Sharpsburg.

FEES   Admission to the battlefield is $2 for adults, $4 per family, and free for those under 17.

VISITOR CENTER   Any trip to the Battlefield should start at the **visitor center** (© 301/432-5124), where you can pay your park fees and pick up a free map. The visitor center also offers historical exhibits, a film shown on the hour, a slide show on the half hour, and an observation room with picture windows overlooking the battlefield. The staff provides free information and literature, and can suggest various touring routes for exploring the battlefield and cemetery. The visitor center is open daily June through August from 8:30am to 6pm and September through May from 8:30am to 5pm. Also important to know: The battlefield officially closes 20 minutes after sunset.

SEEING THE HIGHLIGHTS

The battlefield's quiet hills and limited number of monuments make it a stark and silent contrast to the massive memorials of Gettysburg. The park service offers an 8.5-mile (14km) self-guided auto tour that can also be walked or bicycled.

Be sure to see Burnside Bridge, which crosses Antietam Creek near the southern end of the battlefield. Georgia snipers stalled 4,000 Union soldiers for over 3 hours as the Union tried to secure this stone arch bridge.

Another must-see stop is the observation tower over a sunken country lane near the center of the battlefield. This sunken road, now known as **Bloody Lane,** was the scene of a 4-hour encounter that ended with no decisive winner and 4,000 casualties. The graceful stone arches of Burnside Bridge and the harrowing sight of Bloody Lane are among the most memorable images of the battlefield.

Don't miss the **Dunker Church,** which figures prominently in a number of Civil War photos.

Every year, on September 17, the anniversary of the battle is remembered with ranger-led hikes and special events. The 140th anniversary is in 2002.

In addition, a re-enactment weekend is set on a field near the battleground that same weekend. Some 20,000 re-enactors from around the world are planning to come for this anniversary and up to 100,000 visitors are expected in 2002. (Make your hotel plans now.) Check the website www.antietamreenact ment.org or call Ⓒ **301/791-3065** for more information.

NEARBY ACTIVITIES

CANOEING & KAYAKING   For a different view of the area, **Antietam Creek,** which flows the length of the park and then down to the Potomac, is an excellent novice-to-intermediate-level canoe and kayak run offering views of a small waterfall, Burnside Bridge, the ruins of Antietam Furnace, and the old C&O Canal aqueduct. **River and Trail Outfitters,** 604 Valley Rd., Knoxville (Ⓒ **301/695-5177**), offers a variety of guided float trips down this scenic creek as well as canoe and kayak rental.

ANOTHER MILITARY SITE NEAR FREDERICK

Fort Frederick State Park   Fort Frederick's Civil War history is minor but it protected area residents during the French and Indian War and served as a prison during the Revolutionary War. Its massive stone walls have stood through 3 centuries and three wars.

If you are driving through the area, it's worth a look, especially if you can stop by during one of the encampments with re-enactors or other special events. It's not in Frederick; it about 40 miles (64km) west off I-70. Built in 1756 during the French and Indian War to protect Maryland's colonial frontier, this stone fort (unique when every other fort on the frontier was wooden) was so well built and strategically placed that no one ever attacked it, even during Ottawa chief Pontiac's Native American uprising. British and Hessian soldiers were kept prisoner here during the American Revolution. On December 25, 1861, Confederate raiders fought a skirmish with Union troops who had taken over the fort from a local farmer. This was the only fighting Fort Frederick ever saw.

The interior barracks have been restored to look as they did during the French and Indian War, and a platform installed along the inside of the fort walls so that visitors can look out over the stone walls. Daily during the summer, living history re-enactors show visitors about frontier life and life within these fort walls. Visitors can also see these living history lessons on weekends in spring and fall.

The park also has many opportunities to enjoy the outdoors: campsites (Ⓒ **888/432-2267** for group reservations only); two hiking trails through woods and wetlands; and boat rentals for Big Pool.

11100 Fort Frederick Rd., Big Pool, MD 21711. Ⓒ **301/842-2155**. Admission is $2 for ages 13 and older, $1 for ages 6–12, and free for children under 6. The fort's exhibits are open daily May–Sept 8:30am–sunset but is closed Nov–Mar. The park itself, with its walking trails, is open year-round.

WHERE TO DINE

Because Sharpsburg is so blissfully noncommercial, you may find yourself wondering where to eat besides a fast-food restaurant along I-70. Fear not—there are some excellent alternatives.

The closest dining spot is Shepherdstown, West Virginia, just across the Potomac from Sharpsburg on State Route 64. Shepherdstown is a small college town and has numerous coffee shops and cafes along its main street, East German Street. It also is home to the **Yellow Brick Bank Restaurant,** 3 E. German St.

(© **304/876-2208**), serving lunch and dinner in an old bank. Shepherdstown's other fine dining option is the **Bavarian Inn,** on Route 480, on your right just after crossing the Potomac (© **304/876-2551**), a purveyor of excellent but expensive German food.

Another place offering a meal to cap off your battlefield visit is **Old South Mountain Inn** (© 301/371-5400), located in Maryland at the top of South Mountain ridge on Alternate Route 40 between the battlefield and Frederick. Dinner is served every night but Monday. Lunch service begins at 11 on Saturday with Sunday brunch 11:30am to 2pm and Sunday dinner noon to 8pm.

3 Harpers Ferry (WV) National Historical Site

Harpers Ferry, West Virginia, is a town rich in history, from its early years as a colonial frontier town, to its heyday as a center of industry, to its numerous floods. The town is best remembered most for its role in the Civil War, a part that began over a year before the war itself. On October 16, 1859, abolitionist John Brown (already notorious from a bloody raid against slaveholders in Kansas) enlisted 19 men and raided the federal arsenal at Harpers Ferry, intent on arming the nation's slaves and starting a rebellion. Abolitionist and former slave Frederick Douglass warned Brown that the arsenal, in a town wedged between mountains and the Shenandoah and Potomac rivers, would be strategically impossible to hold with so few men, and, as Douglass had foreseen, the raid failed. Brown and his men captured the arsenal but were unable to raise any significant number of slaves into rebellion. They were soon pinned in the arsenal's firehouse (later to be known as John Brown's fort) and Brown was captured when U.S. Marines under Lt. Col. Robert E. Lee stormed the building. Brown was tried and convicted of "conspiring with slaves to commit treason and murder" and was hanged. To many Northerners, Brown was a martyr. His action polarized the nation and was one of the sparks that ignited the war.

Today, Harpers Ferry National Historical Site is a great place for a day trip or weekend. Many old buildings have been restored, its cobblestone streets are still maintained, and the National Park Service administers vast portions of the town. Historical exhibits abound: There are small museums on John Brown's raid, the town's industry, Storer College (an early African-American college established in town), and the town's direct role in the Civil War, when it changed hands between the Union and the Confederacy eight times. There are also plenty of opportunities for outdoor recreation. The Harpers Ferry area abounds in walking and hiking trails (from easy to strenuous) that lead to intriguing sites and excellent views of the two river valleys. The Shenandoah itself is also a source of adventure as a popular rafting and kayaking run suitable for families.

ACCESS POINTS   To get to Harpers Ferry, take **Route 340** west from Frederick. You will cross the Potomac River Bridge (you'll see the town off the bridge to your right) into Virginia, and then about three-quarters of a mile later, cross the Shenandoah River into West Virginia. The historical park's parking lot is about a mile past the bridge over the Shenandoah on the left.

FEES   Park admission is $5 per vehicle and $3 per pedestrian or cyclist. The fee includes the shuttle ride into town and is good for 3 days.

VISITOR CENTER & INFORMATION   Start at the Cavalier Heights Visitor Center, because that is where the parking is (the park service has removed almost all parking from the lower town) and where the shuttles leave for the lower town. The helpful staff will provide you with a free map of the town and tell you about ranger-led tours (available in spring, summer, and fall). You can contact the visitor center at © **304/535-6298** or by writing **Harpers Ferry National Historical Site,** P.O. Box 65, Harpers Ferry, WV 25425. The park visitor center is open daily from 8am to 5pm.

SEEING THE HIGHLIGHTS

Your visit will probably begin with a short shuttle ride from the main parking lot to the town. There, you'll be surrounded by sites, but a few are exceptional. The **John Brown Museum** on Shenandoah Street offers exhibits and audio-visual displays on the abolitionist and tracks the course of his raid, capture, and conviction. Hours for the museum are the same as the park's hours, and admission is included in the park admission.

The **Harper House** is a restored dwelling that sits at the top of the stone stairs, above High Street. The oldest remaining structure in Harpers Ferry, it was built between 1775 and 1782 by town founder Robert Harper and served as a tavern for such notable guests as Thomas Jefferson and George Washington. If you can make the moderately strenuous but short climb farther up the stone stairs past the lovely **St. Peter's Church, Jefferson Rock** 🎯 offers a view of the confluence of the Shenandoah and Potomac rivers that President Jefferson himself called it "stupendous," and said it was worth crossing the Atlantic to see.

If you don't feel like climbing the stairs to Jefferson Rock, you might enjoy a stroll over the walking/railroad bridge across the Potomac. The view of the Potomac is worth the walk. On the way, you'll pass the old armory fire house, known as **John Brown's Fort,** where Brown and his men took their last stand, and on the other side you'll find the bottom of **Maryland Heights** (see below) and the ruins of **Lock No. 33** on the **C&O Canal.**

WALKING, HIKING & WHITE-WATER RAFTING

Aside from the short walks to Jefferson Rock and across the railroad bridge, **Virginius Island** is the park's third intriguing area to explore on foot. Virginius Island was once a booming industrial center with a rifle factory, an iron foundry, a cotton mill, a granary, and a lumberyard. Now only stone ruins remain. There is a short history trail (about a mile) that offers a great way to walk along the Shenandoah and an opportunity to let curious children explore the ruins.

A more strenuous hike will take you to one of the most spectacular views in the state, the view of Harpers Ferry and the confluence of the Shenandoah and Potomac from atop the cliffs of **Maryland Heights.** The hike takes 3 to 5 hours, and the trailhead is near the railroad bridge on the side opposite the town. The park service provides trail maps for the hike to Maryland Heights as well as to nearby **Weverton Cliffs,** which also boasts a very good view. If you are planning more than a day's hike, the **Appalachian Trail** and the **C&O Canal** join briefly and pass right by Harpers Ferry, on the opposite side of the Potomac, making the town a great stop on a multi-day hike on either of these popular routes.

To experience Harpers Ferry from an entirely different vantage point, **River and Trail Outfitters,** 604 Valley Rd., Knoxville, MD (© **301/695-5177;** www. rivertrail.com), offers half-day white-water rafting trips down the Shenandoah–Potomac, which pass right by the town. Although this can be a harrowing trip during high-water season (Feb through mid-Apr), most of the time it's a fun raft trip through beautiful scenery and a few rapids—in short, a trip suitable for families. Guides lead you down Bull Falls and Washing Machine and through the Upper and Lower Staircases while sharing local history, legends, and corny jokes. Prices depend on the season and the number in your group, but generally run about $45 to $90 per person. River and Trail also offers guided hikes up Maryland Heights, C&O bike trips, and cross-country ski trips in winter. Experienced paddlers can rent a canoe or kayak and lessons are available for every level.

Fishing is permitted in both the Potomac and Shenandoah rivers but adults may require licenses. Check with the visitor center.

WHERE TO STAY

The Historical Park is only about 25 minutes away from Frederick, so you can stay there. Closer to Harpers Ferry, the 50-room **Comfort Inn** (© **800/228-5150** or 304/535-6391), at the corner of Route 340 and Union Street, is within walking distance of the town, about a mile from the visitor center.

WHERE TO DINE

Good dining options are limited. There are numerous overpriced cafes and sandwich shops along Potomac Street. The food is okay but the wait can be interminable on a busy day. If you are looking for something a little more upscale, your better bet is to try nearby Frederick (see earlier in this chapter).

4 Gettysburg (PA) National Military Park ⟨★⟩

34 miles (55km) N of Frederick

Just north of the Maryland–Pennsylvania line, Gettysburg was the "high-water mark" of the Confederate rebellion. Here the 70,000-strong army of Confederate soldiers under General Robert E. Lee faced 93,000 Union men under General George Meade in a 3-day conflict that would change the course of the war. After the battle, Lee's army returned to Virginia and would never again mount an effective attack into Union territory. Later, President Lincoln would use the dedication of the National Cemetery here to deliver his "Gettysburg Address."

The park itself is quite large and almost surrounds the touristy town of Gettysburg. Unlike the town (characterized by fast-food joints and tour companies), the park is defined by rolling hills, fences, farms, occasional cannons, and monuments of marble, stone, and bronze erected in honor of the soldiers who died here.

Gettysburg is the largest and most popular of the area's three major Civil War sites and boasts great facilities and large crowds. The crowds can often be avoided by visiting in autumn, winter, or spring. October to early November is a terrific time of year; crowds are rare and the autumn leaves are beautiful. If you come in summer, try to schedule your Gettysburg time for weekdays, when crowds are smaller, and because schools are out, you will be less likely to run into busloads of field-tripping children.

GETTING THERE   Take U.S. **Route 15** north from Frederick and I-70. After about 30 miles (48km) you'll cross into Pennsylvania; then take the first exit and turn left on Business U.S. Route 15 north. The visitor center is 6 miles (10km) ahead on your right, and the town is just past the visitor center.

FEES & HOURS   Admission to Gettysburg National Military Park is free. The battlefield is open daily from 6am to 10pm; the visitor center and Cyclorama, which has an admission fee, are open daily from 8am to 5pm. The cemetery is open dawn to dusk.

VISITOR CENTER & INFORMATION   The best place to start any visit to the park, the visitor center houses a Civil War museum, an excellent bookshop, and an electric map display, and it is the starting point for all the National Park Service supported tours (see "Organized Tours," below). Rangers are glad to answer questions and offer maps showing hiking trails and the 18-mile (29km) self-guided auto tour, which hits all the major sites. Contact the **visitor center** at © **717/334-1124,** or write to Gettysburg National Military Park, P.O. Box 1080, Gettysburg, PA 17325. For security reasons, backpacks or large parcels are not allowed in the visitor center or Cyclorama.

SEEING THE HIGHLIGHTS

The park has three main indoor attractions: the museum of the Civil War, the electric map presentation, and the Cyclorama. The **Gettysburg Museum of the Civil War** and the **Electric Map Presentation** are housed in the visitor center. The museum contains audiovisual displays and a great collection of rifles, pistols, ammunition, cannons and cannon shot, equipment, and uniforms from both sides of the war. The wide variety of equipment and weaponry on display helps to bring into focus the diversity of people who came together in the Civil War. For instance, on display are several Confederate officers' uniforms, each of which was custom-made (sometimes by the officer's wife). Because they're handmade, often the color and design of the uniforms is not really uniform at all: Some are dark gray, some light gray, and some faded in the sun to a butternut brown.

The 30-minute electric map program depicts the course of the battle in a special auditorium surrounding a very large illuminated map. The cost of the presentation is $3 for adults, $2.50 for seniors, and $2 for ages 6 to 15.

One of the best parts of a trip to Gettysburg is the **Gettysburg Cyclorama** ☞. Housed in a contemporary building next to the visitor center, the cyclorama is a circular oil painting—a popular form of entertainment in the late 1800s. Measuring 356 feet in circumference, the painting offers a wraparound view of Pickett's Charge, the climax of the battle. Completed in 1884 by French artist Paul Dominique Philippoteaux, this work is one of only a few cycloramas left in the world today. Admission is $3 for adults, $2.50 for seniors, and $2 for ages 6 to 15. It includes a viewing of the painting, enhanced by a sound-and-light program narrated by actor Richard Dreyfuss.

After you have toured some of the park's indoor attractions, it's time to head outside. The park is relatively large, so you'll need a car or bike if you want to see most of it. Outside the visitor center is **Gettysburg National Cemetery,** where over 3,000 Union soldiers are buried, and where Lincoln gave the Gettysburg Address on November 19, 1863.

In the park itself, there are over 100 monuments—large and small—dedicated by various states to their military units who fought here. The largest and most often visited is the granite-domed **Pennsylvania Memorial.** Constructed of almost 3,000 tons of cut granite, raw stone, and cement, the monument consists of a dome supported by four arched columns topped by a statue depicting the winged goddess of victory and peace.

Not as frequently visited, but well worth seeing, are the dramatic bronze sculptures of state memorials of the south. Lacking sufficient funds to erect monuments to all of their military units, the defeated states set out to create a single memorial from each state honoring its soldiers. The **Virginia State Memorial** was the first, dedicated in 1917, and is topped by a brass sculpture of General Lee mounted on a house. The **North Carolina, Louisiana,** and **Mississippi memorials** along West Confederate Avenue are particularly dramatic, featuring statuary depicting soldiers in battle.

As you're perusing the monuments, look for the John Burns Portrait Statue. At over 70 years of age, this local constable and veteran of the War of 1812 asked Col. Langhorn Wister for permission to fight with the Union troops. Although initially mocked, he earned the soldiers' respect, fighting alongside several Union regiments at Gettysburg before being wounded and carried from the field.

If you have time, stop by **Devil's Den,** an outcropping of rocks located almost between Little and Big Round Tops (two important high-ground positions during the battle). Then it was a hiding place for snipers; now, these large, rounded boulders are a fun place to climb around and explore.

ORGANIZED TOURS

The Association of Licensed Battlefield Guides, a group set up in 1913 by Civil War veterans to ensure that visitors receive accurate information about the battle, offers park tours out of the visitor center by (for information, contact the visitor center). These guides can tell you about everything from troop movements to who built the Pennsylvania Memorial and how much it cost. A licensed battlefield guide will ride in your vehicle, giving you a personalized tour. The fee for the licensed battlefield guides is $40 for a 2-hour tour for one to five people.

Gettysburg Battlefield Bus Tours, 778 Baltimore St. (© **717/334-6296**), offers battlefield tours on either an air-conditioned or double-decker bus. The tour covers 23 miles (37km) and features a dramatized audio presentation. It costs $16.95 for adults and $11.75 for children.

WHERE TO STAY

Gettysburg has two fine chain hotel options within walking distance of the visitor center. The closest is the 109-room **Quality Inn** (© **800/228-5151** or 717/334-1103; www.gettysburgqualityinn.com), a well-appointed motel next to the visitor center. It has outdoor and indoor pools, a lounge, and an exercise room. Rates ($45–$110 double) include continental breakfast.

Not quite as close is the 102-room **Holiday Inn Battlefield** (© **717/334-6211**), which is a 5-minute walk from the visitor center at the intersection of Pennsylvania Route 97 and Business Route 15.

AN EXCURSION TO NEW MARKET ✩

New Market calls itself the "antiques capital of Maryland." It's a delightful place to stop and browse in the shops along Route 144 (Main St.) and get a bite to eat. The street itself is an antique. The town, 6 miles (10km) east of Frederick on Interstate 70 (Exit 62), was founded in 1793 as a stop for travelers along the National Pike. The blacksmith shops and Conestoga wagons are gone but the buildings remain. The town is listed on the National Register of Historic Places.

The best days to visit are weekends. Every shop is open on weekends, with a number opening as early as 10am. Everything closes at 5pm. About half of the stores have weekday hours. Look for the flags flying to indicate an open store.

Two weekend festivals are worth a visit: during **New Market Days** at the end of September, the town celebrates autumn with local crafts, entertainment, and food. For **Christmas in New Market** in early December the air turns festive with carols, carriage rides, and visits with Santa. The town looks especially pretty, too.

The **New Market Antique Dealers Association** publishes a free guide/map that's available throughout the town, or, before you set out on your trip, visit www.newmarkettoday.com.

The Browsery   Handcrafted furniture and accessories are the focus of this shop. 55 W. Main St. ✆ **301/831-9644.**

Grange Hall Antiques   Housed in a former Grange Hall, this shop offers an eclectic variety of graniteware, jewelry, tools, and country primitives, as well as fishing and sporting antiques and miniatures. Open Tuesday through Sunday from 11am to 5pm. 1 Eighth Alley (off Main St.). ✆ **301/865-5651.** www.grangehall antiques.com.

New Market General Store   The feeling of a 19th century country store continues here among the jars of rock candy, local honey, preserves, potpourri, herbs, and Windsor reproduction furniture from the Lawrence Crouse Workshop. If you're hungry check out the specials at the lunch counter in back. Hours are Monday to Friday 9am to 5pm, Saturday 9am to 6pm, Sunday 10am to 6pm; closed Thursday. 26 W. Main St. ✆ **301/865-6313.** www.newmarketgeneral store.com.

Victorian Manor Jewelry   This shop specializes in antique and estate jewelry. Hours are Saturday to Sunday noon to 5pm. 33 W. Main St. ✆ **301/865-3083.**

WHERE TO DINE

The General Store's breakfast and lunch can be very tempting. And the **Village Tea Room** at 81 W. Main St. (✆ **301/865-3450**) is a dainty little spot for sandwiches, soups, salads, and afternoon tea. It's open Tuesday to Friday 11:30am to 3:30pm and weekends 11:30am to 5pm. But for an elegant full-course meal, there's only one choice in New Market. And that's Mealey's.

Mealey's ✦ AMERICAN   From the moment you step into the pretty parlor, Mealey's staff treats you as a welcome guest. With low-beamed ceilings, pink tablecloths, and stone fireplaces, the dining room is warm and inviting. Want a cozier spot? Ask to be seated in the smaller dining room adjacent. The menu is filled with delicious options at lunch and dinner. Several dinner selections appear on the lunch menu, at lunchtime prices. The crab bisque is rich and filled with crabmeat. Mealey's chicken is marinated in fruit juice and then grilled. Dinner choices include prime rib, fresh fish, and crab, and there's an extensive wine list. They've got a kid's menu, too, with the usual grilled cheese and chicken.

8 Main St. ✆ **301/865-5488.** Fax 301/865-4876 . Reservations recommended for dinner. Main courses $13.95–$28.95; lunch $6.50–$21.95. AE, DC, DISC, MC, V. Tues–Thurs 5–9pm, Fri–Sat 11:30am–2:30pm and 5–9pm, Sun noon–8pm. Free parking in lot on Eighth Alley.

5 Serenity & Apples on Route 15

If you're planning a trip to Frederick or a drive through the Civil War sites and on to Gettysburg, Pennsylvania, reserve a day for the treasures of Route 15. It's a high-speed four-lane highway with too many trucks but many delightful sites awaiting you. As you drive between the orchards and farms, the foothills of the Catoctin Mountains come closer.

The two major towns, charming little places, are Thurmont and Emmitsburg. Thurmont means "gateway to the mountains" and is notable for its two main parks. Emmitsburg was the home of St. Elizabeth Ann Seton and is still the home of Mount St. Mary's College, where a replica of the Grotto of Lourdes is located.

These are great places for a weekend getaway or day trip; both are only about 90 minutes from Baltimore.

SIGHTSEEING

Cunningham Falls State Park (✆ **301/271-7574**) borders **Catoctin Mountain Park** (✆ **301/663-9343**). Catoctin, a national park, has several good trails and is the home of presidential retreat Camp David—whose specific location is top secret. Cunningham Falls also has hiking trails, most of which lead to the beautiful falls as well as Hunting Creek Lake, perfect for swimming and easy canoeing. There's also a guarded beach, a snack bar, and canoe rentals.

Get a guide to the many park trails from the visitor center at the Cunningham Falls State Park's Manor Visitor Center off Route 15 or at Park Central on Route 77. Another trail ends at the **Catoctin Iron Furnace,** the remains of a Revolutionary War–era iron-making complex. The stone casting shed has been rebuilt to help you imagine making iron back in the 18th century.

Four short trails will take you to the base of Cunningham Falls. Three are on the William Houck Area off Maryland Route 77. They range from moderate to strenuous and from a half-mile to 2.8 miles (0.8km to 4.5km). The fourth trail is set aside for the handicapped. A handicapped-only parking lot is right on Route 77 and a boardwalk goes all the way to the falls. It's about 0.3 miles (0.5km), on mostly flat terrain. The waterfall is pretty, and its setting is in a canopy of 100-year-old oaks and hickories, with a floor scattered with huge green rocks, gurgling streams. Stay a few minutes or stay the rest of the day. There are benches set on rock outcroppings for resting or taking in the serenity.

If you want to go off the beaten track (off Rte. 15 and onto Rte. 550 North) for a breathtaking mountain view, take a drive to **Pen Mar Park** (✆ **301/791-3187**). If you're planning to go to Bluebird on the Mountain bed-and-breakfast (see "Where to Stay," below), make sure you take a few minutes and head for Pen Mar Park. The view is worth the short drive past Fort Ritchie and up Pen Mar Road. A dance hall and observation deck have been built right on the edge of the mountain and offer terrific views of the Blue Ridge Mountains. From mid-May to the end of September, free big band concerts (and dance lessons at 1pm in May and June) are held in the dance hall beginning at 2pm. There's a playground for the children who aren't impressed, and hikers can head onto the Appalachian Trail from here. It's 920 miles (1,481km) to Georgia and 1,080 miles (1,739km) to Maine. Call ✆ **301/791-3187** for directions and a schedule of concerts.

Mother Seton's Shrine ★★★ More formally called the Basilica of the National Shrine of St. Elizabeth Ann Seton, the shrine is comprised of a church built in honor of the first American-born saint canonized in the Roman Catholic Church, and several of the buildings where she lived and worked. A young widow who converted to Catholicism, she lived here with her children as she began both the Catholic parochial school system and a new order of religious women. The church is a beautiful monument but the houses where she lived— the Stone House (built about 1750) and the White House (built for her in 1810)—offer a glimpse of her life here in the mountains. Tours of the Seton Way are self-guided and begin in the visitor center and museum. The guides in these hallowed spaces are quite patient with children.

Seton Shrine Center, 333 S. Seton Ave. ✆ 301/447-6606. Fax 301/447-6061. www.setonshrine.org. No fee, donations welcome. Basilica open every day. Other shrine sites open Wed–Sun 10am–4:30pm. Closed on Mon and Tues, also Jan 7–20, New Year's Day, Easter, Thanksgiving, and Christmas. From Rte. 15, turn left on S. Seton Ave. Shrine ¾ mile on right.

The Grotto of Lourdes If you know the story of St. Bernadette, the French peasant girl who saw Jesus' mother Mary in a grotto, but you aren't going to

France any time soon, you might want to stop here. The site has been re-created on a mountain overlooking Mount St. Mary's College. You'll know you're here when you see the 95-foot tall campanile topped with a golden statue of Mary. As you wander through these wooded paths, there are other shrines and the Stations of the Cross. It is said St. Elizabeth Seton came to this site often (although the grotto wasn't built at that time). It's quite pretty. Mass is also often offered here.

On the grounds of Mount St. Mary's College & Seminary. (C) **301/447-5318.** Fax: 301/447-5099. www. msmary.edu/studentsandstaff/grotto/.

National Fallen Firefighters Memorial *(Finds)* This site, which is still being developed at the National Fire Academy next door to Mother Seton's Shrine, holds special significance since September 11, 2001. The firefighters who died at the World Trade Center were honored in ceremonies here last October. President George W. Bush was the first president to visit in the memorial's 20-year history. The firefighters' names will be inscribed on the monument in time for the annual Memorial Day weekend in 2002. The service in tribute to firefighters killed in the line of duty is always held the first day of Fire Prevention Week in October. Plans are underway for construction of a park at this site.

16825 S. Seton Ave. (C) **301/447-6771.** Open daily 24 hours.

WHERE TO STAY

If you think this is the kind of getaway that will last more than a day, stop in one of the few motels on Route 15.

The Cozy Inn This inn has a certain charm in its 21 rooms. Its premium rooms are named after presidents and decorated with things that recall them. President Reagan's room—actually one of four little cottages on the property—features a portrait of the president and horse decorations. The Roosevelt Room has a king-sized bed in a style FDR used. All of the premium rooms have two televisions, fireplaces, and Jacuzzi garden tubs. There are three levels of rooms at the inn, including standard rooms. Continental breakfast is served in the lobby and features homemade breakfasts and New Orleans bread pudding. Call ahead for reservations, especially if the president will be at Camp David; the press corps and president's staff often stays here. The Cozy Inn also hosts special events, including a Strawberry Festival in June, Peace Festival in August, German Fest in October, and Christmas Open House Thanksgiving weekend.

105 Frederick Rd. (C) **301/271-4301.** www.cozyvillage.com. 21 units, including 4 cottages. $44–$150 double; includes continental breakfast. AE, DISC, MC, V. **Amenities:** Cozy Inn Restaurant (see "Where to Dine" below). *In room:* A/C, fridge, coffeemaker, hair dryer.

The Rambler Hotel One of the best features of this hotel is Buddy, a 5-year-old German shorthair pointer who welcomes the guests in his own way. He's been known to carry small bags, and visit guests missing their own pets. He's famous, too, having been on cable TV's Animal Planet channel. The rooms are reminiscent of your mother's guest room: spic and span, with new carpets and bedspreads; and cozy, though with no extra amenities. The end units are much larger. Two double beds and a pullout couch allow a family of five to stretch out.

998 W. Patrick St. (C) **800/245-6701** or 301/271-2424. 30 units. AE, DISC, MC V. *In room:* A/C. Fridge and microwave available for additional charge.

The Sleep Inn and Suites *(Kids)* Just off Route 15 at 501 Silo Hill Parkway, Emmitsburg's first hotel opened in June 2001. Attention, kids! Televisions have Nintendo at $6.95 an hour (plenty of games to choose from). Best of all, you can use your hour in increments—great for waiting for Mom to finish dressing. The Fireplace Suite has a gas fireplace in the seating area and a Jacuzzi for two in the bathroom. Guests can open double doors to enjoy the fireplace and television from the comfort of the tub. That's a sleep sofa in the seating area. Call ahead for reservations since nearby Mount St. Mary's College sends families and sports teams here and the place can be booked solid. Owners of the Sleep Inn plan to build another hotel and two restaurants adjacent to the current facilities.

501 Silo Hill Pkwy. ℂ 800/SLEEP-INN or 301/447-0044. Fax 301/447-3144. www.sleepinn.com. 79 units. $69–119 double; includes continental breakfast. Children free in room with parents. AE, DISC, MC, V. **Amenities:** Pool; exercise room. *In room:* A/C, TV with Nintendo, dataport, coffeemaker, iron.

A B&B

Bluebird on the Mountain ⭐   This delightful place is worth the drive through Sabillasville into Cascade. Besides, it's not really far from Route 15, nor from Gettysburg, Pennsylvania, Hagerstown, or Antietam Battlefield.

This white clapboard turn-of-the-20th-century house has five rooms, including a two-bedroom and bath suite for families. Pets are also welcome. The first-floor all-white room has a wood-burning fireplace. Another room features a cozy down featherbed. The rose garden room has its own sun porch. The family suite isn't fancy but the bathroom has its own whirlpool and plenty of room. The last room has its entrance from the garden, just steps from its own hot tub. Bluebird on the Mountain has an arrangement with a massage therapist who will bring her own table and massage away by appointment. Ask Edie about the spa retreats for small groups, too. A continental breakfast with homemade breads is served every weekday, and hot breakfast on Sundays.

14700 Eyler Ave., Cascade, MD 21719. ℂ 800/362-9526 or 301/241-4161. www.bbonline.com/md/blue bird/. 5 units. $100–$130 double; includes continental-plus breakfast. AE, DISC, MC, V (cash or check preferred). **Amenities:** Garden; massages available by appointment. *In room:* A/C, some rooms have VCRs.

WHERE TO DINE

The Carriage House Inn ⭐ AMERICAN   This historic inn once hosted President Bill Clinton, his wife Hillary, and about 20 of their closest friends. They came for the crab cakes—as many diners here do, unless they choose the prime rib. A big stone fireplace dominates the dining room of this 1857 building. Wide plank floors, Early American–style furniture, and pink and blue linens add to the room's warmth. Special enough for the president of the United States, it's also a place for children. Kids' menus are pasted inside picture books. After your little ones choose between the hamburger or chicken strips for $4.95 or the fried shrimp or petit filet mignon for $8.95, they've got a book to keep them occupied until the food comes. In the fall of 2001, a piano lounge was due to open.

200 S. Seton Ave., Emmitsburg. ℂ 301/447-2366. Fax 301/447-2685. Reservations recommended. Lunch $5.95–$10.25, dinner $15.95–$30.95. AE, DISC, MC V. Daily 11am–9pm, till 10pm on weekends.

Cozy Restaurant *Finds* AMERICAN   Just by looking at the walls, you can tell the Cozy's been around a long time. There's a caboose, memorabilia of summits at nearby Camp David, mementoes of "hoboes" who worked here—oh yes, and they serve food, too; hearty buffet food as well as a huge menu are available in the dining rooms and on the deck in summer. There's room and food enough for quite a lot of people. If you're a root beer fan, try the house brew. New in the fall of 2001 was the fondue room. There's only room for a select few to enter this little nook that recalls the 1970s in decor as well as food. A *prix-fixe* menu includes three courses of fondue and a salad.

103 Frederick Rd., Thurmont. ℂ 301/271-4301. www.cozyvillage.com. Reservations recommended on weekends. Main courses $8.19–$14.99, lunch buffet $5.99–$8.49, dinner buffet $7.79–$$15.99. AE, MC, V. Mon–Thurs 11am–9pm, Fri–Sat 8am–8:45pm, Sun 11:45am–8:45pm.

The Shamrock Restaurant SEAFOOD/STEAKS   This cozy little restaurant proudly proclaims its Irish roots in its decorations and in its celebrations of St. Patrick's Day. You can get Harp Lager or Guinness stout here to go with your hot crab dip, your Illegal Basket of Onion Rings or your crab cake and Wellington Shrimp—shrimp wrapped in pastry and baked. It's a homey place with friendly waitresses and even a few Irish souvenirs for sale at the counter. Oh, and if you want to take your pie home with you, they're on sale, too.

Rte. 15 and Fitzgerald Rd., Thurmont. ℂ 301/271-2912. Reservations recommended on weekends. Main courses $5.50–$17.95. AE, MC, V. Mon–Sat 11am–10pm, Sun noon–9pm.

SHOPPING

If you're in the mood for shopping while on your Route 15 travels, you'll have to be content with the small shops at the Cozy Inn—the **Cozy Shop of Curiosity** (ℂ **301/271-4300**) carries all kinds of antiques, vintage clothing, and small specialties such as the soaps and creams made in nearby Sabillasville.

And you don't want to miss the **orchard stands.** There are several, all with fresh vegetables and fruits grown right in these foothills.

Catoctin Mountain Orchard, on Route 15 (15036 N. Franklinville Rd.), has locally baked pastries and McCutcheon's preserves (produced in nearby Frederick), as well as fresh fruit. Pick your own berries in June and July, pumpkins and Cameo, Pink Lady, and Honey Crisp apples in fall. The orchard is open January 1 to April 1, Friday to Sunday 9am to 5pm; June 1 through October 25, Monday through Thursday 9am to 5pm and Friday through Sunday 9am to 6pm. The rest of the year it's open daily 9am to 5pm. Call ℂ **301-271-2737,** fax 301/271-2850, or check the website www.catoctinmountainorchard.com.

Gateway Farm Market and Candyland not only has produce and fresh cider in season, it has long tables filled with boxes of "penny candy." Pick out your own and fill a bag. A pound was $2.59 in fall 2001. Sugarless candy is $4.39 a pound. (Once your children or grandchildren learn of this place, you can never pass it again without stopping.) They also make and will send fruit baskets and gift packs. It's open daily 9am to 6pm on Route 15 at 14802 North Franklinville Rd.; ℂ **301/271-2322.**

Scenic View Orchards, which truly deserves its name, is actually on Route 550 in Sabillasville. Seven generations of farmers have grown the fruits and vegetables on the farm here. It's open daily 10am to 6pm, June through November, beginning with strawberries and ending with pumpkins, cider, and Christmas trees. They grow their own flowers, too. Pick a bunch. Call ℂ **301/271-2149** or check their website at www.scenicvieworchards.com.

8

Western Maryland

Whether you come for the scenery or to take part in the many recreational activities, Western Maryland is a haven for outdoors lovers in any season. Garrett and Allegany counties offer a number of accessible destinations, and the drive there is a beautiful journey.

Visitors are drawn to the more than 100,000 acres of parkland, including Cranesville Swamp Nature Preserve, Savage River State Forest, and Swallow Falls State Park. There are lakes for swimming, fishing, and boating, including Lake Habeeb at Rocky Gap State Park near Cumberland, and Deep Creek Lake, the centerpiece of Garrett County's outdoor attractions. White-water rafters and fly-fishermen enjoy the region's rivers and streams, such as the Youghiogheny and the Savage.

As remote as it seems, Western Maryland, which stretches from the state's skinniest section at Hancock to the West Virginia border, Western Maryland is easy to reach by way of a interstate highways. To get here from Baltimore, take I-70. Washingtonians can connect with I-70 from I-270. When I-70 turns north into Pennsylvania near Hancock, it connects to I-68, which heads west into West Virginia. I-81 joins I-70 near Hagerstown to bring visitors from Pennsylvania and Virginia. In fact, visitors often combine visits to West Virginia or Pennsylvania with their trip to Western Maryland.

U.S. Route 219 intersects I-68 and heads south to Deep Creek Lake.

For those who prefer a more scenic route, the old U.S. Route 40, the nation's first national pike, connects Frederick to Cumberland and other points west and east. It's slower going but much more interesting.

1 The Great Outdoors in Western Maryland

Western Maryland's gently rolling mountains are part of the Appalachians, with Backbone Mountain (elevation 3,360 ft./1008m) marking the eastern Continental Divide. Outdoor enthusiasts can find endless forests, mountain lakes, and miles of streams and rivers to play on. White-water rafters come to meet the challenges of the Youghiogheny (pronounced "Yok-a-gain-ee"; those in the know just call it the "Yock"). Boaters flock to Garrett's seven lakes. Skiers head for the hills of Wisp, and cross-country skiers glide along the state parks' trails. There's also windsurfing, ATV and snowmobile trails, fly-fishing, mountain biking, golf, hunting, hiking, and camping.

Of the 100,000 acres of protected wilderness in Western Maryland, 40,000 lie in Green Ridge State Forest east of Cumberland and 53,000 are in the Savage River State Forest near Deep Creek Lake.

Recent environmental efforts in the region have paid off, and now, more than at any time in the last 20 years, the area is great for wildlife watching and fishing. Some species, notably hawks and black bears that were beginning to disappear

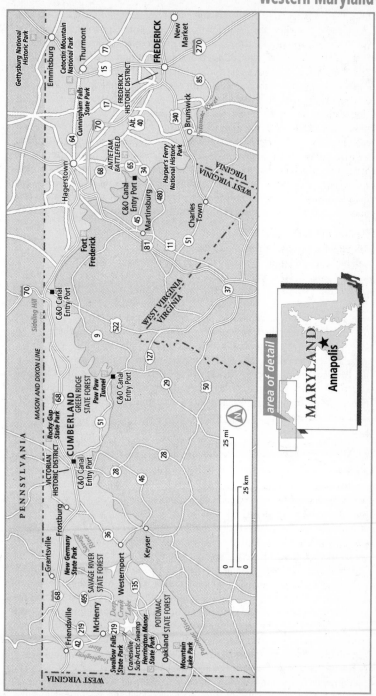

from the landscape are returning in force to the region's parks and forests. Garrett County launched a major effort to reduce the damage to the Casselman, North Branch Potomac, and Youghiogheny rivers caused by years of acid mining in the mountains above them. As a result, these rivers now boast some of the best fly-fishing around and have been featured on national fishing shows.

The state parks and forests, along with a handful of municipal, national, and privately held parks, offer places to hike and watch wildlife, trails for biking and cross-country skiing, fly-fishing streams, and campsites.

In other chapters, this section is organized by activities such as biking and camping. But in Western Maryland, you can do just about anything anywhere. So here instead is a rundown of each of the parks—except Deep Creek Lake State Park, which has its own section—and some of its unique qualities to help you decide exactly where you want to go and what you want to do and see. For more information, call the individual state parks for brochures and maps (see numbers below), or visit the website **www.dnr.state.md.us**.

IN ALLEGANY COUNTY

Allegany has three state parks, plus the terminus of the C&O Canal, which is a national park and quite popular with bikers, hikers, and history buffs.

The scenic **C&O Canal** (✆ **301/722-8226**), whose terminus is in Cumberland, is the ideal place to begin a trip down the canal towpath. The towpath is primarily flat and wide and not trafficked by motor vehicles, except for the occasional forest-ranger patrol vehicle. Both mountain and touring cyclists enjoy all or part of the 184-mile (296km) route along the Potomac River all the way to Georgetown (in Washington, D.C.) from Cumberland. The canal's towpath is a great flat trail for hikers and bikers. The canal passes by numerous sites, including Paw Paw Tunnel, Fort Frederick, Harpers Ferry National Historic Park, and Great Falls. The trip from Cumberland is almost all gently downhill. Any small portion of the canal towpath can make a great 1-day biking trip. Because flooding can make some of the towpath impassable, make sure you check with the park service to see if the route you intend to bike is clear.

At 481 acres, **Dan's Mountain** (✆ **301/777-2139**) is the smallest park in Western Maryland. Located about 9 miles (14km) south of Frostburg, the park is for day-use only and offers features kids will enjoy. The Olympic-size pool has a water slide and views that make you feel as if you're swimming on top of the world. A recycled tire playground will work off some of your energy even if the pool and hiking and biking trails didn't.

Green Ridge State Forest (Exit 64 off I-68; ✆ **301/478-3124**) is the largest park in the county, its 43,000 acres home to abundant wildlife, from deer to wild turkey, and scenic vistas over the Potomac River. New Adirondack-style shelters have been added along the 24-mile (39km) backpacking and hiking trail. The park's roads and most of the 43 miles (69km) of hiking trails as well as a separate bike trail and racecourse are open to mountain bikers. At the forest's southern end you'll find the Paw Paw Tunnel (see "Attractions," later in this chapter) on the C&O Canal. Primitive camping is available at 92 sites ($6 per night). The park's activities include off-road driving, hunting, canoeing, kayaking, and fishing on the Potomac River.

Rocky Gap State Park ✿ (Exit 50 off I-68; ✆ **301/777-2139**) has great trails on which to commune with nature or to enjoy a walk in the forest. Rocky Gap offers views of Lake Habeeb, mountain overlooks, and a stout trail up Evitts Mountain to the remains of a 1784 homestead. Walk along Rocky Gap Run to see the mile-long gorge and hemlock forest. The lake has three swimming beaches, boat rentals, and two boat ramps—come ready for swimming or fishing. The park has 278 **campsites,** including 10 mini-cabins. Camping is very popular, so call ahead for reservations in summer (© **301/777-2138**).

SUPPLIERS, TOURS, GUIDES IN ALLEGANY COUNTY

C&O Bicycle, S. Pennsylvania Ave., Hancock (© **301/678-6665**), rents and sells bicycles in its canalside shop. You'll find all kinds of bikes here, including recumbent and tandems. C&O repairs bikes as well. Rates are $4.50 an hour with a $9 minimum. Reservations are accepted.

If you need a guide for your outdoor adventures, **Allegany Expeditions** (© **800/819-5170** or 301/722-5170) offers guided outdoor experiences in surrounding parks, including hiking, backpacking, cave exploration, canoeing, and rock climbing. Also, call about cross-country-ski packages in New Germany State Park as well as fly-fishing and bass-fishing expeditions. They also rent canoes.

GARRETT COUNTY

Garrett County has a large complex of state parks and forests, some connected to one another. In addition, you'll find a nature preserve run by the Nature Conservancy and a municipal park for swimming and biking. In the state parks, trails are available for hiking, snowmobiling, mountain biking, and horseback riding. To find a park that best suits your interests, visit **www.dnr.state.md.us/ publiclands/trailguide**.

On the eastern side of the county, **Savage River State Forest** (© **301/ 895-5759**) comprises 53,000 acres along the Savage River and the reservoir. Within the state forest, there are two state parks: **New Germany** and **Big Run** (© **301/895-5453** or 301/746-8359). Route 495 off I-68 runs through the state forest and provides access to both parks. For information about all three, write to 349 Headquarters Lane, Grantsville, MD 21536.

Potomac–Garrett State Forest (© **301/334-2038**) is actually two forests run by the same office. Its land, totaling 18,000 acres, is spread out in patches in the southern and western parts of the county. Write to 1431 Potomac Camp Rd., Oakland, MD 21550, for information and brochures.

On the western edge of the state are **Swallow Falls State Park** ★★★ and **Herrington Manor State Park** (© 301/334-9180) both of which provide access to the Youghiogheny and cross-country-skiing in the winter. The parks are connected by a 5.5-mile (8.9km) trail. Swallow Falls has 10 miles (16km) of hiking trails. Follow the Youghiogheny for the views of the Swallow Falls and the even more spectacular Muddy Falls, which drop 63 feet. The walk through one of Maryland's last virgin forests of giant pines and hemlocks shouldn't be missed—you won't forget its quiet beauty.

Swallow Falls State Park features the area's largest camping facility, with 65 improved sites and modern bathhouses with showers and laundry tubs. The camping fee is $11 to $16 per night; reservations can be made up to a year in advance. Pets are permitted on leashes in designated camping areas and in day-use areas in the off-season.

Cross-country skiers come to **Herrington Manor** for the 10 miles (16km) of groomed, marked trails. It also offers equipment rental, cabins, and large stone warming rooms where skiers can grab a snack and hot cocoa. Trails and rental facilities are open from 8am to 4pm during good skiing conditions.

In summer, these same trails appeal to hikers. The 53-acre Herrington Lake has guarded beaches in summer, canoes, rowboats, and paddleboats to rent from May through September. Bring your tennis racquet or volleyball: courts are waiting. Campers can reserve one of 20 furnished log cabins year-round. (Book early, as much as a year ahead.) The park also offers a cross-country-ski race in January, a maple syrup demonstration in March, and an apple butter boil in September.

Savage River State Forest (© 301/895-5759), which surrounds New Germany and Big Run state parks, is the largest of Maryland's state forests, with about 53,000 acres. It features miles of rugged and challenging hiking trails. The longest one, Big Savage, follows a 17-mile (27km) path along the ridge of Big Savage Mountain at an average elevation of 2,500 feet (810m). Another popular trail is Monroe Run, which traverses the forest between New Germany and Big Run. Mountain bikers may use all of the trails at Savage River except Big Savage and Monroe Run. Snowmobiles and off-road vehicles have their own trails. Off-road-vehicle permits are required and available at park headquarters. Trail maps can be found at the park office, including a map delineating 10 miles (16km) of cross-country-ski trails.

Savage River Lake was the site of the 1989 world white-water championships. Only nonpowered watercrafts are allowed on the lake.

Fifty-three primitive campsites, each with a lantern pole, fire pit, and table, are spread throughout the forest—you may not see another camper while you're there. Backwoods camping is also permitted. Camping is permitted year-round at a rate of $5 per night, with campsites offered on a first-come, first-served basis with self-registration. Pets are permitted in all areas on leashes.

If you don't have the time or the inclination to stay for a while, at least drive through the park, as many motorcyclists do on weekends. The roads are public, and the feeling of escape that comes from all those acres of trees is worth the ride.

New Germany State Park ★★ (© 301/895-5453) has 12 miles (19km) of trails, well marked for cross-country skiing. It also offers equipment rental, cabins, and large stone warming rooms where skiers can stop and get a snack. Trails and rental facilities are open 8am to 4pm during good skiing conditions.

New Germany has 39 improved campsites with exceptionally clean bathhouses and hot showers. All sites sit in a wooded glen and are large and private. The camping area is open April through October; the cost is $15 per night. These can be rented up to a year in advance from April through September. From September through October the sites are offered on a first-come, first-served basis. Available year-round are 11 cabins—furnished, with electricity, fireplaces, and room for two to eight persons. These run $70 to $100 a night, depending on size, with a 2-night minimum required. You can reserve the cabins up to a year in advance.

The park also features a 13-acre lake popular with swimmers and row-boaters. Boat rentals are available.

Just down the road, **Big Run State Park** (© 301/895-5453) offers rustic campsites, as well as fishing and hiking along Monroe Run and Big Run. Bring your boat to launch at the Savage River Reservoir.

The park also offers 30 unimproved campsites with chemical toilets and running water. Some of the sites are in wooded areas along Monroe Run and Big Run; others sit on the shore of the Savage River Reservoir. Sites at Big Run are open year-round and cost $10 per night. These are also self-registration and offered on a first-come, first-served basis. Pets are permitted on leashes.

Potomac–Garrett State Forest (© 301/334-2038) is spread over 19,000 acres in two separate tracts in the lower westernmost corner of the county. With plenty of streams, beaver ponds, and cranberry bogs, the forest offers beautiful scenery, including the highest point in any Maryland state forest. Backbone Mountain is in Garrett State Forest near Route 135 and Walnut Bottom Road.

There are has 8 miles (13km) of designated mountain biking trails, as well as designated trails for snowmobiles, dirt bikes, and ATVs. Off-road-vehicle permits are required and can be obtained at each park's headquarters. Hikers can choose from 30 miles (48km) of trails, many of them easy enough for day hikers and many with mountain views that can only be seen off the road.

For hunters, the park offers a 3-D bow range, open April through November. There's a small fee for target practice—allowed here but nowhere else in the forest. Hunting and trapping are permitted during the appropriate seasons. Contact the park office for details.

The forest offers some of the best fishing in Western Maryland, with 21 miles (34km) of first-class trout streams, including 9 miles (15km) of the North Branch of the Potomac River. Here's the place to catch the Maryland Grand Slam: brook, brown, 'bo, and cutthroat trout.

Potomac–Garrett also offers five primitive camping areas, open year-round. Getting to them may take some effort, however: The sites are beautiful and generously spaced, and a few have three-sided wooden shelters, but the roads to the sites are not well maintained. The cost is $5 per night for regular sites, $15 per night for a site with a shelter. Pets are permitted off-leash if they are under control.

Jennings Randolph Lake (© 304/355-2346), covers 952-acres, and has 13 miles (21km) of shoreline. It straddles the Maryland–West Virginia line. On the Maryland side is a boat ramp at Mt. Zion Road via Route 135 and a scenic overlook at Walnut Bottom Road. The lake is open for boating, fishing, and water-skiing in the summer. Hiking trails on the Maryland side start at one of the overlooks with views of the dam and lake.

Located near Oakland, **Boardford Lake** (© 301/334-9222) is a little tamer than the rest. Open March 31 to November 15 during daylight hours, the park features a guarded swimming beach as well as a boat launch and rentals. There are picnic pavilions, playgrounds, and a volleyball court. Pets on leashes are permitted in some areas. Admission is $2 to $3 per car or $1 to walk in.

Cranesville Swamp Nature Preserve ⚐ (© 304/345-4350) is a vestige of the last ice age. Operated by the Nature Conservancy, it's a peatland bog, home to sedges, cranberry, and sphagnum moss as well as tamarack trees—a species usually not found south of Alaska. Visitors can cross the bog on a 1,500-foot (450m) boardwalk or take one of four walking trails to see the unusual plants, including carnivorous ones. The entrance is in West Virginia, however, so it's a bit tricky to find. To get there, head south on Route 219; turn right on Mayhew Inn Road, left on Bray School Road, right on Oakland Sang Run Road, left on Swallow Falls Road, and right onto Cranesville Road. After 0.2 miles (0.3km), turn right at the fork, drive 0.1 mile (0.2km) and it's on the right. The preserve is open in the daylight hours year-round. Admission is free.

THE WILD RIVERS OF GARRETT COUNTY

A massive cleanup effort launched by Garrett County and the Maryland Bureau of Mines has brought fly-fishing back to the rivers known as the "three sisters"— the Youghiogheny, Casselman, and North Branch Potomac. The region has become such a popular area that it's been featured on national fly-fishing shows. The **Casselman River** is a fertile catch-and-release river; anglers here have been known to catch 40 fish a day. The Youghiogheny supports a strong population of brown and rainbow trout, but be aware that dam releases cause substantial increases in the water level below the Deep Creek Lake power plant. Call ℂ **301/387-4111** for a dam-release schedule. Get a brochure from the Garrett County Chamber of Commerce for a basic calendar and map. Call ℂ **301/ 387-4386** or visit **www.flyfishmaryland.com** or **www.dnr.state.md.us/ fisheries**.

Garrett County offers myriad opportunities for white-water rafting, kayaking, and canoeing. The Youghiogheny, the North Branch Potomac, and the Savage are the area's best-known runs. Although they can be challenging all year, they are at their fiercest in spring after snowmelt. In 1976, the Youghiogheny River between Millers Run and Friendsville became Maryland's first officially designated Wild and Scenic River. This portion, known as the Upper Yough, contains approximately 20 class IV and V rapids. Fortunately for the inexperienced paddler, outfitters have sprung up all over the area and are ready and willing to take people down this exciting river. If you'd prefer a little less excitement, the Middle Yough offers class I and II rapids, and the Lower Yough is a class III run. There are also several rivers just across the border in West Virginia—the Cheat, the Gauley, Big Sandy, and Russell Fork—that are rated at class IV+. Much of the river has recently been purchased by the state Department of Natural Resources as part of the river's Wild and Scenic designation.

Kayakers hoping to avoid raft traffic would do well to visit the North Branch Potomac and Savage rivers (both class III/IV); both, however, are only runable after heavy rains or snowmelt. For those looking to do a little open canoeing, the Casselman River (class II) to the west is good in winter and spring.

Most outfitters run raft trips on several or all of these rivers.

SUPPLIERS & GUIDES IN GARRETT COUNTY

Perhaps unique to Garrett County is its **Adventuresports Institute.** This division of Garrett Community College offers an associate's degree in adventure sports, but its classes are open to nonmatriculated students. So if you want to learn how to paddle white water rather than just ride along in a raft, enroll in one of the institute's 2- or 3-day kayaking classes. The institute also teaches classes in sports that you won't readily find outfitters equipped for, like mountaineering and rock climbing or orienteering. For a list of course offerings and prices, call ℂ **301/387-3032** or write to Adventuresports Institute, Garrett Community College, 687 Mosser Rd. (P.O. Box 151), McHenry, MD 21541.

Precision Rafting (ℂ **800/477-3723** or 301/746-4083; www.precision rafting.com), located in Friendsville, offers raft trips down all these rivers, as well as paddling lessons for those interested in learning to kayak. Rafting trips include a riverside barbecue lunch and cost from $90 to $115 per person for an Upper Yough trip. Friendsville is at the intersection of I-68, Maryland Route 42, and the Youghiogheny River; from Deep Creek Lake, take U.S. Route 219 north to Maryland Route 42 and follow it into town.

Several outfitters based in nearby Ohiopyle, Pennsylvania, offer similar trips, including **Mountain Streams** (ℂ **800/RAFT-NOW;** www.mtstreams.com) and **Laurel Highlands River Tours** (ℂ **800/4RAFTIN;** www.laurelhighlands.com). To get to Ohiopyle from Deep Creek Lake, take U.S. 219 north to U.S. 40 west (just past the intersection with I-68). Go into Pennsylvania, and turn right onto

State Route 381 (north), which will take you to Ohiopyle. It's about an hour from Deep Creek Lake. **Allegany Expeditions** (℗ **800/819-5170** or 301/722-5170) offers cross-country-ski packages in New Germany State Park, fly-fishing and bass-fishing expeditions, and a wide variety of other outdoor adventures.

Note: No matter which outfitter you choose, remember to tip your guide: $3 to $5 per person is appropriate.

For tackle and bait, stop by **Johnny's Bait House** on U.S. Route 219 in McHenry (℗ **301/387-FISH**) or **Deep Creek Outfitters** at 1899 Deep Creek Dr. in McHenry (℗ **301/387-6977**).

You can rent bikes or downhill skis at Deep Creek from **High Mountain Sports,** 21349 Garrett Hwy., Oakland (℗ **301/387-4199**). They also sell and service bikes and skis.

2 Cumberland & Allegany County

140 miles (225km) W of Baltimore, 140 miles (225km) NW of Washington, D.C., 113 miles (182km) SE of Pittsburgh

The small city of Cumberland is set on a tight bend of the Potomac River in the heart of the Allegheny Mountains with a portion of the C&O Canal as its centerpiece. Once a mighty industrial city, it is now quieter, with tourism its growing industry. Visitors come to see the canal, George Washington's headquarters, and this city's setting among the mountains.

At the turn of the 20th century, Cumberland was Maryland's "Queen City," second in size only to Baltimore. Many reminders of those days remain: its long street of Victorian mansions, the ornate storefronts of its rejuvenating shopping district, and the black smoke of the coal-powered train called *Mountain Thunder.*

Since the construction of I-68 cut right through—you might say right on top of—Cumberland, the city has become more accessible to the rest of the state. It's not only Cumberland people come to see, but also Rocky Gap State Park, known for Lake Habeeb, as well as a new resort and golf course, or one of the other parks.

The Allegheny Mountains are particularly beautiful in autumn, and the area is becoming popular with bikers and hikers who find Cumberland and nearby Frostburg cheaper and closer to home than Deep Creek Lake to the west.

ESSENTIALS

GETTING THERE **By Car** I-68 runs right through the center of Cumberland and is the fastest route by car from either the east or west. From the east and north, I-70 will take you to I-68. For a more scenic drive, you can get off I-70 or I-68 onto the Old National Pike (U.S. Rte. 40).

The Cumberland Regional Airport no longer serves Cumberland.

By Bus & Train Greyhound (℗ **800/231-2222**) operates regular service into Cumberland, stopping at 37 Henderson St. **Amtrak** operates limited passenger service through Cumberland from points east and west, including a daily train from Washington, D.C., stopping at a station on East Harrison Street. For full information, call ℗ **800/872-7245.**

VISITOR INFORMATION Walking tour brochures, maps, and information about Cumberland and the surrounding area are available from the **Allegany County Convention and Visitors Bureau's** two walk-in locations. The larger one is at the **Western Maryland Station Center,** 13 Canal St., Cumberland,

MD 21502 (② **800/508-4748** or 301/777-5905; www.mdmountainside.com).
It's open daily 9am to 5pm. A center at **Rocky Gap State Park** (② **301/
777-2139**), off I-68, is open Monday through Friday from 9am to 5pm.

If you're coming from the east, the **Sidling Hill Exhibition Center** ⚘, off
I-68 about 20 miles (32km) east of Cumberland, is a great place to stop for
brochures, information, and an incredible view.

SPECIAL EVENTS   The biggest event in Allegany County and maybe all of
Western Maryland is the **Rocky Gap Country/Bluegrass Music Festival** ★★
(② **888/ROCKYGAP** or 301/722-5200), held the first weekend in August each
year at Rocky Gap State Park. An average of 10,000 to 20,000 people attend.
Past performers include Joe Diffie, Sammy Kershaw, Deana Carter, Willie
Nelson, Kathy Mattea, and Travis Tritt.

C&O Canalfest takes place in mid-May at Canal Place and celebrates Cumberland's rich transportation heritage, both boat and train. Stop by for living-
history demonstrations, crafts, entertainment, and food.

WHAT TO SEE & DO
ATTRACTIONS
**Canal Place: Chesapeake & Ohio Canal National Historical Park—
Cumberland Visitor Center**   The C&O Canal opened here in 1850. For
more than 75 years it was an important transport line and had a major impact
on the early development of the town. Visit the Western Maryland Station Center at track level, check out the exhibits on the history of the canal, and pick up
a brochure. Then explore the towpath, a nearly level trail for walkers, hikers, and
bikers. There are remnants of locks, dams, lock houses, and other historical
features along the way. In the works are plans for boat rides on the re-watered
terminus of the canal. Parking is free for visitors to the center in two lots at Harrison and Howard streets.

13 Canal St., Cumberland. ② 301/722-8226. www.nps.gov/choh. Free admission. Daily 9am–5pm. Closed
Jan 1, Thanksgiving, and Dec 25.

Embassy Theatre   This beautiful 1931 Art Deco movie theater has come
back to life as a center for the arts. Its restoration was featured on Bob Villa's
"Restore America" television program. It hosts classic films, live music, theater,
and dance. Call for a schedule and to make reservations.

49 Baltimore St., Cumberland. ② 877/722-4692 or 301/722-4692. new.embassy@att.net.

Emmanuel Episcopal Church   This church is built on the foundations of
Fort Cumberland, where George Washington began his military career; earth-
works from the fort (ca. 1755) still lie beneath the church. Although the
Emmanuel parish dates from 1803, the cornerstone of the current native sandstone building was laid in 1849 and completed in 1851. The church contains
original Tiffany stained-glass windows from three different periods and a scale
model of Fort Cumberland, and the grounds are part of the Fort Cumberland
Walking Trail, signposted with plaques and detailed in a leaflet available from
the visitor center.

16 Washington St., Cumberland. ② 301/777-3364. emmanuel@ang-md.org. Mon–Fri 9am–3pm; services
Wed 5:30pm, Thurs 10:30am, Sun 8am and 10am; open by appointment or prior arrangement at other times.

George Washington's Headquarters   This log cabin, believed to be the
only remaining structure from the original Fort Cumberland, was used by then-
Colonel George Washington as his official quarters during the French and

Indian War. The tiny cabin is not open to the public, but it does have a viewing window and a tape-recorded description that plays when activated by a push button. To visit, park at the nearby tourism office and take a short walk across the footbridge to the park.

In Riverside Park, Greene St. (at the junction of Wills Creek and the Potomac River), Cumberland. ℭ **301/ 777-8215.** Free admission. Open by appointment and on certain holidays. Exterior viewing at all times.

Gordon–Roberts House   Built as a private residence in 1867 for the president of the C&O Canal, this house, formerly called History House, is now in the hands of the Allegany County Historical Society. The 18-room dwelling contains antique furnishings such as a Victorian courting couch and an 1840 square grand piano. Other features include a research room, an early-19th-century brick-walled garden, and a basement kitchen with authentic cooking utensils, fireplace, coal stove, dishes, and pottery. An exhibit showcasing quilts from the 1800s to 1920 will be held through 2002. Reservations are required.

218 Washington St., Cumberland. ℭ **301/777-8678.** historyhouse@allconet.org. Admission $5 adults, $3 over age 12. June–Oct Tues–Sat 10am–5pm, Sun 1–5pm; Nov–Apr Tues–Sat 10am–5pm. Last tours begin 4pm.

C&O Canal Paw Paw Tunnel 🐾   Anyone who starts to explore some of Allegany County's lesser-known attractions will realize that many of them are, well . . . *spooky.* Paw Paw Tunnel, part of the C&O Canal National Historical Park, is the best of them. It all started in 1836 when engineers decided to build the C&O Canal right through, rather than around, an intervening mountain. The result was a tunnel lined with more than six million bricks and passing three-quarters of a mile through the darkness of the hill.

All there is to do at Paw Paw is walk through the tunnel, which takes about 20 minutes (one-way). The park service suggests bringing a flashlight. Walking the tunnel is not for people who are afraid of the dark or the claustrophobic (you must walk down a narrow towpath bounded by a guardrail, with the canal on one side and a sloping brick wall on the other). But if you are up for it, pass through the enormous brick arch into the damp darkness, then head for the light at the end of the tunnel. There is limited accessibility for visitors with disabilities.

Rte. 51 and the Potomac River, south of Cumberland. ℭ **301/722-8226.** www.nps.gov.choh. Free admission. Daily dawn to dusk.

Thrasher Carriage Museum   Housed in a renovated warehouse opposite the steam train depot in Frostburg, this museum houses an extensive collection of late-19th- and early-20th-century horse-drawn carriages, featuring more than 50 vehicles from the collection of the late James R. Thrasher. Highlights include the inaugural coach used by Teddy Roosevelt, several Vanderbilt sleighs, elaborately decorated funeral wagons, formal closed vehicles, surreys, and open sleighs. A new exhibit opening in spring 2002 recalls the days of horse-drawn milk wagons.

19 Depot St., Depot Center, Frostburg. ℭ **301/689-3380.** www.thrashercarriagemuseum.com. Admission $2 adults, $1.75 seniors, $1 ages 12–18. May–Sept Tues–Sun 11am–3pm; Oct daily 11am–3pm; Nov–Dec Sat–Sun 11am–3pm. Closed Jan–Apr.

Western Maryland Scenic Railroad ★★ *(Kids)*   It's worth a trip to Western Maryland to board this vintage steam train and ride the 32-mile (52km) round-trip between Cumberland and Frostburg. The excursion—enhanced by an informative live commentary—follows a scenic mountain valley route through the Cumberland Narrows, Helmstetter's Horseshoe Curve, Brush Tunnel, many panoramic vistas, and a 1,300-foot (390m) elevation change between the two destinations. All trains depart and terminate at Cumberland. The trip takes 3½ hours, including a 1½-hour layover in Frostburg, where you can visit the Thrasher Carriage Museum, a complex of shops, a restaurant, and an active turntable where the train engine is turned for the Cumberland-bound segment of the journey. Admission to the Thrasher Carriage House is included in the price of the train excursion. The railroad also offers group excursions, dinner trains, and Murder Mystery Dinner Trains. Check the website or call for dates and times. *Note:* All Monday, Tuesday, and Wednesday trips, as well as Thursdays May through September, are aboard a diesel train, not the *Mountain Thunder* steam engine. Santa Express trips, offered Thanksgiving weekend through December, are aboard the steam train.

Western Maryland Station Center, 13 Canal St., Cumberland. © **800/TRAIN-50** or 301/759-4400. www.wmsr.com. Tickets $18 adults, $16.20 seniors, $10 kids 12 and under. First class tickets which include lunch cost $30 adults, $27 seniors, and $15 kids 12 and under. Reservations required. Excursions leave at 11:30am. Dinner and special excursions leave at 6pm. From I-68, take the Downtown Cumberland Exit 43C (westbound) or the Johnson St. Exit 43A (eastbound) and follow signs to Western Maryland Station Center.

ORGANIZED TOURS & EXCURSIONS

One of the highlights of a visit to Cumberland is a stroll or a drive through the **Victorian Historic District,** along Washington Street on the western side of town. This area includes the site of the original Fort Cumberland (now the Emmanuel Episcopal Church) and more than 50 residential and public buildings, built primarily in the 1800s when Cumberland was at its economic peak. Added to the National Register of Historic Places in 1973, this street is a showcase of homes with stained-glass windows, graceful cupolas, and sloping mansard roofs. You'll see architectural styles ranging from Federal, Queen Anne, Empire, Colonial Revival, Italianate, and English Country Gothic to Georgian Revival, Gothic Revival, and Greek Revival. Most of the houses are not open to the public, but a self-guided walking tour is available free from the visitors bureau.

SHOPPING

Cumberland's shopping still focuses on the needs of its residents. But a small pedestrian mall along Baltimore Street is worth a stroll. You'll find several antiques stores and gift shops. Most shops are open Monday through Saturday 10am to 5pm, with many open on Sundays, too.

Just off the pedestrian mall is the **Book Center,** 15 N. Centre St. (© **301/722-2284**), where you'll find a large selection of books on Maryland and local history as well as volumes on railroading and canals. They also have postcards, gifts, regional souvenirs, and out-of-state newspapers. It's open Monday from 8am to 8pm, Tuesday through Friday from 8am to 6pm, Saturday from 9am to 5pm, and Sunday from 9am to 4pm.

The **Saville Gallery,** 52 Baltimore St. (© **301/777-2787;** www.allegany artscouncil.org), is operated by the Allegany Arts Council and features the works of Western Maryland artists and craftspeople, with exhibits changing every 6 weeks. It's open Tuesday through Friday 10am to 4pm and Saturday 11am to 4pm.

WHERE TO STAY

The Cumberland–Frostburg area offers an inviting blend of historic inns, modern hotels and motels, and homey bed-and-breakfast lodgings. Most are moderately priced and offer very good value. All have free parking.

Best Western Braddock Motor Inn   A tree-shaded country setting adds to the rural atmosphere of this two-story motel, just off I-68 and east of the historic LaVale Toll Gate. Rooms are furnished in contemporary style. Complimentary shuttle service is provided from the airport, bus station, and train station.

1268 National Hwy., LaVale, MD 21502. © **800/296-6006** or 301/729-3300. Fax 301/729-3300. www.best westernbraddock.com. 108 units. $69–$110 double. AE, DC, DISC, MC, V. **Amenities:** Restaurant; lounge; indoor pool; fitness center; spa; tanning salon; game room. *In room:* A/C, TV.

Failinger's Hotel Gunter ✦ Originally opened in 1897 as the Gladstone Hotel, this four-story landmark was revived and restored several years ago by the present owners, the Kermit Failinger family. The guest rooms are masterfully done, as are the public areas and the main staircase, the hotel's centerpiece. The restoration has added modern conveniences, but hasn't altered the hotel's Victorian style, marked by original oak doors and brass fixtures, claw-foot bathtubs, intricate wall trim, vintage pictures and prints, smoked-glass lantern-style lamps, and delicate wall sconces.

The guest rooms are individually furnished, with canopy or four-poster beds, armoires, laces and frills, and pastel fabrics. The one exception is no. 307, starkly decorated in black and white, and named the Roy Clark Room after the country-western entertainer who stayed here during a 1990 visit.

11 W. Main St., Frostburg, MD 21532. © **301/689-6511**. Fax 301/689-6034. 14 units. $65.95 double, $89.95 suite; rates go down to $42.95 Jan–Mar. Rates include continental breakfast. AE, DC, DISC, MC, V. *In room:* A/C, TV.

Holiday Inn This modern six-story hotel sits at the east end of Cumberland's shopping promenade, providing easy walking access to the downtown area. Rooms are clean and comfortable, as you would expect from a Holiday Inn. Railroad enthusiasts might like a room overlooking the nearby railroad tracks; everyone else will prefer the town side of the hotel, where there's less noise.

100 S. George St., Cumberland, MD 21502. © **800/HOLIDAY** or 301/724-8800. Fax 301/724-4001. www. cumberlandmdholidayinn.com. 130 units. $79–$84 double. AE, DC, DISC, MC, V. Pets accepted; fees may apply. **Amenities:** Restaurant; lounge; outdoor pool; fitness room; fax and copying services. *In room:* A/C, coffeemaker, hair dryer, iron.

Inn at Walnut Bottom ✦ The owners have combined the warmth and charm of a bed-and-breakfast with standard hotel amenities and have added a few niceties of their own, including delicious breakfasts featuring crème brûlée, French toast, ham and egg biscuit pizza, or some other hot delight. You might need to borrow one of their bikes to burn off those calories. Need something more? How about Alfspaending? This relaxation therapy is available to guests, offered by the inn's co-owner, who is trained in the technique. Rooms and bathrooms have recently been updated. Just a block from historic Washington Street, the inn is composed of two restored 19th-century homes: the Cowden House (1820) and the Dent House (1890). Guest rooms are spacious with high ceilings and large windows and are furnished with antiques and period reproductions including four-poster and brass beds, tapestry rugs, and down comforters.

120 Greene St., Cumberland, MD 21502. © **800/286-9718** or 301/777-0003. Fax 301/777-8288. www. iwbinfo.com. 12 units (4 with shared bathroom). $87–$118 double; $140–$200 family suite. Rates include breakfast. AE, DISC, MC, V. **Amenities:** Relaxation therapy; bike rental. *In room:* A/C.

Rocky Gap Lodge and Golf Resort ✦ The newest addition to local accommodations is one of the biggest things to hit Allegany County since the B&O Railroad. An attractive brick structure, the Rocky Gap Lodge overlooks a 243-acre lake and blends seamlessly into its serene mountain setting in Rocky Gap State Park. As you walk into the hotel's expansive lobby, high ceilings, towering stonework, and a panoramic view of Lake Habeeb greet you. Rooms are large and luxurious, ranging from standard doubles to the two large presidential suites.

Many guests come for golf. Rocky Gap boasts an 18-hole Jack Nicklaus Signature golf course set between lake and mountains. Greens fee for 18 holes is $65 for both guests and visitors (rates include cart and GPS system).

Rocky Gap also offers a program of more than 30 outdoor activities and instruction for all seasons, including rappelling and rock climbing, caving, canoeing and kayaking, several horseback riding or horse-drawn carriage or sleigh tours, fly-fishing, and cross-country skiing. Reservations, fees, and a minimum number of participants are required.

P.O. Box 1199, Cumberland, MD 21501-1199. ℂ **800/724-0828** or 301/784-8400. Fax 301/784-8408. www.rockygapresort.com. 218 units. Nov–Mar $110–$130 double, $170–$285 suite; Apr–Oct $135–$155 double, $205–$325 suite. AE, DC, MC, V. Children under 18 stay free in parents' room; 25% discount on additional room for children. **Amenities:** 2 lakeside restaurants; indoor/outdoor pool; fitness center; 18-hole golf course; tennis courts; pro shop. *In room:* A/C, Nintendo, dataport, minibar, hair dryer, iron, 2 phones.

WHERE TO DINE

Au Petit Paris ★ *(Finds* AMERICAN/FRENCH   Au Petit Paris is a find in this rural section of Maryland—a fine, intimate French restaurant, worth the drive from Cumberland. Even other area restaurateurs recommend it. The interior has a Parisian feel, with French murals and posters and bistro-style furnishings. Established 41 years ago, the restaurant is a favorite for such dishes as trout with almonds, duck à l'orange, coq au vin, steak Diane or au poivre, chateaubriand, veal cordon bleu, and a signature dish of lamb noisettes with Madeira sauce.

86 E. Main St., Frostburg. ℂ **301/689-8946.** www.aupetitparis.com. Reservations recommended. Main courses $10.95–$38. AE, DC, DISC, MC, V. Tues–Sat 6–9:30pm. Closed for a week in Jan and July.

Giuseppe's Italian Restaurant ITALIAN   In the heart of town and a block from the Frostburg State University campus, this two-floor dining spot is popular with the college community and is staffed by students and locals. The food is first-rate. Entrees include all the usual Italian favorites, such as build-your-own pizza, pastas, chicken cacciatore, shrimp scampi, and veal parmigiana, as well a few unusual dishes, like crab carbonara and blackened chicken and sausage with red pepper penne. There's also a surprising array of nightly specials, including such fresh seafood dishes as trout stuffed with crab imperial or orange roughy.

11 Bowery St., Frostburg. ℂ **301/689-2220.** www.giuseppes.net. Reservations recommended on weekends. Main courses $7.50–$18.95. AE, DISC, MC, V. Sun–Thurs 4:30–11pm, Fri–Sat 3–11pm.

Mason's Barn, J.B.'s Steak Cellar, Uncle Tucker's 1819 Brew Haus, Uncle Tucker's Pizza Cellar ★ ITALIAN/AMERICAN   Here are four local favorites at one location, a mile east of Cumberland. Mason's Barn was established in 1954 as a roadside diner, and this dependable restaurant has been growing ever since, thanks to the friendly supervision of owners Ed Mason and his son, Mike. As its name implies, it offers a barnlike setting, with a decor of farming tools, antiques, and Maryland memorabilia. Entrees include steaks and seafood dishes as well as barbecued ribs, chicken, veal, and pasta items. All have a home-cooked flavor. Lunch choices range from salads and homemade soups to sandwiches (the crab-cake sandwich is a standout). Breakfast is also available.

To showcase their skills at charbroiled beef and seafood dishes, the Masons opened the saloon-style J.B.'s Steak Cellar downstairs. Here in a slightly more formal atmosphere you can chomp on more expensive fare, including lobster by the pound, grilled jumbo shrimp, and a 20-ounce Angus center-cut T-bone steak.

Two new eateries focus on microbrews. The Brew Haus offers pizza and Italian specialties, while the Pizza Cellar serves wood-fired pizza. Subs and salads are also available. There's free delivery, too.

12801 Ali Ghan Rd., NE Cumberland, just off I-68 (Exit 46E/W). © **301/722-6060** for Mason's and J.B.'s, **301/777-7005** for Brew Haus and Pizza Cellar. www.edmasons.com. For all, main courses $7.95–$22.95; lunch $3.95–$7.95; breakfast $2.59–$6.49. AE, DISC, MC, V. Mason's, daily 7am–10pm; J.B.'s, Uncle Tucker's 1819 and Pizza, daily 11am–1pm.

Oxford House ✪ INTERNATIONAL   This restaurant is a standout in region. The atmosphere is intimate, and the food and service are excellent. The restaurant has three small dining rooms decorated with original oil paintings and reproductions, floral linens, and plants. The menu offers the diner everything from European classics to local Maryland flavors. A unique treat in the mountains is the chicken Annapolis, tender chicken breast stuffed with ham, Swiss cheese and crabmeat. The house salad is exceptional, just as the menu claims. Be sure to check out the wine list.

129 Greene St. © **301/777-7101.** Reservations recommended for dinner. Main courses $12.95–$22.95; lunch $5.25–$8.95. AE, DISC, MC, V. Mon–Fri 11am–2:30pm and 5–9pm, Sat 5–9:30pm, brunch the last Sun of each month 10am–3pm.

CUMBERLAND AFTER DARK

The **Allegany Arts Council,** 74 Baltimore St. (© **301/777-ARTS**), publishes a monthly newsletter detailing upcoming concerts and cultural events in the Cumberland area. You can also stop by the office for an update on events; the council is open weekdays from 10am to 4pm and Saturday from 11am to 4pm.

The **Cumberland Theatre,** 101–103 Johnson St. (© **301/759-4990**), housed in a renovated church, presents a professional program of musicals and comedies as well as mysteries and dramas from June through November. Performances run Wednesday through Sunday, and tickets average $11 to $15.

3 Deep Creek Lake & Garrett County

50 miles (81km) SW of Cumberland, 190 miles (306km) W of Baltimore, 120 miles (193km) SE of Pittsburgh

Garrett County's mountain scenery has beckoned visitors for centuries. Native American hunters combed these mountains a thousand years ago looking for game. In colonial days, this was the American frontier, populated mostly by Indians and trappers. Few settled here until the coming of the Baltimore and Ohio Railroad in the 1850s. Farmers, coal miners, and loggers were the first to arrive. During the Civil War, the railroad provided a needed supply link, and Garrett towns became the targets of Confederate attack. Once peace returned to the country, Garrett became a vacation destination. Three presidents—Grant, Cleveland, and Harrison—vacationed here.

Once the Deep Creek Lake was created in the 1920s and Wisp Ski Resort built in 1944, vacationers had even more reasons to make the trip to Garrett County. In recent years, it has become a four-season destination as well as *the* place for mid-Atlantic residents to buy a second home. It's centrally located between Pittsburgh, Baltimore/Washington, and eastern Ohio cities, a 3- to 4-hour drive from each.

> **Fun Fact Venice in the Mountains**
>
> Okay, nobody's really calling it that, but Deep Creek Lake is trying to get people out of their cars and into boats. Businesses are adding piers to their lakeside establishments and sharing them with neighbors within walking distance of the lake. Visitors can go to the store, the movies, even to church by boat. This only works from April to November, as lake freezes pretty hard in winter. The visitor center (see below) has a "Travel by Boat" map listing all the places with piers.

Visitors can hike or bike the scenic trails; go skiing, snow-tubing, or snow-shoeing; take to the waters and try boating, fly-fishing, kayaking, or white-water rafting; and visit antiques and crafts stores. Or they can do nothing but sit back and enjoy the old-time charm that this region has long been known for.

ESSENTIALS

GETTING THERE   From the east or west, take I-68 to Exit 14 and drive south on Route 219.

VISITOR INFORMATION   The visitor center is on Route 219, near the bottom of Wisp Ski Resort's ski runs. It's open 9am to 5pm with extended hours in the summer. It has brochures on everything from bed-and-breakfasts to fly-fishing schools. Ask for a vacation guide, which contains a calendar of events and information on local history, restaurants, hotels, and shopping. Call ℂ **301/ 4FUN** (4386) or e-mail info@garrettchamber.com.

For up-to-the-minute ski conditions, call ℂ **301/387-4911** or visit www.ski maryland.com.

SPECIAL EVENTS   Garrett County celebrates autumn in grand style with a four-day **Autumn Glory Festival,** usually held the second weekend in October. It also marks the unofficial end of the season—at least until the snow comes. Not only are the leaves in full fall color, the towns are filled with festivities. These include the firemen's parade, the Autumn Glory Grand Feature Parade, and the Oktoberfest celebration in Oakland; a farmer's market, tours of historic sites, antiques shows, music, dinners, outdoor activities, and a Western Maryland Tournament of Bands and the Official Maryland State Banjo Championship. Tours of the Mountain Lake Park Historic District are held all weekend. Call ℂ **301/334-2250.**

Scottish pride shows during the **McHenry Highland Festival,** held annually in early June. Come for the traditional sounds of bagpipe, harp, and fiddle or the dance and athletic competitions. There's bluegrass music, crafts, and even a Kirking 'o' the Tartans. Call ℂ **301/387-9300.**

GETTING AROUND   Businesses in Deep Creek Lake sometimes have mailing addresses in Deep Creek Lake, McHenry, and/or Oakland. Deep Creek Lake and McHenry are, for all intents and purposes, the same place, and you can count on those addresses to be on the lake or close by.

Oakland, the county seat of Garrett County, lies several miles south of Deep Creek Lake. Some businesses maintain mailing addresses there; others are actually just off the lake, outside the Deep Creek Lake/McHenry postal zone. Proximity to the lake resort areas is indicated in the listings.

DEEP CREEK LAKE ✪✪✪

Deep Creek Lake has long been a popular year-round recreational area. It's the state's largest freshwater lake, nearly 12 miles (19km) in length, with 65 miles (105km) of shoreline occupied by private vacation homes and chalets. The northern end is where the action is. The commercial centers, the Wisp ski resort, and the lakefront hotels and inns are located here. The southern end, which begins at the Glendale Road Bridge, is all residential and much quieter. Most of the sailors sail their boats here; look for the weekend regattas.

Summer temperatures, averaging a comfortable 65.9°F, draw visitors escaping the heat and humidity of the big cities. In the winter months, Deep Creek Lake is Maryland's premier ski resort, with an average temperature of 28°F and a yearly snowfall of more than 100 inches.

GETTING AROUND Of course you can drive. But it's faster to go by boat. Local businesses have made it easier for visitors to take their boat to the store, to restaurants, even to the movies. More than 20 businesses have provided piers for their customers; all are listed on a "Travel by Boat" map available from the visitor center. The floating piers stay in the water April 1 until November 1.

If you need a boat, stop by one of the boat rentals on the lake. (You'll have to drive there, though.) For more on that, see "Outdoor Activities," below.

OUTDOOR ACTIVITIES

BOATING Summer activities focus on water sports, with every type of boat, from sailboats to speedsters, on the lake. Nearly all marinas around the lake have craft for rent, 7 days a week. Paddleboats or canoes average $6 an hour; fishing boats, $15 an hour; pontoon boats, from $30 to $40 an hour; and ski boats and runabouts, from $20 to $36 an hour, depending on horsepower. Some of the leading firms at Deep Creek Lake along U.S. Route 219 are **Aquatic Center** (✆ 301/387-8233), **Quality Marine** (✆ 301/387-BOAT), **Bill's Marine Service** (✆ 301/387-5536), **Crystal Waters** (✆ 301/387-5515), **Deep Creek Lake Boat Rentals** (✆ 301/387-9130), and **Deep Creek Outfitters** (✆ 301/ 387-6977). Rowboats can also be rented from the camper/information office at **Deep Creek Lake State Park.**

If you want to sail you'll have to bring your own boat. None are available for rent. Or you can learn to sail at **Deep Creek Sailing School** (✆ 301/387-4497).

FISHING Deep Creek Lake is home to about 22 species of fish, including yellow perch, bass, bluegill, catfish, crappie, chain pickerel, northern pike, walleye, and trout. Four world-class rivers in the area make this fly-fishing heaven. Come for the cutthroat, rainbows, browns, and brooks (wild) trout. Fishing is best April through June, but ice fishing in January and February is becoming popular. Maryland requires a fishing license, which costs $10 for residents and $20 for nonresidents and can be bought at most tackle shops. In addition, a $5 trout stamp is required if you intend to remove trout from nontidal waters. Try **Johnny's Bait House** on U.S. Route 219 in McHenry (✆ 301/387-FISH) or **Deep Creek Outfitters** at 1899 Deep Creek Dr. in McHenry (✆ 301/ 387-6977).

GOLF The **Golf Club at Wisp,** Wisp Resort Golf Course, 296 Marsh Hill Rd., McHenry (✆ 301/387-4911; www.gcnet.net/wisp), is an 18-hole, par-72 championship facility built beside (and on) the ski slopes. Open from April through mid-October, the course welcomes guests 7 days a week. Greens fees are about $48 to $65 per person for 18 holes, $24 for juniors. There is a pro shop

---

Tips **Ditch the Skis, Let's Go Tubing!**

Wisp Ski Resort opened its first **tubing run** in the winter of 2002. If you get tired of skiing, here's another way to speed down a snowy slope. Best of all, you don't have to climb back to the top—a ski lift will take you up. The fee is separate from the lift ticket.

---

and driving range on the grounds. The **Oakland Golf Club,** Sang Run Road, Oakland (© 301/334-3883), invites visitors to play on its 18-hole championship course. Call ahead for greens and cart fees. It is also open April through October.

HIKING   Five hiking trails ranging from easy to challenging are located in **Deep Creek Lake State Park** (© 301/387-5563), south of McHenry on State Park Road. The Indian Turnip Trail, approximately 2½ miles (4km) long, is the most scenic, winding along Meadow Mountain and across the ridge top. Admission is $2 per vehicle; the park is open daily from 8am until sunset in summer, until 4pm in winter. Hikers can also head to Wisp after the snow melts to take a ride up the ski lift for a mountaintop view and a downhill hike.

ALPINE SKIING   Deep Creek Lake is the home of Maryland's only ski area. With an elevation of 3,080 feet (924m) and a vertical drop of 610 feet (183m), the **Wisp Resort** offers 23 ski runs and trails on 85 acres of skiable terrain. Beginners can ski comfortably on several of the long, scenic trails. All you black-diamond skiers can head for the face. It's not pretty, but it's straight down the front of the mountain with lots of moguls thrown in. Trails through the forest can be fast enough for both intermediate and experts. Lift tickets range from $35 on weekdays to $42 on weekends, with reduced rates for night skiing, 2-day tickets, early- or late-season skiing, and children; kids under age 6 ski free. The ski season opens at the end of November and closes in March (or April if it's been really cold). The Wisp also operates an on-premises ski school, a rental service, and a ski shop. Children's programs for ages 3 to 14 offer childcare and ski lessons.

Wisp's new ownership has recently announced plans for proposed additions to the resort: a mountaintop facility with an ice-skating rink, white-water rafting course, natatorium and gym, and up to 20 new ski trails and new vacation homes on the other side of the mountain. A gondola system will take riders from the foot of the slopes to the new center and down the other side of the mountain.

Though all that development is in the planning stages, some new activities are already available. A tubing park opened in December 2001. Chairlifts were extended to make the trails more accessible. Snowshoes and the wild-and-crazy K2 snow bikes are also available.

For information, contact the **Wisp Resort,** 290 Marsh Hill Rd., Deep Creek Lake, MD 21541 (© 301/387-4911; www.gcnet.net/wisp).

SWIMMING   **Deep Creek Lake State Park** (© 301/387-5563) features an 800-foot guarded sandy beach with bathhouses and lockers nearby. It's one of the only public places for swimming. Admission to the park is $2 per vehicle, with seniors and children in restraint seats allowed in free. The park is open from 8am until sunset in summer, until 4pm in winter.

SIDE TRIP TO GRANTSVILLE ⊛

The National Road, which connected the east coast to the Ohio Valley, still comes through here. You can see the tall mile markers along the road. Plan to stop in pretty little Grantsville for some shopping and a home-cooked meal.

To get there from Route 68, take Exit 19 North (Rte. 495) to U.S. 40 East. The first stop is the **Casselman River Bridge.** This stone bridge was the largest single-span stone bridge ever built when it was constructed in 1813. It was closed to traffic in 1953 but you can walk across it (for a glimpse of the Youghiogheny River) to a small park.

At one end of the bridge is the Penn Alps Restaurant and Crafts Shop and the **Spruce Forest Artisan Village** ⊛⊛, 177 Casselman Rd. (© **301/895-3332;** www.spruceforest.org). Old homes, schoolhouses, and shops were relocated here from other parts of Western Maryland; some date from Revolutionary War days. Some 12 of these structures house the studios of local artisans. Stop in to see wooden bird carving. Watch iron being beaten into jewelry or shreds of wood woven into baskets. Operating hours at various studios are variable, but some are open every day but Sunday 10am to 5pm. Also produced here are stained glass, teddy bears, and handcrafted soaps. The village is open Memorial Day through the last Saturday in October, Monday through Saturday from 10am to 5pm.

If you get hungry or feel a need to shop for more crafts, stop at the **Penn Alps Restaurant and Craft Shop** (see listing, below) across the parking lot. Part of the restaurant was originally a stagecoach stop when the National Road was new. The double fireplace from those days dominates one of the dining rooms. Special events are often scheduled, including concerts on Saturdays at 7:30pm, May through August; and Christmas in the Village, the first weekend in December.

Another stop on the National Road is due for restoration. Look for **Stanton's Grist Mill,** along with a visitor center in the mill house, to open in a few years.

Grantsville is also home to **Yoder's Country Market,** 61 Locker Lane, Rte. 669, Grantsville (© **800/321-5148** or 301/895-5148). Started as a Mennonite family farm enterprise in 1932, the market has grown from a one-room butcher shop to an extensive specialty market. It's known for a variety of fresh and natural food items such as jams, jellies, relishes, honey, maple syrup, molasses, fruits, nuts, baked goods, cereals and grains, meats, cheeses, herbs, and spices. In addition, there are cookbooks featuring Amish and Mennonite recipes and Pennsylvania Dutch crafts. It's open Monday through Saturday from 8am to 6pm. Hours may be shorter in the winter.

WHERE TO STAY & EAT IN GRANTSVILLE

The Casselman Hotel and Restaurant (Value MENNONITE/COUNTRY COOKING Walk through the front door of this 1824 inn, and the wonderful aromas from the bakery will capture your attention right away. The dining room is in the back of the inn, a spacious room usually filled with families or senior citizens on day trips. The food here is a bargain and filling. You'll find homemade bread—even in the stuffing—real mashed potatoes, honey-dipped chicken, and grilled ham, along with sandwiches. The children's menu at $4.25 is even available for adults (additional 50¢). Breakfast is served 7 to 11am.

Alt. Rte. 40, off I-68, Exit 19. © **301/895-5266.** www.thecasselman.com. Reservations not accepted. Main courses: breakfast $1.75–$3.85; lunch and dinner $6.75–$9.25. MC, V. Open Mon–Thurs 7am–8pm, Fri–Sat 7am–9pm, closed Sun. Parking on-site, even a hitching post.

Elliott House Victorian Inn ⊛ Away from the hustle and bustle and tourist-laden sights of Deep Creek Lake, the Elliott House is a great place for a romantic weekend away from it all, especially if you choose to stay in one of the inn's cottages. This painted lady was restored in high Victorian style in 1997. Rooms in the main house are spacious, with private bathrooms, and one has a separate sitting room. An efficiency studio, was added in 2002. Complimentary hot and cold beverages are available at all times, and tea is served every afternoon. The inn is on 7 acres along the Casselman River, making it a convenient place for fly-fishing and a lovely place for nature walks. Bikes are also available for guest use. It's across the street from Penn Alps and the Spruce Forest Artisan Village.

146 Casselman Rd., Grantsville, MD 21536. ℂ 800/272-4090 or 301/895-4250. www.elliotthouse.com. 8 units. $85–$135 double; $135–$150 cottage. Rates include breakfast. AE, MC, V. Children under 12 welcome in cottages. **Amenities:** Hot tub; bikes. *In room:* TV/VCR, hair dryer, robes.

Penn Alps Restaurant and Craft Shop ⭐ PENNSYLVANIA DUTCH Remember those old-fashioned restaurants with simple, hearty homemade fare served by the kindest of waitresses? Come for the hearty breakfasts or the substantial lunch and dinner fare. There are buffets every Friday and Saturday night, as well as a Saturday breakfast buffet and Saturday and Sunday brunch. Eat in one of six dining rooms, where Pennsylvania Dutch–style cooking reigns. Dishes include roast pork and sauerkraut and hickory smoked ham, as well as roast beef, fried chicken, steaks, and seafood. Lighter items are also available, including sandwiches, soups, salads, and burgers, plus a children's menu and a seniors' menu. You can buy fresh-baked breads or pies or handcrafted goodies from the craft shop. The restaurant is across the parking lot from the Spruce Forest Artisan Village and an easy walk to the Casselman River Bridge. An 1818 stagecoach inn makes up part of the building. Look for the double fireplace, which has warmed visitors for nearly 2 centuries.

125 Casselman Rd., Grantsville. ℂ 301/895-5985. www.pennalps.com. Reservations not accepted. Main courses $7.95–$22.95; lunch $3.25–$6.95. AE, DISC, MC, V. Nov to day before Memorial Day Mon–Thurs 7am–7pm, Fri–Sat 7am–8pm, Sun 7am–3pm; Memorial Day–Oct 31 Mon–Sat 7am–8pm, Sun 7am–3pm. Closed several days at Christmas.

ATTRACTIONS ELSEWHERE IN GARRETT COUNTY

B&O Railroad Station ⭐ *Finds* The newly restored Queen Anne–style station was rededicated in October 2001. It's a beauty, with its bell-shaped roof and stained glass. This station was built in 1884 for the growing resort clientele. Visitors can climb into the circular tower.

2nd St., Oakland. Sat 10–2pm and Sun noon–4pm.

Church of the Presidents, Oakland Presidents Grant, Harrison, and Cleveland attended services here, as did President Arthur (before he took office). It was built in 1868 as a Presbyterian Church and is made of the same sandstone used for B&O railroad bridges and tunnels.

St. Matthew's Episcopal Church, 126 Liberty St., Oakland. ℂ 301/334-2510.

Garrett County Historical Society Museum This quaint museum, staffed by the friendly volunteers, houses an amazing array of local artifacts. On display are reminders of the old resort days, clothing, furniture, toys, portraits, artifacts of the famous hunter Meshach Browning, an elegant 1908 surrey, and even a black-bordered 1865 newspaper announcing the death of Abraham Lincoln.

107 S. Oakland St., Oakland. Admission free (donations accepted). Open May–Dec Mon–Sat 11am–4pm; Jan–Apr Thurs–Sat 11am–4pm.

Simon Pearce Glass Factory ⭐ Cross the catwalk over the furnaces and workbenches of glass artisans as they create the crystal-clear pieces for which

Simon Pearce is famous. In small teams, the glassblowers share the tasks of blowing orange molten glass into delicate forms. Most of the artisans work until 3pm, but there's always at least one team working until 5pm and on the weekends. A showroom is filled with the elegant, modern wares created here and at the other three Simon Pearce factories around the country.

265 Glass Dr., Mountain Lake Park, south of Deep Creek Lake and Oakland. (♪ 301/334-5277. www. simonpearce.com. Daily 9am–5pm. Take Rte. 219 south to Rte. 135. Turn left and then turn right on Glass Dr. The factory is on the left.

Mountain Lake Park Historic District ★★   Listed on the National Register of Historic Places, these Victorian-era streets look like time stood still in the 1880s, when the town was built as a Chautauqua-style summer resort. It drew thousands of visitors for the next 30 years. The country Gothic and rural Queen Anne homes, as well as the ticket booth from Chautauqua days remain. House tours are offered several times a year, and a self-guided tour brochure is available at the town office on Allegheny Drive or the visitor center in Deep Creek Lake.

Mountain Lake Park. (♪ 301/334-2250. South of Deep Creek Lake. Take Rte. 219 to Rte. 135.

Deep Creek Cellars   Paul Roberts and Nadine Grabania built this little winery in the basement of their home in the farthest northwest corner of Maryland. It manages to produce 12,000 bottles of light, fruity wine every year, and the owners take great pride in their work. (You can find their wines as far east as Baltimore.) Stop by and look at the grapes sparkling on the vines. At harvest time, you can see the juice as it's pressed from the fruit (watch out for the bees!). Best of all, you can taste the final product in the tasting room and buy a bottle of something you like. It's a good 20-minute drive up Route 42, past I-68, but the scenery is worth it.

177 Frazee Ridge Rd., Friendsville, MD 21531. (♪ 301/746-4349. deepwine@qcol.net. Apr 15–Dec 15 Wed–Sat 11am–6pm.

Working Farms *Kids*   If you like bunnies, alpacas, or llamas, or you want your kids to see a real farm, get the brochure at the Deep Creek visitor center *Visit Our Working Farms, Share Our Heritage*. Inside are a map and descriptions of nine farms that welcome visitors. Besides livestock farms, there's a hydroponic tomato farm and a farm specializing in woods-grown crops such as ginseng, walnuts, and shiitake mushrooms. Visit Cove Run Farms, where the family has built a maze into 2 acres of cornfields. The corn is tall and the paths are tricky, but it's fun to hear the kids squealing whether they reach a dead end or the end.

Located all around the western half of Garrett County. (♪ 301/746-8161 or 301/746-6111. www.coverun farms.com. Summer hours: Wed–Thurs 4–8pm, Fri noon–10pm, and Sat 11am–9pm. Aug 10–Oct 27 Fri and Sat only; call for hours.

SHOPPING

A few places in outlying areas of Deep Lake Creek are worth a shopping stop. Just north of Deep Creek Lake, off Route 42, **Schoolhouse Earth,** 1224 Friendsville Rd. (♪ 301/746-8603), specializes in country accessories, furniture, and home decor and carries some interesting garden accessories.

In Oakland, the **Book Market & Antique Mezzanine,** 111 S. 2nd St. (♪ 301/334-8778), is an independent bookshop with a good selection of children's books, literary fiction, history, and biography, as well as antiques and collectibles. If you're looking for furniture, **Unfinished Business,** 114 S. 2nd St. (♪ 301/533-4495), carries all types of unfinished furniture, which they will finish for you if you like, at particularly reasonable prices.

South of Oakland on U.S. Route 219, just past the intersection of U.S. Route 50, is the 12,000-square-foot **Red House School Country Mall** (① **301/ 334-2800**). It carries a variety of antiques, crafts, local Amish wares, and furniture.

WHERE TO STAY
VACATION RENTALS
The Deep Creek Lake area offers plenty of vacation properties—cabins, town homes, and mountain chalets—for rent by the week or in 2- or 3-day intervals. They come in all sizes, from a two-bedroom lakeside cottage or slopeside townhouse to eight-bedroom behemoths with extra everything. Fireplaces, hot tubs, decks, boat slips, and even ski-in and ski-outs are available. Many allow pets. They generally come with all the linens, appliances, and tools you'll need.

Most of the homes are individually owned and rented through real estate/ rental agencies. Two reputable agencies are **Railey Mountain Lake Vacations** (① **800/846-RENT;** www.deepcreek.com) and **A&A/Long & Foster Resort Rentals** (① **800/336-7303;** www.deepcreekresort.com). Railey even has a guest welcome party on Mondays in the summer, so visitors can get to know what's available at Deep Creek, from horseback riding to fly-fishing classes.

HOTELS, MOTELS & B&BS
Carmel Cove Inn ★ This little bed-and-breakfast is tucked in a wooded area off Glendale Road and U.S. Route 219 within walking distance of its own private cove, with dock, along Deep Creek Lake. The inn is the former monastery of the Discalced Carmelite Fathers and has steeples, a clock tower, and a chapel-like facade. The guest rooms have been refurbished—many now have private decks, fireplaces, and whirlpool tubs. A common parlor has a stacked stone fireplace, a TV and video collection, and a billiards table for guest use. Innkeepers Ed Spak and Mary Bender prepare hearty buffet breakfasts, often including Belgian waffles, cheesy sausage mushroom quiche, and griddlecakes with Maryland maple syrup. Guests can use the house fishing poles, canoes or paddleboats, mountain bikes, tennis court, hot tub, and sun deck.

P.O. Box 644, Oakland, MD 21550. ① 301/387-0067. www.carmelcoveinn.com. 10 units. $120–$180 double. Rates include full breakfast. DISC, MC, V. In room: A/C.

Haley Farm Bed-and-Breakfast ★ Situated in a scenic valley 6 miles (10km) south of Deep Creek Lake and signposted off Route 219, this two-story bed-and-breakfast inn, retreat center, and working farm is constantly evolving. In addition to the original rooms, seven suites have been added, all with gas fireplaces and whirlpool tubs, and three with kitchenettes. When Kam and Wayne Gillespie purchased the inn in 1993, it had only five rooms and few of the many amenities it now offers. Guests can enjoy the 65-acre farm, with an orchard, vegetable garden (guests are welcome to take some produce with them), fields of wildflowers, and horses (boarded for a local stable/riding company). The house offers a cozy living area with fireplace, TV, games, books, and videos. Guests can use the inn's bikes, cross-country skis, tubes, rowboats, and fishing tackle free of charge. In the summer and fall, guests can look forward to weekend cookouts, too.

The inn offers a variety of packages and group retreat programs, including a Romantic Weekend package with flowers and dinner at a nearby restaurant. Retreat programs can be arranged on topics ranging from management and conflict resolution to yoga.

16766 Garrett Hwy., Deep Creek Lake, MD 21550. © **888/231-FARM** or 301/387-9050. Fax 301/387-9050. www.haleyfarm.com. 18 units. $130–$215 double. Rates include full breakfast. AE, DISC, MC, V. **Amenities:** Orchard; garden. *In room:* A/C, TV/VCR, whirlpool tubs and fireplaces in suites, 3 with kitchenettes.

Lake Pointe Inn ⭐ Though this cozy inn dates from the 1800s, renovations have kept it looking new and modern. It's only 13 feet from Great Lake, so good views are guaranteed.

Most of the guest rooms have been updated. Seven rooms have new fireplaces; six have Jacuzzi-style tubs. All have private bathrooms. Also new are a boardroom and some spa-like touches. Little extras make this place wonderful, including incredible hot breakfasts. There is also a large collection of videos for guest use, and you can use the inn's bikes, canoes, or kayaks. Or, you can head to the slopes—Wisp is within walking distance.

174 Lake Pointe Dr., McHenry, MD 21541. © **800/523-LAKE** or 301/387-0111. www.deepcreekinns.com. 10 units. $148–$249 double. Rates include full breakfast. DISC, MC, V. No children under 16. **Amenities:** Sauna; steambath; massage room. *In room:* A/C, TV/VCR, hair dryer, ceiling fans, robes, down pillows and comforters.

Point View Inn Right on the shores of Deep Creek Lake, this lodging offers motel-style rooms with porches or private terraces overlooking the lake. Most units have Victorian or antique furnishings, some with fireplaces.

609 Deep Creek Dr. (P.O. Box 100), McHenry, MD 21541. © **301/387-5555.** 20 units. $50–$90 double; $110 double with kitchenette. AE, DISC, MC, V. **Amenities:** Cafe/lounge; full-service dining room overlooking the lake; boat dock; private beach.

Wisp Resort ⭐⭐ *Kids* With rooms looking right onto the slopes and ski lockers just inside the door, Wisp makes it easy on skiers. They also have an indoor swimming pool and whirlpool, tennis court, fitness center, several restaurants, and a child-care facility. A majority of the guest rooms are suites or efficiencies, and all rooms have queen-size bed(s), a sofa bed, a coffeemaker, and a small refrigerator. Some suites have a Murphy bed in the rooms overlooking the slopes to make the rooms more spacious. Some units also have small kitchenettes or fireplaces. Willy Wisp, the hotel's youth center and education facility for ages 3 to 14, makes this resort quite popular with families; the facility runs half- and full-day group skiing and snowboarding classes in winter and golf lessons on its 18-hole championship course after the snow melts.

Wisp specializes in providing vacation packages, so if there's some activity you want to try—mountain biking, white-water paddling, orienteering—let the staff know, and they'll usually be able to make the necessary arrangements.

290 Marsh Hill Rd. (off U.S. 219, on the north side of the lake), Deep Creek Lake, MD 21541. © **800/462-9477** or 301/387-5581. Fax 301/387-4127. www.wisp-resort.com. 167 units. $65–$169 double. AE, DC, DISC, MC, V. Pets accepted. **Amenities:** Restaurant; coffee shop/pizzeria; two lounges; indoor pool; golf; tennis; snowskiing; snowboarding; tubing; concierge; Willy Wisp program for children ages 3–14; arcade; ski shop. *In room:* A/C, dataport in some rooms, kitchenette in some rooms, coffeemaker, hair dryer and iron available.

CAMPING

Deep Creek Lake State Park (© 301/387-5563) offers 112 improved campsites, 25 of which have electric hookups. There are heated bathhouses with showers and a dump station. Reservations are recommended for spring, fall, and summer visits. Pets are permitted in designated loops.

WHERE TO DINE

Note: Garrett County liquor regulations prohibit restaurants from serving any alcoholic beverages, including wine, on Sunday.

Canoe on the Run DELI   This unpretentious sandwich shop serves gourmet sandwiches, coffee, and pastries; there are even a few vegetarian options, a rarity in this area. The dining area is quiet and cozy, with a gas fireplace, and there is an outdoor deck for warm-weather dining. Canoe on the Run serves beer and wine.

2622 Deep Creek Dr., McHenry. ℂ 301/387-5933. Sandwiches and salads $2.95–$6.95. AE, DISC, V. Open daily at 8am; closing varies seasonally.

Deep Creek Brewing Company and Restaurant ★★ PUB GRUB   They serve good food at Deep Creek Brewing Company—hearty stuff that goes well with beer. You'll find a wicked wild stew made with venison, elk, and ostrich as well as a variety of pastas, sandwiches, and salads. It's the kind of grub you want when you come in from the cold. The beer is handcrafted on-site, Youghiogheny Red, Deep Creek Gold, and Beary Wheat among them. This is a family-friendly place—not only is there a children's menu for $4.95, but they have a Stall the Kids Platter with crackers, cheese, and fruit and root beer brewed right here. It's always a fun, casual place, in a beautiful new setting with soaring ceilings, a toasty fireplace, and picture windows overlooking the lake and ski slopes.

Rte. 219 (behind the visitor center), McHenry. ℂ 301/387-2182. www.deepcreekbrewing.com. Main courses $6.50–$24.95. Reservations not accepted. AE, DISC, MC, V.

Deer Park Inn FRENCH   For fine dining in turn-of-the-20th-century atmosphere, it's hard to beat this lovely inn, built in 1889 as a 17-room summer home for Baltimore architect, Josiah Pennington. Although the cottage was left dormant for many years, it was restored several years ago and is now listed on the National Register of Historic Places. Furnished with Victorian antiques, many of which are original to the building and nearby estates, it is now the setting for candlelit French dining with an American flair, overseen by chef Pascal Fontaine. The main drawback is that the inn is in the middle of nowhere, deep in the country (though well signposted), about 9 miles (15km) southeast of the Deep Creek Lake Bridge, off Sand Flat Road and Route 135. To stay overnight, the inn does offer three rooms with private bathrooms upstairs ($115–$135).

65 Hotel Rd., Deer Park, MD 21550. ℂ 301/334-2308. Reservations recommended. Main courses $16.50–$23.25. AE, DISC, MC, V. Mon–Sat 5:30–9:30pm.

Four Seasons Dining Room AMERICAN   Four Seasons is a bit more formal than many of the other restaurants in Deep Creek, kind of like the restaurants you may remember from, say, the early 1960s. Furnishings in this stone-and-glass dining room have that retro flair. But the lake view is beautiful, the burgers are big and juicy, and the menu has plenty to choose from. Order sandwiches, salads, or even a frittata for lunch, and at dinner, the menu includes steak, chicken, lobster, and pecan-crusted salmon. It's a good place to go when you want to get away from the noise of some of the other hopping restaurants in town.

At Will O' the Wisp, Rte. 219 just south of the Deep Creek Lake Bridge. ℂ 301/387-5503, ext. 2201. Main courses: lunch $4.25–$6.45; dinner $13.95–$29.95. AE, DISC, MC, V. Reservations welcome. Daily breakfast 7–11:30am; lunch 11.30am–2pm; dinner 5–9:30pm.

Lakeside Creamery ★ ICE CREAM/SANDWICHES   If you see a crowd outside the Lakeside Creamery in the morning, you know it must be close to opening time. The rich, homemade ice cream draws people by car, by foot, and even by boat. (Climbing the steps from the dock burns off the calories about to be consumed.) The Lakeside offers 24 flavors of ice cream and sherbet, as well as low-fat yogurt. The Muddy Creek sundae, with chocolate ice cream, hot fudge, whipped cream, chocolate sprinkles, and a cherry, is a specialty. Lakeside's vanilla and ice creams have won national awards—and they deserve them. Try the waffle cones, too; they're handmade at the shop.

20282 Garrett Hwy. (U.S. Rte. 219). ℂ **301/387-2580.** Summer Sun–Thurs 11am–11pm; off-season Fri–Sat 11am–11pm, Sun–Mon 11am–9pm. Closed Nov–Mar.

Uno Restaurant *Kids* PIZZA   So what if Uno is part of a chain? It's where everybody goes. It's a family place with a playground and wide lawn by the piers so the little kids can wear themselves out while waiting for their tables. (And there *can* be a wait, especially on weekends.) A deck at the Honi-Honi Bar has entertainment on the weekend. It's a pretty restaurant with a central fireplace and outside seating in season. The food is the usual for Pizzeria Uno: lots of pizza, pastas, sandwiches, soups, and salads and an interesting children's menu. Don't forget Kid's Day at Uno, when pizza and a drink are 99¢. The chain's founder, who lives nearby, has made this restaurant a standout.

19746 Garrett Hwy., Deep Creek Lake. ℂ **301/387-4866.** Reservations not accepted. Main courses $5.95–$20. AE, DC, DISC, MC, V. Mon–Sat 11am–midnight, Sun 11am–11pm.

9

Maryland & Delaware's Atlantic Beaches

A trip to the beach or "down the ocean" in local parlance is the only true vacation for many Marylanders and Delawareans. And though they may choose one beach as their destination, everybody—well, it seems that way—visits the other beaches. Bethany's vacationers can't keep away from Rehoboth's shops and restaurants or Ocean City's amusements. If you're an angler, check out both Ocean City's and Lewes's charter boats. The beaches of Delaware Seashore State Park are the quietest. If you want a party, head for the nightspots of Delaware's Dewey or the boardwalk of Ocean City, Maryland.

Each town has its own character and the Delaware beaches are quite different from Maryland beaches. For one thing, all of the Maryland beaches are public; Delaware has some private beaches. In this chapter, we'll give you a snapshot of each, focusing on the individual delights and differences.

DELAWARE BEACHES

Stretched along 25 miles (40km) of ocean and bay shoreline, Delaware's five beach towns—Lewes, Rehoboth Beach, Dewey Beach, Bethany Beach, and Fenwick Island—have their own personalities, ambience, and repeat visitors.

For information about dinner specials, coupons for fudge, or local news, grab one or two of the free publications piled up in the vestibules of restaurants, real estate offices, and hotels. Some good ones are *The Wave, Sunny Day,* and *Southern Delaware Explorer.*

LEWES With such a quaint little town to keep your attention, you just might forget there's a beach in Lewes. The best beach is at Cape Henlopen State Park (© **302/645-8983**), 1 mile (2km) east of Lewes. There are lifeguards, bathhouses, and lots of parking. Admission is $5 per out-of-state car and it's worth it. The beaches are never wall-to-wall bodies as they can be in Ocean City. Even the water at the confluence of Delaware Bay and the ocean seems calmer. You can take a walk on a nature trail instead of a shopping district and look for shorebirds instead of T-shirts. The public beach in Lewes runs from the Cape May–Lewes Ferry terminal to the Roosevelt Inlet. Public access to this bay beach is at the end of Savannah Road, where there are parking and bathhouses.

REHOBOTH & DEWEY Swimming at Rehoboth's and Dewey's wide sandy beaches is one of the area's top activities. All the beaches have public access and are guarded, but there are no bathhouses.

At Rehoboth, watch out for the NO SWIMMING signs. The signs at the beach between Brooklyn Avenue and Laurel Street warn against swimming near two sunken ships. Though the ships have been cut down to the waterline, there's a ragged edge that can protrude. It's best to avoid this one dangerous spot.

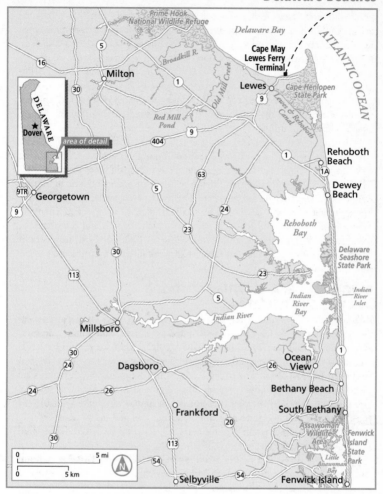

Insider tip: Rehoboth offers "Beach Wheels," wheelchairs designed specifically for beach use, at City Hall. Call ℭ **302/227-4641.**

Just south of Dewey is perhaps Delaware's finest, quietest beach.

A narrow strip of land between the ocean and Rehoboth and Indian River bays, **Delaware Seashore State Park** ✦ (ℭ **302/227-2800**) offers ocean waves and quiet bay waters. Besides 6 miles (10km) of guarded beach, there's a 310-slip full-service marina and boat ramp and 300 sites for RVs and campers. Surf fishermen often set up their poles on these quiet beaches after hours. This is a beach lovers' paradise but don't look for pizza or ice cream stands. You'll have to drive to Dewey or Bethany for those. Admission is $2.50 for Delaware cars and $5 for out-of-state vehicles.

Take your **surfboard** to the beach near the Indian River Inlet on Route 1, just south of Dewey Beach.

BETHANY & FENWICK   Bethany's public beach is small and can be very crowded. Visitors staying in oceanside houses and condos have their own private beaches in most cases and don't have to worry about crowds as much. You'll hear about dolphin sightings all around the Delaware beaches but they're quite common here. Stay a week and you may spot dolphins several times. The beach in front of the boardwalk is free and open to the public. It is guarded Memorial Day weekend to Labor Day Monday to Friday 10am to 5pm, weekends and holidays 9:30am to 5:30pm. Behind the bandstand are large, clean bathhouses.

Bethany Rental Service, 201 Central Ave. (© 302/539-6244), operates a rental concession on the beach, offering 8-foot umbrellas, surf mats, boogie boards, chairs, and more.

Fenwick, on the border with Maryland, is a little more relaxed than Ocean City but not as quiet as Bethany. It has more public beach than Bethany. Its claim to fame is the very narrow but long Fenwick Island State Park (© 302/539-9060), where you can watch the sun rise over the ocean and later in the day, watch the sun set over Assawoman Bay. The beach offers public space for swimming, sunbathing, and surfing. The facilities include shower and changing rooms, a first-aid room, lifeguards, gift shop, picnic tables, and refreshments. Admission is $5 for out-of-state cars and $2.50 for Delaware cars. Admission is free weekdays during spring and fall and all week in winter. Hours are 8am to sunset year-round.

BEYOND THE BEACH: OTHER OUTDOOR ACTIVITIES IN DELAWARE

BALLOONING   The flat terrain, wide, open fields, and wind patterns off the Atlantic make Sussex County well suited for hot-air ballooning. The **First State Hot Air Balloon Team** (© 302/684-2002), will take you up for a 45-minute to 1-hour ride for $100 per person. Because weather conditions have to be just so for the balloon to launch, scheduling a trip can be difficult. Call ahead to let the team know when you'll be in the area, and they'll schedule a ride when the weather permits (it helps if you have several days available). If you live in the area and have a flexible schedule, call and get on their waiting list. When the weather is suitable, the team will go down the list until they find someone who is available.

Visitors can also take a ride in a balloon at the **Delmarva Hot Air Balloon and Craft Festival,** held annually in Milton. Several balloons are often available for untethered rides, for which reservations are necessary, and tethered rides are offered on a first-come, first-served basis. The festival is held in June. For information on the festival and for reservations, call © **302/684-3400.**

BICYCLING   Southern Delaware is a great place to bike. The terrain is flat; the views of the farmland, villages, and wetlands are pleasant; and most roads are wide, with good shoulders. The **Delaware Bicycle Council,** P.O. Box 778, Dover, DE 19903 (© **302/760-BIKE**) produces "Delaware Maps for Bicycle Users." All roads are marked and color coded according to their suitability for cyclists, so there's no guesswork involved in planning your route. Maps can be obtained online from the Delaware Bicycle Council website at www.deldot.net.

Bicycling on your own near the beaches is a breeze because of the level terrain and the wide back roads. Even the trip up Route 1 from Bethany to the Indian River Inlet is easy. The Delaware Department of Transportation distributes free maps designating safe, scenic roads (it also tells you which roads to avoid).

For family excursions, **Cape Henlopen State Park** (see below) has lots of well-marked, paved bicycle trails usually away from park traffic.

Delaware state law requires that children wear helmets.

CANOEING   The creeks and ponds of Sussex County make for lovely canoe excursions. A well-maintained 5-mile (8km) canoe trail along the Hitch Pond and James branches of the Nanticoke River will take you past the two largest trees in Delaware, one of which is estimated to be 750 years old. The trail begins at **Trapp Pond State Park,** R.D. 2, Box 331, Laurel, DE 19956 (© **302/ 875-5153**), where you can rent canoes for $5 an hour if you don't have your own. Launch at the dam, and follow the signs that designate the trail. The trail ends at the state boat launch on Records Pond.

Prime Hook National Wildlife Refuge (© **302/684-8419**) offers 15 miles (24km) of streams and ditches, including a 7-mile (11km) self-guided canoe trail. Electric-powered boats can also use the waterways. There's a boat launch behind the visitor center, but bring your own boat. There are no rentals at the refuge.

Trussum Pond looks and feels more like the Florida everglades or the bayou than Southern Delaware. From Route 24, take Route 449, which goes by the entrance to Trapp Pond State Park, to Road 72, or Trussum Pond Road. There's a small park and parking area next to the pond, and you can paddle among the abundant lily pads and graceful bald cypress. (Sussex County is home to the northernmost stand of bald cypress in the country.) But you'll have to do the navigating yourself; there aren't any trail markers.

A STATE PARK WITH OUTDOOR ACTIVITIES

Cape Henlopen State Park (© **302/645-8983**), with its 3,143 acres bordered on one side by the Atlantic and on another by Delaware Bay, offers beach swimming, tennis, picnicking, nature trails, bay-shore crabbing, and pier fishing, accessible from all the Delaware beach resorts. It's also the home of the famous "walking dunes," most notably the 80-foot **Great Dune** ✿, the highest sand dune between Cape Hatteras and Cape Cod. For those who enjoy a good climb, a refurbished World War II observation tower (115 steps) offers some of the best coastal views for miles. The park is open year-round 8am to sunset. Admission to the park costs $2.50 for Delaware residents and $5 for out-of-state visitors from May through October; it's free the rest of the year.

You can also **camp** at Cape Henlopen, an inexpensive option in a resort area. The 159 campsites sit on pine-covered dunes and have water hookup and access to clean bathhouses with showers. The sites are all fairly spacious, but the ones in the center loops are not terribly private. The largest and most private sites are located in the back loop, but they aren't well suited for trailers or motor homes. (To get to these sites, continue straight along the main road into the camping area until you have to veer left onto the gravel and dirt road.) The campground is open April 1 through October 31 on a first-come first-served basis. Rates are $20 per night. As with all camping on the Atlantic coast, mosquitoes can be a problem (though not nearly as bad as at Assateague), so bring bug repellent.

MARYLAND BEACHES

Ocean City has the most public beaches, and some of the most crowded. If you want to make friends, come here.

The beach near the southern tip of Ocean City is the widest and usually least crowded. A huge parking lot makes this a convenient place for day-trippers.

The beach along the boardwalk actually gets quite narrow in a few places. Beach replenishment efforts have helped. But for those who love the boardwalk and all its shops and restaurants, this is the best beach.

In north Ocean City, land of high-rise condos, the beach widens. Crowds depend on the size of the building but it's easy to find a place for your blanket.

The inlet at Ocean City's southern end divides touristy Ocean City from the wild beaches of **Assateague.** Not a restaurant, gas station, or hotel has made the jump over to the island. It remains a pristine beach, quiet and isolated. It's a great alternative for those who like their beaches as Mother Nature intended.

Although you can see it across the inlet from Ocean City, it's about an 11-mile (18km) drive to the visitor center and parking lots. Most of the 30-odd mile (48km) strip of barrier island is not open to vehicles. It's home to an enormous number of shorebirds, sika deer, and the wild ponies made famous by Marguerite Henry's books. The visitor center and campgrounds are the only buildings here.

The entire 10-mile (16km) stretch of Ocean City beach is open to the public free of charge. Lifeguards are on duty 10am to 5:30pm all summer. Beach chairs, umbrellas, rafts, and boogie boards can be rented for a day or a week. You can't miss the young tanned man or woman watching over a stack of chairs and such. They usually take only cash. Attendants will position your umbrellas and if you rent for the week, umbrella and chairs will be ready when you arrive each day.

Bathhouses are located on the boardwalk at North 1st Street and at Philadelphia and Wicomico, both near the southern end of O.C. Both are privately operated and charge a fee. Public restrooms are strategically located along the boardwalk at Worcester, Caroline, 9th, and 27th.

SURFING   Two stretches of beach are designated as "surf beaches" each day and announced on local radio stations, the newspaper, and signs posted on the beach. Some surf shops in the area are **Quiet Storm,** 74th Street (© **410/723-1313**), and **Endless Summer Surf Shop,** 38th Street (© **410/289-3272**).

SURF FISHING   The big poles usually come out in the evening or early morning since surf fishing is not permitted within 50 yards of swimmers. When the swimmers go home in the fall, surf fishermen take over.

1 Lewes

86 miles (138km) SE of Wilmington, 34 miles (55km) N of Ocean City, 121 miles (195km) E of Washington, D.C., 107 miles (172km) SE of Baltimore

Delaware's northernmost and oldest beach resort, Lewes (pronounced *Loo*-is) is also its oldest town, founded in 1681 as a Dutch whaling station named Zwaanendael. The community maintains strong ties to both its Dutch heritage, which you can learn about at the Zwaanendael Museum, and to the sea—as a beach resort, a boating marina, and a port for dozens of fishing fleets.

Though Lewes is where the Delaware Bay meets the Atlantic Ocean, its main streets are turned away from the water. Not only are the historic sites and Zwaanendael Museum along streets that seem to have forgotten they're so near the ocean, the small shops, restaurants, and inns are there, too. The result is a quaint, friendly little town that also has a beach.

The beach is actually on the other side of the Lewes–Rehoboth Canal. The fishing boats are over there, too. It's an easy walk across the Savannah Road Bridge. Cape Henlopen State Park is so close that many Lewes vacationers head to the wide sandy beaches there.

Lewes is much quieter than the other beach resorts. For those who want a friendly, quiet place with a few good restaurants and shops, this is a good choice. For those who want a break from the other busy resorts, it's a good day trip.

GETTING THERE

BY CAR   From points north, take Routes 113 and 13 to Route 1 and then to Route 9 (Savannah Rd.) into town. From the south, take Route 113 to Georgetown, and then take Route 9 east to Lewes. From Ocean City or Rehoboth, take Route 1 to Route 9. From the west, take Route 50 across the Bay Bridge to Route 404 east, and then to Route 9.

BY FERRY   Many visitors come to Lewes via the **Cape May–Lewes Ferry,** a 70-minute Delaware Bay mini-cruise that connects southern New Jersey to mid-Delaware and saves considerable driving for north- or southbound passengers along the Atlantic coast. In operation since 1964, this ferry service maintains a fleet of five vessels, each holding up to 800 passengers and 100 cars. Departures are daily year-round, from early morning until evening, with almost hourly service in the summer months from 7am to 9pm.

Passenger rates are $6.50 per passenger; vehicle fares, calculated by car length, range from $18 for most cars to $66 for large trucks, with reduced prices for motorcycle and bicycle passengers and off-peak reduced rates from December to March. Reservations are recommended. The Lewes Terminal (© **302/644-6030**) is next to the Cape Henlopen State Park entrance, about a mile from the center of town. The New Jersey terminal is in Cape May, at the end of the Garden State Parkway. Call © **800/64-FERRY** for reservations or © 302/426-1155 for rates and information. Shuttle service is available to both Cape May and Lewes every day in summer and on weekends in the fall for an extra $3.

BY PLANE   Visitors arriving by plane should fly into the **Wicomico County Airport.** See "Getting There" in "Ocean City, Maryland," later in this chapter.

VISITOR INFORMATION   Contact the **Lewes Chamber of Commerce and Visitors Bureau,** P.O. Box 1, Lewes, DE 19958 (© **302/645-8073;** www.leweschamber.com). The chamber's offices are in the Fisher–Martin House at Kings Highway, next to the Zwaanendael Museum. It's open year-round Monday through Friday 10am to 4pm; during the summer the office is also open Saturday 9am to 3pm and Sunday 10am to 2pm. Or get a visitors' guide from the **Southern Delaware Tourism Office,** P.O. Box 240, Georgetown, DE 19947, or visit www.visitsoutherndelaware.com.

GETTING AROUND   The **Seaport Taxi of Lewes,** 306 Savannah Rd. (© **302/645-6800**), operates a taxi transfer service from the ferry terminal to the downtown area, as well as local service throughout the area. Ferry passengers can call for the taxi service from the information station at the ferry terminal.

SPECIAL EVENTS   Lewes hosts one of the strangest sporting events around: the **World Championship Punkin' Chunkin',** held annually the first weekend in November. Contestants enter their own mechanical contraptions (no explosives allowed) to see which can hurl a pumpkin the farthest. The record, set in 1998, is 4,026.32 feet. Aside from the competition, there are food and craft vendors, live bands, and entertainment for kids. Admission is $5 per car or $1 per person. For more information, call the Lewes Chamber of Commerce and Visitors Bureau (© **302/645-8073;** www.leweschamber.com). The event has made *CBS This Morning, Nickelodeon,* and *David Letterman.*

Other less notorious events include the **Great Delaware Kite Festival,** held at Cape Henlopen State Park annually on Good Friday, and **Boast the Coast/Coast Day** weekend, the first weekend in October. Boast the Coast is a celebration of the town's nautical history, sponsored by the Lewes Chamber of Commerce. The highlight is the lighted boat parade in the canal. **Coast Day**

(© 302/831-8083) is sponsored by and held at the University of Delaware College of Marine Studies in Lewes. The fair includes lectures, ship tours, marine aquariums, and a crab cake cook-off. Both events are free, but you may have to pay for parking.

Nearby Milton hosts the annual **Delmarva Hot Air Balloon and Craft Festival** (© **302/684-8404** or 302/684-3400), on the third Saturday in June. Over 20 balloons take flight each year. Visitors can take tethered balloon rides, listen to live entertainment, and shop for crafts, antiques, and food. Admission is free.

WHERE TO STAY

Lewes's accommodation choices include handsome inns as well as traditional motels. Prices are in the moderate-to-expensive range in the summer months and in the moderate-to-inexpensive range at other times of the year. Check what rate is in effect at the time you plan to visit and whether any minimum-night stays are required. Reservations are required in summer months and recommended at other times, since the room capacity in town barely exceeds 300. Parking is at a premium and metered parking on the street may be required at some local inns.

For rentals, call a real estate agent. One reputable company is **Jack Lingo,** 1240 Kings Hwy., © **800/331-4241** or 302/645-2207. Most rentals are houses or town houses in Lewes, some with views of or frontage on Delaware Bay.

MODERATE

Blue Water House Inn ★ *Kids*   Bold new colors, art, and bronze sculptures have remade this fun bed-and-breakfast. Innkeepers Chuck and Karen Ulrich and Charlie and Kayla, their two children, regularly stop by Garage Sale Antiques (see "Shopping," below) looking for new additions. The comfortable guest rooms, all on the second level, are large, have private bathrooms, and open onto a covered porch. The "Lookout" on the upper level provides panoramic views and a good place to relax, play games, and watch TV. The ground-level patio is home to "Captain Chuck's World Famous Conga Bar," where you can lie back in a hammock and sip a margarita.

The Ulrich family has created a casual kick-your-shoes-off atmosphere that makes their guests feel right at home. Families with children are welcome and well accommodated; two or three rooms can be converted to suites.

407 E. Market St. (across the canal on the bay side of town). © **800/493-2080** for reservations or 302/645-7832 for information. Fax 302/644-3704. www.lewes-beach.com. 6 units. $75–$155 double. Rates include continental breakfast. MC, V. Free parking. Children welcome. **Amenities:** Water sports equipment; bikes; beach towels; umbrellas and chairs; massage and babysitting services available. *In room:* A/C, TV/VCR, fax, dataport, fridge, hair dryer, iron.

Inn at Canal Square ★   This four-story inn overlooking its own marina has a casual country-inn atmosphere with the amenities of a large full-service hotel and marina. The generously sized guest rooms are furnished in 18th-century English style, with reproduction headboards, nightstands, armoires, brass lamps, and comfortable armchairs, as well as designer fabrics, waterfowl art prints, and live plants. Best of all, most rooms have a balcony or porch overlooking the water. The modern bathrooms, each with separate vanity area, have sleek black-and-white marble and tile appointments. The newest unit, a two-bedroom canal-view apartment with sun deck and fireplace, rents for $1,800 a week in season.

122 Market St., Lewes, DE 19958. © **888/644-1911** or 302/644-3377. www.beach-net.com/canalsquare. html. 19 units. $90–$195 double. Rates include continental breakfast. AE, MC, V. Free parking. Children under 5 free in parents' room; pets welcome in courtyard rooms for a fee. **Amenities:** Marina with boat slips available for guests. *In room:* A/C, TV.

Wild Swan Inn   This B&B, located a half mile from town and a mile from the beach, opposite the Lewes Library on Adams Avenue, is a standout for turn-of-the-century ambience and 1990s comfort. Built in 1910 as a lightship captain's house in classic Victorian style, it's rich in ornate gingerbread and fancy finials. The common rooms and guest rooms are also Victorian, with high ceilings and vivid colors, lavish wallpaper, antique brass lighting fixtures, and antique furnishings. In honor of the house's name, the innkeepers have filled the rooms with swan-motif accessories, from china swans to swan toilet paper. All the rooms have queen-sized beds. The facilities include a wraparound porch.

525 Kings Hwy., Lewes, DE 19958. © 302/645-8550. Fax 302/645-8550. 3 units (2 with shower only). $85–$150 double. Rates include breakfast. No credit cards. Free parking. **Amenities:** Outdoor pool; bicycles available; garden; gazebo. *In room:* A/C.

Zwaanendael Inn ⭐   Formerly the New Devon Inn, dating from 1926, this restored three-story brick hotel sits in the heart of Lewes. Guests can relax in a modern sitting room with Art Deco tones and a baby grand piano, in the adjacent Music Room, or in the wicker and plant-filled Garden Room. The guest rooms, located on the second and third floors, are individually furnished with local antiques, crystal or brass lamps, and comforters and fine linens. There's even a chocolate on your pillow at the end of the day. Because of the many expensive antique furnishings, this inn may not be suitable for children under 16.

142 2nd St. (at Market St.), Lewes, DE 19958. © 800/824-8754 or 302/645-6466. www.Zwaanendaelinn. com. 23 units. $60–$225 double. Rates include continental breakfast. AE, MC, V. **Amenities:** Cafe serving breakfast and lunch daily, dinner on weekends, coffee in lower lobby 7am–11pm; fitness center. *In room:* A/C, TV in most rooms, dataport, hair dryer, iron available.

INEXPENSIVE

Angler's Motel   One of the oldest lodgings in the area, this well-kept motel is a favorite with fishing guests and families. Most of the rooms have views of the wharf and marina. Outside there's a pleasant sun deck, a pool, grills, and a picnic area. All rooms have a kitchenette or an unstocked refrigerator. Reduced rates are in effect from mid-September to mid-May; closed December to January.

110 Anglers Rd. (at Market St.), Lewes, DE 19958. © 302/645-2831. 25 units. $40–$100 double. 2-night minimum stay on summer weekends. AE, MC, V. Free parking. **Amenities:** Marina; pool; grills; picnic area; sun deck. *In room:* A/C, kitchenette or fridge.

Beacon Motel   This motel near Fisherman's Wharf, opened in 1989, occupies the top two floors of a three-story property, with the ground level devoted to shops and a reception area. The bright and cheery rooms feature standard furnishings, seashell art, and a small balcony with sliding glass doors.

514 E. Savannah Rd. (P.O. Box 609), Lewes, DE 19958. © 800/735-4888 or 302/645-4888. www.lewes today.com/beacon. 66 units. $50–$175 double. AE, DISC, MC, V. Free parking. Closed late Nov to mid-Mar. **Amenities:** Outdoor pool; sun deck. *In room:* A/C, fridge.

Cape Henlopen Motel *Value*   Fishermen alert: this modern two-story L-shaped motel is located directly across from Fisherman's Wharf, and has fully carpeted and wood-paneled rooms, some with beach-style furniture. All second-floor rooms have balconies that overlook the boats in the Rehoboth–Lewes Canal. Plenty of charter boats, restaurants, and watering holes are within walking distance.

Savannah and Anglers rds. (P.O. Box 243), Lewes, DE 19958. © 800/447-3158 or 302/645-2828. www. beach-net.com/henlopenmotel. 28 units. $45–$125 double. 2-night minimum stay and 3-night minimum on holiday weekends in summer. AE, DC, DISC, MC, V. Free parking. *In room:* AC, fridge, iron available.

Savannah Inn   A semi-Victorian brick house with a wraparound enclosed porch, this B&B is in Lewes at the corner of Orr Street. Bedrooms are of varying size and decor, all with shared bathrooms but private basins. Relax in the backyard, or enjoy games, books, and the piano in the parlor. Rates include a breakfast of local fruits, homemade breads or muffins and jams, and a choice of hot beverage. Some rooms can accommodate three or four, at a rate of $55 to $65. Rooms are available at reduced rates without breakfast in the off-season.

330 Savannah Rd. (Rte. 9), Lewes, DE 19958. ℂ 302/645-5592. 7 units (all with shared bathroom). $50–$80 double. Rates include continental breakfast. 2-night minimum stay on weekends and 3-night minimum on holiday weekends. No credit cards. Free parking. B&B Memorial Day through Labor Day; reduced rates, no breakfast off-season.

WHERE TO DINE
EXPENSIVE

The Buttery ✸✸ NOUVEAU FRENCH   The Buttery, in a restored Victorian mansion, is as close as you'll get to a Paris bistro on the Delaware shore. There are candlelit dining rooms set with white linens, a formal bar, and a full wine list. The menu, like most in the area, has a wide selection of seafood—crab cakes, pan-seared yellowfin tuna, and bouillabaisse—with a few beef and poultry options, including oysters in pastry with Pernod-laced champagne cream and caviar. This is also a great place for Sunday champagne brunch. Perhaps the best deal is the early bird three-course fixed-price special, every night until 6:30pm, for $14.95.

102 2nd St. ℂ 302/645-7755. Reservations recommended. Main courses $19–$29; lunch $6.95–$14.95. DISC, MC, V. Tues–Sun 11am–2:30pm and 5–10pm. Open daily June–Aug.

Gilligan's SEAFOOD   One of the unique dining spots in Lewes is Gilligan's. The restaurant is a refurbished diving boat anchored on the marina and attached to a renovated chicken coop on the dock. The result is a charming harborfront structure with a deck bar and a glass-walled dining room, decorated in a tropical island motif. The indoor dining area is rather small and can get crowded and loud at times. Seafood dominates the dinner menu, with such choices as pepita-crusted red snapper and crab cakes with *remoulade* sauce. For landlubbers, there are a variety of chicken, veal, pork, steak, and pasta dishes. The lunch menu has sandwiches and appetizers—but even these come with a twist: honey wasabi aioli on the tuna, fire-roasted corn-tomato salsa on the tarragon chicken salad.

134 Market St. (at Front St.). ℂ 302/645-7866. Reservations recommended for dinner. Main courses $14–$23; lunch $5–$9.50. AE, DISC, MC, V. Apr–Oct daily 11am–11pm.

MODERATE

La Rosa Negra ITALIAN   In a town known for seafood, this storefront restaurant is a change of pace. The decor is highlighted by a black rose (*rosa negra*) etched on stained glass in the front window; the table settings carry on the theme with red-and-white linens and black tableware. Local art enlivens the white walls. Specialties include chicken Florentine Gorgonzola, scampi *alle ceci* (with chickpeas, black olives, and white wine over linguine), and fettuccini puttanesca, as well as vegetarian pastas like manicotti and ravioli with marinara sauce.

128 2nd St. ℂ 302/645-1980. Reservations recommended for dinner. Main courses $7.95–$18.95. AE, DISC, MC, V. Mon–Thurs 11am–2pm and 4–9:30pm, Fri–Sat 11am–2pm and 4–10pm, Sun 4–9:30pm.

Lighthouse Restaurant SEAFOOD   Pleasant views of the marina and a casual nautical decor are the features at this restaurant. There's seating indoors and out, under a covered deck. An all-day menu features soups, salads, sandwiches, and platters; try the seaside salads (greens topped with sautéed shrimp, scallops, and crab). The dinner menu emphasizes a selection of fish dishes, such as crab cakes, combination platters, and lobster, as well as steaks, ribs, and fried chicken. Come for breakfast. You can get pancakes or eggs until 11am on weekdays, 1pm on weekends.

Savannah and Anglers rds. ✆ **302/645-6271.** www.lighthouselewes.com. Reservations accepted for parties of 8 or more. Main courses $13.95–$29.95; lunch $3.50–$15.95. MC, V. Daily 7am–9pm.

Rose and Crown Restaurant and Pub ENGLISH   If you're longing for an evening in an English pub, you can't find a better beach alternative than the Rose and Crown. Plenty of English specialties, including fish and chips, ploughman's platter, and bangers and mash are available. If you want atmosphere but not heavy English food, you can choose from beef, seafood, pork chops, or pasta, or sandwiches. The best beers, however, are American, and microbrews at that. Among them is the locally produced Dogfish Head.

108 2nd St. ✆ **302/645-2373.** Fax 302/645-8605. www.roseandcrown.org. Reservations recommended for dinner. Main courses $8.95–$20.95; lunch $3.95–$7.95. AE, MC, V. Daily year-round 11am–1am.

A COFFEEHOUSE

Oby Lee Coffee Roastery COFFEE   Amy and Oby roast their own beans and have other hot and cold drinks and some yummy baked goods to get you fueled up for a day at the beach. If you have a sweet tooth, try their yummy hot vanilla drink, the Vanilla Dream. It's an interesting alternative to hot chocolate.

124 2nd St. ✆ **302/645-0733.** Daily 7am–5:15pm.

SHOPPING

Lewes is the best shopping destination on the shore for arts and crafts, collectibles, and antiques. All the places listed are in Lewes or close by. Most shops are open daily 10 or 11am to 5 or 6pm, with extended hours in summer.

Auntie M's Emporium   Head here for kitchenware, rare books, including children's books, furniture, and garden sculptures. 116 3rd St. ✆ **302/644-1804.**

Garage Sale Antiques   This is the place that furnished the Blue Water House Inn (see "Where to Stay," above). It specializes in unusual furniture, lamps, garden sculptures, and collectibles. Look for the bright yellow house on the southbound side of Route 1. 1416 Rte. 1 (also called Hwy. One, just south of Rte. 9 into Lewes). ✆ **302/645-1205.**

Kids' Ketch   Get your beach toys here. Or something to while away those rainy days. Lots of fun stuff here. 132 2nd St. ✆ **302/645-8448.** www.kidsketch.com.

Peninsula Gallery   Across the canal below the Beacon Hotel, this gallery displays mainly works by regional artists, supplemented by national and international artists with special exhibitions each month. Open Monday through Saturday 10am to 5pm and Sunday 11am to 3pm. 520 E. Savannah Rd. ✆ **302/645-0551.** Fax 302/645-8124.

Preservation Forge   This blacksmith shop sells the handcrafted ironwork of John Austin Ellsworth—weather vanes, pokers, gates, hinges, hooks, door latches, and more. Stop by just to see the blacksmith at work. Mr. Ellsworth has opened the Preservation Forge Gallery on the second floor of his shop to display his work better. If you go upstairs, stop by **Uncle Phil's Tinsmith Shop** (✆ **302/644-3344**) that shares space there. Open Monday, Tuesday, and Thursday through Saturday 8am to 4pm. 114 W. 3rd St. ✆ **302/645-7987.**

Puzzles   Exercise your brain with the games and puzzles here, including jigsaws, crosswords, brainteasers, mazes, and metal and wooden puzzles. 111 2nd St. © 302/645-8013.

Saxon Swan   Beautiful pottery, calligraphy, and lovely watercolors fill the shelves of the Saxon Swan. Don't miss the holiday items, including nativity scenes and menorahs, all handcrafted. New on the shelves are fabric art and art jewelry. 101 2nd St. © 302/645-7488.

Stepping Stone   Everything in here is the work of American artisans. But the artists keep changing, with something new all the time. Open year-round 10am to 5pm. 107 W. Market St. © 302/645-1254.

Thistles   One of the pricier places in town, this shop carries fine, unusual furniture, including Tiffany-style lamps, pottery, glassware, and silver. The shop carries reproductions and some modern giftware. 203 2nd St. © 302/644-2323.

Union Jack   The gifts here have an English accent: tea and accessories, English food, books, maps, and videos. Open year-round, 10am to 5pm. 107 W. Market St. © 302/645-1254.

OTHER OUTDOOR ACTIVITIES

BIKING   Even if you're not a serious cyclist, bring a bike to Lewes; the historic streets and shoreline paths are ideal for cycling and it's a great way to avoid the parking problem in the shopping district. You can also rent bikes from **Lewes Cycle Sports,** in the Beacon Motel, Savannah Road (© 302/645-4544).

Biking is also one of the best ways to see **Cape Henlopen State Park** (© 302/645-8983). Paved bike routes run through the park and take you places your car can't go. The terrain is mostly flat, with just a few hills on routes to overlooks.

BIRD & WILDLIFE WATCHING   Lewes, with **Prime Hook National Wildlife Refuge** to its north and **Cape Henlopen** next door, is the best base for birders on the Delaware coast. The entire point of Cape Henlopen is prime breeding ground for the endangered piping plover. (Access to the cape is restricted certain times of the year to protect the nesting grounds.) Whales and dolphins appear regularly off the coast of Cape Henlopen, though usually a little farther south. The Prime Hook refuge has a greater variety of wildlife and shorebirds and a 7-mile (11km) canoe trail to get you to those lesser-visited parts of the refuge—though you'll have to provide your own canoe.

About 10 miles (16km) north of Lewes, off Route 16, **Prime Hook National Wildlife Refuge** (© 302/684-8419) is the best place in the area for birding and wildlife photography. The refuge has two hiking trails and a 7-mile (11km) self-guided canoe trail; they're great places to view migrating waterfowl in the spring and fall, and shorebirds, warblers, amphibians, and reptiles in the spring. The refuge is open daily from 30 minutes before sunrise to 30 minutes after sunset; the visitor center is open Monday through Friday 7:30am to 4pm. No admission fee. *Note:* Bring bug repellent, especially in late summer.

FISHING   With easy access to both Delaware Bay and the Atlantic, Lewes offers a wide variety of sportfishing opportunities. The fishing season starts when the ocean fills with huge schools of mackerel in late March through April. Large sea trout (weakfish) invade the waters in early May and June, and flounder arrive in May and remain throughout the summer, as do bluefish and shark. As the ocean warms up in June, offshore species such as tuna and marlin begin roaming the waters. Bottom fishing in the bay for trout, flounder, sea bass, and blues continues all summer, with late August through September often providing the largest catches. October and November also bring porgies, shad, and blackfish. No license is required for tidal water fishing in Delaware.

Headboat ocean and bay fishing excursions can be arranged at the **Fisherman's Wharf,** Anglers Road (© **302/645-8862**), or at **Angler's Fishing Center,** also on Anglers Road (© **302/645-6227**). Call to arrange for full-day, half-day, or nighttime excursion. At the same pier are a couple of other individually owned boats available for charter, as well, such as the *Two-Na Time* (© **302/644-9777**), with Coast Guard certification.

Cape Henlopen is great for shore and surf fishing. There's a **fishing pier** on the bay side of the park right next to **Hoss's Bait & Tackle,** 103 Dock Dr. (© **302/645-2612**), a well-stocked bait-and-tackle shop. In Lewes, try the **Lewes Harbor Marina** at 217 Anglers Rd. for fishing supplies (© **302/645-6227**).

ORGANIZED TOURS & CRUISES

A good way to see the Delaware Bay and the Lewes Canal harbor is to take a tour, by land or by sea. There are no guided walking tours of the historic sites of Lewes, but you can pick up a brochure with a **self-guided tour** from the Visitor Information Center in the Fisher–Martin House on Kings Highway. It covers over 40 sites and gives brief descriptions of each one.

Two companies offer organized sightseeing cruises from Lewes. **Fisherman's Wharf Cruises,** 217 Anglers Rd. (© **302/645-8862**), operates a variety of narrated cruises around the historical harbor of Lewes and the Delaware breakwater areas. Trips include a 2-hour morning dolphin-watching cruise with continental breakfast or midday snack; a 4-hour afternoon whale- and dolphin-watching cruise; a 2-hour sunset cruise; and a 2-hour buffet dinner cruise. Prices range from $10 to $22. Most tours are offered during summer only, but the sunset tours run through September; call for details and departure times. **Jolly Rover,** Front Street, by the drawbridge (© **302/644-1501**), provides 2-hour sailing trips and 3-hour sunset sailing trips cruising the waters of the Delaware Bay in a topsail schooner. Advance reservations are required. The *Jolly Rover* cruises daily from late May through September; call for costs and departure times.

2 Rehoboth & Dewey Beaches 🖈

88 miles (142km) SE of Wilmington, 27 miles (43km) N of Ocean City, 124 miles (200km) SE of Washington, D.C., 110 miles (177km) SE of Baltimore

Rehoboth is the most popular of the Delaware beaches. It combines small-town friendliness with beach-resort casual and a touch of style. Visitors can choose from beachfront hotels, condominiums, and boardwalk, or relax on the porch of an old-fashioned cottage and watch the neighbors stroll or bike by. On the south side of town, grand homes overlook Silver Lake. The town's shops offer a lovely diversion, with everything from home fashions to hippie-style accessories. Just outside of town on Route 1, Rehoboth has become synonymous with outlet shopping. (And Delaware is sales tax free.) When you're hungry you can stop for pizza, a crab cake, or something French.

Rehoboth has also become a popular destination for gay travelers, a mid-Atlantic alternative to Provincetown or Fire Island, with a number of gay-owned and predominantly gay venues, listed below.

Head south from Rehoboth and you hit Dewey Beach. It's a more casual suburb of Rehoboth with a trolley connecting the towns in the summer. Dewey is noted for its nightspots. Ruddertowne, in particular, draws young crowds for its party atmosphere. But the beach is good and the Rehoboth Bay is only a couple of blocks from the ocean.

ESSENTIALS

GETTING THERE   By car from the north, take Routes 113 and 13 to Route 1, and then Route 1A into Rehoboth. From the south, take Route 113 north to Route 26 east to Bethany Beach. From there, take Route 1 north to Rehoboth. From the west, take Route 50 across the Bay Bridge to Route 404 east; then take Route 9 east to Route 1 south. From Ocean City, continue up the Coastal Highway as it turns into Route 1 to Dewey.

Greyhound provides regular bus service during the summer season to nearby Bethany Beach, stopping once daily at Bethany Rental Services, 201 Central Blvd. (© 302/539-6244).

For visitors arriving by plane, the nearest airport is **Wicomico County Airport.** See "Ocean City, Maryland," later in this chapter.

VISITOR INFORMATION   Sightseeing brochures, maps, descriptions of accommodations, and restaurant listings are available from the **Rehoboth Beach–Dewey Beach Chamber of Commerce,** P.O. Box 216, Rehoboth Beach, DE 19971 (© 800/441-1329 or 302/227-2233; www.beach-fun.com). The office, in the old Rehoboth Railroad Station at 502 Rehoboth Ave., is open year-round Monday through Friday 9am to 5pm and Saturday 9am to noon; from Memorial Day through Labor Day there are Sunday hours 9am to noon. Gay and lesbian travelers should check out www.gayrehoboth.com.

GETTING AROUND   By Public Transportation   From Memorial Day through Labor Day, **DARTFirst State** (© 302/739-3278 or 800/553-DART; www.dartfirststate.com) operates daily bus shuttle service down Route 1 from Georgetown to Lewes to Rehoboth to the border with Ocean City. The bus goes down Savannah Road in Lewes and travels along Rehoboth Avenue to the boardwalk in Rehoboth, as well as to the Park & Ride lot and the shopping outlets. It stops in Ocean City so passengers can catch the Ocean City bus. A daily pass is $2.10 per person or $5 per carload, which includes parking at the Park & Ride Lot on Country Club Road off Delaware Route 1. Armed with the pass, you (or your whole carload) can ride the bus all day.

The Jolly Trolley (© 302/227-1197; www.jollytrolley.com) operates a shuttle service between Rehoboth Beach, starting at the boardwalk and Rehoboth Avenue, and south Dewey Beach. The service runs daily from Memorial Day through Labor Day 8am to 2am, on the hour and half hour; in May and September, it operates on weekends only and it's best to call for the schedule. The cost is $1.50 per ride for adults ($3 after midnight) and free for children under 6. Boarding stops are posted.

By Car   Parking in Rehoboth Beach can be difficult. Metered parking is in effect 10am to midnight every day from Memorial Day weekend to mid-September. The meters take only quarters. Change machines are located in the first and third blocks of Rehoboth Avenue.

If you plan to seek out a non-metered parking spot, you need a **parking permit.** Permits for daily, weekly, or seasonal parking are available from stations on the main streets, the municipal building or parking division offices, or some realtors' offices. They cost $25 for a week, $10 for a day on weekends, or $3 for a weekday. The police will explain the rules and even help you get change. Call © 302/227-6181. Once you've parked, leave your car and walk. Almost everything is located within a few blocks of the boardwalk and the main street, Rehoboth Avenue.

SPECIAL EVENTS   The big event in the Rehoboth/Dewey area is the annual **Sea Witch Halloween Festival and Fiddler's Convention,** held at the end of October. This 2-day event features a costume parade, trick-or-treating, a broom-tossing contest, a 5K foot race, and, of course, a fiddling contest. For information, contact the Rehoboth Beach–Dewey Beach Chamber of Commerce (✆ **800/441-1329** or 302/227-2233).

WHERE TO STAY IN REHOBOTH & DEWEY

Most accommodations in Rehoboth and Dewey are moderately priced. In July and August, however, you may encounter difficulty finding any room (single or double occupancy) near the beach for under $100 a night. Even though Rehoboth and Dewey are seasonal destinations, don't expect dramatic off-season discounts like those you'll find in Ocean City. The outlets are a huge attraction for holiday shoppers, so the shoulder season extends through December (but ask your hotel about weekday packages). Sometimes there are significant discounts in the later winter months of January, February, and March, but rates are subject to frequent changes. In any case, reservations are always necessary in the summer and strongly recommended through the holiday shopping season.

House rentals are popular in Rehoboth so they can be tough to get. But for families they can be a good idea: lots of room, kitchens, maybe two bathrooms for about $500 per week and up—way up. Reservations should be made as early as possible—there's so much return business that families put in their request when they return the keys at the end of their vacation. If you would like to rent a house or condo, be sure to call by December. Then again, something, probably older or farther from the beach, could be available in the spring. **Crowley and Associates** (✆ **800/242-4213** or 302/227-6131) is a popular rental agent in the Rehoboth/Dewey area. As with other beach resorts, most condos come well equipped, except for linens, towels, and paper products. Plan to bring those.

REHOBOTH BEACH
VERY EXPENSIVE

Atlantic Sands Hotel and Conference Center ✦   On the boardwalk between Baltimore and Maryland avenues, the Atlantic Sands is Rehoboth's largest hotel—and it has grown in 2001—and the only oceanfront property in town with an outdoor ground-level swimming pool. Its guest rooms, all newly refurbished, have a balcony with view of the water. Some rooms also have a whirlpool, a wet bar, and a refrigerator. In the summer months, the hotel operates a buffet-style restaurant, featuring all-you-can-eat breakfasts and dinners.

101 N. Boardwalk, Rehoboth Beach, DE 19971. ✆ **800/422-0600** or 302/227-2511. Fax 302/227-9476. www.atlanticsandshotel.com. 267 units. $70–$225 double. AE, DISC, MC, V. Free parking. **Amenities:** Restaurant; outdoor pool; exercise room; outdoor Jacuzzi; massage by appointment; babysitting by arrangement. *In room:* A/C, dataport, unstocked fridge, coffeemaker, hair dryer, microwave in suites.

Boardwalk Plaza Hotel ✦✦   With a pink-and-white gingerbread facade, this four-story Victorian-style hotel stands out on the boardwalk. The theme continues inside, with an antiques-filled lobby complete with live parrots in gilded cages and guest rooms decorated with rich, dark-wood antique and reproduction furniture and frilly fabrics. The hotel offers a variety of rooms with different amenities and services. All are a step above the usual ocean hotel. The best rooms have balconies with at least a partial view of the ocean. A few have whirlpools.

Olive Ave. and the Boardwalk, Rehoboth Beach, DE 19971. ⓒ **800/33-BEACH** or 302/227-7169. Fax 302/227-0561. www.boardwalkplaza.com. 84 units. $89–$479 double. Children under 6 free. AE, DC, DISC, MC, V. Free parking. **Amenities:** Restaurant; bar; indoor-outdoor pool; Jacuzzi; exercise room; concierge level; sun decks. *In room:* A/C, VCRs available, T-1 Internet access, voice mail, coffeemaker, hair dryer.

EXPENSIVE

Brighton Suites Hotel ⚄ For families or couples traveling together, this all-suite hotel—a short walk from the beach—is a good choice. Each unit in this sandy pink four-story property has a bedroom with a king-sized bed or two double beds, a large bathroom, and a separate living room with sleep-sofa. Ask about packages, especially if you're interested in staying 3 or more nights.

34 Wilmington Ave., Rehoboth Beach, DE 19971. ⓒ **800/227-5788** or 302/227-5780. Fax 302/227-6815. www.brightonsuites.com. 66 units. $59–$279 suite. 3-night minimum stay on holiday and summer weekends. AE, DISC, MC, V. Free parking. **Amenities:** Indoor pool; exercise room; babysitting in summer. *In room:* Dataport, wet bar, fridge, hair dryer, beach towels in summer.

Comfort Inn ⚄ Within sight of the Rehoboth outlets, this hotel is perfectly located for serious shoppers. Opened in 1996 and expanded in 1997, the guest rooms are clean, comfortable, and spacious. Standard rooms are large and suites are very roomy; many have a refrigerator and/or microwave, and some have whirlpool tubs. Rooms with king-size beds generally have a sitting area with a sofa bed. It's a short drive away from the beach, but the hotel makes up for it by requiring only a 2-night minimum stay on summer weekends (many area hotels have a 3-night minimum). The DART bus to the beach stops right outside.

4439 Hwy. 1, Rehoboth Beach, DE 19971. ⓒ **800/4CHOICE** or 302/226-1515. Fax 302/226-1550. www.rehoboth.com. 97 units. $65–$250 unit. Rates include deluxe continental breakfast. 2-night minimum stay on summer weekends. AE, DC, DISC, MC, V. Free parking. **Amenities:** Outdoor pool. *In room:* A/C, TV with pay movies, dataport, unstocked fridge, coffeemaker, hair dryer and iron available.

Henlopen Hotel ⚄ On the north end of the boardwalk, this beachfront lodging has a tradition dating from 1879, when the first Henlopen Hotel was built here. The present modern structure has 12 oceanfront rooms and 80 rooms with ocean views, each with its own balcony. Families will like the suites with microwave and refrigerator.

511 N. Boardwalk, Rehoboth Beach, DE 19971. ⓒ **800/441-8450** or 302/227-2551. Fax 302/227-8147. www.henlopenhotel.com. 92 units. $60–$300 double. 2-night minimum stay on weekends and 3-night minimum on holidays. AE, DISC, MC, V. Free parking. Closed Nov–Mar. *In room:* A/C, microwave in most, fridge, coffeemaker, hair dryer.

MODERATE

Admiral Motel (Kids) In the heart of the beach district, this modern five-story motel is a favorite with families. Its indoor pool inside a glass pavilion is terrific and the sun deck with whirlpool is lovely, too. Families can opt for six-person suites with kitchens, instead of a standard room. There are also several rooms with hot tubs for those romantic getaways away from the children. All rooms have a partial ocean view; most units have a private balcony. There are supplementary charges for some peak or holiday weekends.

2 Baltimore Ave., Rehoboth Beach, DE 19971. ⓒ **888/882-4188** or 302/227-2103. www.admiralrehoboth.com. 73 units. $55–$240 double. Children under 12 stay free in parents' room. 2- or 3-night minimum stay in summer. AE, DISC, MC, V. Free parking. **Amenities:** Indoor pool; sun deck; whirlpool; hot tub rooms; coffee and tea; microwave in lobby. *In room:* Dataport, fridge.

Heritage Inn and Golf Club Brand new on Route 1, this hotel is right on an 18-hole golf course. Though it's too far to walk to the beach, the DART bus stops in the parking lot. The rooms are all themed and named for American places or traditions. A curio cabinet in each room has artifacts to illustrate the theme. The rooms are decorated in red, white, and blue Early American. In addition to standard rooms, there are six family-sized suites and three rooms with whirlpools.

Rte. 1 and Postal Lane, P.O. Box 699, Rehoboth Beach, DE 19971. © **800/669-9399** or 302/644-0600. www. heritageinnandgolf.com. 86 units. $59–$179 double. Continental breakfast included. AE, DISC, MC, V. Open year-round. Golf fees are $15–$35 and course is open to nonguests. **Amenities:** Outdoor pool; 18-hole golf course; exercise room. *In room:* A/C, TV with free movies, dataport, fridge, coffeemaker, hair dryer, iron.

Oceanus Motel   This L-shaped three-story motel lies 2 blocks from the beach and just off Rehoboth Avenue in a quiet neighborhood. Each room is outfitted with extra-long beds and a refrigerator; most rooms have a balcony overlooking the pool. At certain times, weekend supplements of $10 to $20 a night prevail.

6 2nd St. (P.O. Box 324), Rehoboth Beach, DE 19971. © **800/852-5011** or 302/227-8200. www.oceanus motel.com. 38 units. $69–$205 double. Rates include continental breakfast. DISC, MC, V. Free parking. Closed Nov to late Mar. **Amenities:** Outdoor pool; bikes. *In room:* A/C, fridge, microwave.

Sandcastle Motel ★   You can't miss this hotel, built in the shape of a sugary white sand castle right off the main thoroughfare. Its location, though about 5 blocks from the beach, is ideal for shopping and walking to restaurants. Each of the large and well-laid-out rooms has a private balcony. The motel's facilities include an enclosed parking garage; the pool has a lifeguard on duty.

123 2nd St. (off Rehoboth Ave.), Rehoboth Beach, DE 19971. © **800/372-2112** or 302/227-0400. Fax 302/ 226-9288. www.thesandcastlemotel.com. 60 units. $55–$159 double. Minimum stays during peak season. AE, DISC, MC, V. Free parking. Closed Jan–Feb. **Amenities:** Indoor pool; sun deck. *In room:* A/C, fridge.

DEWEY BEACH

Atlantic Oceanside Motel   This modern three-story structure is on the main north–south beach highway and about equidistant from the bay and the ocean (both about a block away). The rooms are of the standard motel variety but the motel's convenience to the beach and Dewey nightlife recommend it. It's an easy bike ride to Rehoboth. A weekend surcharge is in effect during certain periods.

1700 Hwy. 1, Dewey Beach, DE 19971. © **800/422-0481** or 302/227-8811. Fax 302/227-4039. www.atlantic oceanside.com. 61 units (2 with shower only). $35–$199 double, 3-night minimum stay on summer weekends. AE, DC, DISC, MC, V. Free parking. Closed Nov–Apr. Pets accepted in off-season for fee. **Amenities:** Outdoor pool; sun deck. *In room:* A/C, dataport, fridge, coffeemaker, microwave oven.

Bay Resort *Kids*   It's a little out of the way in bustling Dewey (read: quieter), but this three-story complex on a strip of land between the bay and the ocean is the ideal place to watch the sun set on Rehoboth Bay. The 250-foot pier on the bay is a good place to drop a fishing line or watch the sailboats drift by. Guest units, each with a small kitchenette and a balcony, face either the pool or the bay. There's also a pool, water-sports center, and private beach. Depending on the time of year, there can also be a weekend surcharge of $20 to $50 per night.

126 Bellevue St. (P.O. Box 461), Dewey Beach, DE 19971. © **800/922-9240** or 302/227-6400. www.bay resort.com. 68 units. $54–$199 double. Rates include continental breakfast. Children under 12 stay free. 3-night minimum stay on holidays. DISC, MC, V. Free parking. Closed Nov to late Mar. **Amenities:** Outdoor pool with slide; 250-foot pier. *In room:* A/C, TV with free movies, some kitchenettes.

Best Western Gold Leaf   A block from both the beach and the bay, this modern four-story motel is across the street from the Ruddertowne complex. It offers bright, contemporary rooms with a balcony and a view of the bay, ocean, or both. A comfortable, modern hotel, it is convenient to all of Dewey's attractions. Four king rooms feature whirlpool tubs. Look for reduced-rate packages November through March.

1400 Hwy. 1, Dewey Beach, DE 19971. ℂ **800/422-8566** or 302/226-1100. Fax 302/226-9785. www.best westerngoldleaf.com. 76 units. $129–$249 double. 2- and 3-night minimum stays in summer. Rates include continental breakfast. AE, DC, DISC, MC, V. Free parking in garage. **Amenities:** Rooftop pool; sun deck. *In room:* A/C, dataport, fridge, microwave, coffeemaker, hair dryer, iron.

WHERE TO DINE IN REHOBOTH BEACH
EXPENSIVE

Back Porch Cafe 🍴 INTERNATIONAL   For more than 20 years, a Key West atmosphere has prevailed here, and the emphasis is on fresh foods creatively prepared and presented. There's a little fusion going on here: Indian spice-crusted salmon with eggplant fritters, pork tenderloin with peanut noodles and Szechuan green beans, and Thai green curry duckling. At lunchtime, the menu is just as global, with Jamaica, Thailand, France, and the Eastern Shore all represented in the entrees and omelets. The dining area includes indoor alcoves and three outdoor decks, decorated with an eclectic collection of plants and handmade tables. Live music includes everything from classical to world music.

59 Rehoboth Ave., Rehoboth Beach. ℂ **302/227-3674.** www.backporchcafe.com. Reservations recommended on weekends. Main courses $23–$30; lunch $9.50–$12. MC, V. June–Sept daily 11am–1am; Apr–May and Oct, Sat–Sun 11am–1am. Closed Nov–Mar.

Blue Moon *Finds* AMERICAN/INTERNATIONAL   Located off the main drag, this restaurant is housed in an eye-catching blue-and-mango-colored cottage. The interior features curved banquettes, indirect lighting, and exotic flower arrangements. Bring your sense of adventure because the menu is unlike any other in town. It features things like grilled ostrich tenderloin, marinated bison sirloin, and rock shrimp and smoked chicken apple sausage. Vegetarians: the chef will make something special for you; just ask.

35 Baltimore Ave. ℂ **302/227-6515.** Reservations required. Main courses $16–$30. AE, DC, DISC, MC, V. Feb–Dec Mon–Sat 6–11pm, Sun 11–2pm and 6–11pm. Closed Jan.

Chez La Mer 🍴🍴 CONTINENTAL   Rehoboth is brimming with good restaurants but Chez La Mer skips the beach ambience for that of a French country inn. The three intimate dining rooms fill up quickly with people hungry for veal Marsala; chicken stuffed with leeks, apples, walnuts and gouda; or bouillabaisse. They come for the solid wine list with lots of choices in the $20 to $30 range. Appetizers are intriguing; a crab and wild mushroom cheesecake and a tomato, basil, and mozzarella salad that celebrates the fresh local tomatoes. Special diets, such as low sodium, can be accommodated. Dress up (in your best beach clothes) and bring your wallet and your appetite.

210 2nd St. ℂ **302/227-6494.** Fax 302/227-6797. www.chezlamer.com. Reservations recommended. Main courses $20–$30. AE, DC, DISC, MC, V. June–Sept Mon–Thurs 5:30–10pm, Fri–Sat 5:30–10:30pm; Apr–May and Oct Thurs–Sun 5–10pm. Closed Nov–Mar.

La La Land 🍴 INTERNATIONAL   On a side street off the boardwalk, this acclaimed restaurant specializes in blending California influence with Asian and Southwestern overtones. There's indoor seating in an art-filled pink, purple, and periwinkle-toned dining room and outdoors on a patio with a bamboo garden setting. The menu offers a variety of creative choices: herb-rubbed game hen with sweet corn risotto and summer truffles; butternut ravioli with leek fondue, spiced cranberries, and aged Asiago cheese; crispy duck breast over smoky white beans with duck *foie gras* sausage; or grilled mahimahi steaks in a spicy black bean sauce with avocado and corn salsa.

22 Wilmington Ave. ℂ **302/227-3887.** www.lalalandrestaurant.com. Reservations required. Main courses $19–$32. AE, DC, DISC, MC, V. Apr–Nov daily 6–10pm. Closed Dec–Mar.

MODERATE

Lamp Post AMERICAN/SEAFOOD/STEAK   Far from the boardwalk, this restaurant sits along the highway, 3 miles (5km) north of town. It's a good place to stop on the way to the beach or after a day of shopping. Opened in 1953 by award-winning restaurateur Ruth Steele as the Drexel Diner, this friendly spot has been expanded by three generations of the Steeles. Some tables are crafted from hatch-cover tops from World War II Liberty ships. The dinner menu focuses on fresh local flounder served in a variety of ways, including stuffed with crabmeat, as well as a half-dozen types of hand-cut steaks and prime rib. House specials include chicken Delaware (sautéed breast of chicken topped with a grilled slice of ham, mushrooms, and melted cheddar cheese) and Delaware seafood chowder. Try the seafood buffet that overflows with Mediterranean antipasti, crab bisque and other seafood, prime rib, chicken, and lots of vegetables and desserts, served Wednesday to Saturday in July and August, and Friday October to June.

Rtes. 1 and 24. ℂ **302/645-9132.** Reservations not accepted. Main courses $10.95–$33; lunch $4.50–$16.95; seafood buffet $28 adults, $15 children under 10. AE, DISC, MC, V. Sun–Thurs 11am–9pm, Fri–Sat 11am–10pm.

Obie's by the Sea AMERICAN   You can't dine any closer to the ocean (without being in sand) than at this restaurant, beside the boardwalk between Virginia and Olive avenues. Obie's has an interesting layout: There is indoor dining upstairs and open-air dining downstairs under a few ceiling fans that augment the summer breeze. A casual atmosphere prevails here, with an all-day menu of sandwiches, burgers, ribs, salads, and "clam bakes" (steamed clams, spiced shrimp, barbecued chicken, corn on the cob, and muffins). There's deejay music and dancing on weekends.

On the boardwalk (at Olive Ave.). ℂ **302/227-6261.** Main courses $4.95–$14.95. AE, MC, V. Daily 11:30am–1am. Closed Nov–Apr.

Summer House *Kids* SEAFOOD   Finding this restaurant is the easy part; deciding what to eat is harder. In addition to an array of sandwiches, burgers, and salads, there are plenty of filet mignon, seafood, and chicken choices. One of their standouts is the Filet Bearnaise, two filet medallions on an English muffin topped with sautéed mushrooms and béarnaise sauce. The restaurant is quite casual, with a party atmosphere. But it's a welcome place for children. The menu seems inspired by real-life kids: finger food a toddler can handle; PB&J sandwiches; and chicken, flounder, or filet mignon served with applesauce and fries.

228 Rehoboth Ave. ℂ **302/227-3895.** www.summerhousesaloon.com. Main courses $9.95–$23.95; light fare $5.95–$8.95. AE, DC, DISC, MC, V. May–Oct daily 5pm–2am. Closed Nov–Apr.

Sydney's Blues & Jazz Restaurant ★★ SOUTHERN   Located in an old schoolhouse and run by Sydney Arzt, a former schoolteacher, this restaurant is known for its nightly jazz and blues as well as a grazing menu that allows customers to sample more than one main course. You can enter from the back or the front of the restaurant; the bar (where the bands set up) is in back. The candlelit decor highlights black-and-white photos of Hollywood stars on the walls and a skylit ceiling from which gold and silver mobile ornaments are suspended. Entrees include a jambalaya of crawfish and shrimp with chicken, clams, and mussels tossed with Creole rice; and herb-marinated beef tenderloin with a Merlot glaze and garlic mashed potatoes. New is the Sunday brunch 11am to 2pm. Live music is featured year-round, mostly on weekends.

25 Christian St. © **800/808-1924** or 302/227-1339. www.rehoboth.com/Sydneys. Reservations recommended on weekends. Main courses $15–$24; grazing portions $13–$15. AE, DISC, MC, V. Daily 4pm–1am, Sun 11am–2pm. Hours vary in winter. Closed in Jan.

INEXPENSIVE

Royal Treat ⭐ BREAKFAST/ICE CREAM   The number of breakfast restaurants is dwindling but you can still count on Royal Treat for eggs, French toast, and pancakes. Come back in the afternoon for ice cream. This old-fashioned Rehoboth landmark near the boardwalk must be doing something right. They've been serving breakfast for 2 decades.

4 Wilmington Ave. © 302/227-6277. All items $2–$7.75. No credit cards. May–Oct breakfast daily 8–11:30am; ice cream daily 1–11:30pm. Closed Nov–Mar.

WHERE TO DINE IN DEWEY BEACH

Crabbers' Cove *Value* SEAFOOD   This casual open-air seafood restaurant features a variety of all-you-can-eat specials. Entrees include steak, fried chicken, barbecued ribs, fresh fish, shrimp in a basket, and steamed hard crabs, as well as filet of flounder, grilled tuna steak, baked sea trout, Gulf shrimp, mussels, and crab cakes. The "Little Crabbers" menu offers kids' favorites, some for just $1.

Dickenson St (on the bay in the Ruddertowne complex). © **302/227-4888**. www.deweybeachlife.com. Main courses $9.95–$19.95. AE, DC, DISC, MC, V. May–Sept daily 4–9pm.

Rusty Rudder ⭐⭐ AMERICAN/SEAFOOD   Since 1979, this large California-style restaurant has been a favorite place for young beach-goers. Situated right on the bay, it offers great water views (as well as views of a beach volleyball court) from indoor and outdoor dining rooms, open decks, and terraces. Dinner entrees include chicken cordon bleu, backfin crab cakes, and prime rib, as well as enormous seafood and shellfish platters. The star of dinner here, however, is the salad bar overflowing with fresh vegetables and salads. Lunches range from salads and sandwiches to Cajun catfish and other fish specials. There's also nightly entertainment frequently with better-known acts on weekends.

113 Dickinson St. (on the bay). © **302/227-3888**. www.deweybeachlife.com. Main courses $11.95–$25.95; lunch $5.95–$11.95. MC, V. Daily 11:30am–11pm; Sun brunch 10am–2pm.

The Waterfront AMERICAN   Bayside sunsets and charcoal-grilled meats and seafood are the main draws at this restaurant, which boasts an open deck, a gazebo, and dining rooms overlooking the water. For lunch, it offers shrimp and burgers barbecued in its open-pit grill, as well as soups, salads, and sandwiches. Dinner entrees include ribs, chicken, steaks, and shish kebabs, as well as 1-pound lobsters and a variety of other steamed, baked, and broiled seafood.

136 Dagsworthy St. © **302/227-9292**. Main courses $12.95–$17.95; lunch $4.50–$8.95. AE, MC, V. May–Sept daily noon–1am. Closed Oct–Apr.

REHOBOTH & DEWEY BEACHES AFTER DARK

Sandwiched between the quiet family resorts of Bethany Beach and Fenwick Island to the south and Lewes to the north, Rehoboth and Dewey beaches offer the only consistent nightlife on the Delaware coast.

CLUBS & BARS
Rehoboth

Nationally known jazz and blues artists entertain year-round at **Sydney's,** 25 Christian St. (© **302/227-1339**). Shows are nightly except Wednesday from mid-May through mid-September and on Friday and Saturday nights at other times. Cover charge varies based on the talent on weekends, but there is no cover for dinner guests (see listing in "Where to Dine in Rehoboth Beach," above).

The lilting sing-along sounds of Ireland are heard Thursday through Saturday in the summer at **Irish Eyes,** 15 Wilmington Ave. (© **302/227-2888**). Classic rock-and-roll or deejay music is played on other nights. Cover charge varies.

Dewey Beach

The Washingtonian recently described Dewey Beach's summer nightlife as "Beach Bacchanalia." The two clubs are the **Rusty Rudder,** Dickinson Street and the bay (© **302/227-3888**), and the **Bottle & Cork,** Highway 1 and Dagsworthy Street (© **302/227-8545**). The crowd tends to be 20- to 35-year-olds looking to party. The Rudder usually holds deck parties overlooking the bay but occasionally has bands or other activities, and the cover varies accordingly. The Bottle & Cork is a surprisingly large rock club that hosts both local and nationally known rock bands. Recent acts have included John Popper (of Blues Traveler), Matchbox 20, Los Lobos, Joan Jett & the Blackhearts, and the Connells. This is a neat place to see a band, but in spite of its size, it gets awfully crowded and occasionally out of hand. Cover varies according to talent.

The Starboard, at 2009 Hwy. 1 (© **302/227-4600**), is usually crowded with people looking for a good time. There's a menu, but mostly they have young singles and plenty of beer. You'll know it by the shark bursting out of the roof.

GAY & LESBIAN REHOBOTH

A number of Rehoboth nightspots cater to a gay clientele. A couple of favorites include **The Beach House** at 316 Rehoboth Ave. (© **302/227-4227**), where women flock for late-night dancing and food; and **Blue Moon,** at 35 Baltimore Ave. (© **302/227-6515**), which has a happy hour popular with the men. **Dogfish Head Brewings & Eats** at 320 Rehoboth Ave. © **302/226-2739**) is primarily straight but draws a mixed crowd for its beer and live entertainment. Those who prefer jazz head to **Sydney's Blues & Jazz Restaurant** (25 Christian St.; © **302/227-1339**), which serves up live jazz and R&B.

CONCERT HALLS/THEATERS

The **Rehoboth Beach Memorial Bandstand,** an open-air pavilion at Rehoboth Avenue and the boardwalk (© **302/227-2233**), hosts more than 40 free concerts and other events on summer weekends, starting at 8pm. Check with the chamber of commerce office for an up-to-date schedule.

WHAT TO SEE & DO IN REHOBOTH & DEWEY

Rehoboth and Dewey offer a quieter, more relaxed alternative to Ocean City, Maryland, but both have nightlife and stores that stay open past 5pm, which you won't find at Bethany, Lewes, or Fenwick Island. If the sandy beaches, good restaurants, and intriguing little shops don't interest you, maybe the outlets will.

ESPECIALLY FOR KIDS

Rehoboth Summer Children's Theatre, at Epworth United Methodist Church, 20 Baltimore Ave. (© **302/277-6766**), performs favorites such as *Snow White, Cinderella,* and *Jack and the Beanstalk.* Performances are given on selected weeknights during summer. Curtain time is usually 7:30pm.

The theater also offers morning acting workshops and an apprentice program. Call for information or reservations.

Rehoboth Beach has two summer family amusement areas. **Funland** (© **302/ 227-2785**), on the boardwalk and Delaware Avenue, has rides and games. Funland's rides for the preschool set are varied enough to keep the youngsters busy

Moments **The Life Saving Stations**

Just south of Dewey and beside the Ocean City Inlet are two buildings that memorialize the men of the U.S. Life Saving Services.

The pumpkin and brown **Indian River Lifesaving Station** on Route 1, south of Dewey (© **302/227-6475;** www.irlss.org), has been restored to its 1905 appearance. It was built in 1876 as an Atlantic coast outpost to look out for ships in distress. It was transferred to the U.S. Coast Guard in 1915, decommissioned in 1962, and restored in 1998. Listed on the National Register of Historic Places, its spare interior recalls the lives of the men who lived here. Guides tell the stories of heroic rescuers saving sailors from sinking ships. There's a gift shop, too.

Another station is on the Ocean City, Maryland, boardwalk. The white and red **Ocean City Life-Saving Station Museum,** at the Inlet (P.O. Box 603; © **410/289-4991**), recalls the men who saved 4,500 sailors off these shores and some of the history of Ocean City. You'll see life-saving artifacts, including a restored surf rescue boat and a pictorial history of the storms that have raged here. Admission is $2 adults, $1 under age 12. Hours are June to September daily 11am to 10pm, May and October daily 11am to 4pm, November to April Saturday to Sunday 11am to 4pm.

for hours and the tickets are so inexpensive, parents won't go broke in the process. Rides for older kids (over age 8 or so) are more limited.

About 1½ miles (2.4km) north of town there's **Jungle Jim's Adventure Land,** Route 1 and Country Club Road (© **302/227-8444**). The park offers go-carts, miniature golf, bumper boats, a rock-climbing wall, and outdoor rides. A water park with slides, rides, and a "Lazy River" opens in June 2002. It's open weekends in May and September and daily from Memorial Day to Labor Day, 10am to 11pm.

INDOOR ATTRACTIONS

The **Rehoboth Art League** (© 302/227-8408), at 12 Dodds Lane, is nestled in the Henlopen Acres section of town amid 3 acres of gardens and walking paths and an outdoor sculpture area. The facility includes three galleries, a teaching studio, and a restored cottage. It offers exhibits by local and national artists, art classes, workshops, and performances. Admission is usually free, though for special events there may be a charge ranging from $1 to $10. Open May through September, Monday through Saturday 10am to 4pm and Sunday 1 to 4pm; in October and February through April, weekdays 10am to 4pm (stop by the office first). The Art League is closed November through January.

The **Anna Hazzard Museum** (© 302/226-1119), at 17 Christian St. (on Martin's Lawn, off Rehoboth Ave.), is one of the original tent buildings erected when Rehoboth was a summer resort/retreat for Methodists. It's a good place to learn about Rehoboth and its history. Admission is free but by appointment only.

SHOPPING THE OUTLETS & THE BOARDWALK

Rehoboth Outlets (© **888/SHOP-333** or 302/226-9223; www.shoprehoboth. com) have become a destination in their own right. Stretching for 2 miles (3km) down Route 1, there are 140 stores, including L.L. Bean, clothing stores from Liz Claiborne to Oshkosh, accessories, housewares, china and crystal, sneakers, and handbags at Leather Loft, along with a few restaurants and places to grab a snack. Two outlet centers are on the western side of Route 1 and the third is between them on the east side. You can't walk from center to center—and you have to be dedicated to hit all 140 shops in one day. Get a map to help you plan the most efficient shopping experience. These are popular places, so parking can be a challenge on the weekend or on a rainy day and Route 1 traffic can slow to a crawl. It's so popular, New Jersey residents hop on the Cape May–Lewes ferry to spend a day here. Remember, there's no sales tax in Delaware. The outlets are open January to April, Sunday to Thursday 10am to 6pm, Friday to Saturday 10am to 9pm; and May to December, Monday to Saturday 10am to 9pm and Sunday 10am to 6pm.

In downtown Rehoboth, the shopping is concentrated on the mile-long boardwalk and Rehoboth Avenue, which intersects the boardwalk at its midpoint. Most stores are open 10am to 6pm, with extended evening hours in the summer.

Christmas Spirit   It's Christmas year-round in this shop, stocked with trees, lights, handcrafted ornaments from around the world, angel tree tops, tree skirts, Victorian decorations, candles, nutcrackers, character Santas, lighted villages and figurines, gift wrap, and more. Open daily 10am to 11pm in summer but only to 5pm off-season. 161 Rehoboth Ave. © 302/227-6872. Fax 302/643-5526.

Mizzen Mast   This shop features environmentally friendly and recycled products, such as Birkenstock footprint sandals, nature music, T-shirts, pottery, notepads, stickers, mugs, cards, posters, games, stuffed animals, and hand-painted birds. 149 Rehoboth Ave. © 302/227-3646.

Sea Shell Shop   This shop is a treasure trove of seashell art, lamps, and jewelry, as well as loose shells, sponges, and hermit crab souvenirs. Other stores are at Bellevue Street and Highway 1, Dewey Beach (© **302/227-6695**), and at 4405 Coastal Hwy. (© **302/227-4323**). Little hands, the owners say, are always welcome. 119 Rehoboth Ave. © 302/227-4363. Fax 302/227-8478. www.seashellshop.com.

Ibach's   Head here for chocolates: nonpareils, cashew turtles, cherry cordials. They have salt water taffy, too. It's a pretty shop with a wonderful aroma. 9 Rehoboth Ave. © 877/270-9674 or 302/227-2870. www.dolles-ibachs.com.

OUTDOOR ACTIVITIES

BIKING   With its flat terrain and shady streets, Rehoboth is ideal for bicycling. Bikes are allowed on the boardwalk between 5 and 10am May 15 to September 15 and anytime off-season. Three companies offer rentals: **Bob's Bicycle Rentals,** 30 Maryland Ave. at 1st Street (© **302/227-7966**), rents one-speed touring bikes, mountain bikes, and tandems. Bob's is open Memorial Day through Labor Day, daily from 9am to 6pm or later; hours vary the rest of the year. **Wheels Bicycle Shop,** 318 Rehoboth Ave. (© **302/227-6807**), is conveniently situated on the main thoroughfare. This well-stocked shop rents a variety of cruising bikes. In the peak season, it also operates a rental station on the boardwalk at Virginia Avenue, open daily from 9am to 6pm or later, Memorial Day through Labor Day (hours vary the rest of the year). **Rehoboth Sport & Kite Company,** on the boardwalk at Virginia Avenue (© **800/250-KITE**), also rents bikes. Generally, rates for bike rentals at all shops range from $2 to $7 per hour and $7 to $20 per day, depending on the type of bike.

GOLF A new golf course has opened on Route 1 in Rehoboth. **Heritage Inn and Golf Club** has an 18-hole course open to the public. Call ✆ **800/ 669-9399** or 302/644-0600, or visit www.heritageinnandgolf.com.

PARASAILING See the ocean from 400 feet up while hanging from a parachute towed by a boat. Call **Ocean Winds Parasail,** ✆ **302/227-4359.**

TENNIS There are public courts in Dewey Beach on the bay at McKinley Street, at Rehoboth City Courts on Surf Avenue between Rehoboth Beach and North Shores, and at Rehoboth Junior High School on State Street.

WATER SPORTS **Bay Sports,** 11 Dickinson St., Dewey Beach (✆ **302/ 227-7590**), rents Windsurfers, Sunfish sailboats, and jet skis by the half hour or hour or by the day. Rates for a Windsurfer or Sunfish are $25 to $45 for 1 hour, $70 to $160 for a day; and jet skis are $30 to $65 for a half hour. Sailing and windsurfing lessons can also be arranged.

3 Bethany Beach & Fenwick Island ⭐

100 miles (160km) SE of Wilmington, 130 miles (209km) SE of Washington, D.C., 120 miles (193km) SE of Baltimore

Nicknamed "the quiet resorts," Bethany Beach and Fenwick Island boast the most laid-back atmosphere of the Maryland and Delaware beach resorts. This pleasant stretch of condominium communities, state parks, and public and private beaches offers families and other travelers an impressively calm alternative to the bustle of Ocean City to the south and the sophistication and shopping of Rehoboth to the north. It's a great place just to sit back and enjoy the beach.

You won't find much nightlife here, but outdoor activities abound, from swimming to bicycling to bird watching to a walk on the tiny Bethany Beach boardwalk. For a little more excitement, head for nearby Rehoboth or down to Ocean City, Maryland.

ESSENTIALS
GETTING THERE By **car,** Whether you're approaching from points north or south, it is best to take Route 113 and to avoid the frequently crowded (particularly in July and Aug) Route 1. To reach Bethany Beach, at Dagsboro take Route 26 east; to reach Fenwick Island from the north, take Route 20 south (just outside of Dagsboro); and to get to Fenwick from the south, turn west on Route 54 at Selbyville. From the west, take Route 50 across the Bay Bridge to Route 404 east, then turn south on Route 113 and follow the directions above.

Carolina Trailways provides regular **bus** service during the summer season, stopping daily at Bethany Rental Services, 201 Central Blvd., Bethany Beach (✆ 302/539-6244).

Visitors arriving by **plane** can fly into the **Wicomico County Airport.** See "Getting There" in "Ocean City, Maryland," later in this chapter.

VISITOR INFORMATION The **Bethany–Fenwick Area Chamber of Commerce,** P.O. Box 1450, Bethany Beach, DE 19930 (✆ **800/962-SURF** or 302/539-2100; www.thequietresorts.com), is on Route 1, adjacent to the Fenwick Island State Park at the Fenwick line. The office is designed like a beach house, with wide windows overlooking the ocean and white sands. The chamber publishes a helpful booklet called "The Quiet Resorts" and also stocks brochures from motels, restaurants, and other visitor services. Open year-round Monday through Saturday 10am to 4pm and Sunday in season 10am to 4pm.

GETTING AROUND   Since Bethany Beach and Fenwick Island are within 5 miles (8km) of each other, most people take a car, but bicycles and in-line skates are also useful. Most visitors bring their own vehicles or rent cars from nearby Ocean City. Many Bethany and Fenwick streets are subject to meter or permit parking, and the rules are strictly enforced. Bethany's meters are enforced May 15 to September 30, 10am to 11pm on Garfield Parkway; and 10am to 8pm everywhere else. *Insider tip:* Run out of quarters for the meters? Police carry change, so ask them. All the motels provide free parking for guests, and most restaurants also have access to plentiful parking for customers.

ORIENTATION   If it weren't for the little signs in the median on Route 1, you'd never know there were three communities here. But officially, there are: Bethany Beach, South Bethany, and Fenwick Island, which isn't an island at all. It's really a peninsula and shares a barrier island/peninsula that makes Ocean City. It's surrounded by water, with the Atlantic Ocean to the east and the Indian River Bay, the Assawoman Canal, and the Little Assawoman Bay to the west. North of the town of Fenwick is the Fenwick Island State Park, all beach and parking lot with no restaurants, shops, or hotels.

Bethany Beach and South Bethany are part of the same community. They share shopping, the boardwalk, and the public beach. South Bethany is a residential area with condos and beach houses, a suburb of Bethany Beach that stretches to the public beaches of Fenwick Island State Park to the south.

Fenwick Island is like a hyphen, connecting Ocean City to Delaware. Traveling north from O.C., you hardly know you left the state.

SPECIAL EVENTS   **Bethany Beach Boardwalk Arts Festival,** a juried festival of fine arts and crafts, is held the Saturday after Labor Day, 10am to 5pm.

WHERE TO STAY IN BETHANY & FENWICK

Bethany Beach and Fenwick Island are packed in the summer. More and more people book a condominium unit or bring the extended family for a week in a beach house. Lots of construction in the past few years has expanded the available accommodations. New developments are going up on Route 24, a short drive from the beach, now that almost every oceanfront parcel has been developed.

Bethany has a variety, from oceanfront mansions to houses in tow, to townhouses and duplexes and condos tucked under trees. The **Sea Colony resort** ★★★ is an attractive option. It has a many rental units in the nine oceanfront high-rises and a variety of condos on the western side of Route 1. Some of the buildings are 25 years old, others built in the last year or two. There are pools within walking distance of every unit, along with walking and biking paths. Tennis villas are surrounded by courts, including four indoor courts. There's a fitness center and a children's center, too. Shuttles take Sea Colony West guests to the beach. All this recreation comes at a price, about $25 per person per week.

Look for your rental early. Bookings are accepted beginning in January but you may still find a nice place a few weeks before you arrive. Rentals go for $500 per week for a small unit and up in the thousands for the oceanfront homes with room for extended family.

Some good rental companies to call are **Seacoast Realty** (✆ **800/634-3400** or 302/539-8600), **Moore Warfield and Glick** (✆ **800/234-1777**), **Century 21 Wilgus** (✆ **800/441-8118**), **Tansey–Warner, Inc.** (✆ **302/539-3001**), and **Tidewater Realty, Ltd.** (✆ **302/539-7500**). All of them will send you brochures describing their rental properties.

Hotel rooms for July and August are booked months in advance, cost more, and often come with weekend surcharges and 2- or 3-night minimum stays. Motels that would otherwise be considered in the budget category might charge between $70 and $100 for a double. So if you'd like to keep the cost down, come during midweek or consider a visit in May, June, September, or October, when the weather can be almost as warm.

BETHANY BEACH
Moderate
Bethany Arms Motel and Apts *Kids*   Ideal for families who want to be close to the ocean, this modern complex offers basic motel units with refrigerators, and apartments with full kitchens and ocean views. The complex consists of two buildings right on the boardwalk and three situated just behind the first two, between the boardwalk and Atlantic Avenue. A 2-night minimum is in effect on summer weekends. During holiday periods (such as Memorial Day and Labor Day weekends), 3-night minimums and some surcharges apply.

Atlantic Ave. and Hollywood St. (P.O. Box 1600), Bethany Beach, DE 19930. ℂ 302/539-9603. www.beach-net.com/bethanyarms.html. 50 units. $55–$200 double. MC, V. Free parking. Closed late Oct to early Mar. *In room:* A/C, kitchenettes in 42 units, coffeemaker.

Inexpensive
Harbor View Motel   Located 3 miles (5km) north of Bethany Beach at the southern edge of the Delaware Seashore State Park, this budget two-story motel on the bay side offers views of both the bay and the ocean. Some rooms have whirlpools, and all have balconies.

Rte. 1, Box 102, Bethany Beach, DE 19930. ℂ 302/539-0500. Fax 302/539-5170. 68 units. $49–$119 double; $59–$129 efficiency. There are weekend surcharges. Rates include continental breakfast. AE, DISC, MC, V. Free parking. Closed Nov to mid-Mar. **Amenities:** Restaurant; outdoor pool; sun deck on the bay; barbecue grills. *In room:* A/C, fridge, microwave, hair dryer, coffeemaker and iron available.

Westward Pines   If you want comfort in a secluded setting, consider this ranch-style motel located in a residential area 4 blocks from the beach. Tall trees and leafy shrubs surround it. The guest rooms, all on ground-floor level, have standard furnishings; one has a fireplace, another has a whirlpool. A minimum stay may be required on weekends.

10 Kent Ave. (1 block west of Rte. 1), Bethany Beach, DE 19930. ℂ 302/539-7426. www.westward pines.com. 14 units. $75–$110 double. No credit cards. Free parking. Pets accepted off-season. *In room:* A/C, fridge, coffeemaker, iron available.

FENWICK ISLAND
Fenwick Islander   Situated on the bay side of the highway, just north of the Maryland–Delaware state line, this bright, modern, three-story motel is ideal for families. All of the units are equipped with refrigerator and kitchenette facilities; second- and third-floor rooms have balconies. Weekend and holiday rates are subject to surcharges and minimum-stay requirements.

Rte. 1 and South Carolina Ave. (between South Carolina and West Virginia aves.), Fenwick Island, DE 19944. ℂ 800/346-4520 or 302/539-2333. Fax 302/537-1134. www.fenwickislander.com. 62 units. $36–$159 double. AE, DISC, MC, V. Free parking. Closed Nov–Mar. Children under 5 stay free in parents' room; ages 6–16 stay for $5 each per night. **Amenities:** Outdoor pool. *In room:* A/C, fax, kitchenette, fridge, iron.

Fenwick Sea Charm Motel and Ric-Mar Apartments   The homey Sea Charm, a three-story inn with wraparound porches, is the epitome of a vintage beach cottage. It may be a little time worn, but it's the only place on Fenwick Island with accommodations on the beach. A favorite with families, who come back year after year, it offers motel rooms, oceanfront efficiencies, and one- to three-bedroom oceanview apartments, some with balconies. The 18-unit Ric-Mar Apartments (one- and two-bedroom) is next door. Two units that sleep six rent only by the week in summer. Some surcharges apply on weekends.

Oceanfront and Lighthouse Rd. (just north of the Delaware–Maryland border), Fenwick Island, DE 19944. Ⓒ 302/539-9613. 39 units. $50–$135 double; $80–$180 apt. 3-night minimum stay in-season. DISC, MC, V. Free parking. Closed Oct to mid-May. **Amenities:** Outdoor pool; patio and sun deck with picnic furniture and outdoor grills; discounts to nearby mini-golf. *In room:* A/C, TV with movies, kitchenette, fridge, coffeemaker.

Sands Motel   On the ocean side of the Coastal Highway though not right on the ocean, the Sands offers standard rooms, efficiencies, and apartments.

Rte. 1 (between Indian and James sts.), Fenwick Island, DE 19944. Ⓒed 302/539-7745; Dec–Mar Ⓒed 410/213-2152. sands@dca.net. 37 units. $29–$77 double; $45–$117 apt and efficiency. 3-night minimum stay in-season, holidays, and weekends. AE, DC, DISC, MC, V. Free parking. Closed Nov–Mar. Well-behaved pets accepted. **Amenities:** Outdoor pool and easy access to beach. *In room:* A/C.

WHERE TO DINE IN BETHANY & FENWICK

The restaurants of the Bethany Beach and Fenwick Island area provide a pleasant blend of waterside and inland dining, mostly at fairly moderate prices. Because these two resorts are popular with families, there are also some lower-priced restaurants that offer quality, ambience, and creative cooking. Most restaurants serve alcohol, unless otherwise noted. *Note:* In Bethany, alcoholic beverages are available only in restaurants—there are no bars.

Since most motels in Bethany and Fenwick do not serve breakfast, check some of the places below for breakfast, particularly Frog House, Holiday House, Libby's, and Warren's Station.

BETHANY BEACH

Big Easy *(Finds* STEAKS/CREOLE   I knew this place was a winner when I arrived with seven children and six adults and they seated the children across the room from us and then treated them like adults. I knew the food was good from past visits—they're pushing seafood and steaks, but their Creole and Cajun spiced foods will remind you of New Orleans. Set in the Sea Colony Marketplace, the restaurant tries to have a Mardi Gras atmosphere but the best seats in the house are outside overlooking a fountain where children are always playing. As for the food, they handle shrimp with great care, make a mean shrimp Creole, and never fail to mix in a little Cajun zest. The red beans and rice, BBQ shrimp, and jambalaya are always terrific. It all goes well with their interesting selection of beers. There's also a bar with darts and pool, a light-fare menu, and live entertainment some evenings. A jazz Sunday brunch is new in 2002.

Sea Colony Marketplace, Rte. 1. ⒸC 302/539-7482. www.thebigeazy.com. Reservations recommended, especially for large groups. Main courses $12–$19.95, lunch $5–$9. AE, DC, DISC, MC, V. Daily 11am–1am in summer; in winter Thurs–Mon 4:30pm–1am, Sat–Sun noon–4pm.

Cottage Café AMERICAN   This homey place has a country cottage–style facade and interior. It displays the works of Maryland artist Joseph Craig English (his paintings and prints portray everyday scenes of the region). The menu offers everything from old-fashioned pot roast to meat loaf, steaks, soup and salad combos, sandwiches, and pastas. Breakfast is served Saturday to Sunday 8am to noon. There's a location in Ocean City at 146th Street (ⒸC **410/250-1460**).

Rte. 1, Bethany Beach. ⒸC 302/539-8710. www.cottagecafe.com. All items $2.99–$17.99. AE, DC, MC, V. Daily 11am–1am.

Frog House *Kids* AMERICAN   You can sleep late and still get a hot breakfast at the Frog House, where it is served until 2pm. And it's good, especially the 10 kinds of pancakes, including chocolate chip, pecan, and apple. You won't go hungry at lunch or dinner either. Lunchtime favorites include sandwiches, burgers, and salads; dinner entrees include fried chicken, steamed shrimp, and crab cakes. This is a great place to bring the whole family. Tables of six, eight, or more are quite common. It's casual, friendly, and reasonably priced.

116 Garfield Pkwy., Bethany Beach. © 302/539-4500. Dinner entrees $7.75–$14.50, lunch $3.95–$6.75, breakfast $2.25–$5.35. DISC, MC, V. Daily 7am–9pm.

Grotto Pizza PIZZA   The crowds keep coming to Grotto Pizza. There are outlets throughout Delaware, and Bethany is lucky enough to have two—and at dinnertime, they're both packed. It's no wonder, with the crispy crust, savory sauce, and cheese; and with the perfect White Pizza, which combines spices, onions, and cheese. If you want pizza, Grotto's the place to go. 'Nuf said. Grotto also has restaurants in Dewey and Rehoboth.

793 Garfield Pkwy., Bethany Beach. © 302-537-3278. Also 8-10 York Beach Mall, South Bethany. © 302/537-6600. www.grottopizza.com. No reservations. Pizza $7.95–$17.95. AE, DISC, MC, V. Sun–Thurs 11am–9pm, Fri–Sat 11am–11pm.

McCabe's Gourmet Market DELI   This coffee bar and deli is a local favorite for gourmet deli sandwiches and salads, such as chicken walnut salad, pate, or even bologna. It's perfect food to pack out to the beach. There's a small seating area for those who need a break from the sun. *Insider tip:* Visitors in South Bethany walk from the beach to McCabe's to pick up sandwiches for their beachside lunch. It's that close.

Rte. 1 (in the York Beach Mall, just north of Fenwick Island State Park), South Bethany. © 302/539-8550. Fax 302/539-6392. Sandwiches $4.95–$7.20. AE, DISC, MC, V. Daily 7am–5pm, with extended hours in summer.

Old Mill Crab House ◈ SEAFOOD   In Delaware, this large and popular family restaurant overlooking the Indian River Bay is the place for crabs. From the comfort of your paper-lined table, you can dig into the Old Mill's Crab Special, which includes all-you-can-eat steamed crabs, hush puppies, clam crisps, shrimp crisps, corn on the cob (roasted in the husk), and fried chicken for $22.95. They also have wonderful no-nonsense crab cakes and a children's menu. *Note:* The original Old Mill Crab House, whose reputation launched the Bethany location, is located inland in Delmar on the Delaware–Maryland border, Route 54 West and Waller Road; © **302/846-2808.**

Cedar Neck Rd., Rte. 1, Box 332B, Ocean View. © 302/537-2240. Reservations not accepted. Main courses $7.50–$24. AE, MC, V. Open for dinner only—hours vary. Closed Nov–Mar. Take Rte. 26 west from Bethany Beach; turn right on Central Ave., and then turn left down the long driveway just past Rd. 360.

Sedona ◈ AMERICAN   Offering a little of Rehoboth's sophistication in Bethany Beach, Sedona is a great place to sneak away from the kids and have an adult meal. The sleek interior has room for 79 diners, so during the summer, make a reservation or be prepared to wait. Sedona's has been a hit so it can be crowded and noisy, but the food is worth it. Chef Chris Bunting serves up innovative American foods. The menu changes regularly but two recent standouts were grilled Colorado lamb chops with kalamata olive mashed potatoes, and a grilled loin of ahi tuna with Asian slaw.

26 Pennsylvania Ave. © 302/539-1200. Reservations recommended for dinner. Main courses $21–$32. AE, DISC, MC, V. Hours vary widely so call ahead. Open only for dinner. Closed Nov–Mar.

FENWICK ISLAND

Harpoon Hanna's ★★★ *(Kids)* SEAFOOD   Every summer, our family makes a pilgrimage to this huge, wood-paneled restaurant. We come for the fresh fish cooked any way we choose. The food is always good, including the tropical salad with slices of mandarin orange and tiny shrimp. The waitstaff is young but works hard to please. What we *really* come for is the bread: soft sweet raisin bread, savory rye, and blueberry or coconut muffins. We're not alone in our love for this restaurant. The wait can be long on a summer evening. Make plans to arrive at 4:30pm or so. Or maybe I shouldn't have mentioned this so we'll still have the dining room all to ourselves. Children are very welcome here. There are parties in Hanna's Hideout every night with live entertainment on some evenings.

Rte. 54 (on the bay), Fenwick Island. ✆ **800/227-0525** or 302/539-3095. Reservations not accepted. Main courses $9.95–$32.95; lunch $4.95–$10.95. AE, DISC, MC, V. Daily 11am–9pm with extended hours in summer.

Libby's AMERICAN   Known for its polka-dot facade, this family-friendly restaurant is a favorite for breakfast. Choices include pancakes with personality (royal cherry, Georgia pecan, chocolate chip), buckwheat cakes, waffles, French toast, omelets, and low-calorie fare. Lunch features a variety of overstuffed sandwiches, burgers, and salads. Dinner entrees, which come with a huge salad bar, range from soft-shell crabs and shrimp to steaks and chicken in the basket.

Ocean Hwy. (between Dagsboro and Cannon sts.). ✆ **302/539-7379**. Reservations not accepted. Main courses $6.95–$12.95; lunch $3.95–$7.95; breakfast $2.50–$7.95. AE, DISC, MC, V. Daily 7am–9:30pm. Shorter hours in winter.

Nantuckets ★ SEAFOOD   A New England cottage atmosphere prevails at this restaurant, with its four cozy dining rooms. Chef-owner David Twining is known for innovative dishes, such as Madaket Beach Fish Stew (a potpourri of shrimp, scallops, crab, clams, mussels, and fresh fish in a tomato-saffron broth) and lobster shepherd's pie. Always a favorite is the quahog chowdah (a rich scallop-and-clam chowder with red potatoes and corn). Besides seafood, Nantucket's offers rack of lamb, dry aged New York strip, or filet mignon. Service is top-notch. Early-bird specials are available to those seated by 5:45.

Rte. 1 and Atlantic Ave., Fenwick Island. ✆ **800/362-DINE** or 302/539-2607. Reservations recommended. Main courses $22.79–$34.59. AE, DC, DISC, MC, V. Daily 4–10pm tap room, 5–10pm dining room.

Warren's Station *(Value)* AMERICAN   For more than 30 years, wholesome cooking at reasonable prices has been the trademark of this homey, casual restaurant. Designed to duplicate the look of the old Indian River Coast Guard Station, the decor features light woods, lots of windows, and bright blue canvas dividers. Turkey is the specialty of the house, roasted fresh daily and hand-carved to order, from $7.25 and up for a complete dinner. Dinners with appetizer or soup, salad, two vegetables, and beverage cost only about $10 or so. Sandwiches, burgers, soups, and salads are available for lunch. No alcohol is served.

Ocean Hwy. (Rte. 1, between Indian and Houston sts.). ✆ **302/539-7156**. Reservations not accepted. Main courses $6.50–$15; lunch $2–$6.50; breakfast $2–$6.25. DISC, MC, V. Mid-May to early Sept daily 8am–9pm.

SHOPPING BETHANY

Most of the shopping in Bethany Beach is along or near Garfield Parkway, with a few shops on the boardwalk. Shops are open daily 10am to 5pm with extended hours in summer. **Bethany Beach Books** on Garfield Parkway (✆ **302/539-2522**) is the perfect place to pick up some reading for the beach.

Bethany's premier boutique is the eclectic **Japanesque,** 16 Pennsylvania Ave., Bethany Beach (© **302/539-2311**), which carries a wide selection of Japanese jewelry, home furnishings and decor, and books.

For delicate, handcrafted jewelry, stop in **TKO Designs Art Jewelry** on Garfield Parkway (© **302/539-6992;** www.tkodirect.com). On a rainy day, the place to be is **KilNTime,** a paint-your-own pottery shop and coffee bar at 111 Garfield Pkwy. (© **302/541-4544**). Staff will help you choose a piece, from switch plate to teapot, and then show you how to paint it. Leave it to be fired and pick it up later or have it shipped. For your sweet tooth, stop at the **Fudge Factory** at 3 Town Center (© **302/539-7502**); or follow your nose to the delectable aromas of brown sugar, butter, and popping corn at **Fisher's Popcorn** at 108 Garfield Pkwy., Bethany Beach (© **888/436-6388** or 302/539-8833).

SHOPPING FENWICK

Shopping in Fenwick is limited, but if you like country items, visit the **Seaside Country Store** (© **302/539-6110**). You can't miss it. The big red store on Coastal Highway used to sit all alone, but now commercial strips surround it. Inside, it has room after room of items with a country feel. All kinds of gifts from clothing to home decor to candy and cheese are here.

NIGHTLIFE IN BETHANY

Hanging out on the boardwalk is all the rage—but there really isn't much to do at night. Fifteen years ago, all the young parents brought their children in strollers for a walk before bed. Now young teens gather in the same spots to talk and eat.

Bethany Beach has its own **Bandstand** with shows beginning at 7:30pm. The performances are all family-oriented, with orchestras, bluegrass bands, and puppet shows. Sometimes there are dance lessons or talent shows. The town posts a schedule on the boardwalk and at the town hall on Garfield Parkway.

WHAT TO SEE & DO

Unlike Ocean City or Rehoboth, the 1-mile-long Bethany Beach Boardwalk has very few businesses on it. It's more a promenade, perfect for a leisurely walk near the beach. Most of the shops and fast-food eateries are on Garfield Parkway, perpendicular to the boardwalk, which it intersects in the middle.

Fenwick has no boardwalk between its hotels and the wide-open beach with gentle dunes. Most of the shops and business enterprises are concentrated 1 block inland along Route 1.

ATTRACTIONS

The **Fenwick Island Lighthouse** on the Transpeninsular Line, Route 54, about a quarter mile west of Route 1, built in 1859, is one of Delaware's oldest. The lighthouse is still in operation today; its beams can be seen for 15 miles (24km).

If you've ever wondered what sunken treasure really looks like, head for the **DiscoverSea Shipwreck Museum** ★ (© **302/539-9366**), a small but worthwhile private museum above the Sea Shell City shop at Route 1 and Bayard Street, Fenwick Island. The collection includes jewelry, coins, and china recovered from local shipwrecks and treasure beaches, silver and gold bars, a jeweled dagger, and other weapons. There's a seashell display that will help you figure out what kind of shells you found along the beach. Admission is free. Hours are daily 9am to 9pm, Memorial Day through Labor Day; 11am to 4pm, September through October and April through May; and Saturday and Sunday 11am to 4pm, November through March.

MINIATURE GOLF   The **Viking Golf Theme Park,** Routes 1 and 54, Fenwick Island (© **302/539-1644**), is an inland amusement park across from the Fenwick Island Lighthouse. This summertime attraction features a water slide, miniature golf, and bumper-boat and go-cart rides. Hours are daily 9am to midnight, Memorial Day through Labor Day. Viking miniature golf is open year-round, but hours vary.

    Bethany Beach Country Club on Garfield Parkway (© **302/537-9814**) is actually a teeny miniature golf course squeezed between shops. It's not much to look at but it's certainly convenient for Bethany visitors. And even without all the windmills and babbling brooks, it keeps the kids entertained. (It's fairly easy to win a free game, too.) In the summer it's always open until 9pm.

OUTDOOR ACTIVITIES

BIKING   The flat land along Route 1 in Bethany Beach and Fenwick Island is ideal for bicycling; however, during peak traffic season (July, Aug, and summer holidays) caution is advised. Bethany has bike lanes through town. For a change of scenery, nearby **Assawoman Wildlife Area** offers several sandy but bikable roads that wind through tidal marshland and forests. To reach the wildlife area, take Route 26 west and turn left on Road 361; turn right on Road 362, go about 1½ miles (2.4km), and turn right on Road 363; then turn left on Road 364 and follow the signs for Camp Barnes.

    Birdies and Pars golf shop, Market Place at Sea Colony, Route 1, Bethany Beach (© **302/539-4922**), rents single-speed cruiser bikes by the hour or the week. **Bethany Cycle and Fitness Shop,** Route 26 Mall, Route 26, Bethany Beach (© **302/537-9982**), also rents bicycles. Bike-rental costs are usually $4 to $6 per hour, $12 to $15 per day, or $30 or more per week.

HIKING & BIRDING   During the off-season, Fenwick Island and Delaware Seashore state parks (both on Rte. 1) are great places for a walk along deserted beaches. However, in-season when these beaches are covered with sunbathers, it's best for walkers to head out at sunrise or head a little inland (and remember: bring bug spray). Delaware Seashore State Park's **Burton's Island** boasts a 1½-mile (2.4km) nature trail and many opportunities to spot wildfowl, from the ever-present great blue herons to the rare piping plover.

    Assawoman Wildlife Area (for directions see "Biking," above) welcomes hikers on its few miles of dirt roads through tidal marsh and forests. An observation tower and duck blinds make it easy to view a variety of shorebirds.

SURF FISHING   A major draw in this area, fishing in Delaware's tidal waters requires no license. The Bethany–Fenwick Chamber of Commerce sponsors two surf fishing tournaments a year, in early May and in early October; for information, call © **800/962-7873** or 302/539-2100.

    Fenwick Island State Park has 3 miles (5km) of seacoast beach, much of which is open to surf fishing, and considerable tracts of open bayfront, ideal for both fishing and crabbing. There are also several dune crossings set up for off-road vehicles; a surf-fishing vehicle permit is required. For vehicle permits and maps of surf-fishing areas, call © **302/539-9060.** Similar facilities are also available at **Delaware Seashore State Park** (© **302/227-2800**).

TENNIS   Although there's not much tennis for the general public, Sea Colony Resort (see "Where to Stay in Bethany & Fenwick") is the largest tennis resort on the East Coast, sporting 26 courts, including four outdoor lighted courts, four clay courts, and four indoor courts. If tennis is your game, contact a real estate agent about renting a condo in Sea Colony's tennis villas.

4 Ocean City, Maryland ⭐⭐⭐

For many Marylanders heading "downy ocean," or "to the shore" means only one thing: a summer vacation in Ocean City. It's gotten quite crowded on the beach, in the restaurants, and on Coastal Highway, but it's still Marylanders' favorite place to sunbathe, jump waves, eat, shop, and meet friends or make new friends. On a skinny stretch of barrier island less than 10 miles (16km) long, the attraction is that wide sandy beach, pounding surf, and ocean breezes. By mid-summer, beach blankets cover the hot sand. So many visitors arrive that for 3 months of the year, Ocean City is the second largest city in the state. (Only Baltimore has more people.) Ocean City's entire beach is open to the public. "O.C." (as perennials fondly call it) was named an All-American City for 2001.

The boardwalk, which stretches to 27th Street in the oldest part of Ocean City, is crowded with hotels, some of them dating back to the 1920s. And restaurants, ice cream stands, and shops fill in the gaps. It ends at the fishing pier with amusement rides, including a huge **Ferris wheel** ⭐.

Out on Coastal Highway, shopping centers, restaurants, hotels, and condos demand your attention and your money. Miniature golf courses are exceedingly popular: They're all crowded after dark and there are some dandies. The quieter waters surrounding Ocean City, the bays of Assawoman, Sinepuxent, and Montego, attract fishermen, sailors, parasailers, and kayakers who like their water a little calmer. The inlet at the south end of the island was created during a fierce hurricane early in the 20th century. Its creation spurred the growth of the city's fishing industry since it made the trip to the ocean much quicker.

GETTING THERE

BY CAR **Route 50** goes right to Ocean City. To reach the southern end of town, continue on Route 50 to the bridge that enters O.C. at Caroline Street. For those staying at 60th Street or above, take Route 90 and cross the bridge at 62nd Street. An alternative route is to turn on Route 404 east just past Queenstown; follow it into Delaware. Turn south of Route 113 south. Route 26 east connects with Bethany. Turn south on Route 1 to Ocean City. Or take Route 54 to Fenwick to Route 1. However you get there, avoid Route 1 in Rehoboth, especially on a summer weekend. Traffic slows to a frustrating crawl most of the day.

BY AIR **Wicomico County Airport** (✆ 410/548-4827), 40 minutes west of Ocean City, in the outskirts of Salisbury, handles regular commuter flights to and from Baltimore and Philadelphia via US Airways Express (✆ **800/428-4322**). Private planes also fly into that airport, as well as **Ocean City Municipal Airport** (✆ **410/213-2471**), 3 miles (5km) west of town off Route 611.

Renting a Car Rental cars are available at both airports. **Avis** (✆ **410/742-8566;** www.avis.com) and **Hertz** (✆ 410/749-2235; www.hertz.com) have offices at Wicomico Airport in Salisbury.

BY BUS **Carolina Trailways** has daily service into Rehoboth, Bethany Beach, and Ocean City from points north and south, with nonstop buses from Baltimore, Washington, D.C., and Salisbury. Limited service and no ticketing is available from Lewes. To catch a bus to or from Lewes, call ✆ **800/229-9424.** In Rehoboth, buses stop at Abizak's at 4120 Hwy. One (✆ **302/227-5776**). Bethany's station is at 201 Central Blvd. (✆ **302/539-6244**). In Ocean City, buses stop at 2nd Street and Philadelphia Avenue (✆ **410/289-9307**). For all locations, check schedules and information at www.greyhound.com.

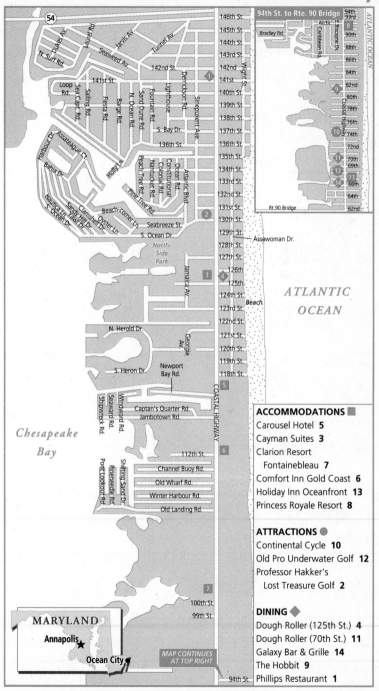

Lower Ocean City

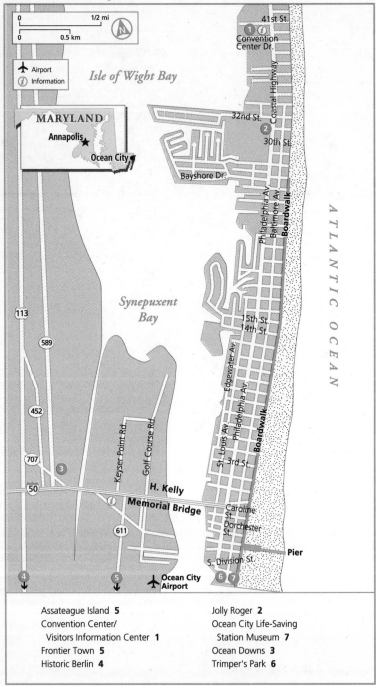

Assateague Island **5**
Convention Center/
  Visitors Information Center **1**
Frontier Town **5**
Historic Berlin **4**

Jolly Roger **2**
Ocean City Life-Saving
  Station Museum **7**
Ocean Downs **3**
Trimper's Park **6**

VISITOR INFORMATION

Ocean City's **Visitors Information Center** stocks information, maps, and brochures. It is located on the bay side in the **Ocean City Convention and Visitors Bureau,** 4001 Coastal Hwy. at 40th Street, Ocean City, MD 21842 (© **800/OC-OCEAN** or 410/289-8181; www.ococean.com), and is open daily all year, Monday to Friday 8:30am to 5pm, Saturday to Sunday 9am to 5pm. If you're heading into town from Route 50, stop at the **Ocean City Chamber of Commerce** Information Center (© **410/213-0552;** www.oceancity.com) at the intersection of Route 707 and Route 50 1½ miles (2.4km) from Ocean City. It's a great place to pick up information and brochures as well as discount coupons for everything from restaurants and shops to miniature golf. Open daily 8:30am to 4:30pm.

Look for discount coupons in *Sunny Day, Beachcomber,* and *Beach Guide.* Pick them up in restaurant, beach apparel stores, hotels, and real estate offices.

GETTING AROUND

BY BUS   During peak season, when parking can be difficult, the bus is the fastest and most convenient way to get around. Buses run 24 hours a day year-round and follow one route from the Delaware border south along Coastal Highway to the inlet and return north along Baltimore Street and Coastal Highway. In the summer months, buses run every 10 minutes; from October 20 through Memorial Day, they run every half hour. The fare is $1 for a 24-hour period and exact change is required. For more information, contact the Ocean City Transportation Department, 66th Street, bay side (© **410/723-1607**).

A new **park and ride lot** on Route 50 in West Ocean City (on the western side of the bridge) has free parking. Visitors can board a shuttle to South Division Street near the inlet to spend the day there or catch a bus to other O.C. destinations. It costs $1 for the whole day.

BY BOARDWALK TRAM   The tram travels from the inlet to the northern end at 27th Street, stopping for passengers who signal the driver to pick them up. It runs every 10 minutes in summer, 7 am to midnight every day. On weekends from Easter to May, and in September and October, it runs every 15 minutes. To get off, raise your hand and the tram will stop. The fare is $1.50 one-way. It's a great ride for parents with tired children and a good way for first-time visitors to become familiar with the boardwalk.

If you need a taxi, call **Sunshine Taxi** (© **410/208-2828**). It serves Ocean City, Ocean Pines, Salisbury, Fenwick, Rehoboth, and the Lewes ferry.

PARKING   Parking is difficult, particularly at the height of the season. Most public facilities, such as shopping centers and restaurants, offer free parking to patrons. There are also eight public lots, mostly around the southern end of Ocean City. The meters must be fed $1 an hour but several lots have change machines: Worcester Street; Somerset and Baltimore; Dorchester and Baltimore; N. Division and Baltimore; and 4th and Baltimore. These, as well as on-street meters, must be fed 24 hours a day, April 15 to October 15. Other times they are free. The largest public lot is the Hugh T. Cropper lot at the inlet, with 1,200 spaces. The first 30 minutes here—90 minutes for handicapped vehicles—are free. Then the rate is $1 an hour, payable to an attendant as you leave. If you plan to park here for nighttime activities, be aware that hundreds of other people have had the same idea and the wait to get in the lot, and later to get out, can be long.

ORIENTATION

Ocean City stretches for 10 miles (16km), with one main north–south thoroughfare, Coastal Highway. It becomes two one-way streets at around 32nd Street: Philadelphia goes south and Baltimore heads north. Cross streets are designated by numbers (from 1st to 145th), with numbers decreasing to the south. It's vital to know the cross streets when looking for a shop or restaurant, though if you have a street number, the first two numbers usually tell you the cross street. Attractions and businesses on the cross streets are designated as either ocean side east of Coastal Highway, or bay side, for those west of Coastal Highway. If you see an address that says Atlantic Avenue, that means it's oceanfront.

 FAST FACTS: Ocean City

Area Code Ocean City's area codes are **410** and **443**.

Camera Repair For repair, photo processing, or supplies, try Atlantic Color Lab, 11511 Coastal Hwy. (℘ **410/723-4687**).

Dentists Emergency work is provided at Atlantic Dental Associates, 105 58th St. (℘ **410/524-0500**).

Doctors Ask for a recommendation from the Physician's Referral Line (℘ **800/955-7762**).

Emergencies Dial ℘ **911** for fire, police, or ambulance.

Eyeglass Repair The local choice is Accurate Optical, 118th St., near the Food Lion supermarket (℘ **410/524-0220**).

Hospitals 75th St. Medical Center, 7408 Coastal Hwy. (℘ **410/524-0075**); Atlantic General Hospital, 9733 Healthway Dr., Berlin (℘ **410/641-1100**); or Peninsula Regional Medical Center, 100 E. Carroll St., Salisbury (℘ **410/546-6400**).

Library The Ocean City branch of the Worcester County Library is at 14th Street and Philadelphia Avenue (℘ **410/289-7297**).

Newspapers **The Daily Times** is Ocean City's newspaper, though dailies from Baltimore, Washington, and Philadelphia are available. **The Baltimore Sun** publishes "O.C.," a supplement covering Ocean City events, weekly from April through October and on the first Sunday of each month during the rest of the year.

Pharmacies Try Bailey's, 8th Street and Philadelphia Avenue (℘ **410/289-8191**); or CVS, 11905 Coastal Hwy. (at 120th St.; ℘ **410/524-7233**).

Police Dial ℘ **911** or **410/723-6610** for Ocean City police, ℘ **410/641-3101** for state police, or ℘ **410/289-7556** for beach patrol.

Post Office The main post office is at 5th Street and Philadelphia Avenue. On the north end of town, the office is located at 71st Street on the bay side, near Bonfire Restaurant (℘ **410/524-7611**).

Radio The local radio stations include WOCQ-104 FM and WKHI-99.9 FM for general programming, and WZBH-93.5 FM for rock.

Taxes The state sales tax is 5%; the county tax is 5%.

Transit Information Dial ℘ **410/723-1607.**

Weather Dial ℘ **800/OC-OCEAN** or 410/213-0552.

SPECIAL EVENTS

O.C.'s party atmosphere is enhanced by festivals throughout the year; below is a selection of the largest and most popular.

Springfest   The first week in May, this 4-day event features crafts, music, and food in the inlet parking lot. Lots of businesses open, as O.C. gets ready for the summer.

Arts Alive   New in 2001, and held the first week of June, this festival features a juried fine art exhibit and sale, along with music and food. It's held at the Northside Park at 127th Street and the bay.

Fourth of July   Some 300,000 people crowd into Ocean City every Fourth. Fireworks over Assawoman Bay top off the family-style picnic held at Northside Park beginning at 11am. A second fireworks display is held at N. Division Street at the south end of the boardwalk. Festivities begin with a concert at 4pm.

White Marlin Open ⚐   Held the first full week in August, some 400 boats register for this annual fishing expedition. The top prize goes for the biggest white marlin, but there are other prizes for blue marlin, tuna, and shark. The purse in 2001 was set at $1.7 million. If you want to see what all the fuss is about (without actually fishing yourself), stop by the Harbor Island Marina on the bay side for the weigh-ins every night from 4 to 9:15pm. They reel in some whoppers. For information, call ✆ **410/289-9229.**

   Note: This is not a good week to try to charter a fishing boat for any other fishing. The boats are all occupied. If you really want to go fishing, call the charter and headboat captains in Lewes.

Sunfest   This 4-day festival held the third week in September officially ends the summer season with crafts, music, and food at the inlet.

Winterfest of Lights ⚐⚐   From mid-November to New Year's, holiday light displays make up this event. The first takes place at the inlet, where you can drive among the lit displays. The second takes place in Northside Park. For $3 for those 12 and older (free for younger visitors), ride the tram through the light displays and then stop to see Santa, have hot chocolate, and browse the gift shop.

WHERE TO STAY

More than in any other part of Maryland, the lodgings in Ocean City depend on a short "high season." Summer (June–Aug) commands the highest rates, often with weekend supplements. In many cases, minimum stays of 2 or 3 nights may apply, so check in advance. Reservations are a must. Every hotel has handicapped-accessible rooms but the accommodations vary.

   If you want to save a little money, consider rooms without an ocean view or a partial view. The rates can be much lower. Or come when the rates are lower. January rates are bargain basement (for good reason) but tariffs in spring and fall are economical, especially packages offered by many hotels. Spring can be damp but September is a terrific month to visit. The beach is nearly empty (except on weekends), lots of restaurants are still open, and the water is still warm. Also look for Valentine's Day and Christmas packages. Christmas is becoming a popular time for a trip to the beach. With hotel packages, light displays, and New Year's Eve parties at area restaurants, the winter holidays are an excellent time to visit.

   For many families, renting a condo or town house is the only way to go. With several bedrooms and bathrooms, full kitchens, and living rooms, these offer a convenient way to take everybody to the beach.

Several local real estate companies offer hundreds of units on both the ocean and bay. They come in every shape and price, starting at $500 a week and taking off from there. Every unit is different so it's a good idea to read the thick brochures detailing available units. Some firms post their listings on their websites. Generally, these units are well kept with fairly new furniture, good appliances, and often a stash of paperbacks and board games for rainy days. Bring your own paper products and linens. Just about everything else is usually provided. (Check the listings to be sure.)

The best units—that is, the newest and closest to the beach—are snapped up by January or February, but if you decide to go to the beach in May, there are usually condos still available.

Moore Warfield and Glick (© 800/289-2821) has rentals in Ocean City, as well as in the "suburbs" of Ocean Pines, a community of homes located on the western side of Assawoman Bay. Or call **Long and Foster,** 11701 Coastal Hwy., Ocean City, MD 21842 (© **410/524-1700** or 800/992-7777); or **O'Conor Piper and Flynn/ERA** at 10401 Coastal Hwy., Ocean City, MD 21842 (© **410/524-6111** or 800/638-1880).

EXPENSIVE

Carousel ⭐   The Carousel continues to be an attractive option for families and couples. It's on of the oldest of north Ocean City's high-rises and one of the most interesting. It has a year-round ice skating rink, and an indoor pool and comfortable, if small, rooms with kitchenettes and oceanfront balconies. If the rooms aren't big enough, 50 two- and three-bedroom condo units are available in the 22-story tower behind the hotel. These are more spacious with two full bathrooms and well-equipped kitchens. The hotel is a conference center and can occasionally be fully booked. Off-season, the hotel offers some great values.

11700 Coastal Hwy., Ocean City, MD 21842. © 800/641-0011 or 410/524-1000. Fax 410/524-7766. 258 units. $49–$309 double; $109–$413 condo. AE, DC, DISC, MC, V. Free parking. **Amenities:** 1 indoor restaurant; 1 outdoor restaurant; 4 bars; indoor pool; lighted tennis court; basketball court; exercise room; Jacuzzi; sauna; indoor ice rink (open to the public); business center. *In room:* A/C, dataport, mini-fridge, microwave, coffeemaker, hair dryer.

Clarion Resort Fontainebleau ⭐⭐   Formerly the Sheraton Fontainebleau, the property is now owned by Clarion, which has kept all the property's best features. It is located on the ocean, far from the boardwalk and in the midst of Condo Row in north Ocean City. It offers oversized rooms and suites, all with views of the ocean and bay. Cabana suites with sitting room and huge bedroom on separate levels are posh. Every room also has its own private balcony, contemporary furnishings, coffeemaker, and refrigerator.

10100 Coastal Hwy. (at 101st St.), Ocean City, MD 21842. © 800/638-2100 or 410/524-3535. Fax 410/ 524-3834. www.clarionoc.com. 273 units. $109–$399 double. AE, DC, DISC, MC, V. **Amenities:** Restaurant and 2 lounges overlooking the ocean; terrace; indoor pool; spa with whirlpool; workout room; steam room; sauna; whirlpool; sun rooms; video game room; hair and nail salon. *In room:* A/C, fridge, microwave, iron.

Coconut Malorie Resort ⭐   With a British colonial name and ambience, this hotel stands out on the bayfront. The lobby features a waterfall, brass chandeliers, marble floors, palm trees, tropical foliage, and an eager staff. The guest rooms are equally distinctive—all decorated with a Caribbean flavor, including a collection of Haitian art. Each unit is a suite: bedroom (often dominated by a four-poster bed), marble bathroom with whirlpool tub and lighted makeup/shaving mirror, and sitting and dining area with a private balcony and kitchen. Facilities include an outdoor swimming pool and sun deck and a full-time concierge desk. A footbridge connects the hotel to **Fager's Island restaurant** and lounge, owned by the hotel (see "Where to Dine," below).

200 59th St., Ocean City, MD 21842. C 800/767-6060. Fax 410/524-9327. www.coconutmalorie.com. 85 units. $73–$278 double. Continental breakfast included in executive or VIP suites. AE, DC, DISC, MC, V. **Amenities:** Outdoor pool; health club included with some suites and offered for a fee to the rest. *In room:* A/C, dataport, kitchen, unstocked fridge, microwave, coffeemaker, hair dryer, iron.

Dunes Manor Hotel ★ *(Moments*   If you like your hotels old-fashioned, the Dunes Manor is for you. On 28th Street in the older part of O.C, this 11-story hotel tries its best to capture days gone by. The wide porch with its rocking chairs, cupolas, and Victorian-style facade are just the beginning. What captures the spirit best is the afternoon tea—so proper in a casual beach resort. Each bedroom and suite is up to date in every way. They all have an oceanfront view, a balcony, two double beds, a decor of light woods and floral fabrics, and a refrigerator. The hotel provides free shuttle service with advance notice to and from the Ocean City bus terminal and Wicomico County Airport.

2800 Baltimore Ave., Ocean City, MD 21842. C 800/523-2888 or 410/289-1100. Fax 410/289-4905. www.dunesmanor.com. dunes@dmv.com. 170 units. $45–$219 double; $85–$295 suite (depending on the season). AE, DC, DISC, MC, V. Free parking. **Amenities:** Restaurant and lounge; indoor/outdoor pool; whirlpool; exercise room; sun deck. *In room:* A/C, TV, dataport, fridge, hair dryer, iron.

Lighthouse Club Hotel ★★   There's nothing like this hotel anywhere else in O.C. It's exceptional to look at: a three-story inn that resembles a screwpile lighthouse, overlooking the Isle of Wight Bay. Inside, the rooms are luxurious with top-of-the-line furnishings, marble bathrooms, wide balconies, and wet bars. Eight rooms have fireplaces and whirlpool tubs. Services include in-room continental breakfast, evening turndown, and VCR rentals. The only drawback to this luxurious, romantic inn is its open and airy design: The cathedral ceiling allows noise from the lobby to drift up to the guest rooms. This hotel is part of a growing community at Fager's Island. The same owners added a new 12-suite hotel, the Edge, in December 2001. Though tiny, it boasts its own luxuries, including its own pool and sun deck. All the buildings are connected to Fager's Island restaurant (see "Where to Dine," below) by footbridge. Several packages make this place attractive even on a mild winter weekend.

Fager's Island, 56th St. (on the bay), Ocean City, MD 21842. C 800/371-5400 or 410/524-5400. Fax 410/524-3928. www.fagers.com. 23 units. $184–$375 suite. Rates include continental breakfast. AE, DC, DISC, MC, V. Free parking. **Amenities:** Restaurant; pool; health club access; Jacuzzi. *In room:* TV/VCR, fax, dataport, fridge stocked with soda, coffeemaker, hair dryer, iron.

Princess Royale Resort ★★ *(Kids*   The rooms are lovely but what makes this the place to stay is its Olympic-sized indoor pool. Even if it rains, this pool is big enough—and not all hotels can say that. It's part of a recreation center, glassed in with games, sauna, Jacuzzis, and a poolside cafe that will keep your children happy. Although the Princess Royale Resort consists of two five-story towers within a 10-story condominium layout, staying here feels more like being on a cruise ship docked on the beachfront. Guest rooms are furnished with light woods and nautical art. One-bedroom suites can sleep two to six people, two-bedrooms sleep six to eight, and three-bedrooms sleep eight to 10 people. Each condo unit has a full kitchen including dishwasher, garbage disposal, microwave, refrigerator, and icemaker. Facilities are well maintained and the staff is gracious.

Oceanfront (at 91st St.), Ocean City, MD 21842. C 800/4-ROYALE or 410/524-7777. Fax 410/524-1623. www.princessroyale.com. 340 units, 24 condos. $69–$309 double; $169–$485 for condos fall–spring,

$2,800–$3,400 only by the week in summer. AE, DISC, MC, V. Children under 12 stay free. **Amenities:** Restaurant; bar; pool; 2 tennis courts; health club; sauna; Jacuzzi. *In room:* A/C, Internet access, kitchenettes with microwave and fridge, full kitchens in condos, hair dryer, iron.

MODERATE

Castle in the Sand *Value*   A good choice for families who don't want to break the bank, this modern hotel with a castlelike exterior is set on the beach at 37th Street not terribly far from the boardwalk. Standard hotel rooms are offered, as well as oceanfront rooms with kitchenettes and balconies. If you'd like something larger, this complex includes condos and quaint cottages that are rented weekly in the summer from about $800 to $1,500. These come with all the amenities you'd expect from any O.C. condo. Outside you'll find the jewel-like Olympic-size swimming pool (one of the largest in Ocean City).

3701 Atlantic Ave., Ocean City, MD 21842. ℂ 800/552-SAND or 410/289-6846. Fax 410/289-9446. www.castleinthesand.com. 179 units. $59–$245 double. AE, DC, DISC, MC, V. Free parking. Closed Nov–Mar. **Amenities:** Restaurant; bar and grill; umbrella and beach rental; arcade; children's activities in summer. *In room:* Most have A/C, TV/VCR with movies, fax, iron. Fridge and microwave in some rooms and condos.

Cayman Suites   Though it's on Coastal Highway, this five-story all-suite hotel is within walking distance of the beach. Each suite has a bedroom with two queen-sized beds or a king-sized bed, and a separate living room with a pullout couch and kitchenette. Most units also have balconies. If you're tired of packing chairs and umbrellas in your car, consider that guests staying 3 nights or more have use of two beach chairs and umbrella and one beach towel per person during your stay (except day of checkout).

12500 Coastal Hwy., Ocean City, MD 21842. ℂ 800/564-0042 or 410/250-7600. Fax 410/250-7603. www.caymansuites.com. 57 units. $59–$209 suite. AE, DISC, MC, V. Free parking. **Amenities:** Indoor pool; exercise room; beach towels/chairs/umbrellas. *In room:* A/C, fax, dataport, fridge, microwave, hair dryer, iron.

Comfort Inn Boardwalk   One of the newest chain properties along the boardwalk, this is a modern five-story complex of two buildings: one directly on the boardwalk and the other next to it. All of the guest rooms are decorated with light wood furnishings and sea-toned fabrics, and each has a sleeping area, kitchenette, sitting area with sofa bed, and private balcony. Facilities include a restaurant, heated outdoor and indoor pools, and a boardwalk deck.

507 Atlantic Ave. (5th St. at the oceanfront; P.O. Box 1030), Ocean City, MD 21842. ℂ 800/282-5155 or 410/289-5155. Fax 410/641-3815. www.comfortinnboardwalk.com. 84 units. $49–$225 double. Children under 12 free in parents' room. Rates include continental breakfast. AE, DC, DISC, MC, V. Free parking. Closed Nov to mid-Feb. **Amenities:** Restaurant; outdoor and indoor pools; deck facing boardwalk. *In room:* A/C, TV with movies, kitchenette.

Holiday Inn Oceanfront   In the center of Ocean City, directly on the beach, this eight-story hotel is convenient to everything and its amenities make it a good choice for a weekend or a week. Each long, narrow room has a balcony and sitting area on one side, sleeping area in the middle, and kitchenette by the door.

6600 Coastal Hwy. (oceanfront at 67th St.), Ocean City, MD 21842. ℂ 800/837-3588 or 410/524-1600. Fax 410/524-1135. www.ocmdhotels.com/holidayinn. 216 units. $54–$254 double. AE, DC, DISC, MC, V. **Amenities:** Restaurant; poolside bar and grill; outdoor pool; tennis court; exercise room; Jacuzzi; sauna; children's programs in summer; game room; business center. *In room:* A/C, TV/VCR, fax, dataport, kitchenette, fridge, coffeemaker, hair dryer, iron.

Howard Johnson Oceanfront Plaza Hotel ✪   A great moderately priced choice on the boardwalk at 12th Street, this modern seven-story hotel has a welcoming lobby with a fireplace. The guest rooms are decorated with light woods, bright but not jarring furnishings, and modern art prints. Deluxe rooms have sleep sofas. Each room has a balcony with full or partial ocean views.

1109 Atlantic Ave., Ocean City, MD 21842. © **800/926-1122** or 410/289-7251. Fax 410/289-3435. www. hjoceanfrontplaza.com. 90 units. $39–$289 double. AE, DC, DISC, MC, V. Free parking. **Amenities:** Restaurant; bar; indoor pool; Jacuzzi; bike rental. *In room:* A/C, fridge, microwave, coffeemaker, hair dryer.

MODERATE/INEXPENSIVE

Comfort Inn Gold Coast *Value*   For value and great location, this bayside hotel is a good choice. Set back from the highway, its bayside rooms have a lovely view and the higher rates to prove it. Though most rooms don't have much to look at, they're comfortable in cheery pastels, and many have whirlpool tubs. The hotel's location near the Gold Coast Mall makes it even better for the shoppers among us. Restaurants and movie theaters are nearby, too.

11201 Coastal Hwy. (at 112th St.), Ocean City, MD 21842. © **800/228-5150** or 410/524-3000. Fax 410/ 524-8255. www.comfortgoldcoast.com. 202 units. $30–$265 double. AE, DISC, MC, V. Free parking. **Amenities:** Indoor pool; bayview sun deck; Jacuzzi; children's play area. *In room:* A/C, fridge, microwave, hair dryer, iron.

Phillips Beach Plaza Hotel   This boardwalk hotel boasts an elegant Victorian lobby with crystal chandeliers, wrought-iron fixtures, open fireplace, and graceful statuary, all contributing to its old-world ambience. Standard rooms and apartments are available. The one- to three-bedroom apartments offer dining/living areas and full kitchens. The big porch with rocking chairs, a throwback to old Ocean City days, is a great place to watch the boardwalk traffic and catch a breeze or wait for your table at Phillips by the Sea restaurant (see "Where to Dine," below). The restaurant also has a cozy piano bar in the lobby.

1301 Atlantic Ave. (between 13th and 14th sts.), Ocean City, MD 21842. © **800/492-5834** or 410/289-9121. Fax 410/289-3041. www.phillipsoc.com. 96 units (2 with shower only). $50–$164 double, $75–$250 apts. Weekly rates available. AE, DC, DISC, MC, V. Free parking. **Amenities:** Restaurant; piano bar. *In room:* A/C.

Talbot Inn *Value*   The Talbot Inn is in the perfect spot for fishermen and those who love the boardwalk. It's an easy walk to the Talbot Street Pier to find a fishing boat or take a ride on the O.C. Rocket, and to the inlet and all those rides, shops, and ice cream stands, and the widest part of the beach. The inn has two three-story buildings, one bayfront and the other without the view. Each unit is an efficiency with stove, microwave, and refrigerator and can accommodate up to six people. They're pretty, with light woods, floral fabrics, and nautical artwork. MR Ducks is right next door, the bar and the sportswear shop.

Talbot St. (and the bay), P.O. Box 548, Ocean City, MD 21842. © **800/659-7703** or 410/289-9125. Fax 410/ 289-6792. www.ocean-city.com/talbot-inn. 36 units. $32–$110 double. 3-night minimum stay on weekends in summer. DISC, MC, V. Free parking. **Amenities:** Restaurant; bar (MR Ducks); marina. *In room:* A/C, TV, kitchenettes with stove, refrigerator, microwave.

WHERE TO DINE

Understandably, seafood is a favorite here. For the most part, a casual atmosphere prevails, although it is always wise to make a reservation in the better restaurants and to check on the dress code.

During summer, restaurants are rarely closed. Some open as early as 5am, dishing up hearty breakfasts, and continue serving through 10 or 11pm.

Most restaurants have full bar facilities. Just to be safe, get a copy of the Ocean City Visitor Bureau's guide to accommodations and restaurants; it gives descriptions, hours, and price guidelines for at least 50 of the best eateries.

Don't want to go out but don't want to cook either? **Takeout Taxi** will bring entrees from 24 restaurants right to your door. Most of the restaurants are moderately priced. Call © **410/524-MEAL** from 4 to 10pm.

EXPENSIVE

Bonfire ⭐ BEEF/SEAFOOD   For more than 25 years, this bayside restaurant has been drawing people for its charcoal-broiled steaks, aged prime rib, and surf-and-turf. The latest addition is a 100-foot-long all-you-can-eat seafood and prime rib buffet. The food is good, especially the beef dishes, but not worth a special trip. This large, elaborately decorated restaurant offers a choice of four dining rooms, filled with captain's chairs, plush banquettes, gas lanterns, and oil paintings. A huge oval bar dominates the center of the restaurant and live music is offered 5 nights a week in summer.

71st St. and Coastal Hwy. Ⓒ **410/524-7171.** Reservations recommended on weekends. Main courses $16–$28. AE, DC, DISC, MC, V. May–Oct daily 4–11pm, Nov–Apr Fri–Sun 5–10pm.

Fager's Island ⭐ AMERICAN/PACIFIC RIM   Fager's Island plays up its bayfront location. Lots of decks, a gazebo, a pavilion, and a pier, as well as all those big windows in the dining room keep the attention on the setting sun. Once it goes down you'll hear "The 1812 Overture" every night, it's a tradition. The menu has taken on an Asian flair with dishes like wok crispy salmon, but you can also get a strip steak with bordelaise sauce or fat crab cakes. If a beer and something light are more your style, Fager's offers burgers, quesadillas, salads, and sandwiches from 11am to midnight. The pricey kid's menu offers tenderloin of beef and fish with lime butter along with the chicken tenders. Stay late and enjoy live entertainment in the bar. Early-bird specials including salmon and tenderloin are offered every day before 6pm.

201 60th St. (on the bay). Ⓒ **888/371-5400** or 410/524-5500. www.fagers.com. Reservations recommended for dinner. Main courses $19–$29; lunch $6–$12.50. AE, DC, DISC, MC, V. Daily 11am–2am.

Galaxy Bar & Grille ⭐ INTERNATIONAL   Although Galaxy can't claim ocean or bay views, this purple and gold restaurant on Coastal Highway can boast a devoted local following. In addition to an innovative menu and sleek interior design highlighted by gold and purple tile, the Galaxy's food is great. Menu standouts include chicken breast stuffed with pancetta risotto, pan-roasted lobster in a charred tomato and chorizo butter sauce and, for lunch, a turkey sandwich topped with bourbon Vidalia jam. Our favorite remains the delicious smoked salmon taco. It's wonderful and filling enough to be a meal on its own.

6601 Coastal Hwy. Ⓒ **410/723-6762.** Reservations recommended for dinner. Main courses $17–$31, lunch $10–$13. AE, DISC, MC, V. Sun–Thurs 11am–3pm and 5–10pm, Fri–Sat 11am–3pm and 5–11pm.

The Hobbit ⭐ SEAFOOD/CONTINENTAL   One of the loveliest places to dine while watching the sunset is this bay view restaurant. The emphasis is on seafood but with a continental flair. In addition to crab cakes and catch of the day, the ever-changing dinner entrees may include roast duckling with a Grand Marnier sauce and veal with Madeira sauce and pistachios. Entrees are showy, but wait until you see the desserts, baked on the premises: chocolate truffle pie, cheesecake, and other fattening delights. The restaurant itself pays homage to J.R.R. Tolkien's beloved characters in its decor. The dinner menu tends to be pricey but the Early Bird Menu offers a few intriguing options at more affordable prices in the $10 to $14 range. It's worth leaving the beach early for some good food and a smaller crowd. Seating is available outside on the decks.

101 81st St. Ⓒ **410/524-8100.** Reservations recommended for dinner. Main courses $19.95–$26.95; lunch $6.95–$16.95. AE, DISC, MC, V. Daily 11am–midnight.

MODERATE

Captain Bill Bunting's Angler AMERICAN   Since 1938, this spacious restaurant has been a favorite on the marina of Ocean City. It features an air-conditioned main dining room with rustic and nautical decor, plus an outdoor patio deck overlooking the bay, an ideal spot to see the fishermen bringing back their bounty. The extensive dinner menu revolves around a variety of daily fresh fish specials, prepared in one of seven different ways, plus steaks and seafood platters. A free evening cruise of the bay at 7 or 9pm is included as part of the dinner price. Lunch focuses on raw-bar selections, fishwiches, salads, and burgers. *Note:* For early risers, doors open at 6am for breakfast.

Talbot St. and the bay. © 410/289-7424. Reservations recommended for dinner. Main courses $6.95–$27.95; lunch $3.95–$7.95. AE, DISC, MC, V. May–Oct daily 6am–11pm restaurant and 11am–2am bar. Closed Nov–Apr.

Harrison's Harbor Watch SEAFOOD   The view from the top floor of this imposing restaurant makes the inevitable wait worthwhile. Besides the view of the inlet and Assateague Island, there's lots of fresh seafood to choose from: the usual crab cakes, stuffed shrimp, and fresh fish. The seafood fettuccini combines pasta with shrimp, scallops, clams, and crabmeat. It's a busy place, quite noisy, and the waitstaff can be a bit overwhelmed. Might as well relax, enjoy the view, and decide whether you want some steamed shrimp from the raw bar.

Boardwalk South, overlooking the Inlet and Assateague Island. © 410/289-5121. Reservations recommended. Main courses $12.95–$22.95; raw bar $5.95–$11.95. AE, DC, DISC, MC, V. Main dining room, May–Oct daily 4:30–10pm; Jan–Apr and Nov Thurs–Sat 5–10pm. Raw bar daily 11:30am–10pm.

Macky's Bayside Bar & Grill AMERICAN   Macky's claims to have the best sunsets in town, and they certainly have the location for it. This comfortable shantylike restaurant sits on its own patch of bay beach with a view of the mainland, the Lighthouse Club, and the Route 90 bridge. You can dine on the sand in white plastic furniture or in the partially enclosed dining area overlooking the beach. Decor is vintage beach house: Napkins and condiments are served in sand buckets, and the beach is strewn with live palm trees and lighted wire palms and dolphins. The menu touches on everything from New Orleans to Florida to the Eastern Shore, with a large number of vegetarian options thrown in (try the black bean burger or the grilled garden sandwich). They even serve a few of the favorites from Tío Gringo's, a Mexican restaurant under the same ownership.

54th St. (on the bay). © 410/723-5565. Reservations not accepted in summer. Main courses $12.50–$22.95; salads and sandwiches $4.25–$10.95. AE, DC, DISC, MC, V. Daily 11am–2am. Closed Jan.

Phillips Seafood Restaurants SEAFOOD   The Phillips family food dynasty began with a small crab house at 21st Street and Philadelphia Avenue. Four decades years later, the first restaurant has taken over the whole block. When it was the only location, families lined up around the block for a table. With two more restaurants in O.C., the lines are a little shorter—except at about 6pm on a weekend. The **21st Street** restaurant is casual: white paper on the tables, which your server will sign, and a huge menu that emphasizes crabs. Phillips's crab bisque should not be missed. Not all tables are created equal here. Most are nice enough, unless you get stuck in the narrow dining room behind the carryout. The food's the same, the ambience isn't.

   Phillips by the Sea ★★ drips with Victorian ambience. A smaller operation in the lobby of the Beach Plaza Hotel, it carries the same crab cakes, crab imperial, and shrimp its fans love. It's the prettiest of the restaurants and offers oceanfront dining on the porch. They take reservations here. The waitstaff isn't as busy and the young men and women are as gracious as the surroundings.

Phillips has also opened an outpost along O.C.'s condo strip. The restaurant at **141st and Coastal Highway** is designed to resemble the original and offers the same menu. The lines at dinnertime look like the original, too. Carryout is available at the 21st Street and 141st Street locations—a good alternative if there's a long wait.

Phillips Restaurant at 21st St., 2004 Philadelphia Ave. ℂ **410/289-6821.** Reservations not accepted. Apr–Oct daily noon–10pm. Closed Nov–Mar.

Phillips by the Sea, 1301 Atlantic Ave. on the boardwalk. ℂ **800/492-5834** or 410/289-9121. Fax 410/ 289-3041. Reservations accepted for dinner. Open for breakfast, lunch, and dinner.

Phillips Seafood House & Seafood Festival Buffet, 141st St. and Coastal Hwy. ℂ **800/799-2722** or 410/ 250-1200. Main courses $9.95–$27.95; lunch $5.95–$10.95. AE, DISC, MC, V. Open only for dinner, 5pm weekdays, 4pm Fri–Sat.

INEXPENSIVE

Dough Roller PIZZA   This pizza parlor has become a popular chain in Ocean City with five locations. If you want pizza or a strawberry daiquiri, come here. The restaurants are decorated with a Victorian theme, including carousel horses, but the attraction is the terrific pizza. Also on the menu are burgers, sandwiches, subs, New England grinders, and Italian entrees such as fettuccini Alfredo and lasagna. If your favorite meal is breakfast, pancakes are served all day.

2 Boardwalk locations, S. Division St. (ℂ **410/289-3501**) and 3rd St. (ℂ **410/289-2599**). 3 on Coastal Hwy. at 41st St. (ℂ **410/524-9254**), 70th St. (ℂ **410/254-7981**), and 125th St. (ℂ **410/250-5664**). No credit cards at boardwalk locations. Entrees $4.50–$23.95. AE, DC, MC, V. Daily 7am until at least 10pm in summer, depending on crowd. Closes at 3pm Mon–Tues off-season.

Dumser's *Kids* AMERICAN/ICE CREAM   An Ocean City favorite since 1939, this eatery began as an ice cream parlor but is now popular as a restaurant. The atmosphere is homey, a "Mom's kitchen" kind of place. Before you indulge in their ice cream, try the comfort foods. You can't go wrong with simple, fresh entrees like fried chicken, Virginia ham, or crab cakes. Lunch choices include sandwiches, salads, subs, and soups. No liquor is served and there are small kids' menus for breakfast, lunch, and dinner. Save room for dessert. Dumser's is still an ice-cream parlor at heart and offers over 20 varieties of sundaes. A second location, **Dumser's Drive-In,** 49th and Coastal Highway (ℂ **410/524-1588**), with a more limited menu, is also open year-round. Both are good options for families with kids. If you want just ice cream, there are three boardwalk locations.

12305 Coastal Hwy. ℂ **410/250-5543.** Main courses $6.60–$16.95; lunch $2.69–$7.95; breakfast $2.95–$6.79. MC, V. Mid-June to Labor Day daily 7am–midnight; Sept to mid-June daily 7am–9pm.

Paul Revere Smorgasbord *Value* AMERICAN/INTERNATIONAL   With eight colonial-style dining rooms, this huge restaurant can accommodate up to 700 diners. One price prevails here for an all-you-can-eat buffet of more than 100 items, ranging from soups, salads, roast beef, turkey, fried chicken, ribs, seafood, and pasta to a tempting dessert bar. Beer and wine are served and there are early-bird specials that offer meal discounts of up to 15%.

2nd St. and Boardwalk. ℂ **410/524-1776.** Buffet $8.99, $5.99 for ages 9–12, $3.99 for ages 5–8. DISC, MC, V. Mid-May to mid-Sept daily 4–9pm. Closed mid-Sept to mid-May.

OCEAN CITY AFTER DARK

From people-watching on the boardwalk, to a game of miniature golf or beach volleyball, to cocktails at the hundreds of beach and bayside bars, in season

Ocean City has almost as much nightlife as it has sand. But if you are looking for standout establishments, there are only a few; and if you are looking for refinement or culture, you might want to check Rehoboth or Dewey beaches (see earlier in this chapter). Here are our votes for the best nighttime haunts in Ocean City. Many are open on weekends in the off-season and you can count on a party for New Year's Eve.

CLUBS & BARS

Fager's Island Fager's Island bar with its dark wood and surrounding Tiffany lamps is a popular watering hole for the well-heeled and over-30 set. In season they have a popular Monday night deck party overlooking the bay. 60th St. (on the bay). ✆ 410/524-5500.

Mackey's Bayside Bar & Grill No live music, no dancing, but also no cover. Mackey's is just one of our favorite laid-back bayside bars in town. 54th St. (on the bay). ✆ 410/723-5565.

Party Block Three clubs in one block have merged into one big party. The Paddock and Big Kahuna's have been around for years. Party Block Rush is the newest club, designed as a South Beach dance club, replacing Dr. Croontoon's. It's one of *the* places for college-age and 20-somethings to meet and dance for one cover (about $5). It's the place to be on summer weekends when the music's pounding and the dance floor is full. 17th St. and Coastal Hwy. ✆ 410/289-6331.

Scandal's Night Club and Sports Bar Located a block from the convention center, Scandal's caters to a crowd of mostly 20- and 30-somethings. Although it has a sports bar boasting two large-screen TVs and lots of smaller ones, on most summer nights after about 10:30, action shifts to the dance floor, where a pretty good light system and a mix of what is typically referred to as "dance" music will help you thump and gyrate the night away. Scandal's is also renowned for its fish bowl draft beers. 44th St. Shopping Center. ✆ 410/723-0500. Cover $5.

Seacrets, Jamaica U.S.A. Seacrets is a Caribbean-themed mega beach bar and grill on the bay side. Once you enter, you are surrounded by a maze of palm trees, dangling lights, bars (at least seven), and sand (it's a good idea to leave the high heels in your room). There is a large covered dancing area where crowds of young and old are treated to live reggae or deejayed party music, ranging from the obligatory "Margaritaville" to tunes by more recent bands. Seacrets also serves food but it's best to come very early and you'll be assured of a good table and good service. We took kids here for an early dinner and they loved the theme park decor, especially the sand on the floor. For some reason, the combination of palm trees and the view of the Isle of Wight Bay from Seacret's beach works, making this a great place to watch the sunset. However, because much of Seacrets is outside, it might not be the best choice if rain is in the forecast. Cover varies but is usually $3 or more. 49th St. (on the bay). ✆ 410/524-4900.

ATTRACTIONS

Wheels of Yesterday Car enthusiasts will enjoy strolling through this relatively new museum, founded in 1997. Curator Jack Jarvis will lead you through the collection of more than 30 classic cars and exhibits, most of which are part of the private collection of Granville D. Trimper, owner of many of the rides and amusements at Ocean City's pier. Favorites include a 1928 seven-passenger Lincoln, several Model T Fords, Jack Benny's Overland, a Model-T fire engine complete with Dalmatian and firefighter, and a replica of a 1950s service station. New in 2001 is the 1952 Chevy used in the movie *Hoosiers*.

12708 Ocean Gateway (Rte. 50). (℃ 410/213-7329. Admission $4 adults, $2 ages 12 and under. June–Sept daily 9am–9pm, Oct–May 9am–5pm. Take the Rte. 50 bridge out of Ocean City. The museum is on the left, across from the shopping outlets.

Ocean City Life-Saving Station Museum On the southern tip of the boardwalk in a restored 1891 life-saving station, this museum focuses on the history of the U.S. Life-Saving Service in Maryland, Delaware, and Virginia, and includes some life-saving artifacts, including a life car and a restored rescue boat. In addition, there are displays of dollhouse models depicting Ocean City in its early years; a pictorial history of the significant hurricanes and storms that have hit the Mid-Atlantic coast; saltwater aquariums with indigenous sea life; a mermaid exhibit; and a unique collection of sands from around the world.

Boardwalk at the Inlet (P.O. Box 603). (℃ 410/289-4991. Admission $2 adults, $1 under age 12. June–Sept daily 11am–10pm, May and Oct daily 11am–4pm, Nov–Apr Sat–Sun 11am–4pm.

ESPECIALLY FOR KIDS: AMUSEMENT PARKS, MINIATURE GOLF & WATER SLIDES

Ocean City claims to be the number one family resort on the East Coast and is home to several amusement parks and child-oriented activities. Before you head for the attractions, stop by the Convention and Visitors Bureau at 39th Street, where they usually have coupons for everything from mini-golf to go-carts.

Ocean City Pier Rides The rides here appeal mostly to older kids and teens who like centrifugal force, but the Ferris wheel is a highlight for all ages. Rising high above almost everything else in old Ocean City, it offers spectacular views of the ocean, the beach, and the boardwalk. It's a wonderful place to be at sunset. The rest of the rides seem to change every season, although the Venetian double-decker carousel is always in its place.

On the Inlet in Downtown Ocean City. (℃ 410/289-3031.

Trimper's Rides and Amusement Park Established in 1887, this is the granddaddy of O.C. amusement areas. It has over 100 rides and attractions for the whole family, including a water flume and a gorgeous 1902 merry-go-round with hand-carved animals. Most rides average $1.50, but a wristband, costing $10, allows unlimited rides between noon and 6pm on weekends and 1 and 6pm on weekdays. The park is open daily, May through September, noon or 1pm to midnight, and on weekends from February to April and October to November. Weekend hours vary outside the summer season.

Boardwalk near the Inlet, between South Division and South 1st sts. (℃ 410/289-8617.

Jolly Roger This park is home to SpeedWorld (the largest go-cart racing complex of its kind in the United States), two miniature golf courses, a water park, and more than 30 rides and other attractions. The go-cart tracks have minimum height requirements. Each attraction is individually priced. SpeedWorld go-cart rides cost from $4 to $6.15; miniature golf is $4.50 to $5; the water park is $17 per half day or $21 a day; and other rides are $2.20 to $3.50 each. The park is open daily Memorial Day through Labor Day; SpeedWorld is open noon to midnight; park rides run from 2pm to midnight; the mini-golf is open 10am to midnight. SpeedWorld and the miniature golf courses are also open March through May and September through October, with reduced hours.

30th St. and Coastal Hwy. (℃ 410/289-3477.

Fun Fact **Mini-Golf Mania**

Ocean City may have the highest concentration of **mini-golf courses** of any barrier island on earth. Here's a rundown of the best on the island:

Old Pro Underwater Golf, 68th Street and Coastal Highway (© 410/ 524-2645). There are eight Old Pro Golf courses at four locations in Ocean City. All are good; two made our "best" list. Underwater Golf is the newest and for our money the best mini-golf in O.C. Although it's not actually under water, the course is entirely enclosed in a hangar-like barn that makes it one of the most fun places to be in O.C. when it's raining. The sets and props include a submarine that you play in and on and a hanging plaster killer whale. The holes, while not always difficult, are well thought out and fun; most include hills and curves, and many include shoots that drop your ball into (sometimes easy, sometimes not so easy) locations on lower greens. Large windows on one side open to let in a cool breeze.

Garden of Eden Miniature Golf, 18th Street and Coastal Highway (© 410/289-5495). If you're looking for a more challenging course in a less childish setting, give Garden of Eden a try. There are no giant plaster whales or gorillas, just a man-made waterfall and pond, and well-kept flowers and shrubbery surrounding a fun and interesting brick-lined course. Many holes offer more than one route to the cup, some involving chutes and one a loop. So put on your thinking cap and tee up.

Jungle Golf, next to Jolly Roger Park, 30th Street and Coastal Highway (© 410/289-3477). If you like fake animals on your golf course, this one's for you. Plastic lions and a rhinoceros look on as you negotiate 18 holes that wrap around and climb the sides of a series of man-made waterfalls. Although this course has one lame hole early on (in essence a flat, straight 10-foot putt), most are fun, and there are a few challenging and steep holes on the back nine that ensure you end your round with a thrill. Since this is part of the Jolly Roger Park, when you're done you can ride in the go-carts.

Professor Hakker's Lost Treasure Golf, 130th Street and Coastal Highway (© 410/250-5678). You can't miss this mini-golf course. It's got an airplane on the roof. There are two courses: Gold and Diamond. The decor is reminiscent of the *Indiana Jones* movies. You'll encounter water traps, caves, and even a bridge. The holes are fairly easy but the theme is what makes this one fun. There's even parking here.

Frontier Town *Kids* The cowboys and outlaws try hard to make you think you're in the Old West—and the stagecoach robbery may scare a younger child. There are train rides, pony rides, can-can shows, bank holdups, gunfights, and swaggering cowboys. Frontier Town has been stuck in the Old West for 40 years.

It was a winner in 1959 and it still is. In a separate park (with separate admission), there's a newer water park and mini-golf. Parking is free. Old West park admission is $10 for ages 11 and older, $8 ages 4 to 10, including all rides and shows. The park is open 10am to 6pm. Water park and mini-golf are $10 for everybody; for unlimited, all day mini-golf, it's $4 for ages 11 and over, $2 for ages 4 to 10. Night mini-golf admission from 6 to 10pm is $4 ages 11 and older, $2 ages 4 to 10. Water park is open 10am to 6pm. Combo ticket for both parks is $16 for ages 11 and older, $13 ages 4 to 10. Parking is free for both parks.

Rte. 611, 4 miles (6km) south of Rte. 50. Take Rte. 50 west and turn left on Rte. 611 toward Assateague. Call ℂ 410/289-7877 for Old West. Call ℂ 410/641-0693 for water park.

BEYOND THE BEACH: OTHER OUTDOOR ACTIVITIES

BIKING An early morning ride down the boardwalk is traditional for lots of families. Cyclists on Coastal Highway share a lane with the buses. A headlight and rear reflector are required on all bicycles on the road after dark. Boardwalk biking is allowed between 5 and 10am during the summer, and anytime in the off-season. Rental rates vary according to the type of bike, but you can expect to pay between $4 and $6 an hour for a two-wheeler, $8 an hour for a tandem. Two of the best sources are **Continental Cycle,** 73rd and Coastal Highway (ℂ **410/ 524-1313**); and **Mike's Bikes,** 1st Street (ℂ **410/289-4637**).

FISHING Since Ocean City is surrounded by the waters of the Atlantic Ocean and four different bays, fishing boats abound. The fishing departures usually run from April to October.

Most boats set sail from one of Ocean City's two main fishing marinas: the **Ocean City Fishing Center** (ℂ **800/322-3065** or 410/213-1121; www.oc fishing.com) at the Shantytown Pier just across the Route 50 bridge in West Ocean City; and the **Bahia Marina** (ℂ **888/575-DOCK** or 410/289-7438; www.bahiamarina.com) on the bay between 21st and 22nd streets. Call either of them for information on the kinds of boats available, as well as their rates and departure times. Another reliable headboat is *The Angler* (ℂ **410/289-7424**), which operates out of a pier at Talbot Street on the bay, just south of the Route 50 bridge. Generally rates range from around $7 to $20 for short sightseeing trips (more for sailboat tours) to $20 to $40 for longer headboat fishing trips. Trips leave as early as 7:30am, so call for departure times. Rod rentals are typically available. Some headboats not affiliated with the Ocean City Fishing Center also depart from the Shantytown Pier area, so it might be worth stopping by to see what is available and if they are offering better rates.

SURF FISHING Surf fishing is permitted on all the public beaches of Ocean City. However, between 9am and 6pm you cannot fish within 50 yards of swimmers or of anyone on the beach, which, in peak season, can be nearly impossible. **Public fishing piers** are located at Inlet Park (this one charges a fee), as well as bay side at the 3rd Street Pier, 9th Street Pier, Convention Center Pier (at 40th St.), and Northside Park (at 125th St.). **Fishing supplies** and tackle can be found at Bahia Marina Inc., 22nd Street and the bay (ℂ **410/289- 7438**); and at Blue Marlin Tackle Co., Ocean City Fishing Center (ℂ **410/ 213-0090**).

WATER SPORTS   From April through October, O.C. is a hotbed of sailing, parasailing, windsurfing, jet-skiing, powerboating, waterskiing, and more. Prices depend on type of equipment and duration of rental, but many boats can be rented for $30 to $70 an hour. Water skis and smaller equipment start at about $10 an hour, jet skis at about $60 an hour. For full information, contact one of the following: **Advanced Marina Boat Rentals,** 122 66th St. and the bay (© **410/723-2124**); **Bahia Marina,** on the bay between 21st and 22nd streets (© **410/289-7438**); or **Bay Sports,** 22nd Street and the bay (© **410/ 289-2144**).

COAST CRUISES   For sightseeing at top speed and splash, *Sea Rocket,* S. Division Street (next to the Coast Guard station; © **410/289-5887**) is a great diversion from the beach and fun for kids. This 70-foot, 150-passenger open-top speedboat zooms along the waters of Ocean City and through the Assateague Island channel. *Insider tip:* People in the very back tend to get very wet (people in the front get less wet, and those in the middle get the least wet). So save this ride for a warm day when a little sea spray is a welcome thing. The trip lasts about 50 minutes and costs $8 for adults, $5 for ages 7 to 10, and free for children under 7 with an adult. Departures run every hour or two from late May to September.

GOLF   Ocean City now promotes itself as a major golfing destination, and there are many courses that welcome visitors (as well as vacation packages designed for people who want to spend time on the links).

The following courses welcome visitors and can be contacted individually or through the **Ocean City Golf Getaway Association,** 6101 Coastal Hwy., Ocean City, MD 21842 (© **800/4-OC-GOLF;** www.oceancitygolf.com).

Most courses in the area use a multi-tiered system for greens fees, which means they vary from morning to afternoon to evening. However, fees generally range from $40 to $96, with cheaper rates in the off-season and on summer afternoons. *Insider tip:* Consider starting a round at about 4pm; the rates don't usually increase in the early evenings and the temperatures have started to drop. Fall rates are usually the highest and if you're a January golfer, you'll find bargains here. All courses are open year-round from dawn to dusk.

The Bay Club   Only 8 miles (13km) from the boardwalk, Bay Club offers two 18-hole par-72 championship courses. Facilities include a clubhouse, driving range, practice green, club rentals, and lessons. Greens fees in summer run $35 to $55, higher in early summer. They include a cart.

9122 Libertytown Rd., Berlin. © **800/BAY-CLUB** or 410/641-4081. www.thebayclub.com.

Beach Club Golf Links   A reserved tee time is recommended at this semi-private club that has two 18-hole par-72 championship courses. It has a clubhouse, pro shop, club rentals, driving range, and putting green. Greens fees range from $37 to $72. Children play for free after 3pm with paying adult.

9715 Deer Park Dr., Berlin. © **800/435-9223** or 410/641-GOLF. www.beachclubgolflinks.com.

Eagle's Landing Golf Course   The lovely scenery here may distract you from your game. This public 18-hole course has some challenges to keep you on your toes. It also features a driving range, club rentals, lessons, pro shop, practice facilities, and clubhouse restaurant. Reservations are recommended. Greens fees in summer run about $65 with cart, $40 without.

12367 Eagle's Nest Rd., Berlin. © **800/283-3846** or 410/213-7277. www.eagleslandinggolf.com.

Ocean City Golf & Yacht Club   Founded in 1959, this club recently rebuilt its two USGA-rated 18-hole championship courses, a seaside par-73 and a bayside par-72. There are a clubhouse, bar, and pro shop. Greens fees range from $40 to $86 in the summer.

11401 Country Club Dr., Berlin. ℭ 800/442-3570 or 410/641-1779. www.ocgolfandyacht.com.

Pine Shore Golf-North   This public course includes a 27-hole mid-length executive golf course, putting green, practice range, pro shop, and clubhouse with snack bar. Tee times are accepted for 18 holes. Summertime greens fees range from $19 to $25 without a cart and $24 to $35 with a cart.

11285 Beauchamp Rd., Berlin. ℭ 877/446-5398 or 410/641-5100. www.pineshoregolf.com.

Pine Shore Golf-South   This public course is an 18-hole mid-length course, completed in the fall of 2001. Summertime greens fees range from $19 to $25 without a cart and $24 to $35 with a cart.

8219 Stephen Decatur Hwy. (Rte. 611), Berlin. ℭ 877/779-3300 or 410/641-3300. www.pineshoregolf.com.

River Run   A Gary Player 18-hole signature course, the par-71 River Run is a favorite in the area. Facilities include gas golf carts, a pro shop, a locker room, beverage carts, PGA golf pros, and a driving range and putting greens. Reserving a tee time is recommended. Greens fees in summer run $35 to $89.

11605 Masters Lane, Berlin. ℭ 800/733-RRUN or 410/641-7200. www.riverrungolf.com.

Rum Pointe Seaside Golf Links   This 18-hole par-72 championship course, designed by the father/son team of P. B. and Pete Dye, is one of the O.C. area's newest courses. Seventeen of the 18 holes overlook Sinepuxent Bay and nearby Assateague Island. Course facilities include a pro shop, driving range and practice facilities, PGA golf pro, clubhouse with full-service restaurant, and beverage cart. Reserving your tee time is recommended. Summer time fees run $55 to $96 and include cart and GPS system.

7000 Rum Pointe Lane, Berlin. ℭ 888/809-4653 or 410/629-1414. www.rumpointe.com.

HORSE RACING   **Bally's** at Ocean Downs, Route 50 (at Rte. 589; ℭ **410/ 641-0600**), 4 miles (6km) west of Ocean City, features harness racing 12 races each night. On Monday, Wednesday, and Thursday in season, and on all nights during spring and fall, there is simulcast TV racing from other tracks. Grandstand admission and parking are free. Clubhouse admission is extra and the rates are subject to change. It's open from early July to early September. Race dates vary; post time is usually 7:30pm but may vary (call to check). The racetrack is a seedy little place but it's very kid friendly. Winning trotters are led to the winner's circle where children gather around and get a close look. A parade of horses starts each evening's races and one horse usually gets close enough for the children to pet. Many of the horses and their drivers are local, too. It's a cheap diversion from the bustle and expense of Ocean City (unless you start betting).

JUST DOWN THE ROAD

Just a few minutes away is the small shore town of **Salisbury,** which hosts a museum and baseball team and is just a short drive or bus ride from O.C.

Ward Museum of Wildfowl Art ★★   Named for Lem and Steve Ward, brothers from Crisfield who turned decoy carving into an art, this museum houses the world's largest collection of contemporary and classic wildfowl art. The building sits on the edge of Schumaker Pond in a small wildfowl sanctuary and habitat, so the flock of resident Canada geese and ducks will set the stage for your visit. The 30,000-square-foot all-white structure houses works of the Ward brothers and has galleries tracing the history of decoy making, from Native American reed figures to the most recent winners of the Ward World Championship Carving Competition, held each spring in Ocean City. Highlights include two life-size tundra swan carved from stumps, several tiny wooden birds perched on branches so small and delicate they would hardly support a real starling, and a spectacular scene of a hawk attacking ducks in which the four birds are suspended in midair among a tangle of reeds. Ask a member of the knowledgeable staff to show you the difference between pieces that use inserted feathers and those made of solid wood. The museum has programs for children and workshops on carving for adults. Even the gift shop is exceptional, with everything from fishing gear to luggage, as well as the usual gift items.

909 Schumaker Dr., Salisbury, MD 21804. ⓒ 410/742-4988. www.wardmuseum.org. Admission $7 adults, $5 seniors, $3 students; $17 family except Sun when admission is $8.50 per family. Mon–Sat 10am–5pm, Sun noon–5pm. From Rte. 50 turn onto Rte. 13 south; turn left onto College Ave., which will veer left and become Beaglin Park Dr.; the museum is on the right.

Delmarva Shorebirds   The Class A South Atlantic League affiliate of the Baltimore Orioles were league champs in 1997 and 2000, and play near Ocean City at Arthur W. Perdue Stadium in Salisbury. Ryan Minor, a former Shorebird, took over Cal Ripken's position when the Iron Man decided to end his streak.

Arthur W. Perdue Stadium. Hobbs Rd. ⓒ 888/BIRDS96 or 410/219-3112 for tickets. www.theshorebirds. com. From Ocean City, take Rte. 50 west to Salisbury. Turn left on Hobbs Rd.

SHOPPING

The shopping in Ocean City may not be high class, but there's a lot of it. The boardwalk, the outlet center, dozens of strip malls along Coastal Highway, and small-town antiques in nearby Berlin are all happy to take visitors' money.

If you enter town from the Route 50 bridge, you can't miss the **Ocean City Factory Outlets** (ⓒ 800/625-6696), a half mile from the bridge, on the mainland at the intersection of Golf Course Road. This complex is home to 40 brand-name outlet stores, including Ann Taylor, Bass, Jockey, Levi's, Mikasa, Nine West, Oshkosh, Reebok, and Tommy Hilfiger. Parking is free and plentiful though, as in the rest of Ocean City, it can be difficult during peak season. The complex is open Sunday through Thursday 10am to 6pm, and Friday and Saturday 10am through 9pm, but it's open until at least 8pm June through August. The other area outlet center is in **Rehoboth, Delaware.** It's considerably bigger, and you save the 5% state sales tax. If you're a serious shopper, you may want to take the short trip north. See the Rehoboth section earlier in this chapter.

Perhaps the most popular and populated shopping destination in O.C. is the boardwalk—27 blocks of souvenir shops, candy stores, restaurants and snack shacks, and, of course, T-shirt shops. You'll find much of the same merchandise in all the T-shirt and souvenir shops, but there are a couple places worth visiting. **Ocean Gallery World Center** (ⓒ 410/289-5300) at 2nd Street is a standout, with its mosaiclike facade of art from around the world. Its three stories are full of art posters, prints, and original oil paintings, all for sale at closeout prices. **The Kite Loft,** at 5th Street and Boardwalk (ⓒ 410/289-6852), has a large selection of kites (from simple to really cool), flags, windsocks, and toys. You may even see a pig fly. They have other stores on 45th and 131st streets.

> ┌ *Fun Fact* **Duck! It's a T-Shirt!**
>
> The unofficial uniform of O.C. is an **MR Ducks shirt.** They're available at
> two stores, one at Somerset and the Boardwalk (℡ **410/289-4510**) and
> another at 140th and Coastal Highway (℡ **410/250-3770**). The MR does
> not stand for "Mister," but for the Eastern Shore way of talking. Two duck
> hunters are talking in the woods: "M R ducks." "M R not." "O S A R. C M
> Wangs?" "L I B—M R ducks." (Translation: Them are ducks. Them are not.
> Oh, yes they are. See them wings? Well, I'll be. Them are ducks.)

If you need something sweet, you can't miss **Candy Kitchen.** It specializes in
fudge and salt-water taffy and has numerous locations. But if you are down at
the inlet end of the Boardwalk, stop in **Wockenfuss Candy** ★★ (Boardwalk &
1st St.; ℡ **410/289-5054**) for their fine chocolates and sublime carmallows. You
can tell the Baltimore-based candy shop by the crowd that never goes away.

5 Assateague Island National Seashore ★★

More than 2.5 million people come to Assateague Island each year to see the
famed wild horses. The small, fat ponies, mottled brown and white, will come
right up to your car if they feel like it. Or they'll ignore you, grazing in the
marshland away from the road. On the Maryland half of this 37-mile (60km)
long barrier island, you can see the ponies up close. They are harder to see on
the Virginia side, where they tend to stay farther from the walking trails.

While it's a worthy destination, Assateague is not without its challenges. First
of all, there are the 2.5 million people. The easily accessible areas of the island are
always crowded in the summer, so if you come here with romantic notions of a
deserted beach, inhabited only by the untamed and free ponies, you'll have to go
a little out of the way, on foot, by small boat, or by off-road vehicle. Then there's
Assateague's second most famous inhabitants—the mosquitoes. They really are as
bad as the brochures, guidebooks, and park rangers tell you, so come prepared
with bug spray, citronella candles, and long sleeves. Compared to nearby Ocean
City, Assateague is still wild and primitive—no hotels, restaurants, convenience
stores, or gas stations. Just people. And ponies. And mosquitoes.

Assateague is in fact two state parks (Maryland and Virginia) and a national
park. We indicate which authority has jurisdiction over which parts in the
descriptions of rules, regulations and activities below. For specific information
about the Virginia side of the island, see *Frommer's Virginia.*

ACCESS   The only access to the Maryland side of Assateague by car is via
Maryland Route 611 south, which meets up with Route 50 just west of Ocean
City. To get to the Virginia side of the island, take Virginia Route 175 west
across Chincoteague Island. You cannot drive from one end to the other.

VISITOR CENTERS   The National Park Service operates a visitor center—
the **Barrier Island Visitor Center** (℡ 410/641-1441), on Route 611 before
you cross the bridge onto Assateague; and the **Campground Office** (℡ 410/
641-3030), which is inside the park. The Barrier Island Visitor Center is the
place to go for brochures, exhibits, two aquariums, three videos about the island
and its wildlife, and a gift shop. It's open 9am to 5pm daily. Maryland also operates Assateague State Park at the northern end of the island. It connects to the
national park but has its own amenities, regulations, and fees.

FEES & REGULATIONS Assateague State Park (© **410/641-2120**) charges admission Memorial Day through Labor Day, Thursday through Tuesday $2 per person, Wednesday $1 per person.

Admission to the National Seashore is $5 per car or $2 per person year-round and is good for a week. Most national park regulations apply. Permits are required for backcountry camping and for use of off-road vehicle areas. Pets are allowed only in the national park and must be on a leash. And, of course, don't feed the ponies.

SEASONS Maryland's state park is open for day use April 1 through December 1. The National Seashore and Chincoteague National Wildlife Refuge are open year-round. There is no daily closing time on the Maryland side of the island, but only surf fishermen and campers who are staying in designated spots are allowed to stay overnight.

AVOIDING THE CROWDS & THE BUGS Weekends during the summer are crowded. If you plan to camp, make reservations in the national park or come early to the state park, where reservations for less than a weeklong stay are not accepted. The human population is not the biggest nuisance: Mosquitoes, biting flies, and ticks are abundant from April through September, and mosquitoes are especially a problem beginning at the end of July and following a heavy or steady rain. They are also much worse on the bay side of the island, so try to get an oceanside site if you're camping in the national park. Your best bet for avoiding the bugs is waiting until it gets cold enough to kill them all off.

The good news is that sea breezes from the Atlantic keep the mosquitoes pretty much off the beach itself. So once you make it to the surf, you're safe.

RANGER PROGRAMS The National Park Service offers a wide variety of ranger-led programs on a weekly basis throughout the summer, including nature hikes, surf rescue demonstrations, canoe trips, campfire programs, and surf fishing and shellfishing demonstrations. For a complete rundown of these activities, pick up a copy of *Assateague Island,* a visitors' guide to activities and events, at one of the visitor centers, or contact Assateague Island National Seashore, 7206 National Seashore Lane, Berlin, MD 21811 (© **410/641-1441**).

SEEING THE PONIES

It may come as quite a surprise to visitors that finding and viewing the famed wild horses takes almost no effort, especially on the Maryland side of the island, where the ponies have virtually free reign. In fact, you'll probably have to stop for a few begging ponies along the side of the road as you enter. (For your own safety, that of the ponies, and your car, roll up your windows and do not feed them.) If you're camping, you may hear a pack of horses stroll by your tent in the middle of the night or see the telltale signs in the morning. For a more picturesque setting, stop by the beach in the evening after the crowds have left; packs of four to six, and an occasional lone pony, roam the beach regularly.

On the Virginia side, the ponies are less accessible; you can generally see them along the paved road called the Wildlife Tour, in the fenced marshes south of Beach Road, and from the observation platform on the Woodland Trail.

The annual **Pony Penning and Auction** ⭐, a unique exercise in population control, is held on Chincoteague Island, a barrier island adjoining Assateague, the last Wednesday and Thursday of July. The Chincoteague "cowboys" round up the Virginia herd on Wednesday, and thousands of spectators watch as the horses swim from Assateague to Chincoteague, where the foals are auctioned off

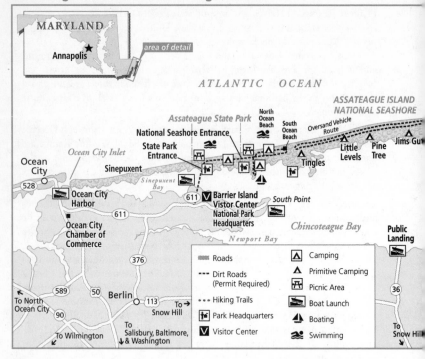

MARYLAND

Annapolis

area of detail

ATLANTIC OCEAN

ASSATEAGUE ISLAND
NATIONAL SEASHORE

Assateague State Park

North Ocean Beach

South Ocean Beach

Oversand Vehicle Route

National Seashore Entrance

State Park Entrance

Ocean City Inlet

Jims Gut

Little Levels

Pine Tree

Tingles

Ocean City

Sinepuxent

528

Ocean City Harbor

Sinepuxent Bay

611

Barrier Island Visitor Center

National Park Headquarters

South Point

Chincoteague Bay

Public Landing

611

Ocean City Chamber of Commerce

Newport Bay

376

589   50   Berlin

To North Ocean City

90

113   To → Snow Hill

36

To Salisbury, Baltimore, & Washington

To Wilmington

To Snow Hill

Roads		Camping
Dirt Roads (Permit Required)		Primitive Camping
Hiking Trails		Picnic Area
Park Headquarters		Boat Launch
Visitor Center		Boating
		Swimming

the next day. Campsites and hotel rooms (only available on Chincoteague and the mainland) fill up fast, so make reservations well ahead of time. If you are staying in Ocean City, get up before dawn and drive the 60 miles (97km) to Chincoteague. You'll make it in time for the pony swim and be back in Ocean City for dinner.

Although it's exciting to see the ponies swim across the channel, be aware that thousands of people come to witness the annual event. You may only see the ponies as tiny dots as you wait along the shore shoulder to shoulder with hundreds of new friends. Traffic on the small island is almost too much to handle.

OUTDOOR ACTIVITIES

CANOEING, KAYAKING & BOATING   The only launch facility on the island is for canoes. It's at the end of Ferry Landing Road on the Maryland side. Larger boats can be launched from **West Ocean City Harbor;** the state park facility off Route 611, across from the Barrier Island Visitor Center; **South Point Boat Ramp;** or the public landing at the end of Route 385 east of Snow Hill.

Waters at the Maryland end of Chincoteague Bay are usually ideal for canoeing, though the tidal currents around Chincoteague Island are strong. The bay is generally shallow, so operators of larger boats should watch for sandbars. During the summer, you can rent canoes from the concessionaire at the end of Bayside Drive. Four backcountry canoe-in campsites are located on the Maryland end of the island. Permits are required and can be obtained in person at the ranger station on the Maryland side or at the Toms Cove Visitor Center in Virginia.

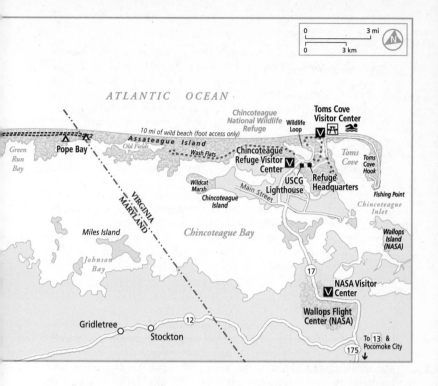

CRABBING, CLAMMING & FISHING Pick up the **"Shellfishing in Maryland"** brochure at the visitor center for a map showing the best places to catch crabs, clams, and mussels. The best time to crab is late summer to early fall, in the morning or early evening. The most common method is the string, bait, and net method. Attach a piece of bony chicken or a fish head to the string (chicken necks are the preferred bait), and cast out in shallow water. When you feel a tug, gently tow the line in. If there's a crab on the end, net it before you take it out of the water, then transfer it to a basket or other container and continue crabbing.

A single collapsible crab pot or trap may also be used, if it is attended at all times. You can purchase a crab pot at bait-and-tackle shops; they look like large chicken-wire boxes. Place bait in the center of the trap, drop it in clear, shallow water, and pull it up as soon as a crab walks in. (On Assateague the crab pot has to be attended; if it weren't for this rule, you could leave the pot out for several hours and maybe get several crabs when you pull it up.) All crabs must measure 5 inches point to point and all egg-bearing females must be returned. Limits are 1 bushel per person per day, or 2 bushels per boat per day. Crabbing is prohibited January through March.

Signing and raking are accepted methods for clamming. The mudflats at Virginia's Toms Cove are more suitable for signing. To sign for clams, walk along the mudflats at low tide and look for small keyhole openings or "signs," indicating the presence of a clam. Then dig it out with a hand trowel or small digging tool. Raking can be done at any tide level, but you need a clamming rake, which has a basket to catch the clams. Drag the rake through the mud until the

---

Tips **Don't Horse Around with the Ponies**

When you see the horses, remember they are wild. Do not be fooled by their gentle appearance and willingness to approach you and your car looking for handouts. The ponies are prone to unpredictable behavior and they will bite and kick, so do not attempt to feed or pet them. Also, please drive carefully; at least one pony a year is hit and killed by a car.

---

tines scrape a shell; then dig up the mud, shake it loose, and catch the clam in the basket. Clams must be 1 inch wide, and the limit is 1 bushel per person per day.

Mussels and oysters are rare in the waters surrounding the island. Oysters are rarely found off the private, leased beds (and trespassing is prohibited). The park service asks that you take only what you will consume in mussels and oysters.

No saltwater license is required for surf fishing on the coast, though an after-hours permit is required on the Virginia end of the island. Fishing is prohibited on the guarded beaches and in the designated surf zones.

HIKING & CYCLING   Conditions and trails for hiking and biking are generally better at the Virginia end of the island, but there are three self-guided hiking trails on the Maryland end: Life of the Marsh, Life of the Forest, and Life of the Dunes. All are short, and all require bug repellent. Cyclists can use the 3-mile (5km) paved bike path along Bayberry Drive and the Oceanside campground.

In Virginia, about half of the 15 miles (24km) of trails are paved for cycling. The Wildlife Tour is closed to automobile traffic until 3pm each day, so hikers and bikers can have it all to themselves. The Woodland Trail, which leads to a pony observation platform, is also paved.

OFF-ROAD VEHICLES   The vast majority of Assateague is not accessible by car; however, off-road (or over-sand) vehicle routes run most of the length of the island. Permits are required and are issued on a yearly basis for a fee of $60. The list of regulations and conditions is long and complex, so contact the Camping Office and request a copy of their off-road vehicles brochure. Detailed information is on the website at www.nps.gove/asis.

CAMPING

Accommodations on the island are limited to the **Assateague State Park campground** (© **410/641-2120** or 410/641-2918) and the two campgrounds and several backcountry campsites run by the National Park Service. The state-run facility, open April 1 through October 31, has 311 sites and offers bathhouses with flush toilets and hot and cold running water, a small camp store, and a snack bar. Reservations are accepted only for stays of a week or longer. All sites are on the ocean side of the island and cost $20 per night.

The **National Park Service** operates an oceanside campground and a bayside campground, which are slightly more primitive than the state park facility (for information, call the office at © **410/641-3030**). They do, however, accept reservations from May 15 through October 31, so you won't end up at the island with no place to camp if you call ahead. And do make reservations; there will not be an empty campsite to be found on the island on a summer weekend (and many weekdays). Both campgrounds have chemical toilets, drinking water, and cold showers. There are also flush toilets and cold showers at the beach bathhouse. If possible, reserve a site at the oceanside campground; the mosquitoes and biting flies are much worse on the bay side. The cost is $14 per night from May 15 through October 31, and $10 per night the rest of the year.

In addition, the park has several backcountry or canoe-in campsites strewn along the Maryland end of the island. Each site has a chemical toilet and picnic table but no drinking water. You must pick up a backcountry permit from the ranger station to use these sites, but there is no fee.

If you don't mind staying off the island, Maryland's **Pocomoke River State Park** (℃ **410/632-2566**) is a less crowded and more comfortable option. It's about a 45-minute drive from the Virginia or Maryland end of the island and offers 250 improved campsites and eight cabins in a wooded environment along the Pocomoke River. In addition to camping, the park at **Shad Landing** offers a few extras: canoe and kayak rentals, a nature center, boat rentals, a swimming pool, and hiking and ORV trails. Best of all, the bugs are not as bad. Sites year-round are $23 for electric, $18 for non-electric, and $35 for sleeper cabins. The park also operates a smaller, more primitive park across the river at Milburn Landing. Its campsites are $18 for electric, $13 for non-electric, $35 for sleeper cabins. It's open from mid-March to mid-December. To make reservations for May 1 to September 30 call ℃ **888/432-2267** and enter the code POC, or visit www.dnr.state.md.us. To get there from Assateague, take Route 611 off the island, then turn left and follow Route 376 until you reach the town of Berlin; from there, take Route 113 south, and you'll hit the park a few miles south of the town of Snow Hill.

WHERE TO STAY NEARBY

For less primitive accommodations, you'll have to stay on the mainland or in Ocean City. The town of **Berlin** offers two good options discussed below. Both are about a 15-minute drive from the island.

SIDE TRIP TO BERLIN, MARYLAND

Barely 10 minutes away from the Ocean City boardwalk is the historic town of Berlin, Maryland. Its quaint stores and antiques shops have long been a favorite excursion for vacationers in Ocean City. It also has two of the best lodgings in the area, an excellent restaurant, and a great little theater. These amenities and a location roughly equidistant from Assateague and Ocean City make Berlin a good choice for travelers looking to split their time between the islands.

To get to Berlin from Ocean City, take the Route 50 bridge out of Ocean City and follow Route 50; take a left on Route 113; from there you'll hit Berlin in less than a mile. As you leave Ocean City proper via Route 50 you'll find the town of Berlin about 7 miles (11km) inland; the city of Salisbury is about 30 miles (48km) inland.

WHERE TO STAY

Atlantic Hotel ★★ Julia Roberts stayed here. So did Richard Gere. Part of the movie *Runaway Bride* was filmed in this hotel. A forthcoming children's movie, *Tuck Everlasting,* was filmed here, too. This three-story Victorian beauty with wraparound porch has plenty of modern amenities along with the old-fashioned charm. Guest rooms are furnished with local antiques and mahogany furniture. The Atlantic offers two sizes of rooms. The smaller rooms can be a bit tight but comfortable enough for $100 during peak season. Larger rooms are almost suites and are quite comfy.

2 N. Main St., Berlin, MD 21811. ℃ **800/814-7672** or 410/641-3589. Fax 410/641-4928. www.atlantic hotel.com. 16 units. July–Aug $85–$185 double; Sept–Oct and Apr–June $75–$135 double; Nov–Mar

$65–$120 double. Rates include breakfast. AE, DISC, MC, V. Free parking. From Ocean City, take Rte. 50 west to Rte. 113 (Main St.), a total of 7 miles (11km). **Amenities:** 2 restaurants; bar with singing waiter; reading parlor; outdoor balcony. *In room:* A/C.

Merry Sherwood Plantation ⭐   This 1859 plantation house underwent 2 years of restoration to turn it into the elegant country inn it is today. The host can tell you about each of the many antiques—from the hand-carved rosewood dining room table and chairs to the inn's pride and joy, a chair made for Queen Victoria. Guests are encouraged to use all the antiques, so go ahead—sit in Queen Victoria's seat or play the grand piano. Breakfast is a formal affair, complete with china, crystal, and silver. After, you can take a guided tour of the inn and get a peek at the other guest rooms. All are large and uniquely decorated. The two that share a bathroom have the most elaborate furnishings. The honeymoon suite is decorated with antique wedding memorabilia and has a whirlpool bath. Even if you can't stay here, it's worth a visit; the house is open for tours when it will not disturb the guests. Just call ahead.

8909 Worcester Hwy. (just south of Berlin on Rte. 113), Berlin, MD 21811. © **800/660-0358** or 410/ 641-2112. www.merrysherwood.com. 8 units (6 with private bathroom). $125–$150 double. Rates include full gourmet breakfast. MC, V. *In room:* A/C.

WHERE TO DINE

Atlantic Hotel Restaurant ⭐⭐⭐ INTERNATIONAL   It's worth the 15-minute drive from Ocean City to dine in this elegant Victorian restaurant, part of the Atlantic Hotel. The waiters in black tie are eager to serve; the lush decor and warm welcome make you want to stay for just one more course. The creative dinner menu often includes such specialties as filet mignon with béarnaise sauce; grilled duck in lemon zest beurre blanc; and rack of lamb with Montrachet goat cheese. In addition, guests are encouraged to personalize menu selections. If you like something a little more casual, try the Drummer's Cafe, which serves some of the excellent entrees of the Atlantic Restaurant as well as pub fare and sandwiches. On weekends, the waiter sings and piano music is featured.

2 N. Main St., Berlin. © **410/641-3589.** Reservations required in dining room. Main courses $26–$31; lunch (Drummer's Cafe) $6.95–$24.95. AE, MC, V. Main dining room daily 6–9pm; Drummer's Cafe daily 11:30am–9pm. From Ocean City, take Rte. 50 west 7 miles (11km) to Rte. 818 (Main St.).

AROUND BERLIN

The **Globe Theatre,** 12 Broad St., right behind the Atlantic Hotel (© **410/ 641-0784;** www.globetheater.com), is a restored movie theater that serves as a cultural center for Berlin. Enter through the bookstore and art gallery for a small cafe and intimate theater and stage. The Globe hosts a variety of nationally known jazz, blues, folk, and traditional artists, as well as readings by local authors, plays, and children's activities. Cover varies according to the artist, and reservations are suggested; call for times and to find out who might be playing.

   Duck Soup, the book/gift shop, is a great place to pick up some beach reading. **The Balcony Gallery** upstairs offers as fine a collection of paintings, sculpture, and other art by regional artists as you are likely to find near Ocean City.

   Berlin supports more than a couple of antiques stores, most notably **Town Center Antiques** (© **410/629-1895**), a small antiques mall that has expanded to two sites, 1 N. Main St. across from the Atlantic Hotel, and 113 N. Main St.

10

Wilmington

Set in a valley filled with America's castles, Wilmington celebrates its industrial nature with its new Riverfront. Although it's a work in progress, it's a lovely 1⅓-mile (2km) walk, dotted with warehouses and other industrial sites reborn as a market, shops, restaurants, offices, and museums. In a whimsical touch, gaily-colored cranes hover above.

As a Baltimorean who has watched the development of the Inner Harbor, I looked forward to seeing what Wilmington could do with its waterfront. Though not as flashy as Harborplace, and with fewer attractions, it's a promising beginning. I spent a few hours walking from the train station through the Tubman-Garrett Park to the Backstage Café, the USA

Riverfront Arts Center, the Shipyard Shops, and the urban nature preserve, and wished I had more time.

Wilmington is known for its museums, theater, restaurants, and well-appointed hotels, including the luxurious Hotel du Pont. Most visitors come for business—but this is a town for pleasure, too. Since Wilmington is very business-oriented, on weekends downtown can seem abandoned. That means weekend travelers can get great deals: hotel rooms at about half price, with free parking, a real value. Spend the day in the city's museums or Riverfront; head to New Castle's historic district or the Brandywine Valley's mansions and gardens; return to the city for a delicious meal and a good night's sleep.

1 Orientation

ARRIVING

BY PLANE Most people flying into Northern Delaware use the **Philadelphia International Airport** (© 215/937-6800), about a half-hour ride from downtown Wilmington. Many Wilmington hotels operate courtesy shuttles to and from the airport. Car-rental agencies at the airport include **Avis** (© 215/492-0900) and **Hertz** (© 215/492-7200).

Shuttle van service is available from **Delaware Express Shuttle** (© 800/648-5466 or 302/454-7800; www.delexpress.com) from the Philadelphia airport to the Wilmington area for about $30. For the most prompt service—and a better price—reserve by phone or online at least 24 hours ahead of arrival. Otherwise, look for the phone near the customer service center near baggage claim.

BY TRAIN Wilmington is a stop on **Amtrak**'s Northeast Corridor line (© 800/USA-RAIL), with Acela, Metroliner, and unreserved trains stopping here several times daily. The Wilmington Amtrak station is at Martin Luther King Boulevard and French Street, on the Riverfront. There's a taxi stand outside.

BY CAR The best way to drive to Wilmington is via I-95, which cuts across the city's center. The **Delaware Memorial Bridge** (part of I-295) connects Wilmington to the New Jersey Turnpike and points north. From southern

Delaware and the Eastern Shore of Maryland and Virginia, Route 13 will bring you into the city.

BY BUS Daily service is provided into the **Wilmington Transportation Center** at 101 N. French St. (© **302/655-6111**) by **Greyhound** (© **800/231-2222**) and **Trailways** (© **800/343-9999**).

VISITOR INFORMATION

A good selection of literature about Wilmington, the Brandywine Valley, and Historic New Castle is available from the **Greater Wilmington Convention and Visitors Bureau,** 100 W. 10th St., Suite 20, Wilmington, DE 19801 (© **800/422-1181;** www.VisitWilmingtonDE.org). For motorists passing through the area, the bureau has a **Visitors Information Center** on I-95 (© **302/737-4059**). It is located south of the city in the service area between Routes 273 and 896 and operates from 8am to 8pm; it also has an automatic hotel reservation system.

CITY LAYOUT

Three rivers surround Wilmington: the Brandywine, the Christina, and the Delaware. The **downtown** business area, wedged between the Brandywine and Christina, is laid out in a grid system, less than 20 blocks wide or long.

Note: Though the downtown area is relatively small, the attractions, restaurants, and hotels are spread out, with most either south of downtown or in the northern suburbs. Aside from a few museums and shops along the Market Street Mall, you really can't or wouldn't want to walk between the major attractions.

Two parts of Wilmington not downtown are worth a visit: the revitalized **Riverfront** area and the more suburban **north side.** The Riverfront is about a 5-minute drive south of downtown between I-95 and the Christina River. Home to outlet shops, an arts center, and other attractions, it can be tricky to get to from downtown (take Martin Luther King St. to Madison St. and follow the signs). Or, head back to I-95 and take exit 6. There's lots of free parking.

North Wilmington (north of Rte. 52 and northwest of I-95 features modest to lavish brick houses, parks, and a trendy neighborhood called Trolley Square. Route 52 and Delaware Avenue are the main thoroughfares, and as you continue out Route 52, north Wilmington gives way to rolling hills and the Brandywine Valley. Though you really can't walk there, you can drive there in a few minutes.

MAIN ARTERIES & STREETS Market Street runs north to south in downtown Wilmington. The east–west cross streets are numbered from 1st to 16th, with the lowest number on the southern end; the north–south streets bear the names of presidents, local heroes, and trees, in no definable order or system. Most streets are one-way, except for Market and 4th streets. I-95 enters Wilmington via two main avenues: Delaware Avenue (Rte. 52) on the north end of the city, and Martin Luther King Boulevard on the south.

From I-95 and downtown, approach Wilmington's north side by using Route 52, which splits into Pennsylvania Avenue (Rte. 52) and Delaware Avenue about 2 blocks north of I-95.

MAPS *Greater Wilmington's Guide to the Brandywine Valley,* a booklet produced and distributed by the Greater Wilmington Convention and Visitors Bureau, has detailed maps of downtown Wilmington and the Wilmington region with all the major attractions marked.

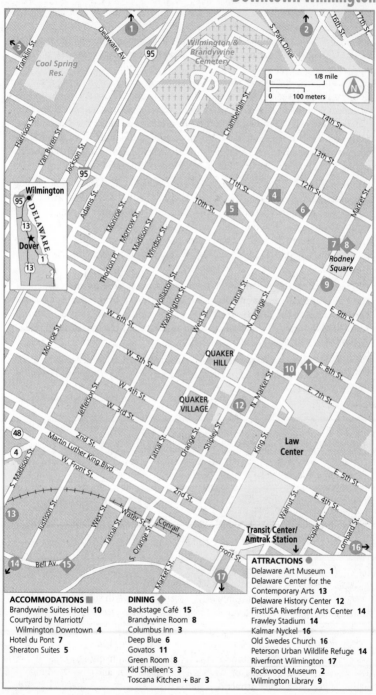

Downtown Wilmington

Cool Spring Res.

Wilmington & Brandywine Cemetery

Franklin St.
Delaware Av.
S. Park Drive
16th St.
17th St.

Harrison St.
Van Buren St.
Jackson St.
Chamberlain St.
14th St.
13th St.
12th St.
Market St.

Adams St.
Monroe St.
Morrow St.
Madison St.
Windsor St.
11th St.
10th St.

Wilmington
DELAWARE
Dover
95
13
1
13

Thornton Pl.
Wollaston St.
Washington St.
West St.
N. Tatnall St.
N. Orange St.
E. 9th St.

Rodney Square

Monroe St.
W. 6th St.
W. 5th St.

QUAKER HILL

E. 8th St.
E. 7th St.

Jefferson St.
W. 4th St.
W. 3rd St.

QUAKER VILLAGE

N. Market St.
King St.
Law Center

Martin Luther King Blvd.
2nd St.
W. Front St.
Tatnall St.
Orange St.
Shipley St.
E. 5th St.

S. Madison St.
Justison St.
West St.
Tatnall St.
Water St.
S. Orange St.
Conrail
2nd St.
Front St.
Walnut St.
Poplar St.
E. 4th St.
Lombard St.

Transit Center/
Amtrak Station

Bell Av.
Market St.

0   1/8 mile
0   100 meters
N

ACCOMMODATIONS ■
Brandywine Suites Hotel **10**
Courtyard by Marriott/
 Wilmington Downtown **4**
Hotel du Pont **7**
Sheraton Suites **5**

DINING ◆
Backstage Café **15**
Brandywine Room **8**
Columbus Inn **3**
Deep Blue **6**
Govatos **11**
Green Room **8**
Kid Shelleen's **3**
Toscana Kitchen + Bar **3**

ATTRACTIONS ●
Delaware Art Museum **1**
Delaware Center for the
 Contemporary Arts **13**
Delaware History Center **12**
FirstUSA Riverfront Arts Center **14**
Frawley Stadium **14**
Kalmar Nyckel **16**
Old Swedes Church **16**
Peterson Urban Wildlife Refuge **14**
Riverfront Wilmington **17**
Rockwood Museum **2**
Wilmington Library **9**

2 Getting Around

BY BUS Wilmington has no subway, but does have a bus system known as **DART (Delaware Administration for Regional Transit) First State.** Blue-and-white signs indicating DART stops are located throughout the city, and regular routes can take you to some hotels, museums, theaters, and parks, as well as popular sights such as Winterthur and New Castle. Those taking the bus to Winterthur should be aware that it stops at the gate and visitors then have a fairly long walk to the visitor center. Fares are based on a zone system; the minimum fare for one zone is $1.15. Exact change is required. You can obtain complete information on schedules and applicable fares at most banks or by calling DART First State (✆ **302/577-3278** or 302/652-3278).

BY SHUTTLE DART operates the **City Circuit,** a 25¢ (exact change) bus that takes visitors from City Hall to the Amtrak Station to the Riverfront. Get a map and schedule from the visitor center or DART. Shuttles run weekdays from 7am to 7pm. The route goes up Walnut Street north via Rodney Square and West Street to 13th Street and down Market Street and King Street to the starting point. Service is provided every 30 minutes. The whole ride takes about 10 minutes.

BY CAR Because downtown Wilmington lacks a real tourist center—its attractions and restaurants are spread across the city—and most people who visit here travel out to the Brandywine Valley, a car is something of a necessity. If you aren't driving into the area, you can rent one from either **Enterprise** (✆ **302/761-4545**) or **Budget** (✆ **302/764-3300**).

BY TAXI There are taxi stands at the Amtrak station, which is across the street from the bus station. If you wish to order a cab, call **Yellow Cab Delaware** (✆ **302/656-8151**).

 FAST FACTS: **Wilmington**

American Express Contact **Delaware Travel Agency,** 4001 Concord Pike (✆ **302/479-0200**).

Area Code Wilmington's area code is **302.**

Camera Repair For camera repair, supplies, or processing, try **Mid-City Camera Shop,** 201 Delaware Ave., at Union St. (✆ **302/654-6241**); **Ritz Camera,** 108 W. 9th St., between Orange and Market (✆ **302/655-4459**).

Emergencies Dial ✆ **911** for fire, police, or ambulance.

Eyeglass Repair The most convenient downtown location is **Wilmington Optical,** 616 Market St. Mall (✆ **302/654-0530**).

Hospitals **Wilmington Hospital,** 14th and Washington streets (✆ **302/428-4410**), or **St. Francis Hospital,** 7th and Clayton streets (✆ **302/421-4100**).

Libraries **Wilmington Library** is at 10th and Market streets (✆ **302/571-7402**).

Newspapers & Magazines The city's daily newspaper is the *News-Journal.* The best monthly magazine is *Delaware Today.*

Pharmacies A local chain is **Happy Harry Discount Drugs,** in Wilmington at 839 N. Market St. (© **302/654-1834**), and Trolley Square Shopping Center, Delaware Avenue (© **302/655-6397**).

Police For non-emergencies, call © **302/654-5151.** For emergencies, dial © **911.**

Post Office The main downtown post office branch is at Rodney Square Station, 1101 N. King St. (© **800/275-8777**).

Taxes There is no sales tax in Delaware, but an 8% lodging tax applies to stays at city hotels.

Transit Information Call **DART First State** (© **302/577-3278**).

3 Where to Stay

No matter where you go in Delaware, when you hear people refer to "The Hotel," they mean the Hotel du Pont in Wilmington. For more than 80 years, this hotel has dominated the Delaware lodging scene. Because Wilmington is a major destination for business travelers, numerous hotels catering to them have popped up in the downtown area. In recent years, several new hotels and motels have sprung up in the surrounding suburbs.

Wilmington hotels, like other city hotels, charge top prices Sunday through Thursday. The best way to save money is to look for a weekend package, which, in many cases, can save you up to 50% off midweek rates.

DOWNTOWN
VERY EXPENSIVE

Hotel du Pont ★★★ Opened in 1913 and owned by E.I. du Pont de Nemours and Company, this is the benchmark for all other Delaware hotels. The 12-story Italian Renaissance structure in the heart of the city is a showcase of polished marble, coffered ceilings, carved walnut, oak paneling, original artwork, and genteel service. Guest rooms have merited an International Gold Key Design Award. Each unit has mahogany reproduction furniture and built-in cabinetry, original artwork, and double-glazed windows. Most of the fabrics, fibers, and fittings are made of the latest DuPont products.

11th and Market sts., Wilmington, DE 19801. © **800/441-9019** or 302/594-3100. Fax 302/549/3108. www. hoteldupont.com. 217 units. $179–$309 double; $499–$599 suite. Weekend packages available. AE, DC, DISC, MC, V. Self-parking $13; valet parking $14. Pets under 20 pounds accepted with $100 deposit. **Amenities:** 3 restaurants; Lobby Lounge for lunch; cocktails and afternoon tea; golf course and tennis nearby; health club; concierge; business center; shopping arcade; 24-hour room service; massage; laundry and dry cleaning. *In room:* A/C, TV with pay movies, dataport, voicemail in 3 languages, minibar, iron, safe.

EXPENSIVE

Sheraton Suites ★★ In the heart of Wilmington's corporate and financial section, this contemporary 16-story hotel offers comfortable, spacious suites. Each has a full bedroom, with a separate living room with large-screen TV, refrigerator, and small sink and desk. The large well-lit bathrooms also have their own TVs, as well as a dressing area. The beds are very comfortable: I never had a better pillow anywhere. **Basil's Restaurant** on-site serves breakfast, lunch, and dinner.

422 Delaware Ave., Wilmington, DE 19801. ✆ **800/325-3535** or 302/654-8300. Fax 302/654-6036. www. sheraton.com. 228 units. $159–$189 double on weekdays, $89–$119 weekends. Weekend packages available, including Brandywine Sampler with admission to local sights $119 a couple. AE, DC, DISC, MC, V. Parking $10 (free Sat night). **Amenities:** Restaurant; lounge; indoor pool; exercise room; self-service laundry and dry cleaning; concierge level. *In room:* A/C, 3 TVs (1 with pay movies), dataport, kitchenette, fridge, coffeemaker, iron.

MODERATE

Brandywine Suites Hotel *Value*   Although the Brandywine Suites may not look like much from the outside—just a small glass entrance wedged between two old brick buildings—this unique little hotel in the heart of Wilmington is one of the area's best values. It is actually made up of three vintage brick office buildings renovated and linked together by a modern atrium and lobby. The ground-floor atrium has a sitting area with a fireplace and a small bistro-style restaurant.

The rooms are all spacious suites, featuring a living-room space with a sofa, a large TV, and a desk. They also sport large, well-equipped bathrooms and bedrooms with king-sized beds and second TVs. Furnishings are of the stock hotel dark-wood colonial type and the rooms generally have at least two telephones. Some rooms not along the front of the building have large cube-glass windows that act as a source of natural light without any loss of privacy. The hotel frequently offers weekend packages and discounts at other low-volume times.

707 King St., Wilmington, DE 19801. ✆ **302/656-9300**. Fax 302/656-2459. 49 units. $169 suite. Rates include continental breakfast. Seasonal weekend packages available. AE, DC, MC, V. Free garage parking across street with validated ticket. **Amenities:** Restaurant; laundry. *In room:* A/C, 2 TVs, dataport, minibar, coffeemaker, iron.

Courtyard by Marriott/Wilmington Downtown   Converted from a 10-story office building, this hotel does not fit the usual mold of the Marriott chain. It does, however, offer good value for downtown. Guest rooms vary in size and configuration, but all have contemporary furniture, wet bar, coffeemaker, refrigerator, and large desk. Some rooms also have Jacuzzis.

1102 West St., Wilmington, DE 19801. ✆ **800/321-2211** or 302/429-7600. Fax 302/429-9167. 126 units. $139–$159 double weekdays, $59–$99 weekends. Weekend packages available. AE, DC, DISC, MC, V. Parking $8.50, free Fri and Sat nights. **Amenities:** Restaurant serving breakfast and dinner weekdays, breakfast only on weekends; coffee and tea bar; fitness room. *In room:* A/C, TV, dataport, kitchenette, coffeemaker, iron.

SUBURBS
EXPENSIVE

Christiana Hilton ✶   This hotel, nestled amid grassy grounds off exit 4B of I-95, is a good choice in the 'burbs. Located in a burgeoning area near Delaware's university at Newark and a variety of shopping malls, it boasts a modern four-story brick exterior, surrounded by topiary gardens with a brick-lined courtyard, gazebo, and pond that a family of swans calls home. The bedrooms are decorated in the Old Williamsburg tradition, with dark wood reproduction furniture and colonial prints and colors.

100 Continental Dr., Newark, DE 19713. ✆ **800/348-3133** or 302/454-1500. Fax 302/454-0233. 266 units. $99–$200 double. Weekend packages. AE, DC, DISC, MC, V. Free parking. **Amenities:** 2 restaurants; lounge; outdoor pool; fitness room; same day valet; free shuttle to downtown Wilmington; concierge level. *In room:* A/C, TV with movies, dataport with high speed Internet connection, coffeemaker, iron.

Inn at Montchanin Village ✶✶   Proximity and atmosphere make this a great place from which to explore the Brandywine Valley and Wilmington. Yet another piece of du Pont history, Montchanin Village was once home to workers in the black powder mills and factories along the Brandywine. What remains of the village, 11 buildings completed between 1870 and 1910, became the Inn at Montchanin Village in 1996. Nine of the buildings, once the workers' residences, have been converted into 27 guest rooms and suites. The blacksmith shop and barn are now the inn's restaurant called Krazy Kat's (see "Where to Dine," below) and the reception area; the railroad station is a gourmet take-out shop.

Each guest room is individually designed and decorated. One- and two-level suites range from one- to two-bedrooms. The six superior suites have king beds, marble bathrooms with double soaking tubs, and fireplaces. All units have access to an outdoor sitting area, and first-level rooms and suites have private gardens. The whole place is warm and inviting.

Rte. 100 and Kirk Rd., P.O. Box 130, Montchanin, DE 19710. © **800/COWBIRD** or 302/888-2133. Fax 302/888-0389. www.innatmontchanin.com. 27 units (11 with shower only). $150–$175 double; $200–$350 suite. AE, DC, DISC, MC, V. Free parking. **Amenities:** Restaurant; lounge. *In room:* A/C, TV, dataport, kitchenette, microwave, iron.

MODERATE

Best Western Brandywine Valley Inn   North of downtown at the gateway to the Brandywine Valley, this modern motor inn is next to a shopping center but set back from the main road. The lobby features a Winterthur reproduction gallery, a collection of 15 furnishings commissioned by the nearby museum. This regional/artistic theme is carried through to the guest rooms, which have Georgian-style furnishings and Andrew Wyeth prints. Many rooms face an outdoor swimming pool and gardens in a central courtyard. Check the inn's website for getaway packages that include museum entrance fees.

1807 Concord Pike (Rte. 202), Wilmington, DE 19803. © **800/537-7772** or 302/656-9436. Fax 302/656-8564. www.brandywineinn.com. 97 units. $69–$115 double. Packages available. AE, DC, DISC, MC, V. Free parking. **Amenities:** Outdoor pool and hot tub; fitness center. *In room:* A/C, TV, dataport, microwave, fridge, coffeemaker, iron.

Courtyard by Marriott   Opened in 1991, this four-story property was the first of Mariott's Courtyards in Delaware. The layout follows the usual Courtyard plan, with sliding glass windows and balconies or patios facing a central landscaped terrace. Guest units are spacious, with a separate sitting area and desk.

48 Geoffrey Dr., Newark, DE 19713. © **800/321-2211** or 302/456-3800. Fax 302/456-3824. 152 units. $124 double; $144–$154 suite. Weekend packages available. AE, DC, DISC, MC, V. Free parking. **Amenities:** Restaurant; lounge; indoor pool and whirlpool. *In room:* A/C, TV, coffeemaker, iron.

Doubletree Hotel Wilmington   Popular with business travelers during the week and families on weekends, this modern seven-story structure is on the busy Route 202 corridor, north of downtown Wilmington and a few miles from the major museums and gardens. The bedrooms have a Brandywine Valley flavor, with dark reproduction furniture and local art. Its location makes it a good choice.

4727 Concord Pike (U.S. Rte. 202), Wilmington, DE 19803. © **800/222-TREE** or 302/478-6000. Fax 302/477-1492. www.doubletreehotels.com. 244 units (45 with shower only). $149 double. Weekend packages available. AE, DC, DISC, MC, V. Free parking. **Amenities:** Restaurant; lounge; indoor pool; fitness room; courtesy limousine service to downtown Wilmington. *In room:* A/C, TV or TV/VCR, fax, dataport, coffeemaker, iron.

INEXPENSIVE

Fairfield Inn *Value*   This three-story property offers comfortable and attractively furnished accommodations at low prices, in a very accessible location. There are three types of bedrooms: a compact single-bed room ideal for a lone traveler, a standard double, and a larger double with a king-sized bed. All rooms have a full-length mirror, lounge chair, and reading light with a work desk. Complimentary coffee and newspapers are available in the lobby.

65 Geoffrey Dr., Newark, DE 19713. 🕿 **800/228-2800** or 302/292-1500. Fax 302/292-8655. 135 units. $59–$79 double. Rates include continental breakfast. AE, DC, MC, V. Free parking. **Amenities:** Outdoor pool; passes for nearby gym. *In room:* A/C, TV with movies, dataport, coffeemaker, iron.

4 Where to Dine

DOWNTOWN
EXPENSIVE

Brandywine Room ★★ AMERICAN/REGIONAL   This is the Hotel du Pont's smaller, more clubby restaurant, with wood paneling, original artwork by three generations of the Wyeth family, and classical music in the background. Although the atmosphere is slightly less formal than in the Green Room, the service is as solicitous, and the food outstanding. The emphasis is on local specialties, such as crab imperial with orange hazelnut Hollandaise sauce, and veal Chesapeake, a thin scallopini topped with jumbo lump crab and béarnaise sauce. For meat lovers, the Brandywine mixed grill offers a combination not often seen on menus—venison chop, sausage, and steak in juniper and rosemary juice. You can hear live jazz nightly, 6 to 10pm.

In the Hotel du Pont, 11 W. Market St. (at 11th), Wilmington, DE 19804. 🕿 **302/594-3156.** www.hotel dupont.com. Reservations required. Main courses $21–$31. AE, DC, DISC, MC, V. Sun 5–10pm, Mon–Thurs 6–11pm. Valet and self parking complimentary.

Columbus Inn ★ AMERICAN/REGIONAL   One of Wilmington's favorites, the Columbus Inn is in one of the area's oldest houses, atop a hill on the edge of the northern suburbs. Because it has both a comfortable semiformal dining room and a more casual, cigar-friendly pub, the Columbus Inn draws both the business lunch crowd and the cuisine-savvy dinner set. Most evenings, the mood in the dining room is relaxed. There are candles on the tables, and the dark wood floors and exposed beam ceilings echo with the sounds of conversation not quite loud enough to be disturbing. The Columbus Inn is known for its excellent wine list, and the menu ranges from gourmet vegetarian to steak. Some highlights include soft-shell crabs, fillet of sole, and grilled vegetable ravioli. Sandwiches and pub fare are always available in the bar.

2216 Pennsylvania Ave. 🕿 **302/571-1492.** www.columbusinn.com. Reservations recommended for dinner. Main courses $16.95–$28.95; lunch $6.95–$16.95. AE, DC, DISC, MC, V. Mon–Fri 11:30am–1am, Sat 5pm–1am, Sun 10:30am–9pm. Complimentary valet and self parking.

Deep Blue ★★ SEAFOOD   How do you like your seafood? Sashimi? Raw bar? Something traditional? A little more Pacific Rim? Deep Blue's got them all. Set in a parking garage of all things, this noisy little restaurant is filled with excitement. The crowd, which tends toward the 30-somethings, fills the bar with loud conversation. The noise spills into the adjacent dining room. In this sleek modern setting nothing can muffle the sound. (Ask for a table away from the bar where conversation might be a bit easier.) As for the food, now there's something exciting. From the Deep Blue raw bar sampler for two to the micro green salad and striped bass over pesto mashed potatoes, the menu is filled with interesting options. The wine list with more than 170 choices takes some time to peruse.

111 West 11th St., Wilmington, DE 19801. ℂ **302/777-2040**. Fax 302/777-1012. www.deepbluebarand grill.com. Reservations recommended for dinner. Lunch $8–$12, dinner $18–$28. AE, DC, DISC, MC, V. Lunch Mon–Fri 11:30am–2pm; dinner Mon–Wed 5:30–10pm and Thurs–Sat 5–11pm. Valet parking $6, self parking $1.50 with validated ticket.

Green Room ★★★ CONTINENTAL/FRENCH   The prices here are steep, but it's not your average restaurant—Delawareans consider this the state's top spot for a memorable meal. The Green Room's impressive decor features tall arching windows, walls of quartered oak paneling, and handcrafted golden chandeliers from Spain. To complete the tableau, tuxedoed waiters provide impeccable service and a classical harpist plays in the background. Best of all, the chefs and the food are top-notch. Entrees range from filet of Black Angus with Madeira truffle sauce to sautéed Dover sole with grapefruit beurre blanc. Even if you can't spend a night at the Hotel du Pont, treat yourself to a meal here.

In the Hotel du Pont, 11th and Market sts. ℂ **302/594-3154**. www.hoteldupont.com. Reservations required. Jackets required for men on Fri and Sat. Main courses $26–$33; lunch $9–$18; Sun brunch $32. AE, DC, MC, V. Breakfast Mon–Sat 6:30–11am, lunch Mon–Sat 11:30am–2pm, dinner only Fri–Sat 6–10pm, Sun brunch 10am–2pm. Valet and self parking complimentary Fri–Sat evening.

MODERATE

Backstage Café ★ *Kids* AMERICAN   Come backstage for a little loud music, a menu with a sense of humor, and memorabilia from entertainers past. Even a gigantic Elvis will greet you near the door. This is Wilmington's answer to the Hard Rock Cafe and Planet Hollywood. And it's fun. The menu is eclectic: Grandma Walton's Pot Roast, Josey Wales's Outlaw Steak, Cecil B. DeMille's brick oven pizza (not a cast of thousands but broccoli, spinach, onion, tomato . . .). There are pastas, soups, salads, burgers, sandwiches, and that's a wrap! Kids will love their own "Bit Players" menu at about $3 an entree. The place is very dark but bright colored spotlights lighten the mood.

100 S. West St. (on the Riverfront). ℂ **302/778-2000**. www.welcomebackstage.com. Reservations accepted Mon–Thurs. Main courses $7.95–$18.95. AE, DISC, MC, V. Open 11am–1am. Free parking in nearby lots.

Kid Shelleen's AMERICAN   Tucked in a residential area on the city's north side (just north of Trolley Square), this lively indoor-outdoor restaurant known for its casual atmosphere and open charcoal grill is always hopping. It's a favorite with the locals. Inside you'll find a pub atmosphere: exposed brick and dark wood and walls decorated with old circus posters. The food is better and the offerings more extensive than your average pub fare. Entrees include grilled salmon, barbecued chicken, baby-back ribs, Black Angus strip steaks, and pastas. Shelleen's also serves a variety of wood-baked pizzas. There is a big, friendly open bar area smack in the middle of the restaurant, where a large-screen TV is usually showing the latest sports action.

1801 W. 14th St. (at Scott St.). ℂ **302/658-4600**. Fax 302/658-7910. www.kidshelleen.com. Main courses $6.95–$16.95. AE, DC, DISC, MC, V. Mon–Sat 11am–midnight, Sun 10am–midnight.

Toscana Kitchen + Bar ITALIAN/TUSCAN   As soon as you step into this restaurant, you'll be assured of both its quality and popularity by the excited din of the customers, the bustle of the waitstaff, the piquant aromas flowing from the open kitchen and the wood-burning oven, and the constant attention displayed by the ever-present owner and chef, Daniel Butler. The restaurant has been completely remodeled to include a new bar, outdoor dining area, and brick oven. Freshly made pastas and individual pizzas with exotic toppings are also on the menu. New is the Sunday jazz brunch.

1412 N. du Pont St. ℂ **302/654-8001.** Reservations accepted for parties of 6 or more. Main courses $13–$25; lunch $10–$15. AE, DC, DISC, MC, V. Lunch Mon–Fri 11am–5pm. Dinner Mon–Sat 5–10pm, Sun 4–9pm.

INEXPENSIVE

Govatos AMERICAN   Established in 1894, this eatery is a Wilmington tradition and an ideal choice in midcity for breakfast or lunch. The menu offers sandwiches, burgers, salads, and hot home-style favorites. The main attractions, however, are the desserts and other confections, since this place produces Delaware's largest selection of homemade chocolates and candies.

800 Market St. Mall. ℂ **302/652-4082.** Breakfast $2.95–$4.95; lunch $4.95–$7.95. MC, V. Mon–Sat 8am–3pm, closed Saturdays from May–Sept.

SUBURBS
EXPENSIVE

Krazy Kat's ☆ CONTINENTAL   If you want a fine dining experience without the formal atmosphere, try Krazy Kat's. In the old blacksmith shop at the Inn at Montchanin Village, Krazy Kat's was once the home of an eccentric cat lover, hence the name and the cat art that adorns the walls. Leopard-print chairs and china with a jungle motif set off the comfortably elegant decor. Menu items focus on fresh local ingredients. Mushrooms of all shapes and sizes pop up everywhere, from the petit filet mignon with grilled portobello mushroom cap to the sautéed escargots with shiitake mushrooms, roasted garlic, and red peppers. The crab cakes and shrimp mousseline are good, and the mixed grill of duck, lamb, and ostrich is superb. The wine list features about 100 carefully chosen vintages. If you're not a wine connoisseur, the staff will gladly help you choose one.

At the Inn at Montchanin Village, Rte. 100 and Kirk Rd. P.O. Box 130, Montchanin. ℂ **302/888-4200.** Fax 302/691-0198. krazykats@montchanin.com. Reservations recommended. Jackets suggested for men at dinner. Main courses $24–$28; lunch $9–$15. AE, DC, DISC, MC, V. Mon–Fri 7–10am, 11am–2pm, and 5:30–10pm; Sat 8–11am and 5:30–10pm; Sun 8am–noon and 5:30–9pm.

EXPENSIVE/MODERATE

Feby's Fishery ☆ SEAFOOD   On the city's southwest side, west of the junction of Route 100 South, this nautically themed restaurant also has a seafood market, a sure sign of fresh fish on the premises. The menu features as many as 18 different fin fish. Feby's is known for good food in a family-style atmosphere. The menu features a variety of crab, shrimp, lobster, and scallop dishes, as well as daily specials and creative combinations, such as salmon with tarragon sauce and crab imperial Florentine. For landlubbers, there's filet mignon and Delmonico steak.

3701 Lancaster Pike. ℂ **302/998-9501.** Reservations recommended for dinner. Main courses $14.95–$21.95; lobster dishes $22.95–$29.95; lunch $5.95–$14.95. AE, MC, V. Mon–Thurs 11am–9:30pm, Fri 11am–10pm, Sat–Sun 4–9:30pm.

MODERATE

Brandywine Brewing Company Restaurant and Brewery ☆ *Kids* PUB FARE   You've got to love a place that serves a good brew and caters to the kids, too. The beers made on-site include a refreshing *Kalmar Nyckel* Ale, spicy Seasonal Ale, and a variety that changes with the day. You can try a rack of four 6-ounce tasters for $4.75. As for the kids, they can have their own homemade brew—root beer—and choose from a variety of kids' items on the Little Brewski's Menu. As for the grown-ups, sit back and enjoy your ale or lager with hard pretzels and a couple of homemade mustards, hot and sweet, while you decide whether to go for the gourmet pizza, the meat loaf and mashed potatoes, or their delicious half-pound burgers. It's all pretty simple, fresh, and relaxed.

9th and Orange sts., Wilmington, DE. © **302/984-2400.** 3801 Kennett Pike, Greenville, DE. © **302/655-8000.** Reservations accepted for 6 or more. Lunch $6.35–$9.25, dinner $6.25–$22.95. AE, DC, DISC, MC, V. Mon–Sat 11:30am–1am, Sun 11:30am–midnight.

Terrace at Greenhill INTERNATIONAL   West of downtown in a residential area off Pennsylvania Avenue (Rte. 52), this restaurant overlooks the Ed "Porky" Oliver Golf Course and is a favorite with local duffers. The decor is bright and airy, with light wood and rattan furnishings, lots of greenery, and walls of watercolors by local artists. Like the setting, the food is fun and varied. Lunch items include turkey burgers and salmon cakes, as well as salads, soups, omelets, pizzas, crab cakes, and sandwiches. For dinner, there's steaks and seafood.

800 N. du Pont Rd. © **302/575-1990.** Reservations recommended for dinner. Main courses $9.95–$17.95; lunch $5.95–$9.95. AE, DC, MC, V. Mon–Thurs 11:30am–2:30pm and 4:30–8:30pm, Fri–Sat 11:30am–2:30pm and 4:30–9pm, Sun 10am–2:30pm and 4–8pm.

5 Attractions

Though most visitors to Wilmington travel out to the Brandywine Valley attractions, Wilmington itself has several museums and sites of interest.

Delaware Art Museum ⭑   Renowned for its holdings of American art (from 1840 to the present), this museum is located north of downtown in Rockford Park. It houses the largest collection of works by Howard Pyle, the father of American illustration and founder of the Brandywine school of painting, and many works by his followers, including various Wyeths, Frank Schoonover, Elizabeth Shippen Green, and Maxfield Parrish. It also contains outstanding examples of American sculpture, photography, and traditional and contemporary crafts, and the largest display of pre-Raphaelite English art in the United States.

2301 Kentmere Pkwy., Wilmington, DE 19806. © **302/571-9590.** Fax 302/571-0220. www.delart.org. Admission $7 adults, $5 seniors and over age 6, $2.50 college students; free Wed evening and Sat morning. Tues and Thurs–Sat 9am–4pm, Wed 9am–9pm, Sun 10am–4pm. From I-95, take Rte. 52 north. Turn right onto Bancroft Pkwy., then left onto Kentmere, and follow signs to the museum.

Delaware Center for the Contemporary Arts   Housed in an impressive new building in the Wilmington Riverfront area, this gallery focuses on contemporary visual arts by local and nationally known artists. A recent exhibit showcased Rick Rothrock's minimalist stone sculptures, "Geometry of Time." As a non-collecting museum, exhibits are always changing. In 2002, 32 shows are scheduled. There's a small gift shop, too. If you like chamber music, the museum hosts the Mid-Atlantic Chamber Music Society series (www.midat music.org).

200 S. Madison St. © **302/656-6466.** Fax 302/656-6944. www.thedcca.org. Admission $3 adults, $1 students, seniors, artists; free to children under 12. MC, V Free Sat 10am–noon. Tues, Thurs, Fri 10am–6pm; Wed 10am–8pm; Sat 10am–5pm; Sun 1–5pm.

Delaware History Center *(Kids)*   In a restored 1941 Woolworths building (once the third largest in America), this museum features changing interactive exhibits on the state's history and social development and permanent displays of regional decorative arts, paintings, children's toys, and items of local interest. The Discovery Room, featuring **Grandma's Attic,** gives children a place to dress up, touch and handle artifacts, and hear storytellers. The gift shop specializes in Delaware-handcrafted items and souvenirs.

504 Market St. (near the south end of the Market St. Mall). ℂ 302/655-7161. Admission $4 adults, $3 students and seniors, $2 under age 18. Mon–Fri noon–4pm, Sat 10am–4pm.

FirstUSA Riverfront Arts Center ★★★   This place is huge and so are the exhibitions. The snaking rope chains, lots of hassock seating for tired visitors, and small displays near the entrance remind me of Disney World crowd control. But that's not to say the crowds will be huge; my own recent visit felt like a private tour. The exhibitions are designed to dazzle. Recent shows focused on Russia's Nicholas and Alexandra, Fabergé's eggs, and ancient artifacts from Syria. Though the space is cavernous, displays are brought down to human size through the use of wall dividers, spotlights, and easy-to-manage groupings of objects. The exhibits are big so plan to stay a couple hours, or make it a day trip all by itself.

Ticket prices generally include timed entry to the exhibit, a short orientation presentation, and an individual recorded tour. Be sure to call ahead to find out what (and if something) is showing. In addition to the blockbuster shows, the arts center has opened a gallery for smaller shows. These have separate ticket prices.

800 S. Madison St. (next to the minor league baseball stadium). ℂ 888/862-ARTS. www.riverfront wilmington.com. $13.50 adults, $12.50 seniors, $6 ages 5–17, free for under age 5. Exhibition Tues, Thurs, Fri, Sat 10am–7pm; Wed 10am–9pm; Sun 11am–6pm (last entry 90 minutes before closing); box office daily 9am–5pm.

Kalmar Nyckel Foundation   On the shores of the Christina River near Old Swedes Church and Fort Christina Park, the _Kalmar Nyckel_ Foundation has re-created the three-masted ship that brought the first Swedish settlers to the Delaware Valley in 1638. Visitors can tour the 139-foot long _Kalmar Nyckel_ and take a look at her 10 cannons, 7,500 square feet of sails, and 10-story high main mast. Occasionally the _Kalmar Nyckel_ sails to nearby ports or takes short excursions, so call to see whether the ship berthed at home or on the high seas.

1124 E. 7th St. ℂ 302/429-7447. www.kalnyc.org. Admission $5 adults and age 13 and over, $3 ages 6–12 at its shipyard or $4 while at other locations. Hours approximate: Thurs–Sun 10am–4pm, Nov–April. If you want to sail on her, call for sailing schedule. To get to shipyard: Take Martin Luther King Blvd. to King St. and then turn right on 4th St. Continue until turning left on Swedes Landing Rd. before the Winchester Bridge, and then turn right on 7th St.

Old Swedes Church ★   Near the Christina River, this is one of the oldest churches in the United States. The church remains in its original 1698 form (and still maintains its extensive genealogical records) and is still used for religious services. Highlights of the interior include stained-glass windows installed from 1885 to 1897 and a church chest dating from 1713, as well as herringbone bricks in the main aisle and a black-walnut canopied pulpit, one of the oldest of its kind in the United States. The churchyard, which predates the church by 60 years, was used as a burying ground for early settlers of Fort Christina and its community. A reconstructed farmhouse nearby depicts the everyday life of the Swedish settlers.

606 Church St. ℂ 302/652-5629. Admission $2, but donations welcome. Mon–Sat 10am–4pm. Take Martin Luther King Blvd. to 4th St. Turn right on 4th St., left on Church St.; church is 2 blocks on right.

Riverfront Wilmington ★   On a bend in the Christina River, Wilmington has built a pretty brick walkway. Beginning at the train station and ending at the Russell W. Peterson Urban Wildlife Refuge, this 1⅓-mile (2km) path takes visitors past some interesting shops, museums, and a series of signs that tell a bit of Wilmington's history. Watch the Wilmington rowing team glide by, discover a Canada goose on the shore nearby, or catch a ride on the River Taxi.

The closest streets are Madison on the west and Water on the north. Market Street will bring you here from downtown. As for parking, it's just about everywhere. Lots are free near the Shipyard Shops and FirstUSA Riverfront Arts Center as well as near the Riverfront Market. Some paid parking and metered parking is near the train station as well.

Once you get to the Riverfront you can start at the Tubman-Garrett Riverfront Park and 21 placards spaced along the walkway tell the history of the Christina River and Wilmington, beginning with the development of industry, shipbuilding, and other transportation here. The efforts of the Underground Railroad, which ran through Wilmington, are recalled here as are efforts to restore wetlands and excavate archaeological sites. Sometimes you can also see the *Kalmar Nyckel,* a reproduction of the ship that brought Wilmington's first settlers, near the Shipyard Shops or by the Tubman Garrett Park. **Dravo Plaza,** with all those huge cranes, recalls the city's shipbuilding history, especially its contributions to World War II.

Stop at the **Riverfront Market** (© **302/425-4454**) for something fresh. Stalls offer sandwiches, coffee, salads, chocolates, and other sweets to eat now, as well as meats, fish, and produce to take home. It's open Tuesday to Friday 9am to 6pm, Saturday 9am to 6pm.

The **Delaware Theatre Company, Delaware Center for the Contemporary Arts,** and the gigantic **FirstUSA Riverfront Arts Center** are all resident arts organizations. For just plain fun, visit the **Backstage Café,** or the stores and restaurants of the **Shipyard Shops.** The Riverfront is fast becoming a place to gather for festivals and concerts at the Dravo Plaza and along the walkway.

Sports fans can see the Blue Rocks play minor league baseball at **Frawley Stadium,** a short walk off the Riverfront.

If you get tired of walking, the **River Taxi** will take you to your next stop. The 40-passenger pontoon boat operated by the **Christina River Boat Company** (© **302/984-2722**) shuttles passengers along a 30-minute loop from the Shipyard Shops to the mouth of the Brandywine River. It stops at the Tubman-Garrett Park, by the Market, by the Backstage Café, and near the Shipyard Shops.

Visitors who make it to the end of the Riverfront will reach the **Russell W. Peterson Urban Wildlife Refuge.** The 225 acres of marshland has become home to many birds and other creatures. Plans have been announced to make the site more comfortable for humans, including an interpretive center and boardwalks.

Rockwood Museum ✦   This Gothic mansion, furnished in 17th-, 18th- and 19th-century decorative arts, has just undergone an extensive renovation and is set to reopen in early 2002. Joseph Shipley, one of the city's early merchant bankers, built the house on 72 tree-filled acres northeast of downtown Wilmington in 1851. The mansion was acquired in 1892 by the Bringhursts, a wealthy family who furnished it with a lavish mélange of 17th-, 18th-, and 19th-century decorative arts from the United States, Britain, and Continental Europe. The elaborate conservatory features a brilliant array of Victorian flora that reflects the 6 acres of exotic foliage and landscape surrounding the manor. Seasonal programs include a summer concert series in May and June, a

---

Finds **Discovering a Famous Castaway**

N. C. Wyeth's illustrations for *Robinson Crusoe* are at the **Wilmington Library** at 10th and Market streets on Rodney Square (✆ 302/571-7402). If you have a few minutes, stop by the library and turn into the reading room to the left of the main lobby. The library is open Monday to Thursday 9am to 8pm, Friday and Saturday 9am to 5pm.

Victorian Ice Cream Festival in July, and a festival of lights with a million lights twinkling on the property.

610 Shipley Rd. ✆ 302/761-4340. www.rockwood.org. Free admission for self-guided garden tour. Call for house tours and admission prices. From I-95 north, take exit 9 (Marsh Rd.); turn right onto Carr Rd., right again onto Washington St. Ext., and then right onto Shipley Rd. The museum is on the left. From I-95 south, take exit 9; turn right on Marsh Rd., right onto Washington St. Ext., and follow directions above.

FORT DELAWARE STATE PARK 🖈

Located on Pea Patch Island, in Delaware City (✆ 302/834-7941), this park is about 16 miles (26km) south of Wilmington, in the Delaware River. To get there, take Route 13 or I-95 south from Wilmington to Route 9 (turn left), which will take you to Delaware City. The park surrounds a five-sided granite fortress that served as a detention center during the Civil War. Inside there's a museum, 19th-century cells and armaments, and an audiovisual presentation about the history of the island. Other facilities include an observation tower for bird-watchers (the island is a popular nesting spot for egrets, herons, and other marsh fowl) and an assortment of nature trails and picnic sites. You can visit the island by taking a 10-minute boat ride from Delaware City. The ferry departs every hour on the hour from Battery Park at the end of Clinton Road. Boat fare, which includes admission to the park, is $6 for adults and $4 for children 13 and under.

When you arrive on the island, a tractor-pulled tram will take you from the dock to the fort, where, if you're visiting during a living history weekend, you'll be greeted by a costumed interpreter playing the part of a Confederate prisoner. The site is open on weekends April through October and some weekdays in summer; call the park for exact hours and the ferry schedule. Reenactments and living history demonstrations are held throughout the summer, so try to plan your visit to coincide with these events. Guided tours by Confederate and Union reenactors and musket, artillery, and cannon demonstrations are great (though a bit loud) for children and adults. Call the park for a schedule of events.

6 Spectator Sports & Outdoor Activities

BASEBALL   Wilmington cheers for the **Blue Rocks** (✆ 302/888-BLUE or 302/888-2015), a minor league baseball team first organized in the 1940s and revived with much fanfare in 1993. It reached the Class A Carolina League championship in 2001. The team plays at the 5,900-seat Daniel S. Frawley Stadium, off of I-95, just south of downtown. Box seats cost $7 and reserved seats cost $6; general admission is $4 and admission for children, seniors, and military personnel is $2. Parking is free.

GOLF   The rolling hills around Wilmington make for challenging golf. The following are a few of the best clubs that welcome visitors:

Delcastle Golf Club, 801 McKennan's Church Rd. (© **302/995-1990**), located southwest of the city near Delaware Park racetrack, offers an 18-hole championship course, pro shop, and full restaurant open 7am to dark. Nearby are a driving range and miniature golf. Greens fees range from $18.50 to $39.50.

Ed "Porky" Oliver Golf Course, 800 N. du Pont Rd. (© **302/571-9041**), is in a residential area west of downtown and off Route 52 (Pennsylvania Ave.). The club has an 18-hole championship course, driving range, pro shop, and restaurant (see Terrace at Greenhill in "Where to Dine," earlier in this chapter); it also provides lessons and group clinics. Tee times are accepted by phone 1 week in advance. Greens fees range from $15 to $40.

The **Three Little Bakers Golf Course,** 3540 Foxcroft Dr. (© **302/737-1877;** www.tlbinc.com), nestled in the Pike Creek Valley southwest of Wilmington, is a semiprivate 18-hole par-71 course open daily to the public except after 3pm on Thursday and Friday. Facilities include a pro shop, club rental, golf lessons, and bag storage. Greens fees are $47 Monday to Thursday and $52 Friday to Sunday.

HORSE RACING & SLOT MACHINES   For half a century, racing fans have placed their bets at **Delaware Park,** 4½ miles (7km) south of Wilmington, off I-95 exit 4B, Stanton (© **800/41SLOTS** or 302/994-2521). Delaware Park, with its tree-lined paddock, offers thoroughbred racing April through November. Post time is 12:45pm. Simulcast racing is offered year-round. A wide variety of coin-operated and video slot machines are available for 5¢ to $10 per play. There are also restaurants and entertainment on weekends. It's open Monday to Saturday 8am to 2am, Sunday 1pm to 2am.

PARKS   Wilmington's playground is **Bellevue State Park,** 800 Carr Rd. (© **302/577-3390**). On the northeast perimeter of the city, this 270-acre park was once the home of the William du Pont family. Facilities include picnic areas, garden paths for walking, and fitness trails for jogging. Admission is free except from Memorial Day through Labor Day and weekends and holidays in May, September, and October, when the entrance fee is $5 for each out-of-state vehicle and $2.50 for each Delaware-registered car.

Southwest of Wilmington is **Lums Pond State Park,** 1068 Howell School Rd., off Route 71, in Bear (© **302/368-6989**). Stretching along the Chesapeake and Delaware Canal, this 1,757-acre park encompasses the state's largest freshwater pond and is home to several beaver colonies and many waterfowl. For humans, the pond offers swimming, fishing, and boating. You can either bring your own boat or rent a rowboat, canoe, paddleboat, or sailboat from the park during the summer and on weekends in May and September. Rates range from $4 to $10 per hour, depending on the type of boat. The surrounding parklands include hiking and walking trails; a nature center; picnic areas; football, soccer, and baseball fields; basketball and tennis courts; and camping sites. Admission charges are the same as for Bellevue State Park, described above, but are in effect from the beginning of May through the end of October. The park is open 8am to sunset year-round.

7 Shopping

The Wilmington area has dozens of malls and shopping centers, such as **Concord Mall,** 4737 Concord Pike (© **302/478-9271**), and **Christiana Mall,** 715 Christiana Mall Rd., I-95 exit 4A (© **302/731-9815**).

The downtown area offers some shopping, mostly on 9th Street and along Market Street Mall. If you happen to be downtown and get a craving for chocolate, stop by **Govatos,** 800 Market St. Mall (✆ **302/652-4082**). Since 1894, this shop has been giving Delawareans a great selection of homemade chocolates and candies. All sweets are available by the piece or by the pound, and the shop is open weekdays from 8am to 5pm and Saturday 8am to 3pm; it's closed on Saturdays, May to September. Govatos has a second candy shop in the Talleyville Shopping Center, 4105 Concord Pike (✆ **302/478-5324**). It is open Monday to Saturday 9am to 5:30pm.

Another downtown shop is the **Ninth Street Book Shop,** 104 W. 9th St. (✆ **302/652-3315**), which offers a large selection of books on travel, Delaware history, and African-American history. Shop hours are Monday through Friday from 8:30am to 5pm and Saturday from 10am to 3pm.

Shipyard Shops on the Riverfront at 900 S. Madison St. (near Frawley Stadium) has 16 outlet stores, including L.L. Bean, Coldwater Creek, and Blair, and a restaurant for lunch and dinner. It's open Monday to Saturday 10am to 9pm and Sunday 11am to 5pm (✆ **302/425-5000;** www.shipyardoutlets.com).

Riverfront Market (✆ **302/425-4454**) is a great place to stop for a quick sandwich or cup of soup, or to get a couple apples or pound of cookies for later. Your conscience might want you to get one of those fresh looking salads but your taste buds will want a pound of nonpareils. Get fresh seafood, meat, and produce here as well. It's open Wednesday to Friday 9am to 6pm, Saturday 8am to 5pm.

8 Wilmington After Dark

For the latest information on area entertainment, consult the Friday edition of the Wilmington *News-Journal,* which features a weekend entertainment guide, *55 Hours.* The city's monthly *Out & About* magazine also lists entertainment events. Both publications are available at newsstands.

THE PERFORMING ARTS

For such a small city, Wilmington has a lively performing arts scene, and the **Grand Opera House** ⚜, 818 N. Market St., is the center of it. Built in 1871 as part of a Masonic temple, this restored Victorian showplace is in the heart of the downtown pedestrian mall. On the exterior you'll see some of the finest examples of cast-iron architecture in America. The facility seats 1,100 and is home to Opera Delaware and the Delaware Symphony Orchestra. It also offers a program of ballet, jazz, chamber music, pop music, and theater. Call ✆ **302/658-7897** for information or **800/37-GRAND** or 302/652-5577 for tickets.

The city's other large venue, **The Playhouse,** on 10th and Market streets, has brought touring Broadway shows to downtown Wilmington for more than 80 years. Located next to the Hotel du Pont, it has a 1,239-seat capacity amid a vintage Victorian decor. In addition, local companies, such as the **Brandywine Ballet,** often perform in the Playhouse. For information or tickets, call ✆ **302/656-4401** or visit www.playhousetheatre.com.

A smaller venue, the **Delaware Center for the Contemporary Arts,** 200 S. Madison St. (✆ **302/656-6466**), features chamber music and classical music concerts, as well as a performing arts series, throughout the year.

CLASSICAL MUSIC

In recent years, under the direction of maestro Stephen Gunzenhauser, the **Delaware Symphony Orchestra** has gained national recognition as a model regional orchestra. The DSO's 90-plus performances a year range from chamber music to pops to classical and chamber with weekend afternoon performances for children, the Lollipop Family Series. Performances are usually held in the Grand Opera House in Wilmington, but chamber music concerts are held in the Hotel du Pont or Winterthur with other concerts at schools around Delaware. For ticket information, contact the Grand Opera House at $\textit{C}$ **800/37GRAND** or 302/652-5577, or visit their website at www.desymphony.com.

How do you like your opera? Grand Italian? Light operetta, or maybe something for the kids? **Opera Delaware** ($\textit{C}$ **800/37GRAND** or 302/652-5577; www.grandopera.org) offers three series with prices ranging from $24 to $64. Family tickets are $9 and $17. Supertitles are provided, those who don't like them can sit in sections where the projections can't be seen.

THEATER

Candlelight Music Dinner Theatre   A big red barn holds Delaware's first dinner theater, started more than 25 years ago. The 2001–2002 productions included *A Funny Thing Happened On The Way to the Forum, Forever Plaid, Grease* and *Murder Medium Rare.* The price of admission includes a buffet dinner. The theater is located in the suburb of Ardentown, near the Hilton Hotel, and is signposted off Harvey Road. Shows are held Thursday to Saturday, with a buffet at 6pm and show at 8pm; Sunday buffet is held at 1pm and the show at 3pm. 2208 Millers Rd., Ardentown. $\textit{C}$ **302/475-2313**. http://candlelightdinnertheatre. com. Tickets $35.

Delaware Theatre Company   At the foot of Orange Street, this 389-seat facility has no seat more than 12 rows from the stage. The theater is home to Delaware's only resident professional company, which presents a program of classic and contemporary plays throughout the year. Call or see the website for show times or to order tickets. 200 Water St. Box office $\textit{C}$ **302/594-1100**. www.delaware theatre.org. Tickets $20–$40.

Three Little Bakers Dinner Theatre   Southeast of Wilmington off Route 7, this theater presents revivals of Broadway shows, as well as celebrity specials featuring stars and bands like Mel Tillis and the Hubcaps (not in the same show). Productions have included *Jekyll and Hyde* and *Singin' in the Rain.* The price includes a buffet dinner with French and Swiss pastries, dancing, and pre-show entertainment. The theater is named after its founders: Al, Nick, and Hugo Immediato, originally bakers by profession. Call for show times. 3540 Foxcroft Dr. $\textit{C}$ **800/368-3303**. www.tlbinc.com. Dinner/show $29–$50.

THE CLUB & MUSIC SCENE

Wilmington's Riverfront is getting to be the place to hear music. **The Big Kahuna,** long a hot spot for local and national live music, is undergoing renovation, and due to reopen in mid-2002. The Backstage Café offers deejays and live bands. Dravo Plaza is the place for outdoor jazz, reggae, classical, and blues. Summertime concerts are held Thursdays. In the rest of the city, the nightlife is pretty mellow, dominated by folk music, blues, and hotel piano bars.

Backstage Café   Primarily a restaurant with lots of entertainment memorabilia, this is also a late night place and a happy hour place and, occasionally, a live band place. Sunday afternoons are mellow with jazz starting at 2pm. A deejay arrives every day at 5pm and then the place starts rocking. Deejays from Newark's WJBR broadcast live from Backstage on Wednesdays. Open 11am to 1am. 100 S. West St. (on the Riverfront). $\textit{C}$ **302/778-2000**. www.welcomebackstage.com. Reservations for dinner accepted Mon–Thurs. AE, DISC, MC, V. Free parking in nearby lots.

Kelly's Logan House Built in 1864 and located in trendy Trolley Square, this place claims to be the oldest tavern in the city. A classic Irish pub with pressed-tin ceilings and exposed brick walls, the house is named for a Union army general, John A. Logan, who instituted Memorial Day; the Kelly family has owned the house since 1889. This is one of the best places in the city for live entertainment in an intimate setting. There is also a nice patio section where you can hear the music in the background and have a conversation under the city lights and stars. There's usually rhythm-and-blues music Thursday through Saturday nights. Pub fare and some lighter, healthier fare are available as well. Hours are Monday to Saturday 11am to 1am. 1701 Delaware Ave. $\textcircled{C}$ **302/65-LOGAN.** Fax 302/642-5285. www.loganhouse.com. Cover $3–$5. AE, DC, DISC, MC, V.

O'Friel's Irish Pub and Restaurant This is the city's classic Irish pub, with beers from the "ould sod" on tap and traditional and contemporary Irish music on many nights. Open Mike Night is the last Thursday of the month, and there are deejays spinning every Tuesday. 600 Delaware Ave. $\textcircled{C}$ **302/654-9952.** Fax 302/ 654-0321. No cover for most sessions.

Epoch Formerly known as Porky's, it's a new Epoch in Wilmington. The club is aiming for a younger crowd. The over-30s already beat a path to their door, especially on Fridays. The music is still mostly rock-and-roll, but some nights are aimed at the 20-somethings: the Thursday rave-music nights, for example. 1206 N. Union St. $\textcircled{C}$ **302/429-6633.** Cover $5–$10.

ESPECIALLY FOR KIDS
The **Delaware Children's Theater,** 1014 Delaware Ave. ($\textcircled{C}$ **302/655-1014**), presents plays based on fairy tales and other stories familiar to children of all ages. Admission is $10, with performances on selected Saturdays and Sundays at 2pm. *Note:* Even for adult visitors, this ornate three-story building is worth a look for its historic and architectural value. Listed on the National Register of Historic Places, it was designed in 1892 by a woman exclusively as a women's club. The building today continues to be owned and operated by women.

11

The Brandywine Valley & Historic New Castle

The Brandywine Valley combines great natural beauty with the best of handmade beauty. Set between Wilmington and the southeast corner of Pennsylvania, the valley's hills, rivers, and expanses of trees make it an eye-pleasing backdrop for the mansions, gardens, and museums that draw visitors to the area.

This is where you'll find the famous homes and gardens of the du Pont family—which give the Brandywine the nickname "Chateau Valley"—as well as where three generations of the Wyeth family have called home and found inspiration to create their art.

New Castle, Delaware's original capital, recalls the First State's first days. Just 20 minutes south of Wilmington, New Castle has preserved its 18th-century past with cobblestone streets, brick sidewalks, and 200-year-old homes. New Castle is also a place to see unique artisans' and antiques shops and enjoy an excellent meal.

1 The Brandywine Valley

10 miles (16km) N of Wilmington, 35 miles (56km) W of Philadelphia, 73 miles (118km) N of Baltimore

Meandering north from Wilmington, the Brandywine Valley has a long and storied history. The river and valley provided for early settlers, powered the first du Pont industry, and inspired a "school" of art. To the Native Americans, the river was the *Wawset* or *Suspecoughwit* and was cherished as a bountiful shad-fishing source. The Swedes and Danes later called it the Fishkill. Quakers and other English settlers renamed it the Brandywine and made it an important mill center in the 18th and 19th centuries. At its peak, more than 100 water-powered mills along the Brandywine produced everything from flour, paper, and textiles to snuff, and black powder, on which the American du Ponts first made their fortune. In more recent times, the valley has been home to a school of artists and illustrators, beginning with Howard Pyle and Frank Schoonover, and including the Wyeth family—N.C.; Andrew, who still lives and paints here; and Jamie.

Mostly in Delaware, the Brandywine Valley begins near Wilmington, and stretches into Pennsylvania. Those who wish to see Winterthur *and* Longwood Gardens can do both, as they are only a 20-minute drive apart. Some Pennsylvania sights are included here because they're part of the area. The Pennsylvania side is also explored in detail in *Frommer's Philadelphia & the Amish Country.*

ESSENTIALS

GETTING THERE The valley's attractions in Delaware are spread out north of Wilmington, but most are along or near Delaware Route 100 or Route 52.

By car, take I-95 into Wilmington to Delaware Route 52 North, which leads to Route 100. The main attractions in Pennsylvania are all along U.S. Route 1. From Wilmington, both Route 52 and 100 lead to U.S. Route 1. If you prefer, take I-95 to U.S. Route 202, which will take you all the way to U.S. Route 1.

Bus service from Wilmington is available from the **Delaware Administration for Regional Transit/DART** (© 800/652-DART or 302/652-3278; www. DartFirstState.com). See "Arriving" in chapter 10, "Wilmington," for information about rail and air transportation.

VISITOR INFORMATION   For maps and brochures, contact the **Greater Wilmington Convention and Visitors Bureau,** 100 W. 10th St., Suite 20, Wilmington, DE 19801 (© **800/489-6664** or 302/652-4088; www.wilmcvb. org), open 9am to 5pm Monday to Saturday; or stop at the branch on I-95 between exits 1 and 3 near Newark, Delaware, daily from 8am to 8pm; or visit the **Chester County Visitors Center,** on U.S. Route 1 at the entrance to Longwood Gardens, Kennett Square, Pennsylvania (© **800/228-9933** or 610/388-2900; www.brandywinetreasures.org). It's open daily 10am to 5pm.

AREA CODE   Brandywine Valley attractions located in the Wilmington suburbs use the 302 area code. Neighboring sights, inns, and restaurants on the Pennsylvania side use the 610 area code.

SPECIAL EVENTS   Longwood Gardens (© 800/737-5500 or 610/388-1000) has changing displays for each season. The **Welcome Spring** indoor display of colorful spring bulbs is a favorite, as is the **Christmas Display** ★★★, featuring hundreds of poinsettias and a lighted outdoor display. The **Old-Fashioned Ice Cream Festival** at Rockwood Museum (© 302/761-4340) is another favorite event, featuring hot-air balloons, baby parades, and, of course, ice cream. It's held the second weekend in July.

THE DU PONT HOMES & GARDENS

If you've seen just one du Pont home, you ain't seen nothing yet.

For sheer splendor, visit **Nemours Mansion.** The tour gives visitors a glimpse into the luxurious lifestyle these people enjoyed.

If your tastes are more of a garden variety, **Longwood Gardens** has the most varied gardens—I've never seen them all in one day. Even if you miss the house, don't miss the conservatories.

The world-famous **Winterthur**'s charms are more academic. Remember, this is more a museum than a house. The room with the Chinese wallpaper has earned its reputation but these rooms tell more about decorative arts than the personality who gathered them together. (Marylanders should check out the Chestertown room and the Baltimore room.) Leave time for the gardens here, especially the new Enchanted Woods garden for children; but if you have time for only one garden in the Brandywine Valley, go to Longwood.

Hagley Museum offers a glimpse of early American life. It's worth visiting to see how regular Americans lived and worked when the country was new. The grounds are naturally pretty, too.

Hagley Museum ★★★ (Kids)   The du Pont fortune got started here, along this wooded riverbank. (It's breathtaking in autumn.) French émigré Eleuthère Irénée du Pont de Nemours built the first of his gunpowder mills here in 1802, and the first du Pont home, Eleutherian Mills, in 1803. The mills grew in number and size, later to include workers' homes and a school. Visitors to the 240-acre site have a lot to see, and a visit can take a couple of hours or a whole

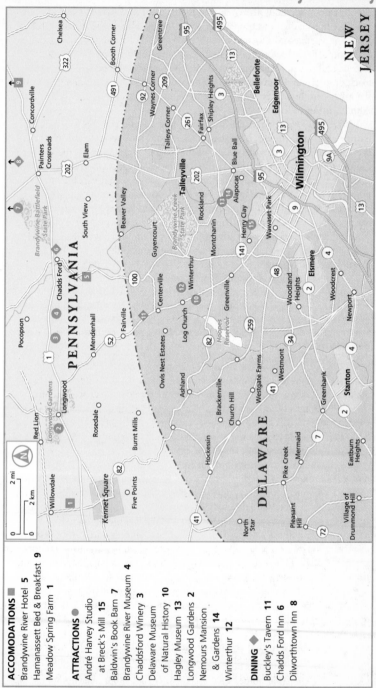

The Brandywine Valley

NEW JERSEY

PENNSYLVANIA

DELAWARE

ACCOMODATIONS
Brandywine River Hotel **5**
Hamanassett Bed & Breakfast **9**
Meadow Spring Farm **1**

ATTRACTIONS
André Harvey Studio
  at Breck's Mill **15**
Baldwin's Book Barn **7**
Brandywine River Museum **4**
Chaddsford Winery **3**
Delaware Museum
  of Natural History **10**
Hagley Museum **13**
Longwood Gardens **2**
Nemours Mansion
  & Gardens **14**
Winterthur **12**

DINING
Buckley's Tavern **11**
Chadds Ford Inn **6**
Dilworthtown Inn **8**

day. Just the walk along the river, past the ruins of the old roll mills, will keep children busy. A visit starts in the Henry Clay Mill—where new exhibits, "DuPont Science and Discovery" and "DuPont: The Explosives Era" are due to open July 2002. Designed to celebrate DuPont's 200th anniversary, these take a look at DuPont past and present. While the first looks at inventions since the black powder days, and includes Jeff Gordon's NASCAR car and a space suit, the other will look at the role of DuPont's black powder in the 19th and early 20th centuries.

Visitors can walk along the river and millrace and see the roll mills, the narrow gauge railroad, and the dangerous steps it took to make gunpowder in the 1800s. Visit the remains of one of the workers' communities, the Gibbons House, the Sunday school, and the Belin House, which also serves as a restaurant. Don't miss the dioramas in the Millwright shop that explain how gunpowder is made. Stop here to see when demonstrations are taking place, too.

Visitors to the du Pont house catch a bus (which stops at several locations on the property), which offers a narrated tour through the powder yards to the Georgian-style residence where five generations of du Ponts lived. Rooms reflect the various periods of the house's history from the 1800s to the 1920s. The French gardens, barn, and First Office are also well worth a look.

Hagley has a series of Family Fun Events, including dollar days, concerts, Christmas events, and bike and hike days. Check the website for specifics.

Rte. 141, Wilmington, DE 19807. ✆ **302/658-2400.** Fax 302-658-3267. www.hagley.org. Admission **$9.75** adults, $7.50 students and seniors, $3.50 ages 6–14. Mar 15 to Dec daily 9:30am–4:30pm; Jan to Mar 14 Mon–Fri 1 guided tour at 1:30pm, Sat–Sun 9:30am–4:30pm. Closed Thanksgiving and Dec 25. From Wilmington, take I-95 to Rte. 202 N. (Concord Pike). Turn left on Rte. 141 S. Hagley is on the right.

Longwood Gardens 🌼🌼🌼   One of the world's most celebrated horticultural displays, Longwood Gardens showcases more than 11,000 different types of plants and flowers amid 1,050 acres of outdoor gardens and woodlands. For sheer size, Longwood is spectacular. But the ever-blooming displays throughout the grounds and conservatory are both creative and delightful, thanks to Pierre S. du Pont, who purchased the existing farm and arboretum in 1906, and from 1907 to 1954 designed most of what is enjoyed today.

Everybody has a favorite spot: mine include the Conservatory's tropical paradise, eye-popping seasonal displays, and the playful children's garden; the flower garden walk which explodes in seasonal color and is one of the original gardens; the understated waterfall and chimes tower (with its newly installed carillon); the idea garden to inspire home gardeners; and the main fountain garden whose 380 fountains and spouts rise over 130 feet high during one of the 5-minute displays throughout the day. There are also illuminated displays in the fountain garden Tuesday, Thursday, and Saturday evenings June through September and fireworks displays on several evenings during the summer (check the website for dates and times). In addition to the Main Fountain Garden, you'll find the Flower Garden Fountains, the Open Air Theater, which also has 5-minute displays several times daily, and a completely restored Italian Water Garden.

Longwood's attractions include seasonal plant displays (the ones at Christmas and Easter are noteworthy) and hundreds of performances. Almost daily events include puppet shows, storytelling, musical performances, carillon concerts, and plenty of garden-related activities. Check the website for the schedule. There is a large museum shop, and the Terrace Restaurant has both a cafeteria (open 10am–4pm, to 5pm on Sun) and full-service dining room (open 11am–3pm daily). The Peirce-du Pont House, on the grounds, is also open to the public.

Rte. 1, Kennett Sq., PA 19348. ℂ 800/737-5500 or 610/388-1000. www.longwoodgardens.org. Admission $12 adults ($8 on Tues), $6 ages 16–20, $2 ages 6–15, free under age 6. AE, DC, DISC, MC, V. Apr–Oct daily 9am–6pm; Nov–Mar daily 9am–5pm; extended evening hours during the Christmas Display and the Summer Festival of Fountains. On Rte. 1, just south of the intersection with Rte. 52.

Nemours Mansion and Gardens ★★★   Only 5 minutes from the Hagley Museum, this 300-acre estate was the home of Alfred I. du Pont and his family. Built in 1909 and 1910, and named after the du Pont ancestral home in France, the 102-room Louis XVI–style château is a model of extravagance. From the staircase dominated by stained glass to the wood paneled game rooms in the basement, the house's opulence never ceases. It was as up-to-date as any home of its day, but also was filled with antiques, paintings, and amazing craftsmanship. Visitors should arrive at the visitor center at least 15 minutes before a scheduled tour to catch the bus to the house. Reservations are a must because tour groups are quite small. The tours of 36 of the house's rooms, led by docents, take about 2 hours. A visit to the gardens could take longer. Extending one-third mile (0.5km) from the house, they include a sunken garden, French style gardens, ponds, fountains, orchards, and natural woodlands. After walking the garden, visitors can return to the bus for a narrated tour of the gardens and a walk through the garage to see the vintage cars, including a couple of Rolls Royces. Those who choose not to walk in the gardens can board the bus at the front door.

Rockland Rd. (P.O. Box 109), Wilmington, DE 19899. ℂ 302/651-6912. Admission $10 adults (under age 12 not permitted). May 1–Nov 30 Tues–Sat, tours at 9am, 11am, 1pm, and 3pm; Sun tours at 11am, 1pm, and 3pm. Take Rte. 202 north; turn left onto Rte. 141 south. Turn left onto Children's Dr. at second light. At first light turn left onto Rockland Rd. Visitor center and parking lot are on right. (Follow the Blue H signs to the A. I. du Pont Children's Hospital—Nemours shares a parking lot.)

Winterthur, An American Country Estate ★★★ *Kids*   Named after a town in Switzerland and pronounced "win-ter-tour," this eight-story mansion and country estate is one of the world's premier collections of American antiques and decorative arts. The estate was the country home of Henry Francis du Pont, a collector of furniture, who in 1951 turned the home into a museum for American decorative arts. The 85,000 objects, including Chippendale furniture, silver tankards by Paul Revere, and a dinner service made for George Washington, are displayed in the 175 period rooms of this museum.

It takes more than one visit to see Winterthur. The Elegant Entertaining tour, which highlights the dining room, sitting rooms, and other period public rooms, only covers one floor. The Winterthur "Estate Passport" is good for 2 consecutive days, and includes the gardens, galleries, and a tram tour of the 966-acre grounds. Forty-five-minute house tours, "Discovery Voyages," cost an additional $5 for adults. Study Visa tours offer in-depth looks at the estate's furnishings and conservation efforts for $15 per tour, with reservations strongly recommended.

Galleries include period rooms, exhibits of furniture styles, life at Winterthur, early American craftsmen, and the famous Campbell Collection of Soup Tureens.

Children (and adults, too) will love the new **Enchanted Woods,** a 3-acre fairy tale garden filled with places to play, including a Faerie Cottage and Troll Bridge. And the rest of the gardens—Azalea Woods, Sundial Garden, Quarry Garden, and the gardens near the house—put on a new show each season.

An annual Yuletide tour is offered from mid-November to December 31. Facilities include two restaurants (afternoon tea is a special treat), an extensive museum store, and a bookshop. Children under 12 are permitted on three of the six Discovery tours, as well as the Yuletide Tour.

Rte. 52, Winterthur, DE 19735. ✆ **800/448-3883** or 302/888-4600. www.winterthur.org. Admission to the galleries and garden $10 adults, $8 seniors and students, $4 ages 5–11. "Discovery Voyages," guided tours of the house and garden, $15 adults, $13 seniors and students, $9 ages 5–11, younger children are free. AE, DISC, MC, V. Mon–Sat 9am–5pm, Sun noon–5pm (last tour at 4pm). Closed Jan 1, Thanksgiving, and Dec 25. 6 miles (10km) northwest of Wilmington on Rte. 52 and 5 miles (8km) south of Rte. 1.

OTHER ATTRACTIONS

André Harvey Studio at Breck's Mill   Housed in an 1814 stone mill building just downstream from the Hagley Museum gates, this studio features realistic bronze sculptures of people and animals by André Harvey. The museum also displays gold sculptural jewelry made in collaboration with goldsmith Donald Pywell. A separate gallery shows the different stages of casting.

101 Stone Block Row, Greenville, DE. Mailing address: Box 8, Rockland Rd., Rockland, DE 19732. ✆ **302/656-7955.** Fax 302/656-7974. www.andreharvey.com. Free admission. Mon–Fri 10am–4:30pm, or by appointment.

Baldwin's Book Barn *Finds*   Okay—technically this is a store, but for true bibliophiles it's a don't-miss experience. With five floors of rare and used books, maps, and prints in a charming stone barn, it's easy to while away hours getting comfortably lost among the stacks.

865 Lenape Rd. (Rte. 100 and Rte. 52), West Chester, PA 19382. ✆ **610/696-0816.** Fax 610/696-0672. www.bookbarn.com. Free admission. Mon–Fri 9am–9pm, Sat–Sun 10am–5pm. From Rte. 1, take Rte. 52 north. The barn is 6 miles (10km) past Rte. 1 on the left.

Brandywine Battlefield   This is where, in 1777, Washington's troops fought unsuccessfully with the British for control of strategic territory near Philadelphia. Though the revolutionaries lost, their courageous stand helped convince the French to form an alliance with the colonists. House tours of two Quaker farmhouses, which served as George Washington's headquarters and the quarters of the newly-arrived French Marquis de Lafayette, are offered throughout the day. There's also a visitor center with exhibits and dioramas, and a museum shop which is open free of charge, as is the battlefield.

Rte. 1 (P.O. Box 202), Chadds Ford, PA 19317. ✆ **610/459-3342.** www.ushistory.org/brandywine. Free admission to battlefield; house tour $8.50 family, $3.50 adults, $2.50 seniors, $1.50 ages 6–12. Tues–Sat 9am–5pm, Sun noon–5pm. Closed Mon.

Brandywine River Museum ✫✫✫   Now a museum, this Civil War–era gristmill was once home and studio to three generations of the famous Wyeth family. Not only are the works of N.C., his son Andrew, and Andrew's son Jamie on display here, but so is N.C. Wyeth's studio where he worked from 1902 until his death in 1945. It's surrounded by a nature trail and wildflower gardens dotted with sculptures. Four galleries display the best of Brandywine area artists, with paintings by Howard Pyle, Frank Schoonover, and the Wyeths, including Andrew's sisters, Henriette and Caroline, as well as works by other American artists and illustrators. One gallery is devoted entirely to the works of Andrew Wyeth, considered one of the most influential artists in American history. The well-stocked museum store offers a large selection of books, reproductions, and posters, primarily Wyeth-related, but other regional artists are also represented.

Rte. 1 (P.O. Box 141), Chadds Ford, PA 19317. ✆ **610/388-2700.** www.brandywinemuseum.org. Admission $6 adults, $3 seniors and ages 6–12. Daily 9:30am–4:30pm. Closed Dec 25. Just south of Rte. 100 on the Brandywine River.

THE BRANDYWINE VALLEY **307**

Kids Wilmington & the Brandywine Valley for Kids

Wilmington and its suburbs, the Brandywine Valley and New Castle, are home to palatial residences, elegant hotels, and immense gardens, not places you'd think of as especially kid-friendly. Fortunately, several sites welcome kids (all are listed above and below, except the Delaware History Center and Fort Delaware State Park, both listed in chapter 10, "Wilmington").

Delaware History Center   This museum of First State history is in an old Woolworths store in Wilmington. It features a hands-on Discovery Room, where kids can hold artifacts and listen to storytellers. See p. 293.

Delaware Museum of Natural History   This has exhibits of birds, shells, mammals, and dinosaur skeletons. There's also a Discovery Room and lots of nature films. See below.

Fort Delaware State Park   Kids will love this Civil War prison fort on an island in the Delaware Bay. Not only is there a boat ride to the island and then a tractor-pulled tram ride to the fort, but reenactors, lead guided tours and give artillery demonstrations in the summer months. See p. 296.

Hagley Museum   The family-friendly museum, set on a beautiful park on the Brandywine River, tells the story of the du Pont family's early gunpowder mill. Kids love the gunpowder testing demonstration, and everyone can explore the lovely grounds, the first du Pont home, and an early workers' village. See p. 302.

Longwood Gardens   This is a sprawling landscape with fountains, animal-shaped hedges, and conservatories. Little children shouldn't miss the children's garden with whimsical fountains and paths just their size. It's expensive, but you can save money by visiting on a Tuesday, when adult admission is discounted to $8. See p. 304.

Winterthur's Enchanted Woods   These 3 acres in the larger gardens will delight the young ones with a labyrinth, fountains, and a kid-sized cottage. Pick up the amusing brochure that tells the tale of the Enchanted Woods. See p. 305.

Chaddsford Winery   Housed in a restored barn, this small winery produces some lovely oak-aged chardonnays, pinot noirs, and cabernets. Visitors are encouraged to tour on their own, free of charge. Guided tours are conducted on the hour on weekends between noon and 5pm, and at 1pm and 3pm on weekdays. Wine classes are held regularly. Check the website for information.

Rte. 1, Chadds Ford, PA 19317. © 610/388-6221. Fax 610/388-0360. www.chaddsford.com. Free admission. *Note:* There is a $5 per person fee to participate in a full tasting session. Apr–Dec daily noon–6pm, Jan–Mar Tues–Sun noon–6pm. 5 miles (8km) south of Rte. 202, just past the Brandywine River Museum.

Delaware Museum of Natural History Kids   On the main route between Wilmington and Winterthur, the Museum of Natural History houses more than 100 exhibits of birds, shells, and mammals, including displays of the Great

Barrier Reef, an African water hole, and Delaware fauna. For young visitors, there's a hands-on Discovery Room, Make-It-Take-It Sundays, and a continuous showing of nature films. The museum has also acquired and assembled for display the skeletal remains of two rare Chinese dinosaurs, making it one of only a few museums in the United States to have them in its permanent collection.

4840 Kennett Pike (Rte. 52), P.O. Box 3937, Wilmington, DE 19807. ✆ **302/652-7600** or 302/658-9111. Admission $5 adults, $4 seniors, $3 ages 3–17. Mon–Sat 9:30am–4:30pm, Sun noon–4:30pm. 5 miles (8km) northwest of Wilmington on Rte. 52.

WHERE TO STAY

Wilmington area hotels are convenient bases from which to tour the Brandywine Valley, so check the "Where to Stay" section in chapter 10 for more places to stay. Below are some of the inns and hotels on the Pennsylvania side of the border. Nearly all the hotels in the area offer weekend packages that include entrance to some of the top area attractions—inquire when you call to make reservations.

Brandywine River Hotel ⟨*Value*⟩   This hotel, perched on a hillside in the heart of the valley, is one of the best values in the area—lots of amenities, good location, comfortable, stylish rooms for the price of an average chain hotel. Designed to meld with this scenic, historic region, with a facade of brick and cedar shingle, it is set beside a cluster of shops, galleries, and an artisans' cooperative. The Chadds Ford Inn restaurant is a few steps away. The lobby has a huge stone, open fireplace and a homey ambience. Guest rooms are decorated with colonial-style cherrywood furnishings, brass fixtures, chintz fabrics, and paintings in the Brandywine tradition. Some suites have an individual fireplace and a whirlpool.

Rtes. 1 and 100 (P.O. Box 1058), Chadds Ford, PA 19317. ✆ **610/388-1200.** Fax 610/388-1200, ext. 301. www.virtualcities.com/pa/brh.htm 40 units including cottage with 2 bedrooms and kitchenette. $125 double; $149–$169 suite. Rates include European-style continental breakfast and afternoon tea. AE, DC, DISC, MC, V. Pets under 20 pounds accepted for $20 per day; must be crated. **Amenities:** Exercise room; Jacuzzi; executive rooms. *In room:* A/C, TV/VCR, dataport.

Hamanassett Bed & Breakfast ⟨★⟩   Built in 1856, this farmhouse has long been a B&B. After more than a century in one family, new owners are redecorating the inn, which is surrounded by 40 wooded acres. The new innkeepers promise lots of luxurious touches, including a billiard room along with new and antique furnishings. The first floor has a comfortable, year-round solarium and magnificent foyer stairway. Breakfast is opulent; afternoon tea is available. The innkeeper will spoil you with her homemade cookies, too.

P.O. Box 336, Chester Heights, PA 19017. ✆ **877/836-8212** or 610/459-3000. www.bbonline.com/pa/ hamanassett. 6 units. $125–$175 double. Rates include full breakfast. AE, DISC, MC, V. No children under 14. Off-street parking. **Amenities:** Refrigerator stocked with complimentary beverages. *In room:* A/C, TV/VCR, coffeemaker, iron.

Meadow Spring Farm ⟨*Kids*⟩   This working 1936 farm is on 125 acres with walking paths and a fishing pond. Rooms come with Amish quilts, and common areas display family antiques and dolls. There is room for children here. Families are welcome; children may collect eggs, feed the animals, swim in the outdoor pool, or fish in the pond. There's also a hot tub in the solarium and a game room. Countryside carriage rides and picnic lunches can be arranged.

96 Violet Dr., Kennett Sq., PA 19348. ✆ **610/444-3903.** 7 units (5 with private bathroom). $85–$95 double. Rates include full country breakfast. $10 per child in parents' room. 2-night minimum stay on weekends. No credit cards. **Amenities:** Outdoor pool; hot tub in solarium; game room; access to nearby YMCA. *In room:* A/C, TV.

WHERE TO DINE

Be sure to check out the dining options listed in chapter 10; Wilmington is very close by and has more varied and, in general, better dining options.

EXPENSIVE

Chadds Ford Inn AMERICAN   With the Brandywine River Hotel just across the parking lot, the Chadds Ford Inn is one busy place on weekends (so be sure to make reservations if you don't want to eat in the bar). Dating from the early 1700s, this sturdy stone building was first the home of the Chadsey family and then a tavern and a hotel. Although it's been renovated, the inn still retains much of its colonial charm, with antique furnishings and century-old memorabilia. Salads, sandwiches, burgers, and pastas make up the lunch menu. Choosing from the dinner menu is tough because of the myriad options. Recommended entrees include Chadds Ford Wellington and Pan Seared Shrimp Provençale.

Rtes. 1 and 100, Chadds Ford, PA. © 610/388-7361. Fax 610/388-3960. Reservations recommended for dinner. Main courses $19–$24; lunch $5.95–$12.95. AE, DC, MC, V. Lunch Mon–Sat 11:30am–5pm; dinner Mon–Thurs 5:30–9:30pm and Fri–Sat 5–10pm; Sun brunch 11am–3pm and dinner 4–9pm.

Dilworthtown Inn ♠ INTERNATIONAL   Located on the road that was once the principal connection between Wilmington and West Chester, this establishment was built by James Dilworth in 1758; because of its strategic position, it soon became a tavern. Restored in 1972, the restaurant has 15 dining rooms, including the house's original kitchen and an outside stable area for warm weather dining. The decor consists of Early American furniture, dark wood support beams, hand-stenciled walls, 11 fireplaces, rooms lit by gas lamps and candlelight, and Andrew Wyeth paintings. The menu includes an array of fine dining options like Dilworthtown Pate (with black truffles), rack of lamb, and venison loin. Pair these choices with an offering from an extensive wine cellar. If you want to learn how to cook these gourmet dishes, the inn has a demonstration kitchen and offers cooking classes.

1390 Old Wilmington Pike and Brinton Bridge Rd. (off Rte. 202), West Chester, PA 19382. © 610/399-1390. Reservations required. Main courses $18.95–$33.25. AE, DC, DISC, MC, V. Mon–Fri 5:30–9:30pm, Sat 5–9:30pm, Sun 3–8:30pm. Closed last week of Aug.

MODERATE

Buckley's Tavern AMERICAN   Even though Buckley's is on the main road (Rte. 52) from Wilmington, you'll begin to feel you're in the middle of nowhere by the time you find this restaurant—but you'll recognize it by the abundance of cars in the parking lot and the general bustle surrounding the place. This old house has a long history dating from 1817. It was first a private residence, then a stagecoach stop with a tollgate in front, later a taproom and bar, and finally an ice-cream store. In 1951, Dennis Buckley turned it into a restaurant. Inside you'll find an old-world atmosphere, the bar hopping with locals and the dining room spacious, quiet, and inviting. The chef serves up an innovative blend of fresh ingredients. Try the grilled pepper-encrusted pork tenderloin or the cornmeal-encrusted catfish. Lighter fare—shared platters and finger food—is also available.

5812 Kennett Pike, Wilmington, DE. © 302/656-9776. Fax 302/656-9752. Reservations recommended for dinner. Main courses $5.95–$19.95; lunch $3.95–$9.95. AE, DC, MC, V. Mon–Wed 11:30am–2:30pm and 5:30–9:30pm, Thurs–Fri 11:30am–2:30pm and 5:30–10pm, Sat 11:30am–3pm and 5:30–10pm, Sun 11am–3pm and 5–9pm.

2 Historic New Castle

7 miles (11km) S of Wilmington, 40 miles (64km) SW of Philadelphia, 70 miles (113km) NE of Baltimore

New Castle was Delaware's original capital and a major colonial seaport. Peter Stuyvesant, who established a Dutch settlement named Fort Casimir, purchased the area from Indians in 1651. (It's said that Stuyvesant designed the town's central Green by "pegging it off" with his wooden leg.) Later captured by the Swedes and then the English, who renamed it New Castle, this stretch of land along the west bank of the Delaware River remains much the way it was in the 17th and 18th centuries. Original houses and public buildings have been restored and preserved, and the sidewalks are still brick and the streets cobblestone.

New Castle is ideal for walking. You can stroll past old homes and churches and such historic sights as Packet Alley, a well-worn pathway named after the many packet boats that came here in the 18th and 19th centuries. If you get tired, take a break on one of the benches by the river and watch the boats go by.

ESSENTIALS

GETTING THERE   From Wilmington, either take U.S. Route 13 south to Delaware Route 273 east to New Castle, or take Delaware Route 9 south directly to New Castle.

VISITOR INFORMATION   You can obtain brochures and information by writing or calling the **Historic New Castle Visitors Bureau,** P.O. Box 465, New Castle, DE 19720 (© **800/758-1550** or visit www.newcastlecity.org).

SPECIAL EVENTS   **A Day in Old New Castle,** held annually the third Saturday in May, gives visitors a chance to tour the town's private homes and gardens, as well as the public buildings, gardens, and museums. The town also hosts several Christmas events, featuring house tours, carolers, carriage rides, and reenactors. Contact the **New Castle Visitors Bureau** (© **800/758-1550**) or the **New Castle Historical Society** (© **302/322-2794**).

WHAT TO SEE & DO

Many of the historic buildings and homes in New Castle are privately owned and not open to the public. However, the Day in Old New Castle Committee publishes a great little guide called *A Day in Old New Castle,* with maps, photos, and descriptions of 105 historic sites of the town. Purchase a copy at the Old Court House on the Green and at several of the local shops.

HISTORIC HOMES & PUBLIC BUILDINGS

Amstel House   Dating from the 1730s, this house, once the home of Nicholas Van Dyke, a state governor, is a fine example of 18th-century Georgian architecture. It was likely the most elegant house in town at the time of its construction. Today, it's furnished with antiques and decorative arts of the period.

4th and Delaware sts. © **302/322-2794.** Fax 302-322-8923. www.newcastlecity.org. Admission $3 (can be combined with a visit to the Dutch House for $5 for both). Mar–Dec Tues–Sat 11am–4pm, Sun 1–4pm.

Dutch House Museum   One of the oldest brick houses in Delaware, this building has remained almost unchanged since its construction around 1700. The early Dutch furnishings include a hutch table and a courting bench. On display is a 16th-century Dutch Bible. During seasonal celebrations, the dining table is set with authentic foods and decorations.

3rd St., on the Green. © **302/322-2794.** Fax 302-322-8923. www.newcastlecity.org. Admission $3 (can be combined with a visit to the Amstel House for $5 for both). Mar–Dec Tues–Sat 11am–4pm, Sun 1–4pm; Jan–Feb Sat 11am–4pm, Sun 1–4pm.

Immanuel Episcopal Church   Started in 1703 and completed in 1820, this building was the first parish of the Church of England in Delaware. Unfortunately, the church caught fire and was extensively damaged in 1980, but it has been carefully restored. Take a stroll through the adjoining graveyard; it has tombstones dating from 1707 with some curious inscriptions. The booklet, *A Day in Old New Castle,* available from the Old Court House, has a map of the graveyard indicating the graves of prominent community members, including the grave site of George Read I, signer of the Declaration of Independence.

2nd and Harmony sts., on the Green. (C) 302/328-2413. Fax 302/322-8923. www.newcastlecity.org. Free admission. Daily 10am–5pm; services Sun 8am and 10pm, Wed 9:30am, Thurs 6pm.

Old Court House ⭐   This building was Delaware's colonial capital and the meeting place of the state assembly until 1777. Built in 1732, on the fire-charred remains of an earlier courthouse, it's been restored and modified over the years, though always maintaining its place as the focal point of town. The building's cupola is at the center of a 12-mile (19km) circle that marks the northern boundary between Delaware and Pennsylvania. Inside you'll find portraits of men important to Delaware's early history, the original speaker's chair, and excavated artifacts. Tours are conducted free of charge, and you must be with a tour to see inside.

211 Delaware St., on the Green. (C) 302/323-4453. www.newcastlecity.org. Free admission, but donations welcome. Tues–Sat 10am–3:30pm, Sun 1:30–4:30pm.

Old Library Museum   This fanciful hexagonal building, erected in 1892 by the New Castle Library Society, is used for exhibits by the New Castle Historical Society. The Victorian design of this house is attributed to the architectural firm of Frank Furriness of Philadelphia.

40 E. 3rd St. (C) 302/322-2794. Fax 302/322-8923. www.newcastlecity.org. Free admission. Sat–Sun 1–4pm, Mar–Dec.

Read House and Garden ⭐   This 22-room Federal-style house, built between 1791 and 1804 near the banks of the Delaware, aimed to be the grandest house in the state, and it's still a must-see in this town of historic homes. Its original owner, George Read II—son of George Read I, a signer of the Declaration of Independence—outfitted the house with unique and eccentric luxuries, including a bathroom on the second floor (water had to carried up), a bell system for ringing the servants, and bedroom doors that can be locked and unlocked from the bed! In addition to these oddities, the house features elaborately carved woodwork, relief plasterwork, gilded fanlights, and silver door hardware, all reflecting the height of Federal fashion. The surrounding 2½-acre formal garden dates from 1847 and is the oldest surviving garden in Delaware.

42 The Strand. (C) 302/322-8411. Fax 302/322-8411. www.hsd.org. Admission $4 adults, $3.50 seniors and students, $2 children. Mar–Dec Tues–Sat 10am–4pm, Sun noon–4pm; Jan–Feb by appointment.

WHERE TO STAY

New Castle provides a charming and convenient base for touring the Brandywine Valley and visiting Wilmington, only 7 miles (11km) away.

Ramada Inn—New Castle   Close to the Delaware Memorial Bridge, between I-295 and Route 13, this busy two-story property is set back from the main roads but within sight of the heavy traffic. Although not in the historic district, it is convenient for those in transit and is popular with business clientele. The building is designed in a modernized colonial motif, the rooms

---

(Finds **Attention HOGs & Other Motorcycle Fans**

Is it a restaurant, a museum, or a motorcycle dealership? Actually, **Mike's Famous** (2160 New Castle Ave., New Castle, DE 19720; ✆ **800/FAMOUS-HD**; www.mikesfamous.com) is all three. Just off the Delaware Memorial Bridge at I-295 South and Route 9 in New Castle, members of the **Harley Owners Group**, and those who love them can visit the **Museum of the American Road**; eat at the **Warehouse Grill**; shop for a new or used Harley, motor clothes, parts, or baby clothes in one place. The grill describes its cuisine as "regional American roadside," and serves what *Delaware Today* calls the "best chili" in the area. The museum (admission $4 adults; children 4–10, seniors, students, military, $3; children 3 and under free) features the Harley ridden around the world. The store, restaurant, and museum hours vary seasonally, but each is open daily. Mike's also hosts bike runs, parties, and other events, and offers motorcycle rental. Check the website for hours and events.

---

decorated with watercolors of local attractions and reproduction furniture, with desks in work areas.

I-295 and Rte. 13 (P.O. Box 647), Manor Branch, New Castle, DE 19720. ✆ **800/2-RAMADA** or 302/658-8511. Fax 302/658-3071. 126 units. $80 double. Small dogs accepted for $20 fee. Rate includes continental breakfast. AE, DC, DISC, MC, V. **Amenities:** Restaurant; bar; outdoor pool. *In room:* A/C, TV, dataport, coffeemaker, iron.

WHERE TO DINE

Air Transport Command INTERNATIONAL   Authentic Air Force memorabilia sets the tone at Air Transport Command, located close to the runways of New Castle County Airport. The flying heroes and heroines of World War II are commemorated with old uniforms, newspaper clippings, pictures, and flying equipment. You can even pick up a set of headphones and listen to the ground-to-air instructions at the nearby control tower. Music from the 1940s adds to the vintage atmosphere. Dinner entrees include simple standards including steak, prime rib, stuffed flounder, and crab cakes.

143 N. du Pont Hwy. ✆ **302/328-3527.** Reservations recommended for dinner. Main courses $12.95–$24.95; lunch $4.95–$12.95. AE, DC, DISC, MC, V. Mon–Thurs 11am–10pm, Fri–Sat 11am–11pm, Sun 9:30am–10pm.

Jessop's Tavern ★★★ AMERICAN   Take the advice of everyone in town and eat here at least once during your visit. If the crowds put you off at dinner, stop by for an early or late lunch. Jessop's strives to reproduce the foods that shaped this region in colonial times; you'll find traditional English pub fare and old American dishes, as well as Dutch and Swedish touches. This is hearty meat-and-potatoes fare—shepherd's pie, turkey potpie, slow-roasted rib of beef with caramelized onions and sautéed mushrooms, and charbroiled rib of pork with colonial pineapple stuffing and Dutch apple butter. Even the sandwiches are excellent, served on thick slices of fresh hearth-baked bread. And try to save room for dessert; the baker selects seasonal fruit and serves up a thick-crusted cobbler of the day. Even the decor is authentic. The owners have created a true colonial seafaring town pub atmosphere—warm, cozy, and a bit raucous at times.

114 Delaware St. ✆ **302/322-6111.** Main courses $10.95–$19.95; lunch $4.95–$10.95. AE, DC, DISC, MC, V. Mon–Thurs 11am–11pm, Fri–Sat 11am–midnight.

12

Dover & Central Delaware

To racecar fans, Dover means NASCAR twice a year. To gamblers, it's a place to play the slots. To history buffs, this town is where the U.S. Constitution got its first "yea" vote.

Set in the middle of this tiny state, Delaware's capital has its share of museums and attractions. Problem is, too many people fail to slow down on their way to the beach! What a shame.

At least the wildlife is smart enough to stop. Bombay Hook National Wildlife Refuge offers migrating visitors 16,000 acres of marsh and wetlands.

1 Dover

45 miles (72km) S of Wilmington, 84 miles (135km) E of Baltimore, 43 miles (69km) N of Rehoboth

Plotted in 1717, according to a charter by William Penn, Dover was originally designed as the Kent County seat. By 1777, however, this rich grain-farming community's importance had increased, and the state's legislature, seeking a safe inland location as an alternative to the old capital of New Castle on Delaware Bay, relocated to Dover. In Dover, Delaware became "the First State" on December 7, 1787, when the state's delegates assembled at the Golden Fleece Tavern on the Green to ratify the Constitution of the United States, the first state to do so.

Today, Dover continues to be a hub of state government and business. The state has opened several museums to showcase its history: a sprawling agricultural museum, a museum of American art stocked with lavish works donated by Delaware's many rich families, the Old State House, and others. On the city's southern edge is Dover Air Force Base, the largest airport facility on the East Coast and home to a museum of its own, boasting several unique aircraft.

ESSENTIALS

GETTING THERE   If you're driving from the north or northwest, take I-95 to Wilmington and head south on Route 1 (a toll road) or Route 13 (also known as the DuPont Hwy.) to Dover. Route 13, which runs the entire length of Delaware, is also the best way to approach Dover from the south. From Washington, D.C., and points west, take Route 50 across the Bay Bridge to Route 301 North. Follow 301 to 302 East, then take Route 454. From 454, take Route 8 into Dover.

Greyhound/Carolina Trailways provides regular bus service into Dover, arriving at 650 Bay Court Plaza (✆ **302/734-1417**).

VISITOR INFORMATION   Begin your visit to Dover at the **Delaware State Visitors Center,** 406 Federal St. at Duke of York Street, Dover, DE 19901 (✆ **302/739-4266**). Located right on the Green, this well-stocked office provides a range of literature on the attractions of the city, Kent County, and the state, as well as two changing exhibits on Delaware history, fashion, and arts and crafts. It also has restrooms, vending machines, and a gift shop. It's open Monday through Saturday 8:30am to 4:30pm and Sunday from 1:30 to 4:30pm. The **Kent County Tourism Office** at 9 E. Loockerman St., Suite 203 (© **800/233-KENT**), also provides information. It's open Monday through Friday 8am to 4pm.

Eleven miles (18km) north of Dover on the road to Wilmington, you'll find the **Smyrna Visitors Center,** 5500 DuPont Hwy. (Rte. 13), Smyrna (© **302/653-8910**). This is an excellent place to stop for brochures and information. It also has restrooms, gardens, and picnic tables, and is open 7am to 5pm.

GETTING AROUND   The most convenient way to get around the city and surrounding areas is by **car.** The major rental agencies with offices in Dover are **Avis,** 3024 N. DuPont Hwy. (© **302/734-5550**), and **Hertz,** 650 Bay Court Plaza (off Rte. 113; © **302/678-0700**). **City Cab of Dover** (© **302/734-5968**) operates a reliable taxi service, with 24-hour radio-dispatched vehicles.

SPECIAL EVENTS   The biggest events in Dover are the two "Monster Mile" **NASCAR weekends** in June and September at Dover Downs International Speedway. The names and lengths of the races vary each year; contact Dover Downs (© **302/674-4600;** www.doverdowns.com) for information. Hotels start booking for these weekends up to 8 months in advance, so make reservations well ahead of time and be prepared for rate hikes. Dover Downs opened a hotel of its own in 2002. (See details in "Stock-car Racing" and "Where to Stay" below.)

Visitors interested in the historical sites should try to visit during **Old Dover Days,** in late April or early May, when several of the city's privately owned historical homes and gardens are open to the public. Costumed guides greet visitors, and maypole dancing, craft demonstrations, refreshments, and general merriment take place on the Green. Contact the **Kent Convention and Visitors Bureau** (© **800/233-KENT**) for tickets and tour information.

EXPLORING DOVER

Most of Dover's historic sites, government buildings, and museums are located around or within walking distance of **the Green.** This is not just a green space in the middle of town; it's where Delaware became the first state to ratify the U.S. Constitution in 1787. From Route 13, follow signs for the historic district and take State Street, which goes right through the center of the Green. Though only those sites open to the public are listed here, many buildings surrounding the Green are historic and are marked with plaques and signs. You can pick up a map of the Green and the surrounding area at the **Delaware State Visitors Center,** located on the northeast corner of the Green, near the State House.

The remaining attractions, along with Dover's hotels and motels, are concentrated east of the historic district, along Route 13, also known as DuPont Highway. This strip, which is home to Dover Downs, the Delaware Agricultural Museum and Village, and the Dover Air Force Base, extends for several miles, so you'll need a car to get from place to place.

MUSEUMS & HISTORIC SITES

The Green   The English-style town square at Bank Lane and State Street was an important site in Delaware's history. William Penn designed it more than 300 years ago. Soldiers gathered here to join the Revolutionary War troops of General George Washington. The Declaration of Independence was read here. And nearby at the Golden Fleece Tavern, Delaware's legislators voted to ratify

Dover

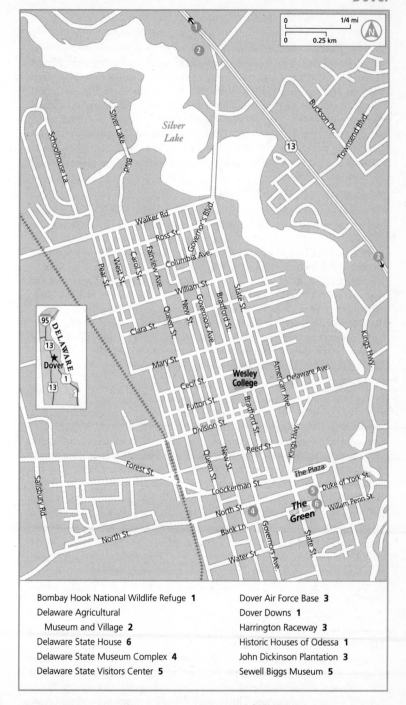

0	1/4 mi
0	0.25 km

Silver Lake

Schoolhouse La.

Silver Lake Blvd.

Walker Rd.

Ross St.

Columbia Ave.

Fairview Ave.

Carol St.

West St.

Pear St.

Governor's Blvd.

William St.

New St.

Governors Ave.

Bradford St.

State St.

Clara St.

Queen St.

Mary St.

Cecil St.

Wesley College

American Ave.

Delaware Ave.

Fulton St.

Bradford St.

Division St.

Reed St.

Forest St.

Salisbury Rd.

Queen St.

New St.

Kings Hwy.

The Plaza

Loockerman St.

Duke of York St.

North St.

The Green

Willam Penn St.

North St.

Back Ln.

Governor's Ave.

Water St.

State St.

Buckson Dr.

Townsend Blvd.

13

Kings Hwy.

Dover Air Force Base

DELAWARE inset

95

13

★ **Dover**

13

1

Bombay Hook National Wildlife Refuge **1**	Dover Air Force Base **3**
Delaware Agricultural	Dover Downs **1**
Museum and Village **2**	Harrington Raceway **3**
Delaware State House **6**	Historic Houses of Odessa **1**
Delaware State Museum Complex **4**	John Dickinson Plantation **3**
Delaware State Visitors Center **5**	Sewell Biggs Museum **5**

315

the U.S. Constitution. The Green remains a popular gathering spot today: on Old Dover Days in the spring, or any pretty day during a Delaware summer.

Sewell Biggs Museum of American Art   The landscapes and still lifes here are a feast for the eyes. The collection includes works by Gilbert Stuart, Frank Schoonover, Albert Bierstadt, and several of the Peales. Decorative arts—antique furniture and fine silver, much of it made in Delaware, and Chinese export porcelain—fill several of the 14 galleries. Delawarean Sewell Biggs has collected these treasures for the past 60 years. Housed on the second and third floors of the Delaware State Visitors Center, the museum also offers a scavenger hunt for children, an evening lecture series for a small fee, and changing exhibits.

406 Federal St. ⓒ 302/674-2111. Fax 302/674-5133. www.biggsmuseum.org. Free admission. Wed–Sat 10am–4pm, Sun 1:30–4:30pm.

Delaware Agricultural Museum and Village ⭐   For insight into Delaware's agricultural heritage, this museum is worth a visit. The main building houses permanent and temporary displays about the last 200 years in the local poultry, dairy, and produce industries. There are more than 6,000 artifacts—including a 1941 crop duster, an 18th-century log house, and a 1912 incubator capable of holding 6,000 eggs—as well as the "Whittlin' Room," featuring the folk art of Jehu Camper, and "A Touch of History," a room full of objects you (and your kids) are encouraged to touch. Behind the main building, there's a re-creation of an 1890s village, with a one-room schoolhouse, church, mill, blacksmith shop, and farmhouse. There's also a gift shop.

866 N. DuPont Hwy., Dover, DE 19901. Across from Dover Downs on Rte. 13. ⓒ 302/734-1618. www.agri culturalmuseum.org. Admission $9 families, $3 adults, $2 seniors and ages 6–17, free for under age 6. Jan–Mar Mon–Fri 10am–4pm; Apr–Dec Tues–Sat 10am–4pm, Sun 1–4pm.

Delaware State Museums ⭐⭐ *Value*   This is a complex of attractions, as well as the visitor center, that highlight the accomplishments and history of the people of Delaware. Five sites are right in Dover but the agricultural museum is out off Route 113, south of town. Together they provide a look at both ordinary and extraordinary Delaware. Admission to all of them is free. Start at the **Delaware Visitor Center** at 406 Federal St. (ⓒ **302/739-4266;** www.destate museums.org). Hours vary so check individual listings.

Delaware Archaeology Museum and Museum of Small Town Life   These two museums are in two historic buildings side-by-side: a 1790 Presbyterian Church and its 1880 Sunday school building. The Archaeology Museum displays artifacts from a Native American burial ground near Bowers Beach. The Small Town Life Museum focuses on Delaware communities and culture of the early 1900s and depicts "Main Street Delaware." This exhibit includes a general store and post office, printing shop, pharmacy, and woodworking shop.

316 S. Governors Ave. ⓒ 302/739-4266. Tues–Sat 10am–3:30pm. 1 block west of the Green, between North St. and Bank Lane.

Johnson Victrola Museum   This unusual museum, which also includes the Meeting House Galleries, is a tribute to Delaware-born and Dover-raised Eldridge R. Johnson, inventor and founder of the Victor Talking Machine Company, now known as RCA. The museum houses a large number of Victrolas (the original record players with the crank and horn) of all makes and models, and a display on Nipper, the RCA dog, including Johnson's copy of *His Master's Voice,* the oil painting that made Nipper famous. One room of the museum is designed as a 1920s Victrola dealer's store and contains an extensive collection of talking machines and early recordings, which a guide will gladly play for you.

Corner of New and Bank Lane, 1 block west of the Green, off Bank Lane and behind the Delaware Archaeology Museum and Museum of Small Town Life. ✆ **302/739-4266**. Free admission. Tues–Sat 10am–3:30pm.

Old State House Built in 1792, Delaware's State House is one of the oldest in the United States. As part of Delaware's bicentennial celebration in 1976, the Georgian-style building was restored to its original appearance and contains the 18th-century courtroom and legislative chambers, a ceremonial governor's office, displays on Delaware history and the history of the building, and county offices. Although the state's General Assembly moved to the nearby Legislative Hall in 1934, the State House still remains Delaware's symbolic capitol.

The Green. ✆ **302/739-4266**. Free admission. Tues–Sat 10am–4:30pm, Sun 1:30–4:30pm.

John Dickinson Plantation The reconstructed boyhood home of John Dickinson, one of Delaware's foremost statesmen of the Revolutionary and Federal periods and a framer and signer of the U.S. Constitution, was originally built in 1740. Destroyed by fire in 1804, the brick house was rebuilt in 1896. Several reconstructed outbuildings and a slave/tenement house stand along with it on the property today. Guides dressed in period clothing give visitors a glimpse of daily life of the Dickinson family, tenants, and slaves.

Kitts Hummock Rd. ✆ **302/739-3277**. Free admission. Jan–Feb Tues–Sat 10am–3:30pm; Mar–Dec Tues–Sat 10am–3:30pm, Sun 1:30–4:30pm. Take Rte. 113 south from Dover to Kitts Hummock Rd., just past the Dover Air Force Base.

NEARBY ATTRACTIONS

Air Mobility Command Museum (Dover Air Force Base) This museum, located in a restored World War II hangar listed in the National Register of Historic Places, houses a collection of vintage aircraft and artifacts. Exhibits reflect the evolution and history of Dover Air Force Base, which has been the hub of strategic airlifts in the eastern United States. The museum's first plane, a C-47A used in the 1944 D-day paratroop drop over Normandy, was rejected in 1986 by other museums as "hopeless to repair." It is now on display, immaculately restored. A more recent addition is an F-16 *Fighting Falcon.* here's a little of everything in between—one of the few remaining B-17Gs from the 1948 Flying Bomb project, an O-2 Forward Air Control plane used in Vietnam, and, when mission requirements allow, the enormous C-5 *Galaxy.* New exhibits focus on the Korean War and Vietnam. The gift shop offers aviation-related books, posters, patches, and souvenirs. *Note:* At press time, due to increased security at the base, advance reservations were required to visit the museum, and drivers of cars entering the base must be prepared to show their license, registration, and proof of insurance. Call or check the website for updates or additional requirements.

1301 Heritage Rd. (off Rte. 113). ✆ **302/677-5938**. www.amcmuseum.org. Free admission. Daily 9am–4pm. Take Exit 93 off Rte. 113/1 to main gate of Dover AFB.

PERFORMING ARTS

Schwartz Center for the Arts This performing arts venue, opened in October 2001, brings back to life a beloved old theater, the Capitol. A wide variety of musicians—country, jazz, symphony, gospel—have lined up to play here. Film, comedians, plays, and ballet are also on the schedule, which can be found on the website. In a town where nightlife is scarce, this is big news.

> **Tips** Put Yourself in the Driver's Seat
>
> Want to ride in a Winston Cup car? Maybe even drive it yourself? **Monster Racing Excitement** (© 800/468-6946) will let you get behind the wheel to "tame the Monster" at Dover Downs. You must call ahead to schedule a drive time. Packages range from $75 for a passenger seat ride with an instructor to $859 to drive a race car for 30 laps, with shorter and less expensive alternatives in between.

118 S. Bradford St., Dover. © 800/778-5078 for tickets, 302/678-3583 for information. Fax 302/678-1207. www.schwartzcenter.com. To order tickets by mail, write to P.O. Box 1449, Dover, DE 19903.

SPECTATOR SPORTS & OUTDOOR ACTIVITIES

HARNESS HORSE RACING   In addition to stock-car racing, **Dover Downs** (© 302/674-4600; www.doverdowns/harness) offers harness horse racing from November through April. Races are run Saturday through Thursday and post time is 4:30pm. A Simulcast Club is open daily noon to midnight. Dover Down's slots casino is also a popular way to while away a few hours. Games range from 5¢ to $20. Check the website for concerts, too, especially if you like pop stars from the past. Recent performers have included Paul Revere and the Raiders, Larry Gatlin and the Gatlin Brothers, and Gladys Knight.

Harrington Raceway, Route 13, Harrington (© 302/398-7223; www. harringtonraceway.com), one of the oldest pari-mutuel racing tracks in the United States, schedules races late April through early November. Harness racing usually runs Saturday through Wednesday with post time at 5:45pm, but call or check the website for an exact schedule. Midway slot machines and "video lottery" are also available at Harrington year-round. The track is located on the state fair grounds, about 15 miles (24km) south of Dover. Admission is free.

STOCK-CAR RACING   Dover's biggest sporting activity is stock-car racing. Fans from far and near flock to the "Monster Mile" at **Dover Downs International Speedway,** Route 13 (P.O. Box 843), Dover, DE 19903 (© 302/674-4600 for information; www.doverdowns.com), the home of two major races, drawing some of the world's top stock-car drivers. The Monster Excitement runs are scheduled May through October. Slots are open year-round. Ticket prices for adults range from $37 for general admission (with limited view) to $165 for the best seats at the Winston Cup featured race. For NASCAR tickets, order online or call **800/441-RACE** or fax 302/672-0100. Mail orders are also accepted.

DART First State offers **shuttle buses** from the Blue Hen Corporate Center south of Dover Downs and Christiana Mall in Wilmington. Tickets are about $15 per carload from the Blue Hen Center and $8 per person round-trip from Wilmington. Call © 302/652-DART or visit www.dartfirststate.com for schedules.

Or avoid driving altogether and take the train. **Amtrak** has begun service on race day from New York to Dover. (Amtrak usually doesn't go to Dover.) Call © 877/835-8725 for details.

SILVER LAKE & KILLENS POND STATE PARK

Dover's beautiful **Silver Lake** is the core of a recreation area in the heart of the city. Biking, swimming, and picnicking draw the most people but the park also has a boat ramp, exercise circuit, volleyball court, and walking/jogging trail. The park has entrances on State Street and Kings Highway, and is open year-round from sunrise to sundown. Complete information is available from the **Dover Parks and Recreation Division** (© 302/736-7050).

Some 13 miles (21km) south of Dover, about a half mile east of Route 13, is Kent County's only state park, **Killens Pond State Park,** 5025 Killens Pond Rd., Felton (© **302/284-4526**). Covering 1,040 acres, with a 66-acre millpond, Killens Pond is a natural inland haven. Its facilities include picnic areas, shuffle-board courts and horseshoe pits, biking and hiking trails, volleyball courts, boat rentals, pond fishing, camping, and the Killens Pond Water Park, which features a guarded main pool, two water slides, a wading pool, and the "Tot Lot," a kiddie water park. Admission to the state park is $2.50 for Delaware-registered cars and $5 for out-of-state vehicles. It is charged daily May through September and October weekends. Entrance to the water park, open Memorial Day to Labor Day, is an additional $1.50 for adults and $1 for children under 16.

Camping facilities at Killens Pond are quite modern, though at times a bit too close for comfort. There are 77 campsites, including 10 cabins and one pond-view cottage. Reservations are taken up to 7 months in advance (© **877/ 987-2757**). Sites cost $14 to $20 for tent sites and $20 to $24 for sites with water and electric hookup. Primitive sites are available for tents only, though quite a few are in an open field rather than in the nearby wooded glen. The park and campground are open year-round; the water park is open Memorial Day through Labor Day.

WHERE TO STAY

Dover doesn't have grand or historic hotels. It has a few modern motels and motor inns, open year-round, with ample parking facilities. The major properties are on Route 13 (DuPont Hwy.).

The rates for accommodations, in general, are moderate. Prices can much higher on NASCAR race weekends at Dover Downs. (If you plan to attend the race, be sure to make your hotel reservations when you get your tickets—hotels in the entire state fill up these weekends.) Dover's hotels also tend to book up on summer weekends, so it's best to make reservations.

Best Western Galaxy Inn   Though situated across from Dover Air Force Base's north gate, at the junction of busy Route 113 and Route 10, this two-story motel is set back from the road on a small hillside. It's a popular motel for businesspeople and tourists interested in easy access to the base.

1700 E. Lebanon Rd., Dover, DE 19901. © **800/528-1234** or 302/735-4700. Fax 302/735-1604. www.best western.com. 64 units. $65–$110 double. Rates include continental breakfast. AE, DC, DISC, MC, V. Children under 16 stay free in parents' room. **Amenities:** Outdoor pool; Jacuzzi. *In room:* A/C, dataport, coffeemaker, iron.

Comfort Inn Dover   Businesspeople and families are attracted to this motel, just off the Route 13 corridor at Loockerman Street. The closest motel to the city's historic district, the brick-fronted Comfort Inn is laid out in two adjoining bi-level wings. The decor and furnishings are typical of the Comfort chain. The facilities include an outdoor swimming pool and an exercise room. A branch of the TGI Friday's restaurant chain is adjacent.

222 S. DuPont Hwy. (Rte. 13), Dover, DE 19901. © **800/228-5150** or 302/674-3300. 94 units. $60–$85 double. Rates include continental breakfast. AE, DC, DISC, MC, V. Pets accepted. **Amenities:** Outdoor pool; exercise room; coffee in lobby. *In room:* A/C, microwave, refrigerator, hair dryer and iron available.

Dover Downs Hotel A brand new 10-story luxury hotel opened adjacent to the slots and racetracks in February 2002. The newest part of the Dover Downs entertainment complex, the hotel is set to pamper guests with luxury rooms, a concierge level, and 12 posh suites on the top floor, as well as a restaurant, lounge, and even a concert hall, the Rollins Center.

1131 N. DuPont Hwy., Dover, DE 19901. © **866/4-RESERV.** www.doverdownshotel.com. 240 units. $125–$175 double. Valet parking $3. Self-parking free. Children under 18 stay free in parents' room. AE, DISC, MC, V. **Amenities:** 4 restaurants; 2 lounges; indoor pool; health club; shuttle service to downtown Dover; concierge level. *In room:* A/C, TV with pay movies, dataport and Internet access, refrigerator, coffeemaker, iron.

Sheraton Dover Hotel ⭐ A favorite spot for business executives and conference attendees, this seven-story hotel is the most complete facility along the north–south corridor. Guest rooms are furnished in a traditional motif with mahogany reproduction furniture. The hotel offers varied dining and entertainment choices: Tango's Bistro, a full-service, upscale restaurant with a casual atmosphere; the Starlight Lounge, a rooftop lounge with a view of Dover; and the Hub Rock Cafe, featuring karaoke on weekdays and a deejay on weekends.

1570 N. DuPont Hwy. (Rte. 13), Dover, DE 19901. © **302/678-8500.** Fax 302/678-9073. www.sheraton dover.com. 156 units. $79–$139 double; $149–$495 suite. AE, DC, DISC, MC, V. **Amenities:** 2 restaurants; lounge; indoor pool; health club. *In room:* A/C, TV with movies, voicemail, dataport, coffeemaker, iron.

WHERE TO DINE

Blue Coat Inn ⭐⭐⭐ AMERICAN/REGIONAL Nestled on Silver Lake just north of downtown in a garden setting, this colonial-style restaurant, originally a private home, offers water views and delicious, moderately priced food. It takes its name from the uniform worn by the Delaware Regiment that marched from Dover Green in July 1776 to join General Washington's army. Four original stone fireplaces, weathered timbers, and antiques enhance the warm atmosphere. At lunchtime, there's wealth of tempting choices both hot and cold, including crab imperial, oyster sandwiches, and filet mignon. Dinner entrees range from seafood combinations of crab, fish, and various shellfish to veal Marsala and prime rib. For a more casual atmosphere, try the new Wolf Creek Tavern. The menu is more casual, too, with burgers, prime rib sandwiches, crab dip, and the like.

800 N. State St. (on Silver Lake). © **302/674-1776.** Reservations recommended on weekends. Main courses $10.50–$33.50; lunch $5.95–$12.95. AE, DC, DISC, MC, V. Lunch Tues–Fri 11:30am–4pm, Sat 11:30am–3pm; dinner Tues–Thurs 4:30–9pm, Fri–Sat 4:30–10pm, Sunday noon–9pm; brunch noon–2:30pm.

Countrie Eatery (Formerly the Blue Coat Inn Pancake House) *Value* AMERICAN/BREAKFAST Do you love breakfast? If you find yourself yearning for some eggs and bacon or creamed chipped beef on toast when other people are set on a hamburger or crab cake, this is your place. Overlooking Silver Lake on the edge of town, the Eatery, a sister operation of the more formal Blue Coat Inn next door, is a good choice for an inexpensive hearty meal in a simple setting. Breakfast—the specialty—is a good choice any time. After traditional breakfast hours, you can get a huge variety of sandwiches, salads, soups, and entrees. There are also daily all-you-can-eat specials. You won't go home hungry.

950 N. State St. © **302/674-8310.** Breakfast and lunch $2.55–$6.95; dinner $6.95–$12.25. MC, V. Mon–Sat 6:30am–8pm, Sun 6:30am–3pm.

Spence's Bazaar MARKET No, it's not a restaurant, but if you like an old-time market this one offers homemade sausages, breads, pies, and preserves, made by members of Mennonite and Amish communities. Hours vary so it's best to call if you have your heart set on shoofly pie. (The market also houses a flea market and auction business.) It has rebounded from a recent fire and is back in business.

South St. and New St. ℂ 302/734-3441. Open Tues and Fri 7:30am–5pm.

Village Inn ★★ SEAFOOD   It's worth the slight detour, about 4 miles (6km) east of Dover past several cornfields, to try this restaurant in the town of Little Creek. Founded 35 years ago and still run by a local family, this restaurant has built its reputation on its always-fresh seafood. The specialties are crab cakes and fresh flounder, served in a variety of ways: stuffed with crab, breaded, poached, or however else you might want it. Don't miss the oysters when they're in season. Lunch consists mainly of sandwiches, salads, chowders, and seafood platters. The interior, with four fireplaces, is decorated in a casual, country style.

Rte. 9, Little Creek. ℂ 302/734-3245. Reservations accepted for dinner. Main courses $10.95–$25.95; lunch $4.75–$12.95. DISC, MC, V. Tues–Fri 11am–2pm and 4:30–10pm, Sat 11am–10pm, Sun noon–9pm.

Villa Paradiso Ristorante ★ NORTHERN ITALIAN   Tucked in a shopping center just west of the Dover Air Force Base, the Paradiso could easily be overlooked by visitors, but it's a favorite of locals. The interior features murals, paintings, and statuary reminiscent of a Roman palazzo. The menu features delicate dishes with a northern Italian flair, such as veal and crab and chicken Marsala. But the owner has bowed to popular demand and added traditional southern Italian dishes, too, including lasagna. Service is what you'd expect at a fine restaurant, and food is expertly prepared and served with pride.

1151 E. Lebanon Rd., Rte. 10 Plaza. ℂ 302/697-3055. Reservations recommended. Main courses $12.50–$26.95; lunch $6.95–$9.95. AE, DISC, MC, V. Mon–Fri 11:30am–3pm and 5–9pm, Sat 5–10pm.

W.T. Smithers ★ INTERNATIONAL   Housed in a Victorian-style building in the heart of Dover's historic district, W.T. Smithers is named in honor of a local hero who was, at various times, a baseball player, a lawyer, a member of the state's 1897 constitutional convention, and one of Teddy Roosevelt's Rough Riders. The interior offers a homey turn-of-the-20th-century atmosphere, with a choice of eight different dining rooms, including a newly renovated outdoor deck and an "anniversary" room, ideal for special dinners for two to four persons. The lunch menu features sandwiches such as the spicy barbecue or crab cake, burgers, pasta, salads, and lots of cheese steak choices. Dinner entrees include a rich vegetable Alfredo, along with lots of beef, chicken, and seafood.

140 S. State St. ℂ 302/674-8875. Fax 302/674-8608. Reservations recommended for dinner. Main courses $5.95–$22.95; lunch $3.50–$7.95. AE, DC, DISC, MC, V. Mon–Sat 11am–1am.

2 Bombay Hook National Wildlife Refuge

Because of its abundance of wildlife refuges, the Delmarva Peninsula is a haven for migrating birds and those who watch them. Bombay Hook, established in 1937 as part of a chain of refuges extending from Canada to the Gulf of Mexico, is the largest of Delaware's refuges. Though the primary (and loudest) inhabitants/visitors of the refuge are wintering ducks and geese, Bombay Hook also hosts herons, egrets, sandpipers, willets, and the occasional bald eagle, as well as a more permanent mammal, amphibian, and reptile population.

If you've visited Maryland's Blackwater National Wildlife Refuge, Bombay Hook will be quite a contrast. The facilities are considerably more primitive—the roads are not paved, the trails are well marked but not well worn, and there are fewer ranger programs and visitor services. This means there are also fewer human visitors, so especially in the off-season, you may have the place all to yourself.

ESSENTIALS

GETTING THERE Take Route 13 north of Dover to Route 42; travel east (left) on Route 42 to Route 9 and then north on Route 9 for 1½ miles (2km); turn right onto Whitehall Neck Road, which leads to the visitor center.

VISITOR INFORMATION The **visitor center/ranger station** (© 302/653-9345; fax 302/653-0684) is at the entrance, off Whitehall Neck Road. It offers displays on the wildlife; maps and information on the trails; and restrooms. It's open weekdays 8am to 4pm year-round and on fall and spring weekends from 9am to 5pm. The visitor center is closed on weekends in summer and winter, when it's off-season, though a map of the refuge is posted outside.

FEES & REGULATIONS The park is open year-round during daylight hours. Entrance fees are $4 per car or $2 per family on bikes or on foot. Hunting is permitted under special regulations on designated portions of the refuge during the regular Delaware hunting season.

SEEING THE HIGHLIGHTS

Like most wildlife refuges, much of Bombay Hook is not accessible to the public. However, the 12-mile (19km) round-trip auto tour route, several nature trails, and three observation towers offer ample opportunity to see birds and other wildlife.

The driving tour route, which can also be used by cyclists, begins and ends at the visitor center and takes you by the three major wetland pools in the refuge: Raymond Pool, Shearness Pool, and Bear Swamp Pool. The roads are well marked and offer plenty of spots to pull off and park. Cyclists should note that the roads throughout the refuge are not paved—they're dirt and gravel—though they are flat. Interpretive audiocassettes for use with the auto tour may be rented at the visitor center. To see the most birds, come in May or June when the shorebird population hits its peak. Or visit in October or November when the most ducks and geese are here. They can number 150,000.

BIRD-WATCHING As you might imagine, the best time to see migratory birds is fall and spring, specifically October through November and mid-February through March. **Canada** and **snow geese** begin to arrive in early October, and **duck** populations—pintail, mallard, American widgeon, blue-winged and green-winged teal, and others—increase through November. **Shorebird** migration begins in April, and their populations in the refuge peak in May and June.

The refuge is also the year-round home to **bald eagles,** though they can be difficult to spot. Eggs begin hatching in April, and in June the baby eagles begin to leave their nests. Shearness Pool serves as their roosting and nesting area. Parson Point Trail will take you to the back of the pool for a closer look. But during mating and nesting season this trail may be closed to protect the eagles. However, if you bring binoculars or stop at the binocular-scope at the observation tower along the auto route, you might see one or two high in the trees.

Birds can be seen all along the auto tour, but for the best vantage point, hike out to one of the three 30-foot observation towers, one overlooking each of the pools. Part of the trail to Bear Swamp Observation Tower is wheelchair accessible, and though the tower itself is not accessible, an observation platform at ground level below the tower provides a good view of the feeding wood ducks, snow geese, egrets, and occasional muskrat. A viewing scope at wheelchair level has been installed on the dock at the end of the path.

In addition to the observation towers, a photography blind is available by advance request.

HIKING Hiking in the refuge is primarily a means of observing and photographing wildlife, so the five nature trails aren't terribly strenuous or long. All the trails are flat, and range from a quarter-mile to a mile long. The Bear Swamp Trail, which leads to the Bear Swamp observation tower, is partially wheelchair accessible. The other two trails are fairly primitive. Mosquitoes, ticks, and biting flies are a problem July through September, so bring insect repellent and wear long sleeves and pants. Parson Point Trail, the longest of the three trails, may be the best place in the refuge to spy bald eagles because it ends at the backside of Shearness Pool, a roosting and nesting area for the eagles. However, it is closed to the public during nesting season (Nov–June). The Boardwalk Trail offers visitors a look at four different refuge habitats—woodland, freshwater pond, brackish pond, and salt marsh—and the widest variety of wildlife. The fifth trail leads to the Raymond Tower set in a meadow.

3 Odessa

23 miles (37km) N of Dover; 22 miles (35km) S of Wilmington

Soon after the town of Cantwell's Bridge was founded in 1731, it became a bustling center of trade, a vital link between Philadelphia and the farmers of central Delaware. The streets were lined with shops and hotels, and the town even had its own tannery and furniture maker. Today, the streets of Odessa, as the town was renamed in 1855, are quiet. There are few businesses, and certainly no trading is done at the little boat landing off Main Street on the Appoquinimink Creek (or "the crick" as the natives call it). But you can still see something of Odessa's heyday in the brick-lined walkways and more than 30 historic and elegant homes and buildings that make up the historic district.

The homes and buildings span 3 centuries and at least four architectural styles, in the village of Odessa, ranging from the modest Collins-Sharp House, a colonial-style cabin dating from the early 1700s, to stately Federal and Georgian homes and Victorians. All the homes and buildings stand within the town's historic district, which begins at Front Street along the banks of the Appoquinimink and extends 4 blocks to 4th Street, an ideal walking tour. Most of the homes are private residences and are only open to the public for special events, but four of the buildings are open for guided tours from March through December. These four are collectively known as the **Historic Houses of Odessa** and are owned and operated by the **Winterthur Museum.** (So when you see a brochure for the Historic Houses of Odessa, it is actually referring only to the homes run by Winterthur.)

ESSENTIALS

GETTING THERE Take Route 13 north from Dover or south from Wilmington or New Castle to Odessa and follow signs to the historic district.

VISITOR INFORMATION There is no official visitor center in Odessa, but the Winterthur Museum staff have brochures for a walking tour of the town at the Brick Hotel on Main Street. Groups can call ahead to arrange for a guided walking tour. For information call **Historic Houses of Odessa** (part of the Winterthur organization), P.O. Box 507, Odessa, DE 19730 (© **302/378-4069**).

SPECIAL EVENTS   The best time to see Odessa is during the Women's Club of Odessa's **Christmas in Odessa,** held annually the first Saturday in December. A number of public buildings and private homes are open for tours. There are daytime and candlelight tours, as well as music, carriage rides, food, and a craft and greens shop available. Tickets are sold at the Old Academy, P.O. Box 254, Odessa, DE 19730 (✆ **302/378-4900;** www.christmasinodessa.com).

The Winterthur houses hold a separate celebration, **Yuletide in Odessa,** from mid-November through December. Decorations in the houses are based on a children's book. For instance, in December 2001, the theme was *Heidi.* Tours are offered Tuesday to Saturday 10am to 4pm and Sunday 1 to 4pm. Admission is $8 for adults; $7 for senior citizens, groups, and students 12 and over; and $3 for children ages 5 to 11. Children 4 and under and Winterthur Guild members are free. Candlelight tours are offered on several days. Reservations for these are required. Contact them at P.O. Box 507, Odessa, DE 19730, ✆ **302/ 378-4069,** or www.winterthur.org.

TOURING THE HISTORIC DISTRICT

If you'd like to see the entire historic district (from the outside), you really have just one option: Pick up a copy of the walking tour guide, and walk, bike, or drive the self-guided tour. Since the tour only covers 3 or 4 blocks, we recommend parking your car along Main Street or Front Street and walking or biking. The brochure maps out the district, labels all 32 structures, and gives a very brief description of each one.

Winterthur's **Historic Houses of Odessa** are open to the public from March through December, Tuesday through Saturday from 10am to 4pm and Sunday from 1 to 4pm. The **Brick Hotel** at the corner of Main and Second streets hosts the museum offices and reception area, as well as the country's largest collection of Belter-style Victorian furniture. Stop in here to buy tickets and begin the tours. You can tour all the properties, or just one or two, and the price varies accordingly. For three houses, the price for adults is $8, and for students and seniors it's $7. Admission for children ages 5 to 11 is $3, and children 4 and under are free. For more information, contact Historic Houses of Odessa, P.O. Box 502, Odessa, DE 19730, ✆ **302-378-4069,** www.wintherthur.org.

The **Collins–Sharp House,** a log-and-frame cabin, is the oldest of the four buildings, dating from the 1700s. The museum uses this building for its educational programs, hosting living history demonstrations on hearth cooking, gardening, and other aspects of early colonial life. It is open to the public only when the museum is sponsoring some special program or demonstration. The cooking demonstrations are lively and fun and you get to eat what they cook, too.

The **Wilson–Warner House,** built in 1769 by David Wilson, a prosperous merchant, is a fine example of Delaware–Georgian architecture. When the Wilson family went bankrupt in 1829, a complete inventory of the family's possessions was made and all the contents of the house were sold at auction. Luckily the inventory survived, and Winterthur was able to furnish the house much as it would have been in the early 1800s.

The **Corbit–Sharp House,** built 5 years after the Wilson–Warner House, is an early example of one neighbor trying to outdo another—surpassing the Joneses, so to speak. William Corbit built his considerably larger Georgian home next door to the Wilsons. It features an impressive frontispiece, a widow's walk, and a view of the Appoquinimink that can't be beat.

Appendix A:
Maryland & Delaware in Depth

For many, the first thing that comes to mind when thinking about Maryland and Delaware is water—the Atlantic coast, and the Chesapeake and Delaware bays, filled with sailboats, yachts, skipjacks, freighters, fishing boats, fish, oysters, and crabs. Cottage-style screwpile lighthouses keep a lookout for vessels too close to shore. This image of maritime life mixes seamlessly with that of the area's bustling ports: Annapolis, a city little changed since Jefferson called its brick-lined streets the best in the colonies; and Baltimore, "Charm City," where the Inner Harbor shimmers under the glass peaks of the National Aquarium. The maritime ways live on in the Eastern Shore's historic towns, from Chestertown to St. Michaels and Smith Island, where James Michener toured while writing *Chesapeake* and watermen still reap the harvest of the bay, just as they have for over 200 years.

For some, the Atlantic beaches are where the action is. Ocean City has its miles of wide, white strand, rippling heat, and almost constant summer parties. Assateague Island boasts 30 miles (48km) of pristine beaches, rolling dunes, grassy marshes, sika deer, and wild ponies. The quieter resorts of the Delaware shore have their star in quiet, sophisticated Rehoboth. Others prefer Cape Henlopen, where you can peer down from the Great Dune at the three light-houses off in the distance, and watch the whales and dolphins swimming in the surf.

But Maryland also had a more turbulent side, when it was the crossroads of the Civil War and saw the war's bloodiest single day of battle at Antietam, where 23,000 men fell. Farther west, the Allegheny Mountains form the state's frontier. These rolling and rumbling hills turn bright red and orange in autumn, drawing visitors to their trails, waterfalls, and steam-powered train, *Mountain Thunder*. In winter, cross-country and downhill skiers explore the quiet, snow-padded forests and hillsides.

Hidden in these hillsides is more water. As the winter snow melts, it feeds the Chesapeake, and, through the Ohio River, the Mississippi—this is wild water. Through deep, forested valleys, the Savage and the Youghiogheny rivers flow through rapids and over boulders, cataracts, and falls, inviting rafters, kayakers, and canoeists to come from all over and test their mettle.

The best thing is that all these images are true to life. They are real. They are as real as the opulent oil paintings on the palatial walls of the du Pont mansions of Northern Delaware, as real as the sweet chocolate desserts in Baltimore's Little Italy, as real as the dappled wild ponies that walk right up to your car window on Assateague Island, and as real as the roar of Great Falls on the Potomac. So pick an image or maybe two or three, come visit, and see how real they are.

1 History 101: Maryland

EARLY EXPLORATIONS & SETTLEMENT

The area that is present-day Maryland was initially settled by Native American tribes including the Algonquin, Leni-Lenape, and Nanticoke. The first European to catch sight of the coast of Maryland was probably Dutchman Henry Hudson as he sailed in from the Atlantic and along the body of water now known as Delaware Bay.

As early as 1629, the Dutch attempted to establish a whaling colony in Delaware. Meanwhile, the English set their sights on Maryland. John Smith explored the Chesapeake Bay in 1608. In 1634, more than 140 English colonists arrived at the mouth of the Potomac River on two ships, *The Ark* and *The Dove*. These stalwart settlers created a community that served as the state's first capital until 1694. Lord Baltimore's brother, Leonard Calvert, named the town in honor of Henrietta Maria, wife of King Charles I, calling it St. Marie's Citty (or St. Mary's City). Among the achievements of this early city was the enactment of the first laws recognizing religious tolerance. By then, Kent Island, now at the eastern terminus of the Bay Bridge, had been established by William Claiborne as an outpost for the colony of Virginia.

PURITANS ESTABLISH A BASE

In 1649, another group from England, the Puritans, arrived, landing first in Virginia, but on encountering religious intolerance there, they moved north to what is now Annapolis and settled at the mouth of the Severn River. These early inhabitants called their new settlement Anne Arundel Town, after the wife of the second Lord Baltimore, proprietor of the colony of Maryland. In 1695, the town was renamed Annapolis in honor of Princess Anne of England, and the colonial government of Maryland was

Dateline Maryland

- **1634** English colonists sail into the Potomac and found St. Mary's City, Maryland's first capital.
- **1649** Puritans find a home in Annapolis.
- **1729** Baltimore founded.
- **1767** Mason-Dixon line completed.
- **1783–84** Annapolis becomes capital of the United States for 9 months; George Washington resigns his commission at Maryland's State House. Treaty of Paris signed at Annapolis in 1784.
- **1788** Maryland ratifies the Constitution.
- **1791** Maryland cedes land for the District of Columbia.
- **1814** "The Star-Spangled Banner" written at Baltimore.
- **1829** Chesapeake and Delaware Canal completed.
- **1845** U.S. Naval Academy founded at Annapolis.
- **1850** Chesapeake and Ohio Canal (C&O) reaches terminus at Cumberland.
- **1852** Baltimore and Ohio Railroad (B&O) reaches Ohio River.
- **1861** "First Blood of the Civil War" shed at Baltimore.
- **1862** Battle of Antietam, Sharpsburg.
- **1875** Ocean City, Maryland, opened as beach resort.
- **1876** Johns Hopkins University founded in Baltimore.
- **1925** Deep Creek Lake created.
- **1952** William Preston Lane Jr. Bridge opens up the Eastern Shore.
- **1960** Baseball "iron man" Cal Ripken born in Aberdeen.
- **1980** Harborplace opens; rebirth of Baltimore Inner Harbor.
- **1992** Oriole Park at Camden Yards opens in Baltimore.
- **1996** Cleveland Browns football team moves to Baltimore, renamed the Baltimore Ravens.
- **1997** Baltimore celebrates its 200th anniversary with expansion of the Convention Center.
- **1998** Wye River Summit—Peace talks between Israel and the Palestinian Liberation Organization—in Queen Anne's County.
- **2001** Ravens win Super Bowl.

moved here from St. Mary's City; it has been Maryland's capital ever since. Shortly afterward, another city began to take shape on the Patapsco River—Baltimore, named after Lord Baltimore of England and founded in 1729.

STRUGGLE FOR INDEPENDENCE   Although Philadelphia was the capital of the colonies for most of the period from 1774 to 1800, during the First and Second Continental Congresses and the major part of the Revolutionary War, Maryland's colonial hub took a turn as capital. As the hostilities of the war drew to a close, Annapolis reigned as the first peacetime capital of the United States (from November 26, 1783, until August 13, 1784). It served as the site of the ratification of the Treaty of Paris, the document in which Great Britain formally recognized the independence of the United States.

After almost 9 months in Annapolis, the capital was once again established in Philadelphia, and in 1787 a Federal Convention of 55 delegates gathered at Independence Hall to debate and revise the Articles of Confederation, and ultimately to write the Constitution of the United States.

STATEHOOD, EARLY GROWTH & A NATIONAL ANTHEM   Maryland ratified the Constitution on April 28, 1788, the seventh of the original 13 colonies to do so. The post–Revolutionary War era was one of growth and expansion for the new states, and farming was pivotal to the development of all the states, including Maryland.

Transportation avenues blossomed—the 19th century became the age of the railroad, the steamboat, and the canal, and rivers were harnessed for milling and industrial use. National roads were built, and Western Maryland, via Cumberland, became a gateway to the West. In 1829, the completion of the Chesapeake and Delaware Canal (C&D) provided a shortcut from the Chesapeake Bay to the Atlantic. The Chesapeake and Ohio Canal (C&O), stretching westward across Maryland from Georgetown, reached Cumberland in 1850, and the Baltimore and Ohio Railroad (B&O) reached the Ohio River in 1852.

Peace reigned until the War of 1812, which began with a British blockade of the Chesapeake and Delaware bays. By 1813, much of the action had shifted westward toward the Great Lakes, but one of the war's most notable events occurred in Baltimore in 1814 as the Americans held off a siege of Fort McHenry. Marylander Francis Scott Key was inspired to write "The Star-Spangled Banner," a poem that, set to music, would become the country's national anthem.

CIVIL WAR YEARS   Maryland got a vivid look at some of the most crucial events of the Civil War (1861–65). On February 23, 1861, Abraham Lincoln passed through Baltimore's President Street Railroad Station on the way to his first inauguration. A few months later, the Sixth Massachusetts Union Army Troops and the Pennsylvania Volunteer Washington Brigade passed through the same station on April 19, 1861, on their way to the nation's capital. While the troops attempted to march to nearby Camden Station, a mob gathered and blocked their passage. The skirmish resulted in the deaths of 4 soldiers and 12 civilians. The incident became known as the "First Blood of the Civil War," and the city earned a new nickname, "Mobtown."

Divided loyalties caused federal troops to be deployed to Baltimore. Guns were set up on Federal Hill to ensure loyalty to the Union so that Washington, D.C., would not become surrounded by Confederate states.

More than a year later one of the war's most significant battles took place at Sharpsburg, Maryland. On September 17, 1862, the Battle of Antietam became the bloodiest single day of the war, with the dead and wounded on both sides exceeding 23,000.

MODERN MILESTONES   In the 35 years from the Civil War's end to the dawn of the 20th century, the United States moved quickly from a war-torn nation to a leading industrial power. Maryland saw the rise of new industries, and the establishment of many new colleges.

The first major tourist destinations in Maryland developed at about the same time on opposite sides of the state. On July 4, 1875, Ocean City opened as a beach resort, and a few years later, the first summer-resort hotel opened in Oakland (Garrett County), along the B&O railroad lines in 1876. Later, in 1925, the construction of the 12-mile-long (19km) Deep Creek Lake would establish Garrett County as a year-round water- and winter-sports playground.

In 1952 the William Preston Lane Jr. Bridge (commonly called the Bay Bridge) was built, stretching from Annapolis to Kent Island, making the Eastern Shore and Ocean City accessible by car. It spelled the end of the romantic steamboat ferries as well as the demise of bay resorts such as Tolchester and Love Point.

The cornerstone of waterfront urban development in Baltimore, Harborplace, was opened in 1980. This spurred further expansion of the waterfront area, with new restaurants, hotels, and attractions including the National Aquarium in 1981, the Pier Six Concert Pavilion in 1991, Oriole Park at Camden Yards in 1992, a $150 million Convention Center addition in 1997, and Ravens Stadium in 1998. The city's development continues with growth in Canton and the new Inner Harbor East development.

2 History 101: Delaware

EARLY EXPLORATIONS   This tiny area was settled by the Leni-Lenape and Nanticoke Indian tribes. The first European to arrive was probably Henry Hudson in 1609, who sailed along the Delaware Bay. He might have stepped off the *Half Moon* to explore, but the dangerous shoals persuaded him to turn his ship north, where eventually he discovered the Hudson River in New York.

The following year, an English sea captain, Samuel Argall, sailed into the same waters by accident en route to Virginia. It is said that he named the body of water in honor of the governor of Virginia, Thomas West, Lord de La Warr (1577–1618). The name "Delaware" was later also assigned to the land around the bay.

FIRST SETTLEMENTS   In 1631, a small group of Dutch fishermen settled on the curve of land between the bay and the ocean. They called their settlement Zwaanendael, or Valley of

Dateline Delaware

- 1609 Henry Hudson explores Delaware Bay area.
- 1610 Delaware named for the governor of Virginia, Lord de La Warr.
- 1629 Delaware's first town is settled by the Dutch.
- 1638 The *Kalmar Nyckel* lands near Wilmington, and New Sweden is established.
- 1655 Peter Stuyvesant establishes Fort Casimir.
- 1664 The English rename Fort Casimir as New Castle and it becomes the first capital of Delaware.
- 1704 William Penn grants Delaware its own assembly.
- 1717 Wilmington is plotted as a city.
- 1777 Revolutionary War battles are fought near Newark and, later, in the Brandywine Valley.
- 1787 Delaware is the first state to ratify the Constitution, December 7.
- 1792 Dover becomes the state capital.
- 1802 DuPont chemical enterprises are established in America.

continues

the Swans. But soon thereafter a misunderstanding arose between the Dutch and the Leni-Lenape, and in the ensuing dispute the colonists were massacred. Now the town of Lewes (pronounced *Loo*-is) lies at the site of their settlement.

In 1637, two Swedish ships, the *Kalmar Nyckel* and the *Vogel Grip,* sailed into Delaware Bay and continued north almost 60 miles (97km), entering a smaller river. The people named it the Christina River after their queen, built a fortress, and called

- 1829 Chesapeake and Delaware Canal (C&D) completed.
- 1937 DuPont laboratories' chemists invent nylon.
- 1940s U.S. Route 13/DuPont Highway is completed.
- 1981 Delaware enacts Financial Center Development Act.
- 1995 C&D Canal Bridge (from Delaware Route 1) opened.
- 1997 *Kalmar Nyckel,* a re-creation of the original ship, is launched.
- 1998 FirstUSA Riverfront Art Center opens in Wilmington.
- 2001 Riverfront Wilmington opens.

their settlement New Sweden. The Swedes adapted well, using local trees to build log cabins, said to be the first in the New World. They raised livestock and grew corn, a staple introduced to them by the Delaware Indians. Although the settlement prospered, it did not remain under the Swedish flag for long. By 1655, the Dutch, led by Peter Stuyvesant, established a stronghold at Fort Casimir, 7 miles to the south. Anxious to extend their power, the Dutch sent warships and soldiers and forced the surrender of the Swedes, but they allowed them to keep their settlement near Fort Christina.

THE COMING OF THE ENGLISH   The tides of history changed in 1664, when the English overpowered the Dutch and took over most of the Eastern Seaboard, with settlements stretching from New England to Virginia. The English, like the Dutch, allowed all previous settlers to stay. They also made a few name changes, and Fort Casimir became New Castle. Because of its location, New Castle evolved into the first capital of Delaware and a major colonial seaport.

Shortly afterward, William Penn crossed the Atlantic to claim extensive lands that were granted to him and his Quaker followers. He dropped anchor first at New Castle in 1682, then sailed farther up the Delaware River to found Philadelphia. At the time, Delaware's territory was considered part of Penn's lands, and so he divided the area south of Philadelphia into three counties: New Castle, Kent, and Sussex. As the three lower counties took shape, they also developed a sense of separateness from the rest of Pennsylvania. Recognizing this, Penn agreed to give them their own assembly in 1704.

As more English colonists poured into the counties, new cities and towns began to develop, including Wilmington (where Fort Christina once stood), named in honor of the earl of Wilmington, and Dover, plotted in 1717 according to a street plan devised by Penn. Dover would become the state capital 60 years later.

THE STRUGGLE FOR INDEPENDENCE   In 1776, as the colonies began their struggle for independence from England, Delaware assumed its part. At one point it was feared that a deadlock would develop in the vote for independence at the Continental Congress, but a Delaware man, Caesar Rodney of Kent County, rode 80 miles on horseback through a storm-filled night from his Dover home to Philadelphia to cast his crucial vote.

As the Revolutionary War got underway, Delaware raised an army of some 4,000 men, who became known for their blue uniforms. In their gear, some of the soldiers carried blue hen chickens (so called because of their blue-tinged feathers), which they used for cockfights. Today, the blue hen is the Delaware state bird.

The battles of the American Revolution largely bypassed Delaware. A large army from England landed near Elkton, Maryland, in 1777, close to the Delaware border, and Washington moved his forces into Northern Delaware to meet it; a short encounter took place at Cooch's Bridge near Newark, after which the British headed north. They met Washington's army at the Battle of Brandywine, one of the largest of the Revolutionary War, north of the Delaware line in Pennsylvania.

STATEHOOD & EARLY GROWTH   The war ended in 1783 with independence from British rule. In Delaware, as in the other former colonies, the citizens felt the need for a new form of government to replace the Articles of Confederation. In September 1787, a Constitutional Convention met in Philadelphia, adopted a new constitution, and then submitted it to the states for approval. Delaware was the first to ratify the document, on December 7.

As the 19th century dawned, Delaware prospered, as did other states on the Eastern Seaboard that had fostered trade with Europe. Early citizens of New Castle County harnessed the fast-flowing waters of the Brandywine River for milling, while the people of Kent and Sussex counties farmed their fertile lands. New immigrants from Europe arrived, among them a Frenchman, E. I. du Pont, who started a black-powder (gunpowder) mill on the banks of the Brandywine in 1802. This establishment was the foundation of a family empire that was to become the largest chemical company in America and a powerful influence to this day on the state of Delaware.

Wilmington, fast becoming Delaware's largest city, was a hub of industrial development and a shipping center. With the coming of the railroads and the steamboat, farm products, from soybeans and corn to peaches, were moved up from Sussex and Kent counties to northern markets. In 1829, the completion of the Chesapeake and Delaware Canal (C&D), a waterway that flows west to east across the entire state, provided a shortcut from the Chesapeake Bay to the Atlantic. In the early 1900s, the du Pont family, branching out into chemical and aerospace enterprises, sponsored a new highway, U.S. Route 13, which runs north to south the length of the state.

MODERN MILESTONES   In recent times, the industrial northern part of the state has taken on an added dimension. The Financial Center Development Act of the 1980s freed banks from restrictions on credit-card interest rates and provided tax advantages for banks moving assets to the state. This legislation drew many of the nation's largest banks to Delaware, as well as other businesses, earning Delaware the title of corporate capital of the world. Currently, thousands of businesses are incorporated in the state, including more than half of the companies on *Fortune* magazine's Top 500 list and more than a third of the companies listed on the New York Stock Exchange.

3 Maryland & Delaware Today

Maryland and Delaware offer great diversity of culture in a rather small region. The states sit astride the Mason-Dixon Line, which traditionally separates the North and the South. While Maryland and Delaware are at identical latitudes, Delaware is considered to be in the North and Maryland in Dixie. A mixture of Northerners, Southerners, and that new category—suburbanites—populates both.

Central Maryland (the Baltimore/Washington metro area) and Northern Delaware around the Brandywine Valley (including Wilmington and Newark) are lands of suburban sprawl, affluence, and big-city culture. They represent what seems most Northern about the area. Both are cities of industry: Baltimore of blue-collar workers and trading, Wilmington of banking and chemicals. If you make the trip from Baltimore to D.C., you get the feeling you're crossing over from a Northern working-class city of industry to a Southern one of politics and gentility.

Baltimore today faces the same difficulties as many large cities, including urban flight. As people leave Baltimore for the suburbs, they create new suburbs farther north and west. According to the last census, the Baltimore/Washington metropolitan area now extends all the way to Hagerstown, Maryland, a 90-minute drive from either city. The ever-growing suburbia is encroaching on traditional farming communities and small historic towns of Western Maryland, and is beginning to move across the bay to Maryland's Eastern Shore.

Baltimore has had some success reinventing itself for a service economy. It continues to draw new industry, especially e-commerce and public service organizations such as the NAACP and Catholic Relief Services. Tourism continues to strengthen the city's economy, and the city is expanding its attractions with new construction planned for the National Aquarium, Baltimore Zoo, and Maryland Science Center. The Baltimore Museum of Art and the Walters Art Museum have done extensive renovation, and new hotel properties continue to add more rooms for visitors, mostly around the Inner Harbor. Attendance is high at sports events, as Oriole fans said goodbye to baseball iron man Cal Ripken, Jr., in 2001, the same year the Baltimore Ravens won the Super Bowl. Sailing enthusiasts have twice welcomed round-the-world racing boats; the Whitbread came to Baltimore and Annapolis amid much fanfare in 1997 and will return for the 2002 race, renamed the Volvo Ocean Race. Culture and the arts have a long tradition in Baltimore, which has an active theater, art, and music scene.

Wilmington has a strong economic base but is only beginning to develop its cultural scene. Banks and the chemical industry keep the town a business center but tourism is picking up with the development of the Wilmington Riverfront. A walkway along a bend in the Christina River, the Riverfront is developing into a destination with shops, restaurants, and museums. In particular, the FirstUSA Riverfront Museum has brought blockbuster shows to town. Restaurants are popping up; smaller museums are expanding, too.

The du Pont family's influence is felt in Wilmington and in the surrounding Brandywine Valley. Mansions and gardens built by the family have developed into tourist destinations while Wilmington can boast of the elegant Hotel du Pont and 19th-century Grand Opera House.

The Delmarva Peninsula, between the Chesapeake Bay and the Atlantic Ocean, draws many tourists seeking outdoor adventures. Maryland's Eastern Shore struggles to maintain its farming and fishing through suburbia's encroachment. Tourism is an economic booster, as bed-and-breakfasts have saved historic homes and charter fishing and boat tours have given watermen a second way to make a living. An interest in the history of the Shore has brought attention and money to places that previously were endangered.

The beaches continue to draw huge crowds—even beyond the traditional Memorial Day to Labor Day season. Ocean City and Delaware's resorts are developing a new population of permanent residents so more businesses are open year-round. Golf courses have developed just west of the resorts, as the area promotes itself as "The Myrtle Beach of the Mid-Atlantic." Construction has brought asphalt and buildings almost to the water's edge. Assateague Island remains a natural refuge, including its wild ponies.

Western Maryland was only made easily accessible to the rest of the state in 1991 when Interstate 68 was finished. Before this, only Frederick and Hagerstown could be reached from Baltimore without spending hours on winding mountain roads. The result of this newfound accessibility is that far Western Maryland—Cumberland, Deep Creek Lake, and the surrounding wilderness—is experiencing a boom in tourism as people discover all the fun to be had on the area's ski slopes, wild rivers, lakes, and mountainsides.

Appendix B:
Useful Toll-Free Numbers & Websites

MAJOR HOTEL & MOTEL CHAINS

Best Western
℡ 800/528-1234
www.bestwestern.com

Clarion Hotels
℡ 800/CLARION
www.hotelchoice.com

Comfort Inns
℡ 800/228-5150
www.hotelchoice.com

Courtyard by Marriott
℡ 800/321-2211
www.courtyard.com

Days Inn
℡ 800/325-2525
www.daysinn.com

Doubletree Hotels
℡ 800/222-TREE
www.doubletreehotels.com

Econo Lodges
℡ 800/55-ECONO
www.hotelchoice.com

Embassy Suites
℡ 800/EMBASSY
www.embassy-suites.com

Fairfield Inns by Marriott
℡ 800/228-2800
www.fairfieldinn.com

Hampton Inns
℡ 800/HAMPTON
www.hampton-inn.com

Hilton Hotels
℡ 800/774-1500
www.hilton.com

Holiday Inn
℡ 800/HOLIDAY
www.basshotels.com/holiday-inn

Howard Johnson
℡ 800/I-GO-HOJO
www.hojo.com

Hyatt Hotels & Resorts
℡ 888/591-1234
www.hyatt.com

Marriott Hotels
℡ 888/236-2427
www.marriott.com

Motel 6
℡ 800/4-MOTEL6
www.motel6.com

Quality Inns
℡ 800/228-5151
www.hotelchoice.com

Radisson Hotels
℡ 800/333-3333
www.radisson.com

Ramada Inns
℡ 888/298-2054
www.ramada.com

Red Roof Inns
℡ 800/RED-ROOF
www.redroof.com

Residence Inn by Marriott
℡ 800/331-3131
www.residenceinn.com

Sheraton
℡ 888/625-5144
www.sheraton.com

Super 8 Motels
℡ 800/800-8000
www.super8.com

Travelodge
✆ 888/515-6375
www.travelodge.com

Wyndham Hotels & Resorts
✆ 800/822-4200
www.wyndham.com

CAR-RENTAL AGENCIES

Alamo
✆ 800/GO-ALAMO
www.goalamo.com

Hertz
✆ 800/654-3131
www.hertz.com

Avis
✆ 800/230-4898
www.avis.com

National Car Rental
✆ 800/CAR-RENT
www.nationalcar.com

Budget
✆ 800/527-0700
https://rent.drivebudget.com

Payless
✆ 800/PAYLESS
www.paylesscarrental.com

Dollar
✆ 800/800-3665
www.dollarcar.com

Rent-A-Wreck
✆ 800/944-7501
www.rent-a-wreck.com

Enterprise
✆ 800/325-8007
www.enterprise.com

Thrifty
✆ 800/THRIFTY
www.thrifty.com

AIRLINES

Air Canada
✆ 888/247-2262 in
  Canada and the U.S.
www.aircanada.ca

Midwest Express
✆ 800/452-2022
www.midwestexpress.com

American Airlines/American Eagle
✆ 800/433-7300
www.im.aa.com

**Northwest Airlines/
  Northwest Airlink**
✆ 800/225-2525
www.nwa.com

American Trans Air (ATA)
✆ 800/I-FLY-ATA
www.ata.com

Southwest Airlines
✆ 800/435-9792
www.southwest.com

British Airways
✆ 800/AIRWAYS
✆ 0845/77-333-77 in Britain
www.british-airways.com

United Airlines/United Express
✆ 800/241-6522
www.united.com

Continental Airlines
✆ 800/525-0280
www.continental.com

US Airways/US Airways Express
✆ 800/428-4322
www.usairways.com

Delta Air Lines
✆ 800/221-1212
www.delta.com

Virgin Atlantic Airways
✆ 800/862-8621
✆ 01293/747-747 (in Britain)
www.virgin-atlantic.com

Japan Airlines
✆ 800/JAL-FONE
✆ 0120/25-5971 in Japan
www.japanair.com (in the
  U.S. and Canada)
www.jal.co.jp (in Japan)

Index